This is the first book to document the origins and early history of environmentalism, concentrating especially on its hitherto unexplained colonial and global aspects. It highlights the significance of Utopian, physiocratic and medical thinking in the history of environmentalist ideas. The book shows how the new critique of the colonial impact on the environment depended on the emergence of a coterie of professional scientists, especially in the Dutch, French and English maritime empires. The prime importance of the oceanic island 'Eden' as a vehicle for new conceptions of nature is emphasised, and the significance of colonial island environments in stimulating conservationist notions is underlined, revealing how, for the first time, the limitability of local and global resources was recognised.

Green imperialism

STUDIES IN ENVIRONMENT AND HISTORY

Other books in the series

Green imperialism

Colonial expansion, tropical island Edens and the
origins of environmentalism,
1600–1860

RICHARD H. GROVE

Institute of Advanced Studies,
Australian National University

Global Environmental History Unit,
Department of the History and Philosophy of Science,
University of Cambridge

Clare Hall, University of Cambridge

CAMBRIDGE
UNIVERSITY PRESS

Published by the Press Syndicate of the University of Cambridge
The Pitt Building, Trumpington Street, Cambridge CB2 IRP
40 West 20th Street, New York, NY 10011-4211, USA
10 Stamford Road, Oakleigh, Melbourne 3166, Australia

First published 1995

Reprinted 1996

First paperback edition 1996

Printed in the United States of America

Library of Congress Cataloging-in-Publication Data is available.

A catalog record for this book is available from the British Library.

ISBN 0-521-40385-5 hardback
ISBN 0-521-56513-8 paperback

For Jean and Dick

Contents

Illustrations

Acknowledgements

This book grew originally from an interest in tropical forest conservation which developed while I was working in Malawi, in central Africa, in 1973 and 1974. It was in 1982, while walking in the forests of Soche Hill in the company of Jim Chapman, a former Conservator of Forests of Nyasaland, that I began to realise the need for a more global approach to the history of environmentalism than was currently fashionable. By then I had already had the good fortune to meet the late Professor Clarence Glacken, the much-missed doyen of Berkeley academic geography. It was at his suggestion that I started to read the extraordinary environmentalist tracts of John Crombie Brown, the missionary and Colonial Botanist of the Cape Colony between 1862 and 1866. This allowed me in turn to appreciate the close intellectual links between the pioneer conservationists of the Cape and Natal and their scientific predecessors in India, St Helena, Mauritius and St Vincent. More generally, it led me to understand the quite disproportionate part played by radical colonial thinkers of the Scottish and French medical and physiocratic tradition in creating a western environmental awareness. My debt to Glacken is at least equalled by my debt to Dr Joan Thirsk for actively encouraging me to look beyond my studies of East Anglian agricultural innovation and Huguenot immigration and embark on an exploration of what were then unfamiliar realms of environmental history and the history of environmental ideas. In fact the change was far less radical than it might seem. We now know that the economic motives and global networks involved in the diffusion of exotic plant and crop species, particularly those of the Dutch, were vital both to the dynamics of agricultural improvement and to the evolution of a global environmental awareness. Huguenots, meanwhile, played as vital a part in colonial botanical experimentation and plant species diffusion as they did in seventeenth-century Europe.

The interdisciplinary nature of tropical environmental history presents some particular challenges. Over a period of years I have thus been very fortunate in being able to consult Dr Mario di Gregorio and Dr Quentin Cronk on, respectively, the lesser-known byways of Victorian science and the intricacies of island ecological history. Similarly, Dr William Beinart has, over a whole decade, been keen to discuss and mull over many of the arguments presented in this book. Without their confident support and enthusiasm my task would have been much more arduous. Professor Barry Supple, first as research supervisor and then as mentor and friend, acted as a perennial source of warm encouragement and tolerance far beyond the dictates of duty. Vinita Damodaran was an ever-enthusiastic and profoundly committed ally in the course of the intellectual journey which this book represents. At several stages Glynnis Reynolds and Ka Kheng Tan spent many laborious hours in helping me to formalise my ideas and actually put a book together.

Many academic colleagues have assisted me with ideas and helpful criticism over the long period of gestation of the book. I am especially grateful to Polly Hill, John Mackenzie and Margaret Spufford, who read early versions of the manuscript, and also to Keith Thomas, Peter Burke, Gillian Beer, and Simon Schaffer, who all went to great trouble to read and comment on later and longer versions of the manuscript. I want to thank, too, those other scholars and friends who have given me their comments, insights and references in the course of my writing. They include Martin Abdullahi, Bridget and Raymond Allchin, David Allen, Robert Anderson, Havovi Anklesaria, Sir Harold Bailey, Philip Barnwell, Chris Bayly, Leon Blusse, Tim Bonyhady, Peter Boomgard, Teresa Brennan, Marlene Buchy, Mary Bullock, Jane Carruthers, Jim Chapman, Dick Chorley, Father Richard Conrad O.P., James Cormack, Alfred Crosby, Selwyn Dardaine, John Dargavel, the late Colyer Dawkins, Robin Donkin, Gina Douglas, Richard Drayton, Beverley Ellis, Toyin Falola, Howard Fergus, Joan Fitzgerald, Elizabeth Flint, Adrian Fraser, Peter Gathercole, Nick Gill, Ram Guha, Polly Hill, Richard Howard, Martin Janal, Nick Jardine, the late Jane Kenrick, John Killick, Ira Klein, Are Kolawole, Shepard Krech, Deepak Kumar, Michael Lacey, Andrew Lightman, Madeleine Ly-Tio-Fane, Helen Maclean, Roy Macleod, Julian Martin, Sir Joseph Needham, Father Patrick O'Malley, Mary Orr, Kings Phiri, Val Pinsky, Father Robert Pollock, O.P., Jacques Pouchepadass, Joseph Powell, Ravi Rajan, Mahesh Rangarajan, Terence Ranger, Jack Ravensdale, John Richards, Chris Rose, Nigel Rubbra, David Sacks, Satpal Sangwan, Jameson Seyani, John Sheail, Ajay Skaria, Ron Smith, Dee Snyman, Emma Spary, Peter Spufford, John Stewart, Peter Stewart, Rachel Stewart, K. K. Sumedathy Sumitra, Ka Kheng Tan, Richard Tucker, Cristina Villalobos, Piers Vitebsky, Adrian Walford, Philip Ward, David Watts, Ken Wilson, Elizabeth Whitcombe, Donald Worster, Peter Wyse-Jackson and Claire Young. The Sprott family of Stravithie, Fife, kindly allowed me to consult the family papers of their ancestor Hugh Cleghorn and to view their pictures. Similarly, the Jenyns family of Bottisham Hall, Cambridge, generously allowed me access to their private library and to the papers and diaries of Soame and Leonard Jenyns. I am especially grateful to the Governor-General of St Vincent and the Grenadines, who volunteered to spend an arduous afternoon with me uncovering and sorting through documents in little-visited and dusty parts of the basement of Government House in Kingstown. Both Dr Vivian Child and Dr Earle Kirby went to great lengths to introduce me to St Vincent and to accommodate me there. Mr Cyril Shallow of Stubbs Village kindly guided me around the King's Hill Forest Reserve, told me the local names for the trees and showed me how to gather American yams in a sustainable fashion. Some of my past teachers have, unknowingly, contributed very considerably to this book. They included John Tanfield and Malcolm Macfarlane at the Perse School, Cambridge, both deeply inspiring and committed men. At a later stage Andrew Goudie and John Patten at Hertford College, Oxford, inculcated a preference for eclectic and sceptical generalism that has proved far more useful than I anticipated. My enthusiasm for conservationist concerns was further stimulated by Andrew Warren, Barry Goldsmith and my contemporaries on the remarkable conservation training course at University College, London.

It is a pleasure to record the assistance given to me by the staffs of many archives and libraries, and particularly the staffs of Cambridge University Library; the Archives of Kings College, Aberdeen; the National Archives of India, New Delhi; the Karnataka State Archives, Bangalore; the Connemara Library, Madras; the Forestry Research Institute Library, Dehra Dun, Uttar Pradesh; the National Library of India, Calcutta; the French Institute, Pondicherry; the National Archives of Mauritius, Coromandel; the Mauritius Naval Historical Museum, Mahebourg; the Mauritius Institute, Port Louis; The South African Library Archives, Cape Town; the Cape Provincial Archives, Cape Town; the Natal Provincial Archives, Pietermaritzburg; the University of Vermont Archives, Burlington, Vermont; the National Archives of St Vincent and the Grenadines, Kingstown; the Public Library, Kingstown, St Vincent; the National Archives of Trinidad and Tobago, Port of Spain; the Public Library and Archives, Plymouth, Crown Colony of Montserrat; the Carnegie Library and National Archives, Roseau, Commonwealth of Dominica; the Archives of the Royal Society of Arts; the Linnaean Society Library and Archives; the Archives of the Royal Botanic Garden, Kew, Surrey; the British Library Manuscripts Room; the National Library of Scotland; the Public Record Office; the Scottish Record Office; the Library of Congress; the Manuscripts section of the Bibliothèque Centrale du Muséum d'Histoire Naturelle, Paris; the Netherlands State Archives, The Hague; the Mitchell Library, Sydney; the Tasmanian State Archives, Hobart; the Hope Entomology Library, University Museum, Oxford; the Indian Institute Library, Oxford; the Lincoln County Archives; and the University of St Andrews Archives.

During the period I was researching and writing this book I held a research fellowship at Clare Hall and then a fellowship and college lectureship at Churchill College, Cambridge. Grants from the Department of Education and Science and the Royal Society and a post-doctoral fellowship from the British Academy provided me with the financial support necessary for the travelling and writing involved in the project. A part of the research was funded by the

Social Science Research Council of the United States. At Churchill College, Sir Hermann Bondi, Professor Alec Broers, Hywel George, and Brij Gupta have all been invaluable soures of friendship and support in recent years. The book was eventually completed during a very pleasant and stimulating one-year fellowship of the Woodrow Wilson International Center for Scholars, at the Smithsonian Institution, in Washington, D.C. Frank Smith, my editor, and Jane Van Tassel, my copy-editor, have both been splendid and meticulous partners in the publishing process.

I have also been lucky to have had the company of some dear friends and relatives during my research. While not directly connected with my work in an academic sense, they were sympathetic to the spirit of it. I should thus like to thank the whole of my wonderful extended family for their support. Sadly, some of them have died long before their time. Jim, Joan and Clare Stewart, who were killed in the course of fighting for a free and just South Africa, were among them and the book is for them. It is also in memory of my great-aunts Gertie Hughes and Vera Kirkland, my grandmother Mary Clark and my cousin Bridget Spufford, who were all unusually courageous women as well as being keen students of nature.

Finally, I owe a great deal to my parents, Dick and Jean Grove. As historical climatologists and geographers with an enormous enthusiasm for field expe-rience, they introduced me, quite unintentionally, to the writing of environ-mental history. They also led me to question orthodoxy. Their own field interests led me, at an early age, to close encounters with the mysteries of Scolt Head Island and Rousseau's beloved Valaisan Alps. Later on, in Ghana, we explored together the Aburi Royal Botanic Garden and the towering forests of the Mampong escarpment. All these places left me with an enduring sense of wonder and a source of hope and inspiration which I trust that they will recognise.

Introduction

In recent years we have seen an explosion of popular and governmental interest in environmental problems. The world is widely seen to be in the throes of an environmental crisis, in which an artificially induced 'greenhouse effect' hangs over humanity like a climatic Sword of Damocles. As a result, environmental matters have become a critical part of the political agenda in almost every country. Increasingly, too, the prescriptions of environmentalists are receiving popular acclaim and support of a kind that, before now, was heard only from a minority. Ideas about conservation and sustainable development, in particular, have become highly politicised. It is clearly right that the environmental future of the earth should be a matter of popular preoccupation. The current fashion has, however, helped to bring about a widespread belief that environmental concerns are an entirely new matter and that conservationist attempts to intervene in human despoliation of the earth are part of a new and revolutionary programme.

While the degree of popular interest in global environmental degradation may be something novel, the history of environmental concern and conservation is certainly not new. On the contrary, the origins and early history of contemporary western environmental concern and concomitant attempts at conservationist intervention lie far back in time. For example, the current fear of widespread artificially induced climate change, widely thought to be of recent origin, actually has ancient roots in the writings of Theophrastus of Erasia in classical Greece.[1] Later climatic theories formed the basis for the first forest conservation policies of many of the British colonial states. Indeed, as early as the mid eighteenth century, scientists were able to manipulate state policy by their capacity to play on fears of environmental cataclysm, just as they are today. By 1850 the problem of tropical deforestation was already being conceived of as a problem existing on a global scale and as a phenomenon demanding urgent and concerted state intervention. Now that scientists and environmentalists once again have the upper hand in state and international environmental policy, we may do well to recall the story of their first – relatively short-lived – periods of power.

---

1 J. D. Hughes, 'Theophrastus as ecologist', *Environmental Review*, 4 (1985), 296–307; see also C. J. Glacken, *Traces on the Rhodian shore: Nature and culture in western thought, from ancient times to the end of the eighteenth century*, Berkeley, Calif., 1967.

Early scientific critiques of 'development' or 'improvement' were, in fact, well established by the early nineteenth century. The fact that such critiques emerged under the conditions of colonial rule in the tropics is not altogether surprising. The kind of homogenising capital-intensive transformation of people, trade, economy and environment with which we are familiar today can be traced back at least as far as the beginnings of European colonial expansion, as the agents of new European capital and urban markets sought to extend their areas of operation and sources of raw materials. It is clearly important, therefore, to try to understand current environmental concerns in the light of a much longer historical perspective of social responses to the impact of capital-intensive western and non-western economic forces. The evolution of a reasoned awareness of the wholesale vulnerability of earth to man and the idea of 'conservation', particularly as practiced by the state, has been closely informed by the gradual emergence of a complex European epistemology of the global environment. The cultural dynamics of this emergence have, to date, been largely bypassed by historians and are therefore central to this study.

Early environmental concerns, and critiques of the impact of western economic forces on tropical environments in particular, emerged as a corollary of, and in some sense as a contradiction to, the history of the mental and material colonisation of the world by Europeans. Until recently most attempts to understand the emergence of purposive and conservationist responses to the destructive impact of man on nature have been largely confined to localised European and North American contexts. Early environmentalism has generally been interpreted as a specifically local response to the conditions of western industrialisation, while conservation has been seen as deriving from a specifically North American setting.[2] Moreover, such Anglo-Americans as George Perkins Marsh, Henry David Thoreau and Theodore Roosevelt have been so securely elevated to a pantheon of conservationist prophets as to discourage the proper investigation of even their earlier European counterparts, let alone those from elsewhere.[3] All this has meant that the older and far more complex antecedents of contemporary conservationist attitudes and policies have quite simply been overlooked in the absence of any attempt to deal with the history of environmental concern on a truly global basis. In particular, and largely for quite understandable ideological reasons, very little account has ever been

2 E.g. see D. Worster, 'The vulnerable earth: Towards an interplanetary history', in Worster, ed., *The ends of the earth: Perspectives on modern environmental history*, Cambridge, 1988, pp. 3–23; and R. Nash, *Wilderness and the American Mind*, New Haven, Conn., 1967.

3 Marsh, *Man and nature; or, Physical geography as transformed by human action*, New York, 1864. This was one of the first texts to explore the history of environmental degradation and to warn of the possible consequences were it to remain unchecked. See D. Lowenthal, *George Perkins Marsh: Versatile Vermonter*, New York, 1958, and M. Williams, *The Americans and their forests: A historical geography*, Cambridge, 1989.

taken of the central significance of the colonial experience in the formation of western environmental attitudes and critiques. Furthermore, the crucially pervasive and creative impact of the tropical and colonial experience on European natural science and on the western and scientific mind after the fifteenth century has been almost entirely ignored by those environmental historians and geographers who have sought to disentangle the history of environmentalism and changing attitudes to nature.[4] Added to this, the historically decisive diffusion of indigenous, and particularly Indian, environmental philosophy and knowledge into western thought and epistemology after the late fifteenth century has been largely dismissed. Instead, it has simply been assumed that European and colonial attempts to respond to tropical environmental change derived exclusively from metropolitan and northern models and attitudes. In fact the converse was true. The available evidence shows that the seeds of modern conservationism developed as an integral part of the European encounter with the tropics and with local classifications and interpretations of the natural world and its symbolism. As colonial expansion proceeded, the environmental experiences of Europeans and indigenous peoples living at the colonial periphery played a steadily more dominant and dynamic part in the construction of new European evaluations of nature and in the growing awareness of the destructive impact of European economic activity on the peoples and environments of the newly 'discovered' and colonised lands.

After the fifteenth century the emerging global framework of trade and travel provided the conditions for a process by which indigenous European notions about nature were gradually transformed, or even submerged, by a plethora of information, impressions and inspiration from the wider world. In this way the commercial and utilitarian purposes of European expansion produced a situation in which the tropical environment was increasingly utilised as the symbolic location for the idealised landscapes and aspirations of the western imagination. William Shakespeare's play *The Tempest* and Andrew Marvell's poem 'Bermoothes' stand as pioneering literary exemplars of this cultural trend.[5] These aspirations eventually became global in their scope and reach and increasingly exerted an influence on the way in which newly colonised lands and peoples were organised and appropriated. The notion that the garden and rivers of Eden might be discovered somewhere in the East was a very ancient one in European thought, one that even predated Christianity

---

4 E.g. see K. Thomas, *Man and the natural world: Changing attitudes in England 1500–1800*, Oxford, 1983; T. O'Riordan, *Environmentalism*, London, 1976.
5 Useful detailed discussions of the idealised new iconography of the tropics can be found in Leo Marx, *The machine in the Garden: Technology and the pastoral ideal in America*, New York, 1964, and T. Bonyhady, *Images in opposition: Australian landscape painting 1801–1891*, Melbourne, 1988.

and could be found in classical Greek writings and myth.[6] Moreover, early Renaissance conceptions of Eden or paradise, which often took concrete shape in the form of the early systematic botanical gardens, were themselves derived from Zoroastrian notions of Pairidaeza and *garōδamān* that had originated in Persia and had been further developed throughout the Islamic world.[7] The developing scope of European expansion during the Renaissance offered the opportunity for this search for Eden and the dyadic 'other' to be realised and expanded as a great project and partner of the other more obviously economic projects of early colonialism.[8] Ultimately the search for an eastern-derived Eden provided much of the imaginative basis for early Romanticism, whose visual symbols were frequently located in the tropics, and for late-eighteenth-century Orientalism, for which the Edenic search was an essential precursor.[9] Parts of Northern India and the Ganges valley had, after all, long been considered as much-favoured candidates for the location of the Garden of Eden in Indo-European mythologies.[10]

Some researchers have suggested that Judaeo-Christian attitudes to the environment have been inherently destructive.[11] Such claims are highly debatable. In fact they should probably be seen as a consequence of a perceptual confusion between the characteristically rapid ecological changes caused by the inherently transforming potential of colonising capital and the consequences of culturally specific attitudes to the environment. In this connection it might be noted, for example, that rapid deforestation of the Ganges basin in pre-colonial Northern India during the sixteenth century does not appear to have been impeded by indigenous religious factors.[12] There were, however, clear links between religious change during the sixteenth century and the emergence of a more sympathetic environmental psychology. Above all, the advent of Calvinism in seventeenth-century Europe seems to have lent a further impetus to the Edenic search as a knowledge of the natural world began to be seen as a respectable path to seeking knowledge of God.

6 S. Darian, *The Ganges in myth and history*, Honolulu, 1978.
7 For detailed discussions of the relevant etymology, see Sir Harold Bailey, *Zoroastrian problems in the ninth century books*, Oxford, 1943, pp. 112–115. See also S. Crowe and S. Haywood, *The gardens of Mughal India*, London, 1972; T. Maclean, *Medieval English gardens*, London, 1981, pp. 125–6.
8 J. Prest, *The Garden of Eden: The botanic garden and the re-creation of Paradise*, New Haven, Conn., 1981.
9 W. Halbfass, *India and Europe: An essay in understanding*, Albany, N.Y., 1988, p. 21.
10 E. Bloch, *The principle of hope*, trans. N. Plaice, 3 vols., Cambridge, Mass., 1986.
11 E.g. see Lynn White, 'The historical roots of our ecologic crisis', *Science*, 155 (1967), 1202–7, and J. Opie, 'Renaissance origins of the environmental crisis', *Environmental Review*, 2 (1987), 2–19.
12 See George Erdosy, 'Deforestation in pre- and proto-historic South Asia', in R. H. Grove and V. Damodaran, eds., *Essays on the environmental history of South and South-East Asia*, Oxford University Press, New Delhi, in press.

During the fifteenth century the task of locating Eden and re-evaluating nature had already begun to be served by the appropriation of the newly discovered and colonised tropical islands as paradises. This role was reinforced by the establishment of the earliest colonial botanical gardens on these islands and on one mainland 'Eden', the Cape of Good Hope.[13] These imaginative projections were not, however, easily confined. Conceptually, they soon expanded beyond the physical limitations of the botanical garden to encompass large tropical islands. Subsequently the colonialist encounter in India, Africa and the Americas with large 'wild' landscapes apparently little altered by man, along with their huge variety of plants (no longer confinable, as they had been, to one botanical garden), meant that the whole tropical world became vulnerable to colonisation by an ever-expanding and ambitious imaginative symbolism. Frequently such notions were closely allied to the stereotyping of luckless indigenous people as 'noble savages'. Ultimately, then, the area of the new and far more complex European 'Eden' of the late eighteenth and early nineteenth century knew no real bounds. Even Australia and Antarctica, in recent years, have not been immune to being termed Edens. The imaginative hegemony implied by new valuations of nature, which had themselves been stimulated by the encounter with the colonial periphery, had enormous implications for the way in which the real – that is, economic – impact of the coloniser on the natural environment was assessed by the new ecological critics of colonial rule.

Paradoxically, the full flowering of what one might term the Edenic island discourse during the mid seventeenth century closely coincided with the realisation that the economic demands of colonial rule on previously uninhabited oceanic island colonies threatened their imminent and comprehensive degradation. Extensive descriptions exist of the damaging ecological effects of deforestation and European plantation agriculture on the Canary Islands and Madeira (Port. 'wooded isle') after about 1300 and in the West Indies after 1560.[14] In the Canary Islands complex irrigation systems formed part of an early technical response to the desiccation that followed on despoilation. In the West Indies, particularly on Barbados[15] and Jamaica, local attempts were made to try to prevent excessive soil erosion in the wake of clearance for plantations.[16] Some of the worst consequences of early colonial deforestation

13 M. C. Karstens, *The Old Company's garden at the Cape and its superintendents*, Cape Town, 1957.

14 R. Bryans, *Madeira, pearl of Atlantic*, London, 1959.

15 P. Ligon, *A true and exact history of the island of Barbados*, London, 1673. Ligon noted that 'mines there are none in this island, not so much of as coals, for which reason we preserve our woods as much as we can'.

16 D. Watts, *The West Indies: Patterns of development, culture and environmental change since 1492*, Cambridge, 1987.

were well documented in the island colonies of St Helena and Mauritius, and
it was on these islands that a coherent and wide-ranging critique of environmental degradation first emerged. It is certainly true that anxieties about soil
erosion and deforestation had arisen at earlier periods in the literature of
classical Greece, imperial Rome and Mauryan India and then in a sporadic
and unconnected fashion in the annals of the early Venetian, Spanish and
Portuguese colonial empires. For example, as early as 450 B.C. Artaxerxes had
attempted to restrict the cutting of the cedars of Lebanon. A little later the
Mauryan kings of Northern India adopted a highly organised system of forest
reserves and elephant protection.[17] Similarly, indigenous strategies for environmental management on a small scale, often involving a considerable understanding of environmental processes, had existed in many parts of the
world since time immemorial. However, it was not until the mid seventeenth
century that a coherent and relatively organised awareness of the ecological
impact of the demands of emergent capitalism and colonial rule started to
develop, to grow into a fully fledged understanding of the limited nature of
the earth's natural resources and to stimulate a concomitant awareness of a
need for conservation.

This new sensitivity developed, ironically, as a product of the very specific,
and ecologically destructive, conditions of the commercial expansion of the
Dutch and English East India companies and, a little later, of the French East
India Company. The conservationist ideology which resulted was based both
upon a new kind of evaluation of tropical nature and upon the highly empirical
and geographically circumscribed observations of environmental processes
which the experience of tropical island environments had made possible. After
about 1750 the rise to prominence of climatic theories gave a new boost to
conservationism, often as part of an emerging agenda of social reform, particularly among the agronomes and physiocrats of Enlightenment France. These
theories, as well as the undeniably radical and reformist roots of much eighteenth-century environmentalism in both its metropolitan and colonial manifestations, have long eluded scholarly attention.

Instead it has been assumed by some historians that the colonial experience
was not only highly destructive in environmental terms but that its very destructiveness had its roots in ideologically 'imperialist' attitudes towards the
environment.[18] On the face of it, this does not seem an extraordinary thesis
to advance, particularly as the evidence seems to indicate that the penetration
of western economic forces which was facilitated by colonial annexation did
indeed promote a rapid ecological transformation in many parts of the world.

17 T. R. Trautmann, 'Elephants and the Mauryas', in S. N. Mukherjee, ed., *India: History and
thought: Essays in honour of A. L. Basham*, Calcutta, 1982, pp. 254–73.
18 E.g. D. Worster, *Nature's economy: A history of ecological ideas*, Cambridge, 1977, pp. 29–55.

This was especially true in the late nineteenth century in Southern Africa, where a particularly exploitative agricultural and hunting ethos at first prevailed.[19] On closer inspection, however, the hypothesis of a purely destructive environmental imperialism does not appear to stand up at all well. In the first place, rapid and extensive ecological transition was frequently a feature of pre-colonial landscapes and states, either as a consequence of the development of agriculture or for other sociological reasons.

Furthermore, it has become increasingly clear that there is a need to question the more monolithic theories of ecological imperialism, which seem to have arisen in part out of a misunderstanding of the essentially heterogeneous and ambivalent nature of the workings of the early colonial state. Many scholars have remained unaware of the extent to which many colonial states were peculiarly open, at least until the mid nineteenth century, to the social leverage and often radical agendas of the contemporary scientific lobby at a time of great uncertainty about the role and the long-term security of colonial rule. Moreover, while the colonial enterprise undoubtedly promoted large-scale ecological change at some periods, it also helped to create a context that was conducive to rigorous analytical thinking about the actual processes of ecological change as well as thinking about the potential for new forms of land control. Ironically, too, the colonial state in its pioneering conservationist role provided a forum for controls on the unhindered operations of capital for short-term gain that, it might be argued, brought about a contradiction to what is normally supposed to have made up the common currency of imperial expansion. Ultimately the long-term economic security of the state, which any ecological crisis threatened to undermine, counted politically for far more than the short-term interests of private capital bent on ecologically destructive transformation.[20] Indeed, the absolutist nature of colonial rule encouraged the introduction of interventionist forms of land management that, at the time, would have been very difficult to impose in Europe.

Colonial expansion also promoted the rapid diffusion of new scientific ideas between colonies, and between metropole and colony, over a large area of the world.[21] The continuity and survival of the kind of critique of the ecological

---

19 For details of this, see J. Mackenzie, *The empire of nature: Hunting, conservation and British imperialism*, Manchester, 1988; and T. Pringle, *The conservationists and the killers*, Cape Town, 1983.

20 D. Washbrook, 'Law, state and agrarian society in colonial India', *Modern Asian Studies*, 15 (1981), 649–721. The highly ambiguous attitude adopted by the early colonial government towards capital and the risks which its uncontrolled deployment entailed is a subject discussed very fully by Washbrook, although he is apparently unaware of the aptness of his arguments to the ecological dimension.

21 To date, only Lucille Brockway (in *Science and colonial expansion: The role of the British Royal Botanic Garden*, New York, 1979) and D. Mackay (in *In the wake of Cook: Exploration, science*

impact of colonial 'development' which had been established by the early
eighteenth century were enabled by, and indeed dependent on, the presence
of a coterie of committed professional scientists and environmental commentators. These men, almost all of whom were medical surgeons and custodians
of the early colonial botanical gardens, were already an essential part of the
administrative and hierarchical machinery of the new trading companies. As
company investment in trade expanded into an investment in territorial acquisition, the members of the medical and botanical branches grew steadily
in number. In 1838, for example, there were over eight hundred surgeons
employed at one time in different parts of the East India Company's possessions.[22] As time passed, more and more complex administrative and technical
demands were made upon these highly educated and often independent-
thinking colonial employees.[23] During the early eighteenth century the urgent
need to understand unfamiliar floras, faunas and geologies, both for commercial purposes and to counter environmental and health risks, had propelled
many erstwhile physicians and surgeons into consulting positions and employment with the trading companies as fully fledged professional and state
scientists long before such a phenomenon existed in Europe. By the end of
the eighteenth century their new environmental theories, along with an ever-
growing flood of information about the natural history and ethnology of the
newly colonised lands, were quickly diffused through the meetings and
publications of a whole set of 'academies' and scientific societies based
throughout the colonial world. Again, the first of these had developed in the
early island colonies, particularly on Mauritius, where the Baconian organising
traditions of the metropolitan institutions of Colbert found an entirely new
purpose. Other colonial societies, such as the Society of Arts of Barbados,
were developed on the lines of the London Society for the Encouragement of
Arts, Manufactures and Commerce, later the Royal Society of Arts.[24] This
was no accident. In many respects the isolated oceanic island, like the frail
ships on the great scientific circumnavigations of the seventeenth and eighteenth centuries, directly stimulated the emergence of a detached self-
consciousness and a critical view of European origins and behaviour, of the
kind dramatically prefigured by Daniel Defoe in *Robinson Crusoe*. Thus the

and empire, 1780–1807, London, 1985) have attempted to assess, on a global scale, the relationship among science, colonial expansion and commerce. Both writers attach exclusively
utilitarian and/or exploitative and hegemonic motivations to the early development of science
in the colonial (especially East India Company) context and ignore the potential for contradictory reformist or humanitarian motivations.
22 H. H. Spry, *Modern India*, 2 vols., London, 1837.
23 D. G. Crawford, *A history of the Indian Medical Service*, 2 vols., London, 1914.
24 S. Pasfield-Oliver, *The life of Philibert Commerson*, London, 1909. The first scientific *académie*
was founded on Mauritius by Commerson in 1770.

island easily became, in practical environmental as well as mental terms, an easily conceived allegory of a whole world. Contemporary observations of the ecological demise of islands were easily converted into premonitions of environmental destruction on a more global scale.

Alongside the emergence of professional natural science, the importance of the island as a mental symbol continued to constitute a critical stimulant to the development of concepts of environmental protection as well as of ethnological and biological identity. Half a century before an acquaintance with the Falklands[25] and Galapagos provided Charles Darwin with the data he required to construct a theory of evolution, the isolated and peculiar floras of St Helena, Mauritius and St Vincent had already sown the seeds for concepts of rarity and a fear of extinction that were, by the 1790s, already well developed in the minds of French and British colonial botanists. Furthermore, the scientific odysseys of Anson, Bougainville and Cook served to reinforce the significance of specific tropical islands – Otaheite and Mauritius in particular – as symbolic and practical locations of the social and physical Utopias beloved of the early Romantic reaction to the Enlightenment.

The environments of tropical islands thus became even more highly prized, so that it may come as no surprise to discover that it was upon one of them, Mauritius, that the early environmental debate acquired its most comprehensive form. Under the influence of zealous French anti-capitalist physiocrat reformers and their successors between 1768 and 1810, this island became the location for some of the earliest experiments in systematic forest conservation, water-pollution control and fisheries protection. These initiatives were carried out by scientists who characteristically were both followers of Jean-Jacques Rousseau and adherents of the kind of rigorous scientific empiricism associated with mid-eighteenth-century French Enlightenment botany. Their innovative forest-conservation measures were based on a highly developed awareness of the potentially global impact of modern economic activity, on a fear of the climatic consequences of deforestation and, not least, on a fear of species extinctions. As a consequence, the Romantic scientists of Mauritius, and above all Pierre Poivre, Philibert Commerson and Bernardin de Saint-Pierre, can in hindsight be seen as the pioneers of modern environmentalism.[26] All of the Mauritius conservationists saw a responsible stewardship of the environment

25 R. H. Grove, 'Charles Darwin and the Falkland Islands', *Polar Record*, 22 (1985), 413–20.
26 Furthermore, all three were early advocates of the abolition of slavery and were highly critical of the corruption and absolutism of the ancien régime. The strong associations between early environmentalism and programmes for social reform were particularly conspicuous. Pierre Poivre's collected works, for example, were published in 1797 as revolutionary tracts. Indeed, the connections between the colonial physiocratic conservationists and Jean-Jacques Rousseau could hardly have been closer. Thus, after he left Mauritius, Bernardin de Saint-Pierre went on to become the confidant of Rousseau as well as the first major French Romantic novelist.

as a priority of aesthetic and moral economy as well as a matter of economic necessity. Tree planting, forest protection, climate preservation and agricultural improvement were all seen as essential components of radical social reform and political reconstruction.

The developments on Mauritius were not, in fact, entirely isolated. A close relationship between French and English science had grown up since the early years of the eighteenth century, largely as a consequence of a strong French interest in English agricultural improvements and technology. In particular, by the 1730s two highly influential French scientists, the Comte de Buffon and H. L. Duhamel du Monceau, both based at the Jardin du Roi in Paris, had begun to take a strong interest in the plant-physiological writings of John Woodward and Stephen Hales and to translate their work into French. Buffon was especially interested by their research into the relationship between vegetation and the composition of the atmosphere. Duhamel du Monceau, taking this work further, wrote extensively on the connections between trees and climate. While his conclusions were not always explicit, they soon received enthusiastic attention in both France and Britain, not least from Pierre Poivre and other physiocrats.

At the same time, however, considerable interest was being shown in climatic and desiccationist theories by a number of Englishmen in the newly founded Society of Arts, some of whom had close links with colleagues in Paris. As a result, by 1764 programmes of forest protection were quickly being put into effect on newly acquired British territories in the Caribbean. The superintendents of the St Vincent Botanic Garden, founded at the behest of the Society of Arts in 1765, played a major role in promoting further forest protection. These initiatives were far less closely associated with the agendas for social reform which characterised Mauritius. Nevertheless, they were sufficiently radical in concept and alarmist in implication to come to the notice of the English East India Company, which was soon persuaded to apply similar forest-protection ideas to St Helena.

There is some irony in this, as the company had in earlier times simply ignored the cries for help of the St Helena governors, isolated as they were in the midst of a fast-moving ecological crisis. Even so, it was conceptually and historically a very significant development. Thus the apparently highly successful results of tree planting and other environmental-protection policies on Mauritius and St Helena eventually provided much of the justification and many of the practical models for the early forest-planting and conservancy systems which developed in India and elsewhere after the early 1830s. Until then the emergence of concerns about the effects of environmental change had been delayed by the sheer scale of the Indian subcontinent, which had served effectively to conceal the effects of soil erosion and deforestation. Even so, the development of a botanical garden at Calcutta, inspired largely by the example of the St Vincent garden, provided a useful base for the precocious tree-planting programmes of William Roxburgh. These too were inspired by climatic fears and further encouraged by the vigorous conservationist lobbying of the Society of Arts in London.

The Edenic, Romantic and physiocratic roots of environmentalism on Mauritius and in the Caribbean and India were strongly reinforced after 1820 by the writings of Alexander von Humboldt. Pierre Poivre, on Mauritius, had already been persuaded of the value of tree planting and protection by his observations of Indian and Chinese forestry and horticultural methods and his knowledge of Dutch botanical gardening techniques derived, circuitously, from the Mughal emperors. Humboldt's environmental writings, however, were guided by Indian thinking in a far more profound way. Much influenced by the seminal Orientalist writings of Johann Herder as well as by those of his own brother Wilhelm, Alexander von Humboldt strove, in successive books, to promulgate a new ecological concept of relations between man and the natural world which was drawn almost entirely from the characteristically holist and unitary thinking of Hindu philosophers. His theoretical subordination of man to other forces in the cosmos formed the basis for a universalist and scientifically reasoned interpretation of the ecological threat posed by the unrestrained activities of man. This interpretation became particularly influential among the Scottish scientists employed by the East India Company. Since these men were mainly medical surgeons trained in the rigorous French-derived Enlightenment traditions of Edinburgh, Glasgow and Aberdeen universities, they were especially receptive to a mode of thinking which related the multiple factors of deforestation, water supply, famine, climate and disease in a clear and connected fashion. Several of them, in particular Alexander Gibson, Edward Balfour and Hugh Cleghorn, became enthusiastic proselytisers of a conservationist message which proved both highly alarming to the East India Company and very effective in providing the ideological basis for the pioneering of a forest-conservancy system in India on a hitherto unequalled geographical scale. The environmental views of the East India Company surgeons were most effectively summed up in a report published in 1852 entitled 'Report of a Committee Appointed by the British Association to Consider the Probable Effects in an Economic and Physical Point of View of the Destruction of Tropical Forests'. This warned that a failure to set up an effective forest-protection system would result in ecological and social disaster. Its authors were able to point to the massive deforestation and soil erosion which had occurred on the Malabar Coast, with the resulting silting up of commercially important harbours, as early evidence of what might happen in the absence of a state conservation programme. The report took a global approach, drawing on evidence and scientific papers from all over the world, and did not confine its analysis to India. Later the forest-conservation system set up in India provided the pattern for most of the systems of colonial state conservation which developed in South-East Asia, Australasia and Africa and, much later, North America.

To summarise, the ideological and scientific content of early colonial con-servationism as it had developed under early British and French colonial rule amounted by the 1850s to a highly heterogeneous mixture of indigenous, Ro-mantic, Orientalist and other elements. Of course the thinking of the scientific pioneers of early conservationism was often contradictory and confused. Many of their prescriptions were constrained by the needs of the colonial state, even though the state at first resisted the notion of conservation. In the second half of the nineteenth century, too, forest conservation and associated forced re-settlement methods were frequently the cause of a fierce oppression of indig-enous peoples and became a highly convenient form of social control. Indeed, resistance to colonial conservation structures became a central element in the formation of many early anti-imperialist nationalist movements.[27] However, despite the overarching priorities and distortions of colonialism, the early co-lonial conservationists nevertheless remain entitled to occupy a very important historical niche. This is, above all, because they were able to foresee, with remarkable precision, the apparently unmanageable environmental problems of today. Their antecedents, motivations and agendas therefore demand our close attention.

However, we need to look further than the motives of a set of environ-mentalist individuals. Any attempt to understand the foundations of western environmental concerns actually involves writing a history of the human re-sponses to nature that have developed at the periphery of an expanding Eur-opean system. This periphery, I argue, became central to the formulation of western environmental ideas. Consequently this book does not fit neatly into any single historiography. It does, however, owe a great debt to Clarence Glacken's magisterial work and to the extraordinarily catholic surveys of John Croumbie Brown, the second colonial botanist of Cape Colony. In questioning some past explanations of the origins of environmental concern, I have stressed instead the significance of the predicament and philosophical identity of the colonial scientist and the influence of indigenous systems of knowledge in colonial constructions of tropical environments and their risks. We need, per-haps, to reconstruct an historical anthropology of global environmental aware-ness. In doing so, we may need to focus more closely upon the history of the discourses of the early environmentalists without being afraid of their geo-graphical marginality. As Marshall Sahlins reminds us,

---

27 R. H. Grove, 'Colonial conservation, ecological hegemony and popular resistance: Towards a global synthesis', in J. Mackenzie, ed., *Imperialism and the natural world*, Manchester, 1990, pp. 15–51.

the heretofore obscure histories of remote islands deserve a place alongside the self-contemplation of the European past – or the history of civ-
ilizations – for their own remarkable contributions to an historical
understanding. We thus multiply our conceptions of history by the diversity of structures. Suddenly, there are all kinds of new things to consider.[28]

Among these 'new things', it appears wise to examine in particular the metaphors and images used by Europeans to characterise, identify and organise
their perceptions of nature at the expanding colonial periphery. When we do
this, two symbolic (or even totemic) forms seem to have proved central to the
task of giving a meaning and an epistemology to the natural world and to
western interactions with it. These were the physical or textual garden and
the island. The significant point is that both were capable of providing global
analogues, one, possibly a narrower one, in terms of species, and the other
offering a whole set of different analogues: of society, of the world, of climate,
of economy. Both were, unlike the real world, manageable in terms of size,
and in that sense, even in a Freudian sense, fantasist. Both offered the possibility of redemption, a realm in which Paradise might be recreated or realised
on earth, thereby implying a structure for a moral world in which interactions
between people and nature could be morally defined and circumscribed. The
specifically religious connotations of formal botanical and other gardens lie far
back in time and are largely beyond the scope of this book. Nevertheless, as
Sir Harold Bailey has demonstrated, the Zoroastrian and Avestan etymology
of both 'Pairidaeza' and 'garden' has a framework of meanings that exhibits
an historical continuity in the textual *meaning* of gardens that runs right
through ancient Iranian, Babylonian, Islamic, Central Asian, Mughal and European traditions.

Thus the process of botanical garden making was highly imitative even in
the colonial period. The pattern and influence of Leiden and Amsterdam, for
example, exercised an extraordinary organising power, at Paris, at the Cape,
at St Vincent, at Calcutta. Aside from the symbolism of redemption and re-
creation, the ruling agendas of the botanical garden continued to be medical
or therapeutic. Hence the underlying analogue of the garden operated within
established Hippocratic ways of defining the well-being or health of man.
From Theophrastus onwards this dictated an interest in climate and its influence on man and ultimately in the human impact on climate and environment.
The garden thus rigidly defined modes of perceiving, assessing and classifying
the world, globally and in terms of a Hippocratic agenda. The structure and
intention of the garden itself were critical to the ways of defining and interpreting human influence on the world and thus to measuring and conceptu-

28 Marshall Sahlins, *Islands of history*, Chicago, 1987, p. 72.

alising environmental risk. The garden itself emerged as an environmental text
and a metaphor of mind, and even literally as a text in the case of the first
Dutch colonial hortus, the *Hortus Indicus Malabaricus* of Hendrik van Reede
tot Drakenstein. However, there was a contradiction in all this: Medical practice in the tropics from the Renaissance onwards dictated the utilisation of
local and indigenous systems of non-European knowledge. This forced
changes in the boundaries of natural knowledge. These changes were arbitrated by the medical botanists who doubled as botanists and garden keepers
in defining and classifying new natural knowledge and, very often, in defining
and classifying people. Increasingly this process of definition took place in
climatic terms, as the easiest way of differentiating exotic cultures and the
landscapes in which they were found.

The garden and the island enabled newness to be dealt with within familiar
bounds but simultaneously allowed and stimulated an experiencing of the empirical in circumscribed terms. The garden organised the unfamiliar in terms
of species. The tropical island allowed the experiencing of unfamiliar processes
in a heightened sense, both because of the symbolic role which the island was
expected to perform and because of the fast rate of geomorphic change in the
tropics.

The landscapes of island and garden were metaphors of mind. Anxieties
about environmental change, climatic change and extinctions and even the fear
of famine, all of which helped to motivate early environmentalism, mirrored
anxiety about social form (especially where the fragile identity of the European
colonist was called into question) and motivated social reform. At the core of
environmental concern lay anxiety about society and its discontents. As we
shall see, there has historically been a very strong correlation between those
advocating environmental protection and those pursuing social reform. But
the conjunction is a very intimate one. In other words, concern about climatic
change, for example, is not simply fear of the effect of man on the environment. Far more the underlying fear is one related to the integrity and physical
survival of people themselves. Many eighteenth-century climatic theorists
were armed with a conviction that change of climate might cause a transformation or even degeneration in man himself. There was no guarantee, for
example, that white Europeans could, in the long term, survive the climate of
the tropics. The possibility of anthropogenically produced climate change was
thus a far more serious business in tropical colonies than might at first appear,
and thus well worth counteracting, even by reluctant capitalist states or companies. These fears were carried on in anxieties and discourses about species
extinctions even before the end of the eighteenth century. The underlying
fear always consisted in the possibility of the disappearance of man himself.
Moreover, as Europeans were deprived of the security of biblical chronology,
the whole potency of man and his capacity for primacy and control might

mentally be lost. Thus from the late eighteenth century until at least as late as 1870, we find that colonial 'ecologists' experienced a measurable and real crisis (in terms of the speed of ecological change) that mirrored an equally real crisis of belief and chronology. Not surprisingly, then, we find environmental sensibilities being articulated particularly by those scientists with ardent or dissenting religious convictions.[29]

Thus it was that Calvinist Holland precipitated much of the process of redescribing and revaluing the natural world as a path to a knowledge of God or as the means to re-create a (social) paradise on earth. Then an erstwhile Jesuit, Pierre Poivre, carried on the logic of this idea, while after 1770 we find a whole procession of Scottish Protestant doctors, missionaries and travellers preaching an environmental gospel. As a result, while one might have expected a growing empiricism to subdue that part of environmental concern which drew on overt notions of moral economy, the reverse seems to have been true.

Colonial states increasingly found conservationism to their taste and economic advantage, particularly in ensuring sustainable timber and water supplies and in using the structures of forest protection to control their unruly marginal subjects. Despite this, the apocalytic environmental discourses of the colonial scientists frequently articulated a vision and a message of a far less cynical kind, and, indeed, one that resonates with us today. In a threatened garden, it appeared, an empirically and experimentally derived awareness of environmental risk could be transformed into a veritable tree of knowledge. Far from the allegorical significance of the Garden of Eden's having died away, the colonial environmentalists felt a steadily growing danger in which, they argued, the whole earth might be threatened by deforestation, famine, extinctions and climatic change. Re-created or not, the human race appeared to face expulsion from the garden altogether!

29 For some of the recent literature on imperialism and science, see David Mackay, *In the wake of Cook: Exploration, science and empire 1780–81*, London, 1985; Nathan Reingold and Marc Rothenberg, eds., *Scientific colonialism: A cross-cultural comparison*, Washington, 1987; Patrick Petitjean et al., eds., *Science and empires: Historical studies about scientific development and European expansion*; Deepak Kumar, ed., *Science and empire; Essays in Indian context 1700–1947*, Delhi, 1991; Satpal Sangwan, *Science, technology and colonisation; An Indian experience, 1757–1857*, Delhi, 1991. For a recent summary of the state of the field, see the critique of Lewis Pyenson's work by Michael Worboys and Paolo Palladino, *Isis*, 84 (1993), 91–102. While useful, none of these works are fully cognisant of the highly innovative nature of science at the colonial periphery, the extent of indigenous influence on colonial science or the colonial impact on the history of environmentalism.

1

Edens, islands and early empires

It seems so natural to man to cross the limits of space with his imagination
and to sense a something beyond the horizon where the sea meets the
sky, that even in an age when the earth was still regarded as a flat disc
or one which was only slightly concave at the surface, people could be
led to believe that beyond the cordon formed by the Homeric ocean there
was another dwelling for mankind, another *oecumene*, just like the *Loka-
loka* of Indian myth, a ring of mountains which is supposed to lie beyond
the seventh sea.

> Alexander von Humboldt, *Personal narrative of travels to the equi-
> noctial regions of the New Continent*, trans. H. M. Williams,
> vol. 1, London, 1819, p. 3.

Environment degradation and conservationist responses before
the age of European colonial expansion

It is very probable that *Homo sapiens*, even in the first millennium of his and
her distinctive emergence as a separate species tens of thousands of years ago,
was capable of promoting very rapid and extensive transformations in the
natural environment. However, the diffusion of any widely accepted and self-
conscious awareness of the potential of the human as a destructive agent of
change in the natural world developed much later in human history, enabled
particularly by the advent of the written word. Nevertheless, deliberate interventions designed to impede or control the deleterious effects of deforestation,
soil erosion or other widespread environmental disruption have been recorded
from very early times. So-called conservation practices cannot, in fact, be
distinguished clearly from the complex web of economic, religious and cultural
arrangements evolved by a multitude of societies to safeguard and sustain their
access to resources. This is particularly the case when one comes to consider
the relationship between 'hunter-gatherer' peoples and their environments all
over the world. Indeed, it may well be futile to try to identify the earliest
instances of consciously conservationist interventions in environmental change.
Instead the approach I have adopted here has been to assume that it is far
more useful to identify the emergence of integrated and relatively 'objective'
thinking about the natural environment, focussing quite intentionally on the
history of the construction of 'western' discourses and policies affecting re-

source use and the idea of conservation. This chapter aims, then, to set out the complex and often elusive antecedents of some of the western environmental attitudes and conservationist policies which have emerged in the last three centuries, both in the context of colonial science and in a broader social setting. Quite intentionally I have tended to focus on the history of responses to deforestation and its consequences.

In the early phases of human evolution, particularly in Africa, induced fires were a major agent of change. Man is known to have used fire since Paleolithic times, so that the distribution of forest cover, especially in subtropical and savannah areas, has been closely associated with his activities. For example, at the well-known Kalambo Falls archaeological site on the Tanzania–Zambia border there is evidence of the use of fire as long ago as 60,000 years, while in Southern Tasmania recent researches have revealed the extensive use of fire to clear forests between 30,000 and 40,000 years ago. As Carl Sauer, one of the great proponents of the role of fire in environmental change, has put it in *Agricultural origins and dispersals* (Cambridge, Mass.): 'Through all the ages the use of fire has perhaps been the most important skill to which man has applied his mind. Fire gave to man, a diurnal creature, security by night from other predators . . . the fireside was the beginning of social living, the place of communication and reflection' (p. 10).

Deforestation was not the only result of such an early humanisation of the landscape. The evolution of extensive pastoral economies radically affected the nature of the world's grasslands and possibly contributed to their early deterioration. Eventually, as arable agriculture made an appearance, the potential for change was further enhanced. Moreover, as we now know, all these changes began to affect the constitution of the atmosphere itself. It was to take a long time, of course, before an appreciation of this last more subtle and imponderable dynamic became socially significant.

The influence of man in tropical forest and rainforest zones has, until comparatively recently, been much more limited than in drier regions. However, outside the wet tropical zones deliberate removal of forest has been one of the longest-continued and most significant ways in which man has modified his environment, whether achieved by fire or by deliberate cutting. Pollen analysis shows that temperate forests began to be removed in Mesolithic and Neolithic times and at an accelerating rate thereafter. Sometimes the removal took place to allow agriculture; at other times, to provide fuel for domestic use, charcoal or wood for construction. Large-scale commercial timber cutting and transport started at least 4,600 years ago with the export of cedars by the Phoenicians and South Indians both to the pharoahs and to Mesopotamia. Urban growth played a major part in this. The first substantial growth of towns and cities started to make a major impact on the cedar forests of the Middle East and the Fertile Crescent by about 7000 B.C. with the emergence of such cultures

as those at Catal Huyuk, Jarmo and Alosh. During periods of climatic warming
after 7000 B.C., a comparatively rich and well-watered vegetal cover may have
developed in parts of the region where Syria, Jordan and Lebanon now meet
as well as in the valleys of the Tigris, Euphrates, Indus and Ganges. Some
writers have regarded specific settlement sites at this period as the archetypal
sources of subsequent Garden of Eden myths, backing up their claims with
detailed and imaginative textual references. Such claims, it should be said,
need to be treated with some caution.¹ Nevertheless, it is quite possible that
the collective memory of the relatively lush landscapes of the fifth to fourth
millennia B.C., later degraded by natural desiccation (or by the effects of deforestation and soil erosion promoted by early urban societies), may have made
their way into literature and tradition in this period.

There is some evidence that deforestation caused the collapse of communities in the Southern Levant as early as 6000 B.C. This collapse may well
have been related not to climatic change but to the effect of human activities
on the environment. In particular, trees were used as fuel for the production
of lime plaster as a building material. Environmental damage was also exacerbated by herds of goats eating seedlings, saplings and shrubs, thereby preventing regrowth and exposing steep hillsides to rapid soil erosion.² In Central
America, by contrast, it was the advent of maize cultivation that had a decisive
effect. Devastating episodes of soil erosion can be dated at around 1500 B.C.,
with further episodes at about A.D. 300 and 1000. Indeed, soil erosion has to
be taken seriously as both a consequence of the growth and a cause of the
collapse of city states and the shifting of power from one political centre to
another in Mesoamerica in Pre-Hispanic times.³

It is difficult to assess the extent to which any distinctive conservationist
or other systematic response developed as a result of major erosion events.
However, as early as the fourth millennium B.C., a written literature had
developed in the Middle East whose first proponents were fully aware both
of the formidable destructive power of the early agrarian and hydraulic empires and of the likely consequences of uncontrolled deforestation. The writer
of the great Epic of Gilgamesh was well aware that drought might follow
deforestation.⁴ According to the epic, Enlil, the chief Sumerian deity, ap-

1 For example, see C. O'Brien and B. O'Brien, *The genius of the few: The story of those who
  founded the Garden in Eden*, Wellingborough, 1985.
2 G. Rollefson and I. Kohler, 'Prehistoric people ruined their environment', *New Scientist*, 125
  (24 Feb. 1990), 29.
3 S. E. Metcalfe, 'Late Miocene human impact on lake basins in Central America', *Geoarchaeology*, 4:2 (1989), 119–41; F. A. Street-Perrott, 'Anthropogenic soil erosion around Lake Putzcuaro, Michoacan, Mexico, during the pre-classic and later post-classic Hispanic periods',
  American Antiquity, 54:4 (1989), 759–65.
4 E. Speiser, 'Akkadian myths and epics: The epic of Gilgamesh', in J. Pritchard, ed., *Ancient
  Near Eastern texts*, vol. 3, Princeton, N.J., 1955, p. 4.

pointed the god Humbaba to 'safeguard the cedar forest' and to protect the interests of nature, and hence of the gods, against the needs of civilization.[5] By the latter part of the third millennium B.C., the depredations of the Southern Mesopotamian city states had made deep inroads into the cedar and oak forests of the mountains to the west of the great river valleys. The cedar wood was easily floated down to urban centres nearer the Persian Gulf. So too, by the end of the third millennium, the growing demand for timber for building construction and shipbuilding meant that hardwoods were being imported from as far afield as Oman and the west coast of India.[6] Surviving records indicate that by the third dynasty of Ur the Sumerian economies were heavily dependent on imported timber.[7] During the early part of the second millennium B.C., a scarcity of large timber in the Euphrates catchment area began to give rise to the introduction of more deliberate measures to protect the remaining forests. The protective measures introduced in the kingdom of Mari at this period are an example of the increasing state interest that had developed in these matters.[8] The reasons for this increased interest in forest protection appear to be linked not only with factors of internal demand but also with the political obstacles that sometimes stood in the way of the long-standing patterns in the trade in valuable hardwood timber between Meluhha (Malabar) in Western India and the Euphrates valley. The complete cessation of this trade during the reign of Hammurabi gave rise to particularly severe forest-conservation measures in Babylonia. Moreover, it is likely that the Mesopotamian states began to rely more on timber from the Mediterranean after the beginning of the second millennium.[9]

The progressive deforestation of Mesopotamia and other parts of the Middle East was closely correlated with the steadily growing capacity of states to consume timber both for construction and for military purposes, in particular for naval shipbuilding. The impact of wars and the ambitions of state builders led in turn to attempts to protect forests, although rarely, it seems, with any clear link being made between deforestation and the steady sedimentation and ecological decline of the great river valleys. It should be noted, however, that

5 J. Hansmann, 'Gilgamesh, Humbaba and the land of the *Erin* trees', *Iraq*, 38 (1976), 23.
6 See P. Steinkeller, 'The foresters of Umma: Towards a definition of Ur III labor', quoted in F. Perlin *A forest journey: The role of wood in the development of civilization*, New York, 1989, p. 40. From this period, too, extensive copper-smelting activity in Oman brought about the destruction of the once widespread forest areas on that part of the Gulf coast. The Phoenicians completed the process.
7 See M. Lambert and J. Tourney, 'Les statues D, G, E et H de Gudea,' *Revue d'Assyriologie et d'Archéologie Orientale*, 47 (1953), 78–141, on the import of wood from Northern Arabia and India and the import of juniper, firs and sycamores from Syria.
8 G. Dossin, ed. and trans., *Correspondance de Iasmah-Addu*, Paris, 1952.
9 G. R. Driver, *Letters of the first Babylonian dynasty*, London, 1924, p. 33; F. Thureau-Dangin, 'le correspondance de Hammurapie avec Samas-Hasir', quoted in Perlin, *Forest journey*, p. 39.

existing knowledge of Mesopotamian archaeological data does not permit very elaborate conclusions to be drawn about the state of environmental knowledge during the period. Moreover, the available sources are not comprehensive enough to allow one to theorise very realistically about the evolution of conservationist concepts at state level. Our access to data on classical Greece, Rome, China and Mauryan India is, however, somewhat less restricted.[10]

In Greece in the first millennium B.C., the association among military activity, state building and deforestation is more evident than in the Euphrates valley. During the Peloponnesian War (431–421 B.C.,) for example, large areas of countryside were transformed into a relatively barren waste, and there are indications that much-increased soil erosion and flooding resulted.[11] These changes made a considerable impression on contemporary observers and particularly on Theophrastus of Erasia, Aristotle's biographer and botanical gardener. Theophrastus was led by his observations of local forest changes to develop a theory which firmly linked deforestation to the decline in rainfall which he believed was taking place in Greece. The climate of Crete, too, he thought, was changing for similar reasons.[12] There is very little evidence, however, that Theophrastus's remarkable theoretical innovation stimulated any serious government restrictions on forest cutting. Indeed, it was only with the Renaissance and the republication of his *Historia Plantarum* in 1483 that this early environmental theorist became influential. At the time that Theophrastus flourished, the forests around Rome were still, in comparison with those of Greece, relatively undisturbed. Even near Rome, Theophrastus records, there were woods of bay, myrtle and beech, while the hill country produced fir and silver fir. Throughout Southern Europe, he wrote, it was only in Italy that timber could still easily be obtained for shipbuilding.[13] This situation did not last long. By the reign of Claudius, the port of Ostia, the main outlet for Rome, had silted up and forced a move by merchants to Civitavecchia. Such developments provoked Pliny and Vitruvius to react in much the same way as Theophrastus had done and warn of the potentially serious consequences of deforestation. The process, they said, would cause

---

10 See R. Meiggs, *Trees and timber in the ancient mediterranean world*, Oxford, 1982, and Ellen Churchill Semple, *The geography of the Mediterranean region: Its relation to ancient history*, New York, 1931. There is an emerging body of research on the development of environmental philosophy and policy in classical China. See, above all, J. D. Hughes, 'Mencius' prescriptions for ancient Chinese environmental problems', *Environmental Review*, 13 (1989), 12–25.

11 Diodorus reports that the Spartans cut down all the trees in Attica during the wars. See also Thucydides, *Peloponnesian wars*, 2.54, quoted in Perlin, *Forest Journey*, p. 91.

12 Theophrastus, *De causis*, (14) 2–4, 5, quoted in Glacken, *Traces on the Rhodian shore*, p. 130n. See also Theophrastus, *De ventis*, in A. Loeb, ed., *Theophrastus' Enquiry into plants*, New York, 1916, p. 379, on the changing climate of Crete.

13 Theophrastus, *Enquiry into plants*, 4.5.5 and 5.8.3.

'devastating torrents' and result in the carrying away of topsoil into rivers. The serious siltation of the River Tiber served to lend their arguments force. However, while such poets as Seneca and Virgil might sing the praises of the lush woodlands, which had almost disappeared by the time they wrote, neither the Roman republic nor the empire sought seriously to control deforestation. Timber sources from further afield, in the outer reaches of the empire, were too easily found. It can be argued, in fact, that the degradation of the land-scapes of Greece and Rome led instead to an increasing literary tendency to speculate about the merits of distant and as yet forested Edens. This was especially so in the case of Greek writers. The imagery of the idyllic and lush conditions of the Isles of the Hesperides in the 'western ocean' developed at a time when some of the Greek islands were still much better forested than the mainland.[14] It was at this period, too, that it became fashionable to idealise much more distant, or even mythical, landscapes, above all those which were imaginatively located in India and the Ganges valley. After the completion of the Alexandrine expeditions, this tendency became even more prominent, as Greek philosophers began to consider the significance of the Oriental ante-cedents of their own systems of thought. The doxographies of Theophrastus played an important initiating part in this, reinforcing the notion of complex, 'civilized' eastern origins and connections with Greek philosophy. These early connections between India and classical western thought are highly germane to the theme of this book. The symbolic significance of India, and of the Ganges valley in particular, as the location of an earthy Paradise found a prominent place in such early medieval texts as the *Alexander Romance*, the *Physiologos* and the *Gesta Romanorum*.[15] These notions resurfaced more fully

14 The great tracts of forest in Germany and Russia were still little known to Greek and Roman writers at this time and also became the subject of a literature of the 'other'; see Simon Schama, 'Primaeval forests and the cult of nature' (manuscript notes of a lecture).

15 Andrea Bianchi, for example, places the terrestrial paradise at 'Kanya kumari' in Southern India.

Most of the early medieval texts drew, in turn, from a Jewish Babylonian text known as *Iter ad paradisum*, which first appeared in about A.D. 500; see Julius Zacher, ed., *Alexandri magni iter ad paradisum*, Königsberg, 1859, pp. 11–32. The *Iter* discusses the links between Indian asceticism and European notions of Paradise. On the connections between Indian myth and early formulations of Paradise (especially the place of the Ganges as the river in the Garden of Eden), see S. Darian, *The Ganges in myth and history*, Honolulu, 1978. Early rabbinical writers, such as Philo and Josephus, both familiar with Megasthenes, show a respect for Indian philosophy. Josephus first established the European tradition that of the four rivers of Paradise, the Phison was the Ganges. Linschoten, at the end of the sixteenth century, quotes Bengalis as believing that the Ganges 'came from Paradise' and was a 'place of pleasant earth, still water and fragrant earth', according to Indian cosmology: *The voyage of Johann Huygen van Linschoten*, ed. and trans. A. C. Burrell and P. A. Tiele, 2 vols., London, 1885, p. 92. F. Bernier in 1671 in *The paradise of Hindostan* describes Kashmiri poets as claiming a Himalayan source for the four rivers of Paradise. Desideri fifty years later dismissed this as a

in the Renaissance and formed the basis for the future development of Orientalist traits in western thought.[16] They then began to provide the symbolic structure for a conceptualisation of nature, and change within it, that had the potentiality to be far more universal in symbolic application and explanatory power than the particularist critiques of the human impact on the environment found in Theophrastus or Pliny. As we shall see, the idea of the botanical garden as a symbolic location for the re-creation of Paradise became central to the changing visions of nature that would later accompany the flowering of the Renaissance. The structuring of natural knowledge implicit in the systemics of the botanical garden encouraged an analytical and organising approach to the whole of observed creation. Theophrastus, as both botanist and natural philosopher, was an early practitioner of this discipline.

The notion of a physical and mental assemblage of human, botanical and medical knowledge in one garden site probably had its origins in classical knowledge of the East. The connection became much more explicit as the Arab kingdoms reached out to the Indus. In the reign of Khalif al-Mansur (754–75), the *Charaka Samhita* and the *Susruta Hamhita*, major medico-

---

Buddhist belief. It was left to Sir William Jones and H. H. Wilson to attempt to complete the gradual reconstruction of a cosmology which had been known to the West in Hellenic times in fragmentary form. Western and eastern notions of Paradise thus appear to have an essential unity. Christian concepts of Paradise were probably informed by the imagery of Indian aesthetics but also by the descriptions of Paradise that pervade Indian mythology. In the earliest relevant text, the *Arthava-Veda* (in which four rivers of Paradise are described), the concept of a *Svarga-Loka* (a heavenly place) is introduced. This was sometimes located on Mount Meru in Northern India. Associated with the notion of a heavenly place was the transition from *Kal Yuga* to *Sat Yuga*, the transition to the latter equating to a transition to a Golden Age. This concept was one that Alexander von Humboldt was particularly aware of. For a fuller discussion of some of these issues, see J. Drew, *India and the Romantic imagination*, Oxford, 1987, and J. S. Duncan, *The city as text: The politics of landscape interpretation in a Kandyan kingdom*, Cambridge, 1990.

16 Ancient knowledge and ideas about India, handed down particularly by Solinus, Orosius and Isidor of Seville, were also included in the encyclopaedic works of the Middle Ages, especially those of Honorius Augustodunensis (who flourished in the twelfth century) and Vincent of Beauvais (thirteenth century). The vital connections between the early Search for Eden and the origins of the later and more structured 'Orientalism' of the late-eighteenth-century Romantic savants are signally ignored by Edward Said in his *Orientalism* (Harmondsworth, 1985). In this work, Said has argued for a post-Enlightenment coherence of ideas about the 'Orient' produced through the colonial experience. In this he falls victim to overgeneralisation, for he almost entirely ignores the highly complex and divergent character of 'Oriental' discourses in the history of ideas before the eighteenth century. The Edenic search does not, either, fit neatly into Said's construction of Orientalism. This is because it was not, of course, confined geographically to the Middle East, India and the Orient, was not culture-specific and was not principally a phenomenon confined to a colonial context. Indeed, the power relations implied in Said's perception of Orientalism do not assist us in explaining the early cultural roots of the Edenic search, critical as it was to the early formation of Oriental perceptions.

botanical works in Sanskrit, were translated into Arabic. Sanskritic botanical knowledge thus entered into the highly innovative and exploratory tradition of Arab botany. There were two major consequences of this mixing of cultural traditions. First, the ancient Persian and Zoroastrian 'Pairidaeza' or 'garōδa-mān', the garden that recreated a religious paradise in an arid physical (or possibly mental) landscape, often became transmuted into more rigorously botanical or experimental concepts.[17] Secondly, systems of Indic botanical knowledge became integrated into the greatest Arabic medical texts, above all the *Kanun* of Avicenna, which also drew from the Greek of Galen.[18] Between 1148 and 1187 this work was translated (in Sicily) into Latin and entered the western tradition. A knowledge of Avicenna was then gradually diffused from Sicily into Northern Italy, where it eventually became an integral part of the innovative Renaissance development of medicine and botanical gardens in the territories of Venice.

There were also more direct connections between the founding of botanical gardens by the Venetians and the older horticultural traditions and skills of the Arabs. The botanical gardens at Cairo were, by the eleventh century, renowned for their complexity and were, according to the poet Nasir-i-Khusrau, the 'most beautiful imaginable'. Furthermore, the eleventh century also saw the prominent development of elaborate tree-planting schemes by Egyptian rulers. These were in response to the gradual disappearance of traditional sources of timber in Syria, Crete, Sicily and other parts of North Africa. By the thirteenth century the Egyptian state was forced increasingly to rely on teak from India and timber traded expensively from the Venetian empire, in the face, it might be noted, of frequent papal prohibitions.

Both in terms of botanical science and in terms of the emerging dynamics and political economy of timber supply for the first modern European colonial state, the environmental histories of the Arab and Venetian colonial worlds were inextricably intertwined. However, it is in the story of the development of Venetian attitudes to nature and to resources that we can find the first clues to the vital connections that would develop between the emergent European colonial empires and the seeds of a global environmental sensibility. At another, more subtle, even subconscious, level lay an old and powerful motivation. This motivation one may conveniently term the 'search for Eden', a phenomenon whose roots lay in a complex mixture of European, Arabic and Indian philosophical traditions. With the Renaissance and the growth of European maritime expansion, this search was sharpened by the pursuit of gold

---

17 For the etymology and associations of *garōδamān* (the Ancient Iranian/Avestan root of Lat. *hortus*, Old Irish *lub-gort*, Persian/Hindi/Urdu *ghar*, Fr. *jardin* and Eng. *garden*), see Bailey, *Zoroastrian problems in the ninth-century books*, p. 113; and Bailey, *A commentary on the 'Bundahisin'*, forthcoming.

18 I. H. Burkill, *Chapters in the history of Indian botany*, Calcutta, 1965, p. 3.

and profits, the settlement of distant island colonies, the garnering of botanical knowledge and, increasingly, the lure of India and China and their riches. At this point in the argument it is worth stepping back a little to consider the intellectual context of the beginnings of European colonial expansion.

Early colonial expansion and the growing significance of island environments in the European mind, 1400–1660

The great expansion of European maritime travel and settlement which took place after about 1400 stimulated the emergence of a new and much more complex way of viewing the relationship between man and nature. This involved at least two main kinds of change. First, a sophisticated awareness developed of the growing capacity of man to radically alter his physical surroundings. Secondly, the experience of encountering new lands, peoples, animals and plants helped to promote the attachment of a new kind of social significance to nature, reflected especially in the philosophies underlying the transfer to, and development of the Middle Eastern idea of the botanical garden in, Europe and in the emergence of the tropical and oceanic island as an important new social metaphor and image of nature on its own account.

During long maritime voyages and particularly in the course of early colonial settlement, the sheer factor of distance meant that perceptions of nature and perceptions of the impact of European visitors on the environment and on the indigenous inhabitants of colonised territories evolved a significant new dualism. The environmental attitudes of Europeans at the temperate metropoles and those settled at the periphery of expansion underwent considerable and divergent transition. While the colonial experience gave rise to a fundamental shift in conceptions of nature, domestic economic and social transitions at the metropole exercised their own influence, which in turn affected the contemporary perceptions of travellers. Overall, however, the circumstances of colonial expansion increasingly exerted the more potent influence on European perceptions of the human relationship with the environment. While there are obvious risks in trying to locate, in chronological order, the kinds of changes in the perception of nature which took place in the context of colonial expansion, some categorisations do seem necessary. Essentially, in conceptualising the relation between man and nature, three kinds of ideas seem to have predominated in the West since classical times: the idea of a designed earth, the preoccupation with those environmental influences which affected the development of man and society and, lastly, the idea of man as a geographical agent.

The first of these ideas owes much to mythology, theology and philosophy; the second, to pharmaceutical lore; and the third, to the plans, activities and skills of everyday life, such as cultivation, carpentry and timber cutting. The first two ideas were expressed frequently in classical antiquity, the third less often, although it was implicit in many discussions which recognised the fact that, through their arts, science and techniques, people had changed the physical environment about them. In the first idea it is assumed that the earth is designed for people alone, as the highest beings in creation, or for the hierarchy of life, with man at the apex. This conception presupposes the earth or certain parts of it to be a fit environment not only for life but for high civilisation. The second idea originates in medical theory; in essence, conclusions were drawn by comparing various environmental factors, such as atmospheric conditions (especially the temperature, the waters and the geographical situation), with the different individuals and people characteristic of those environments and their individual and cultural characteristics. These were not so much theories of climatic influence as theories of airs, waters and places in the sense in which these are used in the Hippocratic corpus. Although environmental ideas arose independent of the argument of divine design, they have been used frequently as a part of the design argument, in the sense that all life was seen as adapting itself to purposefully created harmonious conditions. The third idea was less well formulated in antiquity than were the other two, and in fact its full implications were not realised, according to the argument of this book, until professional natural historians and scientists began to appreciate the full impact of western economic penetration on colonial and largely tropical environments. Like the environmental theory, it could be accommodated in a design argument, for man, through his arts and inventions, was seen as a partner of God, improving and cultivating an earth created for him.

The geographical and economic circumstances of European mercantile and colonial expansion over the period 1400–1900 brought about a much closer connection, and even a coalescence, between these second and third schools of thought: A Hippocratically based interest in environmental influences upon man became fused with the widening perception of man's ability to transform or degrade his environment.[19] When set in the context of two other circumstances – the demonstrable ecological impact of European colonial activity and the growing intellectual concern with the natural world – it can be seen that very specific kinds of responses to artificially caused environmental change might have been expected at the colonial periphery, especially when semi-arid

---

19 Glacken, from whom I have drawn these categorisations, did not regard the third of these schools as having been significant before the publication of *Man and Nature* by G. P. Marsh in 1864. This is particularly puzzling in view of his extensive allusions to the theories of Theophrastus, much quoted during and after the Renaissance, which explicitly linked the process of deforestation to rainfall change. As indicated later, all the essentials of Marsh's ideas had been fully anticipated.

and tropical environments were subjected to agrarian and industrial activities
that had evolved in more ecologically resilient temperate lands.

The substantial eastward movement of populations in Europe which took
place after about A.D. 900 was by the twelfth century closely associated with
forest clearance. By that time an awareness of the extent of the clearance which
had taken place, particularly in Germany, was already leading to notions of
environmental control. Scattered and localised regulations against deforestation began as early as the twelfth century and grew more numerous until, by
the end of the Middle Ages, forest protection was the rule and permission to
clear a special exception.[20] In Henry VII's sharp restatement of King Ru-
dolph's Forest Ordinance of 1289, which specifically concerned the protection
of the Nürnberg Royal Forest, it was said that 'harm had come to him and
the city of the kingdom in the destruction of the forest of the kingdom' and
in its transformation into cultivated land. In this document the transformation
of forest into cultivated land is regarded as a calamity.[21] During the fourteenth
century, both Henry VII and Albert I ordered various 'formerly forested lands'
which had been converted to agriculture to be returned to forest. An order
of 1304, for example, affected the Hagenauer Forest and the Frankenweide
near Annweiler, while others proclaimed in 1309 and 1310 affected the Nürnberg Royal Forest.[22] The 'Nürnberg Ordinance' required the restoration to
forest of lands on both sides of the Pegnitz River which had in the preceding
fifty years been cleared and transformed into cultivated fields. In these regulations, ordering the return of lands to woods, a transition from purely negative prohibitions to positive measures of forest protection took place. Much
later, French and British colonial governments were able to draw upon the
skills and practices that had developed as a part of this early transition in
Germany.

These early controls were limited in conceptual scope. They were essentially
confined to anxieties about the shortage of timber for fuel and construction,
and ideas about soil conservation were rarely involved. Indeed, forest clearance
in Europe before the eighteenth century did not often result in rapid changes
in soil conditions or in run-off. Thus the impact of forest clearance as cultivated area expanded was far less frequently remarked upon in the Europe of
the Middle Ages than it had been in classical Greece, where theories connecting changes in precipitation with deforestation had become well established, particularly in the writings of Theophrastus and Pliny. The relative
aridity and fragility of the landscapes of Greece may help to account for this.[23]

20 A. Schwappach, *Handbuch der Forst- und Jagdgeschichte Deutschlands*, Berlin, 1886, p. 154.
21 E. Mummenhoff, *Altnürnberg*, Bamberg, 1890, pp. 55–7.
22 J. D. Schoepflin, *Alsatia diplomatica*, Mannheim, 1775, vol. 2, p. 500.
23 Theophrastus, *De causis*, (14) 2–4, 5, in Glacken, *Traces on the Rhodian shore*, p. 130n. Also

This generalisation breaks down in one important way in the case of Italy. Here the excessive demands imposed by the Venetian empire in Northern Italy, as well as in several regions of the Mediterranean littoral, provoked an exceptional and early response to environmental stress. As we have seen, the trade in timber with the Muslim world had developed rapidly during the early Middle Ages as the forests of the Middle East and Africa became depleted. The military and strategic demands of the empire implied a need for a continuous supply of wood for ship and barge building, most of it carried out at the Arsenale in Venice itself. Among the first signs of the progressive deforestation of the Venetian hinterland was the movement of the barge-building industry inland from Venice. This was well under way by the second quarter of the fifteenth century. During the 1450s, it appears, the high rate of deforestation became recognised as a danger to the Venice lagoon, since it increased the amount of silt brought down by the rivers. To prevent the filling up of the lagoons, the Council of Ten ordered the replanting of all cut-over woods at the edges of flowing streams.[24] Subsequent to this, between 1470 and 1492, a definite policy designed to conserve and increase the supply of oak from state woodlands was formulated. Although innovative, these measures failed almost entirely to conserve or replenish the timber supply or to curb the ruinous destruction of the oak woods, which continued unabated until the mid sixteenth century. The failure contributed in no small measure to the decline of Venice and to its trading and military displacement by maritime powers with easier access to relatively unworked forests. The Venetian records show that local peasant opposition to state conservation, and even active sabotage and incendiarism, also contributed to the decline of the city state.[25]

After the mid sixteenth century, Venice found that it had increasingly to draw timber supplies from Istria, Dalmatia and other parts of the Adriatic

Theophrastus, *De ventis*, in *Enquiry into plants*, p. 379, on the changing climate of Crete, attributed to no specific cause; and Pliny, *Natural history*, XVII, quoted in Glacken, *Traces*, p. 130. Glacken notes that Albert the Great was also aware of thinking that deforestation might cause climatic change, especially warming. Theophrastus states that in Philippi the clearing of woodland had opened up land, exposing it to the sun and bringing about a warmer climate. Even at the time of Theophrastus, the links between the botanical garden as an institution and environmental thinking were close: Theophrastus acted as the curator of Aristotle's botanical garden; see Hughes, 'Theophrastus as ecologist', and H. Rubner, 'Greek thought and forest science', *Environmental Review*, 4 (1985), 277–96. See also J. Bilsky, *Historical ecology: Essays on environment and social change*, New York, 1980.

24 Venice State Archives: Arsenale, basta 8, ft/9/10. For a wider discussion of these matters, see F. C. Lane, *Venetian ships, shipbuilders and the Renaissance*, Baltimore, 1934.

25 The phenomenon of peasant opposition to imperial forest policy was one that came to be repeated over and over again in the context of much later colonial conservation policy, especially in India and Africa. See Grove, 'Colonial conservation, ecological hegemony and popular resistance'.

coast. These new demands imposed considerable penalties on local economies. In the case of Crete, for example, the Venetian colonial government felt compelled to ban vineyard development during the late sixteenth century.[26] In spite of such measures, by about 1600 a general famine of timber was being experienced throughout the Mediterranean. This assisted the process by which the Dutch and the British were able to move into the Western European and Mediterranean carrying trade. Moreover, Venice was impeded, through the sheer cost of shipbuilding in Italy, from competing for trade and colonies further afield in the tropics.[27]

The economically damaging experience of deforestation and subsequent soil erosion undergone by the Venetian state might conceivably have served as an influential precursor to the later shape of French and British resource policy. The early seventeenth century saw the compilation of several texts published in Italy which surveyed the whole field of deforestation, fire damage to forests and grasslands, and the dangers of soil erosion. The work of Giuseppe Paulini (a major landowner in the Belluo region as well as an intellectual) is particularly noteworthy in this context. Paulini was able to make a pioneering contribution to the emergence of a natural science of geomorphology of a kind that was paralleled at the time only by the geological speculations of Leonardo da Vinci.[28] However, his work, published in 1606, was ignored even by officials of the Venetian government, and there is no evidence that either the French or the British, when they came to be faced with comparable soil-erosion problems in the tropics in the early eighteenth century, were able to benefit from a knowledge of the writings of Paulini. Indeed, it seems that the potentially highly relevant conservation experience of imperial Venice did not diffuse into the limited pool of British environmental knowledge until as late as 1851, when Venetian forest-conservancy regulations were used as a precedent by Indian colonial conservation propagandists.[29] This marked slowness in the dif-

---

26 West Crete was the sole source of supply in Europe for cypress used in furniture, a trade mentioned by Buonditmorti, who visited Crete in 1415. In 1414 the Venetian Senate, under the impression that cypress was being felled for export faster than it was growing, prohibited its export on pain of confiscation of the logs plus a fee equal to their value: Venice State Archives: Delib. Histe, 50.c.131. A. T. Grove and O. Rackham, *Crete: An ecological history*, report to the EEC (DG12), Cambridge, 1990.

27 Semple, *The geography of the Mediterranean region*, chap. 6.

28 G. Paulini, *Un codice veneziano del 1600 per le acque e le foreste*, Rome, 1934.

29 Hugh Cleghorn, the most vigorous proponent of conservation under the East India Company, drew extensively on Italian precedents when compiling his influential report to the British Association for the Advancement of Science, published in 1852 (discussed in Chapter 8). Of the example of Venice he notes: 'As far back as 1475 the subject attracted the attention of the famous Venetian Council of Ten, by which a law was passed on the 7th of January of that year, regulating in great detail the clearance of the forests . . . the mountain forests especially were protected by judicious regulations, which were renewed from time to time down to the

fusion of environmental knowledge can probably be attributed to the lack of any substantial degree of institutional linkage between 'scientists' before the eighteenth century. This meant, for example, that maritime expansion by Europeans into the tropical Atlantic region towards the end of the sixteenth century quickly resulted in forest clearance and soil erosion far more severe than had been the case in the Venetian territories. The move into the Atlantic, and then along the West African coast, involved colonisation of a new kind, facilitated by the development of more sophisticated sailing and navigational techniques. At the Azores, the Canary Islands and Madeira, the early Spanish, French and Portuguese colonists found islands populated by indigenous peoples living under much harsher climatic conditions than prevailed in maritime Western Europe. Large-scale woodland clearance in Spain and Portugal had taken place very much earlier; as a result, early European visitors to the 'Fortunate Isles' were at first struck by the completeness of the forest cover, calling one of them 'Madeira' (the 'wooded isle'). Such terms quickly became inappropriate as both forests and indigenous people were decimated.

The consequences of deforestation on the Canary Islands and Madeira were radical. Most perennial streams dried up, so that the Spanish were compelled to utilise irrigation channels, or *levadas*, of the kind introduced to Iberia from the Middle East by the Moors and their Genoese engineers.[30] Very soon, therefore, the early experience of island colonisation became closely associated with the problem of providing water. Particularly after the introduction of the sugar industry into the Canary Islands and the building of the first sugar mill in 1484 by Pedro de Vera, the archipelago's forests disappeared before the onslaught of a fully developed sugar-plantation economy responding to emerging urban markets for sugar in Europe.[31] On Gran Canaria, which had been heavily forested, an Englishman noted that 'wood is the thing most wanted'.[32] On Tenerife the government had by 1500 started to issue regulations specifically designed to protect the forests from lumbermen.[33] Such measures were,

very year of the extinction of the old Republic. Tuscany and the Pontifical governments were equally provident.' This interest in Italian historical precedent may have originated with Alexander von Humboldt, whose works Cleghorn frequently consulted.

30 Bryans, *Madeira*, p. 30. Concerning the earlier history of irrigation in Europe and its southern peripheries, particularly as regards Islamic influences, see A. M. Watson, *Agricultural innovation in the early Islamic world*, Cambridge, 1983, esp. on the Arabic/Persian influence. Similar irrigation systems occur as far north as the Valais canton of Switzerland, so that the island systems can be seen as part of a much wider response to deforestation and seasonal drought.

31 F. Fernández-Arnesto, *The Canary Islands after the conquest: The making of a colonial society in the early sixteenth century*, Oxford, 1982, p. 70; J. Abreu de Galindo, *Historia de conquista de las siete islas de Canaria*, Santa Cruz de Tenerife, 1977, p. 239.

32 R. Hakluyt, *The principal navigations, voyages and discoveries of the English nation . . .*, London, 1589, IV, pp. 25–6.

33 J. J. Parsons, 'Human influences on the pine and laurel forests of the Canary Islands', *Geographical Review*, 71 (1981), 260–4.

however, largely unsuccessful, so that the use of *levadas* had to be resorted to
in order that sugar production might remain feasible.[34] A lesson had been
learnt, if too late. Deforestation caused major water-supply problems in non-
temperate climates, and it is clear that, in the minds of contemporaries, the
problems of colonial settlement had become intertwined with difficulties in
the provision of adequate water both for settlers and for shipping. The experience of long-distance maritime travel, especially as journeys became much
more extended in the course of forays to the Atlantic islands, had made water
supply a critical strategic problem. Not only was the water supply on long
voyages problematic, but the adjoining continental coast of North-West Africa
offered little in the way of watering possibilities, quite apart from the dangers
that might be involved in encountering hostile coastal peoples. Long sea journeys were physically arduous. When water was short or bad, shipboard disease
became even more prominent than it had been in Mediterranean waters, and
it was in this situation that the medical profession became significant.

Surgeons had long been carried on European fighting ships to tend to the
wounded in battle. During the fifteenth century, however, the need to deal
with tropical diseases widened the role of the surgeon, so that he became
indispensable and of increasingly high status in the commercial world. The
settlement of the Canaries and Madeira, the removal of their forests and indigenous peoples, and the substitution of plantation economies meant that
some of the physical consequences of extra-European colonisation were already
familiar by 1492. In fact, a knowledge of these consequences is occasionally
apparent in statements made by Columbus and in some of his reactions to
particular West Indian islands. It is less well known that on his second voyage,
if not the first, a surgeon or surgeons accompanied the expedition. The presence of the surgeon implied more than simply the presence of a medical
doctor; it also ensured that a relatively highly educated individual capable of
making accurate and informed observations had become an accepted part of
the ship's complement. As Jean Merrier has commented, 'We have no nautical
details of their crossing. We have an account written by Dr Chanca of Seville,
who was an excellent observer, a good botanist, an impartial recorder of disputes, but no sailor.'[35] The quality of the observations made aboard ships
which carried good surgeons was far better than on those without them or
than was often the case on major land expeditions. A second innovative element, already present when Columbus made his first landfall, involved his
preconceptions concerning the relationship between deforestation and rainfall
decline. According to his son Ferdinand, Columbus knew 'from experience'
that the removal of forests that had once covered the Canaries, Madeira and

34 Bryans, *Madeira*, p. 30.
35 J. Merrier, *Christopher Columbus: The mariner and the man*, London, 1958, p. 192.

the Azores had severely reduced the incidence of mist and rain. He was thus led to believe that the afternoon rains of Jamaica and elsewhere in the West Indies were actually produced by the luxuriant forest of the islands and that the actions of European land clearers might directly affect rainfall.[36] Columbus thus provides us with the first documented post-classical instance in a colonial setting of a conscious connection being made between deforestation and a change in rainfall.[37]

As early as 1492 the process of colonisation had become associated with awareness of the potential vulnerability of the colonised territories to outside intervention. Furthermore, awareness of the innate vulnerability of parties of colonising Europeans played a critical part in the development of this apprehension, since at a basic level the destructive potential of man was seen to relate closely to the issue of whether or not Europeans could actually survive in the new territories they sought to control or colonise. In other words, the threat represented by human destructive capability to human survival in the tropics had become apparent in a way which had not been the case in temperate continental Europe, where the possibility of harmful climatic change was less apparent. Moreover, the traditional medical preoccupation with the quality of air and water ensured that climate conditions would attract attention and be monitored wherever medical expertise was carried, and that the medical profession in Europe would quickly become aware of any novel climatic features of newly colonised lands.

The problems of survival on small tropical islands, whether arid or less arid, in the West Indies, in the Atlantic, along the West African coast and on the route to India or in remote coastal settlements were comparable to the problems of survival aboard ship. Food and water and the preservation of health were problematic on both. The experience of travel in the tropics presented Europeans not only with hazardous environments but with landscapes that were as unfamiliar climatically as their peoples, plants, animals, soils and landforms. This unfamiliarity invited comparison and description, framed primarily in terms of the differences of these landscapes from those of Europe.[38]

36 It is possible that Cristóbal Colón (Columbus) had actually read the 1483 translation of Theophrastus' *Historia plantarum*. According to Kirkpatrick Sale, seven of his personal volumes, most with extensive marginalia, have survived and are preserved today in the Biblioteca Combina in Seville. Three of the books are full of travellers' fantasies and descriptions of monstrous beings: Marco Polo's *Orientalium regionum*, Pierre d'Ailly's fanciful *Imago mundi* and other treatises, and Pliny's classic *Historia naturalis* in Italian translation (1489). The acquaintance with Pliny suggests that Columbus may well have known of Theophrastus, even if only by repute.

37 Keen, *The Life of Columbus*, quoted in K. Thompson, 'Forests and climatic change in America: Some early views', *Climatic Change*, 3 (1983), 47.

38 See P. Curtin, 'The environment beyond Europe and the European theory of empire', *Journal of World History*, 1 (1990), 131–50.

The tropical islands which were often the first landfalls and navigational points of reference, and which later became the first colonies, encapsulated an alternative kind of world as well as offering economic opportunities. An insular environment was one which was knowable in terms of the ease with which the island could be mentally circumscribed. Uninhabited islands offered fewer risks to colonists than did the continent of America, Africa or India. Inevitably, then, they became the subject of economic and literary interest, as well as myth, for the navigators of the early period of European expansion.

New worlds, nature and the discourse of islands

The process by which awareness of the New World, American and otherwise, was diffused into the intellectual and cultural currency of Western Europe is difficult to document reliably.[39] Within forty years of 1492 the new 'discoveries' had already made an impact on the imagination of the literate elite, although it is difficult to gauge what impression had been made on the wider social consciousness. The New World had a strong attraction for Renaissance man, and 'discovery', whether in the limited North American sense or in a more global one, gave an opportunity to locate Gardens of Eden, Arcadias, Elysian Fields and Golden Ages in a geographical reality. Indeed, there is some evidence that it was the very strength of Columbus's obstinate conviction that an Indian Eden, or earthly paradise, could be found beyond the Atlantic that gave the explorer the motivation he needed to carry doggedly on westwards in spite of the healthy fears of his colleagues.[40] Similarly, the image of Paradise was important in motivating some of the early 'explorations' of Brazil.[41]

The sheer size of the American continent meant, too, that the newly colonised Americas were most easily conceptualised in the form of an island, real or imaginary.[42] There may have been a particular attraction in islands for the English, being islanders themselves. As a metaphor for retreat and discovery, the island found echoes both in classical literature and in the mental

39 A very valuable attempt to do so has been made by J. E. Gillespie, *The influence of overseas expansion on England to 1700*, New York, 1920. A more controversial, although convincing, attempt to describe the impact of the journeys of Cristóbal Colón on the European mind is made by Kirkpatrick Sale in *The conquest of Paradise: Christopher Columbus and the Columbian legacy*, London, 1991.

40 H. Levin, *The myth of the Golden Age in the Renaissance*, London, 1969, pp. 59–60; V. I. J. Flint, *The imaginative landscape of Christopher Columbus*, Princeton, N.J., 1992.

41 Sergio Buarque, *Visão do Paraiso: Os motivos edénicos no descobrimento e colonização do Brasil*, Brasiliana: Edition Nacional, São Paulo, 1962.

42 Marx, *The machine in the Garden*, esp. chap. 1.

world of the child.[43] Furthermore, the classical desirability of the island had been rediscovered in Italian Renaissance literature. In Dante's *Purgatorio*, for example, an island in the 'southern ocean' offered the possibility of purgatory and redemption, while Dante himself must have been aware of the reality of the newly discovered islands in the Atlantic, the 'Fortunate Islands' of the Canaries and Madeira.[44] The New World, conceived of in island terms, enjoyed the reality of being newly discovered. This desirability was reflected in Columbus's writings: 'The songs of the little birds', he wrote, 'are such that it seems one would never desire to part hence.' Some writers have suggested that the attractiveness of the journey to a tropical island for Columbus consisted in the 'Indies' being a feminized and ultimately eroticised and exploitable symbol to which violent internal male prejudices and oppressions could be transferred. This, it is argued, helps to explain the social and environmental violation of the islands by Columbus and his successors.[45] While this is an intriguing thesis, the known significance to Columbus of ideas about Eden might seem to militate against this theory and tend more towards preservationist notions.

The geography of an island actually offered a contradictory set of opportunities: the social opportunity for redemption and newness as well as an encapsulation of problems posed by the need for physical and mental survival and health. The related emergence, or re-emergence, of the island as a powerful cultural metaphor in Western European thought, particularly in the context of colonisation, can be closely traced in literature. Indeed, the island metaphor could be said to constitute a vital part of the symbolic discourse of early colonialism, albeit an ambiguous part.[46]

Indeed, for Shakespeare, the ambiguities offered by the actualisation of a previously imaginary Arcadian convention on an island were thematically attractive. A brief examination of his dramatic articulation of the contradictions involved in island settlement is, I think, almost essential to any discussion of early colonial environmental perceptions among a literate elite and to understanding the way in which distant lands afforded the mental opportunity to project and objectify discontents and anxieties less palatably dealt with closer to home. The use of the island as a dramatic context in *The Tempest* may have been suggested to Shakespeare by a particular shipwreck in the Bermudas,

43 For a more elaborate discussion on these lines than is possible here, see Bloch, *The principle of hope*, esp. vol. 2, chap. entitled 'Geographical Utopias'.
44 A. Keymer, 'Plant imagery in Dante', B.A. diss., Cambridge University Faculty of Modern and Medieval Languages, 1982, pp. 21–9; and see Charles S. Singleton, *Journey to Beatrice*, Baltimore, 1977.
45 Margarita Zamora, 'Abreast of Columbus: Gender and discovery', *Cultural Critique*, 1990, pp. 127–45.
46 See R. M. Loxley, *The problematic of islands*, London, 1990.

although Italian influences, above all from Dante, may also have affected him. Thus the location of *The Tempest* provided the setting for a bewildering variety of speculation about the Edenic qualities of the island and the potential it offered for erecting an alternative Utopian society on the one hand and for starkly encountering the difficulties of sheer animal survival on the other. Reluctant simply to pour scorn on the idea of Utopia, Shakespeare seems to have chosen instead to highlight the contradictions between the two opposed concepts of the island as an Eden or Utopia and the island as the meeting place between indigenous inhabitant and European colonist.[47] *The Tempest* is realistically complex in that it confronts the contrasting problems of the response to a new physical environment and the response to the indigenous inhabitant, the latter presented in the shape of Caliban, a 'noble savage' character probably inspired by Montaigne's writings.[48] Appearing a century after the publication of Thomas More's *Utopia*, *The Tempest* had moved away from a stereotyped concept of the island as a place where a redemption of European political economy might be tried out and towards a more empirical perception and one more closely reflecting the hard reality of the early American and Caribbean colonies. Instead of laying out a programme for a Utopia, the characters in *The Tempest* debated a whole range of social options. Furthermore, in the play Prospero has to compromise with the overwhelmingly natural features of the colonised island and is to some extent seduced by them. More significant, in so doing and in confronting the reality of the natural world, he successfully weathers the transition from magician to natural scientist. Only a rigorous empiricism, it is implied, can cope with the sheer extent of physical unfamiliarity when there is no culturally received precedent to fall back upon. Moreover, written knowledge would directly assist in the colonist's gaining actual control of the land and thus the means to dispossess the 'savage' Caliban. Caliban's wish to burn Prospero's books emerges as a logical outcome of this power struggle.

In *The Tempest* even social debates are overshadowed by the physical pre-

---

47 A useful development of this theme appears in P. Lindenbaum, *Changing landscapes: Anti-pastoral sentiment in the English Renaissance*, Athens, Ga., 1986. Lindenbaum asserts that Shakespeare, Sidney and Milton all expressed their frustration with the pastoral tradition by subverting its conventions and creating imaginative landscapes which were characteristically not idyllic. The projection of this ambiguity on to an island landscape, therefore, may have offered more complex possibilities than those offered by the botanical garden as surveyed by Prest in *The Garden of Eden*.

48 The comments in this paragraph lean heavily on the interpretation put forward by Leo Marx in *The Machine in the Garden*, chap. 1. The references to *The Tempest* made here are extensive simply because seventeenth-century images of the tropical world are more definitively and comprehensively expressed in the play than in most other contemporary sources. See also H. J. C. von Grimmelshausen, *Simplicissimus: Der abenteuerliche Simplicissimus*, Zurich, 1944, for a popular seventeenth-century discourse on tropical islands.

dicament and the dangers involved in surviving an alien land. A dialogue among Antonio, Adrian, Gonzalo and Sebastian helps to highlight this. A powerful tension, or contradiction, is built up between wishful perceptions of the island as a lush paradise and perceptions of it as a place beset by risks from drought, disease and native people, albeit enslaved. The colonists specifically reject Caliban's holistic vision of the isle, in which 'I lov'd thee / And showed thee all the qualities o' th' isle, / The fresh springs, brine pits, barren place, and fertile'.[49] For the colonists, their need for projection and their strong preconceptions enforce contradictions which cannot encompass the heterogeneous reality of 'barren place, and fertile' but would prefer one or the other:

Adrian:	The air breathes upon us most sweetly.
Sebastian:	As if it had lungs, and rotten ones.
Antonio:	Or as 'twere perfumed by a fen.
Gonzalo:	Here is everything advantageous to life.
Antonio:	True; save means to live.
Sebastian:	Of that there's none, or little.
Gonzalo:	How lush and lusty the grass looks! how green!
Antonio:	The ground indeed is tawny.
Sebastian:	With an eye of green in't.
Antonio:	He misses not much.
Sebastian:	No; he doth but mistake the truth totally.
Gonzalo:	But the rarity of it is, – which is indeed almost beyond credit, –
Sebastian:	As many vouch'd rarities are.[50]

This dialogue continues a little later in a more specific fashion:

Sebastian:	He [Gonzalo] hath rais'd the wall, and houses too.
Antonio:	What impossible matter will he make easy next?
Sebastian:	I think he will carry this island home in his pocket, and give it his son for an apple.
Antonio:	And, sowing the kernels of it in the sea, bring forth more islands.
Gonzalo:	Ay?
Antonio:	Why, in good time.

At least two issues are instructively embarked upon in these exchanges. First, the contradiction between the projection of Edenic or paradisal properties on to the island and the empirical complexity of the island is dealt with. The second dialogue recognises quite explicitly the symbolic or totemic po-

49 William Shakespeare, *The Tempest*, I. ii. 336–8, in W. J. Craig, ed., *The Complete Works . . .*, Oxford, 1905.
50 Ibid., II. i. 49–64.

tential of the island in the mind of Gonzalo, the idealist or dreamer. Meanwhile, the adoption of the apple as an image may evoke echoes of a Garden of Eden, or a state of perfection, but it might also suggest an apple plucked from a tree of knowledge, an act that presages problems and dilemmas. Pocketing the apple implies possibly an awakening to the arrogant power of Europeans as environmental manipulators, moulding an environment for their own material or spiritual purposes. Here, surely, are the early glimmerings of a dyadic view and a capacity to encompass a detached knowledge of an unfamiliar and yet manipulable environment on the one hand and, on the other hand, one that may be appropriated for strictly non-local reasons. In thus projecting his perceptive needs on to the island, Gonzalo is, Sebastian suggests, mistaking 'the truth totally'. Gonzalo makes a most significant remark in starting to comment on the 'rarity' of the island, but leaves the thought unconcluded. This idea of rarity, of the unusual, was to become of critical importance during the eighteenth century as a major motivation in botanical exploration and as a consequence of an emerging global empirical framework of classification against which rarity could be measured; and it was elegantly foreshadowed by Shakespeare in *The Tempest*.[51] As Shakespeare seems to imply, the idea of rarity had more to do with identification with or location of a threatened individual than with an empirical description of the objective frequency of occurrence of an identifiable organism in a new environment. The isolated individual, marooned on an island, was to become a powerful, even Romantic, metaphor.

The play goes on to consider the practical consequences of the possibility canvassed by Gonzalo in his otherwise Utopian plan for a 'Commonwealth': 'Had I plantation of this isle', Gonzalo asserts, 'I would with such perfection govern, sir, / To exceed the golden age.' This mention of a golden age is important. It does not here necessarily contradict the idea of plantation, despite its appeal to the past, the ideal or the Arcadian. Instead it constitutes a reference to the construction of a better world in the future. The implications of Prospero's colonisation of the island consist both in the material economic demands or output or activity that it imposes and in the environmental risks present in human terms on a tropical island. The new material demands made on the colonised are clear-cut from the point of view of Caliban, pressed to carry fuel wood. Having been set to perform this task, he then bewails his fate as an indigene: 'Lo now! Lo! / Here comes a spirit of his, and to torment me / For bringing wood in slowly.' Prospero, however, may also be vulnerable, albeit in a different sense: 'All the infections that the sun sucks up / From bogs, fens, flats, on Prosper fall and make him / . . . a disease.'[52] Dis-

---

51 See Chapter 7 for further discussions of the significance of classification.
52 *Tempest*, II. ii. 1–16.

ease, however, is not the only hostile part of the insular environment to be contended with. As Trinculo observes:

> Here's neither bush nor shrub to bear of any weather at all, and another storm brewing; I hear it sing i' the wind: yond same black cloud, yond huge one, looks like a foul bombard that would shed his liquor. If it should thunder as it did before, I know not where to hide my head: yond same cloud cannot choose but fall by pailfuls.[53]

So while Caliban, struck down by the ague, is also prone to the ills which he has called down on the colonists, the colonists themselves are faced with a deeply unpredictable physical setting. Their main predicament lies in the fact that, however much the island may present opportunities for rebirth or redemption (or for the golden age, as Gonzalo specifically puts it), they find themselves at odds with a place full of risks, the greatest of which relate to climate, disease and the shortage of water. While Caliban harks upon the ability of the island to nurture – 'I'll shew thee the best springs; I'll pluck thee berries; / I'll fish for thee, and get thee wood enough' – the promise of paradisical fertility or present fruitfulness is not enough to deal with the inherent precariousness of the colonists' situation and with its unpredictability. The tropical island was, at a basic level, not a known environment. As an exchange between Sebastian and Antonio suggests, the problem of strangeness is difficult to overcome:

Sebastian: What a strange drowsiness possesses them!
Antonio: It is the quality o' the climate.[54]

Notions of climatic type and water supply relate closely here not only to the material potential for survival but also to notions of morale and mental sustainability. Water in *The Tempest* becomes a context for exploring psychological images of spiritual or emotional well-being, analogous to the flow of water necessary for bodily survival. This is a very important analogy when explored in relation to the island:

Sebastian: Well; I am standing water.
Antonio: I'll teach you how to flow.
Sebastian: Do so: to ebb,
         Hereditary sloth instructs me.
Antonio: O!
         If you but knew how you the purpose cherish
         Whiles thus you mock it! how, in stripping it,
         You more invest it! Ebbing men, indeed,

53 Ibid., II.ii. 18ff.
54 Ibid., II.i. 207–8.

Most often do so near the bottom run
By their own fear or sloth.[55]

What seems to emerge succinctly here is that a discussion about the environmental situation in which the colonists find themselves can develop relatively quickly into a discourse about forms or metaphors of internal alienation or, alternatively, about ways of finding fulfilment. In other words, the internal needs of the colonists may be externalised in the context of external physical forms in water and land. This possibility for projection may be attributed to the physical and mental distance between colony and metropole or mother country and hence perhaps reflects a difficulty in coming to terms with the complexity of a distant colony behind the facade of a projected Eden.

The ease with which the new island as a colonial setting could be appropriated by those with ulterior projective needs was not lost on Shakespeare, even though, as documented above, he digressed into his own discussion of analogies between human and physical 'flows'. He was not alone in his caution, and other writers were also aware of the difficulty of portraying the empirical complexity, if not ordinariness, of the 'New World' to an English audience accustomed to hyperbole and stereotyped, exaggerated images, especially of the tropics. *The Tempest* itself was based on an account of a shipwreck en route to Virginia in 1609. One writer, describing Virginia a year later, appealed to an empirical and critical faculty which he clearly had been led not to anticipate: 'If any man shall accuse these reports of partial falsehood, supposing them to be but Utopian, and legendary fables, because he cannot conceive that plentie and famine, a temperate climate and distempered bodies, felicities and miseries, can be reconciled together, let him now reade with judgment, but let him not judge before he hath read.'[56] The contradictions described here may help us to understand part of the character of sixteenth-century environmental discourse, usefully dramatised by Shakespeare (and others) on a symbolic island but reflecting a very genuine and developing clash between projected icon and the form of colonised, exploited and degrading reality. The Renaissance had promoted a renewed interest in the value and portrayal of the natural world, and this also was reflected in *The Tempest*, which focusses on allegedly civilised Europeans as they attempt to locate themselves in an ahistoric 'wilderness'.[57]

The discovery of the New World and territories along the trade routes to the East helped to stimulate scientific interpretations of the workings of nature. As the pivot of economic power shifted from Southern Europe to the maritime nations, particularly to the Netherlands and England, it is not surprising that

55 Ibid., II.i. 229–36.
56 *A true declaration of the state of Virginia*, quoted in Marx, *The machine in the Garden*, p. 34.
57 See Marx, *The machine in the Garden*, chap. 1.

the process of colonisation by those powers, especially where islands were concerned, should have stimulated literary dramatisations of societies in economic as well as religious transition. Of course the highly sophisticated debates which were set out in the pages of More and Shakespeare were not necessarily typical. On the contrary, they were exceptional and precociously prefigured a philosophical development which took a long time to mature. The insights into the significance and anthropocentric derivation of the idea of rarity which are explicit in *The Tempest* are an instance of the prematurity of some early literary insights into the perceptual consequences of early colonisation. In contrast, most accounts of oceanic islands written by travelers during the sixteenth and the early seventeenth century, whilst reflecting some of the preoccupations of *The Tempest,* were essentially descriptive, and most of them were far from analytical.

While concepts of a social paradise may have been prominent in the writings of theorists in Europe, the language used by many of the travel writers of the sixteenth and the early seventeenth century speaks of paradises of a very practical kind, reflecting the favourable perceptions of many tropical islands as sites of nurturing relief from arduous and disease-ridden sea journeys. As long-distance trade to the Americas and the East became a commercial reality, travel literature, especially that dealing with islands, began to grow in complexity and popularity. Even so, much of it continued to be stereotypical in the selection of descriptive images, dwelling especially on the vegetable products of tropical islands. Furthermore, much of it was of a highly derived kind and based largely on hearsay and secondary material.

The circumnavigation of the world by Sir Francis Drake became especially important in stimulating the entry of images of tropical nature into popular culture in England, particularly in the cheaper street literature. A valuable exemplar of the newly popularised travel writing is to be found in P. Brooksby's book *The Voyages and Travels of That Renowned Captain Sir Francis Drake,* published in 1683. In this chapbook the island of St Iago in the Cape Verdes is described as

> the burning island, called Fogo, continually casting flames, and near to that, lies a pleasant island, always clad with green, exceeding fruitful, abounding especially with Figs, Cocos, Planatos, Oranges and Lemons; it is also replenished with pleasant streams, though the harbours about it are not capable of receiving any ships . . . and in all the island was only one house, supposed to be inhabited by an hermit.

The terminology of fruit, streams and 'hermit' can readily be identified with the image of a Garden of Eden — furthermore, one 'always clad with green' and therefore clearly connected with the idea of a perpetual spring. The latter, hoped for but never found in reality in Europe, could be realised nearer the tropics at, for example, the Canaries, Madeira and the Cape Verdes. Brooksby's rewriting of Drake's circumnavigation thus for the first time makes a clear link between the restored Garden of Eden of the Renaissance botanical garden and the discovered Eden of the tropical island. The stereotyped fruit images help to give us a clue to the main linking ideas involved. The contrast between the availability of water on an island and the aridity of the ocean voyage is also prominently alluded to by Brooksby. 'From this island', he tells us,

> after having taken some of what it afforded, they stood away to the coast of Brazil, but by contrary winds were kept out so long at sea, that provisions grew scanty, and especially water, which in that burning climate was most requisit. But when they desired of obtaining any, God so ordered it that there fell great floods of rain, which supplied their necessity.[58]

To some extent, despite its Edenic stereotyping of language and fruitful image, this kind of literary preoccupation was a product of a very real and emerging awareness of the variety and diversity of the biota of the tropics as it was becoming better known, especially via the printed word.

Andrew Marvell and Edmund Waller, for example, borrowing from the work of earlier writers, frequently took up the island theme. Waller related his island image explicitly to the Garden of Eden, albeit one of classical antecedents:

> That happy island where huge lemons grow,
> And orange trees, which golden fruit do bear,
> The Hesperian garden boasts of none so fair,
> Where shining pearl, coral and many a pound,
> On the rich shore, of ambergris is found;
> The lofty cedar. . .

Captain John Smith was a common source for both Waller and Marvell, while Marvell's 'Bermoothes' (1653) even uses similar imagery.[59] By the time

---

58 London, 1683, pp. 2–3.
59 J. Waller, *The battle of the Summer Islands*, London, 1665; J. Smith, *The generale historie of Virginia, New England and the Summer Isles*, London, 1624. Marvell in 'Bermoothes' writes:

> He makes the Figs our mouths to meet;
> And throws the Melons at our feet
> But Apples, plants of such a price,
> No tree could ever bear them twice.
> With Cedars, chosen by his hand,
> From Lebanon, he stores the land.

(Quoted in H. M. Margoliouth, *The poems and letters of Andrew Marvell*, 2nd ed., Oxford, 1967, p. 17.)

Marvell wrote, the idioms of fruitfulness, whether vegetable, fruit (oranges, lemons, figs) or mineral (pearls, ambergris), were readily identifiable and often repeated. By the 1680s they were present in popular chapbooks of travel writings and became widely disseminated. The semantic was developed even further by Abraham Cowley in referring to the reality of the 'perpetual spring' of the tropics, in a piece written in 1682:

> No cold invades the temp'rate summer there,
> More rich than Autumn, and the Spring more fair.
> The Months without distinction pass away,
> The trees at once with leaves, fruit blossoms gay,
> The changing Man all these, and always does survey,
> Nature some fruits, does to our soil deny,
> Not what we have, can ev'ry month supply,
> But ev'ry sort that happy earth doth bear,
> All sorts it bears and bears them all the year.[60]

This thinking was echoed by John Evelyn, who recommended that a gentleman should plant his dwelling both 'with the taller and the lowest sort of Ever-greens even for some miles about so that he might, even in winter, imagine himself transported to one of the legendary tropical islands in the West Indies, in Ethiopia, or to one of the Fortunate Islands'.[61] Poetic idioms that were far more fantastical than this, or even 'monstrous' in their mythology, continued to find a place in this literature until as late as the end of the seventeenth century, and they continued to fulfil a social need. On the other hand, tropical islands and new colonies were also becoming the context, at a time of social and religious turmoil, for locating New Jerusalems and Promised Lands. Virginia, for example, was a place where 'God's pearl upon our coast was cast . . . even a Promised Land'. It is not surprising, then, that Marvell should have found the island an attractive metaphor during the Civil War period:

> What should we do but sing his praise
> That led us through the watery maze,
> Unto an isle so long unknown,
> And yet far kinder than our own.[62]

Much of Marvell's island poetry conveys a sense of the pilgrimage of the individual in search of truth and in search of self-justification. This was an essential element, too, of the Romantic journey away from the characteristi-

60 *Plantarum. . .* , London, 1721, p. 357.
61 Christchurch College Library, Oxford, 'Elysium Britannicum', vol. 2, pp. 259–60.
62 Marvell, 'Bermoothes', lines 5–8.

cally 'unhappy isle' of England to a more serene island world unalloyed by
social ills. It was closely connected to the idea of the personal pilgrimage of
the Dissenter or Puritan as a 'seeker after truth'. Furthermore the pilgrimage
theme harked back to the early medieval preoccupations of the *iter ad Paradisum*, in which the Alexandrine expedition along a river of Paradise corresponded to a Gangetic pilgrimage to a holy place, or *Svarga-Loka*. Similarly,
the Indic elements of pilgrimage and the notion of the search for mystical
enlightenment, which was so characteristic of the post-Renaissance discourse
of islands, also surfaced freely in poets as diverse as John Donne and John
Milton. Donne, for example, refers to the 'search . . . at the secret parts of the
India or rather Paradise of knowledge . . . launched into the Vast Sea of
Arts'.[63]

St Helena and Mauritius and the insular discourse of nature

The increasing empiricism of travel literature derived simply from the greater
frequency and regularity of long-distance travel. During the seventeenth century, as the work of John Donne suggests, the axis of interest began to shift
away from the Americas towards the East, where a growing intellectual and
Orientalist curiosity was developing alongside commercial concerns. Of course
to some extent the new travel literature continued to use the old Edenic images. It was transferred, however, to a more specifically India-oriented setting,
and particularly to the islands that lay strategically (in both supply and military
terms) on the trade routes to India. It was increasingly practical, empirical
and accurate and exhibited a very distinctive preoccupation with climate and
water supply. Because of their geographical position astride the trade routes,
St Helena and Mauritius became naturally prominent in this literature. Both
islands were important staging posts on the Cape and Indian trading routes.
Being uninhabited, they were peculiarly amenable to the kinds of projection
and Edenic treatment described above. To sailors exhausted and weakened by
long voyages, they were veritable paradises, bowers of untouched woodlands
made up of plant species and inhabited by birds never before seen by man.

Remarks made in 1647 by J. A. von Mandelslo, a Holsteinian traveller, are
worth considering at some length in this connection.[64] They were made in the
context of a journey made by ambassadors from Holstein to India and the

---

63 H. J. C. Grierson, ed., *The poetical works of John Donne*, Oxford, 1971.
64 J. A. von Mandelslo, *The voyages and travels of ambassadors sent by Frederick Duke of Holstein
to the Grand Duke of Muscovy and the King of Persia begun in 1633 and finished in 1634 whereto
are added the travels of J. A. de Mandelslo*, 2nd ed., London, 1669 (trans. of original German
text of 1647).

East Indies during the opening phases of the late-seventeenth-century expansion in Indo-European trade by the East India companies. This was at a time before the oceanic islands along the trade routes had become points of significant territorial contention or seriously considered for colonial plantation agriculture. Hence Mandelslo's descriptions refer to islands that were as yet undisturbed by the demands of early plantation agriculture. At St Helena, he wrote,

> It is so fertile that there is not any province in Europe affords such plenty of excellent fruits and breeds so many creatures as this island. Some affirm, it afforded neither, when it was first discovered by the Portuguese and that the few trees they planted and the little stock of cattle they left there hath so furnished it that it is . . . sufficient to refresh all the fleets that come hither. At this place a man may at any time of year [find] figs and pomegranates; citrus and oranges are there, also goats . . . barbary hens, pheasants, partridges, quails, peacocks, pigeons; and great stocks of all sorts of birds, as also salt for the keeping of them, so that ships may be sufficiently provided with all things if they would stay there any time. The sea supplies with more fish than can be consumed, and the earth brings forth so many excellent herbs, that the Portuguez, unwilling to retard their voyage, leave at this place their sick men, who recover their health within a few days and having only a little Oyl, rice byskets and spice, make a shift to live there till the ships come hither next year. Its mountains are so high that they reach above the clouds and are seen at sea at a distance of 14 leagues. The trees wherewith they are covered bring forth no fruit and are fit only for firing, but the valleys are extremely pleasant. The King of Portugal would not have any establishment to be made upon these reflections; that all ships passing might find refreshment there and that it would be a hard matter to keep the said island against all the other nations who are concerned in its being free, inasmuch as were it not for that vessels many times would be forced upon the coasts of Guiny, where water is not to be had at all times, and where they shall be obliged to stay for rain which would be as great an inconvenience that many of the men would in the meantime droop and die. The fertility of this island proceeds chiefly from the daily rain which falls there, but these are transient showers soon over, so that the sun shining presently after, and that by intervals, it must needs very much advance the maturation of things . . . there are three places where fresh water may be taken in.[65]

Even in this idyllic description, the matter of water emerges as paramount. Mandelslo continued the theme in his references to Ascension Island, which, by contrast, 'affords no water, nay it hath not so much as any verdure'. There are two important points to be made about these descriptions of St Helena

---

65 Ibid., p. 210.

and Ascension. The stereotyped imagery of fruitfulness and plenty found in the more popular writing is certainly present. The role of man, however, is seen at this stage as constructive and even essential to the generous state of the island. Without man, it is implied, the island would have been less fruitful. But the paradisal is directly related to the practical: Ships can be provisioned and watered without the risk of disease that a continental visit would have entailed. Accordingly, the treatment of waterless Ascension is dismissive.

The preoccupation with water supply as a critical determinant of the desirability of an island led, not surprisingly, to closer observation of the circumstances promoting rainfall on a tropical island. Mandelslo refers obliquely to a concern already established in tradition between tree cover and precipitation in his notes on St Thomas Island in the Cape Verdes. This island was, he said, 'a mountain covered with trees, and overspread with a cloud, which supplies it with fresh water – the higher the sun comes over the horizon, the more water falls from the cloud.'[66]

These observations relate to the utilitarian potential of the island. The visions of an apparent Edenic plenty are nonetheless too prominent to be called utilitarian. When we come to Mandelslo's description of Mauritius, it is clear that he had deliberated on something else: the physical beauty of the island and the vulnerability of its creatures to visiting Europeans. Clouds also received attention:

> It hath some mountains which reaching up into the clouds are seen at a great distance and are extremely delightful to the eye, inasmuch as nature maintains them in constant verdure, though some Cocos trees and date trees only excepted, all the other trees are wild . . . in the vallies there are some fruit trees, but such as bear no fruit are not the less esteemed for that . . . the island is not inhabited and whence it comes the birds are so tame that a man may take them into his hand and they are commonly killed with cudgels.[67]

The explicit mention made here of the ease with which birds could be caught and killed on Mauritius foreshadowed the fate of the dodo, which Mandelslo also describes later in the same paragraph as 'a kind of bird of the bigness of a swan which has neither wings nor tail'. The foreshadowing of extinction, however, was only a passing matter for Mandelslo. He was more taken up, despite his images of island plenty, with the vulnerability of any lone individual who might be cast up upon the shores of a desolate oceanic island. Thus he described in detail the shipwreck and torments suffered by a shipwrecked Frenchman marooned on the island in 1601, in an account which

66 Ibid., pp. 210–11.
67 Ibid., p. 195.

was later to exercise the mind of Defoe when he was writing *Robinson Crusoe*.[68] One could, of course, place a straightforward religious interpretation on the early-seventeenth-century interest in the allegorical image of a lone ship-wrecked mariner embarking on his solitary journey through life. However, a more direct connection was also being made with the predicament of Europeans who find themselves in the midst of environments in which they cannot call to aid previous custom or knowledge, either in understanding indigenous peoples and language or in coping with unfamiliar creatures, vegetation and climatic conditions.

While technological sophistication reduced the danger presented by indigenous peoples in the tropics and even allowed their early enslavement, unfamiliarity with a bewildering variety of tropical plants and animals also presented a challenge to empiricism. The older metaphor of an actualised Eden could thus be blended with the image of the island as a new empirical realm of safety amidst an unknown and explorable natural world whose chief characteristic was a lack of connection with all things European.

It is no coincidence that Mandelslo was of Dutch origin. Interest in portraying nature in an empirical and non-religious context had emerged strongly and precociously in the Netherlands towards the end of the sixteenth century.[69] The English perception of the island, on the other hand, had by the mid seventeenth century already diverged significantly from that of the Dutch, so that for the English the image of the island was still utilised more in stark terms of political or psychological escapism or, more important, in terms of straightforward plantation potential. For Marvell, for example, the tropical island clearly constituted a mental refuge from political turmoil. This was to become a commonplace theme in French literature as well. By the end of the seventeenth century the flight of Huguenot refugees from persecution in France had effectively transformed the islands of the Indian Ocean into very real potential refuges. Thus in 1690 the island of Rodriguez, not far from Mauritius, was settled temporarily by Huguenot refugees under the captaincy of Abraham du Quesne.[70] The accounts of the island left by Le Guat, one of their number, are striking both in the detailed annotation of the natural features of the island and in the exultatory and paradisiacal terms in which the island colony is described. However, there are also some novel features of this

---

68 See F. H. Ellis, ed., *Twentieth century interpretations of Robinson Crusoe: A collection of critical essays*, Englewood Cliffs, N.J., 1969. See also Chapter 6.

69 Some writers have placed this transition to the empirical at a much later date; see e.g. B. M. Stafford, *Voyage into substance: Science, nature and the illustrated travel account, 1770–1840*, Cambridge, Mass., 1984. However, the evidence of Dutch painting would appear to be definitive.

70 Abraham du Quesne, *A new voyage to the East Indies in the years 1690 and 1691...*, London, 1696, p. 23.

text which had not at the time been developed by English or Dutch writers. Thus Le Guat wrote that Rodriguez possessed

> a very inviting appearance, both at a distance and on our near approach to it. This little new world seemed to us a source of delight, the aspect of the island was so delightful we could scarce satisfy ourselves by gazing at the little mountains of which it is composed, covered as they were with large and beautiful trees . . . these scenes brought to our recollection the famous Lignon, and the various enchanting spots which are so eloquently described in the Romance of M. D'Urfe . . . we admired the secret and extraordinary operations of Providence which after having permitted us to be ruined in our own country, and to be cruelly driven from it, had at least suffered us . . . this earthly paradise to which we had been conducted.[71]

The explicit reference made here to 'this little new world' was a significant development. With the circumnavigation of the world having become possible, a new sense of the scope within which man might act had developed. The accounts of Le Guat and du Quesne indicate that the islands of 'Mascaregne' were commonly referred to as 'Eden'.[72] 'Be it as it will,' du Quesne wrote, 'it is certain the Isle of Eden is of sufficient extent, to contain easily a long descent of generations of whatever colony will settle there.' He went on to add that 'voyagers have not made mention of any country where the air is more healthy than in this Isle; which is a very important article'.[73] From the language of du Quesne we can deduce that it had become progressively easier for the island to become an analogue not only of a Garden of Eden (with its stereotyped fruits, forests and monsters) or of a single society alone, but of the whole world and of human power over it.

The Le Guat account was remarkable in several ways, but particularly in its consistent lauding of wilderness and a natural state undisturbed by man. This feature links the account very directly to the classical Renaissance tradition of D'Urfe, a tradition which lent itself strongly to the praise of trees and the aesthetics of landscape. The trees of Rodriguez, Le Guat wrote, 'do

71 Quoted in C. Grant, *History of Mauritius; or, The Isle of France and the neighbouring islands from their first discovery to the present time*, London, 1801, p. 104.

72 S. Pasfield-Oliver, ed., *The voyage of François Le Guat of Bresse to Rodriguez, Mauritius, Java and the Cape of Good Hope*, London, 1891, vol. 2, p. 33. There is some debate as to whether the Le Guat account is fictional or biographical. The original version was contained in Maximilien Misson, *Voyage et aventures de François Leguat et de ses Compagnons en deux îles desertés des Indes Orientales*, London, 1721. However, A. W. Secord questions the genuineness of the account; see 'Studies in the narrative method of Defoe', *University of Illinois Studies in Language and Literature*, 9 (1924), 92. Ultimately the debate is not of vital importance. Even if fictional, Misson's *Le Guat* still conveys a valid account of a new and Edenic perception.

73 *A new voyage*, pp. 42–3.

not yield in beauty to the finest trees in Europe'.[74] As refugees from the gross
social distortions and religious bigotry of European society, du Quesne's Huguenots were far more disposed to appreciate beauty in nature untouched by
man. In this they were precocious forerunners of eighteenth-century Romantic
thought and particularly of that important strand pioneered in the Mascarene
islands by Bernardin de Saint-Pierre.[75] Particularly in the context of French
seventeenth-century Calvinist thinking, a fundamental reassessment of the
connection between the Fall of Man and the Fall of Nature was starting to
take place, leading in turn to a tendency to fundamentally disconnect the
'earthly paradise' from the Fall of Man. Furthermore, a new willingness developed during the ensuing century, particularly among travelers in the Indian
and Pacific oceans, to recognise God as 'Creator of a world containing many
wonders and beauties'; that is, to recognise nature's qualities rather than its
'defeat'.[76] By 1690 it was clear that this was already happening in the context
of the Mascarenes. Contemporary illustrations of Le Guat's diary give us an
indication of a very bookish and intellectual sense of paradise or beauty, contrasting considerably with the far more utilitarian illustrations which accompanied accounts of the earliest Dutch settlements in the Mascarenes published
by Van Neck before 1620. These, while intended to convey a sense of plenty,
strangeness and the exotic garden, find no embarrassment in the work of man
in transforming the landscape. In contrast, by the end of the seventeenth
century, at least among dissenters, a well-developed caution about the impact
or desirability of the works of man upon the 'New World' had emerged. This
was not a simple or easy transition, and it was one that took place among the
English more slowly than among the Dutch and French.

Aesthetic transitions in seventeenth-century Europe

The foregoing pages have concentrated on sketching out the changing dynamics of the discourse and language of nature characteristic of early colonial

---

74 Quoted in Grant, *Mauritius*, p. 104.
75 The aesthetic interest in mountains so evident in Mandelslo and exhibited also by Le Guat
   and du Quesne is significant. Van Tieghem finds the interest in mountains in Europe apparently developing much later, as does Nicolson. Thus Mandelslo's perceptions seem to con-
   found existing assumptions about the development of a 'taste' for mountains, e.g. in P. Van
   Tieghem, *Le sentiment de la nature dans pré-romantisme*, Nizet, 1960, p. 159; M. H. Nicolson,
   Mountain gloom and mountain glory, Ithaca, N.Y., 1959, all chaps.
76 D. G. Charlton, *New images of the natural in France*, Cambridge, 1984, p. 114. See also K.
   Thomas, *Man and the natural world*. Much of Thomas's book is taken up with describing a
   similar transition during the period 1550–1750; see his two chapters entitled 'The Subjugation
   of the Natural World' and 'The Dethronement of Man'. In the colonial setting this transition
   is, if anything, more sharply identifiable.

Plate 1. The early Dutch colonists on Mauritius in 1599. In Van Neck's account of
the settlement, the picture is entitled *Comment nous avons (sur l'Isle Maurice autrement
nommée do Cerne) tenu mesnage*. (Reproduced from H. E. Strickland and A. G. Melville,
The dodo and its kindred, 2 vols., London, 1848)

expansion in the tropics and of descriptions of oceanic islands in particular.
These dynamics were not, of course, entirely autonomous, and some assessment of the European domestic background to these developments needs to
be made. It is clear that during the seventeenth century a great transition had
begun in the significance of the natural world in the European imagination, a
transition in which the process of maritime expansion had a part to play, but
which had specific European causes as well. The preoccupation with the island
and its stereotyped form as a descriptive metaphor or device in travel accounts
and more derived literature represented a step on the way to a new evaluation
of the environment. Such changes in emphasis reflected the social traumas
which societies in the European maritime nations were undergoing.

To date, an undue emphasis on the intellectual changes of the eighteenth
century implied in the terms 'Enlightenment' and 'Romanticism' has served
to distract attention from a far more wide-ranging and probably much earlier
transition in attitudes towards nature. This transition became a central part
of a largely secular response to social and economic changes in Europe from

Plate 2. The Huguenot image of the island of Rodriguez in 1692, according to François
Le Guat. (Reproduced from Strickland and Melville, *The dodo and its kindred*)

the late sixteenth century onwards and culminated in aesthetic and moral
critiques of the impact of industrialisation in England in the late eighteenth
and early nineteenth century.[77] In fact, Charlton identifies a fully fledged
'movement' as being far more important than the Enlightenment proper, or
than Romanticism in its early-nineteenth-century phase, in the process of

77 Charlton, *New images of the natural*, p. 114.

shaping environmental attitudes.[78] Both terms, to some extent, identify minority intellectual preoccupations, although they are not less important for that. Instead, the changes in the social significance attached to nature that took place in the context of colonial expansion relate less to late-eighteenth-century economic change than to the transitions which took place in the preceding two centuries in France, England and the Netherlands in particular. Certainly most late-eighteenth- and early-nineteenth-century environmental anxieties and policies owed their foundations to philosophical and practical concepts that were fully developed by the mid eighteenth century. The earlier transitions which gave rise to such fully developed concepts are thus of some importance in understanding later developments in colonial environmental policy.

The most important parts of the seventeenth-century aesthetic transition are probably best explained in terms of a fundamental displacement of social and symbolic meanings away from the confines of religious contexts (such as church buildings) and into more secular settings. In those countries in which religious reform had taken place, it can be said that a distinct degree of social secularisation had already started to emerge by the end of the sixteenth century, partly as a consequence of the wider dissemination of knowledge through the printing press. Associated with this, a growing emphasis on the relationship of the individual to God may in turn have helped pave the way for more individualistic and yet anthropomorphic perceptions of nature.

During the seventeenth century a knowledge of physical creation rather than of purely spiritual notions of divinity was becoming an acceptable path to knowledge of God, especially amongst such radically dissenting groups as the Quakers in England and the Huguenots in France. It is in such developments in religious dissent that we may find parallels between a more questioning approach to a knowledge of the supernatural and a more exploratory and less precedent-based approach to the natural world. This is not to say that acceptance or appreciation of natural works as a route to divine knowledge or grace was an entirely new development; radical doctrinal departures had long been associated with more favourable and open-minded approaches to nature in, for example, the works of Saint Francis, Saint Bonaventure and Saint Thomas Aquinas. However, the connections between religious or political dissent and distinctive shifts in environmental attitudes became increasingly marked after the late seventeenth century.

It is quite possible to argue that the advent of mechanistic, analytical or reductionist interpretations of nature and society stimulated destructive attitudes towards an increasingly objectified environment. The writings of Galileo, Descartes, Hobbes and Newton certainly created a language and an

78 Ibid., chaps. 2–4.

intellectual climate inimical to holism. Some would argue that they brought about a new and essentially masculine discourse inherently hostile to a 'natural', 'sustainable' and more deeply rooted feminine discourse.[79] While such explanations of the antecedents of modern environmental disequilibrium are superficially attractive, they also contain a major flaw. In particular, the growing interest in mechanistic analysis and comparison actually enabled rational and measured observations of environmental change, as well as encouraging an organised conservationist response. As we shall see, the work of a Newtonian such as Stephen Hales, to take one example, provided a vital key to a wider critique of the effects of deforestation. However, there is no doubt that a mechanistic science of the natural world increasingly found itself at odds with traditional belief. Particular totems of cosmic or social import, such as the appearance of comets or other celestial bodies, underwent a very rapid decline in significance.[80] Furthermore, from the early seventeenth century onwards it is possible to detect a wholesale decline in western interest in the specifically magic and supernatural.[81] This had been foreseen, one might argue, by Shakespeare in *The Tempest* as the ability to understand, travel through and control the natural environment grew. Increasingly in the eyes of natural philosophers the physical environment began to acquire the attributes of religious experience and purpose. The idea of a flawed and fallen natural world in opposition to a spiritual heaven became less attractive as the whole globe became technically and economically more reachable and as its extraordinary variety and richness, especially in tropical regions, became apparent and knowledge of it more widely disseminated in printed books. It is true, of course, that some exceptional early oceanic travellers like Columbus had been genuinely sustained by their convictions about the locations of discoverable Edens, Indic or otherwise. In contrast, by the time of Le Guat, the appearance of an earthly paradise is not a surprise to the traveller; it is even anticipated and hoped for. Paradise had become a realisable geographical reality, or so it seemed.

Religious change is inextricably interwoven with economic and social change. The dynamics of the relationships among increasing densities of market connection, the location of capital, and the shifting ideologies of religious conviction have been much debated.[82] During the late sixteenth century, growing volumes of capital started to become redeemable in the developing market

---

79 Carolyn Merchant, *The death of nature: Women, ecology and the scientific revolution*, New York, 1983.

80 The dynamics of this kind of decline have been effectively examined by Simon Schaffer.

81 See e.g. K. Thomas, *Religion and the decline of magic: Studies in popular beliefs in sixteenth and seventeenth century England*, London, 1978.

82 Esp. by Max Weber in *The Protestant ethic and the spirit of capitalism*, trans. T. Parsons, London, 1930.

economies of France, Britain and the Low Countries in connection with agricultural, urban and proto-industrial transitions, and there seems little doubt
that this capital was deeply transforming economically, socially and environmentally.[83] In recent years an increasing number of historians have connected
this transforming power of new capital with the emergence of new cultural
distinctions between town and country and with the growing strength and
powers of control of the state during the late sixteenth and the early seventeenth century.[84] Similarly, the ability to disrupt or control the environment
was vastly facilitated. The activities of the new joint-stock companies which
began to flourish in the early seventeenth century are an instance of this. The
activities of the 'Adventurers' in the East Anglian fens, for example, permitted
the manipulation of areas far larger than the individual estate, in a fashion
paralleled in Europe only in Italy (particularly in the valleys of the Arno and
the Po, where large drainage schemes had operated since the late fifteenth
century) and in the Western Netherlands.[85] By the mid seventeenth century
the colonial plantation investments made by the European trading companies
(especially the Dutch, English and French East India companies) were instrumental, as we shall see, in bringing about rates of soil erosion and deforestation on Caribbean and Atlantic islands that were unprecedented in Europe.
The availability of large amounts of floating capital was directly related to the
new scale of environmental change, both in temperate Europe and, to an even
greater extent, in the tropics. The growth of cities also accelerated changes in
the social construction of the environment. Urbanisation in the Netherlands,
for example, especially when combined with differences in outlook fostered
by religious reform, seems to have wrought very clear changes in preoccupations with natural surroundings. This was seen in a shift away from religious
imagery representative of an older social dispensation towards new kinds of
depiction more closely related to the new physical manifestations of economic
transformation, whether in urban or rural landscape terms.

It is especially significant that the urban middle classes of the Low Countries started to observe and appreciate the transformed reality of their artificial
and often planned cities, ports and drained landscapes. In artistic terms, accurate paintings of the physical manifestations of a new economic dispensation

83 See E. Kerridge, *The agricultural revolution*, London, 1967; J. Thirsk, *Economic policy and projects: The development of a consumer society in England*, Oxford, 1978; H. M. Spufford, *Contrasting communities: English villagers in the sixteenth and seventeenth centuries*, Cambridge, 1974; Simon Schama, *An embarrassment of riches: An interpretation of Dutch culture in the Golden Age*, London, 1987.
84 See in particular R. Williams, *The country and the city*, London, 1972.
85 See H. C. Darby, *The draining of the fens*, Cambridge, 1940; R. H. Grove, 'Cressey Dymock and the draining of the Great Level: An early agricultural model', *Geographical Journal*, 147 (1981), 27–37.

were popular in the Netherlands, and a little later in England, long before such tastes had developed in the rest of Europe.[86] Many of the pastoral images inherited by Claude Lorraine, for example, from Northern Italy also drew inspiration from such vast altered landscapes as the drainage schemes on the Arno.

The first systematically organised Renaissance botanical gardens were first developed in the same geographical context, first in Italy and then in the Netherlands. In the Netherlands a preoccupation with the painterly image of secular reality, in which displaced religious feelings (banished as images from their religious setting) found form in an enthusiasm for the natural, may well have been accounted for as much by religious transition as by the very real growth in the market for paintings of landscapes, buildings, people and the sea which developed in the Low Countries from about 1590. Moreover, the rapid accumulation of convertible capital by a large urban class at a stage when Amsterdam had become the financial capital of the world helped to accelerate the process of aesthetic transition.[87] These developments help one to understand the very striking early portrayals of often 'wild' landscapes, the accurate depictions of 'Little Ice Age' conditions and the growing readiness to move away from the stereotyped image of the Italian pastoral.[88] Such readiness can well be equated with a growing willingness to describe tropical island landscapes in less stereotyped and more dynamic terms.

The accumulation of capital among certain well-defined rural and urban groups able to take advantage of inflation and agricultural innovations, especially in England, was beginning to have a profound effect during the early seventeenth century. It gave rise, for example, to the 'Great Rebuildings' of England and the Netherlands and to significant changes in the age of marriage. However, it also served to promote the growth of literacy, the development of an integrated market economy and the emergence of a market for luxury goods. These last changes led in turn to the growth of the joint-stock overseas trading companies which were shortly to play a critical part in stimulating enhanced environmental degradation in the tropics.

There is some evidence that during this period a detached and relatively objective view of England (or Britain) had evolved, both as an island and as an entity often depicted on maps. Maps of England, displayed on walls or even sold printed on cheap handkerchiefs, had become widely available by the 1680s.[89] Cheap street literature, other printed books and spreading literacy

---

86 For a much more elaborate discussion of the connections among religious change, material wealth and popular art, see Schama, *An embarrassment of riches*.

87 M. M. Kahr, *Dutch painting in the seventeenth century*, London, 1978, p. 82.

88 J. M. Grove, *The little ice age*, London, 1988.

89 L. Weatherill, *Consumer behaviour and material culture in Britain, 1660–1760*, London, 1988.

helped to promote and guide the spread of new ideas and perceptions, not
least of which was a rapidly growing interest in the overseas tropical world.
Demand grew for literature on travel and natural history. So, too, travel in
Britain itself for its own sake became easier and more popular among a certain
group.[90] 'Scenery', and variations in it, became worthy of comment and exploration.[91] Such variations were 'discovered' and appreciated by the end of
the seventeenth century, paralleling the opening up of the wider world by
imperial trading interests. Indeed, by the eighteenth century travel literature
had become the single most widely read and sought-after category of English
literature.[92] In such literature, it might be argued, countries had become com-
moditised, objectified and made subjects for the European traveller, merchant
and scientist.

While in England itself the growth of an intrinsic and objectifying interest
in physical surroundings had not developed in the direction of consciously
organising the environmental impact of human activity in any significant way,
it certainly had done so in the Netherlands. Te Brake argues that the extent
of early land reclamation and the extraordinary degree of control over landforms which the Dutch had begun to exercise had led in turn to a highly
developed form of environmental control.[93] Literacy, it may be argued, led to
a better-defined and more systematic image of geographical space, climate and
the contexts within which colonists travelled and lived overseas. It led also to
a society increasingly open to new and exotic impressions and one which now
possessed the ability to buy books to cater to such new secular interests. A
reading public more aware of the empirical reality of the New World, and
more able to make dyadic comparisons, took a more detached or objective
view of its own society. In this newly literate setting, the flow of information
about the tropics and their natural history increased rapidly during the seventeenth century and then developed into a full flood in the eighteenth, paralleling the growth in trade with the East which had been stimulated by the
new demand for luxury goods. All these developments led to a more empirical
and more informed image of the far tropics, particularly on the part of the
Dutch, to which was added their particular interest in the careful husbanding
and control of scarce and hard-won resources. These concerns were soon to
be projected on to the landscapes of the early Dutch colonies, particularly in
the Cape Colony, where, it was soon realized, a planned Eden could be constructed far more comprehensively than in Europe, not least in the form of a

90 For an extended discussion of this, see E. Moir, *The discovery of Britain: The English tourists,
   1540–1840*, London, 1964.
91 See D. Defoe, *A tour through the whole island of Great Britain. . .* , London, 1724.
92 P. J. Marshall and G. Williams, *The great map of mankind*, London, 1982, pp. 54–9.
93 William H. Te Brake, 'Land drainage and public environmental policy in medieval Holland',
   Environmental History Review, 12:3 (Fall 1988).

colonial botanical garden gathering plant material carried in company ships from the four quarters of the globe.

New ecological pressures on the environment at the centre and periphery in the seventeenth century: The setting for early conservationism

With the growing accumulation of private urban-based capital in northern maritime Europe, it became possible for joint-stock trading companies, and especially the East India companies, to make an increasing and then a dominant contribution to the developing trade with Africa and Asia. Immanuel Wallerstein and Fernand Braudel have both suggested that the history of European expansion, particularly of the kind represented by the growth of the national trading companies, might be seen as the history of an expanding world system which, during the seventeenth and eighteenth centuries, centred first on Amsterdam and then on London.[94] During this period it gradually became apparent, although only to a very limited number of observers, that rapid rates of environmental change were an integral consequence of this expansion process. Braudel has commented presciently that

> even at the end of the eighteenth century, vast areas of the earth were still a garden of Eden for animal life. Man's intrusion upon these paradises was a tragic innovation . . . what was shattered in both China and Europe with the eighteenth century was a biological Ancien Régime, a set of restrictions, obstacles, structures and numerical relationships that hitherto had been the norm.[95]

Braudel's perception of human intrusion was apt, even though his sense of the time scale may have been somewhat tardy with respect to the commencement of large-scale ecological change. Moreover, as we shall see, at the colonial periphery the French ancien régime did in fact attempt to impose its own precocious conservationist restrictions on Braudel's 'intrusion'. As we have already seen, the ability of man to cause very marked ecological changes over wide areas of the globe and then to respond constructively to them has not been confined to the last three centuries. Nevertheless, the scale of ecological change that started to take place in the context of seventeenth-century European expansion was probably unprecedented and, furthermore, elicited very

94 F. Braudel, *Capitalism and material life, 1400–1800*, trans. S. Reynolds, 3 vols., London, 1974, II, p. 106.
95 F. Braudel, *Civilization and capitalism*, trans. S. Reynolds, 3 vols., London, 1981, I, pp. 69–70.

specific and novel kinds of administrative response, often based on systematic empirical observation of environmental processes.

As overseas trade became more significant in volume and competition among the maritime nations more intense, so naval conflicts grew in scale and frequency. This meant that much greater demands came to be imposed on the woodlands of temperate Europe in order to construct and maintain ships of the line of increasing size and number. These new kinds of pressures met with very different kinds of responses on the part of the French and the British. The fact that the British were able to utilise timber sources outside the country with relative ease, especially in the American colonies, made less pressing a situation which had at first seemed urgent. By the end of the eighteenth century this had actually led to a remarkably relaxed attitude on the part of some English commentators, simply because of the relative ease of supply from newly colonised territories. Dr Thomas Preston even told a Commons committee as late as 1791 that the decline of oak trees in England was 'not to be regretted for it is certain proof of national improvement and for Royal Navies countries yet barbarous are the right and proper nurseries'.[96] This was an attitude that helps to explain in part the comparatively casual attitude taken by the English in England towards deforestation until the late eighteenth century, even when attitudes on the Continent had already undergone radical alteration. But there were other reasons for the emergence of a laissez-faire policy.

The wars against Holland and Oliver Cromwell's overseas adventures in the 1650s brought about an urgent need for new vessels and a renewed consideration of state access to timber supplies. Although many hours of Commons debates during the Long Parliament were taken up in discussing appropriate responses to deforestation and the appropriate treatment of seized Royalist land, very little concrete legislative action was actually taken. The issue first made itself felt not only because of the amount of Royalist land taken into Parliamentary custody but more specifically because of the extensive and hurried depredations made by Royalists in the forest of Dean, an area which had normally experienced a very strict governance of timber extraction. The situation was made much more complex and the attitudes of members of Parliament more ambivalent by the revelation that the heaviest despoliation was being carried out on confiscated Royalist land by loyal Parliamentarians, both merchants and those with common rights.[97] Such difficulties were notably absent when it came to the later unilateral imposition of forest regulations by the Crown in the American colonies after 1690 when local rights and local

---

96 Quoted in K. Thomas, *Man and the natural world*, p. 197.
97 J. Thirsk, 'Agricultural policy: Public debate and legislation', in Thirsk, ed., *The agrarian history of England and Wales*, Cambridge, 1985, V, pt II, p. 315.

opposition were at first largely ignored.[98] The anxiety of the Commonwealth government not to antagonise its important political constituency of common-rights holders prevented any serious commitment to a conservation policy. This set a pattern for policy on the part of post-Restoration governments until as late as the mid eighteenth century, at least as far as England itself was concerned.[99] This was despite efforts made by the Royal Society (under whose sponsorship John Evelyn's *Sylva* was written, with its call for extensive tree planting and conservation) to ensure future timber supplies for shipbuilding. Even the political pressure exercised by the Navy Commissioners, whose concern was very evident in, for example, their questioning of the Royal Society in 1662, failed to move the government very far down the path of state forest conservancy.[100]

Most of the Restoration proposals to ensure further timber supplies ran into the minefield of counter-claims between private property and common rights. The fate of the Wood and Timber Preservation Bill of 1674 served as an indicator of the strength of this kind of political obstacle.[101] Riots in the Forest of Dean in 1695–6 against further regulation served to emphasise this problem and make government even more reluctant to act decisively. This was despite continuing heavy pressure from the Navy interest. The high level of naval timber demand over the preceding years had caused increasing anxiety about the security of current supplies. Some very limited local measures were successful, but the New Forest Act of 1696 still spoke of 'great fear for the Navy'.[102]

In view of the apparently insurmountable problem posed by common rights in conserving and enlarging existing woodlands in England, it is not surprising that between 1690 and 1776 increasingly interventionist attempts were made to utilise and secure timber supplies from the American colonies.[103] These were successful in supply terms and did not at first encounter the difficulties of custom and political interest that proved so intractable in England. Suc-

98 R. G. Albion, *Forests and sea power: The timber problem of the Royal Navy, 1652–1862*, Cambridge, Mass., 1926, chap. 2. For details of the growth in local American resistance to British colonial forest policy, see J. J. Malone, *Pine trees and politics: The naval stores and forest policy*, London, 1964.

99 P. J. Bowden, 'Agricultural prices, wages, farm profits, and rents', in Thirsk, ed., *Agrarian history*, V, pt II, p. 78.

100 For more extended discussions of seventeenth-century forest conservancy in England, see Perlin, *A forest journey*, pp. 163–223, and K. Thomas, *Man and the natural world*, p. 198.

101 This discussion is based partly on Thirsk, 'Agricultural policy', pp. 375–6. Thirsk omits to mention that the publication of Evelyn's *Sylva* was in fact probably responsible for passage of the 1668 Forest of Dean Act, which encouraged planting as distinct from the mere imposition of new timber-cutting restrictions.

102 Quoted in K. Thomas, *Man and the natural world*, p. 199.

103 Albion, *Forests and sea power*, chap. 1.

cessive attempts were therefore made to secure exclusive forest rights for the Crown over larger and larger areas of New England. These served to provide administrative and operational precedents for later colonial excursions into state land control in other parts of North America and then in Western India. Only later did these measures provoke political opposition in both territories of the kind that had first developed in England during the reign of Charles I and in the Commonwealth period.[104]

There seems little doubt that increasingly easy access to colonial timber supplies, especially for shipbuilding, ensured that Evelyn's early conservationist ideas received little real commitment from the English government, despite the implicit approbation the Royal Society gave to his views. Evelyn's *Sylva* appealed specifically to a notion of forest science and economics rather than law or custom and quoted freely from the works of Palissy and Francis Bacon.[105] Essentially *Sylva* represented an early attempt to compile a scientific report more concerned with contemporary land deterioration than with historical precedents. It was also far more than simply a text about a strategic timber shortage, although Evelyn was glad politically to stress this latter aspect and to stress as well the patriotic royalist duty of rich men to plant trees, a task for which he probably had other interests and motives. Evelyn even recognised, precociously, the possibility of links between deforestation and changing climatic conditions. However, his familiarity with these ideas, most of them probably derived from classical literature, led him to conclude that forest clearance in Ireland and America had probably been beneficial and the land 'much improved by felling and clearing those spacious shades and letting in the air and sun and making the earth fit for tillage and pasturage [so] that these gloomy tracts are now healthy and habitable'.[106] Evelyn even suggested that the exorbitance and increase of despoiling iron mills should be moved to 'the Holy land of New England . . . it were better to purchase all our iron out of America than thus to exhaust our woods at home although (I doubt not) they might be so ordered as to be rather a means of preserving them'. The concept of America's fulfilling the role of a New Jerusalem or Holy Land (a concept closely related to Arcadia or Eden) did not appear to militate in Evelyn's eyes against the prospect that a mentally unbounded and apparently inexhaustible Arcadia could provide an unlimited supply of raw materials.[107]

This kind of colonial displacement strategy was far less available in France, where by the late seventeenth century the problem of timber supply had

---

104 See Grove, 'Colonial conservation, ecological hegemony and popular resistance'.
105 Glacken, *Traces on the Rhodian shore*, p. 485.
106 Ibid., pp. 485, 490.
107 Evelyn, quoted in Glacken, *Traces on the Rhodian shore*, p. 489. Evelyn's prescriptions for colonial resource use seem to belie his traditionally conservationist reputation.

become just as pressing as in England and a frequently voiced worry on the part of Sully and Colbert in particular. Colbert's Forest Ordinance of 1669 was preceded by a moratorium on cutting throughout the forests of France for an eight-year period, an achievement representing a political commitment to control standing in stark contrast to government attitudes in England at the same period, where common rights were far more politically potent.[108] The 1669 ordinance was instituted in response to a degree of deforestation which was seen as posing an unprecedented degree of risk: A disorder had 'slipped into the waters and forests of our kingdom' and become so universal and rooted that a remedy seemed impossible.[109] The ordinance was the culmination of eight years' practical and legal survey work carried out by twenty-one commissioners under the direction of Colbert. This degree of intervention and planning by the state also contrasts with the response to *Sylva*, which was anyway a brainchild of the Royal Society and not of the comparatively non-interventionist English Crown. As we shall see, *Sylva* ultimately proved far more influential in France than it had been in England. This was largely a result of the interest espoused in it by a group closely associated with the Jardin du Roi, principally the Comte de Buffon and Duhamel du Monceau.

This difference in approach (which might have been less pronounced had Parliament not triumphed in the Civil War) helps to explain the divergent ways in which the two countries responded to environmental deterioration further afield once it became apparent. Major interventions in the control of land use during the mid seventeenth century had already been set in train under state tutelage in France, prominent among them being sponsorship of the construction of the Canal du Midi under the ministry of Colbert and the supervision of Pierre-Paul de Regleur de Bonrepos. Equivalent English projects, such as the construction of the Old and New Bedford rivers, were carried out by private capital and largely at private initiative, utilising, significantly, Dutch rather than English hydro-engineering skills. In part, this was due to the stronger position of the joint-stock institutions vis-à-vis the state in England than in France, particularly after the Commonwealth period. A similar differentiation applies to forest conservation, essentially because there were fewer incentives for English private capital to take a long-term view of natural resources and make the kinds of long-term plans now contemplated by the French state.

Thus one finds that the wording of the French Forest Ordinance of 1669

---

108 Colbert's 1669 Forest Ordinance is discussed in Glacken, *Traces on the Rhodian shore*, pp. 491–4; also in Huffel, *Economie forestière* and 'Les méthodes de l'aménagement forestier en France', quoted in Glacken, *Traces on the Rhodian shore*, pp. 491, 492.

109 Glacken, *Traces on the Rhodian shore*, p. 492, quoting Dalloz and Dalloz, *Jurisprudence forestière*.

made a very clear appeal to long-term posterity rather than to any immediate gain. It was stated that 'it is not enough to have re-established order and discipline, if we do not by good and wise regulation see to it that the fruit of this shall be secured to posterity'.[110] Above all, the ordinance proclaimed the right to prescribe regulations for the exploitation of forests by private persons, and in such form the law remained largely unaltered until 1827.[111] The two most frequent criticisms made of it were the severity of the punishments invoked and the subordination of the interests of the individual to those of the state. In England such subordination remained politically far less palatable.

In summary, then, a comparison of French and English approaches to the emergence of timber shortages in Europe indicates a significant difference of approach to the problem of resource depletion. In England many resource demands were displaced to the colonies, while in France an attempt was made instead to devise a more systematic form of land management. This vital difference in strategy affected the whole pattern of development of the conservation policies of the two countries in their colonial possessions, and elements of this difference of approach can first be distinguished in the evolution of colonial land-use strategies on St Helena and Mauritius. However, attitudes towards risks and changes in the colonial environment actually reflected the broadest and most pressing social preoccupations, particularly in the case of France. Thus by the beginning of the eighteenth century the fundamental divergences in the political systems of the two countries began to show up in yet more developed ways. In particular, the intellectual frustration of the savants in France in their desire for political and social reform started to express itself in terms of natural history, agronomy and attitudes towards climatic theories and fears of climatic change. As a result, ecological changes taking place in French colonies after the seventeenth century acquired more meaning than they did in England at the same period.

The Dutch response to colonial environmental change has so far been left out of this argument. This is not because it was less significant. On the contrary, it exercised a lasting influence on French and British environmental

110 Preamble to French Forest Ordinance of 1669, trans. in J. C. Brown, *The French Forest Ordinance of 1669*, with a historical sketch of the previous treatment of forests in France, Edinburgh, 1873, p. 61. Brown's familiarity with French conservation methods after the 1669 legislation was critically important to the development of conservation precepts in the Cape of Good Hope and hence throughout Southern Africa; the Cape Colony Forest and Herbage Preservation Act of 1858/re-enacted 1888 (and in Rhodesia in 1912) owed much to the earlier French legislation, as did the legislation passed in Mauritius in 1769. See Chapter 5 and R. H. Grove, 'Early themes in African conservation: The Cape in the nineteenth century', in D. Anderson and R. H. Grove, eds., *Conservation Africa: People, policies and practices*, Cambridge, 1987, p. 34.

111 M. D. Dalloz and A. Dalloz, *Jurisprudence forestière*, Paris, 1849, pp. 25–37; opposition to the law is dealt with on pp. 29–32.

policies. However, it was at first rather less constrained by considerations of timber need and much more by the nature of the transition going on in Dutch medicine and natural history. This transition was expressed most clearly and explicitly in the early evolution of the Dutch colonial botanical garden, in botanical networks and in the highly developed interest in indigenous botanical and technical knowledge, a phenomenon not shared until much later by the French and British, and then largely through the medium of a colonial botanical garden 'text' already developed by the Dutch at Leiden, Amsterdam and the Cape.

The colonial environment presented early colonists at the periphery of the new European economic order with a set of problems substantially different from those at the metropolitan core. In Europe, rising population levels, expansion in arable agriculture and demand for timber for urban development and shipbuilding all imposed considerable pressure on the environment. The pressure gradually increased in intensity between 1500 and 1800. By contrast, ecological pressures at the colonial periphery were felt far more rapidly and catastrophically.

For the purposes of the environmental historian, Wallerstein's conceptualisation of the mode of growth of the 'global' European economies can be of some assistance in explaining the consequences of capitalist growth on the relative pressures and rates of ecological change at 'centre' and 'periphery' of a notional 'European world system' during a 'long sixteenth century' between 1500 and 1680. However, in its basic form this model is now increasingly being seen as insufficient to explain the relatively autonomous economic and ecological transformations that were taking place in this period, largely outside the European orbit. The evolution of early merchant capitalism had many more centres than Wallerstein imagined, and episodes of ecological transformation (insofar as they can be related to the impact of capital formation) may be closely related to this multi-centredness. It is certainly true that important population rises, instances of proto-industrialisation, capital formation, urban growth and deforestation can all be identified as having occurred during the period between 1500 and 1700 in parts of India and Japan quite separately from events taking place in Europe; moreover, state building of a fairly complex kind developed elsewhere as well, sometimes with extensive environmental consequences.

By the end of the seventeenth century in Western India, China, Formosa and Japan, forms of state forest conservancy, water control and soil conservation were all starting to appear that were at least as sophisticated as those emerging in the European sphere.[112] Until recently these developments have

---

[112] In China by the sixteenth century the direct relationship among denudation, erosion and flood problems was already recognised as population pressure grew. The Ming scholar Yen

received little attention from researchers. It is clear, however, that pre-colonial Indian excursions into forest reservation, tree planting, irrigation and soil con- servation were relatively elaborate by the early eighteenth century.[113] Similarly, Japanese programmes for forest conservation and soil protection, begun during the seventeenth century, were complex both in ambition and achievement and were based on a thorough understanding of the mechanisms involved in soil erosion.[114] In a pattern which closely resembled the conservationist response of the Venetian state in the 1470s, the Tokugawa shogunate embarked on a far-reaching programme designed to counteract the ecological consequences of a period of rapid economic growth. This served both to reduce levels of soil erosion and to provide for a sustainable timber supply, and also prepared the ground for the highly sylvan nature of the nineteenth-century Japanese landscape. There is no doubt, moreover, that the relatively isolated geograph- ical situation of Japan, broken up into a series of islands, helped to raise the consciousness of the state with regard to the limitability of natural resources and the need for their conservation. Indeed, the significance of the island situation in stimulating conservationist thinking was a common factor in most early conservation thinking, as we shall see.[115]

Wallerstein's world-system theory does, however, offer a useful insight into

Seng-Fang wrote: 'Before the Cheng-Te reign-period [1506–1521], flourishing woods cov- ered the south-eastern slopes of the Shang-chih and Hsia-chih mountains (in the Chhi district of Shanssi). They were not stripped because the people gathered little fuel. Springs flowed into the Pan-to stream, and passing in long waves and powerful sweeps through the villages of Lu-chi and Fen-cha, entered the Fen river at Shangtuan-to as the Changyuan river . . . it was never seen dry at any time of year. Hence villages from afar and in the north of the district all cut branch canals and ditches which irrigated several thousand chhing of land. Thus Chhi became prosperous. But at the beginning of the Chia-Ching reign period [1522– 1566], people vied with each other in building houses, and wood was cut from the southern mountains without a year's rest. Presently people took advantage of the barren mountain surface and converted it into farms. Small bushes and seedlings in every square foot of ground were uprooted. The result was that if the heavens send down torrential rain, there is nothing to obstruct the flow of the water. In the morning it falls on the southern mountains; in the evening, when it reaches the plains, its angry waves swell in volume and break through the embankments, frequently changing the course of the river . . . hence the district of Chhi was deprived of seven-tenths of its wealth.' *Shang Thing Chih*, quoted in J. Needham, *Science and civilisation in China*, vol. 5, pt. 28, p. 245.

113 See Chapter 5 and Chapter 8.

114 C. Totman, *The green archipelago: Forestry and conservation in seventeenth century Japan*, Berkeley and Los Angeles, 1989.

115 A similar awareness of the limited resources of the island of Formosa helped to stimulate the formulation of a timber-protection regime under Chinese rule in the eighteenth century. This was, it should be said, a highly unpopular conservation regime, not least because the cutting of some species of trees condemned the culprit to capital punishment; see J. W. Davidson, *The island of Formosa, past and present: History, people and resources*, Taipei, 1982 (repr. of 1903 original).

understanding the pressures imposed on small island environments during the seventeenth century, especially in the Caribbean and the Atlantic and Indian Ocean areas, where the impact of European capital activity was at first much more immediate than in the Far East. After 1600 Dutch, English and French power steadily displaced the older hegemony of the Portuguese and Spanish over the islands of the Atlantic and the Caribbean area. This was, in part, due to the stable and strengthening pattern of metropolitan demand for sugar and tobacco. This was also a period when oceanic islands such as St Helena were first developed as vital supply points for provisioning and watering the growing India trading fleets. Aridification and soil erosion in the Canary Islands and Madeira served to encourage the westward displacement of sugar production. In this way, between 1580 and 1600 production shifted substantially from the erstwhile Fortunate Islands to Brazil and the Caribbean. Probably the best conditions for sugar production were found on the smaller Caribbean islands and on Jamaica and Barbados. However, even here, after a period of satisfying a sustained and rising demand for sugar and tobacco, the problems of soil exhaustion and erosion started to make themselves felt (by the mid seventeenth century). This was partly because small islands were initially favored over large islands for the establishment of plantations. From the standpoint of transport and defence, the distance from Northern Europe was less, westward islands were more easily defended than those to Leeward, and the high ratio of coastline to land area enabled most plantations to have direct access to sea-going vessels.[116] On the smaller islands there were also more wind for windmills, a less enervating climate and less likelihood of slave insurrections and escapes. The full impact of the new urban market was thus imposed on the fragile environments of the smaller tropical islands. At a similar period and for similar reasons of accessibility, the growing market demand for luxury woods began to be felt on small islands, such as Dutch-held Mauritius, where it had been discovered that very high-quality ebonies and other hardwoods could be obtained with much greater ease than was the case on the coasts of South America, Africa or India.

The degradational impact of new settlement and agricultures exercised in what were now economically peripheral zones was quickly appreciated by local colonists. Very often the first serious difficulties were caused by the introduction of European animals, particularly goats and cattle. In drier regions of Central America and the Caribbean coast, cattle were found to cause serious soil erosion, with results that persist even to the present day. These changes are especially well documented for highland Mexico but probably took place in many other parts of semi-arid Spanish America as well.[117] They were not

116 R. B. Sheridan, 'The plantation revolution and the industrial revolution, 1625–1775', *Caribbean Studies*, 3 (1969), 5–15.
117 E. G. K. Melville, 'The pastoral economy and environmental degradation in highland central

always strictly related, however, to the introduction of a market economy or an entry into the 'world system'. Very often the introduction of a new species of stock or plant was sufficient to provoke changes in the pre-existing ecological equilibrium, while the new subsistence systems of settlers and their collaborators could actually be just as damaging as plantation agriculture adapted to European markets.[118] On the Central and South American mainland, however, the possibility of colonising lands still unaffected by soil erosion or exhaustion tended to discourage the development of effective counter-measures, adoption of new agrarian methods and adoption of forest and soil conservation methods. On the contrary, the decimation of indigenous peoples by disease and genocide that normally followed European colonisation on the Central American mainland often resulted, during the seventeenth century, in forests' reclaiming depopulated landscapes.[119]

Land use on the Caribbean islands was more sensitively adapted to evidence of damage, even if to only a limited extent. It was soon realised, for example, that sugar exhausted the land much less rapidly than did tobacco, so that the main field of activity in the latter was soon moved from the islands to mainland America. By the 1660s the switch was almost complete. As sugar production expanded, so the forests disappeared. The effect was exacerbated by the initially high value which Europeans placed on the removal of the tropical forests. This may have grown out of an historical pattern of forest removal in Europe and more particularly in Britain.[120] For it is the colonisation of the Caribbean islands by the British that we have to consider most carefully, both because of its rapid and uncontrolled impact in response to new market conditions and because the British conceptualisation of environmental degradation in the seventeenth century was so relatively haphazard, particularly in comparison with contemporary Dutch formulations of ecological crisis.[121] Clearing the land

Mexico, 1530–1660', Ph.D. diss., University of Michigan, 1983, and 'Environmental and social change in the Valle del Mezquital, Mexico, 1521–1660', *Comparative Studies in Society and History*, 32 (1990), 24–53.

118 See A. W. Crosby, *Ecological imperialism: The biological expansion of Europe, 900–1900*, Cambridge, 1987.

119 Carl O. Sauer, 'Man in the ecology of Middle America', in Christopher Salter, ed., *The cultural landscape*, Belmont, Mass., 1971.

120 H. C. Darby, 'The clearing of the woodland in Europe', in W. L. Thomas, ed., *Man's role in changing the face of the earth*, Chicago, 1971, pp. 183–216; Marsh, *Man and nature*.

121 Until recently the available literature on the environmental impact of European colonisation on the Caribbean islands has been slight. Before 1987 the principal analyses of the English/British impact were David Watts, *Man's influence on the vegetation of Barbados, 1627–1800*, University of Hull Occasional Papers in Geography, no. 4, Hull, 1966; David Harris, *Plants, animals and man in the outer Leeward Islands, West Indies*, Berkeley, Calif., 1963; and J. S. Beard, *The natural vegetation of the Windward and Leeward islands*, Oxford Forestry Memoirs,

in the British Isles had long been associated with 'improving' it, and by the mid seventeenth century there was a widely held opinion that clearing and tilling the land brought beauty to the landscape as well as economic gain, a notion entirely contradictory, in practice, to the metaphor of the island as the location of an earthly paradise. In early colonial North America, aesthetic delight was taken in creating new vistas in the far and middle distances and meadows in which Europeans could dwell and prosper.

In this way we can see that cultural preconceptions, especially the attempt to reconstruct European-type landscapes in the island colonies, themselves constituted a new kind of ecological pressure on the Caribbean islands quite independent of direct economic motive. This was particularly the case on Barbados.[122] Clearing the land was also important for political reasons. In cases of domestic or international territorial disputes, the clearing and settlement of land with a sufficient labour force to keep it in cultivation provided the soundest claim to ownership. After the French left Montserrat in 1665, several laws were passed to settle disputes amongst major landowners. Fifteen landowners were to have their ownership rights to more than 3,500 acres restored provided the acreage was cleared and settled within twelve months. Once the boundaries were established, each owner was responsible for clearing the land annually. Failure to clear resulted in a fine of 'one thousand pounds of good Muscavado sugar, with one half going to the public treasury and one half to the informer'.[123] Surveyors were also liable for a similar fine if they neglected their duties. With such penalties, it is not surprising that clearing proceeded very rapidly in the mid seventeenth century, and for ideological rather than straightforward economic reasons.

A further cultural construct which initially had the same effect related to contemporary medical theories about forests, climate and disease. Thus the supposed health risks posed by tropical forests provided a further reason for extensive clearing. A common explanation for illness among Europeans was that woodlands exuded harmful vapours which caused fevers and agues. It was thought by some that once the forest was removed the sun would dry out

no. 21, Oxford, 1949. An important little-known study also exists: L. M. Pulsipher on the environmental history of Montserrat, entitled *Seventeenth century Montserrat: An environmental impact statement*, Historical Geography Research Series, no. 17, London, 1986. David Watts's *The West Indies* is a more comprehensive environmental history that does not, however, deal with the global significance of the British Caribbean in the development of climatic theory and environmental policy after 1760.

122 J. P. Greene, 'Changing identity in the British Caribbean: Barbados as a case study', in N. Canny and A. Pagden, eds., *Colonial identities in the Atlantic world*, 1660–1800, Princeton, N.J., 1987, pp. 213–67.

123 Montserrat Assembly Proceedings, 1740:4, quoted in Pulsipher, *Montserrat*, p. 12.

Plate 3. A cleared landscape on Barbados at Hackelton's Cliff in the mid eighteenth century. Landslips caused by deforestation can be seen on the coast at the top right of the drawing. (Reproduced from R. Hall, *A general account of the first settlement . . . of the island of Barbados . . .* Bridgetown, 1755)

the harmful 'miasmas' that were thought to cause disease. In 1677, when Antigua was still heavily wooded, the governor of the Leeward Islands required four thousand slaves to clear the woods for 'more health for the English'. He also noted that in Montserrat, where development had begun much earlier and had proceeded at a faster pace, 'the air is so good that not six here have died'.[124] It should be noted that the debate over the impact on health of forest clearance remained hotly contested over a long period, so that a good deal of ambivalence over the issue is apparent on the part of a number of observers. Embryonic climatic theories started to acquire credence in the island context at the very beginning of European expansion. Oviedo, confirming Columbus's earlier fears about the effects of deforestation on rainfall, noted that the clearance of tropical forest on Hispaniola had indeed caused a decrease in levels of moisture.[125] John Evelyn reported the same phenomenon on Barbados. 'Every year it becomes more torrid', he wrote, as plantations grew at the expense of the island's forests.[126] Evelyn's opinions on the subject were markedly ambivalent. Nevertheless, it seems that this ambivalence may have marked a transition between one climatic school of thought and another, partly as a consequence of the growing alarm over the rate of deforestation on Barbados and Jamaica that developed after about 1660.

Contemporary observations of a whole series of consequences of deforestation and plantation development on Barbados in the 1660s are fairly well documented. They came to the attention of the governor of the colony and were considered important enough to be passed on to London.[127] Soil, it was discovered, rapidly lost its fertility after the original forest was cleared. After thirty years of cultivation, the governor complained, the land now planted 'renders not by two-thirds its former production by acre'. During heavy rain the soil tended to 'run away', and landslides of whole areas of deforested hillside took place. As the 'soil upon these hills is commonly not above eight or ten inches deep and of an oozy or swampy nature underneath', wrote an eighteenth-century visitor to the island, 'it easily separates from the next substratum'.[128] The rapid onset of such conditions and the fact that they received official attention derives from the very rapid rate of deforestation on Barbados between 1627 (when the island was first colonised by the English) and 1665. Inspection of the exceptional increases in sugar imports into England and

124 *Calendar of State Papers, Colonial Ser.* VII, p. 680.
125 G. Fernández de Oviedo y Valdés, *Historia general y natural de las Indías*, 14 vols., Asunción del Paraguay, 1944, bk 6, chap. 46.
126 Evelyn's report appears in J. Houghton, *A collection of letters for the improvement of husbandry and trade*, London, 1707, p. 485.
127 *Calendar of State Papers, Colonial Ser., America and West Indies*, V (1661–1668), p. 586.
128 G. Hughes, *The natural history of Barbados*, London, 1750.

Table 1. *Sugar imports into England and Wales, 1650–99 (000 cwt)*

Years	Ex Barbados	Ex Jamaica	Ex Leeward Islands
1650–4	75	—	—
1655–9	155	—	—
1660–4	143	—	20
1665–9	190	10	33
1670–4	?	10	?
1675–9	?	34	51
1680–4	200	79	66
1685–9	?	129	?
1690–4	183	119	?
1695–9	187	112	?

Source: Data adapted from Watts, *The West Indies.*

Wales over this period (Table 1) tells almost the whole story behind this process.

Through successful catering to the enormous growth in consumption and demand for sugar, the tropical landscape of the Caribbean was transformed in a few years. During the last few years of the 1640s, the immigration to Barbados of Portuguese Jews, who had been exiled from Brazil and were skilled in the production of high-quality sugar, along with the initiative of local wealthy entrepreneurs, caused a revolution in the island's agriculture. The rapidity of plantation expansion defeated embryonic attempts to control deforestation. As a result, by 1665 only one small area of woodland, Turners Hall Wood, survived on Barbados. This was in spite of a number of efforts to control the removal of wood from unoccupied or common land. In 1656 an Act of Council had been passed to prevent abuses of estate boundaries for illegal firewood collection. Its preamble recorded that 'many persons upon pretence that they wanted their proportions of land have encroached upon their neighbour's line and made use of great parcels of their land, and fallen and cut down many of their marked and timber trees of good value'.[129] The penalty for illegal felling of timber or boundary trees was established at five hundred pounds of sugar, and at one hundred pounds of sugar for any other tree. In addition, parish ordinances strictly controlled the removal of timber on unoccupied or common land in an attempt to prevent wastage of wood. Such an ordinance of 29 April 1658 permitted a Mr Lumbard to live on three acres of glebe land for six years and 'in case there be not soe much wood to

129 R. Hall, *A general account of the first settlement and of the leaders and constitution of the island of Barbados written in 1755*, Bridgetown, Barbados, 1755.

complete your quantities of land; whereof he shall not waste, sell or otherwise dispose of any wood without ye consent of ye churchwardens for ye time being, unless it be for ye building thereon, and firewood'. An additional ordinance of 4 November 1661 indicated that at least three acres of this land had been cleared at this time.[130] Despite demands upon the remaining forests for construction timber and firewood, there was no evidence of a severe shortage of wood, especially in the interior, during the early 1660s, although widespread felling continued. Even some lowland plantations retained a large acreage of standing wood: for example, that of Sir Antony Ashley Cooper and Gerard Hawtayne in St George, which in 1652 had a greater acreage under wood than cane; thus, from a total of 205 acres, 95 were retained in standing wood, 60 were under sugar cane, 14 in pasture, 12 under maize, 6 under plantains, 5 each under cassava and potatoes, and 3 under yams, with 5 acres 'run to ruine' and presumably eroded.[131]

Elsewhere on Barbados, forest was still sufficiently common in the interior during 1661 to allow the establishment of different minimum legal widths of road: twenty-four feet in open country, forty feet where woodland was present on one side, and sixty feet where the road passed through woodland.[132] After this date the situation seems to have changed very rapidly, corresponding to the accelerated pace of plantation development. The increasing rarity of good-quality timber foreshadowed the quick removal of most of the remnant forest after 1661. In this way, ideas about timber conservation in glebeland, under strict control by the parish councils, were simply superseded by uncontrolled felling as the demand for timber grew. Similarly, plantation woodlots were cut both for fuel and to increase the acreage of cane. The critical year was 1665, by which time all but the most isolated patches of forest on steep gully sides and in the Scotland district had been cleared. No references to forest (other than to Turners Hall Wood) exist after this date, and a report of 1671 emphasises the almost complete lack of woodland on the island, stating that 'at the Barbadoes all the trees are destroyed, so that wanting wood to boyle their sugar, they are forced to send for coales from England'. In fact, this was a somewhat fanciful notion. Supplies of wood were, in fact, imported after the 1660s from New England and, more often, from neighbouring islands, particularly Tobago. There was to be an important delayed consequence of this pattern of imports. When Tobago was eventually acquired by the British in 1763, its forests, already familiar to the Barbados colonists, were placed

130 Details may be found in 'Records of the vestry of St Michael', *Barbados Museum and Historical Society Journal*, 14 (1947), 136, 173; 15 (1948), 17.

131 G. H. Hawtayne, 'A Cavalier planter in Barbados', *Timehri*, 7 (1893), 16–43.

132 'An act for the better amending, repairing and keeping clean the common highways and known broad paths within this island', quoted in R. Hall, *Barbados*.

under strict protection, in part because of the disastrous experience on Caribbean islands that had been colonised in the preceding century.[133] However, the pattern of rapid change after 1650 was repeated on those other English sugar islands where uninterrupted colonial settlement had been possible. There too any local forest laws and any nascent environmental anxieties were soon overwhelmed by the short-term priorities of a rapacious capitalism, contemporary medical prejudices and the dictates of an imported landscape fashion. The environmental history of Montserrat differs little from that of Barbados at this period. However, some sign of emergent anxiety was apparent from an ordinance passed in 1702 which aimed to protect the streamside (i.e. 'ghaut') forests. Vegetation was to be left twenty feet on either side of the ghauts so that they were shaded from the sun, since 'the laying the same open' was 'oftentimes the cause of their drying up'.[134] Despite this, forest clearance on even the high mountain slopes continued without the early colonists' apparently ever becoming aware of the likely effects of this laissez-faire policy. Instead laws had to be passed to deal with the flash floods that resulted from the increasing lack of any natural upland water-storage capacity. Thus a 1738 Act was introduced 'for repairing Plymouth fort and magazine, and for securing the town from any future eruption of water from Fort Gutt'.[135] By the 1770s Abbé Raynal, the great critic of the social and environmental effects of colonialism, found that the island had lost almost all its original forest cover. His commentary on the colony neatly summarises the effects of a century of unrestrained clearing for sugar and other plantation crops; 'Montserrat', he wrote,

> is in fact but a very high mountain with a gentle slope crowned with tall trees. The plantations rule all around and start at the edge of the sea. They reach almost to the summit. But the further they are from the plains, the more the soil becomes rockier. This island is well watered by numerous brooks. They would be a source of abundance if in times of storms they were not transformed into torrents and did not carry away the soil thus destroying the treasures to which they had given existence.[136]

The impact of sugar-plantation capitalism on the smaller English Caribbean islands was certainly dramatic and even unprecedented in terms of rates of ecological change. While some local appreciation of the dangers of forest clearance had started to develop by the mid seventeeth century, the very speed of clearance meant that any early controls had no time to take effect. After the forests had largely disappeared, some attempts were made on Barbados to

133 Watts, *The West Indies*, p. 399.
134 Montserrat Assembly Proceedings, 1740, 57; see Pulsipher, *Montserrat*, p. 41.
135 Pulsipher, *Montserrat*, p. 41.
136 Guillaume Raynal, *Histoire philosophique et politique*, vol. 5, Amsterdam, 1772, p. 204.

prevent soil erosion on sugar and coffee plantations by contouring and shaping the soil before planting. Some of these attempts have been extensively documented.[137] In general, however, the effects of deforestation on Barbados and Jamaica were remembered, in the official and scientific mind, only in a negative sense. Climate in particular was believed to have deteriorated as a result of forest removal on the smaller islands, and such commentators as Hans Sloane in 1707, Charles Lyell in the 1820s and John Moffat in the 1840s were quick to refer to the case of Barbados in deprecating deforestation.[138] However, most later innovations in colonial forest conservation, at least until the late eighteenth century, came about in areas where the land itself was less economically important, and it was not until after 1750 that the Eastern Caribbean plantation islands started to play a more important role in the evolution of conservationist policies. By that time an external institutional advocacy of environmentalism had become possible based partly on experience and insights gained in East India Company possessions.

Thus, at the same time that evidence was accumulating of the effects of deforestation on Barbados, similar developments were being observed in a markedly different setting on St Helena in the South Atlantic, a very much smaller island. Here, in contrast to the Caribbean case, the colonial response to the ravages of deforestation and soil erosion was relatively structured and interventionist. In part this can be explained by the much smaller size of the island. More significant, however, was the strategic and multipurpose role which the colony played in the plans of the East India Company. St Helena was not alone in this. During the late seventeenth century both the Cape Colony and St Helena became vital watering and provisioning bases as well as sites for a number of projects in plantation agriculture, vineyard de-

---

137 Watts, *The West Indies,* pp. 399–405. According to Watts, most of the significant soil-conservation innovations in the region originated on Barbados in the early years of the eighteenth century. Pulsipher (*Montserrat,* p. 47) records some conservation legislation in Montserrat as early as 1702, referred to in Montserrat Assembly Proceedings.

138 E.g. R. Moffat, *Missionary labours and scenes in Southern Africa,* London, 1840 (repr. New York, 1969), p. 332. Moffat paraphrases Lyell in these terms: 'The felling of forests has been attended in many countries by a diminution of rain, as in Barbados and Jamaica. For in tropical countries, where the quantity of aqueous vapour in the atmosphere is great, but where, on the other hand, the direct rays of the sun are most powerful, any impediment to free circulation of air, or any screen which shades the earth from the solar rays, becomes a source of humidity; and whenever dampness or cold have begun to be generated by such causes, the condensation of vapour continues. The leaves, moreover, of all plants are alembics, and some of those in the torrid zone have the remarkable property of distilling water, thus contributing to prevent the earth from being parched up.' In a rare footnote, Moffat references this text to Lyell, *Principles of geology,* and 'Phil. Trans. vol 2, p. 294'. The latter (an incorrect transcription) appears to refer to observations made on Sir Hans Sloan's estates in Jamaica; see C. Lyell, *Principles of geology,* 3 vols., London, 1830–3, vol. I.

velopment, tank building and irrigation, all of which depended on slave labour. Evidence of deforestation and soil erosion on St Helena was first
noted after the English annexation of the island from the Dutch in 1659, at
a time when East India Company trade was growing and the strategic significance of the island was increasingly being appreciated. As a consequence, the ecological threat to the island evoked a much sharper kind of
official concern and a much more consistent response than was the case in
the West Indies before the mid eighteenth century. At the Cape, by contrast, the Dutch response to environmental change was influenced as much
by a distinctive set of external cultural factors as by local physical exigencies.

This chapter has highlighted the extent to which tropical islands had by
the mid seventeenth century acquired a very specific role as the subject of a
discourse based in large part on archetypal Utopian and Edenic precepts,
many of them with eastern roots. Travellers' descriptions indicate that St
Helena was no exception to this pattern. Indeed, it became prominent in the
discourse, largely owing to Francis Godwin's selecting the island as the fictional and paradisal location for his seminal work *The Man in the Moone*.[139]
Eventually, however, the hard reality of the destructive impact of metropolitan
capitalism on the tropical island at the European periphery served to demonstrate the contradictions between capitalist development and preservation
of the paradisal vision. It was in the context of this contradiction and of the
realisation of it that colonial conservationism began to develop. More important, the formulation of the well-documented response by colonial officials to
the ecological deterioration of St Helena and the Cape Colony marked a major
turning point in European culture as a Utopian aesthetic discourse was transformed into a far-reaching change in attitudes towards European-caused degradation of tropical forests and soils. This change depended, however, on a
major shift in European tropical botany and on a growing empiricism derived
from the incorporation of local indigenous botanical and medical knowledge
into European epistemologies of nature. It is to this phenomenon that we now
need to turn.

139 Francis Godwin, alias Domingo Gonzales, *The man in the moone; or, A discourse of a voyage
thither*, London, 1638.

2

Indigenous knowledge and the significance of South-West India for Portuguese and Dutch constructions of tropical nature

While the growing volume of new long-distance oceanic trade which developed during the fifteenth century helped to stimulate an awareness of the wider world in Western Europe, it also had a much more specific enabling effect on the development of natural history and the status of science in the eyes of governments. A rising interest in empirical fact gathering and experimentation led to growing enthusiasm for experimentation with new types of medical practice and new drugs. Apothecaries' gardens became established at the universities and were increasingly stocked with plants imported from distant lands. These gardens became the sites of the first attempts to classify plants on a global basis. The voyages of the first century and a half after the journeys of Henry the Navigator from 1415 onwards had already begun to transform the science of botany and to enlarge medical ambitions for the scope of pharmacology and natural history.[1] Foundation of the new botanical gardens was, therefore, clearly connected with the early expansion of the European economic system and remained an accurate indicator in microcosm of the expansion in European knowledge of the global environment. The origins of the gardens in medical practice meant that, as knowledge of global nature was acquired, the Hippocratic agendas of medicine and medical practitioners continued to form the dominant basis of European constructions of the extra-European natural world. While the Italians changed the pattern of development of the botanical garden sharply at the end of the fifteenth century, it should not be thought that the Portuguese at the margins of Europe had been inactive. Between 1415 and 1487 they were developing a system of acclimatisation gardens and, long before the Dutch became dominant in this

---

1 See P. E. Russell, 'Prince Henry the Navigator', *Diamante*, 11 (4 May 1960), 1–31. Portuguese sailors actually entered 'unknown' waters when a vessel under Gil Eannes succeeded in rounding Cape Bojador, just south of Lat. 27° N. in what is now the Saharan territory of Rio d'Oro. The Madeira archipelago was occupied in 1418–20 and the Azores in 1439.

field, were carrying out a complex, although not highly organised, series of plant transfers, some of which were to have major economic consequences.[2] In performing such transfers, the Portuguese built on much older patterns of distribution and pharmacological trade in the Indian Ocean region.[3] The main contribution made by the Portuguese was to link such existing systems to the West African, Caribbean and Brazilian regions.[4] The first agencies of plant transfers and the first founders of collecting and medicinal gardens under the Portuguese were the religious houses founded in the first years of settlement.[5]

In August 1487 Bartholomew Dias rounded the southern tip of Africa. Within thirty years, following the establishment of the Portuguese eastern empire in Goa, Magellan's fleet had crossed the Pacific and completed the first circumnavigation of the globe (1521–2). Finally, with the arrival of Vasco da Gama in Malabar in 1498, the scene was set for a global and comparatively accelerated exchange of biological information and biological material, particularly among Asia, Europe and the Caribbean. Such enlarged horizons, perhaps the most significant stimulus and accompaniment to the explosion of mental energy which characterised the Renaissance, had an intellectual counterpart: scholarly exploration of time and text as a consequence of the re-evaluation of Graeco-Roman and Arabic thought that laid particular emphasis on nature and her works. The translation and publication in Venice of Pliny the Elder's *Natural History*, written in the first century A.D., led to a reappraisal of the work of a student of Plato and Aristotle, the Greek naturalist Theophrastus of Erasia (370–285 B.C.). His *Enquiry into Plants* and the *De materia medica* of Dioscorides (first century A.D.) attracted particular attention. This reawakening of interest was also extended into depiction: Leonardo da Vinci (1452–1519) and Albrecht Dürer (1471–1528) made the first truly botanical studies of the Renaissance between 1503 and 1505. This revival of interest in the study of nature and the introduction of exotic plants during the fifteenth century also contributed to the institution of the first acclimatisation and botanical gardens, initially established by the Portuguese on Madeira, São Tomé and Fernando Po and followed a little later by gardens

2 R. N. Kapil and A. K. Bhatnagar, 'Portuguese contributions to Indian botany', *Isis*, 67 (1976), 449–52; K. L. Mehra, 'Portuguese introductions of fruit plants into India', *Indian Horticulture*, 10: 1, 3–4 (1965), 8–12, 19–22, 23–5.
3 P. Maheshwari and R. N. Kapil, 'A short history of botany in India', *Journal of the University of Gauhati*, 9 (1958), 3–32; G. King, 'The early history of Indian botany', *Report of the British Association for the Advancement of Science*, 1899, pp. 904–19.
4 Although it should be said that Asian food plants probably reached West Africa via the old Sahelian trade routes; see Thurstan Shaw, 'Early agriculture in Africa', *Journal of the Historical Society of Nigeria*, 6 (1972), 143–92.
5 Garcia da Orta, for example, knew of Indian plants, including *Cassia fistula*, that were grown in the garden of the convent of San Francisco de la Viega in San Domingo in the West Indies: Orta, *Coloquios*, p. 115 (Markham trans.; see n. 12 for details of this work).

established in Italy on models derived from the major Arabic botanical texts. These Islamic garden models were themselves derived from gardens that had evolved since the eighth century in various parts of Persia, Iraq, Afghanistan and Northern India.[6] The lasting significance of the newly printed Arabic and eastern botanical texts should not be overestimated, however. As we shall see, the empirical agendas of post-Renaissance medicine first took up and then rejected the canons of such authorities as Avicenna as being simply inadequate to deal with the new botanical realms being encountered by Europeans. For after the 1480s the area of these 'known' realms had expanded at great speed. In the course of this process, the problems of classifying and understanding the botanies of South and South-East Asia came to exercise a particular dominance over the pattern of development of European botany and its increasingly empirical character.

By 1550 the world was largely known in outline to Europeans, and the existence of a world flora was being recognised. This was an important development, since a botanical science which was global in scope and exact in its concerns increasingly allowed ecological changes, artificially induced or otherwise, to be accurately recorded. An exultation with the minutiae of the natural world, often apparent in late-sixteenth-century travellers' accounts of the tropics, was paralleled on a small scale in the development of botanical science and natural history in Europe. The new botanical gardens were intended to bring together representative specimens from every part of the world. As such, the gardens themselves acquired a meaning as symbols of an economic power capable of reaching and affecting the whole biological world. As landscape 'texts', they signified a particular type of ecological control that had not previously been available. Earlier herbal gardens and herbal books had been confined to a far narrower Indo-European and Arabic field of knowledge and plant collection. Since printed Arabic botanical texts and Islamic garden models appeared as a product of the same renaissance of learning and broadly from the same textual sources, the significance of the relationship between the hortus (plant collection) as printed medico-botanical text and the hortus as planned botanical garden cannot be ignored.[7]

At another symbolic level the new botanical gardens also played a role as re-creations of Paradise, as John Prest has recently demonstrated.[8] The Edenic

6 See John Brookes, *Gardens of Paradise: The history and design of the great Islamic gardens*, London, 1987.

7 George H. M. Lawrence, 'Herbals: Their history and significance', *History of botany: Two papers presented at a symposium at the Clark Memorial Library, UCLA*, Los Angeles, 1965.

8 Prest, *The Garden of Eden*. The titles of some popular late-seventeenth-century English books on botany indicate that this purpose could also be fulfilled in a less elaborate way by the domestic garden, which developed rapidly in popularity between 1600 and 1700. Thus at least one book marketed in England in the 1650s was entitled *The Garden of Eden*, and many other

terminology associated with the mental and actual constructions of post-
Renaissance botanical and other gardens tends to show that the innovations
involved in the emergence of systematic botany were actually strongly connected with the inherent religiosity of much natural history, however empirical
and accurate its practitioners might have been.

Commercial pressures also helped to bolster botanical empiricism. From
the late sixteenth century onwards, apothecaries' gardens were starting to undergo the transition from being repositories of plants collected only for medical
reasons to being botanical gardens cultivated from motivations of science and
curiosity as well as for their commercial potential. Rural agricultural innovation during the seventeenth century was increasingly closely associated with a
growth in empirical botanical knowledge and an interest in the transfer of crop
plants from one country to another. Whilst the results of this kind of innovation have been extensively investigated in England, particularly by Joan
Thirsk, very little attention has, until recently, been given to the more global
aspects of early crop transfers, particularly in the context of the spice trade.[9]
The role of the expansionist colonial empires in promoting botanical gardens
played a critical part in this development.

The direct involvement of European governments in botanical garden development began in Renaissance Northern Italy at the universities in Pisa and
Padua with the official patronage of botany by the governments of Florence
and Venice. The universities developed teaching gardens and pioneered the
preparation of 'books' of mounted dried plants, known as *horti sicci*, or 'dry
gardens'. Padua had a live garden in 1545, Pisa by 1547 and Bologna in 1567.
The teaching method quickly spread northwards: Leiden and Amsterdam had
gardens by 1587, Montpellier from 1593 and Heidelberg in 1597.[10] From the
outset, such gardens were directed by physicians who were also specialists in
botanical study. Many of them, however, especially in Germany and the Netherlands, sought to express ambitious political and religious messages in the
layouts of their gardens. The organisation of the Heidelberg garden is a good

garden and herbal instruction books stressed similar themes. See H. Plat, *The Garden of Eden;
or, An accurate description of all flowers and fruits now growing in England*, London, 1653, and
the account of the rise in popularity of seventeenth-century gardens in K. Thomas, *Man and
the natural world*.

9 Thirsk, *Economic policy and projects;* the main major exception to this rule are the works on
the spice trade by Madeleine Ly-Tio-Fane, especially *Mauritius and the spice trade*, 2 vols.,
Port Louis, 1958–70.

10 A. G. Morton, *A history of botanical science: An account of the development of botany from
ancient times to the present day*, London, 1981, p. 121. A fuller account of the early history of
botanical gardens in Europe can be found in Burkill, *Chapters in the history of Indian botany*,
pp. 3–4.

example, especially in the way in which a new knowledge of the tropics was spatially expressed and new religious dispensations were symbolised.[11]

Travellers were soon advised to observe indigenous practice and collect material to extend the European materia medica. It was counsel such as this that elicited the first major European book on Asian botany. This was compiled by Garcia da Orta, a Portuguese physician who lived in Goa and who intended to compile a description of plants in the East and India from which medicines sold in Europe and in the Portuguese colonial possessions were extracted. His book, *Coloquios dos simples e drogas he cousas medicinais da India*, was published in Goa in 1563.[12] It was quickly translated into Latin (in 1567) by Charles d'Ecluse (Clusius), who also included with the Orta text a translation of a medicinal history of the New World.[13] Clusius went on to establish both the Hortus Medicus of Emperor Maximilian in Vienna and, in 1593, the Leiden botanical garden. His contacts and travels were unusually extensive, and he introduced into Europe many plants (tulips, narcissi etc.) from West Asia, the region from which the concept of the quadripartite European botanical garden was directly derived. Through his English friends he also introduced many plants from the Americas, in particular the potato, which had been brought from Peru by Drake. Clusius's contacts with England were built upon by his successor, Paul Hermann (who had travelled extensively in the Cape and South Africa), in his contacts with the Chelsea Physic Garden and with the Oxford Botanic Garden, through a friendship with William Sherard. Many students from the British Isles flocked to the medical school at Leiden to hear the lectures of the great teacher Hermann Boerhaave, who also continued Hermann's work in the Leiden garden. The influence of the Leiden garden, with its strong Asian collection and network of contacts, spread as far as Vienna, where the Schönbrunn gardens were being established by Maria Theresa and her husband. Further afield, the establishment of Dutch power in Cochin on the decline of Portuguese power in Malabar was marked in

11 See Richard Patterson, 'The Hortus Palatinus at Heidelberg and the reformation of the world', *Journal of Garden History*', 1 (1981), 67–104. For a useful related discussion of gardens and female power, see Sheila Ffolliot, 'A queen's garden of power: Catherine de Medici and the locus of female rule,' in M. A. Di Cesare, *Reconsidering the Renaissance*, Binghamton, N.Y., 1992.

12 Garcia da Orta, *Coloquios dos simples e drogas he cousas medicinais da India comportos pello Doutor Garcia da Orta*, published in Goa on 10 April 1563. This was the third book printed by the Portuguese in India; it was first published in English as *Colloquies on the simples and drugs of India by Garcia da Orta*, ed. and trans. Sir Clements Markham, F.R.S., London, 1913. All page references are to the 1913 translation.

13 The *Coloquios* was a text included in Clusius's book on exotics entitled *Exoticarum, libre decem*, Antwerp, 1605.

botanical terms by the preparation of the *Hortus indicus malabaricus* as a personal project initiated by Hendrik van Reede tot Drakenstein.[14]

The close association between Clusius and Garcia da Orta and the connections between van Reede and the Dutch botanical establishment ensured that the diffusion of botanical knowledge between South-West India and the Leiden botanical garden became central to the whole relationship between European and Asian constructions of nature. Because of this, two main texts can be said to lie at the core of the relationship between European colonial expansion and the diffusion of botanical knowledge: the *Coloquios* of Orta and the *Hortus malabaricus* of van Reede. In these texts, contemporary Hippocratic emphases on accuracy and efficacy tended to strongly privilege Ayurvedic and local Malayali medical and botanical (and zoological) knowledge and to lead to effective discrimination against older Arabic, Brahminical and European classical texts and systems of cognition in natural history. Inspection of the mode of construction of the *Coloquios* and, even more, of the *Hortus malabaricus* reveals that they are profoundly indigenous texts. Far from being inherently European works, they are actually compilations of Middle Eastern and South Asian ethnobotany, organised on essentially non-European precepts. The existence of European printing, botanical gardens, global networks of information and transfer of materia medica, together with the increasing professionalisation of natural history, seem actually to have facilitated the diffusion and dominance of a local epistemological hegemony alongside the erosion of older European and Arabic systems. As a direct consequence of this, almost all subsequent substantial 'European' texts on South Asian botany retain the essential indigenous structure of the *Coloquios* and the *Hortus malabaricus*.

A word on research methodology may be appropriate here. The historiography of botany is not highly developed, despite the recent appearance of some very important biographical works, and natural history in general has tended to be the poor relation of other disciplines in the history of science. Because of this, the increasingly vigorous field of environmental history probably represents a more appropriate area of debate within which to set surveys of the history of contact between notionally discrete Asian and European bodies of knowledge about nature and botany in particular.[15]

As yet, however, we have no overarching accounts of the connections among ecology, science and society for South, South-East or East Asia, although a

---

14 H. A. van Reede tot Drakenstein (1636–91) (referred to here as 'van Reede'), *Hortus indicus malabaricus, continens regioni malabarici apud Indos celeberrimi omnis generis plantas rariores*, 12 vols., Amsterdam, 1678–93 (henceforth *HM*).

15 The work of Alfred Crosby on 'ecological imperialism' represents one especially useful approach to studies of interactions among botany, ecology and colonising societies, but one concentrating mainly on the colonisation of the 'white' New World by 'European' food plants.

modest literature is accumulating.[16] Both the biographical approach taken by Heniger and the analytical approach to the study of colonising institutions taken by Bruno Latour are helpful to those attempting histories of cultural constructions of nature.[17] Debates about the mode of diffusion of botanical knowledge are perhaps most relevant and interesting in addressing a rather more conventional and specific historiography: that which investigates the nature of colonial power in Asia in terms of the epistemological and representational dimensions of societies subject to European colonisation. In this light the botanical 'texts' of the sixteenth and seventeenth centuries are of particular value. An essential dimension of historical practice lies in attention to the context in which the knowledge and assumptions of our predecessors were produced. In the Indian case, caste has been seen as playing a central part in structuring European knowledge of the colonised society. Brahminical interpretations and texts have, it has been argued, been reinforced by the colonial situation and have strongly affected European perceptions and discourses.[18] By contrast, the diffusion of medico-botanical knowledge has tended to privilege non-Brahminical epistemologies and impose an indigenous technical logic, thereby transforming European botanical science. There are sound reasons for this apparent deviation from the mainstream (where colonised societies are dominated through arms, discourse and text), relating primarily to the shared Indo-Arabic-European roots of medical and biological knowledge and to the effective technical supremacy of indigenous systems in regional botanical terms. Considerations of the derivation of texts, location of 'centres of calculation' and the evolution of knowledge networks thus become the most appropriate tools for understanding the diffusion of biological knowledge in the first centuries of contact.

The technology of the printed book does, of course, have some significance in the codification of both European and Asian systems of biological and natural knowledge, but more in offering us a text than in providing a real explanation for epistemological dominance.[19] The number of available or relevant texts involved is very small, while, correspondingly, each has a life of extraor-

16 E.g. Mark Elvin and Marika Vicziany, 'Ecology and the economic history of Asia', *Asian Studies Review*, 1990, pp. 39–72; J. Kathiramby-Wells, 'Socio-political structures and South-East Asian ecosystems: A historical perspective up to the mid-nineteenth century', in Ole Bruun and Arne Kalland, eds., *Asian perceptions of nature*, Nordic Institute of Asian Studies, Copenhagen, 1992; J. Baird Callicott and Roger T. Ames, eds., *Nature in Asian traditions of thought: Essays in environmental philosophy*, Albany, N.Y., 1989.

17 J. Heniger, *Hendrik Adriaan van Reede tot Drakenstein and 'Hortus Malabaricus': A contribution to the study of Dutch colonial botany*, Rotterdam, 1986.

18 See e.g. Rosalind O'Hanlon, 'Cultures of rule, communities of resistance: Gender, discourse and tradition in South Asian historiographies', *Social Analysis*, no. 25 (Sept. 1989).

19 C. R. Boxer, *Exotic printing and the expansion of Europe, 1492–1840*, Bloomington, Ind., 1972.

dinary influence and longevity, far more than is the case with, for example, narrative histories. Far from imposing European systems of classification and perception on South Asia, the invention of printing and the collation of regional botanical knowledge actually provided an opportunity for the diffusion of indigenous South Asian methodologies of classification throughout the European world, rather than the reverse. The division between European and Asian botanical systems is anyway an arbitrary one. A more logical division might be between Arabic and Hindu/local botanical systems. Taking a broad perspective, the epistemological, textual and cognitive origins of written accounts of South Asian botany between about A.D. 700 and 1800 find a centre of balance well to the east of Venice.[20] Initially, perhaps, one needs to explain the resilience and potency of Avicenna and the Alexandrine school in accounts of South Asia.

The dominance of low-caste epistemologies and affinities in the diffusion of Asian botanical knowledge after 1534

These questions all arise in a textual analysis of Garcia da Orta's *Coloquios*. The original text of 1563 (later transformed in the Latin translation by Clusius)[21] is highly ambivalent and self-revelatory, simultaneously heavily relying on and critically evaluating the classical and Arabic authorities. Orta's emphasis on personal medical experience, local field observation and indigenous knowledge was not typical of the time. This aspect of Orta's text was first recognised and approved of by Clusius and has more recently been recognised by Boxer for its wider historical value.[22] The privileging of European learning and preconceptions, as Garcia da Orta makes clear, can only lead to medical failure. The text is also, however, affected by the delicate balance in power relations among the European physician, the Muslim patron and the local Arab or Persian doctor. Orta's scientific insights are gained through becoming part of this pattern of patronage and subordination as well as through personal friendship. This last factor is not a slight one (as we shall see much more in the case of van Reede), since friendship may allow critical entry into guarded and compartmented local systems of knowledge. Characteristically, Orta's sources are multifarious, while he does not neglect a healthy estimation of his own experience, based in part on the utilisation of drugs in his own experimental fruit and drug gardens (these being essentially a Mughal innovation

20 See Burkill, *Chapters in the history of Indian botany*, p. 3.
21 Clusius's own annotated copy of the *Coloquios* is held by Cambridge University Library.
22 C. R. Boxer, 'Two pioneers of tropical medicine: Garcia d'Orta and Nicolas Monardes', *Diamante*, 14 (1963), 1–33.

in India). Through the efficacious treatment of important patrons, Orta gained access to new knowledge from other, mainly Arab, physicians. This accumulation of new knowledge, balanced against older texts, created the conditions for a reasoned critique of the kind which Clusius, purchasing Orta's text in Lisbon in 1566, found particularly attractive. The book was intended for sale, significantly, in both India and Europe.

The structure of the *Coloquios,* in the form of a dialogue between Orta and an imaginary interrogator sceptical of new and indigenous knowledge (possibly himself as a young student), actually creates a dialectic and a creative tension and invites internal debate about the relative merits of entirely different sources of medico-botanical knowledge. In general the text is remarkably subversive and even hostile to European and Arabic knowledge, regarding it as superfluous in the face of the wealth of accurate local knowledge. The reader becomes aware of a dialogue developing at several levels, some more hidden than others, in which Orta allows his own position to remain publicly indeterminate. We may be allowed, I think, to make a connection between the subversive element of the text and the personal problematic and ambivalence in Orta's status as a hidden Jew, a status he retained only with difficulty and which his family failed to retain.[23]

Orta soon shifted his basic allegiance away from the Portuguese government (in the person of Martin Afonso de Sousa) to Burhan Nizam Shah ('Nizamoxa' in the text) and hence interacted with the other physicians employed by the Shah at 'Balagate' (Ahmadnagar or Palghat), to whom 'he gives large rents'.[24] These doctors, Orta notes, knew 'Hypocras, Galen, Aristotle and Plato'.[25] 'I was taught', he tells us, 'by the Khorasani physician in his [the Shah's] employment.' However, eventually Orta's own knowledge, he implies, is better, essentially because it is more pluralistic. Occasionally, he says, 'small people like me reveal things which great people . . . could not explain'. Rather than relying on the static learning of antique authorities, Orta thus advocates a continual accretion of new learning. 'Please God', Orta adds, 'we will continue to search for and enquire about medicines.' Far preferable to the position of the Arab doctor, he asserts, is the position of the Indian doctors 'who do not know physic through the Arabic books'. 'Dr Orta', he says of himself in the dialogue with Ruano, 'often knows better than all of us, for we only know the Gentoos, but he knows Christians, Moors and Gentoos better than all of us.' However, given the choice between Christian and Arab authorities, Orta un-

---

23 There is a further element, gender, which should not be ignored. Some of the collecting and most of the cataloguing of Orta's specimens were carried out by Antonia, a local Konkani 'slave-girl': Orta, *Coloquios,* p. xiii.

24 Ibid., p. 7.

25 Ibid., p. 10.

hesitatingly chooses the latter: 'Now let us examine', he proposes, 'the writers commencing with the Arabs, for with them we are on more certain ground . . . the Greeks having more learning and the invention of good letters'. 'I have friendly relations', he goes on to remind the reader, 'with physicians of Cairo and Damascus.' Finally Orta makes a startling attack on the lack of any scientific agenda on the part of the Portuguese establishment:

> The Portuguese, who navigate over a greater part of the world, only procure a knowledge of how best to dispose of that merchandise, of what they bring there and what they shall take back. They are not desirous of knowing anything about the things in the countries they visit. If they know a product they do not seek to learn from what tree it comes, and if they see it they do not compare it with one of *our* Indian trees [*sic*], nor ask about its fruit or what it is like.[26]

Garcia da Orta's personal identification with India is reflected, too, in the approbation he grants specifically to Malayali doctors and their medicine. 'I will take you', he suggests to Ruano, 'to see patients cured by Malayalims and Canarese, that you may know it [physic] more thoroughly.' He adds an important caveat, warning that it is very difficult to obtain information from Malayali doctors.[27] This difficulty in acquiring access to privileged information arose later, too, for van Reede in the course of the compilation of the *Hortus malabaricus*, although he seems to have dealt with the difficulty more successfully. Orta was probably too closely identified with Muslim power to attain such access.

Orta's initial dependence on Arabian classification systems reflects the centre of gravity of the international trade in materia medica based on Venice and the Levant. 'Much comes to India', Orta says, 'from Arabia and Abexim [Axim in Ethiopia].' 'I was taught', he constantly reiterates, as though trying to locate his professional identity, 'by the Arabian and Khorasani physicians' in the Nizamoxa's employ.[28] Correspondingly, European knowledge is further marginalised by Orta himself. Even Northern India, in practice, becomes of marginal significance to the reality of medical practice in Southern India. 'At Goa', he states, 'doctors are very little conversant with things in Delhi.'[29] What does this amount to? Essentially that Orta himself, based in Goa (but, we should note, isolated on his own land on an island at Bombaim), relies on the patronage of a Muslim prince to achieve access to knowledge, but, having occasional access to Malayali medicine, emerges in his own text as an ambiv-

26 Ibid., pp. 86–7.
27 Although he adds (p. 97) that 'we stick to the Malayali names, because this was the first land we knew'.
28 Ibid., p. 306.
29 Ibid., p. 483.

alent and even autonomous actor. His position is symbolised by the the device of the dialogue in the text itself, with its harsh critique of the West and western systems of classification and its assertion of the value of the empirical and the situational and, in essence, its presentation of the case for local ethnobotany. Orta's situation is also symbolised by his position on Goa, physically adjacent to his own botanical garden. This garden, and Orta himself (isolated without any academy as such), emerge, then, as a single personal centre of calculation, suspended between botanical traditions, drawing from many sources, often arbitrarily, and dissatisfied with most of them, continually debating their value but always favouring local knowledge. The testimony of an eye-witness, we are told, 'is worth more than any other authority'.

Incidentally, this was a view that sat uncomfortably with Brahminical teachings, so that we cannot simply equate 'empirical/technical knowledge' with Hindu or Indian knowledge. One is left with a somewhat tantalising question: To what extent did Orta ever gain access to Malayalim and especially non-Brahmin medicine and plant knowledge in South-West India? The answer appears to be that he achieved very little substantial access. And despite his protestations, Orta gained little from other 'Gentoo' contacts during his travels in other parts of India. As O. M. Jaggi has noted, the flow of medico-botanical knowledge 'between castes' would have been very limited in this period.[30] Indigenous technical knowledge remained firmly compartmented in the sixteenth century. Orta was, indeed, peculiarly aware of caste insofar as it affected presumptions of power over the natural world, dwelling at one stage in the *Coloquios*, in his description of Baccaim (Bassein), on the precise roles of Curumbis (kumari [shifting] cultivators of the Western Ghats) and Malis, the latter being of great interest to him in their role as gardeners and fruit-tree cultivators.

Orta was probably too closely identified with the establishment of the Muslim Sultan Bahadur for him to gain easy access to Malayali knowledge.[31] Even so, his position as personal physician to the sultan and the Nizamoxa do allow us to explain the relatively autononous nature of Orta's text. In terms of power relations, the imbalance lies not in the way in which the *Coloquios* is structured as a discourse, for it represents an amalgam of Arabic and local knowledge, but in the mode by which the text is transmitted: as a printed book (perhaps the most important ever published by the Portuguese in India, according to C. R. Boxer) and as information inserted into a relatively privileged pre-existing network, the elements of which were the Portuguese colonial botanical (or acclimatisation) gardens and an established pattern of plant and drug transfer. At this stage the network was not at all exclusively dominated by Euro-

30 *Ayurveda: Indian system of medicine*, Delhi, 1981.
31 Orta, *Coloquios*, p. 474.

peans, except on the longest routes between India, West Africa and the West
Indies. Essentially, the Portuguese networks were marginal extensions of an
existing Indian Ocean system of plant transfer. The *Coloquios*, then, is an early
exercise in ethno-botany. Similarly, Orta's role as a doctor utilising contemporary plant knowledge in India (with an unwilling bias towards Muslim systems) prefigured the pioneering role played by other lone European doctors
employed by Indian potentates in promoting and utilising indigenous technical
knowledge, Hönigsberger and Johann Koenig being the two outstanding examples in the first decades of East India Company rule.[32]

Burkill has described the critical part played by Clusius in exploiting this
phenomenon by evaluating Orta's text and using it as part of his attempt to
move towards the empirical and indigenous in both European and tropical
plant knowledge.[33] More important, Clusius's early adoption of Orta reinforced the primacy of the Leiden garden in tropical botany. Jacob Bondt, for
example, relied heavily on the *Coloquios* for his pioneering excursion into tropical medicine, the *De medicina indorum*, published at Leiden in 1642.[34] Reliance
on indigenous local knowledge in Europe came significantly later, however,
than was the case in the colonial context, being pioneered particularly by
Commenius at the University of Sarospatak in Eastern Hungary. However,
while Garcia da Orta was able very quickly to discard the intellectual baggage
of Dioscorides and other ancient authorities, it proved far more difficult for
such men as Clusius to do the same in Europe.

Thus when van Reede, in the aftermath of the displacement of the Portuguese in South-West India, took an independent decision to compile a new
materia medica for the region, largely in response to Vereinigte Oost-Indische
Compagnie (VOC) medical needs, he was unable to rely on any pre-existing
European template or model of technical organisation for assembling South
Asian plant knowledge. A variety of exhaustive accounts now enable us to
chart the ideological and practical history of the compilation of the *Hortus
malabaricus*, the accounts by Heniger, Manilal and Fournier being the most
significant.[35] However, it needs to be very clearly stated that these writers have

32 For details of Hönigsberger and König, see Chapter 7.
33 Burkill, *Chapters in the history of Indian botany*, pp. 5–6.
34 See *An account of the diseases, natural history and medicine of the East Indies, translated from the
    Latin of James Bontius, physician to the Dutch settlement at Batavia, to which are added anno-
    tations by a physician*, London, 1769. Pp. 165–231 of this book constitute an 'animadversion
    on Garcia de Orta'. For the impact of Orta on Bontius, see D. Schoute, *De Geneeskunde in
    den dienst de Oost-Indische Compagnie in Nederlandisch-Indie*, Amsterdam, 1929, pp. 119–30.
35 Heniger, *Van Reede;* K. S. Manilal, C. R. Suresh and V. V. Sivarajan, 'A re-investigation of
    the plants described in Rheede's *Hortus malabaricus:* An introductory report', *Taxon*, 26
    (1977), 549–50; K. S. Manilal, ed., *Botany and history of 'Hortus malabaricus'*, New Delhi,
    1989; K. S. Manilal, 'The epigraphy of the Malayalam certificates in *Hortus malabaricus*', in
    Manilal, *Botany and history*, pp. 113–20; M. Fournier, 'Hendrik van Reede tot Drakenstein

not really been concerned to identify the wider historical significance of the power of the Ezhava affinities in the text of the *Hortus malabaricus*, with all that it implies for assertion of Ezhava classificatory superiority. There is little doubt that Hendrik van Reede was largely responsible for thus elevating Ezhava knowledge, with the straightforward aim of acquiring the highest quality of indigenous expertise.

Van Reede's father had been a chief forester in the Netherlands, and the emotional and aesthetic impact of the Malabar forest environment played a vital role, according to van Reede himself, in encouraging him to embark on a project on the enormous scale of the *Hortus malabaricus*.[36] As he makes clear, the commercial and medical potential role of the *Hortus* was almost entirely subordinate to the aesthetic when it came to motivation.[37] Accuracy of depiction of the plants became a priority for van Reede. This may give the game away. The project of the *Hortus* was strongly connected with the strong contemporary shift which took place in the Netherlands towards a concern to describe the empirical and accurately depict an increasingly highly valued natural world. Van Reede's own account is very helpful here in actual spelling out the close associations in his own mind between an aesthetic appreciation of the Malabar forests and a wish to compile indigenous knowledge about them. On his tours of Malabar he often had occasion to travel through 'large, lofty and dense forests'.[38] They were pleasing, he adds, 'through the marvellous variety of the trees, which was so great that it would be difficult to find two trees of the same kind in the same forest if one were to search for this'.[39] Significantly, he describes the forests in the language of Dutch urban architecture. 'One might regard one such tree', he writes,

> as a magnificent, elegant and delightful palace, whose vaults were supported by as many columns as one could discern branches. And in such a palace a great many people could easily be sheltered in order to shun the inclemency of the climate, for instance excessive showers and the heat of the sun; and thus these forests were like a house of very elegant structure rather than virgin forests.[40]

The connection made here between palace and forest is especially vivid. But the simile also expresses an underlying fear about the ferocity of an unre-

---

en de *Hortus malabaricus*', *Spiegel Historiael*, 13 (1978), 577–8, and 'The *Hortus malabaricus* of Hendrik van Reede tot Drakenstein', in Manilal, *Botany and history*, pp. 6–21.
36 Heniger, *Van Reede*, p. 3.
37 Van Reede, Preface to *HM*, vol. 3, p. v.
38 Ibid.
39 Ibid.
40 Ibid.

strained climate. In other parts of his preface, van Reede remarks on the ability of the forest both to moderate the climate and colonise an otherwise hostile rocky landscape. 'The most barren rocks', he remarks, 'abounded nevertheless with the splendour of a rich vegetation of trees and herbs.'[41] Van Reede went on to extend the metaphor of the palace out into the garden. Indeed, he actually conceptualised Malabar as a garden. 'Every land and field', he recalls,

> extending into the plains abounded so much with plants and trees of every
> kind, (as I have said of the above forests), and radiated such fertility, that
> indeed every piece seemed to have been cultivated by the careful hand
> of some gardener and planted in a very elegant order. Indeed even the
> pools, and one may wonder about this, the marshes, nay the very borders
> of the rivers which carried salt water displayed several plants with which
> they were almost completely covered. There was no place, not even the
> smallest, which did not display some plants.[42]

Malabar, then, was a garden for van Reede, and, more than just that, a 'garden of the world'. 'This had led me to believe', he said, that 'this part of India was truly and rightly the most fertile part of the whole world and that it was largely similar to the island of Taprobana (which nowadays is called Ceylon), especially to that part which is situated in the same climate as the Malabar region.'[43] The connection was thus made between Malabar and an island, a connection that van Reede seemed unable to resist. His mental construction of the landscape as a garden persuaded him towards a more comprehensive set of connections between landscape and people and among forests, people, medicine and health. Such associations were to have a decisive impact on Dutch colonial responses to deforestation, especially when van Reede encountered the Cape environment in 1685.

In this kind of thinking, too, plants took on a value other than purely medicinal or economic, as even a cursory inspection of contemporary paintings makes clear. This may help us to explain why, in the course of organising the appropriately named *Hortus malabaricus*, van Reede moved quickly through three chronological project stages, at the end of each of which he moved farther from European precepts and nearer to a wholly Malayali classification of plants, largely a consequence of the search for botanical accuracy

---

41 Ibid. Van Reede refers here to a trip he made from Tuticorin to Travancore through high
   mountain areas (Netherlands Colonial Archives, Ref: Inv. no. 1142, pp. 702–831, quoted in
   Heniger, *Van Reede*, p. 43).
42 Van Reede, *HM*, III, p. v (translation by J. Heniger).
43 Ibid.

and medical efficacy, but also as a consequence of an emerging attitude to nature.[44]

Working more than a century after Orta wrote the *Coloquios*, van Reede went through the same process of rejecting Arabic classification and nomenclature and European knowledge in favour of a more rigorous adherence to local systems of classification.[45] His own attempts at running an experimental garden had not been very successful. That his approach was innovative and experimental was already demonstrated by his founding a laboratory, against company policy, to process cinnamon oils.[46] This willingness to experiment is also reflected in the way in which van Reede was able to adapt indigenous institutions to the medical and broader scientific agenda of the *Hortus malabaricus*. It took him only two years to reject the methodologies of plant description represented by the *Viridarium orientale* of Father Mathew of St Joseph, a European botanist. Initial meetings between the two had taken place in 1673 and 1674.[47] By April 1675, however, certificates published in the *Hortus malabaricus* itself indicate that van Reede had already shifted entirely to a reliance on Malayali sources and, initially, to the professional expertise offered by three 'Brahmins', Ranga Bhatt, Vinayaka Bhatt and Apu Bhatt, as well as a Malayali physician, Itti Achuden, who was an Ezhava doctor of the Mouton Coast of Malabar.[48] Van Reede's own writings show quite clearly that Achuden played a major role as ultimate arbiter of botanical accuracy and correct identification. This was because the Dutchman soon found that the botanical learning of the Brahmins was in fact quite weak and entirely dependent on the restatement of dictums from old texts.[49] For any useful field identification or collection of particular plants desired by van Reede and the *Hortus* board, the Brahmins were forced to rely on the much greater field knowledge of their low-caste servants. Their knowledge of natural science was, as far as van Reede was concerned, merely academic. It thus made sense to bypass the Brahmins. For field collection, therefore, complete reliance was placed on

> certain men who were experts in plants, who were entrusted with collecting for us finally from everywhere the plants, with the leaves, flowers and fruit, for which they even climbed the highest tops of the trees.

44 Ibid., pp. iv–v.
45 Heniger, *Van Reede*, pp. 42–3.
46 Ibid., p. 41.
47 Ibid., p. 40.
48 Ibid., p. 43.
49 Ibid., p. 147: see also M. Fournier, 'Enterprise in botany: Van Reede and his *Hortus Malabaricus*', *Archives of Natural History*, 14 (1987), 123–58, 297–338.

Having generally divided them into groups of three, I sent them to some
forest. Three or four painters, who stayed with me in a convenient place,
at once accurately depicted the living plants readily brought by the collectors. To these pictures a description was added nearly always in my
presence.[50]

From this passage one may conclude that van Reede never made a herbarium
of Malabar plants.[51] It was van Reede's contact with these Ezhava collectors,
of the 'toddy-tapper' caste, adept both at tree climbing and plant identification,
that seems to have awoken him to the wider value of the knowledge possessed
by this caste.[52] Among them were families of Vaidyar traditional doctors,
highly esteemed Ayurvedic medical practitioners, whose occupation was
passed down a lineage from father to son, along with bulky collections of
books and papers containing hundreds of years' worth of accumulated medico-
botanical knowledge. Itti Achuden was probably the best-known of these low-
caste Vaidyar physicians.

The epigraphy of the Aryazuthu and Kolezuthu Malayalam script certificates appended to the original printed editions of the *Hortus malabaricus* provides us with a surprising amount of further data on the identity of Achuden
and his sources of skill.[53] A translation of what Emmanuel Carneiro wrote
(originally in Aryazuthu script) states that the certificate is

> as intended by Emmanuel Carneiro, the interpreter of the Honourable
> Company, born, married and residing at Cochin. According to the Com-
> mand of Commodore Henrik van Rheede, the trees, shrubs, twiners and
> herbs and their flowers, fruits, seeds, juices and roots and their powers
> and properties described in the famed book of the malayalee physician
> born at Carrapurram, of the Ezhava caste and of the name Colladan, have

50 Van Reede, *HM*, III, p. viii (trans. Heniger, *Van Reede*, p. 47).
51 See the discussion of the 12-vol. herbarium *Plantae malabaricae* (at Göttingen) by N. Johnston,
   'Still no herbarium records for *Hortus malabaricus*,' *Taxon*, 19 (1970), 665.
52 The Ezhavas were a Sudra caste whose traditional occupation was toddy tapping. Many of
   them had an extensive knowledge of the medicinal value of plants and, like Itti Achuden, were
   Ayurvedic physicians very highly regarded by the community. Known as Vaidyars, these
   physicians based their knowledge on the works of their ancestors, who were also physicians,
   and the knowledge was thus handed down from generation to generation. Itti Achuden's texts
   were written in the Kolezuthu script that the lower castes used, for they were prevented from
   learning the more Sanskritised Aryazuthu script which was the preserve of the upper castes
   of Nairs and Nambudris. For details of the Malayalam of the period, see A. Govindakutty,
   'Some observations on seventeenth century Malayalam', *Indo-Iranian Journal*, 25 (1983), 241–
   73.
53 See van Reede, *HM*, vol. 1. The translation is that provided in Manilal, *Botany and history*,
   pp. 113–20.

been dictated separately in Portuguese language and Malayalam language. Thus, for writing this truthfully, without any doubt, my signature . . . [Attested 20 April 1675]

Achuden's own certificate (originally in Kolezuthu script) gives more information:

> As intended by the hereditary Malabar physician born at Collada house of Coddacarapalli village of Carrapurma and residing therein. Having come to Cochin fort on the order of Commodore Hendrik Van Rheede and having examined the trees, shrubs, twiners, herbs and seeds varieties described in this book, the descriptions of and the treatment with each of them known from our books and classified as in the illustrations and notes and explained in detail to Manuel Carneiro, the interpreter of the Hon. Company, clearing doubts [sic] thus supplied the information as accepted without any doubt by the gentlemen of Malabar. [Attested 20 April 1675]

Achuden appears to have given an overmodest account of himself. Careful investigation allows one to conclude that the content of *Hortus malabaricus* was far more influenced by van Reede's Ezhava collaborators than his own accounts suggest. In practice, Achuden and his fellow Ezhava tree climbers actually selected the plants that were to be drawn and hence included in the book and disclosed their names for the plants and so contributed their knowledge about the virtues and uses of the plants. Most important for the subsequent history of tropical botany, the insight of the Ezhavas into the affinities among a large number of plants in the *Hortus malabaricus* are revealed by the names they gave to those species which have the same stem and to which one or more prefixes are added: for example, Onapu, Valli-onapu, and Tsjeri-onapu.[54] The names also give us a considerable amount of incidental sociological material. For Onapu, Onam is the harvest festival in which this particular flower would be used. The names thus preserve the true social affinities of the plant name instead of isolating them in a contextless arbitrary category, as well as probably allowing a truer affinity in terms of pharmacological properties.[55] As Arnold Syen and Jan Commelin in Leiden so arranged the sequence of plants in *Hortus malabaricus* that those which the Ezhava assumed to be related were treated successively (even if the Europeans knew this to be contrary to their own classificatory system),

---

54 Van Reede, *HM*, IV, pls. 47–9.
55 Correspondence with K. K. Sumitra, Vachaly Koroth House, Tellicherry.

the knowledge of the Ezhava has directly influenced the classifications of *Hortus malabaricus.*[56]

Similarly, it has directly influenced the many historically and botanically important texts that have relied heavily on the *Hortus*. Linnaeus, in particular, in 1740 fully adopted the Ezhava classification and affinities in establishing 240 entirely new species, as did Adanson (1763), Jussieu (1789), Dennstedt (1818) and Haskarl (1867) in their work.[57] In India, Roxburgh, Buchanan-Hamilton and Hooker all relied on the same Ezhava structures. Unfortunately, despite the searches of Manilal and his colleagues, the ancestral papers of Itti Achuden at Collada House seem to be permanently lost.[58] Unless they are found in future, the *Hortus malabaricus* appears to remain the only faithful textual record of the accumulated Ezhava botanical knowledge of the seventeenth century. It needs to be stressed that this was made possible only through the innovative and diplomatic ability of van Reede in establishing the board of fifteen botanical 'experts' on the indigenous lines of the Royal Council of Cochin, of which he had at one time been a member. Continuity and survival of local knowledge in a printed text were therefore closely associated with the survival and successful co-option of an indigenous institution.

Ultimately about 780 species of the most important plants of Malabar were described in *Hortus malabaricus,* supported by 794 illustrations. Although botanical explorations were being undertaken in many parts of the world at that time, almost no reliable information was available on South or South-East Asia, so that with *Hortus malabaricus* van Reede could fill that huge gap at a stroke. Together with the *Herbarium amboinense* of Rumphius (1628–1702), the *Hortus malabaricus* immediately established Holland as the centre of tropical botany.[59] This was further strengthened by the arrival of Linnaeus at Leiden, where he completed his studies under Johannes Burmann and Boerhaave. Burmann in particular encouraged the study of the *Hortus malabaricus* and also brought about the establishment of a botanical garden in Java.[60]

56 Arnold Syen (1640–78) and Jan Commelin (1624–92) collaborated closely in Leiden in assembling materials for the *Hortus malabaricus,* adding their own extensive commentaries and emphases.

57 C. Linnaeus, *Flora zeylanica sistens plantus indicus zeylonicae insulae,* Stockholm, 1747; A. W. Denstedt, *Schlüssel zum 'Hortus malabaricus'; oder, Dreifaches Register zu diesem Werk,* Weimar, 1818.

58 D. H. Nicolson, C. R. Suresh and K. S. Manilal (*An interpretation of Van Rheede's 'Hortus malabaricus',* Königstein, 1988, pp. 1–22) state that the papers at Collada House, in Allepey district, were alleged to have been lost 'seven years ago'.

59 See E. M. Beekman, ed., *The poison tree: Selected writings of Rumphius on the natural history of the Indies,* Amherst, Mass., 1981.

60 Before this the gardens at Kaap Stad, Mauritius and Peredeniya were the only realisations of

Further developments in the eighteenth century: The establishment of Dutch, French and British botanical networks

The achievement of the Dutch–Ezhava alliance at the colonial centre of calculation in Cochin and the botanical network based on Leiden, the Cape, Malabar and Batavia provided both the intellectual and informational base and the model for subsequent botanical developments in the British and French colonial empires of the next century. The Dutch, and more particularly the Leiden, intellectual background was indispensable to the emergence of new networks of acclimatisation gardens under the direction of the Comte de Buffon and Sir Joseph Banks and their colonial correspondents. The links with Leiden were very direct in terms of economic botany. Antoine de Jussieu, for example, first described the coffee plant from seed grown in the Leiden garden. The deliberate reliance on the best sources of indigenous botanical knowledge presaged in Orta and put into effect by van Reede, as a direct consequence of the medical rather than commercial significance of much plant knowledge, continued to exert a critical influence on colonial botany. It led, above all, to the direct employment, in situ, of professional naturalists by the French and English as well as Dutch East India companies. These naturalists, following Dutch methods, were often instructed to collect as much indigenous information as possible. Their postings, often as supervisors of botanical gardens, ensured that indigenous knowledge as exhaustive as the Ezhava tradition co-opted by van Reede would continue to find its way into the floras and materia medica of the colonial states, albeit frequently turned to more mercantile uses.

Not surprisingly, it was the Leiden and Amsterdam gardens that soon established a very distinctive dominance in the whole field of European and colonial botany and a pattern soon imitated in other countries. In this way the main botanical gardens and medical schools at Paris, Oxford and Edinburgh were all founded on the Leiden model, and the Chelsea Physic Garden was much strengthened through its contacts with Leiden.[61] The remarkable religious tolerance of the University of Leiden was one reason for this, since it encouraged students of any creed – Jewish, Roman Catholic, Anabaptist, Anglican, Calvinist, Lutheran, Quaker etc. – to come to study medicine in a country little ravaged by war after the attainment of independence and at this period the most learned in Europe.

---

the kind of hortus that Van Reede seems to have had in mind. Their networking, however, was vastly inferior to that later set up by the French.

61 W. T. Stearn, *The influence of Leyden on botany in the seventeenth and eighteenth centuries*, Leidse Voordrachten 37, Leiden, 1961.

Perspective View of the Cape of Good Hope.   Sherwin sculf

Plate 4. An engraving of Cape Town made shortly after the first Dutch settlement. The enclosed Company Garden can clearly be seen beside the church, occupying a very prominent site in the town.

By the 1630s the commercial as well as teaching potential of the Leiden botanical garden was realised sufficiently for the French government to take an interest in the establishment and support of the Jardin du Roi in Paris. The foundation of the Jardin du Roi and the extent of government commitment to it was to prove a critical factor in the subsequent development of environmental perceptions, particularly in view of the unprecedented opportunity which it gave individual scientists not only to acquire a global biological knowledge but, through the connection with government, to exercise their knowledge and interpretations of the dynamics of the natural world in political terms. In this connection, the foundation of the first colonial botanical gardens was particularly significant.

The most noteworthy first step of this kind was the foundation of the 'Company Garden' at Cape Town (Kaap Stad) in 1654.[62] The botanical collections of the company gardens, drawing on a global range of plants, some

62 For details of the history of the Cape botanical garden, see Karsten, *The Old Company's garden.*

of them intended specifically for medical or commercial use, represented an accurate analogue of the current state of botanical knowledge and endeavour, one that was symbolic of the degree of economic or colonised control which was being acquired over the global environment. The exercise of environmental control was already well developed in the Netherlands, and it was no coincidence that the Dutch should have pioneered the colonial botanical garden. The implicit aim of acquiring a comprehensive and increasingly classified knowledge of the botanical world was comparable to the contemporary interest in the acquisition of knowledge of the workings of the human body as a whole system.[63] In the VOC service, medical surgeons were responsible for knowledge of both bodily and botanical systems. Such 'global' knowledge made particular sense in the context of an island colony. Thus, as Du Quesne made clear in his account of the Mascarenes, the analogue of the island as 'a whole world' had become increasingly attractive to Protestants.[64] In France and in Huguenot émigré communities in Norwich and in the Cape Colony, the accumulation of detailed botanical knowledge by Huguenots became an integral part of the local intellectual culture. Similar associations developed in the context of early Quakerism, particularly in Norfolk. At the same time as commercial development facilitated the assembling of plant species from all quarters of the world, the early scientific societies, especially in Britain and France, sought increasingly to systematise the collection of botanical and other knowledge. Thus the newly formed Royal Society went so far as to issue instructions for the use of travellers in this respect as early as 1666 and then again in 1704.[65] Its intervention went some way to redress the relative lack of direct interest in this respect by the English government.

In hindsight it can be seen that the acquisition of a global knowledge of plant and faunal occurrence and distribution constituted a first step towards an ability to determine the influence of man on the environment, particularly where his activities impinged on the existence of species whose rarity, and thus particular value, could only be assessed in the context of a reasonable degree of knowledge gleaned on a global basis. The accumulation in Europe of a global knowledge of plant and other life – and the active role played by institutions and governments in promoting such knowledge – was important. It coincided with the opening of a period when the ecological impact of European maritime and trading expansion first became apparent and com-

---

63 Harvey's discovery of the mechanism of the circulation of the blood in 1616 is a case in point. Both Stephen Hales and François Quesnay (who were key eighteenth-century figures in the development of plant physiology and economics, respectively) were much interested in the circulation of the blood.

64 Du Quesne, *A new voyage to the East Indies*, p. 23.

65 Marshall and Williams, *The great map of mankind*, pp. 45–7; J. Woodward, *Brief instructions for making observations in all parts of the world* . . . , London, 1696.

mented upon. It was in this context that the first well-developed awareness of ecological constraints came about with the Dutch colonisation of the Cape of Good Hope. In particular, the presence of the botanical garden there, with all its paradisal antecedents, combined with emerging Dutch sensibilities about the value of indigenous and local medico-botanical knowledge to produce a response to environmental degradation which French and English colonists were only later able to emulate. The Dutch response was based, above all, on the capacity of local colonists to utilise a developing network of botanical knowledge based on the structures and active participation of the VOC. Such reinforcement was not available at the time to English colonists on St Helena.

3

The English and Dutch East India companies and the seventeenth-century environmental crisis in the colonies

At the core of the developing economic system in metropolitan Europe, environmental anxieties were for a long time confined almost entirely to the prospect of a timber shortage – with the notable exception of the Venetian colonial state. By contrast, the situation at the colonial periphery, especially in the tropical island colonies, evoked a necessarily far wider range of land-management and eventually conservationist responses. Furthermore, the tropical island had become a focus for understanding natural processes and a metaphor for handling new ideas about nature, 'new worlds' and social Utopias. In literature, the island was also serving as a vehicle for a discussion of issues about climate, disease and threats to health. Within this overall cultural context, a comparison of the colonial environmental 'policies' of the English and Dutch East India companies shows that the different abilities to utilise botanical networks and to professionalise knowledge of nature led to very different environmental outcomes.

Fighting ecological decline: Local conservationism on St Helena, 1660–1790

The small size of St Helena and the heavy reliance which the East India Company placed upon it as a supply base meant that environmental and health risks necessarily became the special concern of the island's governors and administration. While the island was initially described by travellers in predictably paradisal terms, the effects of new economic and ecological pressures soon gave rise to a much more critical and pejorative descriptive language. St Helena was the first territory in which the English East India Company became acquainted with the consequences of land degradation – long before such problems became apparent in India itself. As a result, later responses made

95

by the company to ecological degradation in India were strongly influenced by early experiments with land management on St Helena. The environmental policies developed in the island colony therefore deserve a degree of historical investigation quite disproportionate to the size of the territory. St Helena was also noteworthy in a negative sense. A local conservationist response to its ecological problems developed without a structured scientific or professional critique's being developed by the home authorities in London. Because of this, the conservationist response to degradation was idiosyncratic and dependent on the initiatives taken by individuals. Practically no external policy precedents were available to the actors.

St Helena had first been sighted by the Portuguese in the year 1502. At that time, as Alexander Beatson records, 'its interior was one entire forest – even some of the precipices, overhanging the sea, were covered with gumwood trees'.[1] Subsequent to the first Portuguese landing, the main agent of anthropogenic change was the goat, much as it would be on Montserrat and Mauritius and many other islands. The first settler was Fernando López, a political refugee from Portuguese India, who arrived on the island in 1533.[2] López cultivated 'gourds, pomegranates and palm trees and kept ducks, hens, sheep and she-goats with young, all of which increased largely, and all became wild in the woods'.[3] He also tended a large plantation of orange trees, the first of many fruit-tree plantations developed by the Portuguese (they had done the same in Malabar). When López died he left a multiplying inheritance of introduced animals, which soon caused very rapid changes in the original ecology. By 1582, Cavendish tells us, 'there were thousands of goats and they were seen up to 200 together and sometimes in a flock almost a mile long'. Goats probably constituted the single most effective agent of deforestation and landscape change. As Beatson rightly pointed out in 1816, 'to the goat, therefore, is solely to be ascribed the total ruin of the forests, an evil which is now sorely felt by every individual [living on the island]'.[4] However, before the onset of permanent settlement in the mid seventeenth century, the goat on its own was able to bring about only a relatively slow pace of ecological change; ultimately the activities of colonial settlers precipitated a far more rapid transition. Since the time of its first sighting, St Helena had been considered a paradise by mariners, and it managed to retain this reputation until the 1670s, not least among the Dutch. In 1589, for example, Linschoten recorded that 'on the 12th of May, in the morning betimes, we discovered the island of St

1 *Tracts relative to the island of St. Helena, written during a residency of five years*, London, 1816, p. 1; see also Osorio da Fonseca, *Narrative of the voyage of João da Nova in 1502*, trans. J. Gibbs, London, 1752.
2 H. Clifford, 'The earliest exile of St Helena', *Blackwood's Magazine*, 173 (1903), 621–33.
3 Correa, quoted in P. Gosse, *St Helena, 1502–1938*, London, 1938, p. 5.
4 Beatson, *Tracts*, p. 1.

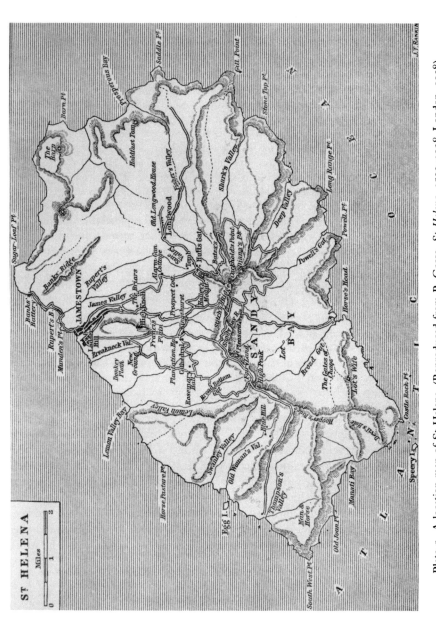

Plate 5. A location map of St Helena. (Reproduced from P. Gosse, *St Helena, 1502–1938*, London, 1938)

Helena, whereat there was great joy in the ship, as if we had been in heaven'. He goes on to describe the merits of the island very concisely:

> The water is excellently good and falleth down from the mountains and so runneth in great abundance by small channels to the sea, where the Portuguese fill their vessels with water and wash their clothes . . . [and there was] a great abundance of fish . . . that it seemed a wonder wrought by God . . . it is an earthly Paradise for the Portuguese ships and seemeth to have been miraculously discovered for the refreshing and servicing of the same, considering the smallness and highness of the land, lying in the middle of the Ocean seas, and so far from the land or any other islands that it seemeth to be a buoy placed in the middle of the Spanish seas. For if this island were not, it were impossible to make any good or prosperous voyage. For it hath often fallen out that some ships have missed thereof, have endured the greatest misery in the world and were forced to put into the coast of Guinea, there to wait the falling of the rain to get fresh water and afterwards come, half dead and spoiled to Portugal.[5]

A little later, in 1601, the French traveller Pyrard de Laval added in similar terms that he thought

> that God has been pleased to fix [St Helena] in this place as a half-way house in the midst of the great ocean, so that we should give to all Indian peoples a knowledge of the faith and obtain knowledge of all the wondrous things to be seen in these far distant lands. To this end has Providence bestowed upon it all that is best of air, earth, water; and nowhere in the world I believe will you find an island of its size to compare with it.[6]

On a later visit, in 1610, Pyrard found that the once-plentiful fruit trees had all but disappeared and now had to be searched for. Apparently the crews of passing Portuguese ships had taken to cutting down the fruit trees while they were still in flower, on the pretext that it was better to do this than leave them for the Dutch or English. The first destructive phase on St Helena, then, seems to have resulted from competition between ships' crews of the maritime nations once the pleasant monopoly of the Portuguese on St Helena had been disturbed. This wanton destruction was commented on by Tavernier when he visited St Helena in 1649. 'There are quantities of lemon trees', he wrote,

> and a few orange trees, planted originally by the Portuguese. For these people have one thing to their credit, that wherever they go they attempt to improve the place for those that come after. The Dutch do just the

5 A. C. Burrell, ed., *The voyage of John Huygen van Linschoten to the East Indies, the Maldives, Moluccas and Brazil, from the translation of 1598*, 2 vols., London, 1885, II, pp. 250–1.
6 A. Gray, ed., *The voyage of Francis Pyrard to the East Indies, trans. from the 3rd French edition of 1619*, London, 1887, p. 18.

Plate 6. St Helena in about 1570: Portuguese ships at anchor in the Jamestown roads at the time of Linschoten's visit. The scattered nature of the tree cover is clear; even during the Portuguese period, depredations by goats were already severe. (Reproduced from Jan Huygen van Linschoten, *John Huighen, van Linschoten, his discours of voyages into Eeste and West Indies*, London, 1598, vol. 1)

reverse and destroy everything, so that those who follow after them shall find nothing left. It is true that this is not due to their leaders, but to the sailors and soldiers who, knowing that they are not likely to return to the place, combine together to cut down trees, so as to get all the fruit with the least trouble.[7]

Until the mid seventeenth century, however, the few accounts of deforestation on St Helena were still outshone by accounts of the island as a paradise or even as a social Utopia. The first and most important, but fictional, account of this kind was written by Francis Godwin at some time between 1627 and 1632 and published in 1638.[8] In it St Helena appears as the paradisal setting

7 J. B. Tavernier, *Six voyages into Persia and the East Indies*, London, 1676, pp. 310–11.
8 *The man in the moone.*

for what is largely an allegorical treatment of the new astronomical information
brought to light by the discovery of the telescope. It was particularly concerned with discussion and use of new beliefs which followed Copernicus,
Kepler, Gilbert and Galileo. In other words, Godwin confronted the new
mental world created at the beginning of the seventeenth century by the rise
of modern astronomy and physics.[9] However, the work was also concerned
with contemporary debates about censorship and, as a very early exemplar of
the tropical desert island genre, exercised a great influence over the shape and
agendas of later island and Utopian literature, and a particular influence over
Cyrano de Bergerac. Jonathan Swift and Daniel Defoe, among other 'island
Utopian' writers, were undoubtedly keenly aware of *The Man in the Moone*.
Furthermore, this main book was published by Godwin nine years after a
traditional Utopian work which he entitled the *Nuncius inanimatus*.[10]

In the 1638 text, Godwin's hero is landed on St Helena voluntarily and
finds himself in 'the only paradice, I thinke, that the earth yieldeth'. 'I cannot
wonder', he remarks, 'that our King in his wisdome [ambiguously, either
Portugal or England is intended here] hath not thought fit to plant a Colony,
and to fortifie in it, being a place so necessary for refreshing of all travaillers
out of the Indies.' The island, Godwin says, was 'a miracle of nature, that
out of so huge and tempestuous an Ocean such a little piece of ground should
arise and discover it selfe'.[11] This enigmatic reference to self-discovery was
unusual and significant. Otherwise, Bishop Godwin seems to have relied
closely on the texts of Linschoten and Pyrard for descriptions of an island he
never actually visited. The native and imported fruits, plants and animals are
all adequately listed, very much in the repetitive and cliché-ridden pattern
familiar at the time. However, Godwin makes much of the very limited supply
of victuals available to his hero and to his 'negro' companion. They are forced
to live separately, 'because being alway together, victuals would not have fallen
out so plenty'. These are interesting perceptions of the limits to the available
resources of the island. But Godwin then goes much further in his use of the
island as an allegory. Deploying some co-operative swans, or 'gansas', to power
a flying machine, Diego Gonzales leaves the limited confines of the island
world to fly around the earth and visit the moon. From the moon he thus
observes the earth as another 'mere' but colourful moon. While concerned to
dramatise the new astronomical knowledge, Godwin also manages to dramatise

9 See Marjorie Nicolson, 'A world in the moon', *Smith College Studies in Modern Languages*,
   17:2 (1936), 23–55.
10 H. W. Lawton, 'Bishop Godwin's *Man in the moone*', *Review of English Studies*, 7 (1930), 23–
   55. First printed in English in 1638, the book was published in French translation in 1648,
   in Dutch in 1651 and in German in 1659. At least a dozen Continental editions had appeared
   by 1718.
11 P. 16.

a further consequence of the new knowledge, that is, an emerging consciousness of the limits of the earth itself and, potentially, the relative power of man
in relation to it. The drama was achieved, it seems, by the imaginative coun-
terpointing of island, moon, earth and universe, in ascending order. In constructing this new cosmology of astronomical consciousness, Godwin also
managed to underline the dramatic part that the isolated oceanic island, and
St Helena in particular, would play in the emergence of insights into the
destructive dynamics of human relationships with the world of nature, and
insights into the nature of peoples and species and their evolutionary histories.
Later imitators of Godwin were much more explicit in representing these
insights. But by the time he wrote, the environment of St Helena was already
undergoing great alterations to the 'Paradise' described by Linschoten and
others. These were much accelerated by the increasingly competitive ambitions of the European East India companies.

The decision taken by the Dutch to occupy the Cape prompted the English
East India Company (EIC) to establish a comparable permanent colony on St
Helena, thus putting into practice a suggestion made by one John Boothby in
1644.[12] The intentions of the EIC were not limited to establishing a supply
base. In contrast to the early Dutch objectives at the Cape, the company was
concerned to reap the advantages of a plantation economy, based on West
Indian models, at the earliest possible opportunity. A minute of December
1658 records that the Court of Directors,

> having several times very lately taken into their consideration the great
> conveniency and concernment that it might be . . . both to the Company
> and the nation . . . to fortify the island of St Helena, whereas (it is be-
> lieved) many good plantations may in tyme be made, did it again this day
> reassure the serious consideration of that business. And finding so much
> reason to engage them in this work, as well as encouragement, after a
> long debate of the whole business, resolved, by a general erection of hands
> to send 400 men with all expedition to remayne on the island, with con-
> veniences to fortifie and begin a plantation there.[13]

Company instructions in 1659 additionally stipulated that 'while this is going on you are especially to have regard to the first season and opportunitie
that God shall grant unto you to proceede to planting of your provisions, but
especially your plantains and cassava'.[14] A little later Barlow remarked upon
the early stocking of the island in an account of the activity of the first settlers:

12 In *A true declaration . . . in a briefe discovery and description of the most famous island of Madagascar or St. Lawrence in Asia neare unto East India*, London, 1646. In fact, Boothby initially
   suggested an English colony on Madagascar.
13 Quoted in Gosse, *St Helena*, p. 45.
14 Ibid.

> Since then our East India Company has taken it into possession and have
> transported people thither to till it, and keep it for them, sending out of
> England a stock of cattle with them, which they have increased very much
> through our people's industry, for the island produceth nothing of itself
> [*sic*] only some few oranges and plenty of fresh water, for it is over very
> mountainous and rocky; yet there are some valleys which are full of low
> stubby wood and very good grass in some places which keep the cattle
> very fat and in good case, they multiplying very much on it.[15]

A similar portrait was provided by a Dominican, Father Fernández Navarette, visiting the island in 1673:

> The Portuguese discovered that island; had they kept possession of it and
> the Cape they might easily have lorded it over India, for where should
> ships take in fresh water or provisions? The Dutch took it, but then fixing
> on the Cape, the English made themselves masters of it; the Dutch retook
> it and the English again beat them out of it. The island is so small, all
> encompassed in rocks rising up to the clouds, it looks like a great fort or
> castle, it has no harbour, but there is good anchoring and safe from the
> winds, because at that season they come over the island. The place where
> the English were is a little valley, not a musket shot in breadth, without
> a tree or bush, or a foot of strand, but there is an excellent spring which
> God had provided for the benefit of the sailors . . . there is no wood which
> would have been a great help [*sic*] . . . in that place there is a little town
> of English who till the ground, sow rice, make butter and cheese; there
> are some sorts of fruit, swine and goats that were put in by the Portuguese
> so there is refreshment enough there at present.[16]

Navarette's observation that 'there is no wood', probably referring to the James
valley, seems to suggest that substantial felling had already occurred and that
it was noticeable to a visitor.

A part of the problem was the failure of the EIC to appreciate the results
that might ensue from the rapid establishment of plantation agriculture in a
small area of very high relief, with variable rainfall. The basis of the difficulty,
it would seem, lay in the transplantation of an agricultural system which was
effectively a hybrid of a freeholder English agriculture and a plantation system
established in the North American colonies and in the West Indies. The Dutch
were far more cautious, at least in the Cape Colony, in embarking on this
kind of activity. Agriculture among the first Cape settlers was at first confined
to producing certain supplies for ships, through intensive market gardening
within the fort area of Cape Town. This was linked to a policy of purchasing

15 Ibid., p. 46.
16 Quoted in A. Churchill and J. Churchill, eds., *A collection of voyages and travels*, 4 vols.,
London, 1704, I, p. 239.

and stealing meat from the indigenous population. The EIC, by contrast, failed to separate supply and plantation objectives on St Helena.

This uncertainty of purpose at the St Helena settlement, which derived partly from anxieties about the costs of running the colony as a supply station, continued to pose problems for the local administration throughout company rule. Associated with this ambivalence was the idea that in the course of clearing the forest and planting crops a purely beneficial process of 'improvement' would be achieved. It is striking, in this connection, that the company seems to have remained entirely unaware, until well into the eighteenth century, of contemporary experience in the West Indies, which was already showing that forest clearance for plantation purposes could lead to some very undesirable environmental effects. These effects, and some of the early attempts to counter them, had been referred to in Royal Society publications as early as 1675.[17] It would be untrue to say that the EIC was institutionally isolated from such advances in knowledge. In 1676, for example, the company was directly involved in funding and hosting the six-week expedition to St Helena organised by Edmund Halley for the purpose of observing the transit of Venus. Furthermore, Halley, whose main astronomical objectives were much impeded by the local seasonal cloud cover, spent most of his time theorising about the nature of the hydrological cycle. This research, which drew attention to the relative water-storage capacities of bare soil, rock and vegetation, was written up using data from locations on St Helena as the main field evidence.[18] Despite this, and despite the fact that Halley's observations constituted some of the first systematic studies of environmental processes, the East India Company persisted with its blinkered refusal to appreciate the environmental effects of developing a colonial island economy. The results of this policy were not slow to appear.

As we have seen, Fernández Navarette had already referred, in 1673, to early difficulties with the supply of wood.[19] From about this date, too, the deleterious consequences of establishing land-use methods and stocking den-

17 See 'An extract of a letter of Mr Lister's containing some observations made at Barbados by Mr Ligon', *Philosophical Transactions of the Royal Society*, 1675, p. 399. These remarks were in fact based on comments made by Ligon on forest clearing and water shortage in Barbados in his book *A true and exact history of the island of Barbados*, London, 1673. Lister noted that 'the springs here are all near the sea so that those who live up in the country have no benefit of them. They made ponds formerly to receive rain, which served well enough, being kept cool by a broad-leaved weed . . . but now almost every sugar plantation has a well, that gives very good water.' In fact the remaining forests seem to have been systematically conserved to some extent; as Ligon stated (p. 101), 'mines there are none in this island, not so much as of coal, for which reason we preserve our woods as much as we can'.

18 Edmund Halley, 'An account of the circulation of watry vapours of the sea, and of the cause of springs', *Philosophical Transactions of the Royal Society*, 192:17 (1694), 468–73.

19 Navarette, quoted in Gosse, *St Helena*, p. 49.

sities imported from England began to be observed. These were felt in a variety of ways and over the years presented steadily more complex and pressing difficulties. These were all well documented in the Council records and EIC correspondence on St Helena, especially between about 1673 and 1730.[20]

It was the introduction of large domestic animals on St Helena which provided, on the one hand, the basis for some of the first glimmerings of awareness of the limitations of the island and, on the other, the ease with which it could be transformed. In late 1673, the year in which Navarette had recorded his impressions, the Directors ordered that 'no female cattle are to be killed for three years until the island could be sufficiently replenished'.[21] The idea of manipulating the existing livestock population extended quickly to the prospect of introducing new kinds of livestock. In March 1676 the Directors referred to the purchase of eight Carmenian goats 'sent from India for 132 rupees being all we can procure which are to keep apart from their breed that it be not lost as it seems some formerly hath by running amongst the ordinary'.[22] This measure complied well with a policy which had developed by 1676 of actively promoting the plantation economy as an enterprise in its own right. However, an initial investment in a new species of goat was somewhat ironic: The goat population had been the main cause of the substantial woodland clearance which had already occurred by the time of the first English settlement in 1659. The company sought to encourage the planters by subsidising them, as, for example, 'planters are informed that their produce of sugar will be bought to encourage them'.[23] Despite this the company met, at best, with only limited co-operation from the settlers in their plans for arranging a model plantation economy. More often they met with what amounted to passive resistance. In 1678 the Directors complained that

> several persons have many times neglected the planting and improving of ye lands allotted them and have taken a liberty to hunt and kill many of the goats that are wild and under pretence of killing wild have killed some tame altho the said persons have no more right unto ye goats than to any cows or other cattle that are wild . . . on said island all the wild goats and cattle being the property of the Company who are sole lords of the island where the said wild goats and cattle breed and feed.[24]

So started a whole series of accusations and counter-accusations in which the company sought, increasingly ineffectually, to assert its wishes and 'rights'

20 Council records and correspondence in H. R. Janisch, ed., *Extracts from the St. Helena records and chronicles of Cape commanders*, Jamestown, St Helena, 1908 (henceforth *SHR*).
21 *SHR*, Court of Directors (henceforth CoD) to Council, 19 Dec. 1673, p. 1.
22 *SHR*, CoD to Council, 8 Mar. 1676, p. 5.
23 Ibid.
24 *SHR*, Consultations, 30 Sept. 1678, p. 9.

and a degree of control over a setting in which local imperatives grew increasingly dominant in influencing the way in which the settlers made their decisions about land use. Ever-present local fears of food and water shortages were a major factor in the divergence of views. Disagreements were arbitrated, often with bitterness, through the governor and Council, who were by no means always disposed to take a company view.

In August 1679 it was minuted that 'a great scarcity of lemons had arisen by reason of disordering [*sic*] persons that gather them wherever they find them . . . to the great inconvenience of the ships that touch here expecting refreshments, ordered a penalty of four dollars if any presume to take lemons from any private land or from the Companies plantation or betwixt their house called the Hutts and the place called the money tree ground'.[25] Here we can already see quite clearly a conflict developing between the company and the colonists with regard to the ownership of a 'wild' resource. The potential conflict between the basic requirements of the colonists as they adapted their activities to the physical exigencies of the island and the demands of the visiting company ships soon made itself felt in connection with the provision of water. Thus on 27 October 1679 swine were reported 'running loose up and downe Chappel Valley besides coming into and annoying the fort and frequently going upon the batteries root up along the water course that runs to the spouts where the ships take in their fresh water'.[26] This is the earliest specific reference in the island records to anxieties about water supply, a topic which was to become a constant worry to the authorities.

The company at this time was also concerned enough about the delineation of ownership to commission an accurate map of the island lands, to be draughted by Captain Antony Bealle, 'who hath measured all the lands that hath been distributed and disposed to the inhabitants'. He was 'to draw up and prepare as exact and punctual a draught Mapp of every man's land on the Island with that due and just Buttals and Boundrys as possibly as he can to be transmitted to the Company'.[27] Efforts made by the company to control and improve the colony in this way began increasingly to contradict notions of landholding which had emerged on the part of the colonists, in particular with regard to common rights and rights of forest use, especially where stock were concerned. In essence, the *de facto* assertion of common rights by the planters militated strongly against company ambitions to enclose the landscape fully and, indeed, against the whole idea of a plantation economy. The conflict between colonists and company faithfully reflected in microcosm many of the debates about enclosure which had long been familiar in England. At such a

---

25 *SHR*, Council minutes, 11 Aug. 1679, p. 12.
26 Ibid., 27 Oct. 1679, p. 12.
27 Ibid.

prodigious distance, however, it was far more difficult for the company to assert control than it would have been for a contemporary improving and enclosing landlord in England. Furthermore, the St Helena governors were almost always far more disposed to compromise with the colonists and to see the logic of common resource use of pasture and woodland as it had evolved on the island. This conflict of interest between nascent colony and mother country emerged sharply in a letter from the Court of Directors to the governor in 1683. 'Lands are to be fenced in', the letter stated, 'in three years or forfeited – no cattle to stray on commons except such as are first marked with the Company's hand . . . not that we intend to allow of any common hereafter when the island's fully improved which are but nurseries for thieves and beggars, though we borrow the method from a custom used upon commons here.'[28]

A clear connection was being made here between undesignated or unregulated land use of unestablished ownership and anxieties about social disruption and social disorder. Such fears were not entirely unjustified, as military mutinies and rioting became increasingly frequent on St Helena during the eighteenth century. It was a logical step, therefore, for the company Directors to extend their anxieties about social disorder to the regulation of woodland and commons. The forests were already under heavy pressure for purposes of fuel supply and grazing, so that the Directors, noting that 'we think the Great Wood is the fittest place for the Companys use', ordered that 'we would have you fence in the full extent of the Great Wood which we understand is two miles square'.[29] By the 1680s the scarcity of wood and other resources had become a matter of such anxiety to the colonists that the Directors' orders went almost entirely unheeded, even by the local administration. This was partly because of an insufficiency of labour for fencing. More important, the realities of island politics simply did not permit enclosure. Nevertheless, the Directors persevered in their grandiose and far-flung projects. In a letter dated 25 April 1684 they pressed the case again for sugar plantations with the words

> The soil and climate of the island is fit for productions and commodities of a richer nature than cattle or potatoes, yams, plantains etc. and being willing that our inhabitants and free planters should not only live but grow rich as we know they will if they may have hands [slaves] to cultivate their plantations as they have in Barbados, Jamacoe and other worse places we have thought fit to take off that restraint.

28 *SHR*, CoD to Governor, 16 Aug. 1683, p. 17.
29 Ibid.

While plantation developments in the West Indies provided the model for these ideas, an equivalent awareness of the potential for resultant soil erosion did not, for some reason, undergo the same diffusion.

Nevertheless, from the West Indies the Directors had begun to learn of other ecological hazards. Worries about species introductions and crop pests led them to warn the St Helenans, very belatedly and probably to the irritation of the island Council, that 'you must be careful and diligent in destroying rats, for which purpose we shall send 20 lbs of impalpable powdered glass'.[30] In the mind of the island government, other concerns were uppermost. By the 1690s the shortage of firewood and depredations in the company forests meant that new and stiffer regulation was contemplated locally. In May 1694 the governor ordered 'that none of the Company's timber trees [the indigenous St Helena redwood was intended here] be sold for private use'.[31] The timing of this species-selective sanction is intriguing. It was almost exactly contemporaneous with the beginnings of the Crown's reserving particular timber species for exclusive Royal Navy use in the neighbourhood of towns in Massachusetts – a type of reservation which was soon to generate conflict between Crown and colonial interests in the American colonies.[32] The power of the Crown on St Helena, as mediated by the EIC, was far more limited than it was in North America. In particular, the attempt to do away with common land had to be abandoned. A Council minute of April 1695 refers without comment or surprise to the status of 'The Commons', indicating that their status as such was now not questioned.[33] Part of the reason for this simply related to the clear failure of the company to establish plantations on anything like the commercial basis it had hoped for. Indeed, a note of desperation began to creep into some of the Directors' missives on the subject of projects after about 1695. This was especially so in connection with proposals to start vineyards on the island, an idea which may have been influenced by comparable developments at the Cape and which was given additional stimulus by the arrival of a number of Huguenot refugees and in particular Jean Poiryer, later to become governor and already a skilled botanist, as many Huguenots were. At this time it was recorded that 'after divers attempts to make some profitable productions upon the island we have at length fixed upon the planting of vines and the making of wine and brandy which all men of quality soever that ever were upon the island that we have conversed with do unanimously agree to be a feasible attempt'.[34] In fact, as one observer noted in 1700, 'the success in

30 Ibid., 25 April 1684, p. 17.
31 *SHR*, Diary, 3 May 1694, p. 57.
32 See Albion, *Forests and sea power;* Malone, *Pine trees and politics.*
33 *SHR*, Council minute, 11 April 1695, p. 17.
34 *SHR*, CoD to Governor, 5 April 1689, p. 42.

ye vineyards hath not been altogether what was desired', part of the reason
being climatic; 'I am satisfied', he continued, 'that this place as well as India
hath for some years past had reason to complain of ye irregularity of ye seasons
which we have more felt in Europe.'[35]

Some vines were eventually planted, although the number of rats on the
island did not bode well for such a project. Rats and goats were not least
among the obstacles to establishing a viable colonial agriculture, and by the
1690s both animals had reached plague proportions. Moreover, goats continued to compete with domestic cattle for grazing. In October 1698 it was noted
that wild goats were 'greatly increased and cattle endangered by total ruin –
hunting allowed of them every Wednesday'.[36] Attempts to control the goat
population were an important first step on the road to wider environmental
regulation. Goats had long had an extremely destructive effect on the vegetation and on the ability of the forests to regenerate. However, they also constituted a direct threat to the survival of other and more valuable domestic
stock. The problem was not confined to colonial possessions such as St Helena
and islands in the West Indies where precisely the same problems had developed. By the end of the seventeenth century the spread of goats in the wake
of European expansion was creating ecological difficulties on a global scale,
and legislation against them was being attempted in many parts of the world,
including South-Eastern Europe.[37]

Soon after 1700 fears began to be expressed about the likely risks of drought
on St Helena. This was directly due to observations that clearly demonstrated
the effects of deforestation on the regularity of stream flow on the island.[38]
The yam, a staple food in the colony, especially for the slaves, and imported,
like the slaves, largely from the Gold Coast, required large amounts of irrigation water for successful cultivation. Despite this, the plant was referred to
in 1699 as 'to be looked upon as the main stuff'.[39] Any loss of perennial
streams threatened this crucial food source. Deforestation was by 1700 already
being considered on St Helena a hazard which might bring unpredictable and

35 Ancaster Deposit, Lincolnshire Archives, Lincoln: 'Report on St Helena'.
36 *SHR*, Consultations, 5 Oct. 1698, p. 65.
37 Strenuous efforts were being made, for example, to legislate against goat keeping in a number
   of regions in Dalmatia and Bosnia, where the geomorphological consequences were in fact
   already far worse than on St Helena. Similar problems were developing on Cyprus, where
   goat keeping was becoming an entrenched part of the local economy. See P. Nikovski et al.,
   'The effects of placing a ban on goats in the forests of Yugoslavia', unpublished paper, p. 1.
38 By 1700 deforestation was already seriously affecting water quality on the island and giving
   rise to complaints from ships crews. Halley, after his second visit to the island in 1700,
   recorded that he 'went to St Helena, where the continued rains made the water so thick with
   a brackish mud, that when settled it was scarce fit to drinke': Letter from Bermuda, 8 July
   1700, in E. F. MacPike, ed., *Correspondence and papers of Edmond Halley*, Oxford, 1932.
39 *SHR*, CoD to Governor, 5 April 1689, p. 42.

dangerous consequences in its wake, quite apart from scarcity of firewood. Such forebodings were soon to be amply borne out. Before the turn of the century it had become apparent that the distillation of arrack, the main island spirit, entailed the burning of large amounts of wood. As a result, the process had come to represent a serious risk to the survival of the forest cover. One observer noted that 'the hourly occasion of great fires under the Yamme pot, with the great consumption that was lately made by their distilling of Arrack from potatoes hath in a manner destroyed all wood of the island, what is remaining being left in those remote places that it is little less than half the employ of slaves to bring it to their respective families'.[40] In 1701, by imposing a heavy duty on arrack sales, the Council sought to 'prevent ye distilling trade which we understand is grown very ripe in the island to the general destruction of the wood'.[41] This was a radical measure. However, the provision of firewood had by this time become such a logistical problem that slaves had to be despatched several miles to collect wood for Jamestown. Deforestation meant, too, that crops were now frequently being blasted and destroyed by the dry winds of drought periods and on the hottest summer days.

As the perceived consequences of deforestation developed from irritant to obvious risk, very little was done, effectively, to reverse the process, even though at least one visitor to the island put forward a well-considered plan for its reafforestation. It was suggested that the shortage of firewood demanded

> a speedy redress, which in my opinion cannot be better effected than by the Company's planting 10 or 12 acres of ground yearly for about fifty years to come, which parcelled into 1, 2 or 3 acres about the island according to their necessity will in that space of time all through supply to Futurity; especially if seconded with liberty to the planters to take and fence in a acre or two (according to their families) of the Companys Commons adjoining to them, which under penalties shall be employed to the increase of wood and no cattle to be turned into them.[42]

Such measures were delayed too long, however. By 1708 the onset of serious soil erosion on the steeper deforested hill slopes had become only too apparent. On 24 August of that year a new governor, John Roberts, arrived. By the time of his installation, the consequences of deforestation began to appear to the inhabitants to be practically irreversible. For Roberts, the soil-erosion problem amounted to a baptism of fire. During the first two years of his governorship he grew steadily more anxious about the supply of firewood and basic construction timber. In particular, he was surprised to find that the Great Wood, now much reduced, was still unenclosed, and he proceeded to embark on the

40 Ancaster Deposit, Lincs. Archives: 'Report on St Helena'.
41 *SHR*, CoD to Governor, 1 Jan. 1701, p. 67.
42 Ancaster Deposit, Lincs. Archives: 'Report on St Helena'.

island's tree-planting programme. In a letter to the Court of Directors he explained that 'we shall be encouraging the people to plant for their necessary uses about their plantations'. If the Great Wood were fenced, he added, 'it would be wood enough for the whole island'.[43] Roberts was at first relatively complacent, even claiming that 'about wood we do apprehend that there can be no want this fifty year'.[44] However, by May of the next year his perception of the problem had been transformed. In a letter to the Court he contrasted the considerable investment in fortification being undertaken by the company with the simultaneous ruin of the rest of the island. The very changed and critical tone of his letter is readily apparent. 'Considering the vast charge that Hon. Masters are at in fortifying the island', he pointed out, 'at the same [time] the inside is going to ruin and has been decaying for fifteen years past especially in that article of wood.' A new approach was clearly now necessary, and in specifically rejecting almost all of the company's enclosure ideas Roberts resolved that

> the inhabitants shall enclose and plant one acre in ten within two years. The Company have ordered the enclosure of the Great Wood but the inhabitants having represented to us what a damage to them enclosing it would be, we will intercede that they may have liberty of the Great Wood provided they enclose their own land one acre in ten – ordered that no person do presume to cut any live wood until such time the vast quantity of Deadwood that lays in the Companys woods be first used.[45]

The proposal that each landholder should conserve a fixed proportion of land was an innovation entirely of Roberts's creation. At the same time he embarked on his own plantation programme, planting both gumwood and lemon trees. Furthermore, he stipulated that planted trees were to be not more than seven feet apart, 'and if not planted in two years the lands to be seized by the Company'.[46] At this time, as a purely administrative innovation, Roberts also invited islanders to submit proposals for reforming the island's legislation on a variety of subjects. A group of islanders did submit some propositions with a formal 'address to the Governor and Council' on 14 June 1709. Anxieties about the island woodlands and the depredations of animals were strongly reflected in these propositions, forming the basis for at least six out of twenty grievances presented to the governor. Roberts's views on the subject had clearly made themselves felt and were shared by many of the inhabitants, as their general submission to the governor made clear:

43 *SHR*, Governor to CoD, Nov. 1708, p. 85.
44 Ibid.
45 *SHR*, Diary, 19 July 1709, p. 88.
46 Ibid., 31 May 1709, p. 88.

And whereas your Worship and Council having represented to us the necessity we are in for the good of ourselves and successors to use means for the preservation of wood, which grows very scarce, and will inevitably be, at last, the undoing of the island and the inhabitants of it, if due care is not taken for the maintaining of wood in planting the same we, making serious reflections on this account, came to the conclusion viz. . . . that every planter possessed of twenty acres of land shall be obliged to enclose one acre and plant it with wood, and so proportionally for more or less; and to take care that no cattle or hoggs shall come to graze on the said land, that the said wood so growing may not be spoiled. And also that every planter shall from the time of this resolution, be obliged to fence the said piece of land in three years time. This is to be understood of those planters that have no wood growing on the land, to take in any more land for the same purpose . . . and we hope that every one of us and all together will do our utmost endeavours to do anything for the preservation of this island, and the good of the Honourable Company.

Roberts, not surprisingly, agreed to most of these proposals, which he had skilfully done a good deal to solicit. However, he felt unable to accommodate the islanders' reluctance to fence off their land over the long term, arguing that the company would eventually order land seizures and that he could intercede for the islanders versus the company in this matter for only a temporary period. He suggested that, providing the fencing were to be installed in some form, he might be willing to permit limited access to the Great Wood for commonage (which would include firewood use).[47] The diplomatic skill shown by the governor in eliciting some active role from the islanders themselves in initiating a new policy was paralleled by his perseverance in tracking down the real causes of forest destruction, a task for which he had developed a considerable enthusiasm. On 11 July he reported that

the Redwood and Ebony trees are most of them destroyed by the Tanners that for laziness never took pains to bark the whole tree but only the bodies. We find that Ebony wood will burn lime and being informed that there is huge quantities of that wood which lies dead in the hills near Sandy Bay the Governor and Captain Maribone went there to view it and found the report true.[48]

This entry gives some indication of the extent of Governor Roberts's interest in the mechanisms of the island's deforestation. He feared, however, that his attempts at restoration might be too late and in vain. This was not altogether surprising, for given the kind of restoration he projected and the seriousness of deterioration that had already taken place, he could expect to

47 Annexes to address to governor, appended to Gosse, *St Helena*, pp. 388–92.
48 *SHR*, Diary, 19 July 1709, p. 88.

find little in the way of precedent from which to draw instruction or experience. As he minuted pessimistically in March 1710, the island was 'brought
to that pass that should the law of planting wood prove abortive the island in
20 years time will be utterly ruined for want of wood, for no man upon St
Helena can say there is one tree in the Great Wood, or other wood, less than
20 years old, consequently it will die with age'. At this stage the spread of
soil erosion throughout the island was being observed; it was recorded, for
example, that 'there is no wood on Bowmans land and the yam ground is
worn out . . . the Governor says this is a plain demonstration of the decay of
the island as on this land there formerly lived three families that now won't
maintain one although it is in the very heart of the country'. The soils of the
island, it appeared, were quite simply disappearing into the sea.[49]

The governor's pessimism at this stage was due partly to the high rate of
failure of the early replanting schemes. This had been occasioned by the dry
wind blast which the loss of tree cover elsewhere permitted, as well as the
constant depredations of goats. Most of the young trees died. Even where
plantations were successful, soil erosion still seemed to be continuing, and it
was recorded that 'the ground wears away strangely for notwithstanding we
have made several new plantations within this three years [but] by the decay
of the old plantations we can't say we are increast'.[50]

Between the end of 1709 and the termination of his term of office, Roberts
set out to convince the company of the extent of the crisis on the island and
its likely long-term consequences for the survival of a viable colony. Simultaneously he continued to try to restore the forest cover and safeguard the
perennial water supply, and in one letter (written in December 1710) assigned
blame for the situation equally to the failure of successive governors to carry
out any attempts to protect the existing woodland (especially by enclosing the
Great Wood) and the company's failure to intervene more effectively. In this
letter Roberts showed that he understood that these past administrative failures had resulted in a high and rising expenditure by the company, both in
terms of direct costs and labour needed:

> We say that the Antient Old Company has been very ill served – there
> was never a stone laid [to enclose the Great Wood] or had Governor
> Poiryer [his predecessor] . . . fenced in the wood about him which was so
> thick that they could hardly find their way to the place and now they can
> hardly find a tree; or had he fenced in the ground that nearly costs as
> much money to keep the cows out as the value of the grapes amounted,
> or indeed done anything to prevent the island going to rack and ruin we
> should have the less needs of hands [slaves] and our labour and time been

49 Ibid., 7 Mar. 1710, p. 90.
50 Ibid., 7 Mar. 1711, p. 93.

employed to much better service. Whatever that gentleman [Poiryer] had done is a secret to every soul upon the island.

As we have seen, Poiryer had in fact taken a professional interest in the botany of the island as well as in the possibilities of vineyard development. However, these efforts had not impressed Roberts, since Poiryer had remained quite oblivious to the erosive consequences of the plantation projects which he had supported.[51]

Both the difficulties of communication and the apparent unwillingness of the Directors to appreciate the gravity of soil erosion and deforestation problems eventually provoked the island Council to express itself in a very explicit way. It objected specifically to orders from the Directors allowing individuals title to the enlargement of their estates, explaining in one instance that 'if your honours should give George Hoskins his estate at the home pasture again we must bid farewell to most part of the island and expect no wood from thence, we shall not have wood to boil your yam [for the company slaves] and it will render your island useless after all your great charge'.[52] The rest of the letter backed up the Council's plea for understanding with the threat that the difficulties into which planters had been compelled by events might persuade them to contemplate migration. A specific connection was made in the letter between environmental deterioration and the poverty of the populace. 'The young trees we have planted', Roberts wrote,

> does not answer expectation as we would wish. We pray your Honours to hearken what we say for we regret to tell you that your island is almost ruined. Without your encouragement in general we can have no hopes for if we are not plentifully supplied with stores so we may be able to put your plans in execution these two most important articles of fencing and planting should they prove abortive there is an end to it; for a great many planters which are very poor and much indebted to you care not which end goes foremost and even challenge us to send them where we

51 *SHR*, Council to CoD, 1 Dec. 1710, pp. 91–2. Poiryer collected plants on St Helena for James Petiver, a professional collector in London, transferring them via EIC marine medical officers such as Samuel Brown (d. 1703?) and Edward Bulkley (1651–1714); see P. I. Edwards, 'Sir Hans Sloane and his curious friends', in A. Wheeler, ed., *History in the science of systematics*, London, 1981, pp. 27–35, for further details of Petiver's methods. This connection between Poiryer, as a French Huguenot, and the emerging community of naturalists surrounding Sir Hans Sloane may well mark the beginning of a period in which the plants of St Helena became recognised as specifically endemic to the island, an awareness that was inherited by Burchell, Roxburgh and Darwin and on which all commented during their respective stays on the island. The sending by Poiryer in 1704 of a plant named *Wahlenbergia liniflora*, recognised later as being confined to St Helena, may be said to have marked the start of this process (Q. C. B. Cronk, pers. comm.). The recognition of endemism on St Helena was a key step in understanding the vulnerability of species to human activity on a global basis; see also Chapter 4.

52 *SHR*, Diary, 7 Mar. 1711, p. 93.

will for it cannot be they say to a worse place for here they neither get cloathes to their back nor a dram to drink.[53]

Roberts embarked during the following month on an adventurous scheme to channel water on to Prosperous Bay Plain in an effort to obtain a larger area of irrigated arable ground. But these early irrigation efforts, entered into in an attempt to make up for the decline in perennial stream flow, were brought to an abrupt end when the governor left the island in December 1710. His departure marked the end of a first phase of attempts to come to terms with the ecological crisis into which the island had declined. Meanwhile, the company had contrived to remain quite unable to grasp the difficulties of contending with long-term degradation even when confronted with the facts by official despatch. Roberts was aware of this official blindness, and there is some evidence that on his return to England he made it his business to further publicise the parlous condition of St Helena. In particular he tried to convince the Directors that tree planting would be of little help until goats were controlled and more land fenced off. Despite these efforts, no attempt seems to have been made by the company to inform Roberts's successor, Governor Boucher, of the situation he might have to confront.

During 1712–14 matters came to a head both because of severe maladministration during Governor Boucher's term of office and the incidence of a very long and severe drought, which began in July 1712 and continued until at least April 1713. The extent of deforestation by this time meant that the effects of the drought were much worse than they might have been in earlier years. Furthermore, with Roberts's departure most of the soil- and forest-conservation programmes seem to have been abandoned. Most seriously, nothing was done to tackle the goat problem. While rigorous and organised goat control might have resulted in long-term benefits, individual landowners were not prepared to sacrifice the cheap supply of meat on the hoof which goats represented. There was a lack of official resolution in other areas as well, despite the growing evidence that the indigenous redwood, the principal timber tree, was facing extinction. These attitudes were made clear in a letter from the Council sent in answer to points put by the Directors in response to Roberts's campaign:

> As to what Governor Roberts says in his letter that the goats destroy all the trees and the island speedily ruined if they were not killed we don't think this is feasible or beneficial either for that goats range generally in the out parts of the island next the sea where nothing else can, or few trees grow except shrubs which is no use, and they live with lesser care than anything else and is very ready meat and saves the killing of cattle

53 Ibid.

... its impossible to fence the Great Wood and had we never so many hands the charge of doing it would be more than the advantage and as to these trees being barked for tanning leather (they never grew in the Great Wood but under the main ridge) called Redwood trees the best and most proper for building houses of which theirs but very few now the nature of these trees seldom producing younger ones although enclosed, whereas Gumwood doth.[54]

This confused and defeatist letter was, if nothing else, an indication of how much conservationist efforts depended on the convictions of an enthusiastic individual. By June 1713 the continuing drought had put paid, anyway, to much of Roberts's restoration effort. Most of his plantations were 'merely burnt or scorcht up and little of any sort to be seen above ground, besides the great dearth and consumption of cattle which has reduced most of the inhabitants stocks very low'.[55] During the serious droughts of 1712–14 more than two thousand cattle died.[56] The resulting privation seems to have provoked a resumption of arrack drinking, and a letter from the Directors in March 1713 notes that 'excessive drinking of arrack has grown up upon all the people strangely of late and shews their oppression or some other discontent made them careless how matters went for such excess necessarily tends to beggary'. A similar comment was made on 15 March 1715: 'We are surprised at the large demand for arrack. The people are grown sottish and the place is less healthful than formerly and diseases more rife.' Somewhat to the surprise of the company, then, Roberts's warnings were being borne out, and as the Council minutes recorded tersely, the island was 'in a very bad and deplorable condition'.

With the arrival of Governor Pyke in 1715, attempts at reafforestation were recommenced, utilising imported *Pineaster* species for the first time. These grew well, and it was reported that 'the seeds of the trees came well out. The first to all appearance will be of extraordinary service.'[57] On his arrival, Pyke, like Roberts, inspected the island minutely with a view to increasing or stabilising the still non-eroded area, paying particular attention to Rupert's Valley, which contained 'more than 200 acres of good land which has never been occupied . . . [but] . . . the whole valley wants water'.[58]

Pyke considered extending Robert's irrigation plans by building an irrigation channel across the island watershed into the valley in order to permit its use for agriculture. He seems to have become psychologically overwhelmed,

---

54 *SHR*, Council to CoD, 9 April 1713, pp. 105–6.
55 *SHR*, Diary, 4 June 1713, p. 107.
56 Ibid., 18 Jan. 1715, p. 113.
57 Ibid., 1715, pp. 114–15.
58 Ibid.

however, by the limitations of the island and its deteriorated state. It was
against this background of the general ecological decline of the island that
Pyke's thoughts appear to have wandered away from the immediate and frus-
trating context. He embarked on a long and somewhat whimsical interchange
with the Directors which recommended, in essence, that consideration be
given to the idea of seizing the island of Mauritius, recently vacated by the
Dutch, and resettling upon it a selection of the younger and more destitute
St Helenans. The letter is interesting in a number of ways, but more especially
in the way in which, implicitly, the state to which St Helena had been reduced
was compared with a land as yet, so Pyke believed, relatively untouched by
European activity or settlement and one which stood in tempting and attractive contrast to St Helena. In fact Pyke had previously visited Mauritius and
so clearly thought back to it with regret. Almost undoubtedly, too, the severity
of the droughts of 1712–15, as well as the ravages of soil erosion and the
relative impoverishment of the islanders, had heightened the perceptions of a
distant land of well-being, indeed one that was still a paradise of the kind that
St Helena remained in the memories of its older inhabitants. Pyke's analysis
reads as follows:

> We have had a sickly season lately here but we hear that a general sickness
> has ranged both at the Cape of Good Hope and all these coasts [referring
> to the trade forts on the Gold and Slave Coasts]. We hear that the fruitful
> island called Mauritius that was lately left by the Dutch is yet uninhabited
> and has not had any dearth upon it but abounds plentifully. There is
> deer and other cattle both of the Indian and European kinds with fruit
> of every sort and plenty of many sorts of timber with commodious har-
> bours for ships and a fine temperate air which usually preserved the
> former inhabitants to a very great age. But now 'tis wild, the land un-
> occupied and almost overgrown with wood as well as overstocked with
> cattle – be pleased to pardon us for this freedom who had not troubled
> your Honours with such accounts as this but Captain Litten making this
> report and our Governor having formerly been in several parts of the
> island from the flatts about the North and NW down to Black River which
> is above sixty miles and being able of his own knowledge to confirm all
> that Capt. Litten has said about the Mauritos [sic,] was desirous of writing
> your Honours concerning this place for the following reasons: First that
> we have several young people here more than we can supply with plan-
> tations that because of their way of living here would be very proper
> inhabitants to settle in that place, and because that place is naturally so
> well supplied that it would maintain a very great colony without any
> charge to their Patrons more than sending them out and the place lies in
> the Root or Tract of all homeward bound shipping. But out great and
> principal reason is that the Government and people of the Don Mascar-
> enes [Madagascar] say they have sent to France for libertie to transplant

themselves to this neighbouring Island which is not only more commodious than Mascarenas in regard to shipping but it exceeds it so much in fertility that it is as a Paradise to the other. The consideration of keeping out the French or the Indian Pyrates from an island of such consequences as the Isle Mauritos may be to us will, we hope, excuse us to your honours for making this digression because we believe ourselves bound by the Tyes of gratitude and duty to acquaint your Honrs with whatsoever has an appearance of yours and our countrey's interest.[59]

The letter neatly sums up a central paradox in the history of St Helena during the first half-century of the English settlement. It tends to confirm the parallel retention of two different types of image of the colonial island environment. Persistent attempts had been made to improve and develop the island as a profit-making plantation economy. These had been dependent on the kind of intensive and unsustainable agriculture permitted by the use of slave labour. This had by 1715 been shown to exert a most unexpected consequence in the form of rapid deforestation, firewood shortage, drought and soil erosion. The migration and resettlement proposal was itself an indicator of this deterioration, and the comparison made between a ruined St Helena and the wild 'Paradise' of Mauritius was quite explicit. Indeed, as late as 1715 Mauritius had remained a fertile paradise by comparison with St Helena. It had been abandoned by the Dutch in 1710 and was colonised by the French only in 1721, a full six years after Pyke's appeal to the Directors. The language in which Mauritius is described indicates the resilience of the paradisal image of the island colony, a setting that could provide a new beginning and an economic redemption for men who had despoilt an erstwhile Garden of Eden in only one generation.

During the years 1715 to 1795 the difficulties involved in arresting the environmental decline on St Helena became gradually more apparent, and its symptoms, despite valiant attempts at restoration, more acute. A subtle shift also took place in the rationale behind plans for investment in island projects. In a sense, this had started under Roberts's governorship. Roberts himself had remained somewhat ambivalent. Economic projects for new crops, mineral extraction and water supply had originally been put forward on their own merits as profit-making ventures or as ideas designed to reduce company expenditure on imported supplies. After about 1715 such proposals were made specifically with a view to arresting the physical decline of the island. Apart from perennial problems of public order, deforestation and inadequate water supply now became the central preoccupations of the St Helena government. This change in emphasis was summed up in a letter to the Directors in January 1716:

59 *SHR*, Council to CoD, 19 Feb. 1715, p. 113.

We propose also to carry the water over the saddle of the mountain that parts this place from Ruperts Valley which will improve that whole valley and make it fit for garden ground. The place only wants water to make it the fruitfulest place on the island being two miles long and very near a plain . . . we would not trouble your Honours with any of these notions, which to your greater judgements may seem like projects, but that we seeing the island in a declining state and in some parts constantly decaying being every year in a worser state, in some gutts or narrow valleys the grounds worn out so as to be no longer fit for Plantation land and wants a general recruit being too properly compared to an old ship that must have a thorough repair to hold out long, or else will never be in order tho' a continual charge . . . but with a good number of useful hands the whole country could have a new face.[60]

Implicit in this letter with its vivid ship simile was an appeal for extra supplies of slaves. This was somewhat ironic in view of the fact that the intensity of land use associated with the use of slaves had contributed directly to the rapidity of deforestation and erosion. Frequent remarks were made at this time about the changes that had taken place in the woodland area 'within our memories'.[61] A direct connection between deforestation and the deteriorated state of the island landscape was now often made. 'We are told', it was recorded, 'by all the planters, and partly know it ourselves, that formerly the country before the wood was destroyed was much fruitfuler than it is now.'[62] A fortnight after this comment was made, heavy fines were introduced for illegal wood cutting, and early in the next year the woods were reported after the rains to be 'in a flourishing condition'.[63] By the early 1720s, however, construction timber had become very scarce,[64] so that by 1724, for example, timber was actually being ordered from India for use in building fishing catamarans.[65] The council minutes and letters to the company during this period exhibit meticulous attention to the state of the island tree cover and a considerable determination to enforce regulations in this respect. A survey of October 1726 showed that '583 acres' had been planted and that during the month '23 persons were summoned for neglect, several fined and the rest excused upon promises to plant'.[66] A little later the felling of several 'fine trees', probably redwoods, resulted in trespassers' being fined, and it was

60 *SHR*, Letter to CoD, Jan. 1716, p. 134.
61 *SHR*, Diary, 16 Oct. 1716, pp. 134–5.
62 Ibid., 8 May 1717, p. 143.
63 Ibid., Jan. 1718, pp. 145–6.
64 Ibid., 5 Mar. 1722, p. 162.
65 Ibid., 16 July 1724, p. 164. These were almost certainly built on the lines of those used up until today in Tamil Nadu. Today wood for catamarans on the Madras coast is imported from Kerala.
66 Ibid., 31 Oct. 1726, p. 167.

'ordered that all persons going for wood should pass by the Great gate and no other way'.[67]

The increased incidence of environmental litigation soon became part of a more general deterioration in the relationship between the island government and its colonists, slaves and soldiers. This tension manifested itself both in passive forms of resistance and in periodic government attempts to assert control through regulation and punishment. To some extent such attempts in the resource field represented a median course negotiated between the barbarous treatment meted out to military mutineers and the more hesitant attitude normally taken in cases of environmental misdemeanour. The pendulum swung to and fro between complacency and overreaction, increasingly reflecting the development of considerable economic inequalities among the island population.

The zeal shown, for example, in punishing illegal fellers of redwoods was a reflection of a very specific anxiety that developed during the early 1720s, especially on the part of Governor Byfield, a 'diligent man' with a eye for detail, that the redwood species might become extinct altogether. Clearly this would represent a straightforward economic loss. Significantly, the more basic kind of loss was also anticipated. Byfield later recorded that the redwood 'was nearly lost to the island, but about five years ago [1722–3] the Governor got a couple of young plants, neither of them above an inch high and set them in his garden, took great care of them and they now produce seed in great abundance'.[68]

This was an important act, as it indicated an appreciation of the threat of extinction that had developed for a particular species of tree. More significantly, it represented a highly manipulative attempt to preserve a species which was restricted to the island and by this date actually known to be endemic. The heightened awareness of the vulnerability of species that were native to St Helena may well have developed in response to the evidence of deforestation. It was also associated, however, with the deliberate importation of alien species for experiments in restoration, as had happened, for example, in 1726 when a request was made from Fort St George in Madras for specimens of margossa and banyan trees.[69] The apparent emergence of an awareness of endemism on St Helena was almost certainly related to contemporary attempts to develop classification systems that could accommodate the enormous flow of plants into Europe as well as a growing interest in importing and experimenting with new plant species acquired on a global basis. Comparable interest in species differences may be read into the pointed comments

---

67 Ibid., 14 Nov. 1726, p. 167.
68 *SHR*, Council to CoD, 29 May 1717, p. 167.
69 *SHR*, Diary, 4 July 1716, p. 133.

made in Council minutes in October 1729 of visits by unfamiliar bird species, probably blown off migration routes during storms. Thus it was reported that 'birds of a different species lately came hither, the bodies of which are as large as a pheasant, their legs long and black but thicker and longer in proportion to the bulk of their bodies'.[70]

Such comments revealed a new enthusiasm for exact empirical description. It was this emerging interest in the details of biological processes which assisted Governor Byfield in making the link between the increasing difficulty encountered in achieving natural regeneration in St Helena's tree species (especially in the redwood) and the incessant depredations of goats on the island. He had already ordered annual surveys to be made to document the extent of areas in which tenants were planting furze (an innovation introduced by Governor Pyke in an attempt to ease firewood problems – furze was used as a fuel in contemporary England). Byfield was also interested in discovering whether tenants were keeping up their fences and planting the number of trees stipulated in their leases. Few defaulters escaped his eye, and 'it was not long before the tenants perceived that until the depredations committed by goats and sheep upon the plantations were prevented, they must be perpetually liable to be fined'.[71]

While for pragmatic political reasons Governor Roberts had wished to be rid of the goat population, he had found it impossible to legislate to that end. By 1730 the situation had changed enough to make Byfield's task much easier. Forty inhabitants presented him with a petition urging the destruction of all goats and sheep over a period of ten years. This was to commence from 1 February 1731, 'so allowing the owners time to reduce their flocks' naturally.[72] The Court of Directors agreed to this proposal, relayed by the governor. Once the law had been confirmed, the number of indigenous trees started to increase in number. Gosse records that an inhabitant who died in 1805 at the age of eighty had informed Governor Brooke that many parts of the island where no trees had grown for many years became covered with wood after the enforcing of the St Helena Forest Act of 1731, one of the first pieces of colonial conservation legislation.

The reasons for this somewhat surprising turn of events probably had less to do with the governor's actions than with the geomorphic consequences of denudation, which, with tree planting but in the absence of controls on goats, had grown steadily more obvious and concentrated. Thus from the early 1730s there were a growing number of reports of potentially catastrophic change rather than gradual deterioration. While reports of soil erosion and 'worn-out'

70 Ibid., Oct. 1729, p. 168.
71 Ibid.
72 Ibid., 30 Jan. 1730, p. 169.

ground first appeared in about 1700, by the 1730s the problem had become more entrenched. In July 1732 it was said that 'a late slip of 7 or 8 acres had fallen in Lemon valley and altered the taste and colour of the water there. The slip was 600 yards long by 901 deep.'[73] For an island the size of St Helena, such a large landslip amounted to a considerable economic setback and renewed past fears about the stability of both soil and the water supply.

Observations of rapid geomorphic change had already been made in 1717, when it was observed that 'the weather breaks and washes away the soil till the naked rocks appear'.[74] It was on this occasion that a connection was first made between the physical deterioration of the island and the possibility of disease:

> As to the healthiness of the place we believe the same thing we have alleged for the decay of trees has in great measure contributed towards diseasing the body too. For we have sometimes a pestilent sulphorous air comes down the valleys which divers have got sudden sicknesses and particularly one Ripon Wills and Mrs Coles have each lost an eye by such a sudden blast.

Identification of environmental risks with bodily risks to the individual in such an explicit fashion serves to emphasise the anxiety which the physical degradation of the island had caused by this stage. There is little doubt that the entire economic basis of the island economy was genuinely threatened. The 'pestilent . . . air' mentioned in the report was probably air carrying a heavy dust load from parts of the island so devegetated and destabilised that winds could simply lift the dry topsoil and scatter it in a manner familiar to students of the desertification phenomenon in the Sahel regions.

An increased awareness of disease risks also characterised the second administration of Governor Pyke, between 1731 and 1738. Such thinking reflected new interpretations, based on empirical observation, that were being made between health and environment in contemporary Europe.[75] Pyke possessed a wide-ranging knowledge of contemporary medical thinking and was, for instance, familiar with current debates about the causes and correct treatment of mental illness. On St Helena he correctly identified links among stagnant water, mosquitoes and the incidence of fevers. The water regime of the island received constant attention for this and other reasons during Pyke's tenure. Additionally, the regular flow of water and the effect of major rainfall events remained a permanent preoccupation. This was because large areas of the island continued to suffer from almost unchecked soil erosion, despite

73 Ibid., 26 July 1732, p. 169.
74 Ibid., 12 Jan. 1717, pp. 135–6.
75 Some of these had originated in the new theories of Stephen Hales and were stimulated by the publication of his *Vegetable Staticks* in 1727.

government tree-planting efforts. Bad flooding was reported in 1734 (when the whole of an old gun battery was washed away) and again in 1736.[76] In 1737 springs which had been perennial within living memory dried up completely, and this was reported again in 1747.[77] In 1756 serious flooding again occurred, destroying several houses.[78] The effects of storms which took place in March 1787 were even worse, 'the flood flooding over the whole extent of the line'. At Banks's 'a new Beach [was] form'd by the wash of rubbish from the Flagstaff hill gullies'.[79] This incident was sufficiently pronounced to merit pointed mention in a letter sent to the Directors the following day, when they were told that 'at a moderate computation the damages to your property alone must amount to thousands of pounds exclusive of the injury done individuals in many parts of the island . . . before the works gave way the whole of Ruperts Valley was one entire sheet of water'.[80] The vivid description of this flood, the most destructive described in the island records during company rule, is consistent with the sorts of mass overland flow which typically follow on prolonged deforestation and slope destabilisation. Exacerbated by the effects of gullying in deforested upper parts of the catchment, run-off would have occurred in a disastrously short period of time.

The response of the Court of Directors to this kind of report was remarkably negative, and in some areas it actually continued to countermand cattle destocking measures taken by the governor himself in the interest of sustainability of the island's agriculture. Such indifference to the perceptions of the local government had gone on for a long time, and sometimes the Court of Directors went so far as to overturn penalties awarded for environmental misdemeanours in the island court. Thus, for example, in October 1745 two individuals, Thomas and James Greentree, were arraigned for refusing to impound their goats when ordered to do so. According to the official record in this instance, the penalty imposed was intended to 'deter others from daring to offer the least contempt for the future'.

> We ordered that each of the Greentrees should be fined ten pounds . . .
> We told them they ought to look upon this fine as a very mild punishment
> for so great a crime . . . that disobeying lawful authority was much the
> same as resisting it and resisting authority was the beginning of a Rebel-
> lion which was a capital Crime. . .[81]

The connection made in this arraignment between ecological crime and rebellion needs no emphasis. Nevertheless, when the Directors heard of this

76 SHR, Diary, 16 Mar. 1736, p. 174.
77 Ibid., 3 May 1737, p. 176.
78 Ibid., 29 June 1756, p. 187.
79 Ibid., 31 Mar. 1787, p. 200.
80 SHR, Council to CoD, 22 Mar. 1787, and Diary, 31 Mar. 1787, p. 200.
81 SHR, Diary, 23 Oct. 1745, p. 183.

harsh exaction, they took a critical view of the governor's action, and the Council was forced to retreat, reporting acidly that 'we have repaid the Messrs Greentrees their fines according to your orders, and as you're of opinion that the Goats are of more use than Ebony they shall not be destroyed for the future'.[82]

This incident demonstrated the failure of the EIC in London to understand the basis on which successive St Helena governments had been proceeding, with the broad approval of many landholders, since the time of Roberts in 1709. It is the more surprising in view of the repeated attempts made by governors to establish and document the high cost to the company of the kind of soil erosion and flooding which followed unchecked deforestation and neglect of tree planting. Even though the policy of successive governors since Roberts represented a precocious programme of interventionist conservation and land management, it was still a policy of an entirely indigenous variety. It owed nothing to an understanding by the Court of Directors of conditions in the colony but was, on the contrary, actually repeatedly impeded. Instead, the continuance of successful plantation and soil-conservation measures relied heavily on the insights and observations of the colony's governors, reinforced intermittently by the island landholders. Almost all the conservation initiatives undertaken to import alien tree species, for example, were originated by the island governors without the knowledge or comment of the Court of Directors. Perhaps this is not surprising. After all, the chronic environmental instability induced by the colonial economy on St Helena had no parallel, before about 1780, in any other territory about which the company possessed detailed knowledge.

The very singularity and novelty which St Helena's problems entailed were thus the main reason for a lack of response on the part of the company. When the company did finally intervene to legislate on deforestation in 1794, it did so only under pressure from Sir Joseph Banks and in the knowledge of legislation already passed on Mauritius and St Vincent. Until that time the local administration on St Helena had to respond to its specialised problems quite autonomously.

The active role which the island governors found themselves forced to play had the eventual effect of making them into environmental propagandists, caught between short-term company interests on the one hand and long-term island or indigenous interests on the other. Whilst able to threaten the islanders themselves with the law or with the logic of long-term consequences, the governors, in the eyes of the company in environmental as in other matters, had a very weak position, at least on paper. They could not by their environmental arguments threaten the integrity or safety of the company itself

82 *SHR*, Council to CoD, 19 July 1745, p. 186.

(as later scientists in India were successfully to do) to any serious degree, nor did they wield any telling moral or intellectual authority. There is some irony in the fact that the greatest recognition acceded to any eighteenth-century St Helena governor by the EIC was to Byfield, not on the basis of his reafforestation campaigns but on the basis of his success in cutting down the day-to-day running expenses of the island, an achievement for which he was duly rewarded financially. Typically, the concerns of the company on St Helena rarely extended further than the short term for most of the eighteenth century. However, after 1778 the company did begin to take up ideas espoused by the governors long before. Thus in January 1778 the Directors ordered that large-scale furze planting should be started on waste lands, 'such lands not to be let out but reserved entirely for fuel for the general use of the inhabitants'.[83] When, sixteen years later, the Directors did seek to intervene on their own initiative in environmental matters on St Helena, the rationale for intervention was not really based on the environmental history of St Helena at all. Ironically, the reasoning advanced in support of intervention was couched precisely in the terms so often used by the governors to them. Thus in March 1794 the Court advised the island Council, without any forewarning, that

> We are of the opinion that encouraging the growth of wood is of the utmost consequence to this island not only from the advantages to be derived from it as fuel but because it is well known that trees have an attractive power on the clouds especially when they pass over hills so high as those on your island and we are inclined to believe that the misfortunes this island has been subject to from drought might in some measure have been avoided had the growth of wood been properly attended to. We have been uniform in our directions for keeping Longwood securely fenced ... should there be any parts of this enclosure that are not at present planted we direct that you immediately order the Governor to plant as many young trees there as possible.[84]

In a further letter the Directors added, apparently unaware of the irony:

> On perusing the minute of the Lieutenant-Governor and the Gardeners Report on the estate of Longwood we lamented the lack of attention, not to say total neglect, that has prevailed for more than 70 years past with respect to an object of the highest importance to the welfare of the island, namely the cultivation of wood, and if a steady perseverance is not observed to promote it in the future the present inhabitants will afford their posterity as just a reason for condemning their conduct as they have now to deplore that of their ancestors.[85]

83 *SHR*, CoD to Governor, 23 Jan. 1778.
84 Ibid., 7 Mar. 1794.
85 Ibid., 25 Mar. 1795. The botanical garden on St Helena, an acclimatisation garden, had been established by the EIC at the suggestion of Dr George Young, the first curator of the St Vincent Botanic Garden, and Patrick Anderson, an EIC surgeon-naturalist.

This appeal to posterity was something quite new. A more important innovation lay in the specific raising of the suspected links between rainfall and the presence of a forest cover. However, an understanding of the new-found interest of the East India Company in climatic concepts must await a later stage in this narrative and an acquaintance with events taking place on Mauritius and in the Caribbean.

The environmental history of St Helena between 1660 and 1790 illustrates clearly how an isolated oceanic island that had significant strategic value to the colonial state could become the subject of close observation and the location of attempts to conserve its resources and species. Nevertheless, in hindsight the ecological decline of St Helena can also be said to have powerfully affected the development of an ecological theory in the observations made by Halley on vegetation and the hydrological cycle in 1676 (although these were not published until twenty years later) and in his remarks on the reasons for the catastrophic removal of the soil of St Helena into the sea in 1700.[86] By contrast, the lack of any institutional 'scientific' continuity clearly contributed to the relative lack of success in controlling deforestation, and there was a clear lack of any meaningful way of systematically referring to comparable experiences of erosion elsewhere in the world.

While at a later stage St Helena did emerge as central to the development of conservationist ideas and methods, its main role in the history of environmental ideas up to the 1760s was simply as a documented site of environmental decline whose sad state made a great impression on contemporaries, and (most importantly) on Sir Joseph Banks. However, for purposes of this account, the story of St Helena is significant as an historical lesson in the failure of a conservation policy, even if a closely observed failure.

The development of Dutch colonial conservationism at the Cape and on Mauritius

The differences between the land-management strategies adopted by the English colonists on St Helena and by the Dutch at the Cape became apparent to contemporary observers during the late eighteenth century. Sir Joseph Banks was one such observer. In 1771, on a visit to St Helena in the course of his return voyage to England, he wrote in scathing fashion about the English treatment of the island. Despite what he considered the vastly superior natural endowments of St Helena in comparison with the Cape, the English had allowed the island to degenerate into what he felt was a sorry state, in stark contrast to what he had seen of Dutch management of their colony in the face

86 Halley, 'An account of the circulation of watry vapours'.

of all its natural deficiencies. This was a rare observation coming from an outsider and is a useful indication of the way in which the deterioration of the island could be perceived by a visitor after a hundred years of occupation. Banks felt that the laziness of the inhabitants was largely to blame for the state of the island. 'Here', he reported,

> are plantations, Peaches, Lemons, Apples, Guavas and I believe scarce any other fruits, tho' probably very few kinds exist in either Indies which might not be cultivated here and brought to at least a degree of perfection. But while their pasture lay as they really do, as neglected as their gardens, there can be little hopes of amendment; in short the custom of the Indies Captains who always make very hansome [sic] presents to the families where they are entertained besides paying any extravagant prizes for the few refreshments they get, seems to have inspired the people with a degree of Lazyness. Were refreshments cheap they would probably receive not much more money for them by the year and the present would be the same, so at least they seem to think. In short the Cape of Good Hope which tho' by nature a mere desert supplys abundantly refreshments of all kinds to ships of all nations who touch there, contrasted with this island, which though highly favoured by nature, shews not unaptly the Genius's of the two nations in making colonies, nor do I think I go too far in asserting that was the Cape now in the hands of the English it would be a desert as St Helena in the hands of the Dutch would as infallibly become a Paradise.[87]

In fact the environs of the Cape were far more climatically hazardous than St Helena. The Cape peninsula and some adjoining areas formed an island of relatively high rainfall and lush vegetation adjacent to areas of much greater aridity at an increasing distance from Cape Town, particularly to the north and north-east. This regional difference was so pronounced that the botanical and environmental history of the South-West Cape can, for most practical purposes, be considered an island history.[88] In this way, too, the story of the Dutch colonial response to deforestation and environmental change in the Cape and their other early colonial possessions provides a striking comparison with the situation which developed on St Helena and with the relatively ad hoc English response to ecological change on the West Indies sugar islands.[89]

In order to understand the nature of the Dutch response, one needs to

87 Sir J. Banks, diary entry dated May 1771, in J. C. Beaglehole, ed., The 'Endeavour' journal of Sir Joseph Banks, 1768–1771, vol. 2, Sydney, 1963, pp. 265–6.

88 D. F. Kokot, An investigation into the evidence bearing on recent climatic changes over Southern Africa, quoted in A. J. Christopher, Southern Africa, Folkestone, 1976, p. 20.

89 There are few studies of ecological crisis under Dutch colonial rule. For an important exception, see L. Blusse, 'The story of an ecological disaster', Strange company: Chinese settlers, mestizo women and the Dutch in VOC Batavia, Dordrecht, 1986, pp. 15–35.

appreciate the derivation and subsequent history of the Dutch construction of the tropical environment. This response was constrained and influenced by the development of a very particular set of cultural traits. As we have already seen, these had evolved and were evolving in the Netherlands itself and in other parts of the Dutch mercantile empire, above all in Malabar and Cochin in South-West India, during the seventeenth century.

The experiences and perceptions of a remarkably small number of colonial officials and experts were essential to the formulation of a specialised construction of nature and a particular kind of state-sponsored environmentalism. The significant difference in this respect between England and the Netherlands at the end of the seventeenth century was that, whilst the English East India Company showed no concern at all about the extent of ecological decline on St Helena, the government of the United Provinces (the Lords XVII) took on a highly interventionist role. This meant that eventually effectiveness in tree planting, forest protection and botanical-garden maintenance in the colonies came to be seen by the metropolitan authorities as a precise measure of the effectiveness and prestige of the colonial state.

Indeed, from the outset, the newly independent Dutch state showed signs of an inclination towards careful observation and management (if not protection) of the natural world. For example, the new heraldic crest of Holland consisted in a lion above a walled garden.[90] This use of the garden as symbol or sign was central to Dutch constructions of nature both at home and in the colonies which the Netherlands accumulated during the seventeenth century. The environmental and social intention which the garden represented was derived both from a long-developed attitude towards the management of created or safeguarded land and from the new secularisation of paradisal notions and their transfer to the outside world and to the landscape.[91]

There was a potent additional perceptual and strategic factor involved in the management of colonial landscapes. This related to the need to achieve effective control over medical expertise and pharmacological supply. This allowed and gave particular power and sanction, within the colonial state framework, to the medical profession, its views and its Hippocratic notions. This primacy had originated in a pragmatic recognition of the advisability of co-opting local indigenous pharmacological and botanical expertise for European purposes. It is difficult to date this recognition precisely, but it was clearly closely connected with the timing of Dutch mercantile expansion. More specifically, the steps involved in recognising the need to collect and incorporate indigenous knowledge and materia medica can best be elucidated by reference

90 Schama, *An embarrassment of riches*, p. 71.
91 For an effective discussion of this kind of transference, see Patterson, 'The Hortus Palatinus at Heidelberg'.

to the intellectual relationship among Garcia da Orta, Clusius and Hendrik
Adriaan van Reede and the development of a flow of botanical and environmental ideas among Amsterdam, Leiden, the Cape, Malabar and Batavia.

Within this set of interlinked factors, the Malabar environment of forest
and cultivated landscape had emerged as pre-eminently significant. The incorporation or utilisation of indigenous constructions of nature and a recognition of their significance underlay almost the whole structure of the Dutch
response to the tropical environment and changes induced within it. Moreover, a Hippocratic recognition of the potential medical value of a vegetal cover
was directly associated with a broader-based and aesthetic valuation of the
forested landscape.

A major new perceptual element was thus involved in the development of
an active environmentalism at the Cape as it had evolved by the mid 1690s.
This was a less situational and arguably more imported element, involving the
accumulated typology of Dutch aesthetic and technical responses to the tropical natural world. For van Reede in particular, by his own confession, the
'primaeval' forests of Malabar provided a major and even overwhelming emotional stimulus. This in turn affected his policies for the Cape forests when
he eventually found himself in a position to affect policy. In short, Dutch
conservationism at the Cape can in part be explained by biographical reference
to van Reede and by reference to the institutional arrangements facilitating
his activities, policies and potential. The most basic institutional counterpart
and precondition of van Reed's environmental project was the mental and
physical structure of botany and natural history in the Netherlands itself. As
we have seen, this was in turn contingent on the broader context of Dutch
colonial expansion. It was, of course, its geographical position in relation to
India and the East Indies that defined the importance of the Cape (like St
Helena and Mauritius) as a supply base and then as the site for an acclimatisation garden. This role defined, too, the physical significance of the garden.
The need to maintain the Cape as a provisioning base meant that, much as
at St Helena under the English, considerable efforts were made from the
outset to sustain the physical and biological viability of the whole colony.
Between 1652 and 1700 we can observe the painstaking development of a
botanical garden and a pattern of protective forest and land management
which, once evolved, constituted a model which was then replicated by the
Dutch themselves in Ceylon and Java and, at least in part, by the French and
British in their respective possessions in the Indian Ocean region.

The initial development of this system was primarily the achievement of
three men, Joan Huydecoper van Maarseveen, Hendrik van Reede and Simon
van der Stel. Their lives and involvement with the Cape environment spanned
a period between 1652 and 1690 in which the approach to colonial land management went through a significant transition. The two most decisive historical

events in this transition were the foundation of the Amsterdam botanical garden (Hortus Botanicus) in 1682 and the return of van Reede from the Cape
to Malabar in 1685. At first, however, the environmental mind-set of the
earliest Dutch colonists in tropical territories did not, in fact, differ very
greatly from their English contemporaries. The first settlement of Mauritius
is a case in point, since the Dutch settlers of the first fifty years of occupation
saw the island primarily as a source of tropical forest products and provisions
for supply stops.

Despite the development of Leiden by Clusius in 1593, no really significant
colonial botanical information network seems to have developed before the
1640s. Nevertheless, there are some signs that, much as at St Helena, anxieties
about the impact of settlement and human use did develop shortly after the
first Dutch encounter with Mauritius. The environmental history of the first
fifty years of Dutch settlement are worth exploring, since during the mid
seventeenth century the political management of Mauritius became closely
linked to that of the Cape. Developments after about 1680 need to be treated
separately, as after that time the Cape and Mauritius both became parts of a
much wider system of exchange of environmental knowledge and insight.

The Dutch and Mauritius, 1599–1655

Mauritius had been well known to Arab and Hindu merchants over many
centuries, as had been the adjacent islands, the Mascarenes and Seychelles.
One may speculate that it had first been encountered, in an ecologically undisturbed state, in the course of the long Arab searches for teak and other
wood on the southern coasts of the Indian Ocean.[92] It is even possible that
the Arabs made commercial use of the ebony forests. If they did so, the impact
does not appear to have been very great. It has been suggested, too, that the
island was made use of as a base by both Indian and Arab pirates from the
earliest phases of Indian Ocean trade. By 1500 charts or sketches of the island

92 A very basic approach to the ecological history of Mauritius is found in A. W. Diamond, ed.,
   Studies of Mascarene island birds, Cambridge, 1987. Mauritius is a volcanic island, the remains
   of a huge shield volcano built up in the course of the Pliocene with the last of the lava flows
   of Pleistocene age. It is 40–50 km across and is 840 km east of central Madagascar in Lat. 20°
   S. Réunion (Bourbon) lies about 164 km to the WSW, and Rodriguez 574 km to the east. The
   islands supported specialised faunas and floras with biota long adapted to the specialised island
   conditions. Amongst the animals, tortoises and flightless birds were especially prominent.
   Some of the original creatures, known from fossil remains first excavated by Edward Newton
   in the 1870s, were not described in the first accounts of visitors and may have been the victims
   of rats from shipwrecks long prior to settlement.

are reported to have existed, some of which may have been utilised by European ships on their first Indian Ocean journeys.[93]

The incorporation of Mauritius into a European economic world system can be said to have been begun by the Portuguese shortly after their first landing on St Helena. A fleet of fourteen Portuguese vessels, commanded by Tristan da Cunha and Alfonso d'Albuquerque and sent to Melinda, anchored off Mozambique early in 1506.[94] Diego Fernández Pereira, the first pilot of the fleet, taking charge of the *Cirne*, desired to cruise farther into the Indian Ocean. On 9 February he encountered Réunion and called it 'Santa Appolinia'. He landed on Mauritius a few days later and called it 'Cirne' after his vessel. A little later on, Pereira came across Rodriguez and named it 'Diego Fritz' after himself.[95] Much as in the case of St Helena, the Portuguese do not seem to have attempted to make a permanent settlement on the island, since they were not seriously threatened strategically during the sixteenth century and were able to concentrate their resources on colonies farther to the east. Ecologically, however, the Portuguese must have had some influence and certainly introduced deer, goats, monkeys and pigs.[96] Subsequently the Spanish visited Mauritius and made formal claims to it. However, with the loss of the Netherlands Provinces in 1598 all Indian Ocean trade was abandoned to the Dutch.

On 1 May 1598 a fleet of eight Dutch vessels under the command of Admiral Cornelius van Neck and Rear-Admiral Wybrandt van Warwick left Texel Island for Bantam in the East Indies. Soon after passing the Cape of Good Hope, the fleet was separated by a cyclone. Three vessels, the *Mauritius*, the *Holland* and the *Over Yesel*, continued their voyage under the command of Admiral van Neck, while the five others, the *Amsterdam*, the *Zeeland*, the *Guelderland*, the *Utrecht* and the *Vriedland*, all under the orders of van Warwick, sighted Mauritius while sailing eastwards in the afternoon of 17 September. Two boats were sent to study the coast. Van Warwick anchored in the south-eastern bay on the 19th and allowed the crew to land on the 20th. The Dutch are recorded as having admired the dense forests, especially the palms, ebony trees and giant tree-ferns. They found the island inhabited by birds of many species and of a remarkable tameness. On the beaches was

93 S. B. de Burgh-Edwardes, *History of Mauritius*, London, 1921, p. 1.

94 Of these fourteen Portuguese vessels, the names of only seven are known. These were the *San Iago*, the *Cirne*, the *Santo Antonio*, the *Santo Afonso*, the *Santo Maria das Virtudes*, the *Santa Maria*, and the *Galagea*.

95 In fact there is evidence that a year later the Portuguese had become aware of the much older Arabic names for the islands. One map of 1508, drawn by Ruych, includes these names, with Portuguese notes appended. On this sketch Madagascar is called 'Comorocada', Bourbon 'Margabin', Mauritius 'Dinarobin' and Rodriguez 'Dinanora'. The Portuguese notes adjust the Arab names to those given by Pereira.

96 Burgh-Edwardes, *History of Mauritius*, p. 2.

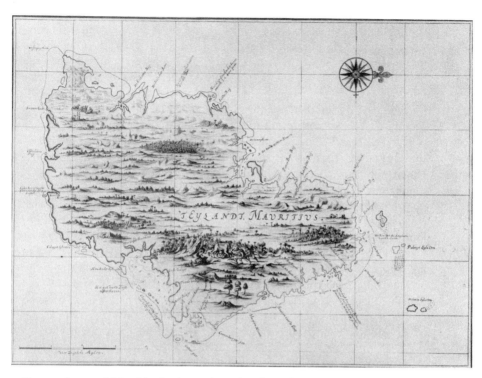

Plate 7. A map of Mauritius in about 1670, taken from the 'secret atlas' of the Dutch East India Company. The coastline is highly accurate for navigational purposes; the interior, little better than fantasy. (Reproduced by permission of Cambridge University Library)

evidence of the wrecks of several ships. The sick were landed and soon re-covered their health, and the chaplain of the vessel celebrated a thanksgiving service. Parties of the crew were detailed to examine different parts of the island, and it was found to be uninhabited. Van Warwick then took possession of the island and named it 'Mauritius' in honour of the Stadtholder of Holland, Prince Maurice of Nassau. He then named the bay in which they safely anchored 'Warwick Haven'. A board bearing the arms of Holland, Zealand and Amsterdam, under which were cut the words 'Christianos Reformados', was nailed to a tree. A plot of ground was then cleared in which fruit trees, beans and peas were planted, and the whole surrounded by a wooden pali-sade.[97]

Van Warwick's largely symbolic construction of a garden belied the real

97 Ibid., p. 5.

aims of the Dutch. The central attraction of Mauritius for the new colonists lay in its potential as a source of ebony and other heavy tropical timbers, which were already in great demand in Europe, Batavia and the Cape by the mid seventeenth century.[98] Timber-supply difficulties encountered when the Dutch later came to occupy the Cape only made the role of Mauritius as a source of raw timber, rather than as a place of settlement, more pronounced. Furthermore, during the Dutch period the rate of deforestation on the island became closely correlated with the state of the European market for luxury goods. The island's initial management, therefore, was the very opposite of conservationist. This was in spite of the fact that, as suggested above, the Dutch were rather more aware than their Portuguese, English and French competitors of the advantages of careful land management. Very large quantities of ebony were exported from as early as 1640 when van der Stel (later governor at the Cape) despatched 1,132 large ebony logs from the island.[99] During the ensuing five years of van der Stel's administration, as many as five or six thousand large 'pieces' of ebony were sent to Batavia alone.[100] Fearing competition from the French and English, whom they could not easily exclude from the island, the VOC decided quite deliberately to cut all exploitable ebony trees as quickly as possible. This unusual policy attracted some comment even from contemporary European observers. In 1644, for example, it was said that ebony had been cut so heavily near the coast that it was

> now so scarce that they are forced to pull, as [they] themselves report, 2,600 Dutch paces counting an English yard to each pace, so that the trouble and travail in gaining so gross a commodity is considerable, and doth somewhat stagger judgement to reason what in future they intend to do here, when, as it must necessarily follow, their charge and trouble will with their work be increased.[101]

Exploitation was so rapid in Grand Port, for example, that soon areas farther north at Mapon and Flacq, 'prodigious forests of ebony', were being exploited. There is some evidence that by 1645 the speed of deforestation had already become a matter of concern. A report on the matter by one Frans van Beverwyk is recorded as having been submitted to the Lords XVII in that year.[102] The Baie aux Tortues had already been 'devastated' by 1646. Nevertheless,

98 N. R. Brouard, *A history of the woods and forests of Mauritius*, Port Louis, 1963, p. 2.
99 Ibid., p. 3.
100 Ibid., p. 5.
101 Ibid.
102 A. Toussaint, ed., *Dictionary of Mauritius biography*, 5 vols., Port Louis, 1941–84, p. 472 (henceforth *DMB*). Van Beverwyk arrived on Mauritius in May 1644 as a commissary for the Indies to Rodriguez and Mauritius to enquire into the fate of the English ship *Henry Bonaventure* and into ebony cutting.

cutting continued to be quite uncontrolled in subsequent years, and Pitot in his *T'Eylandt Mauritius* writes of a 'destructive urge' that swept the island.[103] A further report in 1654 dealing both with the problems of runaway slaves and with the high rate of deforestation made observations on both matters but proposed no long-term solutions.[104] In the event, a glut in the Dutch market for ebony seems to have slowed the pace of forest cutting, and eventually, between 1657 and 1664, the Dutch abandoned the island altogether. However, the matter was not forgotten, and it was during this interregnum that the governor-general at the Cape commented that 'in twenty years time not a single Ebony tree worth exploiting will be found in the whole island'.[105] It may be significant that this comment was made from the Cape rather than locally on Mauritius. Mauritius was formally a dependency of the Cape, and it is clear that at quite an early stage in the process of ebony extraction the obvious profligacy of a commerce catering largely for the urban Dutch market was causing some disquiet and even resentment in the new timber-hungry colony at the Cape.

Managing 'Het Paradijs': The evolution of Dutch attitudes to the environment, 1600–1770

The growth of the Dutch East Asia trade during the first decades of the seventeenth century soon made the need obvious for a permanent provisioning base at or adjacent to the Cape. St Helena seems to have been specifically rejected for this purpose in 1633. It has been suggested that van Riebeeck himself was responsible for the decision not to consolidate earlier Dutch claims on the ground that, despite the superficially fruitful appearance of the island, it could not sustain the demands of provisioning that might be made on it. This kind of calculation appears to be confirmed by the highly regulated approach to land management adopted at the Cape from the beginning of settlement in 1652. Indeed, until the 1640s most reports had described the Cape as being most unsuitable for settlement, both in terms of the potential productivity of the land and the apparent hostility of the indigenous inhabitants. By contrast, the absence of indigenous populations on Mauritius and St Helena made them appear far more secure for settlers. Some observers, how-

---

103 Brouard, *Woods and forests*, p. 4.
104 The Hague, Algemeen Rijksarchief, Verbalen der Haagsch Besoignes en van eenige generale commissien uit e Oost-Indische Compagnie (1653–1796): Mauritius Files, no. 300, Report on runaway slaves and deforestation, cited in A. Toussaint, *Bibliography of Mauritius*, Port Louis, 1956, p. 627.
105 Brouard, *Woods and forests*, p. 4.

ever, viewed the Cape in a more favourable light. In 1649 one Captain Janssen, shipwrecked on the Cape peninsula, noted that

> the soil of the said [Table] Valley is very good and fruitful and in the dry season all the water one could wish for could be led through the gardens with little toil. Everything will grow there as well as anywhere in the world . . . since everything is to be had there in sufficient quantity, abundance of fish and . . . further Elands and Steenbok are abundant there . . . while there are all sorts of birds there in thousands.[106]

While this optimistic description helped to bring about van Riebeeck's settlement, most descriptions from 1550 onwards had indicated that woodland was limited. These descriptions recorded the presence of indigenous people and their herds and spoke of the extensive grass fires deliberately set by the herders.[107] In April 1608 Cornelis Matelief wrote that he found firewood along the banks of a small rivulet that emptied itself into Table Bay, but John Jordain, who stayed at the Cape in the same year, complained that the only drawback of his stay had been shortage of wood. 'Only timber', he wrote, 'will be somewhat tedious in fetching, which is about three miles.'[108] Nicholas Downton had a similar experience when in July 1610 he found 'none but small green wood' at a distance of three miles from the ships.[109] These impressions of timber scarcity are confirmed by van Riebeeck's journal, in which we read that wood was 'scarce in the vicinity of the fort'. Even before he came to the Cape, van Riebeeck was aware of this fact, for his ship, the *Drommedaris*, carried a cargo of pine beams, planks from Norway, rafters, small joints and plank from Sweden, and rough planks, with which the first dwellings were built.[110] During his first year at the Cape, van Riebeeck undertook much exploration himself. On 21 April he explored the kloof between Table Mountain and Lion Mountain. There he found only clayey soil and no trees.[111] On 27 April he described Lion's Head as having slopes which were 'dry and stony'.[112] However, on 6 May, exactly a month after his arrival, four men whom he had

106 R. Raven-Hart, *Before van Riebeeck: Callers at the Cape from 1488 to 1652*, Cape Town, 1967, pp. 25–9.

107 For example, the crews of the sailing vessels *Pensée* and *Sacre* gave a description of large herds of cattle guarded by many people: Edward Strangman, *Early French callers at the Cape*, Cape Town, 1936, pp. 17–18.

108 Raven-Hart, *Before van Riebeeck*, pp. 25–9.

109 Ibid., p. 49.

110 The Hague, Koloniaal Archief, Ref. no. 396: Brieven en Papieren ingecomen 1653: Journal van Negotie.

111 D. B. Bosman and H. B. Thom, eds., *Journal of Jan van Riebeeck*, vol. 1, *1651–1655*, Amsterdam, 1952, p. 33. This part of Lion's Head was nine miles from the fort and gives an indication of the extent of forest clearance even at the time of the Riebeeck settlement.

112 Ibid., p. 35.

sent out on an inspection tour reported finding behind Table Mountain 'a fine, large forest of very tall and straight growing trees'. On 9 June he himself went to see this forest and described it as being 'full of large, tall, straight heavy, medium and small trees, suitable for the largest construction one could desire, but so far and difficult to convey that it would be less expensive to buy timber in Holland or Batavia and have it sent here than to have it brought down from this forest'.[113] Imported wood, however, grew damp and warped on the long voyage, and van Riebeeck was within a few months driven to use timber from the high mountain valleys even though it was 'heavy and difficult to transport'.[114]

Only five months after the 'Free Burghers' were settled on their small-holdings along the Liesbeeck River, van Riebeeck began to realise that he would have to protect the indigenous plants and trees against destruction. A first 'placaat' was issued in July 1657, but it was in fact more of a warning to those burghers who trampled fruit trees and plants in gardens and destroyed wild plants.[115] The first placaat issued specifically for the protection of indigenous forests was proclaimed in October 1658 and summarily forbade the Free Burghers to fell trees for domestic use in the forests. Only two Free Burghers, known as 'free woodcutters', would be allowed to chop wood in certain parts of the forest, and everyone, officials of the VOC as well as Free Burghers, would have to buy their timber from these two sawyers.[116] At this period van Riebeeck also restricted the right to sell firewood. The Free Burghers could still sell firewood from their own holdings, but for every other wagonload they would have to pay the company ten stuyvers. Also the cutting of timber anywhere along the Liesbeeck River was prohibited.[117] Ten days later van Riebeeck went a step further when he issued orders for the protection of yellow-wood, which he described as 'the best wood for making planks, being scarcer than any other kind of wood in the Cape forests'.[118] No one was allowed to fell these trees, apart from the two official woodcutters, each in his own delimited area and for no other purpose than to make planks.[119] These placaats were not reissued during van Riebeeck's administration. The commander, farming at Bosheuvel, kept a vigilant eye on the woods of Leedert Cornelisz van Zevenhuysen and Pieter Paulus Cley, the two woodcutters.

Only seven years after van Riebeeck's first settlement, the clearly perceived

113 Ibid., p. 44.
114 Ibid., pp. 59–60.
115 M. K. Jeffreys, *Kaapse argiefstukke: Kaapse placaatboek*, pt 1, *1652–1707*, Cape Town, 1944, pp. 29–30.
116 Ibid., pp. 37, 41.
117 Ibid., pp. 41–2.
118 Ibid., p. 43.
119 Ibid.

paucity of resources was already stimulating a great deal of formal boundary making. Thus on 7 November 1659 Placaat 8 stated that all freemen on the other side of the River Liesbeeck 'are ordered to enclose their lands with pega-pegas and to plant them with wild almonds'. This idea was later extended to enclosing the whole area of the settlement, effectively creating an administrative island with a permanent timber shortage. Apart from use as building material and firewood, the indigenous trees and shrubs were easily employed in this boundary making, creating a highly symbolic hedge between the white settlement and the Hottentots. On 25 February 1660 it was decided to plough a semi-circular piece of land 3,673 roods long and 1 rood wide and to plant thereon 'bitter almond trees and all kinds of brambles and thorn bushes'.[120] The work was completed before the end of the year, and the wild almond trees began to grow with 'reasonable success'.[121]

In spite of all the laws and proclamations forbidding the unnecessary use and waste of wood and the damaging of forests, the demand for timber was still so great that van Riebeeck and his successors could not prevent the slopes of Table Mountain and the surrounding area from being denuded of timber. Moreover, timber imports started at an early stage. An important pattern began when ebony was imported to the new colony from Mauritius in 1666; Jacob Granaet brought in 944 logs. In April 1673 a request was made for 1,350 planks and 90 teak beams from Batavia. Further imports of teak were also made from Malabar. The cost involved in importing timber served to focus attention on the vulnerability of the Cape to uncontrolled deforestation. As a result, throughout the period of Dutch rule, proclamations and placaats were frequently issued to try to retain some control over the process.[122] Some of the stiffest rules were those intended to protect trees growing in or adjacent to the Company Garden. The first one, dated 21 December 1653, fixed the penalty for robbing or damaging the garden at two years in chains. A further placaat, of 21 February 1660, fixed the penalty for injuring trees at twelve months' hard labour. This emphasis on protecting the garden was, of course, significant.

At the time of Hendrik van Reede's first visit to the Cape on his way to Malabar in 1656, the Company Garden was still essentially a provision garden. However, it also specialised in providing anti-scorbutic vegetables and fruits and in that limited sense was already fulfilling some kind of medical role as well as being the chosen location for experiments in tree planting. After 1669,

---

120 Bosman and Thom, *Journal of van Riebeeck*, vol. 3, *1659–1662*.
121 Ibid., 20 Dec. 1660: 'met wilde amandelboomen tot een lantweer al beplant is die oocq met redelijcq succes beginnen te wassen'.
122 For details of these, see T. R. Sim, *The forests and forest flora of the Cape Colony*, Cape Town, 1907.

however, the medical function of the garden was much expanded. In that year Andries Cleyer, director of the VOC medical store at Batavia, started to encourage the administrators of the Cape to develop the Cape garden. He also urged the administrators at company factories in Bengal, Coromandel and Ceylon to undertake research on and collect medical plants. The research consisted essentially in the gathering of both plant specimens and indigenous medical and plant knowledge. The frequent contacts between Colombo and the Cape, in particular, meant that the Cape governors soon became responsible for a medical acclimatisation garden of an increasing size and strategic importance. In 1677 Johannes Bax, the new Cape commandant (lately transferred from Ceylon), commanded his agents in Hottentots Holland to 'shift as best you can with indigenous medical herbs'.[123] The transfer of Bax to the Cape had been secured by Maarten Huydecoper van Marseveen, a VOC director and mayor of Amsterdam. In 1676 Huydecoper had already despatched a medical botanist, Jan Hendriksz de Beck, to superintend and develop the Cape garden. This was a major step, as it institutionalised the role of medical expertise and the place of natural history in the colony for the first time. More than sixty years were to elapse before the same process took place in the French colonial context (on Mauritius) and over one hundred years before a comparable development took place in the territories of the British East India Company. As in these later cases, the onset of professionalisation in natural history in the context of the botanical garden facilitated a new stage in the development of an embryonic conservationism. The renewed encouragement of tree planting and preservation was an early sign of this. Thus, as soon as he had been appointed superintendent of the Cape garden, de Beck set about developing a second garden, at Rustenberg in Rondebosch.[124] Here, as Huydecoper had intended, de Beck planted several species of European trees, principally hazelnuts, oaks and beeches.[125]

Between 1669 and 1677 two important developments took place in the history of the Cape garden. The first consisted in a re-evaluation of the garden and its hinterland as a source of medicinal plants. This in turn focussed attention on the nature of the indigenous vegetation and its ethno-botany. Secondly, Huydecoper and Bax secured a sophisticated network for the exchange

123 The Hague, A. S.: VOC 4013, 190–190v, letter of 17 April 1677, Bax to Laurens Visser. Hottentots Holland is a mountainous region east of Cape Town.

124 A. Hulshof, 'H. A. van Reede tot Drakestein, journal van zijn verblijf aan de Kaap', *Bijdragen en Mededeelingen van het Historisch Genoolschap* (Utrecht), 62 (1941), 1–245; F. Valentyn, *Oud en niew Ost-Indien*, vol. 2, Dordrecht, 1726, p. 135.

125 Rijksarchief Utrecht [Utrecht State Archives; henceforth RAU]: Records of Huydecoper family, 56, Letterbook 1675–6: Letter of 30 November 1676, Huydecoper to Bax. In 1695 Beck reported on the impressive size of the Rustenberg plantations: VOC 4034:250–3, inventories dated 5 May 1695.

of botanical and medical material and information. At exactly this time Hendrik van Reede was planning and beginning to implement the arrangements for his *Hortus malabaricus*, a project which was representative of a new interest in empirical data and indigenous knowledge and which had been stimulated, according to van Reede, by his own admiration for the beauty of the Malabar forests and the extraordinary medical skills of their Malayali and Ezhava inhabitants. At this time, too, the Cape was acquiring steadily greater prominence among the major Dutch botanists at Leiden and elsewhere. Paul Hermann, for example, visited the Cape in 1672 and 1680 in the course of his longer journeys to Malabar and Ceylon.[126] The formation of Huydecoper's informal natural-history networks (formed, incidentally, in outright contravention of official company policy) can be said conveniently to mark the maturation of the new Dutch valuation of the tropical environment, partly in a medical sense, but also in an increasingly aesthetic or environmental sense. The continuing problems in securing firewood and wood for construction at the Cape had stimulated this sensibility and ensured that the Cape remained the focus of conservationist and arboricultural concerns. The official sanctioning of tree-planting programmes after 1675 became progressively more marked, and on 10 July 1676 a further placaat was passed, yet again strictly penalising illegal woodcutting.[127] On the death of Commandant Bax in 1678, Huydecoper used his growing influence in the VOC to appoint his nephew, Simon van der Stel, as Cape commandant.[128] From the outset, Huydecoper expected van der Stel to supply his gardens in Amsterdam with bulbs, seeds and animal specimens from the Cape. This process had in fact already begun with the appointment of Isaac Lamotius as administrator of Mauritius in 1676. At the time of the appointment, Huydecoper sent instructions for Lamotius which desired him to construct a 'herbarium' on the island. Huydecoper made it clear that he was particularly concerned to receive detailed drawings of plants and trees from both the Cape and Mauritius.[129] Huydecoper's objectives were quite clearly very complex. Certainly a major part of his project consisted in building up sufficient material to develop a new botanical garden, and, indeed, in 1682 he was able to open the new Hortus Botanicus in Amsterdam. At the same time, Simon van der Stel was encouraged to develop a new

---

126 However, Hermann's promised *Prodromus plantaris africanus* never appeared, a fate shared by the hoped-for *Hortus africanus* of van Reede. Instead, regions farther east, particularly in Ceylon and Malabar, consumed the energies of these botanists, leaving the African field open for the German, Swedish and British botanists of the late eighteenth and the early nineteenth century.

127 Sim, *Forests and forests flora of the Cape Colony*, p. 77: Placaat no. 161.

128 The Hague, AR: VOC 108: Resolution of Lords XVII 1675–80, 18 March 1679.

129 RAU, Records of Huydecoper family, 57, Letterbook 1679–82: Letters of 22 May and 20 Oct. 1679, Huydecoper to van der Stel.

Plate 8. Ebony cutting in progress on the east coast of Mauritius in 1677. This drawing, now in the Netherlands State Archives, is one of the earliest portrayals of colonial
deforestation in the tropics. At least one of the birds depicted is a dodo and represents
the only known illustration of the species in its natural lowland ebony-forest habitat.
(Reproduced courtesy of the Algeneen Staatsarchief, The Hague)

function for the Cape garden, namely as a site for centralising live specimens
of what were now understood to be 'rare' plants.

However, Huydecoper was also interested in a more extensive kind of survey project. He began to encourage the agents in his network to carry out
large and accurate landscape drawings, carefully surveying the state of the
vegetation and the details of the plants and trees making up the landscape
surface. Such requests were carefully carried out by Isaac Lamotius, a man
already skilled in botanical and medical matters. As a result, Lamotius has
left us with a very important indication of the state of Mauritius at a time
when it was being heavily exploited for ebony timber for the Cape and European market, in the form of a coloured drawing probably executed in 1677.
The drawing is remarkable both for the care shown in portraying the details
of deforestation and for the attention given to the physiological details of the
plants and trees, which are even shown in a cross-sectional diagram. It is

probably the earliest pictorial evidence we have of tropical deforestation in the Indian Ocean region. The extent of this deforestation had, however, been known for some time at the Cape and may to some extent have stimulated the passing of forest laws at the Cape soon after the Riebeeck settlement. It may even be possible to explain Simon van der Stel's tree-planting interests as being connected to his knowledge of Mauritius and to his status as the son of Adriaan van der Stel, one of the early Mauritius administrators. Within a year of van der Stel's arrival, a further placaat had been passed respecting the licensing of firewood cutting. At this stage, however, such restrictive legislation was not effectively reinforced by the active pursuit of plans for tree planting. Van der Stel preferred instead to carry out more esoteric natural-history collecting to serve his own narrow enthusiasms. While his idiosyncrasies would eventually, in the 1690s, result in his ignominious dismissal, there is no question that his long survey expeditions into the Eastern and Northern Cape were scientifically and geographically significant. His expedition to Namaqualand in 1683 was especially valuable. Meanwhile, the deforestation of the Cape progressed.

The decisive event in the emergence of a strong and centralised Dutch conservation policy at the Cape was undoubtedly the return of Hendrick van Reede to the Cape after an absence of nearly twenty-five years. In the intervening period, as we have already seen, van Reede's views about nature had been transformed, largely by his experiences in the Malabar forest and his labour in building the *Hortus malabaricus*. During his few months' stay at the Cape, he reviewed the whole status of the colony and the management of its botanical garden and forests. Van Reede's first point of call after alighting from his ship in April 1685 was, significantly, the botanical garden.[130] In the preceding year the garden had been much damaged by the attentions of Rekloef van Goens, an administrator and life-long enemy of van Reede's. Van Goens had ordered much of the topsoil removed from the garden for other purposes and had had all the many cinnamon trees at the edge of the garden cut down. His hostility to van Reede's *Hortus malabaricus* had been of the same kind. By April 1685, however, van Goens was safely removed from the Cape, largely through the influence of Huydecoper. As a result, van Reede was able to tour the Cape and make his conservation plans for the colony without fear of disruption.

Even his first observations at the garden revealed a new sensibility to the processes of environmental change and the dynamics of their human causation over time. Conditions in the garden, van Reede perceived, reflected the wider environment. The garden, he observed, was not sited on level ground but on a steep slope. As a result, its soil was composed of a fertile black earth up to

130 Hulshof, 'Van Reede', pp. 169–70.

a foot and a half deep. But, he suggested, this merely showed that the soil was derived from the washing away of the surrounding deforested highlands during heavy rain.[131] Otherwise van Reede found reason to praise the gardens. 'Nothing can be compared', he said,

> with the pleasant and nice aspects of the Company's garden, the mere sight of which is able to comfort and refresh a man coming from the wild, raw and merciless sea in a land without trees and bare highland. For the footpaths, which extend further than the eye can reach, are planted on either side with high walls of pleasant green trees, where one can be safe in the heaviest south-easterly winds; the whole garden is divided into a great many square sectors or beds, planted with all sorts of fruit trees and vegetables which, protected against evil winds, grow and flower plentifully, so that benefit and pleasure are combined here.

He was also impressed by the now full-grown European oaks at Rustenberg in Rondebosch. These trees, planted by Beck at the behest of Huydecoper, were 'about 20 years old, and . . . about as thick as a man's waist'. They 'had no tall trunks, being as it were polled, and . . . spread their branches very far from each other, and bore much fruit, clear evidence that the earth and the air might produce such trees'.[132] While the gardens and their tree plantations were thus praised by him, van Reede was far more critical of the overall state of the Cape Colony's woods. Already, under van Riebeeck, the area of woodland had been much decreased.[133] Van Reede found an almost entirely deforested Table Valley and in his early tours began to wonder where the company had ever obtained sufficient wood. Moreover, even the wood that remained appeared to be wastefully managed. South of Rondebosch, for example, he saw a vast tract of tall felled trees, which had apparently been found useless as timber. The youngest trees had also been cut down. Van Reede greatly deprecated such profligacy in a country that already had so few trees and commented that 'those who have neglected it so much have provided only for themselves and not at all for the future'. This was an important advocacy of a sustainable policy of woodland use, and it coloured all van Reede's subsequent observations.[134] At Houtbaai, van Reede found a spectacle similar to that at Rondebosch: plains full of the stumps of recently felled trees. Van der Stel, while asserting that the woods were capable of regeneration from seed,

---

131 The average slope of the garden was in fact 20%.

132 J. Heniger, *Hendrik Adriaan van Reede tot Drakenstein (1636–1691) and 'Horlus malabaricus': A contribution to the history of Dutch colonial botany*, Rotterdam, 1986, pp. 70–7.

133 Karsten, *The Old Company's garden at the Cape*, pp. 64–6.

134 These details of van Reede's comments on the deforestation of the Cape are taken from Heniger, *Van Reede*, and from van Reede's reports of 5, 21 and 25–28 May 1685 in Hulshof, 'Van Reede', pp. 72–3, 129–30, 139–46.

was forced to admit to van Reede that the original policy developed to preserve the woods for the company had entirely broken down. Even areas long planned for plantations of European species, using laboriously imported European seeds, had been largely neglected, and for this van Reede was forced to take full blame. One such area, between Table Mountain and Devil's Peak, had optimistically and symbolically been named 'Het Paradijs' and had been intended, as such, to be a plantation of European alder. Van Reede found that it had reverted to indigenous woodland. He was less disturbed by this than by the discovery that the woodmen employed by the VOC were in the practice of giving the names of European trees to what were, quite patently, indigenous specimens. This conflicted with every principle that van Reede had learnt in his days in Malabar. His comments made in the course of one exploring expedition expanded more fully on this notion, explicitly linking the particularly and aesthetic value of the Cape plants and trees to their medical potential:

> It should be added to this that this protruding corner of the countries of Africa is also notable with regard to plants and trees, for wherever one goes, on low and moist, high and dry lands, everywhere one finds great plenty of fragrant flowers of the most brilliant and beautiful colours that one might imagine, most of which have bulbs such as they are not found in any other countries in the world. Nay, there is no mountain or rocks or stones so barren, bearing nay green foliage, but there are found the most beautiful flowers, fragrant plants, even various kinds of heather which are fragrant in their leaves or flowers, so that doubtless that soil brings forth many strong herbs serving man's health if they were known and used in the right way, which will also be profitable for the Honourable Company to be examined.[135]

This statement was, of course, highly reminiscent of the charged language used by van Reede in describing the Malabar forests. The connection is an important one, with the difference that in the Cape these emotions soon led to practical policy.

Through his enthusiasm for the natural history of the Cape, van Reede encouraged van der Stel in his collecting and surveying activities. He also stimulated the future development of the botanical garden.[136] But his greatest impact derived from his strictures on forest conservation and tree planting. He thus instructed van der Stel to plant, wherever the Cape woods had been

---

135 Ibid., p. 151.
136 Also through the influence of van Reede and Huydecoper, van der Stel was supplied after 1687 with the services of Bernard Oldenland as superintendent of the botanical garden. Oldenland, a fully trained physician, had been a pupil of Paul Hermann's at the Leiden garden.

destroyed, plots of ten to twelve roods with new saplings. With respect to woods still existing, he ordered that during felling circular or square sectors of six to seven roods should be spared, so as to make natural regeneration possible. In doing so van Reede transferred the practice of tree planting, which had previously been confined mainly to the precincts of the botanical garden, to the whole hinterland of the colony. The poor condition of the Cape forests had in fact provoked van Reede's main criticism of van der Stel's activities. As a consequence, and through van Reede's intervention, Huydecoper took great pains to improve the situation at the Cape. In his letters of 1686, 1687 and 1694, for example, he gave van der Stel detailed advice on the cultivation of a variety of European woods: abeles, pines, spruce-firs, poplars, beeches, elms, lime trees, oaks, olive trees, chestnuts, walnut trees, plane trees etc.[137] By the late 1680s the Lords XVII had become fully converted to the importance of tree planting, largely through the efforts of van Reede. Unfortunately, this told against the energetic and scientifically minded van der Stel, and during the early 1690s the Lords issued a stream of complaints about the supposed lack of successful arboriculture at the Cape. It seems that they had not fully appreciated the difficulties involved in growing European trees in Southern Africa. Van der Stel, it is true, was far more interested in collecting and cultivating indigenous species. Moreover, van Reede had died in April 1692, leaving van der Stel politically defenceless. Eventually, in 1696, he was dismissed from the service of the company, despite his historic role in promoting natural history, scientific botany and forest protection at the Cape. It was a considerable irony that he should have been dismissed by a colonial state structure now fully convinced of the value of state forest protection.

However, the anxieties expressed by the Lords XVII are relatively easy to understand. Despite the conservationist efforts of van Riebeeck, van der Stel, Huydecoper and van Reede, the small forests of the Cape peninsula 'island' had proved inadequate for the demands made on them. Indeed, the restrictions placed on the use of the small area that was conserved actually encouraged the search for forests at a greater distance and the movement of the settler population away from Cape Town and the Cape peninsula. New forest patches were found along the lower slopes of the Riviersonderend and Swellendam mountains, and these soon fell to the uncontrolled attentions of woodcutters. Felling then spread further to the Grootvadersbosch between Swellendam and Heidelberg. In 1711 reports reached the Cape of large forests in Outeniqualand in what is now the George–Knysna region. However, these forests were not exploited until after 1770, when the Riviersonderend and Grootvaders-

---

137 RAU, Records of Huydecoper family, Letterbook 1686–7: Letter of 26 Nov. 1686, Huydecoper to van der Stel: 'Mr Commelin and I are engaged in sending you everything that is in your list, and also a botanist and a dauber.'

bosch forests had been exhausted. What, then, had become of the earlier state commitment to conservation?

It had, it appears, come to an abrupt end with the discovery by the Dutch of the Riviersonderend forests. In 1712 the Council of Policy had despatched a survey mission to the forests, composed of *Ondercoopman* van Putten and state gardener Jan Hartogh. These men had reported finding large numbers of yellow-wood trees, assegai, white and red pear, alder, ironwood and stink-wood trees, all suitable for timber and wagon wood. They recommended the establishment of a sawmill in the forests and, most important, reported that the forests contained enough wood for a hundred years' worth of consumption. With this statement the psychologically insular status of the Cape settlement came to an end, at least temporarily. At a basic level the location of the colony at the tip of a seemingly limitless continent would eventually permit out-migration as a logical response to resource scarcity. Indeed, in 1711 the first trekboers reached the forests of the George–Knysna–Tzitzikama area, lying in a band two hundred kilometres long between the sea and the Outeniqua and Tsitsikama mountains. It would be fifty years before these forests were much exploited. However, the economic motivations behind these movements had more to do with soil conditions than with timber shortage. In arable areas of the Cape, long fallow periods had been found necessary to maintain fertility. This, of course, put pressure on remaining woodland areas. More significant, as early as the 1720s complaints were being voiced about the extent of soil exhaustion and soil erosion. This was partially eased by the development of regular patterns of migration to seasonal pastures in the interior. Furthermore, the evolution of such patterns militated against the static pattern of resource conservation that had developed as a response to local shortage in the Cape peninsula in the late seventeenth century.

In the other VOC colonies, however, forest protection continued to be a matter of established state concern, particularly in the island colonies of Java and Ceylon.[138] In both colonies the VOC adapted indigenous forest-management systems to their own use, especially in Ceylon.[139] Here the task of tree planting and the subsequent care of saplings was allotted to individual village headmen. For this and other duties entrusted to them, the Dutch government distributed patches of unoccupied, or 'chena', forests, according to the pattern built up by the Kandyan kings.[140] This was even the case when

138 See P. Boomgard, 'Forests and forestry in colonial Java, 1677–1942', in J. Dargavel, ed., *Changing tropical forests: Historical perspectives on today's challenges in Asia, Australia and Oceania*, Canberra, 1988, pp. 54–88, and Nihal Karunaratna, *Forest conservation in Sri Lanka from British colonial times, 1818–1982*, Colombo, 1982.

139 This use of indigenous methods was later echoed by the British in their adaptation of the pre-colonial forest-reserve system of Sind to the requirements of other parts of India.

140 Samuel Wood, the British superintendent of government forests, wrote to Alexander Wood

teak species were introduced to Ceylon from Java in the 1680s, almost certainly at the suggestion of van Reede.[141] In Java the VOC teak-forest conservation system had become relatively complex at an early date; the first formal reserves can be dated from about 1722. This approximates to the period at which conservationist practices started to be neglected in the Cape, and there may in fact have been a dynamic relationship between these developments. Certainly by the mid eighteenth century the VOC was maintaining a relatively sustainable teak-forest system in Java, from which the company was able to supply the shipbuilding needs of its other colonies as well as the European market.

Ultimately the forest-conservation systems set up by the VOC in the Cape, Ceylon and Java remained self-contained in concept and did not at first directly affect the conservationist strategies of the other colonial powers. The pattern established in the management of the Cape garden was a quite different matter. Indeed, in shaping the development of future French and British colonial environmental policy, the sophisticated development of the Cape botanical garden would, like St Helena, exercise an influence out of all proportion to its small area.

The growing importance of Mauritius in European environmental thinking

Like the Cape garden, Mauritius started to acquire a disproportionate significance in the history of European colonial environmental policy, particularly after the annexation of the island by France in 1716. Even before that, however, Dutch governments and French travellers had started to chart a significant place for the island in European perceptions and in a fashion easily traceable in company documents and the diaries of individual voyagers. It is to this prescient location in environmental history that we shall now return for the main thread of our story.[142] As early as 1645 Frans Beverwyk had voiced anxieties about the excessive speed of deforestation which he had wit-

in 1810 that 'these lands, which were termed *accommodisans*, have since been resumed by [the British] government, with them, I supposed, the right of calling on the headman for gratuitous service': Sri Lanka National Archives, 6/285, 18 May 1811, quoted in Karunaratna, *Forest conservation in Sri Lanka*, p. 67.

141 F. D. A. Vincent, *Report on the conservation and management of the Crown forests of Ceylon*, Colombo, 1882, p. 54.

142 Two major primary sources for the study of pre-French Mauritius are the correspondence files of the VOC and the diary of François Leguat. The official VOC day-book compiled by Isaac Lamotius between 1677 and 1688 is also of great value in constructing the environmental history of the island. [Held at Cape Provincial Archives, Cape Town]

nessed on Mauritius in 1644.[143] His worries did not, however, lead directly to
attempts to control the process. Similar expressions of concern, originating at
the Cape in 1654, coincided with a glut in the ebony trade and were, anyway,
related more closely to perceptions of shortage in the Cape environment than
to conditions on Mauritius itself.[144]

The earliest attempts at conservation on the island did not, in fact, relate
to the ebony trade at all but to the control of hunting and feral species. During
the rule of Governor Hugo (1673–7), legislation was introduced to control the
wild dogs, which were harassing deer and cattle, and to curb domestic pigs,
which had run wild on the island. The large land tortoises were already being
massacred for the small deposits of fat found on their backs, and they soon
became extinct on the Mauritius mainland, despite some desultory attempts
to control their slaughter by ships' crews.[145] By 1670 the dodo, too, was known
to be extremely scarce, a casualty of the first phase of felling in the lowland
forests which were its chief habitat. Indeed, Lamotius's 1677 drawing appears
to be the last extant representation of the dodo actually drawn from life; the
last definite sighting of the bird took place in June 1681.[146] The dodo had, in
fact, become a potent symbol of rarity very much earlier. There are indications
that Clusius himself, for example, was well aware of the very unusual physi-
ognomy of the bird and its highly restricted range, and it is certain that by
the end of the seventeenth century Mauritius was already closely associated
with the idea of rarity in the minds of both English and Dutch naturalists.[147]
It is hard to say at exactly what date this perception actually developed. Sir
Thomas Herbert visited Mauritius in 1627, a time when it was still largely
uninhabited by man. He described the dodo and made a fairly clear statement
about its rarity. Only on Mauritius, he said 'and in Dygarroys [Bourbon?] is

143 See entry under 'Adriaan Van der Stel', compiled by Barnwell in *DMB*, p. 472. Van der
Stel had commenced the large-scale despatch of ebony trees in the early 1640s. Slaves from
Madagascar and Batavia were imported to assist in the ebony cutting. Van der Stel himself
was killed in Ceylon in 1646.
144 The Hague, Algemeen Rijksarchief, Verbalen de haagsch Besoigne en van eenige generale
commissien uit e Oost-Indische Compagnie, 1653–1796: Mauritius Files, no. 300, Report on
runaway slaves and deforestation.
145 See A. North-Coombes, *Histoire de tortues de terre de Rodrigues et le mouvement maritime de
l'île*, Port Louis, 1986, pp. 2–15.
146 H. E. Strickland and A. G. Melville, *The dodo and its kindred*, vol. 1, London, 1848, p. 26.
Strickland utilised British Library, Sloane MSS.3668.Plut.cxi.F: Benjamin Harry's Journal.
147 The dodo (derived from Port. *doudo* [foolish, simple]) is listed in Clusius's *Exoticarum*, published in Antwerp in 1605. Clusius had seen parts of a dodo specimen in a Leiden collection.
This specimen was lost, however, and does not appear in the *Catalogue of all the chiefest
rarities in the publick Theater and Anatomie Hall of the University of Leiden*, Leiden, 1678.
(This is bound in Bodleian Library, Linc.F.l.3l.) With such a lack of specimens, it was easy
for the dodo to take on mythic proportions, a fact which may have blunted the impact of
accurate reports of its extinction.

Plate 9. Late-seventeenth-century engraving of the dodo; taken from Strickland, *The Dodo and its Kindred*. The appearance of the bird (drawn from a captive and overfed specimen) should be contrasted with the much trimmer and more accurate depiction in Plate 8.

generated the Dodo, which for shape and rareness may antagonize the Phoenix of Arabia'.[148] As early as 1656 the dodo was also included in Tradescant's catalogue, *Collection of Rarities Preserved at South Lambeth near London*.[149]

Two years later the dodo appeared as a 'rarity' in James Bontius's *Account of the Diseases, Natural History and Medicine of the East Indies*, book 6.[150] This book would undoubtedly have been known to a naturalist like Isaac Lamotius. It thus seems reasonable to infer that Lamotius, and other Dutch naturalists

---

148 T. Herbert, *A relation of some years travaile begunne anno 1626 into Afrique and the greater Asia, especially the territories of the Persian monarchie, and some parts of the Orientall Indies and Iles adjacent*, London, 1634.

149 We here find the entry 'Dodar from the island of Mauritius; it not being able to flie being so big' (p. 4).

150 This was contained in Piso's edition entitled *Gulielmi Pisonis Medici, Amstelaedamensis de Indiae utriusque re naturali et medici, libri quatuordecim*, published in Amsterdam in 1658.

with a knowledge of the Mascarene Islands, would have associated the idea of rarity very directly with Mauritius. Moreover, Bontius made a direct connection between the dodo and an island 'celebrated for its ebony'.[151] It is thus not surprising to find that Lamotius, appointed governor in 1677, seems to have been the first resident official to worry himself about the effects of ebony extraction. The changing status of the dodo would, it seems, have been well known to him. It would not be wise, however, to exaggerate the significance of the dodo in stimulating conservationist attitudes among Dutch officials. Only some decades later, when Buffon took a renewed interest in the dodo, did the full significance of its extinction start to enter a wider scientific consciousness.[152]

As a naturalist and a trained surgeon, Lamotius also became interested in the botany of the island and described the different ebony species for the first time.[153] During his first year as governor, Lamotius toured the island coasts on foot and later discovered a fine plateau in the centre of the island. He can be credited with producing the first detailed map of Mauritius and, as we know, soon provided the drawings and specimens requested of him by Huydecoper van Marseveen. In 1690 Lamotius followed this up by sending a detailed report and survey of the colony to Governor van der Stel at the Cape. As a consequence of his professional training and dedication to natural history, he was able to form a far more accurate impression of the ecological impact of colonial occupation than any previous administrator. The rate of unregulated ebony extraction represented, Lamotius thought, a potential loss to the state, and he proposed a fee for every plank (or per one hundred planks) to cover the bare administrative costs of government. This was an interesting development. Having no personal financial stake in rapid timber extraction, Lamotius seems to have been more inclined to be hostile to deforestation. Indeed, he may have been an early exemplar of the later tendency of colonial governments, in contrast to colonial commercial interests, to take a critical view of rapid change in land use, particularly as it affected the viability of resources and government income in the long term. However, the fact that Lamotius had medical and botanical interests was probably equally important. His links with Huydecoper and the Cape establishment certainly encouraged him to construct a botanical garden, probably at Flacq. However, his early efforts to cultivate European trees in the garden, and the failure of these efforts, seem to have discouraged him from developing the garden further.

---

151 The Bontius text reads 'Inter insulae orientalis, censetur illa quae ab iliis Cerne dicitur, a nostratibus Mauritii nomen audit, ob Ebenum nigrum potissimum celebris': chap. xvii, p. 70.

152 Buffon, in his *Natural history of birds*, quoted in Strickland and Melville, *The dodo*, p. 27.

153 Isaac Johannes Lamotius, governor of Mauritius from 1677 to 1692: Barnwell in *DMB*, pp. 458–9).

Moreover, Huydecoper did not encourage or provide for the installation of a professional botanist on the island, so that Lamotius would have remained intellectually isolated. His interests in safeguarding the ebony forests did not, therefore, outlive his tenure as governor, and even the botanical garden as an institution did not survive him. The lack of professional backing might be deemed unfortunate, for there is plenty of evidence that Lamotius was a person possessed of remarkable insight and powers of observation, as the drawings he made for Huydecoper clearly reveal. His day-books help to confirm this impression.[154] But the intellectual isolation in which he found himself meant that the governor became increasingly frustrated and tense in his relationships with his fellow colonists. In 1692 he was arraigned for a variety of 'offences' and removed from Batavia. These offences, it appears, were mainly associated with his overfriendly relations with visiting English ships' crews and other political activities that caused offence to the VOC. Little has been discovered about the course of his life after a period spent in jail in Batavia, although it is known that he spent the years from 1711 to 1715 at the Cape before returning to the Netherlands.[155] Deodati, Lamotius's successor as governor, was, by contrast, apparently an uninspiring character. He did, however, acquire a considerable understanding of the hydrological importance of the rainforest on the island and its powers of water retention, a property that was later to become a focus of French interest in the island forests. Thus in 1696 Deodati described the upland forest as 'wet forest', noting that 'there is here a place called the "wet forest" and though no more rain falls there than elsewhere the forest consists of a short and twisted undergrowth, the trunks of the trees being covered with moss and their crowns entangled into each other. During the rainy season the water remains in the moss and gradually drips down so that the ground is wet and marshy.'[156] The water-holding quality of the Mauritius forest was important in a practical sense. When it came to be cut down, the hydrological and flow properties of the exposed ground were radically changed and would have given rise to contemporary comment.[157] One needs to be sceptical about Deodati. Any insights he had about the importance of the forests were most probably derived directly from the doctrines espoused by van Reede and van der Stel at the Cape. The shallowness of his views are reflected in his remark 'Wood is so abundant in the forests [of Mauritius] that 2000 men continually felling trees for 200 years would never see an end to it.'[158] For the VOC, the sacking of Lamotius, like the sacking of van der Stel

---

154 Cape Town, Cape Provincial Archives: Lamotius's Official Day-books.
155 *DMB*, pp. 458–9.
156 Ibid., p. 5.
157 Ibid., p. 239.
158 Ibid.

at the Cape six years later, turned out to be an expensive mistake. Deodati's regressive views were bound eventually to prevent the development of any notion of achieving a sustainable timber yield and thus to affect the commercial value of the colony itself. In 1709 Momber van de Velde, the last Dutch governor of Mauritius, wrote that 'ebony is hard to come by, having been cut down everywhere'. In this way van de Velde was, belatedly, struck by the inherent destructiveness of the Dutch occupation. He was especially critical of one of the last major biological interventions of the Dutch colonists, their releasing of wild dogs in large numbers at the port of Black River on the west coast of the island. This meant, he remarked, that 'the great part of the island would be so full of wild dogs . . . that in two or three years time the island would be devastated, there being left neither game nor cattle'.[159]

In just over a century of occupation the Dutch had managed to bring about great changes in the ecology of Mauritius. Nearly all accessible black ebony trees of commercial size in the coastal lowlands had been taken. The coastal palm community, which was of very limited distribution, had been destroyed by fire, used for food and thatching material, and tapped and burnt for arrack production.[160] Javanese deer had been introduced, as had been many 'useful' food plants and cash crops (sugar cane, tobacco and sweet potatoes, above all), as well as fruit trees. Goats, pigs, dogs, cats and rats had all run wild, bringing about the decline and extinction of many indigenous plant and animal species. The land tortoises and a few large birds, such as the dodo and aphanapteryx, had been made rare or extinct. In addition, the opening up of a limited road system linking up the logging camps, settlements, harbours and loading stations soon laid the foundations for future depredations. Finally, in 1709 the first major planting of sugar cane took place, the growing of which was to become the major cause of deforestation during the eighteenth century.[161] By the end of the century human activity had already caused a considerable amount of forest clearance and was also beginning to cause the extinction of some endemic animal species to an extent sufficiently obvious to attract contemporary comment. By 1700 land tortoises on mainland Mauritius had become extremely rare or extinct (although surviving on neighbouring Rodriguez), and game and wild cattle were said to be scarce. The island had become infested by 'thousands of millions of rats', undoubtedly the single most destructive influence on the indigenous bird, animal and plant species.

It is significant that the most acute observers of the processes of forest

---

159 Momber van der Velde, quoted in Brouard, *Woods and forests*, pp. 11–12.
160 The same utilisation which had proved so damaging on St Helena.
161 Brouard, *Woods and forests*, p. 9. Burgh-Edwardes asserts that Governor Reynier Pory introduced sugar cane in April 1648. However, the experiment seems to have failed and was not continued by Pory's successors, Maximilian de Jongh and Abraham Evertz: *History of Mauritius*, p. 7.

destruction and species extinction on Mauritius at the end of the century were the French Huguenots of the expedition commanded by Abraham Du Quesne. In 1691, shortly before the departure of Lamotius, François Leguat, a member of the expedition, is recorded as remembering that 'this island fairly abounded with Wild Geese and Ducks, Moorhens, Quails, Sea and Land Tortoises, but now all these are become scarce. The Sharks also and divers other sea animals have forsook it, since the natives have been accustomed to lay nets for them.'[162] Leguat had a shrewd idea as to the main agency of destruction and remarked, 'Here . . . are hogs of the China kind . . . these beasts do a great deal of damage to the inhabitants, by devouring all the young animals they can catch.'[163] Leguat's perspicacity with regard to the extinctions on Mauritius was by no means an accident. It derived from a very specific kind of naturalistic cosmology that, arguably, individuals such as Lamotius may only partially have shared. Human disruption, measured by species extinctions, represented a highly symbolic incursion on the Edenic image of an island wilderness so beloved of Leguat and which he and his Huguenot refugee colleagues had found it so necessary to construct. Each extinction represented a step further away from a God-given Eden and a step towards imperfection and corruption. Species extinctions, one may suggest, represented for Leguat a major artificial, or even sinful, disruption in a particular kind of constructed and highly visual natural moral economy. To some extent, the same kind of moral or religious connotations had attached themselves to nature in the context of Dutch natural history and Dutch Calvinist sensibilities about the natural world.

Calvinism was an abiding common factor in both Dutch and Huguenot naturalism. As a doctrine it encouraged the individual to take a personal and unmediated responsibility for a relationship with God and for the consequences of that relationship. Furthermore, a decline in the significance of the Fall and a consequent willingness to accept a knowledge of nature (and its species) as a path to a knowledge of God was a further characteristic of many seventeenth-century strands of Protestantism. The assumption of responsibility for human actions in nature was a logical development from these changing tenets of religious belief and religious dissent, particularly when an unspoilt and remote nature could represent the beliefs of a 'chosen' and dissenting few.

However, Leguat and his Huguenot colleagues seem to have taken the process a stage further. For them, as we have already seen in Leguat's ecstatic response to the physical appearance of Rodriguez, the undisturbed island actually represented a restoration and the end of a spiritual journey away from danger and religious conflict. The unspoilt island even stood, one may surmise, as a symbol for the reformation of society and the world. In a very real sense, then, Leguat's ecological observations symbolically mark the transition between emergent Dutch environmental sensibilities and the far more structured and ideological response that would come to characterise the French reaction to colonial deforestation after the mid eighteenth century.

In contrast to the older Dutch empiricism, French conservation ideology would fully incorporate the findings of the seventeenth-century scientific revolution and adapt them to the construction of a fully developed and reformist social ideology. Above all, French environmentalism depended on a growing body of climatic theory of a kind that had not been available to van Reede and his colleagues and which drew much of its inspiration from Newtonian physics. Mauritius, however, remained central to the intellectual development of this new climatic environmentalism, as it had to the earlier evolution of environmental anxiety.

4

Stephen Hales and some Newtonian antecedents of climatic environmentalism, 1700–1763

Until the end of the seventeenth century, conservationist policies in the colonial context were associated closely with the development of an Edenic discourse that broadly encouraged some European colonists to attempt a project
of restoring or rebuilding Paradise in the landscape of islands and botanical
gardens. The projection of restorationist, Utopian or Orientalist social programmes on to the insular landscapes of a dyadic 'other' played a part in this.
This was augmented, as we see clearly from the company responses to the
ecological problems of the Cape and St Helena, by the agendas of colonial
medicine and economic botany, the growth of natural history and a growing
interest in empirical observation that was typical of the European scientific
revolution of the seventeenth century. In the Dutch colonies a keen awareness
of the value of indigenous botanical and medical knowledge had also played
a part in co-opting non-European environmental epistemologies into a more
global *Weltanschuung*.

After 1700 these factors continued to exert an effect. However, at this stage
a new intellectual development started to transform and inform the western
colonial response to a rapidly changing environment. This consisted in the
burgeoning influence of climatic theories and the emergence of a distinctive
'desiccationist' discourse linking a deforestation cause to a climate or atmospheric effect. The practical implications of the new climatic theory were, it
may come as no surprise, first put into effect on colonial island colonies in
the 1760s. However, the origins of the new theories had much earlier antecedents and were closely related to the diffusion of Newtonian principles in
England and France during the early eighteenth century. The local scientific
renaissance taking place in Cambridge between 1690 and 1720 was especially
important in the unfolding of this process – so much so, indeed, that the
primacy of the Leiden and Amsterdam scientific establishments began to fade
into the intellectual background as a factor in the development of western
environmentalism. They were replaced by the savants and salons of Cambridge, Paris and London.

As we have already seen, desiccation theories linking deforestation with rainfall decline and climatic change had had a long history in western thought, with their antecedents in the books of Theophrastus. But there had been little intellectual continuity in the theme, even after its Renaissance revival in the writings of Columbus and his associates. With Columbus, however, climatic and desiccation theories had become firmly located in the vital geographical periphery of western expansion. After Columbus, the growth of a western interest in climatic theories as European expansion took place arose as a natural consequence of increasingly frequent contact with peoples previously unknown to Europeans. Such contact demanded questions as to the origins and migrations of peoples over the earth, and about the origins of species in general. Climatic explanations were easily seized upon to explain cultural behavior and differentiation. Ideas about environmental influence, and about the influence of climate on culture in particular, increased in effectiveness as European expansion proceeded in all parts of the world. This became an even more potent influence as Europeans began to be able to see themselves, objectively and self-consciously, as modifiers or destroyers of apparently primeval (and mainly tropical) landscapes, and even as destroyers of the cultures they encountered.

Towards the end of the sixteenth century, especially in Latin America, these issues came to a head, so that there began to develop a comparatively complex critique of the impact of European-caused deforestation on indigenous peoples, on the forests in which they lived, on health and on local climates.[1] For example, in a *relación* of 1579 Diego de Esquivel describes the deleterious effects of colonisation on the life and health of Mexican Indians in a passage distinctive for its mixing of climate, health and deforestation issues:

> They live less long and have more illness than formerly because the country was then more thickly populated with Indians who cultivated and tilled the land and cleared the jungle. At the present time there are great jungles and forests which make all the region wild, swampy and unhealthy. The Indians being now so few and scattered over more than fifty leagues of territory and the region being so damp and raining . . . eight months of the year and they are not able to clear the ground so that the wind may spread over it and dry it as of old.[2]

1 To date, changing critiques, perceptions and treatments of indigenous peoples by Europeans, especially in Latin America, have received detailed attention from scholars. By contrast, shifting European perceptions of the health and climatic consequences of this destabilisation have received much less attention.

2 Diego de Esquivel, 'Relación de Chinantha', in Francisco del Paso y Troncoso, ed., *Papels de Nueva España*, 2nd ser., vol. 4, Madrid, 1905, pp. 56–68, trans. and included as appendix in Bernard Beran, *The Chinantec and their habitat*, Instituto Panamericano de Geografia y Historia, Pub. 24, Mexico City, 1938, pp. 139 ff.

A connection is implied here between high rainfall and the maintenance of a forest cover, even if the forest cover (in contrast to slightly later commentaries on islands) is not considered desirable by the writer. It is perhaps not surprising that remarks such as this were made in the context of Mexican deforestation, as early European settler degradation of the pastures and forests of Central America had been extensively documented and commented upon by contemporaries. What is more noteworthy in Esquivel's text is the linkage made between environmental disturbance and social disruption.[3] Esquivel does not, however, see European settlement as posing a threat to forests in general. Moreover, he reaffirmed existing negative prejudices by which forests were perceived as disease-ridden and dangerous environments. Such prejudices began to disappear only in the early eighteenth century as forests began to be seen as climatically beneficial. One may also suggest that such anti-forest feelings died away in direct proportion to the growing incidence of deforestation in Europe and to the rising influence of tree-planting ideologies (often stimulated by shortages of naval timber) and Germanic nature cults.[4] A scientifically based belief in the climatic desirability of forests was probably much more important, however, in dispelling the old associations made between trees and disease, which, it should be said, took a long time to die, particularly in North America, where they hung on until the mid nineteenth century.

It is difficult to pinpoint any more sophisticated development of the desiccation themes in the century after Esquivel's commentary. This situation was rapidly altered in the western context by the foundation of scientific societies on Baconian lines and particularly by the institution of the Royal Society and the Académie des Sciences. It was these two associations that provided the intellectual infrastructure for the formulation of many important desiccation and climatic theories, much as they provided a setting for wider discussions about tree planting and agricultural improvement. In France the reorganisation of forest management by Colbert in the 1660s, again on Baconian lines, also stimulated climatic and physiological thinking. Given these institutional preconditions, the critical catalysts to the creation of theory were the colonisation of oceanic islands, the formulation of responses to their rapid ecological transformation and the increasing interest taken by the medical pro-

3 His commentary can be compared with the slightly later and stronger remarks of Montaigne, who warned that 'we shall have greatly hastened the decline and ruin of this new world by our contagion', quoted in K. Sale, The conquest of Paradise: Christopher Columbus and the Columbian legacy, London, 1991, p. 567.

4 Simon Schama, 'Primaeval forests and the cult of nature', lecture given at Christ's College, Cambridge, 8 May 1991, to be published in a book of similar title. Schama suggests that the association between the French revolutionaries and the 'tree of liberty' was also based on a Germanic naturalistic lineage. This may be partly true, but the connections between revolutionary ideology and climatic theory were probably equally important.

fession in factors affecting health and disease in tropical climes. Desiccation-ism, in other words, became clearly linked to developments in tropical medicine.

In the Royal Society itself there is some evidence that deforestation–climate links were receiving attention as early as the 1670s, when Richard Ligon wrote his *True and Exact History of the Island of Barbados*. This in turn may have encouraged Edmund Halley in his observations on the hydrological cycle, made on St Helena in 1676 but not published until 1694.[5] The notion of atmospheric circulation, as put forward by Halley, was no doubt encouraged by Harvey's work on the circulation of the blood, which had first been pub-lished in the 1630s. When combined with Newtonian theory, these ideas would exert a potent influence and were a further reason (besides the new concerns of tropical medicine) for the increasing involvement of the medical profession in making climatic theories. Theoretical connections between the dynamics of atmospheric and bodily circulation were also integral to the dis-coveries of John Woodward and Stephen Hales, the two Cambridge specialists whose work (along with the later insights of Pierre Poivre and Joseph Priestley) formed the basis of the desiccation theory that was to become so important in cultural and scientific terms in the tropical colonies during the late eigh-teenth century. Increasingly, too (and especially in the work of Hales), the principles of the new Newtonian physics made an important contribution.

John Woodward and ideas about the atmosphere

Trained as a physician by Peter Barwick (physician to Charles II), John Wood-ward commenced a series of experiments on plant nutrition in 1696. His conclusions, the first important essays on transpiration, were published in 1699.[6] Probably the most important result of this investigation was a clear demonstration that the greater part of the water absorbed by a growing plant is exhaled through its pores into the atmosphere. Woodward also claimed that the food of plants was not water but the mineral substances dissolved in it. In a publication of 1708 he developed these ideas further. Countries having many trees, he said, were damper and more humid and had more rainfall. As the first settlers in America overcame these disadvantages by burning and destroying woods and groves 'to make way for Habitation and Culture of the

5 Halley, 'An account of the circulation of the watry vapours of the sea, and of the cause of springs'.
6 J. Woodward, 'Some thoughts and experiments concerning vegetation', *Philosophical Transac-tions of the Royal Society*, 21, (1699), 196–227; repr. in E. Halley, ed., *Miscellanea Curiosa*, vol. 1, London, 1708, pp. 230–30.

Earth, the Air mended and clear'd up space, changing into a temper more dry and serene than before'.[7]

Woodward's thoughts on these matters arose from a deep interest in geological chronology and from an awareness of processes taking place on a global scale, not least in the colonies. His other projects included attempts to produce a 'universal' natural history of fossils and works on epidemiology and the state of medicine. He was thus intimately concerned with rates of environmental changes over time and environmental influences on disease and extinctions.[8] His knowledge of North America and of contemporary American debates about the climatic effects of deforestation seems to have been derived from his correspondence with a considerable number of colonial naturalists.[9] This cosmopolitanism typified Woodward's approach to science. A global approach to the gathering of data and the construction of theory characterised almost all of his work and clearly influenced his views on the relations among plants, atmosphere and climate. In 1696 he had published *Brief Instructions for Making Observations in All Parts of the World, as Also for Collecting, Preserving and Sending over Natural Things*. This later became the basis for Royal Society instructions to 'scientific' travellers, first published in 1704. In this way Woodward both exemplified and himself consciously acted upon the connections between the stimulation brought about by the gathering of a welter of new data from all parts of the world and the formulation of new theories and models of the natural world. Desiccation theories were one major outcome of this development. Nevertheless, while Woodward's pronouncements on a forest–rainfall relationship were made with conviction, he actually had no firm mechanical or physiological or even statistical data to back up his assertions. The advent of Newtonian physics transformed this situation. Even so, it was still twenty years before Stephen Hales (1677–1761), an early disciple of Newton's, was able to emulate Woodward's speculations on the relations between vegetation and atmosphere.[10] Hales was very conscious of his debt to Woodward, stating in 1727 (with some exaggeration), 'I pursued this experiment [on transpiration] no further, Dr Woodward having long since given an account of the plentiful perspirations of this plant.'[11]

7 Woodward in *Miscellenaea Curiosa*, Vol 1, pp. 220–230, quoted in Gilbert Chinard, 'The American Philosophical Society and the early history of forestry', *Proceedings of the American Philosophical Society*, 89 (1945), 444–8; see also Chinard, 'Eighteenth century theories on America as a human habitat', *Proceedings of the American Philosophical Society*, 91 (1947), 27–57.

8 Unpublished MS of Woodward's preserved in the Royal Society Library, the British Library and the Bodleian.

9 R. P. Stearns, *Science in the British colonies of North America*, Urbana, Ill., 1970, pp. 405–26.

10 A. Clark-Kennedy, *Stephen Hales, D.D., F.R.S.: An eighteenth century biography*, Cambridge, 1929.

11 *Vegetable staticks*, London, 1727, p. 20. Hales owed a good deal, too, to the pioneering chemical

Stephen Hales and the rise of climate theories

Stephen Hales had entered Bene't Hall, Cambridge (later Corpus Christi College), in 1696.[12] As a student he soon came under the influence of several Newtonians, as well as William Stukeley, a young physician. A minor renaissance was going on at the time in Cambridge. Hales was thus able to attend lectures in experimental physics given by thinkers as prominent as William Whiston and John Cotes at the observatory in Trinity College. Cotes, in his share of the lectures, demonstrated the experiments of Torricelli, Pascal, Boyle and Hooke.[13] Cotes made frequent references in his works to Newton's *Opticks*, and it was in this intellectual setting that Hales would first have become familiar with Newtonian ideas. Particularly after the first publication of *Opticks* in 1704, Newton's influence was far more strongly felt in England than elsewhere in Europe. However, there were other major non-English works that would have affected Hales, too. We know from Stukeley that students at Bene't Hall read the Cartesian *Physics* of Jacques Rohault, but in the edition of Samuel Clarke, who appended Newtonian footnotes to 'correct' the text.[14] At this stage in his career (between about 1707 and 1712), Hales spent much of his time devising models of the motions of the planets; after 1712–14, he concentrated on the circulation of the blood.[15] A multiple, but linked, preoccupation, on different scales, with planetary and bodily circulation thus emerges in his mind. From this point it was only a logical (and short) step to move on to consider the dynamics of atmospheric circulation.

Hale's work was recognised in 1717 by his election to the Royal Society, and his contacts after this in the society probably encouraged his catholicity of experiment. While conducting experiments on animal blood, Hales wrote, 'I would I could have made the like experiments, to discover the force of sap in vegetables' but 'despaired of ever affecting it.' In fact, he soon discovered a way of investigating the mechanisms of sap flow in plants.[16]

work of the Leiden establishment and cited Hermann Boerhaave's *New method of chemistry*, translated into English by P. Shaw and E. Chambers and published in London in 1727. So the Dutch influence was not entirely lost at this stage.

12 *Gentleman's Magazine*, 34 (1764), 273.

13 Robert Smith, ed., *Hydrostatical and pneumatical lectures by Roger Cotes*, Cambridge, 1738.

14 W. Stukeley, *The family memoirs of the Rev. William Stukeley, M. D.*, 3 vols., Durham, 1882–7, vol. 1, p. 21.

15 Clark-Kennedy, *Stephen Hales*, pl. W.

16 Hales explains his breakthrough thus: Early in 1719, 'by mere accident I hit upon it, while I was endeavouring by several ways to stop the bleeding of an old stem of Vine, which was cut too near the bleeding season, which I feared might kill it. Having, after other means proved ineffectual, tied a piece of bladder over the transverse cut of the stem, I found the force of the sap did greatly extend the bladder; whence I concluded that if a long glass tube were tied there in the same manner, as I had before done to the arteries of several living animals, I

By 1726 Hales had finished the experimental work forming the basis of his *Vegetable Staticks* and possessed the basics of a chapter entitled 'The Analysis of Air'. In 1727 the book was published, and it rapidly made an impact. Besides quantifying and emphasising the significance of the relations between vegetation and air, Hales's experiments also implicitly underlined the ability of man to affect the constitution of the atmosphere. This was an essential step to a more credible advocacy of desiccation ideas. Moreover, Hales's theories reinforced current medical ideas about the relationship among diseases, 'miasmas' and 'bad' or 'wet' air. Logically, it seemed, the constitution of such air might be manipulated through vegetal change. As a committed public-health reformer, Hales himself also started to develop the implications of some of his experimental findings with his invention of 'ventilators' designed to circulate clean air into prisons and so, he hoped, prevent disease.

By applying Newtonian ideas about motion and the conservation of energy within systems to plant–atmosphere relations, Hales laid the groundwork for critiques of the human impact on air quality and changes in vegetation. In particular, his findings tended to reverse previously held assumptions about the unhealthiness of forests. The full implications of these findings took some time to percolate into a wider intellectual context, especially in the tropics. Thus even in the 1770s reputable colonial writers were still treating Hales's views as providing revolutionary insights into medical and climatic questions. Edward Long, for example, in his *History of Jamaica*, a very influential text for colonial advocates of forest protection, utilised Hales's arguments without any apology for their age. 'The incessant vitiation of our atmosphere', he wrote,

> by the decay of vegetable bodies, by fires, and by volcanoes, made it reasonable to conclude that some provision must be made in nature for correcting this depraved state and restoring the air to purity. Dr Hales seemed to think no other agent necessary for this purpose than motion . . . he finds that the effluvia of vegetables are endued with the power of reviving common air, that has been vitiated or fouled by fire or respiration.[17]

Clearly, any theory that could convincingly argue that vegetation possessed the power to cleanse air and prevent the spread of disease agents, possibly through increasing the clean-water content of the air, would eventually acquire some popularity. Even so, Hales's ideas as put forward in *Vegetable Staticks* at first experienced a far more rapid and favourable impact in France than they did in England. This was largely due to the alertness and attitudes of

should thereby obtain the real ascending force of the sap in that stem': *Vegetable staticks*, p. iii.

17 *A history of Jamaica*, 3 vols., London, 1774, III, pp. i–iv.

individuals working in the Académie des Sciences and, more especially, in the Jardin du Roi. Since the time of Colbert's reorganisation of French forestry, the Jardin had always had the staffing and outlook to respond quickly to new concepts affecting botany, and particularly to ideas emanating from England. John Evelyn's *Sylva*, for example, had already had a far more popular reception in France than in England.

The French savants would have been alerted to the significance of Hales's work by their interest in following the great controversies between Cartesianism and Newtonianism. Their enthusiasm for following English trends of thought in botany, zoology and chemistry was developing, by the time of *Staticks*, into a broader interest in the methods of English agriculture and arboriculture. This was to have long-term consequences, not least in the colonies, and also ensured that Hales and his successors continued to be carefully read by climatic theorists in France.[18] The institutional preoccupation of the French with English science was particularly well developed by the late 1720s, and some understanding of its foundations is necessary. It can probably be said to have begun with the tours made by Du Fay, keeper of the Jardin du Roi, in the Netherlands and England at the beginning of the eighteenth century. On his return, Du Fay remodelled the garden on the basis of precepts developed at Leiden and Oxford and continued to maintain contacts with these establishments.[19] Following in this tradition, the brothers de Jussieu came to England to purchase plants in 1727, the very year that *Vegetable Staticks* was published. The value of England as a location to train the experts increasingly desired by the French state (and generally far less by the comparatively non-interventionist English state) was thus becoming well established, particularly by the growing establishment at the Jardin, which by 1726 included such men as the Comte de Buffon, Duhamel du Monceau, Bernard de Jussieu and Etienne-François Geoffroy.[20]

It was on this basis that Duhamel du Monceau, later known as one of the greatest French writers on agrarian matters, arrived in England in 1729 to study shipbuilding and timber treatment. This training introduced him both to the problems of timber shortage (far more acute at this stage in England than in France) and to a whole variety of new literature in science, agriculture and arboriculture.[21] One of the earliest results of this intensified contact between French and English scientists was the decision taken by Buffon, as head

18 For a detailed analysis of the French enthusiasm for English agricultural methods and innovations, see A. J. Bourde, *The influence of England on the French agronomes, 1750–1789*, Cambridge, 1953.
19 L. F. Maury, *L'ancienne Académie des Sciences*, London, 1872, p. 28.
20 Bourde, The *Influence of England*. p. 11.
21 For details on French 'training visits' to England at this time, see J. Ballet, 'La fondation de Creusot', *Revue d'Histoire des Doctrines Economiques et Sociales*, 1912, p. 30.

of the Jardin du Roi, to translate *Vegetable Staticks* and encourage the pursuit of Hales's plant physiology in France.[22] After Duhamel's return to the Jardin and his resumption of a close working relationship with Buffon, it seems likely that Hales's writings would have acquired an intellectual prominence for both men at a time when the Jardin was beginning to extend its collecting, informational and institutional role both in France and in the wider world. Soon after his return, Duhamel began to work on the relationship between rainfall and rates of vegetation growth, a task in which he was clearly affected by his reading of Hales. According to Bourde, some of his other literary enterprises (and they were very numerous even as early as the mid 1730s) were also closely influenced by Hales.[23] Duhamel keenly debated, too, the works of such other 'new' English agricultural writers as John Grew and William Ellis and, as a result, began to formulate French agricultural writing as a science.[24]

Hale's new theories and Duhamel's training visits to England exerted an increasingly pervasive influence on the Jardin establishment and especially on the growing interest in timber shortage, forestry methods and vegetation–atmosphere connections. Although one should not exaggerate the speed with which these latter concerns developed in France, there is little doubt that the French began to set the pace in applying the implications of Halesian and Newtonian thinking to land management, albeit continuing to rely on English scientific insights. At least a third of Duhamel's writings continued to be in the field of botanico-meteorology, while Buffon in the late 1730s wrote extensively on forestry practice, relying heavily on the works of John Evelyn, Stephen Hales and William Ellis. In two essays, published in 1739 and in 1742, Buffon dwelt at length on the risks incumbent on deforestation.[25] In these essays, reflecting on the apparent failure of the 1669 Forest Ordinance, he concerned himself with the security of state access to a naval timber supply and with changing perceptions of woodland decay. He did not, however, show much interest at this point in the climatic consequences of deforestation. This is somewhat surprising in view of his later long-term preoccupation with climatic influences on cultures and species.

22 See Philip Sloan, 'Buffon's preface to the *Vegetable Staticks* of Stephen Hales (1736)', in J. Lyon and P. R. Sloan, eds., *From natural history to the history of nature: Readings from Buffon and his contemporaries*, Notre Dame, Ind., 1981, pp. 35–41.

23 Bourde mentions in this connection Duhamel's works on grafting and on 'layers and slips'.

24 See W. Ellis, *The timber tree improved; or, The best practical methods of improving different lands with proper timber*, London, 1738.

25 Comte de Buffon (G. L. Leclerc), *Sur la conservation et le rétablissement des forêts*, Paris, 1739, pp. 140–56, and *Sur le culture et exploitation des forêts*, Paris, 1742, pp. 232–46, both in *Histoire naturelle Générale et particulière*, 44 vols., Paris, 1749–1804. These essays were translated into English by G. Hamilton and J. Balfour in *A treatise on the manner of raising forest trees . . .*, Edinburgh, 1761.

The rise of climate theories in France

In the years between 1696 and 1740 a steadily more mechanistic and systematic analysis of vegetation–atmosphere relationships became both possible and well defined in both England and France. This provided a new theoretical and empirical basis for much future work in plant physiology and for wider environmental debates, especially those relating to the climatic consequences of deforestation. This development of theory did not lead by itself to an environmental critique of human disruptions of the landscape, even though, as we shall see, the intellectual and personal influence exerted by Stephen Hales may well have produced a decisive effect in the application of theory to colonial land-management ideas in English and French colonies. Instead, something more was needed before scientific thinking became incorporated in the wider scope of changing environmental attitudes.

During the 1740s and 1750s the likelihood that the seeds of an environmental message would fall on favourable ground was much increased by the rapid growth in popularity of a number of social theories relating climatic influence to social evolution. It is difficult to account for the growth of these theories with great confidence, even though Clarence Glacken made a brave attempt to do so in his 1967 book.[26] What we can say with certainty is that the political atmosphere of mid-century France was far more conducive to the popularity of climatic theory than that in Britain at the same period, largely because discussions about relations between climate and society became a surrogate for more direct criticisms of a corrupt and oppressive polity. Furthermore, the rise of climatic theorising was encouraged by the extraordinary growth of the travel-account genre during the early years of the eighteenth century.

With this genre, Europe was deluged with accounts of the habits, appearance, social organisation, religion, agriculture and other details of 'exotic' societies, as well as corresponding accounts of the local climate, natural productions, animals, plants, minerals, drugs, food and so on. All of these accounts implicitly compared European society with the cultures and countries with which they were concerned and explicitly ascribed differences in custom to differences in climate. Such accounts were a major source for essayists and naturalists throughout the eighteenth century. A view developed that both moral and physical differences within a species and between species could be ascribed to the effects of climate. It was this perception that underlay the development by Buffon and his contemporaries at the Paris Jardin du Roi and Société d'Agriculture of a programme for the investigation of acclimatisation and naturalisation among living organisms – in other words, the investigation

26 *Traces on the Rhodian shore.*

of ways of preventing the climate of one country from causing the 'degeneration' of the living beings of another.[27] Such notions were not entirely confined
to French intellectuals. On the contrary, there is some evidence that the fashion for explaining historical and social phenomena in terms of climatic theories
flourished in the early Enlightenment circles of Scotland as soon as it did in
France. David Hume, for example, wrote extensively on the relations among
climate, society and population, publishing an influential essay on the subject
in 1741.[28] A few years later, Montesquieu's widely read *Esprit des lois* of 1748
stressed the influence of climate in determining the kinds of institutions to be
found in different countries. This claim formed the basis of his justification
of the necessity for the reform of French society in line with natural laws. As
d'Alembert's analysis of the work argued, 'No-one can doubt that the climate
influences the habitual disposition of the body, and thus the character; that is
why laws must conform to the nature of the climate in indifferent things and,
on the contrary, combat it in its negative effects.'[29]

In the first volume of his *Histoire naturelle*, published in 1749, Buffon developed these ideas to construct a far more charged climatic theory relating
climate change to the highly controversial concept of 'degeneration'. 'Everything', Buffon asserted,

> goes to prove that the human type is not composed of species with es-
> sential differences between them, but that, on the contrary, there was
> originally only one species of man, which having multiplied and spread
> out over the whole surface of the earth, underwent different changes by
> the influence of climate, by the difference of nourishment, by the manner
> of living, by epidemic diseases, and also by the infinitely varying mixture
> of individuals resembling one another more or less.

Buffon's writings went on, eventually, to stress what he saw as the 'degenerating' effects of particular climates on individual species. The process of
degeneration, he felt, could occur in several ways: by variations in temperature, altitude, wind direction and nature of soil. Climate, he thought, could
also affect animals via their food, and this he stressed as being one of the most

27 For an account of Buffon's interest in climate, see Glacken, *Traces on the Rhodian shore*, and
    E. Spary, 'Climate, natural history and agriculture: The ideology of botanical networks in
    eighteenth century France and its colonies', unpublished paper presented at the International
    Conference on Environmental Institutions, St Vincent, West Indies, April 1991.
28 'Of the populousness of ancient nations', in T. H. Green and T. H. Grose, eds., *Essays moral,
    political and literary*, London, 1882, pp. 356–60.
29 J. le R. d'Alembert, 'Analyse de L'esprit des lois', *Encyclopédie*, vol. 5, 1755. Diderot's article
    entitled 'Climate' in vol. 3, published in 1755, refers to the Baron de Montesquieu (writer,
    political thinker and landowner) as the originator of the social 'theory of climate'. In fact,
    Hume might have a prior claim to such recognition. The d'Alembert translation is from Spary,
    'Climate, natural history and agriculture'.

important determinants of differences within species: 'It is from that same temperature that, in consequence, the difference in men's nourishment derives, a second cause which greatly affects their temperament, nature, size and strength.'[30] Moral (or as we might say today, behavioural) and physical differences between individuals, between cultures and between species, Buffon argued, could be ascribed directly to the effects of climate. Clearly, by elevating climate to such significance as a cause of and as a vehicle for the discussion of social and political morality, Buffon also elevated the study of climate and its causes to new heights as well. In this latter field, however, the French continued in the 1750s and 1760s to rely on the English Newtonians for their fundamental scientific insights.

This dependence was directly reflected in the appointment in 1753 of Stephen Hales as a foreign associate of the Académie des Sciences in Paris, in direct succession to Sir Hans Sloane. The primacy, to the French, of Hales's plant and atmospheric work was thus underlined. It was at this precise point in time, however, that Hales started to exercise a more political role in England itself, principally through his involvement in co-founding and then running the new London Society for the Promotion of Arts, Manufactures and Commerce. From 1754 onwards, the flow of ideas between the two intellectual establishments became remarkably intense and close, in fact so close that one may even characterise the Académie des Sciences and the Society of Arts as component parts of what was effectively a single intellectual community or 'centre of calculation', at least for the purpose of the ongoing debate about the causes and effects of different climates. Thus there was a significant French membership of the Society of Arts, matching the older-established English membership of the Académie des Sciences. For example, both L. F. Turbilly (the author of a work translated into English in 1762 as *A Discourse on the Cultivation of Waste and Barren Lands*) and the Comte d'Abeille, another well-known French agricultural writer of the 1760s, were listed as corresponding members of the Society of Arts in 1761.[31]

Partly because of this degree of intellectual cross-fertilisation, climatic theories underwent a major sea-change. Until the 1750s most climatic theorists had, with the notable exception of John Woodward, implicitly envisaged man as a passive actor (or even victim) in the face of monolithic or even global climatic forces over which he had no control. Processes of 'degeneration', it was implied, could not be forestalled in any way, and humanity could take no overall responsibility for the nature and consequences of climate change. In this context one can clearly observe the critical nature of debates about the

30 Buffon, *Histoire naturelle*, suppl. to vol. 4, 1777, p. 555; translations from Spary, 'Climate, natural history and agriculture'.
31 Archives of the Royal Society of Arts, John Adam St, London: 'Sponsored members' files.

relation of forest cover and rainfall levels to wider climatic arguments. Having accepted, on the 'scientific' basis provided by the Newtonians, that forests could be directly linked to atmospheric moisture, the theorists could further propose that man might control the constitution of the atmosphere through his control of forest cover. There are some indications that this critical proposition was beginning to achieve tentative support in the arboricultural writings of Duhamel du Monceau, particularly in the books published after 1753.[32] His most explicit statements on the subject were made in *Des semis et plantations des arbres et de leur culture*, a book published in 1760. The second chapter of this work, entitled 'Du climat, et de l'exposition, relativement aux arbres', comes very close to making a direct connection between deforestation and rainfall decline and is clearly much influenced by Hales. Even so, despite his great interest in forest conservation, Duhamel did not foresee any very broad implications of his climatic observations. Instead he was probably attempting to summarise the experience of twenty years' daily records of temperature and barometric pressure and additional data on crops, floods and plant growth in general. Above all, he remained limited by a lack of any real appreciation of the more extreme consequences of deforestation outside the temperate zone. Despite this, his remarks on bio-meteorology were precocious for the time.[33]

A shift away from the 'passive' view of man's position may also have started to occur, ironically, through a series of events in which humanity emerged even more decisively as the victim of earthly hazards. Specifically, the London earthquakes of 1750 and the great Lisbon earthquake of 1755 served to highlight the vulnerability of man to natural processes. Indeed, like Daniel Defoe some decades before him, Stephen Hales became so preoccupied by the London earthquakes that he wrote a book about their causes, which was published

32 H. L. Duhamel du Monceau's impressive and polymathic output of work included *Traité de la fabrique des manoeuvres pour les vaisseaux ou l'art de la corderie perfectionne*, 2 vols., Paris, 1747; *Traité de la culture des terres suivant les principes de M. Tull*, 6 vols., Paris, 1750–61; *Eléments d'architecture navale*, Paris, 1752; *Avis pour le transport par mer des arbres, des plantes vivaces, des semences, et de diverses autres curiosités d'histoire naturelles*, Paris, 1753; *Traité de la conservation des grains et en particulier du froment*, Paris, 1753; *Traité des arbres et arbustes qui se cultivent en France en pleine terre*, Paris, 1755; *Mémoires sur la garance et sa culture*, Paris, 1757; *La physique des arbres*, Paris, 1758; *Moyens de conserver la santé aux équipages des vaisseaux*, Paris, 1759; *Des semis et plantations des arbres et de leur culture*, Paris, 1760; *Eléments d'agriculture*, Paris, 1762; *Histoire d'un insecte qui dévore les grains dans L'Angoumois*, Paris, 1762; *Du transport, de la conservation et de la force des bois*, Paris, 1767; *Traité des arbres fruitiers*, Paris, 1768; *Traité général des pêches, et histoire des poissons qu'elles fournissent*, 3 vols., Paris, 1769–77.

33 See Theodore S. Feldman, 'Late Enlightenment meteorology', in T. Frangsmyr, J. L. Heilbronn, and R. E. Rider, eds., *The quantifying spirit in the eighteenth century*, Berkeley and Los Angeles, 1990, pp. 143–79.

in 1750.[34] In much the same way, Voltaire's anguished commentaries on the cosmic lessons of the Lisbon earthquake dealt a heavy blow to the perception, purveyed by Buffon and his colleagues, of a powerful and beneficial control exercised by man over nature. Moreover, after 1755 natural hazards were seen to affect Europe and Europeans as much as the catastrophic forces that had been observed at work in North America and the tropics. Within ten years of 1755 active attempts were being made to control climate change in the tropics. How and why did this rapid (and revolutionary) trend towards the assertion of attempts at control (that is, towards an active climatic conservationism) actually start to take place?

The Newtonian insights brought by Woodward and Hales into plant–atmosphere dynamics and the rise of climatic social theory could not by themselves have brought about this change within the confines of England and France. The constraints acting on men as perceptive as Duhamel du Monceau indicate that a further critical, and situational, element was needed. This new element consisted, I would argue, in a learned encounter between the new social and 'Newtonian' climatic theories and the realities of a rapidly changing and closely observed tropical forest environment in which rainfall reduction would be seen to have a devastating potential for economic disruption and decline. Such an encounter would then require the presence of a European traveller and administrator in the tropics well versed in current scientific thinking on the 'causes' of climate.

Such a person was Pierre Poivre, a naturalist and botanist who had travelled widely in the East and had a particular knowledge of Mauritius and its vegetation, as well as of many other tropical environments. In early 1763 he gave a speech in Lyons to the new agricultural society of that city in which he very explicitly preached the dangers of deforestation in bringing about rainfall changes, and the particular dangers of such changes for a tropical colony. In the same speech he drew particular attention to the care taken by the Dutch at the Cape to reafforest their colony. The implication was clear: The French must both protect the existing forests in their colonies in the 'Indies' and the Indian Ocean and plant more trees to stabilise the climate.[35]

As we shall see, it was this speech of Poivre's which laid the foundation (less than six years after 1763!) for the forest-protection policies set up in both French and British colonial island territories. These early policies became the direct forerunners and models for almost all later colonial forest-protection policies and those of other territories in Europe and North America. In Poivre's case, he followed his own precepts in the forest rules of the *Reglement*

---

34 *Some considerations on the causes of earthquakes*, London, 1750.

35 Paris, Archives of the Bibliothèque centrale, Muséum national d'histoire naturelle (henceforth BCMNHN), MS 575, fol. 74, pp. 27–9: Poivre's speech at Lyons.

Économique imposed on Mauritius in 1769. The political traumas and territorial exchanges wrought by the Peace of Paris in 1763 accelerated this process. Almost certainly coaxed into action by the news of Poivre's speech, the British acted even faster, incorporating rain reserves into their plans for developing the 'Ceded Islands' of the Grenada governorate (Tobago, Grenada, St Vincent, St Lucia and Dominica) in late 1763. This British scheme (which we shall consider in Chapter 6) was at least partly derivative of Poivre's environmentalism. It therefore seems appropriate to consider the antecedents and history of the environmental policy implemented under Poivre on Mauritius before we try to understand the rather more superficial and less politically integrated British climatic environmental policies in the Caribbean that started in the same decade and were derived from the same Anglo-French roots.

5

Protecting the climate of paradise: Pierre Poivre and the conservation of Mauritius under the ancien régime

> To contemplate the progress of a rising colony is a spectacle worthy of a philosopher, for it is there that the culture of man forms a striking contrast with that of nature.
>
> J. H. Bernardin de Saint-Pierre[1]

Under French rule between 1722 and 1790 Mauritius became the location for the flowering of a complex and unprecedented environmental policy. This policy started to acquire a particularly innovative and deliberate character between 1767 and 1772 as a result of the personal intervention of Pierre Poivre. In part this development can be attributed to the systematic way in which Poivre marshalled the climatic arguments against deforestation which had emerged by the 1760s and then persuaded the French colonial authorities of their importance. There is no question that this task of persuasion was made much easier for Poivre by the Newtonian rationales of Hales and others and by their previous acceptance by Duhamel du Monceau and his colleagues at the Jardin de Roi. However, it would probably be a great mistake to assume that the rationales of the climatic environmentalism aspired to by such Newtonians as Hales, Duhamel and others played a central part in the formation of Poivre's views. Certainly there is little doubt that he successfully co-opted arguments which had, by virtue of the influence of Stephen Hales in France, become convincing for those in government circles, and particularly for the physiocratic circle of which Poivre and Duhamel du Monceau were leading members. Nevertheless, many of his own views on deforestation, climate change and man–nature relationships were strongly affected by an acquaintance with the Indian, Zoroastrian and Chinese systems of knowledge that he had encountered during his long years as a travelling naturalist. This chapter is intended to outline the practical and theoretical consequences of the het-

---

1 *Harmonies of nature*, 3 vols., London, 1815, I, p. 177.

erodox heritage of environmental ideas that was effectively personified in Poivre and his colleagues.

Poivre's actions during the period of his power in Mauritius, in which he implemented his environmentalism, were constrained mainly by the needs of the spice transplantation schemes which were his major policy objective. They were also affected by the previous history of response to the deforestation taking place on the island. After about 1757 an increasing state interest in the economic advantages of crop transfer became further developed in the agrarian ideologies of the physiocrats, with their particular emphasis on the application of science to agriculture and forest management and indeed to the whole rural economy. When applied to the colonial context and allied with the philosophies of Poivre, this physiocratic ideology stimulated the emergence of an overtly conservationist policy linked to a whole set of broader economic and social objectives. What was the historical and institutional background to this development?

The economic basis of the French settlement on Mauritius

The French interest in annexing Mauritius originated in part in the increased competition between Britain and France in their attempts to build up spheres of influence in India and the East Indies.[2] In this respect Mauritius had a good deal to offer, both as the location of two well-protected harbours, at Port Louis and Grand Port, and as an entrepot and forward base at which ships could be revictualled and repaired on their way to and from the French Indian factories and possessions. It was also a useful base to counter British interests in India in naval, military and commercial terms and was considered by the French to be a part of the 'Indies'. Besides, the French were already settled on nearby Bourbon (Réunion). Mauritius had, to begin with, a much more elaborate role to fulfil for the purposes of the French than St Helena had for the British or the Cape had for the Dutch. Although the connection with the island was at first mediated through the Compagnie des Indes (CoI), Mauritius occupied a strategic position in French thinking and soon invited the prospect of direct intervention by the French Crown. There is, in fact, a good deal of evidence that the main motive for colonising Mauritius in the first place consisted in a desire to use the island to displace the Dutch in their monopoly of the spice trade.[3]

2 See A. Toussaint, *A history of the Indian Ocean*, trans. J. Guichemand, London, 1966, *A history of Mauritius*, trans. W. E. F. Ward, London, 1977, *La route des iles: Contributions à l'histoire des iles Mascareignes*, Paris, 1967, and *L'Océan Indien au XVIII siècle*, Paris, 1974.

3 The following discussion of the significance of the spice trade to the French on Mauritius is based on Madeleine Ly-Tio-Fane, *Mauritius and the spice trade: The odyssey of Pierre Poivre*, 2 vols., Port Louis, 1958, and Paris, 1970.

Plate 10. The physiocrat Pierre Poivre (1719–86). As commissaire-intendant of Mauritius from 1767 to 1772, Poivre was responsible for introducing forest- and climate-
protection measures to the island. (Collection of the Royal Society of Arts and Sciences
of Mauritius, Mauritius Institute, Port Louis)

Almost from the beginning of European participation in the lucrative spice
trade, the French had tried to secure their share of the profits. The exploits
of Jean Ango's pilots had had the effect of drawing their attention to the great
possibilities of eastern trade.[4] The merchants of St Malo were even more
enterprising; in 1617 they had already established an entrepot in Bantam, but

4 Sonia Howe, *Les grands navigateurs à la recherche des épices*, Paris, 1939.

the Dutch took energetic measures to expel these rivals, and the establishment was short-lived.[5] Towards the middle of the century the Dutch carried out a new offensive against the interloper trade, destroying all spice-bearing plants in the territories belonging to vassal sultans, and concentrated the cultivation on Amboina and Banda. This, however, did not stop the brisk trade of the natives with Mindanao and Kedah. They travelled to buy spices in regions unknown to the Dutch, and this in fact provided the opening for the other nations which were attempting to end the Dutch monopoly.

For some time the French had been examining the possibilities of growing spice plants in their tropical territories, especially nutmeg and clove plants, the latter being the most highly valued. A close connection thus developed between the colonial spice-growing plans of the French, their plans to reorganise the colony of Bourbon and their plans to occupy Mauritius after it had been abandoned by the Dutch. The perceived potential of Mauritius as a site for spice plantations clearly encouraged proposals for colonisation. This is confirmed by a letter written in 1716 by Dulivier, the governor of Pondicherry, to Pontchartrain in which he voiced doubts as to the feasibility of spice cultivation on the island in view of the threat posed by marauding monkeys.[6]

The Compagnie des Indes, which came into being in May 1719 under the impulse of Law de Lauriston, adopted the policy of the old company with regard to the spice trade and concentrated its efforts on obtaining plants for acclimatisation. The correspondence of the Board of Directors with the Council of Pondicherry gives us some information about this search. The earliest reference occurs in a letter of 9 November 1719 in which the councillors were advised to bring clove and nutmeg plants for Bourbon. Not overkeen on this scheme, the councillors replied that the expedition was dangerous and might require the use of force. As absolute secrecy was necessary, and as that could not be ensured in a place like Pondicherry, where the destination of every ship was known as soon as it was fitted out, it was better for the success of the venture to send the expedition out from the Mascarenes. Apparently nothing further was done, for the project figured in a list of undertakings capable of restoring the credit of the company after the collapse of Law's system. The order was reiterated on 20 February 1722, and on 2 March 1723 the Council

5 Charles de la Roncière, 'Les précurseurs de la Compagnie des Indes Orientales – La politique coloniale des Malouins', *Revue Historique Col. Fr.*, 1 (1918).

6 Albert Lougnon, *L'île Bourbon pendant la Régence*, Paris, 1956, pp. 63–9: orders of Pontchartrain of 31 Oct. 1714. Dulivier was responding to a plan to acquire coffee plants from Moka for Bourbon and pepper and cinnamon plants from the Malabar Coast, and to acquire Mauritius for plantation purposes. It seems that the whole proposal had been sparked off by the ideas of a certain Sieur de Vauvre, who solicited from the government the concession of Bourbon, asserting that in future years it would produce enough spices and coffee to meet all the needs of France.

of Pondicherry decided that on the return from Canton of the *St François*, a ship engaged in local Asian trade, they would send it to the Moluccas on a reconnaissance expedition.[7] In 1726 the Directors sent a special agent, La Rivière, to India, but after examining his plans, Pierre Lenoir, governor of the CoI, decided that they were too vague and risky to carry out. Thus for the time being the spice-transfer projects came to an end. However, before they did so, the directors drew up a formal plan for a spice-gathering expedition to the Moluccas.[8] It was this document which was to provide Poivre with the blueprint he needed to plan his own series of spice expeditions in 1747–70 and which laid the basis for his particular interventions in the land management of Mauritius.

The relative political and economic importance of the Mauritius colony to the French was crucial to the development of any reaction to the environmental changes which took place as a result of settlement. Moreover, as a rule, those personalities who became closely involved with environmental policy on Mauritius were relatively far more eminent in French society, in literature, and in the metropolitan state apparatus than those involved with the island colonies of Britain or Holland. In this sense, the environment of Mauritius was relatively accessible and easily affected by changing economic conditions and aesthetic and social fashions in Europe, and in France in particular.

This interaction was not one-sided. Before the end of the eighteenth century, Mauritius had come to occupy a central and innovative place across the whole field of new thinking in French philosophy, botanical science and literature. It became especially important in the early literature of the French Romantic tradition. In many ways, Mauritius became at least as significant in this sense as the later discoveries of the South Sea islands are conventionally supposed to have been to French culture. This pre-eminence was reflected, not surprisingly, in the way in which the Mauritius environment was perceived, evaluated and then managed by colonial officials. Indeed, the new name for the island, the 'Isle de France', was no idle misnomer. Mauritius was also the location of more active investment and political intention as a straightforward plantation and slave economy than either St Helena or the Cape and was, perhaps, more comparable to the possessions acquired by the British in the Caribbean after 1763.

Its vaunted and apparently favourable soils and climate, no less obvious to the French than they had been to St Helena's Governor Pyke in 1715, could only encourage commercial ambitions. However, after the initial collapse of the spice-plantation plans, an alternative crop had to be found. This soon

---

7 Lougnon, *L'ile Bourbon*, p. 81.

8 'Plan for the acquisition of spice plants', document dated 7 July 1729, reproduced in Ly-Tio-Fane, *Mauritius and the spice trade*, I, p. 39.

presented itself in the form of sugar cane, the plant which had already caused, and would continue to cause, such spectacular environmental deterioration in the West Indies. The contradictions between the economic potential of the colony and the ecological consequences of sugar-cane plantation investment on the island were to dominate the context within which its environment was valued and attempts at ecological control were tried out. Above all, sugar-cane plantations entailed the rapid clearance of large areas of forest. Growing demands for naval, construction and furniture timber also speeded up the impetus towards deforestation, particularly during the naval wars of the 1740s.

However, the problems of dealing with deforestation had, in fact, been given some thought much earlier, as soon as the CoI had assumed control in 1721.[9] In January 1722, M. de Nyon, appointed governor of the colony in April 1721, arrived with a force of 210 soldiers, 180 settlers and 30 slaves. From the beginning, Nyon encouraged the cultivation of Mocha coffee, and large clearances of forest were made accordingly. Nyon had brought with him in his entourage a botanist known as 'Brother Adam'. The friar was directed to supervise the new plantations and the cultivation of new crop species. However, he was drowned during a hurricane in June 1722, so that any chance of building up a botanical tradition or of monitoring land-use changes was temporarily lost.[10] The principle of employing a professional botanist had, nevertheless, been initiated in the French settlement.

Land concessions were offered without fee to whoever was willing to settle and work the land, while slaves were imported by the company from Madagascar, Mozambique and West Africa. The use of these concessions was constrained by the company in a number of ways. By the terms of the 'Concessions Regulations' of 1723, a 'Reservation' was established which forbade timber cutting for a width of fifty paces in a 'cordon sanitaire' around the entire circumference of the island.[11] This regulation probably derived in part from practices initiated in France through the enforcement of the 1669 Forest Ordinance. The Concessions Regulations were followed by comparable restrictions regulating hunting which were imposed in 1726 as a response to the widespread and uncontrolled pursuit of game by company officers.

The Game Law as gazetted on 31 May 1726 accordingly stated that 'it has been generally decided that all kinds of hunting would be prohibited to soldiers and inhabitants' and that 'hunting wild pigs and goats would be prohibited' even to army and naval officers. All dogs in the island were 'to be killed except for ten which will be held by the Company'.[12] Rather than al-

---

9 The island had been formally claimed for the French Crown six years before.
10 Burgh-Edwardes, *History of Mauritius*, p. 13.
11 Brouard, *Woods and forests*, p. 11.
12 Ibid.

lowing free enterprise in hunting, the governor would organise shooting parties in order to supply the colonists with basic food needs. In this way the
company began to relive some of the problems which the Dutch had begun
to encounter and to which they had eventually failed to respond. The significance of the hunting regulations was simply that the perceptually strictly finite
nature of the island's resources, whether of land or game, helped to give rise
to a mentality encouraging further regulation. Already the imposition of the
1726 rules meant that any lingering ideas of limitless bounty had already been
superseded at the beginning of the colonisation process.

    The agricultural potential of the island soon came in for closer inspection,
partly because of a policy decision to allocate development of coffee plantations
to the neighbouring island of Bourbon and the development of pepper and
medicinal plants to Mauritius. From the start, the Council of Government
took a somewhat pessimistic view, admitting in 1730 that

> carefully examining the soil of this island in all its aspects, it is essentially
> dry, gravelly, hard and heavy; very few small areas differ more or less
> from this description, which you may accept as general, without even
> excluding the middle of the island, which had been described to you as
> being marvellous. It is true that wherever it is covered with forests and
> before being worked, it looks deceptive because of a sort of soil which is
> formed by the rotting of leaves and trees spreading to a depth of a few
> inches over a more or less large area, but as soon as it is cleared and
> worked it takes a reddish and fiery tinge which is found below.[13]

This well-observed account of the rapid nature of laterisation and the fragility of the tropical forest soils displays an empirical approach which contrasted with the initially more ecstatic and unreal accounts of the St Helena
setting and its fruitful soils.[14] The impression conveyed here is of a developing
awareness of the fragility of the apparently lush Mauritius landscape. This
may help to account for the decision taken by the CoI in 1730 to restrict all
land sales and impose a land tax on cultivated land. But by a regulation of
December 1730 it was stipulated that any concession holder who did not clear
land within three years would forfeit the uncleared portion.[15] This actually
had the effect of stimulating deforestation, although this does not appear to
have been the official intention. Instead it allowed the company, at least in
law, to retain a tight hold on land. Moreover, unlike the St Helena authorities,
the CoI had no popular agitation for 'common' land ownership to contend
with.

13 Ibid.
14 The term 'laterites' was first coined by Buchanan-Hamilton in Malabar in a similarly erosive
    context: pers. comm. from Sir Joseph Needham.
15 Brouard, *Woods and forests*, p. 12.

The arrival of Mahé de Labourdonnais as governor in 1735 marked the start of a period of rapidly increasing pressure on the Mauritius forests and soils. As they became better known, many of the island timbers were found to be unusually durable, very suitable for shipbuilding and, in the opinion of Labourdonnais, especially suitable for export to French territories in mainland India. Both slaves and oxen were now imported specifically to expedite timber-cutting operations.

Although early and somewhat impractical attempts were made to introduce exotic fruit trees, such as peach and mulberry, more basic problems were experienced with basic food crops, and serious food shortages were recorded in 1735, immediately after the arrival of Labourdonnais, and again in 1741. These were due partly to the rapid increase of the slave population in the early 1730s. Labourdonnais was compelled to organise shooting and fishing expeditions simply to feed the population, probably as a result of crop failures and insufficient planting. This early acquaintance with dearth on the island seems to have awoken him to its basic limitations and also to have stimulated him to consider more specific kinds of 'improvement'. For immediate purposes, resort was had to the neighboring island of Rodriguez, and tortoises were brought from there as a meat supply for Mauritius, where they had already been hunted to extinction by the 1740s.[16]

Labourdonnais and the significance of the botanical gardens

More significantly for the long term, Labourdonnais embarked on a series of attempts to introduce and breed new crops on his estate, 'Mon Plaisir', at Pamplemousses. This crop-trial garden formed the basis of the later botanical garden at Pamplemousses. Labourdonnais had particular success with one crop, manioc, which had been introduced from Brazil, and it proved a useful staple food for the slave population. The success of this innovation, and more especially the idea of cultivating new crops in a specialised garden on a trial basis, meant that his initiative became widely known among English as well as French botanists and later provided part of the inspiration for the introduction of the botanical-garden system in India.[17] Labourdonnais himself, however, may well have been influenced by the use of the VOC garden at the Cape as an acclimatisation garden, although there is no firm evidence for this. Most of his political initiatives related to the military function of the colony. In 1746 he was successful in capturing Madras, using ships constructed of

16 *DMB*, p. 154.
17 In particular for the foundation of the Calcutta Botanic Garden.

Mauritius timber. This strategic use of the island woods was the cause of a further increase in the rate of deforestation.

Labourdonnais's successor as governor, Pierre David (1711–95), chose a different site, at La Reduit, for a further botanical, or acclimatisation, garden, ensuring that the relationship between the colonial state and botanical science would continue to be close.[18] This relationship had clear economic advantages and even constituted a necessity on an island where commercial plantations were an objective of settlement. Although dearth had first encouraged Labourdonnais in the enterprise, the development of the botanical-garden idea on Mauritius seems to have combined elements of two related traditions: the acclimatisation garden long established at the Cape and the more academically orientated Jardin du Roi in Paris. It is difficult to say which influence was the more dominant.[19] Simply by virtue of its presence as an institution, the botanical garden directly promoted the gathering of information about plant distribution and status on the island and encouraged comparisons of the Mauritius environment with environments in other parts of the tropics. Although the immediate commercial motives for establishing a garden were important, they were by no means the only or even the most important motives behind the concept.[20] Broadly, there were two other main types of motivation. The first related essentially to the connection between the establishment of a highly formalised garden comprehensively stocked with plants from as many parts of the world as possible and the idea of re-creating a Garden of Eden, or an earthly paradise. This was a common factor behind the establishment of both domestic gardens and more elaborate apothecary and scientific botanical gar-

18 In fact David founded the garden as a direct response to Poivre's plans to open a commerce in spice plants between Cochin China and Mauritius. David promised the directors that as soon as Poivre sailed he would set about preparing a garden to receive the spice plants at Le Reduit, where he had built himself a large country residence. See *DMB*.

19 However, the Dutch interest in tree planting undoubtedly played a part in the way the deforestation issue was later dealt with on Mauritius. This transference of ideas was occasioned by the very far-ranging travels of French botanists at this period, of whom the most outstanding was Pierre Poivre. Poivre travelled extensively in China and the East Indies, as well as in the Indian Ocean, between 1749 and 1755 in search of spice plants that might profitably be transplanted to Mauritius. In 1752 he remarked that 'oak trees which I have brought from the Cape [to Mauritius] have been successful and are promising because they were left to grow in the very soil with which I had brought them' (Brouard, *Woods and forests*, p. 12; source unknown. For references to Poivre's early work on spice-tree transfer, see Ly-Tio-Fane, *Mauritius and the spice trade*, I). This intimate concern with soil conditions, engendered by a professional interest in crop transfers, was to have long-term relevance in Poivre's career. Here one may simply note that in two conceptual ways – in the development of a botanical garden and in promoting the idea of tree planting – the Dutch settlement at the Cape had been a fertile source of ideas and examples. The significance of the former in particular is difficult to overestimate.

20 See Brockway, *Science and colonial expansion*, for a purely 'utilitarian' analysis of this.

dens in Europe.[21] Moreover, it was also closely related to the Dantean conceptualisation of the tropical island as an earthly paradise. The Jardin du Roi,
the Chelsea Physic Garden and the VOC garden at the Cape were all founded
at least partly on this basis and at the same period (1630–70), during a time
of considerable social and religious travail and upheaval in Europe. All were
dependent, however, on the growing frequency of trading voyages to supply
them with plants of a worldwide provenance. As Valentyn's description indicates, the VOC garden was visually as well as conceptually spectacular, and
its imitation on Mauritius was predictable.[22] Apart from the needs of the spice-
transfer programme, a second major motivation for establishing a permanent
state botanical garden on Mauritius was medical, and it was here that the
influence of the Paris Jardin du Roi was most closely felt. In Mauritius this
took a very specific form with the arrival of Jean-Baptiste Fusée Aublet in
1753.[23]

Aublet arrived, at the age of thirty-three, during the absence of Poivre on
his first major spice-gathering expedition. He had trained in Lyons under the
direction of Christophe de Jussieu, a skilled pharmacist with a great interest
in botany. Aublet later studied in Montpellier and was then accepted into the
Jardin du Roi in Paris to complete his training as 'apothicaire-botaniste'.[24] The
staff of the Jardin du Roi had the right at this time to make a direct appointment to the Isle de France and, through the influence of Bernard de Jussieu,
Aublet was appointed 'apothicaire-compositeur' of the Isle de France and
Bourbon. On arrival on 25 August 1753, he started to search the island for
medicinal plants. These he cultivated in the garden of Mon Plaisir at Pamplemousses, the botanical garden founded by Labourdonnais. Eventually finding this site unsuitable, he moved his collection to an estate owned by the
Compagnie des Indes in the Quartier de Moka known as Le Reduit.[25] This
was a botanical garden developed on a very secluded, well-watered site, and
it catered exclusively to Aublet's research interests. The holdings of this garden are well documented and represent Aublet's botanical and horticultural
work over a period of ten years, the first documentation dating from 1754.[26]

21 Prest, *The Garden of Eden*, p. 22.
22 F. Valentyn, *Oud en nieuw Oost-Indien*, vol. 1, Dordrecht, 1724, pp. 4–8.
23 Brouard, *Woods and forests*, p. 11. For a biographical account of Fusée Aublet, see *DMB*, pp.
   2–3. Aublet also provides a biography in the preface of his *Histoire et plantes de la Guiane
   francaise*, Paris, 1775, pp. ii–xxix. A useful summary of his work as a predecessor of the
   botanist Pierre Sonnerat appears in M. Ly-Tio-Fane, *Pierre Sonnerat, 1748–1814: An account
   of his life and work*, Port Louis, 1976. I have leant heavily here on Ly-Tio-Fane's interpretation
   of Aublet's work.
24 His teachers were Guillaume-Francois Rouelle (the 'démonstrateur de chimie' at the Jardin
   du Roi) and Bernard de Jussieu for botany.
25 Ly-Tio-Fane, *Pierre Sonnerat*, p. 50.
26 Paris, Archives of the BCMNHN, MS 452, fol. 1. Two sheets without description, probably

A later 'précis' indicates that the garden contained plants from as far afield as Europe, St Iago (Cape Verde Islands), the Americas, India, China, Senegal, the Cape of Good Hope, the Seychelles (Isle des Trois Frères), the Near East and the Malay peninsula.[27] This document constituted the basis for a paper entitled 'Indication des plantes qui se trouvent à L'Isle de France, tout indigènes ou naturelles à cette isle, que naturalisées ou apportées de diverses régions', which was published in London in 1775 as part of the second volume of the *Histoire des plantes de la Guiane française*.

While laying the practical groundwork for later French botanists working on the island, such as Commerson and Charpentier de Cossigny,[28] Aublet also promoted a much wider dissemination of the botanical knowledge of Mauritius. Later this was reinforced by his correspondence with Sir Joseph Banks and by the contact he established with the Royal Society through Jacinto de Magalhaens, a botanist and Fellow of the Society. It was the latter who was responsible for advising Banks eventually to buy Aublet's herbarium.[29] More important, Banks's acquaintance with Aublet's highly detailed and extended work on Mauritius influenced him in promoting the idea of stationing resident 'colonial botanists' or 'naturalists' in as many parts of the colonial territories in the tropics as possible.[30] Aublet himself also symbolised the direct link between the metropolitan focus of developments in French botany and the growing awareness of the changes taking place in the Mauritius environment. This link ensured that whatever changes took place, the components of its biota would be intensively studied and known, so giving a new quality and urgency to subsequent anxiety about deforestation. At the outset, therefore, the response to deforestation differed substantially from the ad hoc response which was developing simultaneously on St Helena, even though the causes of deforestation were substantially the same. To some extent, the dynamic link between botanical science in Paris and events on Mauritius can be seen as the product of a chronological coincidence between the settlement of Mauritius and the contemporary revolution in botanical science taking place through debates about classification and early thinking (for example, on the part of

drawn up in refutation of the minutes drawn on the orders of Commissaire-Ordonnateur Poivre and entitled 'Conduite du Sieur Aublet, anciennement chargé de cette Pharmacie', dated August 1767.

27 Aublet, *Histoire des plantes de la Guiane*, pp. 139–60.

28 Charpentier de Cossigny's dates are 1736–1809. Author of *Lettre à M. Sonnerat* (1784) and *Moyens de'amélioration des colonies* (1803), Cossigny also imported the bois noir tree (*Albizzia bebek*) from Malabar and Bengal to Mauritius in 1766: *DMB*, p. 11.

29 Letter of 28 Dec. 1778: British Library, Add. MS 8094, 136, and 33977, pp. 38–9, 86–7; *Banks letters*, 242–3.

30 It may also have been important in Banks's lobbying of the East India Company in his efforts to promote the installation of professional naturalists in India.

Buffon) about species mutability. The rich flow of material from places like Mauritius had helped to promote this revolution by permitting global taxonomic comparisons to be made and forcing new thinking about plant classification to take place. The stationing of a botanist on a permanent basis on Mauritius only made this relationship more significant.

Aublet also provided at least part of the empirical basis of research into the distribution and characteristics of the island's plants from which Pierre Poivre was able to profit. This was despite the fact that an intense antipathy existed between the two, deriving ostensibly from the suspicion nurtured by Poivre that Aublet had actively sabotaged the successful transplantation of the spice plants he had imported with such effort to Mauritius from the Moluccas.

Rising anxieties about deforestation, 1750–64

Although Pierre Poivre visited Mauritius on two occasions during the 1750s, he was not to return to reside on the island in an official capacity until 1767. Nevertheless, during this period a good deal of unease was expressed on the part of several observers as to the state of the tree cover. This was partly a consequence of the effective abandonment of the initially cautious attitude adopted by the Compagnie des Indes as its administration came under pressure from the more rapacious landowners, both resident and absentee. The progressive deterioration in the company's economic fortunes was a related factor. In 1752 the company confiscated 204 concessions on the ground that their owners had not complied with the terms of their contracts, especially the provision stating that all land except for the 'reserves', which were rather loosely defined, should be brought under cultivation within three years. A surveyor had been appointed and two types of concession granted, according to a regulation of 1734: the 'petite habitation' and the 'grande habitation', which was twice as big. The concession boundaries usually followed a straight line, regardless of terrain, and a strip of six feet either side of the line had to be kept open by the owner at all times for access and demarcation.[31]

Even at this stage, the island forests were still thought of as substantial and were perceived by only a few observers as imminently threatened. This impression is given in the descriptions of the Abbé de la Caille, a famous French astronomer, mathematician and geographer who visited Mauritius in 1753 as probably the first representative, apart from Aublet himself, of the many members of the French scientific establishment to visit the island during the eighteenth century. La Caille was able to make the first accurate survey and map of the island. This was significant, as it enabled accurate stock to be taken,

31 Brouard, *Woods and forests*, p. 14.

Plate 11. The topography of Mauritius in 1801. This map of the island as Decaen (governor 1803–10) would have known it shows how forest clearance was still limited to the northern plain and to the environs of Port Louis and to the region of Grand Port and Mahebourg in the south-east of the island. Road building had developed substantially since the Revolution and it facilitated much faster deforestation in subsequent years. (Map published by Charles Grant, Viscount de Vaux, in 1801 and reproduced by permission of Cambridge University Library)

for the first time, of the whereabouts of the island's forests. Lozier-Bouvet,
the governor, was most impressed and wrote that 'this academician has carried
out the operation in less time than was taken by the engineer-geographer to
measure the base-line according to his instructions'.[32] La Caille's map remained the standard basic map of the island for ten years. He found that the
island was

> almost entirely covered with woods, which are of handsome appearance,
> particularly those on the south-east side; but a passage through is ren-
> dered very difficult and troublesome from the quantity of fern and creep-
> ing plants. These plants, whose branches are like those of our ivy, wind
> about and interlace themselves with the shrubs and deadwood and render
> the forests in a great measure impassable. Nor can a passage be obtained
> in any part of them but by circuitous ways, which are also . . . few. These
> forests are the refuge of Maroon negros.[33]

The frequent use of fire to clear the land was causing alarm by 1756, particularly to Governor René de Magon, who thought the burning of a grass (*Ther-
mida quadrivatus*) which could be used for haymaking very wasteful. The
governor, an enthusiastic horticulturist, was keen on fodder and haymaking.
Grass fires, he considered,

> dry up trees every year and kill them. Consequently today all the plains
> and slopes of the depression and surrounds of the port of St Louis [Port
> Louis] are completely denuded of trees and going northwards along the
> coast as far as the Pointe des Roches [Cap Malheureux] and in the leeward
> side of the island, the coast is bare for a considerable distance, which is
> a great loss.[34]

In a memoir to the CoI in 1757 a M. de Saint-Muan accused Magon of
having allowed the planters to cut trees without any controls. 'It is untrue',
he said,

> that trees do not regenerate in the Ile de France . . . each inhabitant who
> clears up a well-wooded piece of land sets fire to it; how then can one
> expect trees to regenerate . . . there are many streams in the island colony
> where 'teak' would grow very well. It is easy to obtain seed of it from
> the Malabar coast. Everybody knows that it is the best timber in the

32 Ibid.
33 Pasfield-Oliver, *Voyage of Francois Le Guat*, II, p. 208, quoting Abbé de la Caille, *Journal
historique du voyage*, Paris 1763. See esp. chap. entitled 'Plain and Forest', where La Caille
has marked 'Forêt très Epaissé, NW of the Montagne de Créoles in the Municipality of Grand
Port'. See also N. Pike, *Sub-tropical rambles in the land of the Aphanapteryx*, London, 1873, p.
203.
34 Brouard, *Woods and forests*, p. 14.

world. It is better than oak for shipbuilding and it only takes 30 years to
reach a size for this purpose.[35]

In fact, it seems to have been the shortage of naval timber in France that was
uppermost in the mind of M. de Saint-Muan. He was exasperated with Magon's fatalistic attitude towards deforestation – not an unusual one.[36]
    Some of the earliest French policy initiatives on forest clearance arose from
anxieties about the defence of the island. These worries are well evidenced in
a secret report on the island's military capabilities made to the East India
Company Council at Fort William in Calcutta in May 1761. The report referred specifically to the situation which prevailed less than two years after
the completion of La Caille's map and marked the beginning of a long period
of intense British interest in the governance of Mauritius.[37] Particular attention
was paid to French anxieties about the island forests, in a passage remarkable
for its attention to detail:

> They first recommend the division of lands into final parcels among such
> as choose to become planters and to let each follow the bent of his own
> genius, whether it is tilling corn, breeding horses, bullocks, poultry and
> for planting cotton or coffee trees but for the advantage of refreshments
> to shipping, and to reduce the price of labour, and they particularly rec-
> ommend breeding carriage and draft beasts of all kinds. The next atten-
> tion is devoted to the cutting of wood, which it seems was formerly
> supplied by contractors, who on account of the early conveyance no doubt
> cut that nearer the shore. The Company looking on this practice preju-
> dicial to the defence of the island Mauritius whose shore is in many places
> guarded against descents by the woods positively forbid the cutting of
> any wood there in the future and say there are two places which require
> the most immediate attention; the first is the shore between the West Bay
> and the bay of the Tomb (Bay de Tombeau) it would be more preferable
> to abandon the making of lime there after the antient custom than to
> continue the stripping of the shore of wood in the neighbourhood of the
> port which is defended thereby. In the second place there in the adjacent
> country to the East Bay where there is a considerable . . . workhouse for
> cutting wood, it must be forbad (if it is not too late) that they do not
> strip the seashore in the neighbourhood of that point, and render it def-
> enceless as they have done the north west harbour if the [?] toil is begun
> it must be stopd. Mr St David has in that place a large carpenters yard
> managed by Sieur Routtier. (p. 210)

35 Ibid.
36 P. W. Bamford, *Forests and French sea power, 1660–1789*, Toronto, 1956, Introduction.
37 'Remarks on the French East India Company's Instructions given to Mon. Magon, one of the
    Directors who was sent out Governor to the Islands of Mauritius and Bourbon 4th May 1755':
    National Archives of India, New Delhi, Foreign and Political Department Records: Select
    Committee Proceedings, vol. 7, 1761, Jan.–Dec., pp. 210–60.

This passage is especially interesting, as it appears to mark the earliest occasion on which the English East India Company showed a real interest in forest matters. The report was made at a time when a firewood shortage was being experienced in Calcutta.[38] By 1760 timber for ship and construction purposes was being exported again from Mauritius, and Charpentier de Cossigny mentions a 'sawmill which produces more in twenty-four hours than sixty pit sawyer slaves in two days'. The company started to take over concessions adjoining the sawmills, and in 1761 it responded to the opinions of Saint-Muan and others and forbade the felling of trees around the two harbours (Grand Port and Port Louis) for defence reasons. Deforestation and cultivation continued elsewhere. In a letter to the company in September 1762, Governor Desforges-Boucher explained this decision, noting:

> The Council sends you a copy of a notice which has been published regarding the prohibition of all felling and logging operations. At the same time you will receive a provisional regulation which the Council has thought fit to make to prevent wholesale destruction. It is based on essential needs and on local knowledge . . . everything concerning the control of waters and forests had been included in it, and apart from an area with a distance of 2–3 leagues around this port, all the rest of the island being still covered with forest, you will appreciate the necessity of allowing the clearing and cultivation of lands there.[39]

This communication stimulated a growing awareness on the part of the company of the scale of clearing that was now beginning to take place and led to fear that it might be losing its assets in terms of tradable timber. The linking of water and forest controls is intriguing and appears to reflect a growing appreciation of the relationship between the two, although whether this realisation was inspired in Paris or on Mauritius is hard to say. Desforges-Boucher sought to reassure the company and made explicit mention of initial attempts at tree planting, which probably owed their inspiration to Poivre's observations at the Cape, although it is difficult to establish this conclusively. He was also frank about the extent of destruction and observed:

> All kinds of trees are planted; the oak and chestnut grow wonderfully well; I had more than 4000 oaks planted at Le Reduit . . . they are doing fine and taller and bigger at three years than they would be in France at seven or eight. I had some planted at Monplaisir where they are doing well; they are planted in all the districts, and it would appear that they are doing best on the driest soils, though in general they are successful everywhere. There is no longer any doubt that oaks could be planted to replace all woods which have been devastated near the port . . . at Le

---

38 See Chapter 8.
39 Brouard, *Woods and forests*, p. 15.

Reduit there are plants of nearly all the fruits of Europe, Asia, Africa and America . . . in the interior of the island there are very large ponds and marshes . . . these have been reached by surveys of the Court of Concessions . . . what wonderful wealth could be obtained from these marshes if they were all cultivated and planted with rice![40]

Other criticisms of reckless felling by planters were made in 1764, as for example those by one M. de Landevisian that

the island in general is covered with big trees suitable for shipbuilding, but this has been neglected. In order to clear the land the planters burn the trees and often the soil underneath as well . . . two thirds of the island are still uncleared and uncultivated . . . it is important to prevent clearing of all the land and to preserve woods which are nearest to the two ports because of the ease of transport. In addition to the specially reserved areas each settler should be compelled to surround his habitation with trees.[41]

It was in 1764, too, that Charpentier de Cossigny remarked on the very high quality of the woods which were being so recklessly incinerated.[42]

Pierre Poivre and the geographical origins of a climatic environmental policy on Mauritius, 1719–66

In 1764 Mauritius and Bourbon were sold by the CoI to the French Crown. A final transfer of the territory did not take place until 1767, when Daniel Dumas was sent out as governor and Pierre Poivre as commissaire-genéral-ordonnateur (and subsequently 'intendant') of the 'Isle de France'. This major change in the governance of the colony brought about an equal change in perceptions of the status of the island forests. While anxieties about deforestation had been expressed before, they now acquired a far more critical character and faithfully reflected the concerns of a much wider and more 'scientific' community. This sense of crisis was well expressed in the set of instructions written for Pierre Poivre by the Duke of Praslin in 1766. 'Monsieur Poivre', he promised,

would immortalise his administration if he were able to make the colony compete with the Moluccas in the production of spices. Cinnamon is already established at the Isle de France, but it is not of good quality . . . it is easy to obtain pepper for trials, but with nutmegs and cloves there are great difficulties to be overcome . . . *if the forests do not regenerate in*

40 Ibid.
41 Ibid., p. 16.
42 Ibid.

*the island rain will be less frequent and the overexposed soil will be burnt by
the sun . . . timber should be given particular attention. It is necessary for the
navy and for military works. Complaints have been made that this very important matter has not received all the care and attention which it deserves.
Messrs Dumas and Poivre should hasten to control it with a good policy; they
will examine existing regulations on this subject, study the exact condition of
the forests, exploit and utilise them in the most economical way possible and
only allow people to cut them if they ensure their conservation.*[43] This will be
the object of a provisional regulation after which . . . a general forest policy and laws will be set for all the forests of the two islands. The best
forests should be declared 'Royal Reserves' . . . such as at Jacotet [Bel
Ombre Forest] and elsewhere . . . it is necessary to keep stocks of building
timbers for the repair of ships which His Majesty may send to India.[44]

The duke also mentioned checks on concessions to prevent abuses and,
finally, suggested that any existing regulations should be studied and amended
if they were deficient.[45] These instructions were very specific in their intention
and, in their explicit mention of climatic anxieties, marked a completely new
departure in French colonial policy. During his intendancy Poivre followed
them in detail and considerably developed them. This was to be expected,
since the evidence indicates that the minister's instructions were themselves
inspired by Poivre's writings and by the lectures which he had given in France
to some of the new agricultural societies, if not by his direct lobbying. They
also arose, though less directly, from the close interest espoused by members
of the Académie des Sciences in the climatic theories of Buffon, Duhamel and
Stephen Hales. Poivre, who had been made a member of the Académie in
1756, had stimulated this preoccupation in a 1763 speech in which he linked
long-standing fears about climate change directly to the increasing rate of
tropical forest clearance taking place in the French colonies.[46] The colonists
on Mauritius, Poivre stated, 'profit by pasturing their flocks . . . and burning
the vegetation . . . so that nothing remains on the ground but a straw too hard
for the animals to nourish themselves on . . . soon the fires brought by a thousand accidents among this straw consume it and with it a part of the virgin
forests'. But 'the greatest fault that has been committed in this island', he
went on, and that which most prejudiced the success of agriculture, is 'their

---

43 My italics.
44 From the 'Mémoire du Roi pour servir d'Instruction aux Sieurs Dumas, Commandant Général, et Poivre, Commissaire Général de la marine, faisant fonction d'Intendant aux Isles de
   France et Bourbon', Versailles, 28 Nov. 1766, quoted and trans. Brouard, *Woods and forests*,
   p. 16.
45 Ibid.
46 Paris, Archives of the BCMNHN, MS 575, fol. 74: Lecture to the Agricultural Society of
   Lyons, pp. 27–9.

having reclaimed the forests by fire without leaving any woods at intervals between the clearings'. This would have direct climatic results, he believed, since 'the rains which in this island are the sole amendment and the best that the earth can receive . . . follow the forests exactly, but cease and do not fall on cleared lands; also these lands have no shelter against the violence of the winds which often destroy all crops'. There was ample theoretical evidence for this, Poivre asserted, as 'we have seen before now that the Dutch, who had no wood at the Cape, have since planted it to guarantee their rain'. By contrast, 'the Isle of France was covered with [forest] and our colonists have destroyed it'.

Poivre's role as an enthusiast for forest conservation was not confined to his period as a colonial official on Mauritius, which was relatively short. A wider survey of the development of his philosophical ideas is therefore necessary in order to account for the character of his environmental policy before embarking on an account of Poivre's interest in the desiccation problem.

Poivre had became a commentator on the horticulture and land use of Mauritius long before being given any official licence to intervene in the processes of environmental degradation. His unusually decided and deliberate views about land use and about the relationship among citizens, arts, sciences and the land were all stimulated by an unusually well-travelled early career and training, made possible in the main by the nature of French commercial ambitions of the period. Born in 1719 at Lyons, Poivre was educated by the Missionaries of Saint Joseph at Lyons and the Jesuit Missions Etrangères in Paris.[47] Contact with the Jesuit community probably gave him his connection with the colonial experience, and it was probably in this period that he first learnt of the problems encountered by the Jesuits in South America in their uncomfortable relationship with the Spanish colonial power. As a Jesuit novice, Poivre began to develop a highly critical view of colonialism in Latin America and elsewhere, and it was a subject to which he frequently alluded in his later philosophical writings.[48]

Having finished an initial period of training as a Jesuit but still too young to enter full orders, Poivre took the decision to travel to China. It was on this voyage, on the vessel *Mars*, that he paid his first visit to Mauritius. During

---

47 *DMB*, pp. 343–4. Useful biographical notes on Poivre's early life are also provided in Yves Laissus, 'Note sur les manuscrits de Pierre Poivre (1719–1786) conservés à la Bibliothèque centrale du Muséum national d'histoire naturelle', *Proceedings of the Royal Society of Arts and Sciences of Mauritius*, 4:2 (1973), 31–56. The most useful contemporary guide to Poivre's life is the biography by his son-in-law, Pierre Samuel Dupont de Nemours, entitled *Notice sur la vie de Poivre, Chevalier de L'Ordre de Roi et l'Intendant des isles de France et Bourbon*, Philadelphia, 1786. This very rare book was revised and edited by L. Malleret as an extract of the *Bulletin de la Société des Etudes Indo-Chinoises* (Saigon), no. 5 (July–Sept. 1932).

48 See esp. *De l'Amérique et des Américains* . . . , Berlin, 1771.

the ensuing two years, the young ordinand was first held under house arrest in Canton and then managed to acquire the political favours of the Viceroy of Canton. As a result, he was able to acquire a working knowledge of Chinese and consequently an unrivalled familiarity with Chinese writings on natural history, forestry and agriculture. It seems likely that it was at this stage that Poivre began his life-long interest in tree planting and water management. Already by the sixteenth century extensive Chinese texts existed on the relationship among denudation, erosion and flooding, and it seems likely that Poivre gained some knowledge of these ideas while in Canton.[49] More important, he developed a very open attitude towards the value of eastern learning at a time when few Europeans possessed any insight at all into Chinese or Indian technical knowledge. Poivre was particularly interested in the aesthetics and horticultural technologies of Chinese gardens, an enthusiasm that helps to explain his later role in setting up the Jardin du Roi on Mauritius.[50] After his long sojourn in China, Poivre went on to spend a period in Annam (Vietnam), where he botanised widely, eventually embarking on the Dauphin, on 16 January 1745, intending to return to France. On 5 February 1745 the ship was captured by a British vessel, during which encounter Poivre lost an arm, his botanical collections, and (apparently) his vocation as a Jesuit. Ten days later he was landed by the British at Batavia, which, quite fortuitously, allowed him to broaden his new-found horticultural interests and acquire a very specific knowledge of the Dutch culture of spice-tree species and to come to estimate very highly (probably far too highly) the value of the spice trade to the Dutch. It was during this stay that his injuries persuaded him finally to leave the priesthood and offer his services instead to the Compagnie des Indes to found a base in Cochin China in order to attempt to break the Dutch spice monopoly. This task, Poivre had already concluded, might be of great value to the French on Mauritius. Eventually returning through Pondicherry, he arrived back on Mauritius with Labourdonnais's victorious fleet on 10 December 1746. Some time after leaving Mauritius in the following March, Poivre's ship was once again captured, and he was forced into another sojourn at Pondicherry.

In June 1748 he arrived back in Paris bearing a letter of introduction from the governor of Mauritius (Pierre Bartholémy David) to his father, a director of the CoI. At this stage the company agreed to back Poivre in two objectives: the founding of a company base in Indo-China and the project to acclimatise

49 For details of some of these texts, see Needham, *Science and civilization in China*, vol. 5, pt 28, p. 245, and a forthcoming volume in the same work on the history of Chinese forestry by Nicholas Menzies.

50 In 1763, for example, he published an essay on the beauty of Chinese gardens, in *Le citoyen du monde; ou lettres d'un philosophe chinois à ses amis dans l'Orient*, Amsterdam, 1763. See esp. p. 202, where he advocates a less prejudiced attitude towards eastern technical knowledge.

East Indies spice trees on Mauritius. On 23 October 1748 Poivre embarked
for Mauritius once again. On this occasion, however, he called at the Cape
Colony and stayed there for at least three months, arriving back in Mauritius
only on 13 March 1749.[51] There is no detailed surviving account of his lengthy
stay in the Cape Colony. However, there is little doubt that his experiences
there exercised a decisive influence over the rest of his career. At the Cape,
Poivre learnt both the manifest value of a state botanical garden and the transforming influence of a tree-planting programme and conservation ethos. Both
notions fitted well with his main interest in the acclimatisation of spice trees.

Between March 1749 and April 1756 Poivre was occupied almost entirely
with the planning and execution of three major voyages between Mauritius
and the East Indies.[52] None of these voyages resulted in a fully successful
transplantation of spice trees to Mauritius, for which the enmity of Fusée
Aublet can probably be held to account. Nevertheless, the attempts to trans-
plant new species did serve to introduce Poivre to an acute awareness of
variations in soil conditions, modes of soil formation, the significance of variations in rainfall and drainage, and the relationship between vegetation and
soil type. Moreover, his travels enabled him to make well-informed comparisons between soil types in a number of different countries. At the Cape he
had become particularly interested in the ability of soils to retain moisture
and fertility and the extent to which the vegetal cover was related to this
factor. Thus in 1752 Poivre wrote that 'oak trees which I have brought from
the Cape have been successful and are promising because they were left to
grow in the very soil with which I had brought them, whereas the others
which were planted out in the natural soil have not shown any sign of natural
growth or vigour'. Poivre attributed this difference to the fact that the soil
from the Cape was well-watered, composted and improved, while the local
island soil was 'burnt and liable to desiccation by the first rays of the sun'.[53]
He was here beginning to learn something of the fragile nature of the Mauritius forest soils, which, while initially appearing highly fertile, were in fact
very vulnerable to erosive forces and dehydration after forest removal. By the
time Poivre left Mauritius in 1757, he had acquired a working knowledge of
soil conditions and horticultural methods in various parts of Indo-China, the
Moluccas, the Philippines, Malabar, Mauritius, Bourbon and the Cape Colony. He also believed himself qualified (with far less justification) to comment

51 Laissus, 'Manuscrits de Pierre Poivre', p. 34.
52 A full account of this enterprise is to be found in Ly-Tio-Fane, *Mauritius and the spice trade*,
   vol. 1, and 'Pierre Poivre et l'expansion francaise dans l'Indo-Pacifique', *Bulletin Economique
   Francaise d'Extrême Orient*, 53 (1967), 453–511, and in Malleret, *Un manuscrit de Pierre Poivre*.
53 Brouard, *Woods and forests*, p. 13. The difference was probably due to the inoculation on
   Mauritius of micro-organisms from the Cape necessary for the good development of oak.

critically on agricultural techniques used on the west coast of Africa and was uniformly disapproving of them.

Poivre was forced to leave Mauritius in 1757 in the face of opposition to his spice-transfer projects from the new governor, René de Magon.[54] His work on spices had, however, become well known to Bertin, the new comptroller-general of France. Bertin's domestic agricultural policy reflected the physiocratic ideas which were becoming prevalent at the time, and it was at his express suggestion that Poivre was granted a state pension. This enabled him to retire temporarily to his estate at La Fréta near Clermont-Ferrand to 'lead the life of a gentleman farmer and to indulge his love of rare plants'.[55] He also widened his social circle and became a friend, for example, of Malesherbes. The latter came greatly to respect Poivre and wrote detailed notes on his conversations with him, in the process acquiring a life-long interest in botany and arboriculture.[56] Despite his pension, Poivre did not retire at all in an intellectual sense. Elected president of the Royal Agricultural Society of Lyons and a member of the Royal Society of Paris, he proceeded to deliver a series of lectures on his foreign travels and his hard-won agrarian and botanical knowledge.[57] The timing of his return to France closely coincided with the onset of rapid growth in the influence of the physiocratic school of thought. One immediate result of this ascendancy had been the appointment of Bertin. The new philosophy of physiocracy, which laid great stress on the virtues of agriculture, drew its inspiration largely from the abundant earlier English literature on economic subjects.[58] The prestige of the physiocrats created and fostered the seminal idea that the prosperity of its rural workers was necessary to a nation and that 'agriculture' (a new word which now began to appear in

54 René de Magon was appointed governor of the Isle de France in May 1755 and administered the colony from December 1755 to January 1759.

55 Ly-Tio-Fane, *Mauritius and the spice trade*, I, p. 9.

56 Paris, Archives of the BCMNHN, MS 575, 'Notes sur Poivre'.

57 These lectures were first published in Yverdon, France in 1768 under the title *Voyages d'un philosophe; ou observations sur les moeurs et les arts des peuples de l'Afrique, de l'Asie et de l'Amérique*. Further editions were published in 1769 in London and Leipzig, in 1770 in Dublin and Glasgow and in 1773 in Danzig. In 1778 a first American edition was published in Philadelphia as an appendix to a life of David Hume. Two separate translations were published in London in 1769; I have used the Dublin edition of 1770, entitled *Travels of a philosopher; or, Observations on the manners of various nations in Africa and Asia*.

58 E. Baker, G. Clark, and P. Vaucher, *The European inheritance*, vol. 2, London, 1954, p. 365. See also Bourde, *Influence of England;* M. Beer, *An enquiry into physiocracy*, London, 1939; J. F. Bell, *A History of economic thought*, London, 1907, chap. 6; N. J. Ware, 'The physiocrats', *American Economic Review*, 21:4 (1931), 607–19; G. Weulersse, *Le mouvement physiocratique en France de 1756 à 1770*, 2 vols., Paris, 1910; Joseph Schumpeter, *The history of economic analysis*, London, 1955, chap. 4; and E. Fox-Genovese, *The origins of physiocracy*, Ithaca, N.Y., 1976.

the French language) was something which could be improved and transformed by human progress. But physiocracy was hostile to the mercantilist
emphasis on the accumulation of bullion ('capital' in more modern parlance)
and laid stress instead on the value of an efficiently working agricultural economy. This encouraged the growth of agricultural associations, like the one of
which Poivre became president in Lyons, and after 1755 these associations
sprang up almost everywhere in France at the rate of several a year.[59] The
British influence in this direction continued in the work of Adam Smith,
whose *Theory of Moral Sentiments* was translated into French in 1764, representing an important evolutionary link between mercantilist theories and
those of the physiocrats.

The social diffusion of physiocracy can be said to date from the meeting
between the royal physician, François Quesnay, now the recognised founder
of the school, and Victor Riqueti, the Marquis de Mirabeau (1715–89). This
meeting took place in 1757, the year Poivre had arrived back in Paris. By that
time Quesnay had already written *Fermiers* (published in 1756) and *Grains*
(published in 1757), two treatises for the *Grande encyclopédie*. These writings
radicalised Poivre's views on taxation, tenure and many other matters.[60] The
influence of *Grains* in particular goes a long way towards explaining his ob-
jections to cash-crop plantations of cotton, coffee and sugar. In 1758 Quesnay
followed up these works with his economic masterpiece, the *Tableau économique*. In this major work he stressed the interrelationship between different
parts of the industrial and agricultural economy and held that commerce and
trade were subservient to agriculture. Of the last three activities, agriculture
alone, he suggested, really added to the nation's wealth. Quesnay feared, pro-
phetically perhaps, that these ideas might lead to a revolution and so tried to
restrict the circulation of the *Tableau*. However, they quickly became known
to Poivre and formed much of the basis of his philosophy. The Hippocratic
basis of Quesnay's reasoning seems to have held a particular attraction for
Poivre. The medical strengths of the work were to be expected: Quesnay had
been a trained physician and surgeon of high repute and was elected secretary
of the Académie des Sciences in Paris in 1731. His first publications had been
in the medical field, and he soon became an authority on the systemic aspects
of the body, as then conceived, and the interrelations among its functions. He
was particularly interested in the theories of blood circulation first put forward by William Harvey in 1616 and held strong beliefs in the creative and
healing powers of nature and the effectiveness of particular plant remedies.
Both these interests deeply affected the structure of his physiocratic and

59 Baker et al., *The European inheritance*, II, p. 315.
60 H. Higgs, *The physiocrats: Six lectures on the French économistes of the eighteenth century*, Lon-
    don, 1897, p. 25.

economic theories.[61] The connections between 'disease' and the normal functions of a natural system, whether medical, agricultural or moral, were also central to the thinking of Quesnay. In fact, in this field he had derived most of his ideas indirectly from Richard Cantillon's *Essai sur la nature du commerce en général*, published in France in 1755.[62]

Cantillon's writings, it has been argued, mark the transition between a national preoccupation with government regulation of trade and a far more global, supra-national and cosmopolitan approach to economics of the kind Adam Smith was to show in his *Inquiry into the Nature and Causes of the Wealth of Nations*.[63] This cosmopolitanism was also present in the writings of Poivre. It was an approach which helped to stimulate universalism in social theory and also bring about professionalism in economics and natural history. A major part of Cantillon's work was devoted to advocating the interests of the small cultivator. The idle consumer he viewed with disapproval. Luxury he defined as the abuse of wealth. An unequal distribution of wealth was prejudicial to production, for the very rich are 'like pikes in a pond' who devour their smaller neighbours. Great landowners, he said, should live upon their estates and stimulate their development and not lead an absentee life in the metropolis. This last point was a central part of Poivre's thinking on Mauritius and contributory to the anti-urban bias of his philosophy. Cantillon thought that interest rates should be reduced, public debts extinguished, and a ministry of agriculture created to bring to agriculture the succour of applied science and to facilitate the development of canals, communications, drainage and so on. The most significant part of this discourse for the likes of Poivre concerned Cantillon's concept of the structure and function of the state. The state, he said, was a tree, agriculture its roots, population its trunk and arts and commerce its leaves.

In this revolutionary naturalistic image, the vivifying sap came from the roots of the tree, drawn up by multitudinous forces from the soil. The leaves, the most brilliant part of the tree, are the least enduring. A storm may destroy them. But the sap will soon renew them if the roots maintain their vigour. If, however, some invading insect attack the roots, then in vain would one wait

---

61 Quesnay's publications included five books on medical and anatomical subjects published between 1730 and 1753. His economics essays were largely published anonymously.

62 Paris, 1755. This book offered the first comprehensive analysis of the financial interactions of a complete economy. Until very recently Cantillon's contributions to economic and political thought have been little recognised. Mirabeau believed that only 5 per cent of Cantillon's writings survived. Mirabeau himself used Cantillon's unpublished work as the basis for his own largely plagiarised *L'ami des hommes*, and it was from this book that Quesnay derived his knowledge of Cantillon: A. E. Murphy, *Richard Cantillon: Entrepreneur and economist*, Oxford, 1986, p. 16.

63 Higgs, *The physiocrats*, p. 16.

for the sun and the dew to reactivate the withered trunk. To the roots must
the remedy go, to let them expand and recover. If not, the tree will perish.[64]

It was this kind of philosophy which encouraged Poivre to advocate the
protection of soil and trees from wind and the elements. Cantillon's themes
combined elements of antiurban thinking (as part of the persistent town-
versus-country theme so prevalent in French literature), with a disposition to
view nature in terms of bodily functioning, transferring ideas and anxieties
about human vulnerability to nature. This transference was reflected, too, in
Poivre's outlook. Essentially, it implied and permitted the penetration of Hippocratic concepts of the bodily system into newer environmental concerns.
Much physiocratic thinking in this connection involved questioning land-
tenure traditions, leading to a far-sighted critique of landholding in French
agriculture and to an idealisation of peasant and resident landholders. It was
in terms of a debate about landholding that Poivre's conservation ideology was
developed – that is, in terms of a debate about the social control of land.
However, the influence of physiocracy upon Poivre went much further than
this. Quesnay's texts had been innovative in encouraging intellectuals to think
in terms of an essential interdependence among the many groups in society
and between man and nature. We can see Poivre as having inherited these
notions both in his environmentalism and in his crusading efforts against
slavery and notions of European superiority.

By contrast, it should be noted that his interest in promoting the arts and
natural history (for which he was famed in the Mascarenes) places him somewhat apart from the bulk of the physiocrats, as his biographers after 1792
seem to have realised.[65] Above all, Poivre's tropical experience set him apart.
Nevertheless, it was his familiarity with the basic technical problems of tropical crop transfer which gave him an appropriate introduction to physiocratic
thinking and an unusual perspective informed by his experience of agricultural
systems in a variety of societies. In his lectures in Lyons and Paris, therefore,
he was able to marry his expertise with the new physiocratic enthusiasms.
The descriptions of different agricultural methods practised in the countries
through which he had passed acquired, at the very least, a distinct moral tone
but one leavened by an empirical approach and one, atypically for the period,
prone to find value in largely alien indigenous systems. It may well be that it
was his early Jesuitical background and his long residence in China which
enabled him to disown both conventionally racist assertions of the supremacy
of the European and contradictory but still fashionable evocations of the 'noble
savage'.[66] 'Throughout the world', he wrote,

64 Ibid., pp. 21–2.
65 See esp. Dupont de Nemours, *Notice sur la vie de Poivre*.
66 Poivre's willingness to experiment with eastern perceptions of European attitudes is especially

man has forgotten his destiny and his origins; everywhere he has a heart, but acts as if he had only a body. In China just as in Europe, his customs are everywhere corrupted. From burning equatorial regions to the polar regions the Indian, the Tartar, the Negro, the American, the 'civilized man' and the 'savage' are all enemies of virtue and run after nothing but lies.[67]

This was an extremely telling statement. Above all, it marked out Poivre as having rejected the fashionable 'degeneracy' theories espoused by Buffon and his poorly travelled colleagues at the Jardin du Roi. These theories located white Europeans as the original undegenerate race, implicitly threatened by the hot climates and corrupted customs of tropical races. By rejecting this concept, Poivre was, like van Reede before him, correspondingly able to elevate indigenous non-European epistemologies on their merits alone and then adapt them for his own purposes. This fact alone helps to account for the evolution of a new philosophy of environmental management on Mauritius, allowing it to incorporate aspects of Chinese and Indian knowledge. However, for Poivre the personal dimension of this may have become even more developed with regard to his attitude towards interventions in the natural world in general. Dupont de Nemours, for example, asserted that Poivre was much attracted to Zoroastrian concepts of balance and harmony in nature and to the Zoroastrian stress on the prime importance of agriculture to the well-being of man. Poivre, he added, 'thought that ways of life should not ideally too closely resemble those of men mainly interested in consumption alone. Instead, informed by the thinkers of Asia and by his own common sense, he thought that one could not be more agreeable to God or useful to the world than by planting a tree or cultivating a field; these were precepts of Zoroaster which he followed for their own intrinsic value and reward.'[68] These opinions link Poivre directly to the Zoroastrian meanings implicit in the etymologies and philosophies of garden and paradise which we explored earlier.

Poivre's sceptical view of European cultural supremacy also encouraged him to make useful cultural comparisons, in a manner familiar to mid-nineteenth-century ethnography. Much of the material in his *Travels of a Philosopher*, for example, relates to a comparison of the horticultural methods which he had encountered on his travels, the moral purpose used to justify such a survey being expressed in the opening sentence of the book, that 'the general hap-

---

apparent in his essays entitled *Le citoyen du monde; ou lettres d'un philosophe chinois à ses amis dans l'Orient*. The term 'citoyen du monde' is significant here. The writings precede his lecturing on agricultural topics, but the latter seem to have incorporated the same 'citoyen du monde' radicalism.

67 Malleret, *Un manuscrit de Pierre Poivre*, pp. 25–6.
68 Dupont de Nemours, *Notice sur la vie de Poivre*, p. 32.

piness of every nation must depend on agriculture'.[69] The main significance
of the *Travels*, in the light of Poivre's involvement in the planning of land
use on Mauritius after 1767, relates to the way in which, by making a survey
of a variety of agricultural systems, he was able to show up the deficiencies
of the agricultural system operated by the Compagnie des Indes on Mauritius.
Secondly, the *Travels* indicates the very important influence of both Dutch
agricultural methods (as they were practised in the Cape) and South Indian
tree-planting and irrigation ideas on the formation of his attitudes to colonial
agricultural policy.

For Poivre, the agricultural traditions of different nations were a unifying
subject more worthy of debate and learning than all the other traits which
distinguished nations. All peoples, he wrote,

> however barbarous, have gifts peculiar to themselves; the diversity of
> climate, whilst it varies the lot of mankind, offers to their industry dif-
> ferent productions in which to exercise it. Every country, at a certain
> degree of distance, has fabrics so peculiar to itself that they could not
> have been the fabric of other nations, but agriculture, in every climate,
> is the universal art of mankind . . . the state of agriculture has ever been
> the principal object of my researches among the various people I have
> seen in the course of my voyages.[70]

The significance of Poivre's visit to the Cape in 1749 has already been
emphasised. Clearly, for someone who was concerned with the technicalities
of transplantation, the activities pursued by the Dutch in and adjacent to the
Cape Company Garden would have been of great interest. More specifically,
Poivre had become aware of the work of Rumphius and in particular of his
Herbarium amboinense, prepared by Johannes Burman between 1741 and
1750.[71] Poivre wrote with admiration of Rumphius in 1752, 'I believe that we
can trust the opinions of Rumphius, since this able naturalist stayed longer
in the Moluccas and had more experience and knowledge of this matter than
anyone else.'[72]

In his more specific references to Cape agriculture, Poivre gives credit to
the Huguenots for the developments which had taken place in Dutch horticulture at the Cape, noting that 'they have enriched their adopted mother

69 P. Poivre, *Travels of a philosopher*, Dublin, 1770, p. 1. Much of this book was based on lectures
given at Lyons in 1763.
70 Ibid., p. 2.
71 Poivre's enforced stay in Batavia during 1745 may help account for the onset of this interest.
72 See Poivre's observations on the nutmeg tree, 12 Feb. 1752, in Ly-Tio-Fane, *Mauritius and
the spice trade*, I, p. 46. Even Commerson was obliged to refer to Rumphius in his identification
of spice plants brought to Mauritius in 1770: Commerson's report on the plants brought to
the Isle de France, documented in ibid., p. 93.

by their industry'.[73] What seems to have struck Poivre most was the way in which Cape agriculture had been adopted as a constructive response to what he saw as an inherently hostile environment. His remarks in this respect need to be considered here at some length, since the topic bulked large in his own writing; he was especially interested in the deliberate use of tree planting and noticed that 'in all their pasturages they have an eye to groves of trees, where the herds and flocks may shelter against the heat of the sun'. He commented on this in more detail:

> The Cape is exposed for the greater part of the year to violent hurricanes which blow greatly from the north-east. These winds are so impetuous that they would beat down the fruits of the trees and sweep to destruction the labours of the farmer had they not been provided with high palisades of oaks and other trees, planted very close to one another, somewhat resembling a chemille designed for ornament of a garden. These palisades they cut every year as they grow, their height being commonly from twenty feet to thirty feet; every separate field in consequence is enclosed like a chamber. It is by this industry alone that the Dutch have rendered their colony not only the granary of all their settlements in the West Indies but the most commodious place for vessels to touch at for refreshments and provisions of all kinds.[74]

Poivre went on to make the connection between this type of agriculture and the care lavished by the Dutch on the VOC garden at Cape Town:

> Independent of the garden of the colonists which is kept in as fine order as any in Europe the India Company have caused to be laid out two or three gardens extensive and magnificent which they support with an expense worthy of a sovereign Company. Fifteen or twenty European gardeners, whose abilities are approved before they are embarked, are employed in the cultivation of each of these vast gardens, under the direction of a principal gardener whose place is . . . honourable. It is in these gardens that all the experiments are made in every new species of culture, and it is there that every private individual is provided gratis with such plants and seeds as he may have occasion for, together with the necessary instructions for their cultivation. These gardens furnish in the greatest abundance herbage and fruits of various kinds for the Company's ships.[75]

It was the adaptive and experimental aspect of the Cape garden which most fascinated Poivre and which was ultimately to influence him in establishing the objectives and priorities of the botanical garden on Mauritius after 1767:

73 Poivre, *Travels*, pp. 6–7.
74 Ibid., pp. 13, 17.
75 Ibid., p. 12.

Travellers cannot but with pleasure and admiration observe large enclosures consecrated to the study and improvement of botany, in which the
most rare and useful plants from every quarter of the world are arranged
in the most excellent order. The curious [Poivre surely refers to himself
here] have the additional satisfaction also of finding skilful gardeners who
take pleasure in describing and pointing out their virtues. These beautiful
gardens are terminated by large orchards, where are to be found all the
fruits of Europe, together with several natives of Africa and Asia.[76]

Poivre found the garden an aesthetic attraction as well as worthwhile in
agricultural terms and added that 'nothing is more agreeable than to see in
different expositions even in the same enclosure, the chestnut, the apple and
other trees which are natives of the torrid zone'. In contrast, Poivre took the
opportunity in the *Travels* to dwell on and to recall the forces he saw at work
on Mauritius. Again and again Poivre visualised Mauritius as a garden. 'The
island', he wrote, 'is as fertile as is Bourbon; rivulets, which are never quite
dry, water it like a garden, notwithstanding which the harvests often fail, and
scarcity here is almost perpetually felt.' Despite this, the garden of Mauritius,
Poivre felt, was being cultivated in a most inappropriate manner. While praising Labourdonnais, 'who governed the island for ten or twelve years and ought
to be regarded as the father of the colony for his introduction and patronage
of agriculture', he castigated those in the company who had subsequently
planned its agronomy. They had, he said, 'wandered incessantly from project
to project, attempting the culture of almost every species of plant without
properly prosecuting them. The coffee, the cotton, the indigo, the sugar cane,
the pepper etc., all have been cultivated by experiments but in such superficial
manner it could never ensure success.' In the wake of economic failure, the
company was succeeding, he believed, in gradually destroying the natural assets of the island. Indiscriminate grass burning, as Magon had observed, was
partly responsible. Hay and straw 'left lying, is kindled here by a thousand
accidents, consumes this straw and with it frequently part of the neighbouring
forests. During the remainder of the year, the herds wander about and lan-
guish amongst the woods.'[77] He noticed that land was cleared for cultivation
quite deliberately through the reckless use of fire rather than by deliberate
felling. It was this, he thought, that led to desiccation:

The greatest fault which has been committed in the island, and which
has proved most prejudicial to cultivation is the method of clearing the
woods from off the ground by fire; without leaving groves and thickets
at proper distances; the rains in this island conduce most to the amelioration of the grounds; but the clouds being stopped by the forests there

76 Ibid., p. 19.
77 Ibid., p. 30.

the rains fall; whilst the cleared lands are scarce watered by a single drop. The fields at the same time, being thus deprived of defence are exposed to the violence of the winds which often entirely destroy the harvests.[78]

In Poivre's eyes, the contrast with the Cape was stark: 'The Dutch, as we have before observed, found no trees at the Cape, but they have planted them there, as shelter for their habitations. The Isle de France, on the contrary, was covered with woods and the colonists have entirely destroyed them.'[79] This was in fact a considerable exaggeration of the true position on the island, as Poivre well knew, but for his Lyons lectures and his book it served his propaganda purposes extremely well. His implicit criticism of the objectives of commercial plantation agriculture, as promoted most unsuccessfully and fitfully by the CoI, is somewhat difficult to interpret, although it is predictable from a physiocratic viewpoint. Poivre had an underlying feeling that plantation cropping, of tobacco and sugar in particular, was unsuitable for Mauritius. Instead, he thought, 'the cultivation of grain . . . neglected and badly understood, is that which succeeds the best – without the intervention of one fallow year and without the least improvement, or any other mode of labour, than that which is practised in Madagascar'. Already, he observed, manioc was 'now the principal source of the colonists for the nourishment of the slaves'.[80]

There is little doubt that through genuine conviction, as well as for more political reasons, Poivre saw fit to make direct criticism of the CoI, already in financial crisis by the early 1760s through the exigencies of war. The company had given insufficient attention to 'agriculture', by which Poivre meant food production and not the capital-intensive production of plantation crops. It was more important, he said, to ensure that the land would 'be a certain resource against those dearths which too frequently distress . . . these islands [Mauritius and Bourbon]'. Clearly, a plantation policy which actively promoted careless forest clearance and outright forest destruction would not serve the ends of agriculture. Such carelessness, Poivre had implied in his 1763 Lyons lectures, threatened the security of the state. Only if the agriculture of the island was properly maintained would 'our squadrons bound for India put into the Isle of France for refreshment . . . [and] would not thus be subject to the necessity of losing their time at the Cape'.[81]

The warnings conveyed by Poivre in his lectures and writings after his 'retirement' to La Fréta found a ready audience among his physiocratic col-

---

78 Ibid.
79 Ibid., p. 31. It should be noted that these remarks by Poivre in the 1770 *Travels* closely resemble the text of his original lecture given at Lyons in 1763 (see n. 46).
80 Ibid., p. 32. Manioc is the same as cassava. It had been used widely by the Portuguese in West Africa and by the English on St Helena.
81 Ibid., p. 24.

leagues, and above all with the Duc de Choiseul and Bertin, the comptroller-general. With the loss of other colonies and interests in India, Mauritius had came to assume a new importance, while the mismanagement of the affairs of the CoI came to be treated with less tolerance. With the increasing military dominance acquired by the British in the Indian peninsula, the French were now forced to look instead at commercial expansion in the Indo-Pacific region farther to the east.[82] Mauritius became the keystone for such plans, so that any warnings Poivre made about the ecological state of the island were bound to be taken as seriously as his proposals for French expansion in the spice trade. By 1766 Poivre's wide-ranging writing were well known in France, although he was thought of more as a philosopher than as an agricultural specialist. It was his specialised knowledge of Indo-China which was the main factor in his appointment as commissaire-général-ordinnateur of the Isle de France on July 1766. Praslin's instructions to Poivre on his appointment reflected the three main preoccupations of the new intendant, the promotion of crop transfer (spices), the desirability of soil and forest conservation, and the fear of rainfall decline. That all these interests were now effectively part of French colonial policy indicates Poivre's success as a propagandist. Praslin does not, however, seem to have appreciated the extent to which the appointment of an individual of such vigour and convictions as Poivre might promote internal dissension and opposition, particularly to his conservation ideas, once he had arrived on Mauritius.

Poivre himself was interested in a tropical environment in which, in contrast to temperate regions, the implications of a desiccationist theory were potentially serious. In the tropical zones with which he was familiar, the amelioration, warming or rainfall reduction which might seem desirable in North America could clearly threaten agricultural adversity: Rainfall was scanty or seasonal and the balance between satisfactory irrigation and disastrous drought very finely tuned in practical terms. With his experience of the practicalities of crop transfer and replantation, Poivre was more sensitive to the danger posed by artificially enhanced drought than other contemporary European observers of tropical climates. A reading of his *Travels* makes this quite clear. He had already taken a deep interest in the way in which the indigenous population of China, and more especially South India, had learnt to cope with the vagaries of heat and drought and had developed irrigation systems, on the one hand, and tree-planting customs, on the other, all designed to reduce the blast of the overhead dry-season sun. In the *Travels* Poivre dealt in detail, in a section entitled 'Method by which the Malabaris irrigated their lands', with the irrigation systems employed in Malabar. 'In spite of the excessive heat', he wrote, 'the country is kept green.' The most delicate trees were watered,

82 Ly-Tio-Fane, 'Pierre Poivre et l'expansion française', pp. 455–8.

and the soil was kept irrigated even when the heat was at its greatest. He understood the problems that had been encountered in achieving this degree of control: 'The irrigation systems of India involve the complex construction of earthen terraces.'[83] It was this sophisticated response to seasonal aridity that had come to occupy a central place in the perceptions of Poivre. The vulnerability of agriculture in the seasonally arid tropics meant that theories concerning the desiccational consequences of deforestation that were accepted without a great deal of excitement or comment in Europe itself held quite a different message for colonists in the tropics. For example, deforestation in North America was, until well after 1850, generally seen as a positive process. This was a consensus reversed in the United States itself only after the publication of *Man and Nature*, by George Perkins Marsh, in 1864 and by what was beginning to be known about forest-protection problems on Mauritius and in India. On Mauritius the implications of artificially induced desiccation had already been taken to heart a century earlier. Poivre, in particular, realised that the threat had to be responded to in a comprehensive fashion. Leaning heavily on his observations of hydrological control in Southern India, he set about comparable kinds of intervention on Mauritius after 1767 with some vigour.

The conservation programmes of Pierre Poivre, 1767–72

Poivre's enforced early retirement ended abruptly with the collapse of the Compagnie des Indes, ruined by war. The French Crown was compelled to take on the bankrupt administration of the whole Mascarene island group and did so under a royal edict of 1764, placing Mauritius under the supervision of the naval ministry, headed by the Duc de Choiseul's cousin the Duc de Praslin. Choiseul and Praslin then sought the advice of Poivre on the reorganisation necessary to save the colonies and bolster up the fragments of the French empire after the Peace of Paris in 1763. Finally, Poivre was urged to accept a post as commissaire-general of the Mascarenes.[84]

The appointment of Poivre as intendant by the Duc de Choiseul under the supervision of Praslin was part of Choiseul's new reform policy in defence, colonial policy and trade and also part of his flirtation with a somewhat am-

---

83 Malleret, *Un manuscrit de Pierre Poivre*, pp. 113–14.
84 I rely here on the brief reconstruction of the appointment of Poivre which appears in Ly-Tio-Fane, *Pierre Sonnerat*, pp. 5–7. The objectives of policy were defined, after consultation between Poivre and Praslin, in the 'Mémoire du Roi' dated 28 Nov. 1766: Ly-Tio-Fane, 'Pierre Poivre et l'expansion française', p. 453. In this article Ly-Tio-Fane does not deal with Poivre's achievements in forest protection. To date, his conservation activities have either been ignored or seen as an idiosyncratic adjunct to his other enterprises.

biguous set of physiocratic principles.[85] Poivre's enthusiasm for Chinese agriculture and for the potential offered by development of the spice trade and other specialised crop transfers had attracted the attention of the minister. While Choiseul's enthusiasm for experimenting with exotic political and economic philosophies was eventually to play a part in his downfall, he was not as complete a convert to physiocracy as Poivre, and he did not appreciate the extent to which Poivre's physiocratic concerns would bring him into conflict with the more aggrandising and conventional approach of the colonial officials with whom he was expected to work. On the other hand, it has been suggested that Poivre was in fact expected to spy on Governor Dumas, among others, on behalf of the minister.[86] On 14 July 1767 Poivre arrived again on Mauritius, more than ten years after his last departure. Between then and August 1772 he embarked on a series of initiatives in agricultural and forest policy and in natural history and pharmacological research.

In striving for a new environmental and moral order, Poivre can be said consciously to have rejected the corrupt social and urban mores of France. On Mauritius this was far more difficult to achieve in practice than in theory. Almost from the start, Poivre's desire to rectify the island economy and environment placed him in direct confrontation with the short-term economic objectives of Daniel Dumas, the governor, whom he had accompanied on the outward voyage to the colony. Dumas realised at an early stage that Poivre was developing a policy which derived only in part from the orders of the Duc de Choiseul. His fears were confirmed when Poivre proceeded to outline his policies and plans to all the colonists of the island in a series of public speeches, the policy details of which he confirmed to the minister only in letters written long afterwards. He was able to do this knowing that he enjoyed the tacit support of the minister in his radicalism. Dumas's suspicions could only grow stronger.

Shortly after his arrival, the intendant launched into his first public speech to the crowd assembled to meet him at Government House in Port Louis, presumably realising that he would need to rely for support for his policies on the effectiveness of his own propaganda and on a personal approach to the island planters. The opening speech constituted a polemic on the need to make a new beginning after a period of company corruption and decline and the need for a new agrarian and moral economy.[87] It contained a skilful mixture of criticism of, and praise for, the colonists.[88] Poivre first announced the

85 Higgs, *The physiocrats*, p. 78.

86 Pasfield-Oliver, *Life of Commerson*, p. 162.

87 Poivre, 'Discours prononcé par P. Poivre à son arrivée à l'Isle de France aux habitants de la Colonie assemblées', in J. Salles, *Oeuvres complètes de Pierre Poivre, précédées de sa vie*, Paris, 1797.

88 Liberal quotation is made of this opening speech. Far more than the legal aridity of the

creation of a new Tribunal Terrier (Land Court), one of the main planks of
the Duc de Choiseul's reforms and one which threatened those many colonists
who had been allowed by the company to abuse the concessions stipulations.
He then told the colonists that they were 'the cherished children of the kingdom – His Majesty desires that, above all, you should be happy'.[89] But such
happiness might prove to be demanding, for Poivre told the colonists that
they would be rewarded 'by cultivating your lands with more care and more
intelligence than you have ever done up to the present'.[90]

In the past, Poivre maintained, the colonists had 'regarded this colony as
nothing other than a temporary abode and with no significance other than as
a place to make a fast fortune and return as quickly as possible to France'.[91]
This was the wrong attitude, he affirmed. The colony, he said, was far less
oppressed by regulation than the motherland. 'Permit me to say to you, sirs',
he warned them, 'that someone as lucky as a colonist on this island, living on
such fertile land, exempt from all impositions and onerous duties, and in the
middle of all the riches produced by land and seas . . . would never be found
in France.'[92] In short, Poivre told the colonists that they lived in a physical
and social paradise and one which, climatically, enjoyed a 'perpetual spring'
– the term used by Dante to describe the island of 'earthly paradise' and
evoked frequently since the writing of *Purgatorio* by the makers of early botanical gardens in Europe.[93]

While influenced by physiocracy, these admonitions amounted to more than
just the doctrinaire propaganda of a physiocrat. Instead Poivre was permitting
himself the luxury, or the delusion, of projecting a Utopian vision of a tropical
island upon its three thousand planters. His message was clear: a sanitary and
climatic Elysium such as the Isle de France was not to be squandered. But
he believed it was being squandered, and for reasons closely associated with
a physiocratic critique of the colonial economy. In the Isle de France, multiple
cropping was possible, while in France itself multiple taxation was the norm,
and by 'a horde of men more terrible in the countryside than all the insects

language of the Conservation Ordinance, Poivre's public speeches give a reliable indication of
his perceptions of the tropical world and his expectations for it.

89 'Vous êtes les enfans chéris de la patrie – Sa Majesté desire, sur toutes choses, que vous soyez
   heureux': Salles, *Oeuvres*, p. 203.

90 'Rendez-vous heureux en cultivant vos terres avec plus d'ardeur et plus d'intelligence que
   vous ne l'avez fait jusqu'à présent': ibid.

91 ' . . . n'a regardé cette colonie que comme in lieu de passage et ne s'est attaché qu'aux moyen
   de faire une rapide fortune par toute suite retourner promptement en France': ibid., p. 204.

92 'Permettez-moi de vous le dire, Messieurs, le colon qui sous un ciel aussi heureux que celui
   de cette île, habitant une terre aussi fertile, exempt de toute espèce d'impositions et de droits,
   au milieu de toutes les productions de l'univers que la mer lui apporte, n'a pas su se procurer
   le bonheur qu'il cherche, ne le trouvera jamais en France': ibid.

93 Ibid., p. 205.

which even in France are nearly as great in number as those you complain of
here'.[94] These were sentiments to become more familiar in France after 1789.
But for now, the benefit of distance from Europe had allowed the islanders
to forget 'the misfortunes which afflict humanity'. Poivre advised them to
realise their good fortune and dedicate themselves to cultivating the land to
'perfection'. As he pointed out, the company and the state had both spent
enormous sums of money in promoting the commerce and agriculture of the
island: sixty million livres since colonisation, Poivre computed. But this had
not been the only cost. There had been indirect costs as well, and Poivre made
no bones about them. 'Reckless and ignorant men', he said, 'thinking of nothing but themselves, have ravaged the island, destroying the trees by fire to
make a fortune at the expense of the colony, leaving nothing for their successors but arid lands abandoned by rain and exposed without relief to storms
and the burning sun.'[95] In his view, nature had done everything for the island,
and men had done everything to destroy it and make their fortunes at the
expense of posterity. In this speech Poivre was specifically not relying solely
on a utilitarian argument, although it was certainly an element in his exposition. Moral and aesthetic arguments came foremost. Thus the forests he
talked of were 'magnifiques', and they also determined, he thought, where a
'fertilising rain would fall'. 'The land', he added,

> which is still uncleared has not ceased to receive the blessings of nature,
> while the plains which were first to be cleared and were made so through
> fire and without any woodland being saved and without any contact with
> the forest, are now of surprising aridity, and consequently much less
> fertile. Even rivers have declined, and cannot supply water any longer to
> their hinterlands. Thus we see that the sky, by refusing to provide rain
> in these areas, seems to have taken revenge for the damage done to nature
> and to reason.[96]

Allowing for Poivre's love of eloquent metaphor, his real conviction could not
easily be disguised; aridity and sterility were seen as revenge wrought upon a
people unwilling to obey either the laws of nature or the reasoning of man.
At least part of the root of the problem, Poivre admitted, returning to the
more mundane, lay in the mode by which the company had granted land

94 '. . . une foule d'hommes bien autrement terribles dans les campagnes que tous les insectes
   qui même en France sont presque en aussi grands nombres que le sont ici ceux dont vous
   vous plaignez': ibid., p. 207.
95 'Des hommes avides et ignorans ne pensant que pour eux-mêmes, ont ravagé l'île, en detruisant
   les bois par le feu, empressés de faire aux dépens de la colonie, une fortune rapide, ils n'ont
   laissé à leurs successeurs que des terres arides abandonées par les pluies et exposées sans abri
   aux orages et à un soleil brulant': ibid., p. 210.
96 Ibid., pp. 210–11.

concessions, 'sans économie, sans discernement'. But the damage was done, and the fertile land left would have to be allocated to feed the inhabitants and visiting garrison soldiery. He gave a warning, too, that with a few more years of the old destructive ways the island would become completely uninhabitable.

> It will become necessary to abandon it. Here we have a state which for forty years has endeavoured to establish a colony . . . the treasures of France, Messieurs, are the sacred fruit of the labour, sweat and blood of our fellow countrymen. Long enough, and too long, they have been employed apparently quite uselessly. Their work has been dissipated and pillaged by sacrilegious hands.[97]

Here Poivre was making a complex set of practical and political connections. Underlying his desire to establish a new moral economy of nature in the colony was the sense that an exploitation of human exertion and capital had gone on in the past, and one that closely paralleled the overexploitation of the material assets of both the home nation and a 'God-given' colony by a 'sacrilegious' minority. He thus equated the moral order quite firmly and deliberately with an imperative to maintain a natural order in nature itself. It is not surprising, then, to find Poivre ending the first part of this exhortatory address to the colonists with the definitive words 'The disorderly times are over.'[98] While this may seem a commonplace of political metaphor, it was seriously meant in this case and had direct policy implications in environmental terms: The success of the colonists in conserving the forests, soils and rainfall would secure for them the approbation and protection of the state. However, by terming past treatment of the landscape sacrilegious, Poivre was asserting the importance of a spiritual order in nature, in which the landscape itself was sacralised or sanctified. It would be wrong to attribute a single origin to this avowedly religious attitude towards the landscape which Poivre so clearly indicated in his inaugural speeches to the colonists. Even so, one would be unwise to forget Poivre's long Jesuit training. It is quite possible that the fate of the Mauritius landscape attained a personal allegorical quality in his own mind. Indeed, one might go further and argue that his proposals for restoring earlier damage to the island forests had a resurrectionist significance. Thus he told the colonists that

> the uncultivated lands will be assigned their full potential everywhere [on the island], but those which have to be cultivated must be cleared with the maximum economy in the destruction of woods. When lands are to be cleared it must be in small portions, with each plot separated and bounded by windbreaks of full height, so that by sheltering your crops

---

97 Ibid., p. 211.
98 'Les tems du desordre sont passés': ibid., p. 212.

from the violence of the wind you will conserve all the soil, keep it moist and retain a healthy connection with the woodland.

'I will let you know later', he went on, 'the intentions of the government on the manner according to which clearing shall be carried out, which will be the only one permitted, as well as the method to be used in replanting the woodlands properly in those lands formerly devastated by fire.'[99] But the interventions of the new government did not stop at conservation and forest restoration. They were intended instead to restructure the whole economy on physiocratic lines. For example, the state would decisively discourage the coffee and cotton production in which the old company had specialised. It would simply require a minimal production of food crops. It was important, Poivre stated, that the French should be seen to be able to maintain a colony efficiently, to show 'all other nations, jealous of our good fortune, and who accuse us of inconstancy and slowness, that the French are capable of building a powerful colony that the mother country looks on with approbation'.[100]

In this opening speech, Poivre's social viewpoint emerged as radical in several ways. The colonists, he said, 'should be as citizens drawn from the labouring classes of the metropole'.[101] This kind of class language is a little hard to fathom in the context of Mauritius in 1767 but is probably best understood in terms of the hostility Poivre felt towards the kinds of speculative landholders who had moved into the island, burnt the forest for plantations or resold their concessions, and then left for France. He equated such speculators with the 'terrible men' he saw plaguing the peasantry in France, and associated reckless deforestation directly with their class objectives.[102] It may seem ap-

99 Ibid., p. 213.
100 Ibid., p. 214.
101 Ibid., p. 218.
102 There is some irony in this. A. Cobban, in *The social interpretation of the French Revolution*, Cambridge, 1964, has found that the exploitation of forests to the detriment of the peasantry was one of the most general grievances; see his extensive notes on regional variations in forest grievances on pp. 100–1. News coverage on the French situation in *The Times* during 1789–93 frequently refers to incendiarism and agitation over forest rights, and the issue was perceived as important even in England. There is currently much debate about the timing of extensive soil erosion in late-eighteenth-century France, and there are some reasons for suspecting that much of it in fact predates the Revolution. A useful recent treatment appears in P. Blaikie and H. Brookfield, *Land degradation and society*, London, 1987, pp. 124–42. Essentially two possible types of explanation are possible for the late-eighteenth-century Franco-German soil-erosion events: climatic and agrarian. Blaikie and Brookfield argue for the latter, contending that growing commercialisation and attendant differentiation and hardship account for increased erosion: 'It is the social condition of those who work most of the land that is relevant' (p. 140). This is an important, although as yet very young, debate of some applicability to the late-eighteenth-century Indian situation. Whatever the causes, by the early nineteenth century the experience of erosion in France was serious enough to promote active environmental thinking, just as it did in India thirty years later. The onset

propriate that the first publication of Poivre's early speeches in the colony should have taken place in Paris during 1797, when they were circulated as radical physiocratic and revolutionary tracts worthy of imitation and study.[103]

The apparent wish to identify the problems of the colonists with the concerns of the French peasantry and urban working classes is reconcilable too with a physiocratic way of thinking. However, Poivre's radical stance had far deeper roots than those of most of the leading physiocrats and was further stimulated by the existence of slavery on Mauritius. Slavery was a practice about which he felt strongly but, even as intendant of Mauritius, was practically powerless to eradicate or reform. It underlay his disaffection with Dumas and Desroches as successive governors during his tenure. Poivre's anti-slavery sympathies may have had simple humanitarian roots in his philosophical preoccupation with the Americans. This preoccupation was part of a more generalised French intellectual fashion in the mid eighteenth century and one which had its roots in the work of Montaigne. It had already led Poivre to enter into debate about the character and status of indigenous Americans.[104] As noted above, his views on this matter were coloured by his Jesuit training as a child and then as a seminarian, when he had come into contact with men who had witnessed the plight of indigenous Indians under Spanish rule.

This awareness had also made him critical of Buffon's thinking on the degeneracy of American indigenes, flora and fauna. Poivre took a different view of both. He was, for example, impressed by the sheer size of American trees and was inclined to consider the culture and characteristics of American Indians in the same favourable way. Scornful of the degenerative thesis, he emphasised instead the travails of the Peruvians and Mexicans at the hands of the Spanish and found the barbarity of the colonials extraordinary in men 'who call themselves so civilised, so soft and so Christian'.[105] Here we have a clue to Poivre's own anti-slavery stance. The whole discussion of the differences between peoples raised other related questions. From the time of Jean Bodin in France, the influence of climate on the development of human and natural traits had been a perennial theme of debate.[106] Poivre himself had written a monograph on the influence of soil and climate 'on the character of the English nation'[107] as part of a work in which he chose, by assuming the

of conservationism on Mauritius appears to predate that in France, but the intellectual connections require further research.

103 Posthumously Poivre's life and works were considered worthy of imitation by the more revolutionary-minded physiocrats, and his biography was written up by one of the leading later physiocratic figures, P. S. Dupont de Nemours, as *Notice sur la vie de Poivre*.

104 *De l'Amérique et des américains*.

105 Ibid., pp. 30–1.

106 For a fuller discussion, see Glacken, *Traces on the Rhodian shore*.

107 *Citoyen du monde*, p. 84.

imaginary role of a Chinese philosopher, deliberately to step outside Euro-centric perceptions. His period in China must have encouraged this openness to other cultures. Above all, Poivre was an empiricist who believed in the sanctity of 'judicious observations' when characterising both human and environmental phenomena.[108]

To Poivre, then, the European treatment of indigenous peoples and the colonial treatment of the environment were deeply interconnected matters. In his first address to the island council in 1767 he referred to the 'land in servitude' when discussing deforestation.[109] The new moral economy he outlined to the colonists thus contained two essential underlying elements: the restoration and protection of nature and the restoration and protection of the slave population. In both cases, great damage had already been done, but 'fortunately not without the possibility of remedy'.[110] There are good grounds for thinking that, in realising the formidable political obstacles to humanitarian reform, Poivre was driven to tackle the problems of environmental degradation with an equivalent and genuine passion. Such a symbiosis of humanitarian and naturalistic motivations can rarely have been expounded before, and yet Poivre, with his eloquence, found it quite possible to justify such a concept. In what amounted to a manifesto in his appeal to the colonists for a new moral order, he declared that 'it is for you to demonstrate your attachment to all that nature, religion and society prescribe . . . in this way Providence will respond with blessings on a culture formed by clean and innocent hands, and you will all find great abundance'.[111]

It is quite clear that in his first speech in the colony in July 1767 Poivre was guilty of some exaggeration in his descriptions of the extent of rainfall change and deforestation in the colony. He had, after all, been absent from the island for more than a decade. Nevertheless, the changes which had taken place in the meantime had been considerable. Bellin's survey of 1763, made only four years before, shows that most forest clearance had in fact taken place around Port Louis itself and along the river valley to the south-east of the city.[112] This kind of clearance would have been highly visible, in contrast to the still forested mountain tops – a contrast still present in a picture painted by Ganneret as late as the 1840s.[113]

---

108 On the value of empirical observation to the European in understanding the Orient, see
      Poivre, 'Utilité d'un voyage dans l'Orient', *Citoyen du monde*, p. 172.
109 Salles, *Oeuvres*, p. 239.
110 Poivre, 'Discours', 15 July 1767, in Salles, *Oeuvres*, p. 220.
111 Salles, *Oeuvres*, p. 232.
112 'Carte de l'Isle de France', drawn by M. Bellin, Ingenieur de la Marine, 1763, in Ly-Tio-
      Fane, *Pierre Sonnerat*, facing p. 6.
113 Hong Kong and Shanghai Bank Collection, Hong Kong: Painting of Port Louis approaches
      by J. Ganneret.

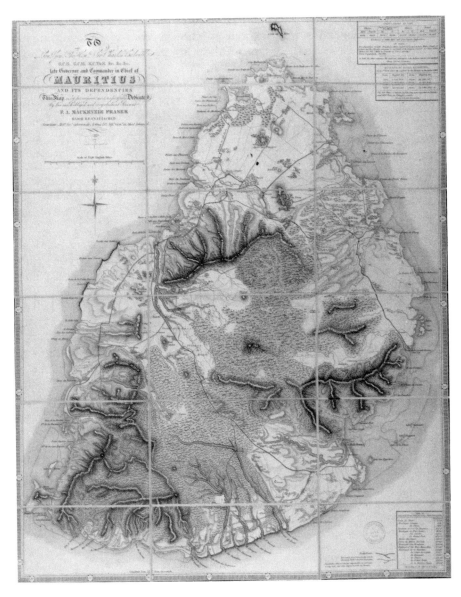

Plate 12. Map of Mauritius in 1835, by F. A. M. Fraser. The extent to which the early forest reservations had prevented clearance, especially in the south-east of the island, can clearly be seen. (Reproduced by permission of Cambridge University Library)

Some months after arriving, the new intendant started to convey a more accurate picture of the environmental state of the island in his reports to Minister Praslin. Most of them were couched in terms of the agricultural setting and the choice of crops, matters which were of some consequence for future forest clearance and soil status, as Poivre well knew.[114] In November 1767 he reported that he was surprised to find that since the time of the French settlement, crop production had made very little progress, in spite of the fertility of the soil.[115] The colonists had come more with a view to commerce and profit than with any useful knowledge of agriculture, he said. Since Labourdonnais had departed, project after project had been sponsored by the CoI. The cultivation of several species of plants had been attempted, and none had been successful. Coffee, cotton, indigo, sugar cane, cinnamon, tea, annatto and pepper had all been attempted without real success. If Labourdonnais's policy of relying on the growing of basic foodstuffs had been followed, Poivre believed, the colony would have been 'flourishing'. Where food crops had been cultivated, they had succeeded well, giving two crops per annum, one of wheat, oats or beans from June to October, and another of maize or rice from November to May. But the soil was not rested or recovered and had had no fertiliser applied; the colonists were content to exhaust the soil, he complained. But with the best methods of agriculture, Poivre averred, the ground could be made to produce well. However, there were many natural hazards to be faced. Birds took much of the crop and rats of all types a great deal, and monkeys took much of the rest. Scared off one field, they were driven into another. In three to four years, he thought, the situation would end in disaster. Another important hazard, he thought, was drought, which had come about since management of forests had been abandoned in favour of enclosure and clearance. Rain had become less frequent and the rivers less full, so that, overall, sterility threatened. In that part of the island which remained un-

---

114 I have made some use here of the documents collected in L. Malleret, *Pierre Poivre*, Paris, 1974 [cited as 'Malleret'], and *Un manuscrit de Pierre Poivre*. Since these documents have not been available in English before, I have included the original archival references exactly as they are footnoted by Malleret. These refer to letters between Poivre and Dumas on Mauritius and Praslin and de Boyne in Paris. My own translations of these are supplemented by the rendering given of some of Poivre's letters in Brouard, *Woods and forests*. It should be pointed out that Malleret, like Ly-Tio-Fane, largely ignored Poivre's environmentalism and also neglected the critical political and scientific support given to Poivre by Commerson and Saint-Pierre in his conservation campaigns. The only explicit recognition to date of Poivre's unusual environmental viewpoint appears in J. Benot's introduction to *Voyages a l'Isle de France par Bernardin de Saint-Pierre*, Paris, 1983, p. 12: 'Poivre was disturbed by the degradation of the "environnement".' However, Ly-Tio-Fane and Malleret should by no means be censured, as both started to write on Poivre before modern environmentalism reared its head in the 1970s.
115 Poivre's report in Montauban Archives. 89, no. 41, du 30 Nov. 1767 (Malleret, p. 369).

cleared, it rained every day, while in other parts there was no rain from June to December.[116] It would be necessary to act firmly against reckless deforestation, and he proposed to publish an ordinance to regulate clearing and to conserve the forests.[117]

Poivre then examined what consequences might arise from different sorts of cropping. Manioc, imported from Brazil by Labourdonnais, merited encouragement because of the ease with which slaves and troops could be supplied with it and because it was successful in the driest soils. The culture of coffee had taken several years to develop, some colonists having been discouraged from producing grain because of lack of space in the company storehouses. These plantations were still not properly developed, and Poivre told the minister, as he himself had recognised, that it would be best to persuade the colonist to cultivate spices efficiently in the long term and to concentrate on essential grain production in the short term. The culture of cinnamon and pepper was still in its infancy; some had been cultivated, but without the necessary knowledge or care. In order to inspire some order in the colony, Poivre proposed to set a personal example in the cultivation of these species. Cotton cultivation was unprofitable and undesirable and should be abandoned.

He estimated that of about 40,000 arpents, the majority of the cultivated land in Mauritius, only one-eighth was productive. This tiny area produced 1,200 units of wheat, 600 units of rice, 2 units of maize and 300 units of beans. During the recent war, slaughter of stock animals had taken place, and he proposed to restore stocking levels. At present there were only 6,000 cattle, a few sheep and a large number of goats. His objective was to raise stocking levels to 12,000 head by importing cattle from Madagascar, and he requested two new large-capacity ships to carry cattle from that island, as the two state ships already in use were not suitable for carrying cattle. Two years would suffice to build up the herds.[118]

The significance of these measures lay in Poivre's hostility to the concept of making use of the island purely as a source of profit for absentee landlords and overseas investors interested only in making a profit, regardless of the soil, the capacity of the island to feed itself and the needs of the colonial enterprise in India. This was the situation which had prevailed under the CoI.

---

116 This was no fanciful observation on the part of Poivre to justify his desiccationist thinking. The very real discontinuity in seasonal rainfall distribution due largely to rain-shadow and altitudinal effects of the prevailing winds meant that the areas first cleared on the island did in fact receive less rain; but, then, they always had received less rain. The net effect was to confirm theories linking deforestation to rainfall decline on Mauritius in the absence of rainfall records, which would have told a more complex story. Rainfall recording was introduced in the colony only in 1860.

117 The ordinance was eventually put into effect on 12 Nov. 1769.

118 Malleret, *Pierre Poivre*, p. 369.

Instead Poivre sought to re-establish the island as a supply base and as an economy dominated by small resident landowners and labourers – a visionary and unlikely scenario but one which reflected physiocratic principles. A more innovative element related to formal land-use planning. The intendant sought actively to plan the structure of the island's agronomy and its land-use patterns as meticulously as possible. Even the position assigned to the development of spices had the advantage that it was specifically a state project rather than a private speculative one. Planning would also favour the protection of forests, which was one of Poivre's main concerns. State control of land use on a rational basis would be the main outcome.

He wrote to the minister much more specifically on the subject of forests,[119] dealing particularly with the problem of the consumption of timber for construction. Of 400,000 arpents of cultivable land, 350,000 arpents were still covered in forest. Most clearing had taken place on the coast, exactly the zone in which it was considered (as it had been by the CoI) necessary to conserve wood for defence purposes. Apart from some limited areas, all the coast between Grand Port and Black River had been cleared. He thus proposed to pursue the conservation of forests without delay with a clause in concession agreements obliging the reservation of a strip of forest by the sea (the future 'pas réserves') and restrictions on clearance in the interior and by the edges of rivers. House construction at Port Louis and the 'Camp' involved the excessive use of ebony and other hardwoods. So Poivre planned to prohibit the use of wood in construction, as enough masons and stonecutters were available for alternative methods. Moreover, stone for building abounded, as did coral. In police regulations he had introduced measures prohibiting the use of wood in palisades and had authorised the use instead of live saplings and hedges, simply to save forest trees. He also gave orders to plant trees along all roads. This was a practice Poivre had noted with approval in Malabar.[120] At the same time, he recorded, he had set up tree plantations to encourage others to do the same. Everything, he emphasised to the minister, depended on a wise and far-sighted administration. The colonists, he observed, cut wood and cleared recklessly and showed little interest in maintaining the forest. Cut areas were rapidly invaded by grasses, which became a permanent fire hazard. Vagabonds, maroons (runaway slaves) and the 'relentless' wind did the rest.[121]

To counter these problems more directly, Poivre planned to order half of each concession to be conserved along the coastal zone, and in the interior to limit felling to 20 arpents per concession, with orders to leave a belt of forest around all cleared areas to protect crops against the wind and to maintain

119 Montauban Archives 89, no. 57, 30 Nov. 1767 (Malleret, p. 369).
120 Malleret, *Un manuscrit de Pierre Poivre*, pp. 113–14.
121 Archives Nationales (AN) C(4)18; Col. 30 Nov. 1767, no. 37 (Malleret, p. 543).

moisture and rainfall.[122] At the same time, a belt of woodland would be protected along all the rivers. This last measure may have reflected the belief
current in some contemporary medical writings that low-lying areas along
rivers were particularly unhealthy if cleared.[123] However, it is also possible
that Poivre had observed the kind of soil erosion and gullying which developed
along stream sides when trees were felled down to the water's edge and their
roots washed away. Such empirical observation coloured his approach to regulation. Poivre realised that he had a major re-education task ahead of him if
the behaviour of the colonists was to be altered. He felt it necessary to develop
an awareness of the advantages and aesthetics of tree planting and a consciousness of the negative factors involved in not having trees. Thus the report
noted in connection with the tree-planting orders that he had 'ordered tree
planting along all streets to accustom people to the idea and diminish the
horror to the eye of those places that were without a single tree, in which the
prospect was frightful'.[124]

In his acknowledgement of Poivre's first report, Praslin approved most of
the proposed measures without much comment, whilst observing that the
intendant would not be able to carry them through entirely on his own. They
required the authority of intendant and governor together.[125] A system for
inspecting the forests would have to be set up, and this would be forthcoming,
although the minister did not specify when. However, he could not grant
Poivre the title and authority of Inspecteur des Eaux et Forêts, which had
been asked for, as this would be contrary to the constitution of the French
colonies.[126]

Praslin seems to have hesitated to take the further steps towards interven-
tion which Poivre believed to be necessary. Clearance for cultivation was not
the only pressure on the forests, and the minister had not appreciated this.
The state itself required timber for shipbuilding and construction at Grand
Port. There were other demands too. The ironworks owned by one Monsieur
Hermans consumed a great deal of timber which Poivre thought would more
properly be used for naval purposes and for construction.[127] Nevertheless,
Poivre was impressed by Hermans's successful and pioneering attempts to

122 AN C(4); Col. No. 42, 30 Nov. 1767 (Malleret, p. 543).
123 See e.g. J. Arbuthnot, *An essay on the effect of air on the human body*, London, 1733, pp. 64,
    72, 89, 206. Arbuthnot was the first authority after Woodward to make specific connections
    between mountain vegetation and rainfall incidence and the corresponding likelihood of de-
    cline if clearance were to occur. His work would undoubtedly have been familiar to Buffon
    and Poivre.
124 AN C(4); Col. no. 42, 30 Nov. 1767 (Malleret, p. 538).
125 Quimper 12 bis, fol. 12A, p. 252 (Malleret, p. 544).
126 Quimper 12 bis; fol. 39R, 15 Aug. 1768 (Malleret, p. 544).
127 Ibid.

acquire a sustainable supply through the use of coppice. The activities of three timber merchants were more of a worry, and Poivre acted quickly to fix a common timber price at a rate sufficiently low to discourage unnecessary cutting. This was to the chagrin of Dumas, the governor, who had hoped to reap the benefits of the timber trade on his own disputed holdings at Trois Islots. Poivre's relations with Dumas were already poor, and his determined action to forestall timber speculation hardened the governor's antipathy towards him and set the scene for future disputes within the administration. Praslin backed the intendant on this occasion.[128]

The extent of Poivre's excursion into land-use planning during his first months in office met with some resentment, especially among the coffee planters, whose clearance activities Poivre bitterly opposed, largely on doctrinaire physiocratic and not on practical grounds. The growing of coffee did not contribute directly to the functioning of the island as a source of food for the military authorities, and its marketing was not subject to state control.

A deliberately anonymous document despatched by a group of colonists to Praslin on this subject made the point that there was very little logic in the restriction of coffee cultivation if soil fertility was to be a major issue. In France, complained the anonymous writers, there was a free choice with regard to which crops or land one might cultivate, and the Crown did not overly interfere in such matters. In the Isle de France, the letter continued, soil was indeed being eroded, both in the course of droughts and in heavy rain, in spite of attempts to prevent it which were superficial and heavy-handed in their administration. In less than twenty years the land would be reduced to a state of sterility. It would be better to produce coffee rather than corn, as Poivre wanted, since coffee trees provided shade and conserved moisture. It was, the document argued, actually the only way of keeping cleared land on the island fertile and protected from erosion. The proof of this was to be seen on neighbouring Bourbon, where the best land for wheat growing was that which had at one time been covered in coffee trees.[129] Subsequently Poivre was forced, not by the minister but through domestic political lobbying during 1769, to concede most of these points. Moreover, the difficulties of actually storing surplus corn, in contrast to the options available for keeping coffee beans, helped the cause of the coffee planters.[130]

Crops were not the only route to profits on Mauritius. Some, as Poivre quickly discovered, enriched themselves by speculating in land concessions,

128 AN C(4)22; Col. 27 April 1771 and Quimper 12C(2)A4, pp. 81–4 (Malleret, p. 544).
129 AN C4/23, entitled 'Extrait des lettres des gens les plus sensées de l'Ile de France', 17 June 1768 (Malleret, p. 544).
130 AN C(4)22; Col. 12 July 1769, extrait d'un lettre de Poivre du 13 Jan. 1768; no. 6 (Malleret, p. 544).

buying and selling them on Mauritius and in France, and coupling this with speculation in silver coin, which was in short supply. Such activities were a challenge to the intendant. The problem of concession speculation was especially difficult to solve. The concessions had been liberally distributed by the CoI 'without principle and without any fixed plan', according to Poivre. Some individuals had been illegally allocated very large areas and others small areas, but most holdings had not been measured out properly at all. Some had been allocated along the coast, while other persons were granted holdings on what were technically strategic reserves where clearing was illegal.[131] No lands at all had been assigned to parishes, to churches, to the care of a priest or to communes, as had been intended.[132] Moreover, many lands had been semi-legally allocated by the company after the Company Termination Edict of 1764 had been promulgated.

Poivre formed the idea of amalgamating all such concessions made since 1764 which remained unproductive, probably with the impression that such land would then revert to the Crown. Its management and conservation would then be more enforceable. A simple difficulty prevented him from achieving this aim at first: The surveyor appointed by the Crown failed to arrive in the colony. This difficulty was compounded by uncertainty about the extent of the intendant's authority. A contract had been made with Messrs Harambure, de Commerville and Chantilly, who proposed to set up an association with a concession of 2,808 arpents, a very large unit. Poivre could not afford to alter this arrangement as he would have wished because of the embarrassing intervention of Governor Dumas, who had an interest in a similarly large concession. This latter was a concession Poivre had judged useful to the Crown and of which the Crown had effectively been deprived by the governor. And this was only the tip of the iceberg. In 1767–8 Poivre received more than two hundred requests for land, most of them from individuals who, like Dumas, had no intention of working the granted land but intended to sell it. Poivre had suggested to Praslin that such sales should be prevented, but he was not granted that power.[133]

Dumas then raised the stakes by proposing to take for himself a concession of 10,000 arpents in a part of the island called Trois Islots, the best land in the colony, where there were already sixty 'habitations'. On it he wished to install slave labour and cattle imported from Madagascar. This was too much

---

131 Concessions were mostly allocated in Port Louis by drawing lines on a map: a 'grande habitation' or a 'petite habitation', the boundaries being described roughly according to previous adjoining concessions. E.g. in the 1730s the Brouard family were allocated a concession at Rivière du Rempart, most of which was on the Plaine des Roches, a barren lava field (Jean Brouard, pers. Comm., 1991).

132 Quoted by Malleret, p. 538.

133 AN C4/22; Col. 30 Nov. 1667; no. 43 (Malleret, p. 538).

for Poivre. As he saw it, ever since Dumas had landed on the island he had spent his time looking after his own interests and attempting to accumulate a fortune. The intendant absolutely refused to countenance further abuses of his authority by the governor or to tolerate his other projects, as he reported to Praslin. Accordingly, he asked the minister to back him on the detailed terms of his original commission, which had specifically sought to control land speculation and to protect forests; failing which, Poivre demanded to be re-called to France.[134] On the margin of this ultimatum from Poivre, in connec-tion with the proposal of Chantilly and his associates, Praslin inscribed, 'Restrict this concession to a standard allocation according to the regulations' and, more decisively, 'Terminate the Dumas concession altogether.'[135] Later, in a diplomatic attempt to be even-handed, Praslin offered both men royal authorisation for a single new concession each (which Poivre had not re-quested) for purposes of agricultural demonstration and personal use, to com-pensate them for the modesty of their respective salaries. However, by the time this offer came through, the situation had developed further.[136]

Clearly perturbed by the reports of the intendant, Praslin himself decided to take a tougher line. In a letter of 15 August 1768, addressing Poivre and Dumas jointly, he asked for a complete reassessment of concession allocations, to ensure that the grants had complied with regulations. If they had not, they were to be reincorporated as state land, especially if they remained unworked. They could then be administered as communal land by the governor and intendant. This, he said, had been the practice in other colonies.[137] Dumas himself would not be conceded any private estate. Moreover, the king revoked permission for the governor or the intendant to possess any holdings rightfully belonging to the Crown.

A month earlier Poivre had written to the minister objecting to the holding of lands assigned to such nobles as the Comte de Polignac and other absentees. Such lands, owned by court worthies, differed little from the kinds of duchies and baronies which were rarely visited in France itself and which were shortly to cause the king more severe domestic problems.[138] In this respect Poivre had contrived to nail his colours, precociously, to a very radical mast indeed. In the matter of absentee landlordism, Dumas, oddly enough, seems to have sided with Poivre; three days after Poivre, he wrote against the granting of land to individuals in Paris. Large estates, which such landlordism encouraged, tended to be put down to coffee or cotton; furthermore, there was also a labour

134 Ibid.
135 Brest M89; no. 56 (Malleret, p. 538).
136 Montauban 123, no. 1, p. 3 (Malleret, p. 538).
137 Quimper 12 bis; fol. 28R; 15 Aug. 1768 and Compiegne 12AA, pp. 224–6 (Malleret, p. 539).
138 AN C(4)22; Col.; 27 July 1768 (Poivre de Ministre), no. 88 (Malleret, p. 539).

shortage, which might thereby be exacerbated. Poivre had been anxious to end the practice of slave corvée in this connection for humanitarian reasons, and absentee landlordism threatened this initiative.

In January 1769 Dumas was finally summoned back to Paris.[139] Although Poivre's relations with Desroches, the succeeding governor, were little better than they had been with Dumas, he managed in the interim to strengthen his position and freedom of action considerably. This was owing largely to his success in gathering around him a small group of like-minded intellectuals and scientists who broadly shared his vision of how the colony and its natural resources might ideally be administered. They also shared his enthusiasm for its beauty and for its unusual natural history. On his return to the island, Poivre had been shocked at the state of Aublet's botanical garden at Le Reduit. Most of the trees in the surrounding area had gone, and the plants and trees imported from other parts of the world had either disappeared or were in poor condition. The state of the cinnamon and pepper trees especially shocked Poivre, who had taken so much trouble to obtain good strains of these plants. The restoration of the botanical garden thus became a central concern for the intendant. The garden was also essential for his plans to continue to introduce spice trees from the East Indies.[140]

In his speech to the 'little colony of virtuous men' on 3 August 1767, Poivre had talked of the 'perpetual spring' which prevailed on the island.[141] In his treatise 'De Amazonas' he had expatiated on a related theme. The Garden of Eden might be found, Poivre thought, 'in a corner of Asia' and not, he had decided, in America.[142] Although Poivre put this sentiment in the mouth of an imaginary commentator, the idea was clearly one that had a good deal of serious meaning for him.

Such concepts might seem to have conflicted with a distinctively empirical and unfanciful approach to natural phenomena. However, Poivre was innovative in the sense that he contrived to combine older European and Zoro-

---

139 Brest M90; 30 July 1768, no. 53 (Malleret, p. 539).

140 J. Macintosh, *Travels into Europe, Asia and Africa*, London, 1782, quoted in P. J. Barnwell, *Visits and despatches: Mauritius, 1598–1948*, Port Louis, 1948, p. 170. His success, and the success of Nicholas Céré, in restoring the botanical garden was widely attested to in later years, not least by the English. In 1778, for example, it was recorded by Macintosh that 'the spiceries of Ceylon and Amboyna promise to flourish on this island. In the parish of Pamplemousses, the King of France maintains at considerable expense, and in good condition, a spacious botanical garden, divided into four parts, representing the great quarters of the earth, in which the trees, shrubs, plants, flowers, herbs, roots and so on of each are respectively planted, pieces of wood fixed on the ground by each describing its name, native country and qualities. In this garden cinnamon and cloves thrive amazingly.'

141 Poivre, 'Discours', in Salles, *Oeuvres*, p. 210; Dante, *Purgatorio*, quoted in A. Keymer, 'Plant imagery' in Dante, B.A. diss., University of Cambridge, 1982, p. 26.

142 Poivre, *De l'Amérique et des américains*, p. 14.

astrian notions of the possibility of attempting, in an earthly sense, to recreate a paradise or Garden of Eden within the convenient mental confines of a botanical garden, with a rather stronger sense that the whole tropical island on which he found himself could be termed a land of 'perpetual spring'. Peter Mundy had asserted of Mauritius that 'there is not under the sunne a more pleasant, healthy and fruitful piece of ground for an island inhabited',[143] and Poivre certainly shared his opinion. However, until the arrival on the island of Philibert Commerson and Bernardin de Saint-Pierre, it was a perception he was not able to voice to much effect. When his future collaborators in the physiocratic and conservation enterprise did finally arrive, he found that they also shared his critical opinions of domestic French society. It was Commerson who seems to have been most instrumental in reinforcing Poivre's perception of the island as a site for the construction of a social, natural and agrarian Utopia in which the protection of nature would play a major part. It is to the story of this collaboration between the two visionaries that we now turn.

Pierre Poivre and Philibert Commerson: Co-operating in the development of conservationism

On 8 November 1768 Philibert Commerson disembarked from the *Boudeuse*, flagship of the Bougainville expedition. One week later, on 15 November, Bougainville himself signed the certificate which relieved Commerson of his obligations as a naturalist of the expedition and gave him permission to stay in the colony.[144] In his instructions Commerson was required to 'carry out observations and investigations in the natural history of the different coasts and interiors of the countries the officer will find himself in; and report on the significant details of all the animal, mineral and vegetable specimens which he may encounter'.[145] Poivre had taken the decision to acquire the services of Commerson from Bougainville so that he could 'acquaint himself with the natural history of the island' and so that he might 'teach the planters the best way of employing the territorial riches that their vigilance had preserved and was still procuring'.[146]

In this way Poivre intended to employ Commerson specifically as a scientific

143 R. Temple, ed., *The travels of Peter Mundy in Europe and Asia, 1658–1667*, 8 vols., Cambridge, 1897, I, p. 9.
144 Certificate delivered to Commerson by Bougainville on 15 Nov. 1768: 'Sur la demande que m'a faite par M. Poivre nous lui avons permis de s'y débarquer . . .', reproduced in A. Lacroix, *Figures des savants*, vol. 4, Paris, 1938, pl. III; quoted by Ly-Tio-Fane, *Pierre Sonnerat*, p. 58 n. 3.
145 Ser. Col. E., Commerson's file, fol. 1, quoted by Ly-Tio-Fane, *Pierre Sonnerat*, p. 58 n. 1.
146 C. Pridham, *England's colonial empire: Mauritius*, London, 1846, p. 47.

expert. He was probably aware that in this way he would be able to pursue his chosen policies with a much increased conviction and persuasive power vis-à-vis those interests which opposed him on the island and in Paris. In so doing Poivre had found a powerful ally in the person of Poissonier, the physician to the king and 'Inspector-General of medicine, surgery and pharmacy in the colonies', as well as in Bougainville himself. Indeed, Poissonier and Bougainville made it their business to ensure that the somewhat unorthodox manner in which Commerson entered the service of the intendant was properly legitimated upon Bougainville's return to France. That this was successfully achieved was made clear in a letter to Praslin in April 1770 in which Poivre intimated that 'Monseigneur [Poissonier] has given permission that Sr. Commerson the medical naturalist, who accompanied M. de Bougainville on his journey, should stop for some time at the Isle de France to reconnoitre the medical plants that are found on the island, to facilitate their use in hospitals and thus supply in greater numbers those which one is obliged to send to France.'[147]

It seems clear that this justification of Commerson's employment on the island, ostensibly to carry out a survey of its medicinal resources, was considered by Poivre and Bougainville to carry a mark of credibility that other more purely academic reasons might not have done, for there was no doubt that Poivre's motives for employing Commerson were by no means limited to medicinal research, if they included it at all. Nevertheless, the cachet of authority and respectability which medical men and medical research were acquiring in this colonial setting is quite manifest.[148]

Commerson was well aware of these difficulties in justifying his employment to the authorities in Paris and in disguising the fact that he was actually fulfilling a rather different and innovative professional role designed by Poivre.[149] Thus in one letter he reveals that Poivre envisaged a grand natural history or natural resource survey of the whole Mascarene island area, to be conducted on a scale that had probably not been envisaged before, except

147 Letter to Ministre de la Marine, 7 April 1770, AN Ser. Col. E, Commerson's file, fol. 8, quoted by Ly-Tio-Fane, *Pierre Sonnerat*, p 54 n. 1.

148 Commandant to Secretary of State, 16 Feb. 1771; A Dept., Réunion; Ser C, Régistre de l'Ordinnateur no. 35, F, pp. 80–2, quoted by Ly-Tio-Fane, *Pierre Sonnerat*, p. 55. When in April 1770 orders were issued for Commerson to return to France, the commandant and *ordonnateur* on Bourbon wrote to the Minister for the Navy, again putting forward a medical justification (which by this time was far from the truth) for Commerson's retention, stating that 'it is proposed to make an extensive collection of the best specimens of plants and simples which can be found on the Isle de France, Bourbon and Madagascar . . . the researches which he has already carried out . . . have concerned plants which are absolutely unknown and of great utility [potential?] for medicine'.

149 P. Cappe, *Philibert Commerson: Naturaliste-voyageur*, Paris, 1861, p. 163, citing Commerson to Lemonnier, 1 May 1772.

perhaps in the embryonic schemes of Sir Joseph Banks, whose participation
as naturalist on the *Endeavour* voyage coincided with the first year of Commerson's employ by Poivre. The pioneering role which Commerson had performed as surgeon-naturalist on the Bougainville voyage was thus to be
repeated on land. Even though the employment of a naturalist in a professional
capacity by government was as yet a relatively novel concept, there is no doubt
that Poivre had a clear vision of what he wanted. Certainly Commerson would
have performed a useful practical function in identifying imported spice trees
and other species whose identification was often disputed by Poivre's enemies,
who still had some influence in Port Louis and Paris. But for most of the
time Poivre left Commerson to design his own programme of investigation as
an independent scientist. In the words of François Beau, 'this generous patron
gave Commerson a huge apartment in his house where he could prepare and
conserve his plants, birds, insects . . . for four years he hosted him at his table,
lent him his servants, and rewarded his talents in the most generous possible
way'.[150]

In short, Poivre had set about the business of state patronage of natural
science more on the basis of the value of the study itself than on the possibility
of an immediate utilitarian outcome. Moreover, there seems little doubt that
at least part of the sense of the expression 'préparer et conserver les plantes'
used here by Beau represented an attitude of mind easily transferred to the
whole of the living portion of the island, which both men valued so highly.
For Poivre, the recording of unique and hard-collected data by an acknowledged expert was of obvious and unquestionable merit. Specifically for the
purpose he provided Commerson with a skilled draughtsman, Paul Philippe
de Jossigny, at the expense of the colonial exchequer.[151] Poivre also took the
opportunity to have his nephew Pierre Sonnerat trained specifically as a
draughtsman and naturalist under Commerson, partly to ensure the continuity
of such expertise on the island.

Commerson commenced his work with a project not paralleled in scale by
a botanist in the tropics until Alexander Buchanan-Hamilton started his surveys in Mysore nearly forty years later. In particular, he began work on an
ambitious treatise based on an initial survey of the island plants.[152] Poivre was
keen that Commerson should also carry out botanical fieldwork in Northern
Madagascar during 1770. Commerson had no illusions about the nature of
Poivre's Madagascar enterprise, believing that his plan to establish new French

150 Ly-Tio-Fane, *Pierre Sonnerat*, p. 58, citing letter from François Beau to Turgot.
151 Jossigny had arrived in Mauritius in 1768 as aide-de-camp to Desroches: Ly-Tio-Fane, *Pierre Sonnerat*, p. 59, citing AN Ser. Col. E, Jossigny's file, fol. 116 and fol. 102.
152 Philibert Commerson, *Insularum borbonicarum florilegium* . . . , Paris, 1768.

bases on the island was mainly a pretext for the prosecution of the intendant's botanical enthusiasms.[153]

Between the departure of Dumas in November 1768 and the arrival of Desroches in June 1769, Poivre administered the Isle de France without undue interference. It was during this period that the most innovative developments in land-use control started to take place. As we have already seen, Poivre's ideas about the relationship between deforestation and desiccation were well developed long before the arrival of Commerson or Bernardin de Saint-Pierre. At some stage, however, Poivre focussed his attention on the possible connections among deforestation, soil erosion and the silting up of rivers and harbours. The silting problem was a considerable development of the desiccation theme.[154] Moreover, it was one of the factors which decided Poivre on the promulgation of the first ordinance dealing specifically with the prevention of erosive processes and with the installation of a framework of conservationist legislation. The ordinance covered the planting and protection of trees and the planting of acacia (*Leucaena glauca*) 'hedges' and live hedges of bamboo. The tree-planting provisions of the ordinance reflected the practices that Poivre had observed in the Cape and Malabar in the 1740s. The species he recommended for planting were tamarinds, bananas, mangosteens and peaches, all of which were imported South Indian species. They were to be planted, as was the practice in Pondicherry, sixteen to eighteen feet apart.[155]

With the approval of Poivre, Commerson and another botanist, Charpentier de Cossigny (who had been responsible for importing the South Indian *bois noir* into the colony), commenced a systematic survey of the state of the woodlands and forests of the island, paying particular attention to the potential of the local woods for shipbuilding. The results of the survey were carefully annotated and presented in a formal report.[156] The report, as Poivre must have anticipated, recommended rigorous forest protection and gave him a cast-iron case for bringing forward a comprehensive set of conservation measures. These became law on 15 November 1769. Before the submission of the Commerson–Cossigny report, Poivre had hesitated over such draconian attempts at land-use control, through a sensible fear of the very real opposition he expected to all his land-use planning schemes, in spite of the backing he knew he had from Minister Praslin. However, political backing at such a distance was of only limited use. By calling in aid a scientifically sanctioned and properly

153 Cappe, *Philibert Commerson*, p. 106, citing Commerson to Georges-Marie (his brother), n.d.
154 Brouard, *Woods and forests*, p. 18.
155 Ibid.
156 Ly-Tio-Fane, *Pierre Sonnerat*, p. 40. Cossigny had botanised extensively in the region of Pondicherry and had thus acquired a knowledge of the trees that might be transplanted to Mauritius.

documented assessment of the impact of forest depredations on vital naval
timber supplies, Poivre was able to initiate controls which were, in truth,
guided by quite other motivations, however real may have been the fear of a
timber shortage.[157]

The *Reglement économique* of 15 November contained nineteen major provisions. Implicit in the legislation was an understanding of the dynamic processes of change at work on the island environment as a consequence of
deforestation. It incorporated a specific set of measures intended to inhibit
and then reverse the most damaging of those processes.[158] Three articles of
the ordinance (nos. 4–6) were designed specifically to prevent soil erosion and
encourage land restoration.[159]

The regulations were highly innovative, and they were quite distinctly different from the kinds of measures which had been current in Europe since
the early Middle Ages; these had been designed solely to secure a sustainable
timber yield or hunting area. The 1769 ordinance specifically recognised and
attempted to redress the complex impact of destructive artificially induced
environmental change, including processes, such as soil erosion, which were
little known in Europe but highly characteristic of denuded tropical lands.

The three most significant of the rules of 1769 were those that concerned
'reserved' areas and provisions to replant denuded parts of the island, two
proposals that Poivre had first promised in his 1767 inaugural speech to the
colonists. Thus Article 4 set up the future 'mountain reserves', formalised by
Governor Decaen in 1804 and much later emulated by the British in India.
This restriction recognised the importance of stabilising steep upper slopes
and so preventing destructive levels of run-off and silting lower down in the
stream catchments. Article 5 laid down requirements for tree planting on
denuded areas, specifying preferred species and penalising delays in replanting. Article 6 set up the 'river reserves', designed specifically to prevent silting
in rivers and estuaries.

---

157 For details of the serious shortages affecting the French navy at this time, see Bamford,
Forests and French sea power.
158 The main provisions of the 1769 ordinance are in Brouard, *Woods and forests,* pp. 18–20.
159 '4. One-quarter of the area of all concessions must be reserved under forest, especially rocky
ground and areas unsuited to cultivation, cliffs, mountain tops and steep slopes. [These were
the future 'mountain reserves'.]
   '5. Trees must be planted in denuded areas – the owner will be required to sow within 15
months – penalty: 1000 livres – with plantation trees of all species, either exotic or native to
the island, and will preferably use in the case of native seeds those of *bois de natte, bois puant,
tacamahaca, benjoin* etc.
   '6. Trees must be protected over 10 perches or gaulettes [about 200 ft] along streams, and
restocking is ordered if they are destroyed with 4 or 5 rows, either of bamboos, or fruit trees,
cinnamon trees, vacoas or others. [These were the future 'river reserves'].' (Brouard, *Woods
and forests,* pp. 18–20)

All three regulations recognised the chronic soil erosion on the island and the relationship between deforestation in one part of the catchment (especially on mountain-sides vulnerable to gullying or soil erosion) and damage in another part of the catchment. This was an approach which owed much to empirical observation of the impact of clearance in virgin tropical forest. It also owed a great deal to the central tenets of the physiocrats, who stressed the interdependence of land, crops and society and consequently the interdependence of groups within a society deriving from their common reliance on the products of the soil.[160] The state, as Cantillon had proposed, was a tree with its roots in the land. The circular flow or cycle of wealth within an economic 'system' (the society) was a dynamic concept. When applied to an environment such as Mauritius, where the dynamics of human impact were so demonstrable, this was an approach which offered a convincing justification for conservation.

The report made by Commerson and Cossigny on the natural resources of Mauritius had lent authority to this legislative initiative, as had Poivre's effective transformation of the whole of the island into one taxonomic laboratory. Commerson, a man who had become a physician largely because of the botanical training which that profession conveyed, was also a scientist whose skills were recognised even outside France when he was still a young man. In 1754 Linnaeus himself had commissioned him to investigate the marine plants, fishes and shells of the Mediterranean at the request of the Queen of Sweden. The work had resulted in Commerson's being rewarded with associateship at the universities of Stockholm and Uppsala.[161] The relationship between Uppsala and Montpellier, Commerson's alma mater, was an important one. Boissier de Sauvages, Linnaeus's mentor in the construction of disease and plant classifications, had also taught Commerson. Linnaeus was thus well aware of developments at Montpellier and of the course of Commerson's career. The innovative botanical-garden establishment at Montpellier endured a very troubled relationship with the more conservative Paris Jardin – an antipathy which ultimately drove it to depend more on its Huguenot links with English naturalists than with the French establishment. The English–Huguenot influence (with its distinctively Baconian content, one may speculate) could help to account for Commerson's attitude to the role of the state in controlling the environment. Indeed, Poivre's idea that Commerson should carry out a complete survey of all the island in all its aspects was in an essentially Baconian tradition. The same may be said of the thinking behind Colbert's 1669 Forest Ordinance, which had clearly helped to inspire Poivre's conservation laws.[162]

160 Bell, *History of economic thought*, chap. 6.
161 Ly-Tio-Fane, *Pierre Sonnerat*, p. 57, citing An Ser. CIE, Commerson's file, fol. 296.
162 For relations between Linnaeus and Sauvages and the intellectual links between Montpellier

However, it was not only Commerson's scientific reputation which Poivre found intellectually congenial.

Behind his advocacy of conservation, Poivre sustained a vision of a renewed moral economy as an antidote to the corrupt life of France, the social habitat which had reared the monopolists and the profiteers with whom he constantly contended and who so anxiously sought his downfall. The star at the centre of Poivre's new Garden of Eden, with its climatically genuine 'perpetual spring', was the new Mauritius Jardin du Roi.[163] Arcadian as Poivre's vision was, it was also severely practical, to be attained by the regulation of land and the safeguarding of forests and by the encouragement of the arts among what he had hoped was 'a virtuous people'. This was a naturalism tempered by the practicality of physiocracy.

Defoe, Rousseau and Commerson: The island motif and the Utopian antecedents of Romantic environmentalism

In the first part of this chapter I characterised the conservation ideas of Pierre Poivre fairly narrowly as an outcome of a physiocracy constrained by the empirical conditions of an island colony and the extensive and idiosyncratic influences that formed Poivre's own opinions, particularly through his contact with Dutch, Indian and Chinese land-use methods and philosophies. I did this advisedly, as I believe these factors predominated in his views and are evidenced by his own writings. What I have left unsaid or neglected thus far is the less specific influence exercised by changes in attitudes to nature that were taking place in France. The influence of these is difficult to assess properly, although the language of Poivre's 1767 speeches suggests that he was at least partially affected by the formulations and expressions of Jean-Jacques Rousseau. However, Poivre's views and his shaping of Mauritius environmental legislation were more immediately affected by his contacts with Philibert Commerson and Bernardin de Saint-Pierre.

We need, therefore, to consider carefully the rather distinctive origins of the views of Commerson and Saint-Pierre, which were substantially different in character from those of Poivre and which were strongly affected by a Utopian naturalism dominated by the thinking of Rousseau but which also represented the culmination of a variety of other strands in the corpus of French

---

and Newtonian and Baconian thought in England, see J. Martin, 'Sauvage's nosology: Medical enlightenment in Montpellier', in A. Cunningham and R. French, *The medical enlightenment of the eighteenth century*, Cambridge, 1990, pp. 111–37.

163 The gardens were purchased from Poivre by the French Crown in 1772: Pridham, *England's colonial empire: Mauritius*, p. 372.

responses to the natural world, especially in the tropics. This Romantic environmentalism, while distinctively different from the more rationalised approach of Poivre, did serve to buttress his policies.

For Commerson and Saint-Pierre, the island acted as a symbolic vehicle for the formulation of ideas about nature and environmental change and also about science and society in general. In this way the island (especially the tropical islands of the South Pacific and the Indian Ocean) became the central motif of a new discourse about nature which we can safely characterise as environmentalist rather than simply conservationist. This insular discourse became so strong in the Romantic tradition that it allows us to trace many of the central features of early western environmentalism back to the pattern established by the French on Mauritius. The discourse emerged as part and parcel of a much more generalised and extensive engagement between French thought and the islands and island societies of the southern oceans, an engagement which was central to the Romantic cult of nature as well as to the Romantic reassessment of European society. Indeed, one could even say that environmentalism was, to a great extent, born out of a marriage between physiocracy and the mid-eighteenth-century French obsession with the island as the speculative and Utopian location for the atavistic 'discovery' of idyllic societies or the construction of new European societies. Moreover, the Romantic cult of islands and tropical nature which environmentalism implied was, with physiocracy, an essential part of the Romantic reformism that lay behind the French Revolution. Without the Romantic cult of islands (itself the outgrowth of much older Utopian and paradisal traditions), a fully fledged environmentalism, rather than a rather utilitarian shadow of it, could not have emerged. The convergence between physiocracy and climatic and insular Romanticism took place on Mauritius partly as a consequence of the strategic economic importance of the island environment, one that became politically important enough to attract the likes of Poivre, Commerson and Saint-Pierre. But Mauritius had also attracted all three men simply by virtue of being an island; and all of them had deliberately chosen to go there.

The apparently decisive synchronic historical moments in the drama of an emerging environmental consciousness on Mauritius were enabled, appropriately enough, by Bougainville's circumnavigation of the globe, bringing Philibert Commerson first to Otaheite and then to Mauritius, or, one might say, from Utopia to Eden. It seems worth looking both at the immediate and even haphazard conjuncture that led to the development of environmentalism on Mauritius and at its deeper roots, some of which were hinted at in earlier chapters. In particular, one needs to consider the social and literary influences on Rousseau, the one absent but critical participant on physiocratic Mauritius. Rousseau was the most important single personal influence on Commerson and Bernardin de Saint-Pierre, above all in affecting the way in which the two men appropriated and strengthened the island motif for their own purposes.

Environmentalism, then, emerges as an integral part of the French intellectual response both to the tropical world and to the encounter with indigenous peoples. In its attempts at projection and idealisation, the older 'insularist' imagery which French environmentalism co-opted was soon articulated and coalesced with early scholarly Orientalism. This is not surprising, since many early French specialists on Indian texts, topography and natural history, such as Pierre Sonnerat, set out from Mauritius on their Indian excursions, while Saint-Pierre would site his novels both on Mauritius and in an imagined India, which he never actually visited. The island, like the 'Orient', could be distanced, objectified or romanticised.

The idea that the roots of environmentalism are closely connected with Romanticism and with Jean-Jacques Rousseau is not, of course, entirely new. A number of writers have rightly suggested that Rousseau's writings were significant stimulants to and antecedents of 'modern' environmentalism. LaFreniere, especially, regards Rousseau as a 'pre-environmentalist'.[164] In reality, Rousseau himself was much more sharply and directly connected with a fully developed and practically oriented environmentalism expressed in a conservation policy (and in a series of explicitly environmentalist texts) than LaFreniere realised. For his part, Commerson can be identified not simply as an early conservationist (like Poivre) but much more as the major practical initiator of the South Pacific island cult and instigator of its incorporation as one of the main motifs of Romantic literature, philosophy, science and art. Commerson transformed the rather vague and book-learned perorations of Rousseau on tropical islands and their societies into a fully fledged fashion among the French elite, initially in a letter written to the Paris journal *La Mercure* in February 1769.[165]

Both Rousseau and Commerson adopted the aesthetic potential and isolated aspects of a tropical island as eminently suitable for representing a 'pure' or 'virtuous' environment untouched by the imprint of European hands and customs, as the location for an ideal or uncorrupted society or else as the projected location for a new society, for which an 'untouched' environment would be essential. While Commerson supplemented a predetermined literary vision of an island with empirical science, Saint-Pierre went a stage further, first to

164 Gilbert F. LaFreniere, 'Rousseau and the European roots of environmentalism', *Environmental History Review*, 14 (1990), 41–73. See also David Pepper, *The roots of modern environmentalism*, London, 1984.
165 See Yves Giraud, 'De l'exploration à l'Utopie: Notes sur la formation du mythe de Tahiti', *French Studies*, 31 (1977), 26–41, and P. Commerson, 'Lettre de M. Commerson, docteur en médecine et médecin botaniste du Roi à l'Isle de France, sur la découverte de la nouvelle Cythère', *La Mercure*, 25 Feb. 1769, pp. 196–205.

theorise on the natural world in his *Studies of Nature* and his Platonically inspired *Harmonies of Nature*, and then to refictionalise his island experiences in *Paul et Virginie*, thus further reinforcing the island motif.

Before exploring the crystallisation of these ideas as a consequence of the arrival of Commerson in Otaheite and Mauritius in April and November 1768, it is worth recalling again in detail the historic collusion of the exploring and literary genres which helped to give rise to this intensive focussing on the island motif, particularly by referring to the overwhelming influence of the fashion for 'robinsonnades' on the later development of 'insularism' and Romanticism.

During the sixteenth and seventeenth centuries a growing acquaintance with the landscapes of remote tropical islands (partly a consequence of their increasing importance in the production of cash crops for European markets and their colonisation for this purpose) had stimulated the development of a whole genre of popular literature on islands, particularly after about 1620. While initially this literature had portrayed perceptions of remote islands as paradisal, it grew increasingly diverse and ambivalent in theme during the seventeenth and the early eighteenth century. Like travel literature in general, the island genres even became global in reference and perception, and frequently emerged as the chosen medium for debates about natural processes and the new cosmological knowledge that had come about as a consequence of the work of, for example, Copernicus, Newton and Halley. This new knowledge tended to decentre man and make him appear increasingly subordinate and insignificant – even vulnerable – in the face of large cosmological systems. Instead of being simply a paradise, the island became the medium or metaphor for a much more fundamental questioning of the nature of existence, societies and the self and consequently for fictional or experimental constructions of new societies and analyses of old ones. The strength of the island metaphor as a basis for such questioning was particularly augmented by the use of the island as a convenient vehicle for religious dissent or reformism as well as Utopianism.

Thomas More, Shakespeare and Marvell had all created instances of this phenomenon. However, it was not until Bishop Francis Godwin wrote *The Man in the Moone*, published in 1638, that the themes of dissent, isolation and social experiment were combined in popular literature with more overtly 'ecological' commentaries that expressed an awareness of the limitations of resources available to the European on the real or fictional 'desert' island. As we saw earlier, Godwin's fictional hero, Diego Gonzales, and his companion, a 'negro', were 'constrained to live separately' on the island of St Helena 'because, being always together, victuals would not have fallen out so plenty'. They had to share resources, so that 'if the hunting or fowling of the one succeeded well, the other would finde means to invite him'.

Discussion of the problems confronting the survival of stranded semi-Utopian communities dominated the themes of two further fictional works, Henry Neville's *The Isle of Pines,* published in 1668, and Denis Vairasse d'Alais's *The History of the Severambians,* both of which combined the desert-island theme with the theme of Utopia.[166] They also added the more familiar discussion of the problems of survival on a desert island to explorations of the meaning of gender, new relations between the sexes and new kinds of social hierarchies.[167] It is significant that the island context appeared to permit (perhaps through a psychological distancing) otherwise socially unpalatable experiments in the meaning and social control of gender. It has been suggested that as far back as Columbus the encounter with the tropical island of the Western Ocean was synonymous with the exploration of, search for or conquest of a female other.[168] Later Utopias both before and after Defoe experimented with alterations in the social and political roles of women.[169] This association between island literature and the possibility of movement in the social dynamics of gender and attitudes to sexuality became steadily more important during the eighteenth century and was an essential component of the 'return to nature' which the island allowed, particularly when the island genre acquired Pacific locations. The island context then became increasingly closely connected with critiques of the extinction process and the destructive power of (male?) man, as a threat to wholeness and the unhindered working of 'natural law'.

Probably the first major literary work in French in a desert-island genre was the 'diary' of François Leguat.[170] It was also one of the first works to explicitly decry the threat posed to unspoiled landscape by human intervention and to describe and criticize the process of extinctions. As we have seen, these concerns arose directly out of a dissenting Protestant world view in which the distant unspoilt island served as a location to build 'an earthly paradise' in which an effectively 'unspoilt' society might be attempted, far from the imprint of the society that had persecuted the Huguenots. 'This little new world', as Leguat had called it, 'seemed to us a source of delight.'[171]

Shortly after 1700, the Pacific island was added to those remote real islands

166 For a discussion of the authorship of the latter, see Geoffroy Atkinson, *The extraordinary voyage in French literature before 1700,* London, 1922, p. 39.
167 For a comparable discussion (although one which disregards the crucial island influence), see G. K. Hall, L. F. Jones and S. W. Gooden, eds., *Feminism, Utopia and narrative,* Knoxville, Tenn., 1990.
168 Zamora, 'Abreast of Columbus'.
169 For a comprehensive list of these, see L. T. Sargent, ed., *British and American Utopian literature (1516–1985): An annotated bibliography,* New York, 1988.
170 For a discussion of the disputed veracity of this work, see Chapter 1.
171 See Chapter 1 at n. 71.

of the Atlantic, Caribbean and Indian oceans (St Helena, Mauritius, Ascension and the Caribbean islands) as a favourite literary location for the desert-island genre, with the appearance in popular literature of Juan Fernandez, off the coast of Chile. William Dampier, in *A New Voyage Round the World*, told the story of a Moskito Indian left behind on the island who stayed there for three years living on goat's flesh and fish. This was followed by the much more famous episode in which Alexander Selkirk, having quarrelled with the captain of his ship and expecting it to sink in the course of further voyages, asked to be put ashore on the same Juan Fernandez Island, 'where he continued four years and four months, living on goats and cabbages that grew on trees, turnips, parsnips etc.'[172]

Several accounts of Selkirk's experiences were published, more than one of which emphasised the value of solitude and a simplified and healthier lifestyle. However, one account stands out as making far more specific comments about the relations between consumption and available resources. Richard Steel, writing in 1713, believed that the main applicability and significance of Selkirk's island sojourn could be conceived of in precisely those terms. 'This plain man's story', he writes, 'is a memorable example, that he is happiest who confines his wants to natural necessities; and he that goes further in his desire, increases his wants in proportion to his acquisitions.' Steele went on to demonstrate the superiority of a state of nature over 'civilized' life. Selkirk, he reported, 'frequently bewailed his return to the world, which could not, he said, with all its enjoyments, restore him to the tranquillity of his solitude'.[173]

Thus the theme of life on a desert island was, from the start, invested with environmental, cultural, religious and moral significance made explicit in particular texts by the narrator's comments and generalisations. In other words, the set of motifs that later came to define the general identity of the French (and German) 'robinsonnades' had already by Defoe's time become associated with a definite range of cultural meanings, making up the basis for a distanced 'other' or 'insularism'.[174] These different literary themes of travel and Utopian tales were freely drawn upon by Defoe. He also, however, conveyed a kind of overt commoditisation of the environment that reflects the processes at work in oceanic island and plantation colonies and in some of the 'settlement' literature used to expedite early venture capitalism. Indeed, Robinson Crusoe's physical context appears to have been closely modelled on the descriptions of

172 Edward Cooke, *A voyage to the South Seas and around the world*, London, 1712, p. 37.
173 Richard Steele, 'Talia monstrabat relegens errata retrorum', *The Englishman*, no. 26 (3 Dec. 1713), 121–4.
174 Artur Blaim, *Failed dynamics: The English Robinsonnades of the eighteenth century*, Lublin, 1987, pp. 9–43.

Tobago in one example of this commercial literature, John Poyntz's *The Present Prospect of the Famous and Fertile Island of Tobago*, a book which had been published in 1683 and which was essentially an exercise in highly coloured colonial real-estate advertising. The transformation of the landscape by artificial means which such literature promised was a major theme of *Crusoe*, and Defoe clearly took a great interest in describing the working of natural processes and itemising natural objects. However, Defoe was also clearly interested not only in gradual processes but in the working of catastrophic events as they affected people and the landscape. His book on the 'Great Hurricane' of 1703 and his essay on 'the destruction of St Vincent' are clear indicators of this interest in vast and elemental forces far beyond the control or, more critically, the understanding of man.[175]

Defoe's 'The Destruction of the Isle of St Vincent', an island located just north of Tobago, is particularly important, as it was written at the same time as he was completing *Robinson Crusoe*. It recounts 'the entire destruction of the island in the West Indies by the immediate hand of Nature, directed by Providence, and in a manner astonishing to all the world, the like of which never happened since the Creation, or, at least, since the destruction of the earth by water in the general Deluge'. Defoe noted with concern that hitherto the 'Caribbees have many villages where they live pleasantly, (without being cannibals, we may note!) and without any disturbance'. But they had apparently undergone extinction when the island 'was blown up out of the very sea with a dreadful force, as it were taken up by the roots and blown up from the foundation of the earth'.

We can see here a clear connection between the matter of the survival of the isolated individual in Crusoe and the topic of extinction with respect to an indigenous society – and one about which Defoe speaks favourably. In both cases the vulnerability of man to the power of natural processes is underlined. It was, of course, this retreat to the elemental that was part of the well-known attraction of *Robinson Crusoe* for Rousseau. Even the theme of cannibalism is elemental, even if it can be characterised as a 'colonialist' construction justifying annexation and subjugation, since it relates to a fear of the consequences of resource shortage as well as a fear of the unknown 'other'.

But above all *Crusoe* emphasised the theme of isolation, the struggle for survival by a community or an individual, and, as a corollary, the possibility of extinction. These themes led to a preoccupation with natural processes and, implicitly, to an examination of the meaning and minutiae of society reduced to its bare essentials. Correspondingly, the connection was made between Providence (a critical idea in *Crusoe*) and nature, and the vulnerability of the lone human being to both. As a form of early novel, *Crusoe* dramatised these

175 See Defoe, 'The destruction of the isle of St Vincent', *Mist's Journal*, 5 July 1718.

problems and even objectified them (in the sense that a novel can be a dramatic objectification). By first examining Crusoe's culture objects and beliefs in great detail, Defoe created a kind of one-man anthropology of the self, inviting comparisons with the other non-European cultures which emerge in the story. The predicament of Crusoe also stressed the significance of the relations between him (the lone man) and nature, and consideration of the natural processes operating on him in his isolation and on other living things and cultures. The sheer length of Crusoe's confinement means that the long-term operation of processes and changes *over time* becomes an issue in itself.

The literary and commercial success of *Crusoe* meant that a cult of 'robinsonnades' was created at a time when travel literature was entering an extraordinary period of growth, very much in parallel with the process of territorial colonisation by European maritime powers. *Crusoe* became especially fashionable in France, possibly as an escapist response to a relatively rigid political context. Moreover, the cult of *Crusoe* became so well developed and its themes so frequently imitated that it was probably fundamental to the formulation of the tropical island as the location for complex Utopias and a focus for ideas about social reform and even revolution in mid-eighteenth-century France. Already in Montaigne, in *The Tempest* and in Godwin's *Man in the Moone*, the encounter with non-European peoples had been symbolised as taking place with single individuals or with small groups, who were often characterised as black Africans or American 'Indians'. Sometimes, as in Godwin, newer and more equal relations with non-Europeans were experimented with. But after the ambivalent treatment of Friday in *Crusoe*, such indigenous representation began to offer far more serious models for alternative societies. This transition as it began to take place in Defoe's writings (particularly in 'The Destruction of the Isle of St Vincent') is important, since the response of Commerson and Saint-Pierre to Tahiti and Mauritius was very closely constrained by their exposure to the 'robinsonnades' and to the work of Rousseau, and since both Commerson and Saint-Pierre can be identified as the founders of the French cult of the South Sea island. Their intense need to construct Tahiti and Mauritius in Utopian fashion as a desired 'other' untouched by European society or, alternatively, as sites for nurturing 'better' societies, had considerable practical consequence in terms of land management. For an island to be a Utopia and to be the appropriate setting for a 'harmonious' society, the 'laws of nature' had to be obeyed and human intervention and artifice minimised.

Following this logic, environmentalism (which we can define in part as the safeguarding and nurturing of the natural order) therefore became a vital condition for sustaining a physical and social Utopia. This may well have been a hidden agenda for Poivre, too, for whom the preservation of climate (again, 'obeying the laws of nature') was the atmospheric equivalent of a 'more earthly nature', as his 1767 speeches make clear. In this sense the physical confines of the island attained significance as being contiguous with a cosmic order in which the 'Providence' of nature was exercised through, for example, the control of rainfall. By contrast, Commerson and Saint-Pierre were far more frank as to their motivations and agenda, in which extinction, whether of 'natural' people or 'natural' organisms, is an evil directly to be combated. Furthermore, obedience to 'natural law' implied both an attempt to approach and understand natural society and the self, as well as the necessity to retain and safeguard 'pure' and 'virtuous' nature. The two tasks of the French Utopians, one social, the other environmental, were thus inseparable.

In order to understand the sequence of events in the construction of an environmentalist discourse in the South Seas during the 1760s and the reason why Commerson and Saint-Pierre (and Poivre) so clearly latched on to islands with a predetermined fervour, one needs to understand the power which the island had already acquired as a social motif in French society, and to understand what reformist agendas it implied. To do this one has, above all, to appreciate the role which Rousseau had played by the early 1760s (and continued to play) in strengthening and popularising the island motif and using it to unite and dramatise a whole series of social themes and prescriptions.

By understanding the power and significance of the island motif, one can begin to understand why islands played a vital role in stimulating environmental concern and in provoking thinking about natural processes and then in provoking much more specific theorising about the formation and survival of species. This in turn is connected with the increasingly sophisticated attempts made in the late eighteenth century, particularly by the French, to locate the individual himself, cosmologically, socially and biologically, at a period when an acute sense of existential isolation was developing with the discovery of 'deep' time.[176] The development of a Utopian island literature (especially in the 'robinsonnades') played an important part in this process of the examination of the self, society and the species. Through a simple transference, it led, too, to a particular awareness of extinctions and the part played by human action in ecological change.

Crusoe and Rousseau

Ian Watt has suggested that Robinson Crusoe was 'harassed by fear and ecological degradation'.[177] These two threatening themes related the intertwined

176 See Stephen Jay Gould for a closer discussion of the discovery of deep time in *Time's arrow, Time's cycle: Myth and metaphor in the discovery of geological time*, Cambridge, Mass., 1987.
177 In Ellis, *Twentieth century interpretations of 'Robinson Crusoe'*, p. 150.

problematic of the psychological and physical survival of the individual human being. In this sense Defoe reflected a contemporary religious predicament. As Max Weber has written, the religious individualism of Calvin created among its adherents an historically unprecedented isolation.[178] Undoubtedly the isolation of Crusoe reflected the isolation of Defoe's own life and religious sensibility. One may hazard, then, that Rousseau's obsession with Crusoe reflects the similar inheritance of a Calvinist background. In constructing his own social critique and new society, Rousseau experimented with a variety of natural and Utopian structures, something one might have expected from an adherent of a religion which set specific store by an earthly paradise. Indeed, one may surmise that it was natural for Rousseau, as a Calvinist by origin, to be interested in earthly Utopias as such and therefore to identify very closely with Crusoe. Rousseau took particular pride early in his career in calling himself a 'citizen of Geneva', a city which had been imbued for two hundred years with a Calvinist creed that implied an intrinsic holiness. Geneva had seen itself as a New Jerusalem, a New Zion set amidst a corrupt Europe. In 1755 Rousseau had considered it 'an idyllic city', but afterwards he rejected this notion and moved on to other symbols to support his social idealism and narratives, especially in *La nouvelle Héloïse*.

In his enthusiasm for *Robinson Crusoe* and in his implicit sympathy for Defoe's way of thinking, Rousseau found himself the inheritor of an innovative and complex set of ideas. Defoe had been, like Rousseau, a dissenter in a broad sense as well as an outspoken critic of the corruptions of English court life in the first three decades of the eighteenth century, which he saw as a return to the amorality of Charles II's reign. He saw the 'natural order' as being threatened by this reversion.[179] One may legitimately argue that Defoe's critical vision of his own social background found an appropriate fictional form in the context of an island. There the writer found an imaginative retreat from worldly evil and a setting which offered the opportunity for restoration and even conversion and spiritual deliverance. An essential part of this restoration was a changed valuation of worldly goods, money in particular, as well as a renewed appreciation of the gifts and merits of nature and the moral goodness of a more basic interaction with it. In undergoing this transition Crusoe effectively created a new society, even if it was only a society of one, of a solitary, and of a kind that Rousseau repeatedly professed himself to want to constitute. In essence, then, Crusoe represented 'natural' man.

Two main elements, it may be argued, are present in Crusoe: detachment and a journey. The element of detachment, enabling the observer to see a

178 See James F. Jones, *La nouvelle Héloïse: Rousseau and Utopia*, Geneva, 1977.
179 See D. Blewett, *Defoe's art of fiction: Robinson Crusoe, Moll Flanders, Colonel Jack and Roxana*, Buffalo, N.Y., 1969.

society from the outside, even in a fantasy, was essential in the sense in which
Defoe was a novelist, even if a heavily autobiographical one. He was also a
pioneer in the art of travel writing. This discourse, too, permitted an element
of detachment and the sense not only of an appreciation of variety in scenery
and variety within a society, but a sense of a search for a better society that
might actually have been lost. The roots of this detachment lay, it seems, in
rejection or criticism of the corrupt world of the city and the resort to a
journey to the country, towards nature. Even on the island itself Defoe replicated this division of town and country, symbolising an innate alienation of
the urban, capitalistic, money-bound condition (a condition about which Defoe was highly ambivalent) from the country. Crusoe has his 'town house' on
the shore and his 'country bower' secluded in the middle of the island. All
these innovative elements appealed strongly to Rousseau: the encapsulation of
social commentary and fantasy in the novel, rejection of the city in favour of
the country and the action of spiritual journey towards a new society. These
were elements which Defoe and Rousseau (in fantasy) and Poivre, Commerson
and their colleagues (in reality) actively sought to realise.

Rousseau and Defoe both wrote works characterised by accounts of journeys
to an earthly paradise in which the individual or a small group encounters
wild nature and speaks highly of it in terms of spiritual deliverance. Defoe's
work may have been seminal in provoking the transition between rather limited conceptual notions, in which the botanical garden or the tropical island
passed as a milieu for the recreation of the paradisal, towards a more comprehensive discourse in which untouched nature as a whole becomes the location of non-urban redemptive potential.

This dynamic shift away from the idealised city and ultimately to the symbol of the tropical island is dramatised with precision in *La nouvelle Héloïse*.
To some extent the conflict in Rousseau's mind between the ideal city and
the ideal island remained endemic, perhaps as a continuation of a clash between the urban idea of Plato's *Republic* and the more rural image of More's
Utopia, two works to which he had long been attached.[180] But there were other
major literary themes that had led Rousseau towards the island motif expressed in *La nouvelle Héloïse*. Not least of these was the early pastoralism of
Honoré d'Urfé's *Astrée*, the work which also featured so prominently for the
writer of the diary of François Leguat in inculcating the novel taste for a
pristine nature, one previously untouched by Europeans. Rousseau hoped, in
some senses, to reconstruct a better past or Golden Age *in the present*. Féne-
lon's *Telemachus* (a work which fascinated Rousseau) featured a Golden Age,

180 Although one might note that in 1765 Rousseau chose to carry out a commission to draw
up a new constitution not for a city state but for the island of Corsica. See Jones, *La nouvelle
Héloïse*, p. 22.

but it may well have been the island setting of Vairasse's *History of the Sev-erambians* that sharpened the social significance of the island for Rousseau.

In *La nouvelle Héloïse*, perhaps the most important and widely known topos in French eighteenth-century literature, Rousseau's hero Saint-Preux moves from Geneva to the capital of the Valais canton at Sion (Zion). Here Rousseau postulates his hero's experiencing a Utopian garden at Etange and a second Utopian structure, the complex of mountains, valleys and peasant people of the Valais. And yet for Saint-Preux these were not sufficient, and Rousseau goes on to explore a third set of Utopian structures, the tropical desert islands of Tinian and Juan Fernandez in the Pacific. Tinian (actually an island close to Guam in the Western Pacific and north of the Solomon Islands) had been described in accounts of Anson's Pacific voyages of 1745 and seems to have fascinated Rousseau to the extent that it emerges as the favoured Utopian topos in *La nouvelle Héloïse*.[181] From accounts of Anson's voyage we know that on the occasion of arrival at both Juan Fernandez and Tinian the ship's crew was desperate for sustenance and exhausted and sick from a long and dangerous journey. Rousseau clearly identified with these accounts in a pro-jective sense. New social and physical vistas were needed, he appears to have thought, as a relief from the moral and social exhaustion of European urban life. Juan Fernandez had, of course, been Selkirk's desert island. In *Héloïse* Rousseau makes a specific link between the imagery of an 'Elysium' garden in the Valais and the environments of the two Pacific islands. In fact, it was the 'wildness' of the islands visited by Anson (as told by his biographer Walter and specifically illustrated in his account of the voyage) that most attracted Rousseau and that he wished to reintroduce into Europe – or, more specifi-cally, into the enclosed garden context of Etange or elsewhere (see Plate 13). This reintroduction symbolised a wider attempt to rebuild a 'virtuous' or 'natural' society by restoring and elevating its suppressed and innate 'wild' elements, a core theme of Romanticism.[182] But if Romanticism such as this was derived from an 'imperial' journey and involved the contradictory co-option of tropical images, how much better it must have seemed to revert to a natural order or society outside Europe! In fact, this was a main part of the project of Commerson and his colleagues. It is remarkable, however, how prominent Crusoe's island remains as the core inspiring image of Rousseau's Romantic constructions and fiction. But there were deeper reasons for this than the merely aesthetic or voyeuristic aspects of the Defoe tale.

Robinson Crusoe had enjoyed a far more enthusiastic reception in France than it had in England, a reception to which Rousseau added the weight of

---

181 Christopher Thacker, ' "O Tinian! O Juan-Fernandez!": Rousseau's 'Elysée' and Anson's desert islands', *Garden History*, 5:9 (1977), 41–7.
182 Christopher Thacker, *The wildness pleases: The origins of Romanticism*, London, 1983.

A View of the Watering Place at Tenian.

A View of the Commodores Tent *at the Island of* Juan Fernandes.

Plate 13. Illustrations of the Pacific islands of Tinian (Top) and Juan Fernandez (Bottom) published in *A Voyage to the South Seas and to Many Other Parts of the World Performed from 1740 to 1741, by Another of the Squadron* (London, 1744). These were the drawings that proved so influential in stimulating Rousseau's articulation of a Romantic discourse of tropical islands, the forerunner to Commerson's cult of the South Pacific island.

his approval. Indeed, in *Emile* he indicates that he considers it to be the one book that should be required reading for all children.[183] As Crusoe had done, so the child could learn in a utilitarian sense, and Crusoe's concern was with things, sensations and feelings, not with words and abstractions. The island offered the opportunity for a new collective childhood and the hope for a new kind of society, one in which a new rational unity might replace the instinctive unity of the primitive state.

For the Romantics, mountains, clouds, the sea, thunder and lightning, forests and wild animals had all, like islands, become objects of idealisation and preoccupation, representing elements in the human condition threatened or alienated by the increasingly complex pressures on the individual imposed by European society. In their discourses a very firm differentiation became established between the European urban world and the 'other' of the tropical world, integral to which was the adoption of a whole new series of natural symbols or preoccupations. But the most important of these was the island. The direct influence of Defoe in effecting this kind of transition, particularly through Rousseau and his disciple Bernardin de Saint-Pierre, should not be underestimated.

The image of the island gradually became more complex in its role as a major cultural metaphor in western and Romantic thought, far beyond the symbolism of the 'robinsonnades'. However, it also became more complex as metaphor in Rousseau's own thinking. For him the island seems to have become the ultimate refuge, even to offer symbolic return to the comfort and security of the womb.[184] More important, Rousseau further developed the connections between the 'purity' or 'virtue' of an oceanic island and the virtue of the garden which he had first made in *La nouvelle Héloïse*. These connections go some way towards explaining the similar and extraordinary symbolic significance of islands and botanical gardens in the minds of Poivre, Bernardin de Saint-Pierre and Philibert Commerson. Rousseau went some way in his *confessions* to expand on the connections between the older symbolism of the botanical garden and the related one of an island. During September 1765 he had lived on a small island in the lake of Bienne in Switzerland, where,

> taking the entire island as my botanical garden, whenever I needed to make or verify some observation I would run through the woods or across the meadows, my book under my arm; there I would lie prone on the ground next to the plant in question in order to examine it in its site. This method was a great help to me in getting to know the plants in their natural state, as they are before they have been cultivated and denatured

183 R. Niklaus, *A literary history of France: The eighteenth century, 1715–1789*, London, 1970, p. 201.

184 Ibid., p. 204.

by the hand of man . . . sometimes I would cry out with tears in my voice: 'O Nature! O my Mother!'[185]

This passage is useful for gaining some insight into part of the psychological significance of the botanical garden and its now established connection with island refugia. First Rousseau equates the island with the female part and with the return to woman, a theme which Commerson would soon act out in reality in a very distinctive way. But Rousseau also related the female gender to the natural and, more specifically, to the botanical.

This connection foreshadows a connection between the discovery of an apparently innocent, uncomplicated society on Tahiti and the discovery of new plants by Commerson. Certainly in the case of Rousseau, plants in their unspoilt habitats stood as anthropocentric representations of a natural human order, one which had not been 'denatured . . . by the hand of man'. Rousseau was an authoritative contemporary commentator on the merits of various plant classification systems, and it seems apparent in this context that his attempt to analyse and classify the societies and interactions of plants was directly analogous to a critical analysis of human society and himself – his other main interests. Voyages such as that made by Bougainville were necessarily enriching botany with a treasure-house of new information as well as stimulating more systematic methods of classification. 'Lost in this mere labyrinth', Rousseau observed in letters written specially to 'a young lady', 'the botanists were obliged to sew a thread to extricate themselves from it . . . they attached themselves therefore at last seriously to method.'[186]

The island as an object of study short-circuited difficulties of global classification while satisfying most of the requirements of a Utopia. Moreover, it possessed advantages a garden might not have, in the sense that a garden was something contrived. Indeed, a garden might be considered denatured, to use Rousseau's term.

Rousseau had a good deal more to say about the two months he spent with his family on the Ile de Saint-Pierre in the lake of Bienne. 'I was allowed to pass', he tells us, 'only two months on this island, but I could have passed there two years, two centuries, and the whole of eternity without being weary for one moment . . . I count these two months as the happiest time of my life and so happy, that it would have sufficed me throughout life, without for a single moment allowing in my soul the desire for a different state.'[187]

In the *Reveries* Rousseau was far more specific about the vulnerability of the island in a practical sense and in the role it could play as a surrogate location for the restoration of the individual or as a place where integrity or

185 *The reveries of a solitary*, trans. J. C. Fletcher, London, 1927, p. 104.
186 *Letters on the elements of botany addressed to a lady*, trans. T. Martyn, London, 1782, p. 9.
187 *The reveries of a solitary*, p. 105.

truth might be sought. This latter was the very motive, incidentally, which had driven him to seek truth in the minutiae of botany, conceived on a global scale of classification. Thus he described the basin of the lake of Bienne as having 'a form almost round, containing two islands in its midst, one inhabited and cultivated . . . the other more small, desert and fallow, which will be destroyed in the end by the transportations of earth which are being carried out incessantly in order to repair the damage which the storms do to the greater island. It is thus that the substance of the weak is always employed to the profit of the powerful.'[188]

A direct connection was being made here between the erosion of the recreative potential of the individual and the erosive damage caused to the valued island environment: precisely the phenomenon which had concerned Poivre, who had hesitated in making an explicit connection between the integrity of the individual and the physical environment but instead had drawn a parallel with the moral economy of the state. This option, it might be argued, was not available to Rousseau in view of his prior criticism of the state.

This, then, was the kind of thinking which both directly informed Commerson and in a less direct way moulded the intellectual background against which other Frenchmen viewed tropical islands, not least among them Bernardin de Saint-Pierre and Pierre Poivre on Mauritius – although it should be emphasised that Poivre was also the inheritor of a physiocratic tradition which was disliked and vigorously contested by Rousseau.

Commerson and Utopian science on Mauritius, 1768–72

Two important arrivals during 1768, at Tahiti and at Mauritius, set the scene for the concretisation of the French South Sea island cult and its concomitant environmentalism. By November 1769 both arrivals were being widely discussed in Paris. The second, the arrival of Philibert Commerson in Mauritius in November, represented the culmination of an extraordinary physical and mental journey which had reached its most significant point in an earlier arrival and encounter between Bougainville's expedition and the inhabitants of Otaheite (Tahiti). This earlier encounter made a great impression on Commerson, and there is little doubt that it deeply coloured his perceptions of the socially very different Isle de France, peopled by his own countrymen and served by slaves, and that his opinions found a receptive audience in Pierre Poivre. Bougainville had named Tahiti 'La Nouvelle Cythère' when the islands were first sighted and even before *La Boudeuse* had actually attained an anchorage. By using the name 'Cythère' (Gr. *Kythera*) Bougainville was making

188 Ibid., p. 104.

deliberate reference to classical visions of an idyllic island society. More specifically, he was alluding to the island dwelling of Aphrodite, Greek goddess of beauty. This idea had been popularised in France at the end of the seventeenth century by Watteau in his painting *The Embarkation for Cythera*, and it may have been this image that Bougainville was rediscovering. Philibert Commerson, however, was puzzled and apparently unhappy with the use of the name Cythera and preferred 'Utopia', a term more fitted to his own wishful but more modern preconceptions of the island and its society. His own responses to Tahiti were summarised in a letter written to the Paris journal *La Mercure* in February 1769.[189] This long letter, written when Commerson had already been in Mauritius for three months, was based on his own (still unpublished) diaries of the voyage.[190] As a text it provides us with a short but eloquent guide to his ideas about Tahiti and to his state of mind. Like Bougainville, Commerson was much taken up with the island in its 'female' manifestations, especially with regard to open displays of unashamed sexuality, which to Commerson were an acceptable and entirely suitable part of a distinctive projected polity. 'I can assure you', he wrote,

> that it [Tahiti] is one spot upon the earth's surface which is inhabited by
> men without either vices, prejudices, wants or dissensions. Born under
> the loveliest of skies, they are supported by the fruits of a soil so fertile
> that cultivation is scarcely required and they are governed rather by a
> sort of family father than by a monarch . . . they recognise no other god
> save Love. Every day is consecrated to him and the whole island is his
> temple . . . the women are meet rivals of the Georgians in beauty; they
> are full of . . . the graces and are entirely without clothing.[191]

Tahiti was, Commerson said, a 'real Utopia', a term which, he explained, 'Thomas More gave to his ideal republic'.[192] The cynical observer, he warned, might fail 'to recognise the condition of natural man, tainted by no Prejudice and following without remorse the sweet impulses of his instincts, always sure guides, for they have not yet degenerated with reason'.[193] Incidentally, even the worldly Bougainville was overwhelmed by Tahiti and delighted by its beneficence and thought that he had been 'transported into a Garden of Eden . . . we crossed a plain of grass', he remembered, 'covered with beautiful fruit

189 Commerson, letter in *La Mercure*, 25 Nov. 1769, pp. 196–205. I am indebted to Adrian
   Walford for his translation.
190 Paris, Archives of the BCMNHN: MSS nos. 2214 (pp. 1–700) and 699. MS 2214 has two
   sections of relevance here, entitled 'Fertilité de l'isle et ses productions' and 'Description des
   sauvages qui habitent les isles: le 29/30 juin 1768'.
191 MS 2214, p. 197.
192 Ibid., p. 124.
193 Ibid., p. 125.

trees and intersected with rivulets that maintained a delightful coolness in the air, without any of the disadvantages produced by humidity'. The climate was so healthful, he added, 'that despite the hard labour we undertook . . . none fell ill'.[194] It is significant that a description of Eden could actually provoke a description of its micro-climate, and that a healthful climate should be the supreme test of the acceptability of a newly encountered land. However, this was becoming typical of contemporary French travellers in the tropics, who were sensitive both to the practical problems posed by arduous climates and to current theories about the societal implications of particular climates.[195] Noteworthy too are Commerson's specific allusions to the fruit trees of Tahiti. Fruit trees were the appropriate accoutrement of Eden, and Commerson went into horticultural detail on this score. 'Everything in their homes', he noted, 'manifests the greatest intelligence . . . their navigator is directed by observation of the stars . . . their fruit trees are so planted at judicious intervals that they have not the tiresome monotony of orchards, though retaining all that is agreeable and pleasant in the latter.'[196]

The Tahitians were, he added, 'prudent in all matters'. Here, it seems, lay at least part of the inspiration for the emphasis on tree planting in the first Conservation Ordinance promulgated little over a year later in Mauritius and the main inspiration for the regulations directing the planting of fruit trees.[197]

Commerson chose to draw a specific comparison between the generous Tahitian temperament, insensible, so he thought, of property rights, and the suspicious and grasping inclinations of the French sailors on the *Boudeuse.* 'Of such a nature', he asserted, 'is the sailor's soul (indeed, as for it, J.-J. Rousseau judiciously places a mark of interrogation and of doubts about its existence!).'[198] Commerson made this remark as an adjoinder to a discussion in which he surveyed the whole field of property rights, the concept of a 'state of nature' and 'natural equity', a discourse which clearly owed a good deal to a reading of Rousseau but which also betrays a conviction that arose out of something more than the dictates of literary fashion. To avert any likely censure of the unfavourable comparisons he made between a corrupt society in France and the society of Tahiti, Commerson observed in *La Mercure:*

> It was not my intention to entertain people . . . every person sees and
> observes in his own way. I am a missionary naturalist. I ought to speak

194 L. A. de Bougainville, *A voyage around the world performed in the years 1766–1769,* trans. J. R. Forster and G. Forster, London, 1772, p. 156.

195 See Chapter 4.

196 Pasfield-Oliver, *Life of Commerson,* p. 126.

197 However, one should not forget that contemporary French agricultural writers, such as Duhamel du Monceau, had been equally keen to imitate the methods laid down in dictums of John Evelyn on the desirability of large-scale fruit-tree planting.

198 Pasfield-Oliver, *Life of Commerson,* p. 131.

correspondingly. I have seen peoples still happily enjoying their primitive instincts; I have represented them by the light of truth. They wore nothing but floating gauze; should I have dressed them like Lapps or Eskimos?[199]

Commerson was, however, clearly strongly influenced by Rousseau, and to some extent his reactions had been anticipated by Rousseau in *La nouvelle Héloïse* when Saint-Preux gives an account of his protracted journey across the oceans with Anson's expedition. Rewarded after the travail of journeying, Saint-Preux reaches a distant place where 'I stayed for three months on a deserted and delightful island that offered a gentle and moving image of the age-long beauty of nature and that seemed to have been confined to the end of the world in order to provide a refuge for persecuted innocence and love.'[200]

Nevertheless, Commerson's standpoint was genuine enough on its own account, and his statement 'I am a missionary naturalist. I ought to speak accordingly' is an important one, not least in understanding his dedication to his later work on Mauritius and the tendency to deify nature which he shared with Poivre and Bernardin de Saint-Pierre. The expression 'missionary naturalist' epitomised a combination of religiosity and valuing the search after the empirical natural truth that was relatively new in European thought. Whilst owing much to Rousseau, Commerson's thinking represented a philosophy far beyond Rousseau's in action and practical implication. Thus Commerson extended the older notion of re-creating a botanical Eden encapsulating species in a single hortus to develop a much more complex view of the tropical world. This was an approach which extended the idea of an unfallen paradise out beyond the realm of the botanical garden or small island to embrace the totality of the natural world that remained, as Commerson had found the southern oceans, almost entirely untouched by western man. The whole tropical world which he had circumnavigated in the course of his botanical and taxonomic work was one in which an individual might retreat from the personal disappointments and social corruption of modern French society. According to this construction, the unspoilt nature and society of the tropics were a redemptive refuge. 'My plants', he wrote, 'my beloved plants have consoled me for everything; I found in them Nepenthes, curare, dulce.'[201]

For this redemptive purpose the island was the ideal allegorical, practical and botanical symbol and desired place of abode. As Commerson frequently pointed out, the prospect of knowing and itemising the whole of the plant kingdom was well outside the bounds of possibility:

199 Ibid., p. 133.
200 Rousseau, *Oeuvres complètes: Avec des notes historiques*, 8 vols., Paris, 1834, II, p. 413.
201 Pasfield Oliver, *Life of Commerson*, p. 202.

I venture to say, however, that I have already made my own hands a
collection of 25,000 species and I am not afraid to declare that there exists
at least four or five times as many species on the earth's whole surface,
for I cannot reasonably, so far, flatter myself that I have gathered a fourth
or fifth part of the world's vegetation.[202]

By contrast, then, Commerson's residence on Mauritius offered the possibility
of knowing the entire flora of the whole island, or a whole small world. For
the island had by this time, as Commerson exemplified, come to represent an
increasingly powerful and frequently employed metaphor of the world or of
a new way of life chosen in preference to a rejected older one. Within such a
concept, the search for truth, mediated through an acquisition of botanical
knowledge, could well have been ascribed as the appropriate task of a 'missionary naturalist'.

For Commerson, the outstanding feature of Tahiti had consisted less in its
natural history than in the society he observed there. Nevertheless, the project
of preconceiving and perceiving an idyllic society was closely bound up with
the project of empirical observation and analysis of the non-human species
with which Commerson was more professionally concerned. Quite simply, the
observations of a 'different' human society focussed attention on real (cultural
and natural) differences and therefore on the operation of natural processes
over time, the essential step to understanding and criticising the human impact
and to questioning the fixity and mode of the formation of species. These
topics arose in the *Mercure* essay directly out of a description of the qualities
of the *human* society. The sequence and underlying semantic of this essay is
therefore worth close attention. Overall the essay shifts rapidly from the Utopian to the strictly empirical. First, Commerson describes the island as Utopian and thus possessing a meritorious polity. Above all, the people of
'Utopie', he says, have no kings, but merely a paterfamilias. The allusion here
is obvious. Other qualities of the society are mentioned, all diametrically opposed to those of France. The motif of naturalness is twofold, represented in
a 'natural' uninhibited exercise of public sexual freedom and in the social
position of women: They are apparently 'not at all subjugated'.[203] This was a
matter very close to Commerson's heart, by virtue of his own wife's very
unusual personal history. On their first disembarking on a beach in Tahiti, it
was pointed out by the Tahitians that 'Jean Bart', Commerson's 'manservant',
was actually a woman. The real Jeanne Baret had in fact boarded the ship at
Le Havre in disguise with the intention of sailing around the world. She had
become Commerson's paramour. She was socially restored to her sex, appro-

202 Ibid., p. 203.
203 Ibid., p. 198.

priately, only on arrival at Tahiti. Later she became the royal botanist's wife, collaborator and archivist.[204]

Even language on Tahiti, Commerson asserts, was 'natural', clear and without guile. Similarly, the Tahitian agricultural and arboricultural technology was appropriate and carefully crafted. Finally, the Tahitians, he believed, were pacifist and even detested metal because of its connection with weapons. This wishful construction of a desired society (which actually bore little relation to any objective or social reality) led, perhaps logically in the essay, to a discussion of the *origins* and *affinities* of such a *different*, clearly untypical and (above all) insular and isolated society. Here Commerson as the questioning naturalist finally steps out as a distinct and analysing persona from the disguise of the 'projecting' Utopian. In using Tahitian society to cast light on Europeans, Commerson found that he had raised a related question, that is, how could the Tahitians have come to be so very different? In other words, by creating and promoting the exotic dyadic as a way of criticising European society, the problem of process and origins had, inevitably, to be addressed.

The critical problem for Commerson was to address the role of migrations and displacement (extinctions) in explaining *variation* as an alternative to simply postulating spontaneous generation of species. 'It will doubtless be asked', Commerson begins his questioning,

> from what continent, what people have these islanders come? As if it were only from emigration to emigration that the continents and the isles could have been peopled. As if we could not in the very hypothesis of emigrations, which we cannot avoid admitting from time to time, suppose over the whole earth a primitive people, which received and incorporated the emigrant people, or which was chased out, or destroyed by them. For myself, considering this question as a Naturalist, I would willingly admit, everywhere, these Protoplast peoples, of whom despite the physical revolutions that have occurred on the different parts of our globe, there has always been preserved at least a couple on each of those [parts] that have remained inhabited, and it is only as a historian of human revolutions, that I could deal with all these true or supposed emigrations; I see, besides, very distinct races of men. These races together could well have produced variations; but only a mythologist could explain how the whole would have emerged from common stock: thus I do not see why the good Tahitians might not be sprung from their own soil, I mean, descended from ancestors who have always been Tahitians, going back as far as the people most jealous of its antiquity. Still less do I see to what nation we

204 A full account of this amazing episode is to be found in ibid., pp. 83–7. Jeanne Baret was probably the first woman to circumnavigate the world, certainly the first on a scientific expedition.

should ascribe the honour of the colony of Tahiti, always maintained
within the bounds of simple nature.[205]

There is little doubt that the island situation and motif, in conjunction with
an ideologically 'differentiated' people, stimulated Commerson to consider the
role of migration in bringing about variation in 'races'. Of course it is clear
that his hostility to the innate corruption of a European race inhibited him
from allowing explicitly here an evolutionary or migratory connection with
the characteristics of Tahitians. But one does not need to take this *ideological*
difficulty too seriously. Commerson had, partly through his own voyaging
(migration) via islands and partly through his unrivalled knowledge of species
numbers and variations, stumbled on the significance of migration over time
in explaining the incidence of variation. This was a concept extraordinarily
close to that put forward nearly thirty years later by Cuvier, and very specific
and innovative in the thinking of Commerson. Through his influence on Lamarck and Geoffroy Saint-Hilaire, Cuvier has generally been thought of as
the originator of this 'migration' concept, in which a single stock is postulated
as the ancestor of later variants. However, it seems that Commerson may well
have anticipated Cuvier. Moreover, his personal relationship with Bernardin
de Saint-Pierre (himself a close associate of Cuvier, Lamarck and Saint-
Hilaire) suggests that Commerson's thinking on this subject may actually have
had some impact.

The significance of the passage on race or species variation in the *Mercure*
letter is that Commerson had drawn attention for himself to the connections
between *process* and species. This can provide one with important clues in
explaining his later interest in species protection and the prevention of deforestation on Mauritius. However, there was another important connection between species and 'race differentiation' (with regard to corrupt Europeans and
'idyllic' islanders). 'A society of men once corrupted', Commerson says, 'cannot be regenerated in its entirety . . . colonies take with them everywhere the
vices of their metropolis.' The implications of this statement can be guessed
at, at the very least. By preventing alterations to the 'naturalness' of an island
in terms of species, forests, climate and an economy (physiocratic) organised
according to 'natural laws', the virtues of a non-European and non-corrupt
Utopia could be maintained. This would be Commerson's particular contribution to Poivre's project on Mauritius.

However, in transferring the concept of either a social or natural Utopia to
Mauritius there were glaring differences to be tackled. Far from being a Uto-
pia, the colony was a slave state of 18,000 blacks and 2,000 Europeans.[206]
Bernardin de Saint-Pierre pointed out with some irony that when Aoatorau,

205 Ibid., pp. 201–3.
206 Toussaint, *History of Mauritius*, pp. 38, 53.

the Tahitian exhibited in Paris, passed through Mauritius he was amazed to see men of his own colour in chains. This in itself was an oblique reference to Poivre's failure, in spite of some effort, to improve the condition of the slaves to any serious extent.[207] For Poivre, who had characterised the colonists as a 'virtuous people', the disillusionment he experienced in this respect was a bitter blow. But it was a disillusionment that may have encouraged him to pursue his conservation objectives more doggedly than otherwise. As Bernardin de Saint-Pierre wrote in 1772, 'Nature compensates for our disappointments in the study of mankind, as we cannot but trace throughout the whole the harmony with which intelligent beneficence unites to render the system complete.'[208] Where Commerson, the scientist, found his solace in contemplation of what he conceived of as a harmonious botanical system, Bernardin de Saint-Pierre was compelled, on an island that was actually the antithesis of a social Utopia, to take refuge in a natural harmony, or 'ecology', possessed of its own 'beneficence'. In fact it was Poivre himself who taught Bernardin de Saint-Pierre the elements of the natural history of the island, a training that permitted him not only to write the natural history of the island but eventually to succeed to the directorate of the Jardin des Plantes in Paris during the Revolution at the same time as being appointed professor of ethics at the University of Paris.[209]

An examination of the careers and preoccupations of Commerson and Bernardin de Saint-Pierre demonstrates the very permeable divide between enthusiasm for the study of natural history and enthusiasm for the study of society, along with the extent of the interdependence between the two. In Bernardin de Saint-Pierre's case this easy osmosis was directly related to what he saw as the imminent destruction of the Mauritius environment and the disappearance of its species. In contrast to Poivre, who concentrated almost entirely on the threat of deforestation, Bernardin de Saint-Pierre concerned himself with species disappearance. 'Formerly', he recorded, 'a great many flamingoes were also found about this isle; this is a large and beautiful sea fowl of a rose colour; they say also that three of them did yet remain, but I never saw one.'[210] The seashores, he noted, 'formerly abounded with turtles, which are now but rarely found'.[211] But he also observed the changes wrought by deforestation. 'The rivers marked in this plain were entirely dried up', he remarked on one occasion, referring to a phenomenon to which he had drawn

207 J.-H. Bernardin de Saint-Pierre, *A voyage to the Isle of France*, trans. H. Hunter, London, 1800, p. 208.
208 Ibid., p. 143.
209 *DMB*, p. 196; Niklaus, *Literary history of France*, p. 359.
210 *Voyage to the Isle of France*, p. 175.
211 Ibid., p. 77. See also North-Coombes, *Histoire des tortues*.

the attention of Poivre and interpreted as a result of deforestation.[212] Bernardin de Saint-Pierre's main concern, however, lay in the fate of the individual specimens of flora and fauna, to which he afterwards attached much meaning in his literary works.[213] Part of this enhanced meaning originated in the very anthropomorphic nature of Saint-Pierre's perceptions of species. This was transparent in his use of simile. 'I had much rather look upon a tree as a republic', he wrote on one occasion,[214] alluding to his youthful aspiration to found an ideal republic, an idea which had surfaced shortly after he finished his training in engineering.[215] Nature, for Saint-Pierre, had become a solace and possibly a substitute for or an allegory of a deity. This deification of nature meant that, when the life of bird or animal species could be closely identified with the human condition, the possibility of extinction on an island such as Mauritius attained an enhanced significance. Buffon, the first main discussant of extinction, had been strongly influenced by his knowledge of the fate of the dodo on Mauritius at the hands of the Dutch, and Bernardin de Saint-Pierre almost certainly knew of Buffon's remarks on the subject.[216]

Growing awareness of the process of species extinction and the feared impact of deforestation were decisive in motivating attempts to control the depredations of European settlers on Mauritius. As we have seen, the response to both phenomena was closely linked to social preoccupations and anxieties, for which practical solutions must have seemed elusive, if not impossible. Perceptions of species extinction (comparable to the 'denaturing' mentioned by Rousseau) certainly related, at one level, to notions of the threat posed to the individual within a society. Deforestation, on the other hand, through its believed connection with climate, threatened both the moral and the colonial economy in a far more direct way. It therefore remained more politically significant for a physiocrat like Poivre.

The tendency towards a Rousseauist deification of nature involved, almost inevitably, a new stress on the inherent value of investigations of scientific and empirical truth in the 'natural' system. Nevertheless, conventional religious conviction remained important for such men as Commerson, for whom the defence of scientific truth was directly analogous to the search for religious truth.[217]

---

212 Saint-Pierre, *Voyage to the Isle of France*, p. 173.

213 Ibid., pp. 175–6.

214 Ibid., p. 91.

215 Niklaus, *Literary history of France*, p. 359.

216 See Strickland and Melville, *The dodo and its kindred*, and Glacken, *Traces on the Rhodian shore*, pp. 667–9.

217 Pasfield-Oliver, *Life of Commerson*, p. 236. Furthermore, Commerson put this forward in the course of defending the right to question secondary causes and in particular to question notions of species non-mutability.

The greatest problem for the embryonic scientific community on Mauritius was a lack of assured institutional continuity. By his own efforts as intendant and through the temporary support of the Ministére de la Marine during the Choiseul period, Poivre had secured an unprecedented professionalisation of science and natural history as an integral part of government policy and economic planning. This was, one could argue, a logical culmination of the physiocratic programme of a kind that had never been attained by its originators in France.

But this professionalisation, unparalleled in any European country, had little in the way of institutional backing and was instead dependent on the personalities of Poivre and his friends. In 1770 an awareness of this deficiency encouraged Commerson to propose the idea of an 'Académie' for the Isle de France. It was to concern itself with exotics, the history of tropical diseases and everything in natural history which could not be investigated in Europe. Tropical agriculture and economic botany were to be important features of its work. Such an institution would both safeguard specialised knowledge and secure the functions of such trained scientists as Commerson. Poivre, of course, looked favourably upon the idea.[218] Even so, the project did not see the light of day during the lifetimes of the two men, although it did provide the seed for the emergence on Mauritius in later times of scientific societies which had the same objectives.[219] Commerson's 'Académie' project anticipated by eight years the founding of the Batavia Society of Arts and Sciences, by fifteen years the foundation of the Asiatic Society of Bengal and by twenty-six years the Linnaean Society of London.

In the event, Commerson failed to live long enough (he died in 1773) to be able to persuade the state to bridge permanently the conceptual gap between the accepted role of the scientist in accompanying maritime exploring expeditions and a role for the scientist in a sense that went beyond temporary patronage. As a result, the lack of institutional permanence that persisted on Mauritius made it hard for Poivre to ensure the future of his conservation programmes after his departure. They were too closely connected with individualistic scientific interpretations of the impact of man on the tropical environment, which had not as yet become widely accepted by scientists, let alone governments. The arrival in 1769 of Desroches, the new governor, high-

218 Ibid., p. 176.
219 See M. Ly-Tio-Fane, 'Joseph Hubert and the Société des Sciences et Arts de l'Isle de France, 1801–1802', *Proceedings of the Royal Society of Arts and Sciences of Mauritius*, 11 (1961), 221–46. This paper discusses the origins of the first scientific society in the Mascarenes, created in 1801 under the initiative of the scientific staff of Commodore Baudin, the explorer of the Terres Australes, and of the colonial savants Lislet Geoffroy and Joseph Hubert. In 1811 Charles Telfair founded the Royal Society of Arts and Sciences of Mauritius on similar principles.

lighted this problem. Poivre was forced to fight a running battle with him, much as he had with Dumas, to ensure that the concessions regulations were adhered to. The one measure that did ensure some continuity, the existence in law of the 1769 Forest Ordinance, strengthened his position with the Ministère de la Marine. In February 1770, for instance, the ministry agreed to strengthen the provisions for protecting a proportion of forest cover in concessions, securing the protection of half the area of a concession instead of only the quarter laid down in the 1769 ordinance. This was a major achievement.[220] Even so, other land-use proposals made by Poivre were now watered down by Praslin, under direct pressure from the mercantilist Desroches.[221] In retrospect, Poivre seems to have relied heavily on Commerson's support, as most of his concessions to Desroches occurred during the absence of Commerson from Mauritius between October 1770 and November 1771. These difficulties were reported by Poivre in August 1771. Conscious of the probable consequences of his political isolation, he wrote that 'the ensuing deforestation will be irredeemable'. Poivre was given considerable support by the garrison commander, Steinauer, and by Bernardin de Saint-Pierre as chief engineer, in his attempts to prevent new bouts of reckless clearance. Nevertheless, his conservation efforts were now sharply contested, despite his refusal to sign almost all the forest-clearance concessions advocated by Desroches.[222]

The political demise of Choiseul and his cousin Praslin marked the end of support from a ministry with physiocratic sympathies and left the position of Poivre as intendant much weaker than it had been in 1768–9. However, on his return to France Poivre was able to vindicate himself with regard to his conflicts with Desroches when a commission of enquiry was set up to investigate the allocation of concessions on the island. For his part, the responses given by Desroches to the commission were considered unsatisfactory. The commission members agreed with Poivre that the failure to reincorporate illegally granted concessions was due solely to the governor's misdeeds and not to any lack of diligence on the part of Poivre.[223] For all practical purposes, however, the brief period during which a pioneering conservation ideology had reigned had, at least temporarily, come to an end.

Bernardin de Saint-Pierre and his four environmentalist texts

Although physiocratic conservationism suffered a temporary loss of political support after 1771, the visionary policy initiated by Poivre soon developed an

---

220 Brest M91; 1 Sept. 1769, no. 48 (Desroches et Poivre à Ministre) (Malleret, p. 540).
221 Quimper 12 bis; fol. 204: Copies des 12A, pp. 304–55 (Malleret, p. 540).
222 Brest M93; 24 Aug. 1771 (Poivre à Ministre) (Malleret, p. 541).
223 Quimper 12A/4, pp. 154–61 (Malleret, p. 542).

equally innovative philosophical offspring in the thinking of Bernardin de Saint-Pierre. As a direct consequence of his experiences on Mauritius and his exposure to the physiocratic doctrines espoused by Poivre, he developed an apparently holistic and environmentalist theory of nature grounded in an understanding of the interdependence of processes and objects in the environment. These insights found their way into four remarkable texts: *A Voyage to the Isle of France*, the *Studies of Nature*, the *Harmonies of Nature* and, not least, the novel *Paul et Virginie*. Through these very personal discourses Saint-Pierre was able to exercise a long-term influence on attitudes to nature and to the European impact on the tropics of a kind which Poivre and Commerson could emulate only in the much narrower definitions and precedents of state policy. Indeed, Saint-Pierre's two texts specifically on nature stand out as among the earliest fully developed, fully argued and fully evidenced critiques of the European impact on tropical nature; they have few rivals in style or scholarship. The insights presented in the two works, many of them derived from Commerson (especially in their stress on extinctions and the potency of the human impact), later influenced Lamarck and Cuvier, although with quite different consequences for the theorisings of those two.[224] As with Poivre and Commerson, it was awareness of the destruction of the endemic fauna and flora of Mauritius which stimulated Saint-Pierre's particular discourse on nature, quite apart from a physiocratic interest in the interdependence of various elements within a society. His main preoccupation, apart from an adulation of the form and 'truth' of the natural world, concerned the steadily increasing power of western man to change nature as he colonised the world.

For Saint-Pierre this involved consideration of a long historical perspective involving the impact of technologies much more 'primitive' than those of eighteenth-century France. The means of migration of people or organisms to remote uninhabited islands again arose as the critical stimulant to theory, as it had with Commerson (and later did with Darwin). 'It was thus in canoes', Saint-Pierre suggested, that man 'first found the means to people islands and to commence that course of navigation which put it eventually in his power to circumnavigate the globe.'[225] Over human history, this expansion was eventually deleterious, since Europeans in particular 'brought hither more and greater evils than Nature herself'.[226]

The environment of an island exercised an imaginative and intellectual appeal to Saint-Pierre to an even greater extent than it had for his two colleagues, possibly as a consequence of his much closer association with Rousseau. More-

---

224 See F. Burckhardt, 'The inspiration of Lamarck's belief in evolution', *Journal of the History of Biology*, 5 (1981), 413, 418.
225 *Harmonies of nature*, I, p. 176.
226 *Voyage to the Isle of France*, p. 24.

over, he is quite explicit in his later writings about his adherence to the 'robinsonnades' and even regretted that 'we [the French] have not had a romance on the plan of *Robinson Crusoe*'.[227] Thus the Defoeian theme, in which man undergoes a personal transformation or conversion through contact with nature, was extensively reinterpreted by Saint-Pierre in his writings. Natural history, he felt, lent insights into the nature of being. A human preoccupation with nature, Saint-Pierre asserted, might develop in direct proportion to the degree to which man felt alienated from nature or, presumably, from his own nature. Human artifice was thereby condemned. It was, he said, 'really in the same proportion as the arts became naturalised among us that nature is estranged'. By contrast, a study of natural history and any attempt to understand the components of nature would lead to spiritual insights, and he thought that 'we should rather particularise the several parts of His work, than give a general definition only of it. Nature presents to us relations so very ingenious, intentions so beneficent, and scenes which though mute and one might say imperceptible, are so expressive, that they might influence the most inattentive mind and exact an exclamation of, surely there is a GOD!'[228]

The investigation of this divine natural order, which Saint-Pierre saw essentially as a good and not a fallen one, could best be carried out on an island. The island, he stated explicitly, was his 'motto', and to reinforce the point he used an illustration of an island as the frontispiece of his *Studies of Nature*.[229] The explanation he gave for the selection of this frontispiece was a striking declaration of classical image and empirical, functional insight. It represented

> a solitude in the mountains of the island of Samos; an attempt has been made notwithstanding the smallness of the field to introduce and display some elementary harmonies peculiar to islands and to lofty mountains. Clouds of vapour formed by the winds on the shores of the island, and by water pumped up by the sun from the bottom of the sea, are wafted towards the summits of the mountains, which arrest them by their fossil and hydraulic attractions.[230]

227 *Harmonies of nature*, III, p. 196.

228 *Voyage to the Isle of France*, p. 300. This passage in *Voyage*, while published in 1770 just after Saint-Pierre returned from Mauritius, actually formed part of a letter (no. XXVII) written to France in 1768, shortly after his arrival.

229 *Studies of nature*, trans. H. Hunter, 5 vols., London, 1796. Although the *Studies* was written and published at the express instigation of Rousseau, the feeling about islands certainly predated Saint-Pierre's period of close association with his intellectual mentor. The intellectual relationship between the two men grew close after Saint-Pierre's return to France. Indeed, one of his first acts after his return was to contact Rousseau. As a consequence, Rousseau seems to have had his own interest in the tropics much strengthened. The influence of these two men upon each other, important for the work of both, is an underresearched topic.

230 Ibid., I, p. 2.

This picture of a hydrological cycle, powered by the sun and driving the circulation of water from sea to clouds, to precipitate in mountains and run again to the sea, was the basis of the flow or 'harmonies' through which Saint-Pierre began to see natural processes interacting. Quite happy mentally to transpose northern species to a tropical island, he explained this system of interdependence in microcosm:

> The squirrels are playing along the stem and among the boughs of the fir; and the female of the heath-cock makes her nest in the moss which covers the roots. The beavers, on the contrary, have built their habitation at the foot of the birch and a bird of that species which eats birds is fluttering around the branches. The fir accommodates its quadrupeds in its boughs; and the birch finds lodging for its creatures . . . upon its roots. The habits of their respective birds are equally contrasted.[231]

These notions of interdependence are reminiscent of modern ecological 'niche' theory, in which species are seen as adapted to utilise a particular part of the environment. The 'supreme intelligence', Saint-Pierre asserted, was manifest in this 'harmony of vegetables'. In other words, ecological interdependence could be directly equated with a quality of the divine. Saint-Pierre moves in the *Harmonies* from the general to the particular lesson of Mauritius, and to an explicit critique of the ecological impact of European colonial rule. While an island, he explained, might teach the harmony of nature, it could also reveal the destructiveness of European man.

> To contemplate the progress of a rising colony is a spectacle worthy of a philosopher, for it is there that the culture of man forms a striking contrast with that of nature. That contrast was frequently brought before my eyes, in the pedestrian journey which I made in 1770 . . . I entered spots lately brought into cultivation, where monstrous trunks of trees overturned by the axe and sometimes by gunpowder, lay along the ground.[232]

The problem was that modern man had come to value the wrong things in nature. It was here that Saint-Pierre diverged dramatically from the physiocratic view when he asked, 'To what degree have our speculations and our prejudices degraded her? Our treatises on agriculture show us, on the plains of Ceres, nothing but grain; in the meadows, the beloved haunt of nymphs, only bundles of hay and in the majestic forest only cords of wood and faggots.'[233]

There is no sympathy for colonial agriculture of any kind here. Agriculture, commerce and capital were all held equally responsible for the damage. 'What should we say of the violence done to her by Pride and Avarice?' Saint-Pierre

231 Ibid.
232 *Harmonies of nature*, I, pp. 177–8.
233 *Studies of nature*, I, p. 36.

asked; 'how many charming hills have been reduced to a state of villainage by our laws? . . . what majestic rivers degraded by our imports?'[234] In equating the transformation of nature by deforestation and cultivation with 'villainage', the writer was offering a striking social simile, and one that closely resembled Poivre's 1767 reference to a land in 'servitude'. As for the second image, it had been Saint-Pierre as an engineer who had first warned Poivre of the problem of river and harbour silting on Mauritius.

In the eyes of Saint-Pierre, man had become destructive and had allowed commerce to run its destructive path because he had himself become denatured and been 'universally dissected, and now nothing is shown of him but the carcase. Thus the masterpiece of Creation, like everything else in nature, has been degraded by our learning.'[235] As man had come to manipulate nature cruelly, he increasingly acted 'the part of the tyrant of Sicily, who fitted the unhappy traveller to his bed of iron; he violently stretched, to the length of the bed, the limbs of those who were shorter and cut short the limbs of those who were longer. It is thus', Saint-Pierre added, 'that we apply all the operations of nature to our pitiful methods, in order to reduce the whole to our common standard.'

These quotations indicate the extent to which Saint-Pierre recognised the workings of a particularly destructive colonial economic system. In the face of this destructiveness, all the 'repositories of Arts and Sciences' were worth little. All working knowledge of nature was lost, and even the 'savage' remained more capable of empirical observation. It was to him that 'we are indebted for our first observations, which are the sources of all science'.[236] Empiricism and non-European knowledge could, then, be associated with a return to the merits of untouched, unsullied nature, a state which Saint-Pierre confessed he had never seen. 'I have not had the felicity,' he wrote, 'like the primitive navigators, who discovered uninhabited islands, to contemplate the face of the ground as it came from the hand of the Creator.'[237] Here, then, were a rationale for wishing for wilderness and an aspiration, perhaps, to revisit or relive the world before the corrupting fall of western man. Even Mauritius, cruelly treated by the colonists, could not now be regarded as a wilderness.

The logic and direction of this long argument, which forms the bulk of the first volume of *Studies of Nature*, did not end in this pessimistic mode. Instead, in building up a picture of human mistreatment of wild nature and the misuse of human ingenuity (which attained distinctly anti-intellectual overtones in

234 Ibid.
235 Ibid.
236 Ibid., p. 40.
237 Ibid., p. 280.

the *Studies*), Saint-Pierre was moving towards a personal prescription for a future harmony between man and nature. However, it was a prescription with a sting in its tail. The first stage of the conclusion of the argument dwelt quite specifically on the topic of extinctions, or at least extinctions from known ranges.[238]

Strikingly, Saint-Pierre linked his sermon on extinction not only to deforestation but to the idea that the interdependence of one part of nature with another meant that destruction in one part would have deleterious consequences for the whole. To support this argument, he preferred to rely on another authority as well as on his own observations. Significantly, he chose a colonial example, revealing that

> Denis, Governor of Canada, relates in his *Natural History of Canada* that the cod, which in shoals used to frequent the coasts of the Island of Misson, disappeared in 1667 because, in the year preceding, the forests had been destroyed by a conflagration. He remarks that the same cause had produced the same effect in different places. Though he ascribes the disappearance of these and is in other respects a very intelligent writer, we shall demonstrate, by other curious observations that it might have been occasioned by the destruction of vegetables which used to attract them to the shore. Thus everything in Nature is in strict alliance.[239]

Reverting to his classical imagery, Saint-Pierre found an apt metaphor to describe this interdependence. 'The Fauns, the Dryads and the Nereids', he asserted, 'walk everywhere hand in hand.' Nature was ultimately entirely vulnerable to man in modern times and 'seconds his effects and seems to invite him to prescribe laws for her'.[240] Man had thus acquired a formidable responsibility to cultivate a harmony with nature. 'If it were possible for me to show humanity to man', Saint-Pierre suggested,

> then it were possible to enlarge this humanity with respect to nature . . . man has been in every age the friend of nature, not merely from the interests of commerce but by the sacred and more indissoluble bonds of humanity. Sages appeared two or three thousand years ago, in the East, and their wisdom is now illuminating us in the remotest corners of the West.[241]

238 The unwillingness to postulate complete extinction reflects Saint-Pierre's uncertainty about his own breadth of knowledge in natural history rather than an uncertainty about the ability of man to destroy species with a known range, about which he had little doubt.

239 *Studies of nature*, I, p. 280.

240 Ibid., p. 63.

241 Ibid., p. 70.

He finally saw a hope of restitution not in the 'West', which he dispar-
agingly terms as 'remote', but rather in the more ancient philosophies of the
East, where, as he was clearly aware, the interdependence of man with nature
as a unity rather than as a separate superior entity, had been long assumed.
We have here a glimpse of Saint-Pierre's Orientalist leanings, which had
probably been strengthened through Poivre and his acquaintance, through
the Jesuits, with Chinese and Indian ideas about nature and the landscape.
A regard for Oriental ideas appeared in this writing as a form of reaction
equivalent to the retreat to 'Nature' and as part of the same search for new
and absolute values. To this extent, Saint-Pierre's vision was prophetic in
scientific terms; the conception of unity between man and nature promoted
later by Alexander von Humboldt, and seminal to much early-nineteenth-
century environmental philosophy, derived at least some of its inspiration
from an interest in Oriental texts as they were understood by Schelling, Herder, Goethe and William von Humboldt.[242] Moreover, the Oriental theme
was one which Saint-Pierre had himself utilised in his novel *La chaumière
indienne*. This novel managed to combine an adulation of wild nature with a
supposed rural Indian Arcady, in which a civilisation lived in perfect harmony with nature. It was notable also for its pioneering advocacy of vege-
tarianism, an idea also carried over from a growing European interest in
Indian society. However, it was in *Paul et Virginie* that Saint-Pierre probably
made his longest-lasting contribution to fictionalising and thus implanting the
island motif in Romantic culture. He was successful in the novel in resolving
some of the practical and thematic tensions between the isolation (as it is
dramatised in *Crusoe*) of the individual European (man) on an island and the
idyllic society, and between European and noble savage. In some respects one
can also argue that *Paul et Virginie* reinforced and fictionalised a 'gender balance' restored when Jeanne Baret's real gender was revealed on Tahiti.[243]
Prior to 1768 desert-island literature had tended to contemplate isolated communities of either men or (less frequently) women but had rarely put them
together. This was changed radically by the Bougainville expedition and the
incorporation of a newly constructed sexuality as part of the same return to
nature which underlay environmentalism. By fictionally reconciling wild nature and the new European notions about gender that had been outlined in
La nouvelle Héloïse, Saint-Pierre strengthened both nature and the island as
motifs in popular and scientific culture.

242 J. W. Sedlar, *India in the mind of Germany: Schelling, Schopenhauer and their times*, Washington, D.C., 1982, pp. 25–51. See also Chapter 7.
243 Although the novel is also believed to have dramatised Saint-Pierre's own illicit relationship
  with Madame Poivre.

With Bernardin de Saint-Pierre's departure from Mauritius in 1770, Poiv-re's resignation in 1772 and the death of Commerson on the island in 1773, all the main intellectual participants in the physiocratic and Rousseauist environmentalism of Poivre's intendancy ceased to direct events on the island. A remarkably innovative and short-lived period of experimentation had thus come to a close. The conservation ideas and policies developed during that period were enshrined, nevertheless, in a variety of ways, not least in the elaborate formulations of the 1769 Forest Ordinance and its legislative successors. While these were only patchily enforced, they were not entirely neglected. As Saint-Pierre remarked enigmatically, 'Various laws, relative to the planting business exist . . . no people in the world know their own interest better than the inhabitants of the Isle de France, nor what is best suited to the soil they possess.' In spite of the decline of the physiocratic party in France (the Duke de Choiseul had been removed in 1770), the role of the colonial state in forest and soil conservation had been accepted in a broader fashion, and in the sense which Poivre had intended. In 1777, for example, an 'Inspecteur des Forêts de L'Ile de France' was appointed to head a forest service.[244] Lartigue, the new inspector, had to cope with 'checking abuses of all kinds all over the island'. In addition to his police duties, the inspector was responsible for continuing the planting of *bois noir* trees on the slopes around Port Louis and in the north of the island and for the enforcement of legislation regarding the erection of wooden buildings in Port Louis.

The Ministère de Marine continued to maintain an interest in the desiccation issue alongside its more predictable worries about the supply of naval timber. Thus in a memoir of 1781 the ministry urged Souillac, the governor, to take all steps to conserve woods and forests for use in shipbuilding, artillery works and civil buildings, as well as for firewood. In addition, 'intense protection' was required 'for defence purposes, to maintain a fresh atmosphere and to prevent the drying up of rivers and streams without which the soil would soon lose its fertility'. Finally, no land was to be awarded inside the Royal Reserves, and it was laid down that 'badly utilised lands should be returned to the domain and reconceded to other settlers who would use them better'.[245] This repetition of the novel arguments of 1769 seems somewhat surprising. It tends to indicate the continued role of Pierre Poivre in colonial policy long after his return to France (where he died in 1786).[246]

244 Brouard, *Woods and forests*, p. 20.
245 Ibid., p. 25.
246 This would not be surprising, since Poivre successfully lobbied to keep Nicholas Céré, his own appointee, in place as the highly successful curator of the now vast botanical garden at Le Reduit, described by Milon as 'one of the wonders of the world' (Pridham, *England's colonial empire: Mauritius*, p. 217).

Environmental legislation during the Revolution and the Franco-British wars

Despite the onset of the Revolution and a British blockade of Mauritius, coffee and tea plantations continued to be developed on the island in the face of official discouragement. Forests also continued to be cleared for agriculture. The government, virtually independent of Paris after 1789 and feeling itself increasingly vulnerable and isolated from sources of external supply, acted quickly, although largely ineffectually, to control the increased pressures on the forests.[247] An arrêté of 1803, for example, ruled that no concession could extend beyond two-thirds of the way up a mountain slope – even less in some cases.[248] The events of 1789 had encouraged the legislative effort, principally through the installation of a Colonial Assembly in 1790. In November 1792 the Assembly itself published two arrêtés relating to the perennial struggle against grain-eating birds.[249] These stipulated that planters should kill off one bird per arpent per year and present its head to the local authority.[250] The birds to be spared were 'martins, messanges, merles, tourterelles'. The categories of 'messanges' and 'merles' were probably meant to cover all endemic birds. This was an interesting excursion into selective forms of biological control, possibly based on a developing awareness of the significance of endemism, although this cannot be firmly established.[251] A second arrêté was passed in 1798 relating to the conservation of fish stocks. Both measures reflected growing wartime anxiety about the long-term reliability of food stocks, although, as the riders to the bird-control regulations show, other motives were creeping in as well.

The precocious resort to legislation of this kind by the Colonial Assembly stemmed partly from the precedent established by Pierre Poivre. It also owed something to an increasing readiness by the state to try to counter environ-

---

247 Brouard, *Woods and forests*, p. 27.
248 Ibid.
249 Pers. comm. from R. V. d'Unienville, Port Louis, to P. J. Barnwell, Downing College, Cambridge, 21 Nov. 1986.
250 R. V. d'Unienville, *Histoire politique de l'Ile de France*, Port Louis, 1975, p. 23. The insular biotas of the Indian Ocean were already under heavy pressure by this stage, the exploitation of the atolls having begun in consequence of the scarcities occasioned by the prolonged wars of the Revolution. Thus in 1793 a factory was established on Diego Garcia for the export of copra and oil to Mauritius; then in 1808 Laurent Barbe and Céré (the son of Nicholas Céré) obtained a concession to exploit the rich coconut groves on Agalega, the nearness of the atoll to Mauritius rendering it a more promising commercial venture: M. Ly-Tio-Fane, 'Indian Ocean islands: Some account of their natural history as depicted in the literature', paper presented at 2nd International Conference on Indian Ocean Studies, Perth, 1984, p. 20.
251 The anomaly here, according to d'Unienville (see n. 249), is that 'tourterelles', an endemic species, were also pests and voracious seed eaters.

mental risks by legislative means. Once this pattern was established, it was easily resorted to again when new kinds of risks appeared. The development of the indigo industry posed a new kind of risk in exactly this way. The indigo factory process, which catered primarily to European export markets, produced a peculiarly unpleasant and poisonous effluent. This was at first allowed to drain away into the rivers and irrigation canals, creating an early form of industrial pollution on the island. While in other parts of the world, including Europe, such early industrial pollution remained largely unrestricted for many years, the traditions of control and legislation which had developed on Mauritius, together with an inherent sense of risk nurtured by the obvious limitations of the island environment, ensured that positive attempts were made to control the problem. The industry was new, but its impact was noticed almost at once in a society where an adequate water supply was such a sensitive matter. However, it was a local council and not the Colonial Assembly which took the initiative. It fell to the municipal council of Moka to ask the Colonial Assembly to legislate (on 13 February 1791) on 'the unfortunate accidents which have resulted from the very close proximity of indigo works to rivers, springs and canals'.[252]

These pioneering anti-pollution measures were in fact contiguous in theme with other legislation, such as the 1798 fisheries-protection measure and other provisions designed to protect fisheries, which had been incorporated in the 1769 *Reglement économique*. As Saint-Pierre had suggested in his reference to Denis's *Natural History of Canada*, changes in water quality, whether occasioned by deforestation or by other causes, were already thought to be deleterious to the island fisheries.[253] Clearly the possibility of risks from indigo effluent would have presented a more direct issue of contamination of the drinking water, which, since most settlements were sited where streams entered the sea, was a matter of very genuine concern. Thus the concern about water quality, as well as the impact of land-use change as it affected run-off and stream flow, was one that grew rather than lessened as time went on. It formed a central part of the legislation gazetted by Decaen in 1804.

Decaen, governor-general of all French possessions in the Indian Ocean, with headquarters on Mauritius from 1803 to 1810, was a 'very able administrator' and keenly aware of the environmental threats which faced the is-

---

252 Quoted in d'Unienville, *Histoire politique de l'Ile de France*, p. 62. Accordingly, 'elle arrêta, le 22 février que les citoyens, qui ont établi ou établissent des indigoteries sont fermés de prendre toutes les mesures nécessaires pour éviter que même par infiltration des eaux qui ont servi à la fermentation ne se ineffluent avec celles des rivières, canaux, sources qui les avoisinnent, et qu'à cet effet serait creuses des fosses ou ... destinés à récevoir l'eau de fermentation'. The municipalities were charged with enforcing these regulations 'avec le plus grand soin'.

253 J. Denis, *Natural history of Canada*, quoted in Saint-Pierre, *Studies of nature*, p. 64.

land.[254] His arrêté of 14 Vendémiaire An XIII (the 'Decaen rules' of October 1804) reinforced the provisions of Poivre's *Reglement économique*, which included the 1769 Forest Protection Law. But Decaen's rules also contained important innovations with regard to enforcement. A 'conservateur des eaux et forêts' was appointed long before this title, with its emphasis on 'eaux', was used in any other French colonial territory. The 1804 laws greatly reinforced the protection of river-banks, declaring a strip 120 feet wide on either side of the river to be sacrosanct – a radical measure which encountered immediate opposition.[255] Both the intentions and the emphasis of the Decaen legislation differed from what the fledgling republic had tried to impose in 1795.[256] The latter had required 'pas réserves', or 'pas géométriques', a strip of land along the coast, to be reserved without compensation, uninhabited and uncultivated, for the free passage of troops and artillery.[257] The 'Réserves de la Republique' were not the central part of the 1804 laws, which attended far more to domestic than military needs or metropolitan wishes. Indeed, after the ejection of the republican representatives from the colony (due largely to the wish of the colonists to retain slavery) it is clear that domestic conservation objectives took precedence, especially with regard to water. For the government in Paris, whose writ effectively ceased to run during the Napoleonic wars, naval security matters were paramount. By contrast, for the colonial government threats to agricultural production and fisheries during the British blockade far outweighed matters of military security.

Another innovation of the Decaen laws was the formal reservation of the top two-thirds of all mountain slopes on the island, a draconian measure which Poivre had hesitated to take. However, this measure was simply a consequence of the government's continuing adherence to Poivre's desiccation ideas and relates especially to perceptions of the supposed relation between precipitation and the ability of mountain forests to attract rain-clouds. The institutional continuance of Poivre's conservation rationale in the Decaen laws is partly explained by the evidence of notes left by Governor Magallan for General Decaen on his assumption of the governorship. These make it quite clear that the main intention of the legislation related to soil and crop protection rather than to timber conservation.[258] By the time Decaen became governor, the

---

254 Brouard, *Woods and forests*, p. 27. On Decaen, see H. Prentout, *L'Ile de France sous Decaen*, Paris, 1907, and *DMB*.

255 In 1880 a visiting official of the Indian Forest Service recommended that the idea of the river reserve developed on Mauritius should be introduced in India: R. Thompson, *Report on the forests of Mauritius*, Port Louis, 1880.

256 Brouard, *Woods and forests*, p. 26. This was the arrêté of 13 Messidor (July 1795).

257 Arrêté of 14 Vendémiaire, in 'Extrait des registres des arrêtés du Capitaine-Général "au nom de la République" ' (i.e. Decaen as 'C-G des établissements français a L'est du Cap de Bonne Espérance'): Mauritius Archives, 1804, Decaen file, n.p.

258 Prentout, *L'Ile de France sous Decaen*, p. 198. Magallan's notes directly recall Poivre's state-

Poivrean conservation rules were already becoming known outside the confines of the French colonial system. For example, an East India Company intelligence report of 1794 about land use on Mauritius, compiled by Captain Alexander Beatson, referred explicitly to the forest-protection rules.[259] They were similarly mentioned in the painstaking record of events on the island made by Matthew Flinders, the explorer of Australia, who was held in captivity on the island for several years during the Napoleonic wars. Flinders was sufficiently impressed by the Decaen laws to make notes on the reasoning behind them in his diary in the course of describing a trip he had made outside Port Louis in August 1805 to climb the hills near the town. He noted that 'it has lately been forbidden to cut down any of the wood in the upper part of the mountains, the rains having been found to decrease in late years, owing as it is thought to the hills being stripped of their covering'.[260]

A supplement to the Decaen rules, published in October 1804, unlike the 1769 *Reglement économique*, set out a whole system of enforcement by eight white 'gardes particuliers des eaux et forêts' and seven free blacks ('chasseurs des eaux et forêts') with two additional forest guards appointed so that the chief public-works officer might supervise the supply of water to canals feeding the Jardin d'Etat (Poivre's botanical garden), the Powder Mill at Pamplemousses and the Grandes Réserves forest at L'Asile.[261] Further arrêtés of 1807 redefined the Réserves de la Republique along the coast and referred to them as 'inalienable', a term which was to be transferred to India after 1810.

The global context and the later influence of Poivre's environmental policy

Matthew Flinders's familiarity with the thinking behind the idea of mountain forest reserves was to be important in that it was one of the routes by which knowledge of the conservation practices of the Isle de France governments became known to British naturalists. A knowledge of the same practices appears to have been temporarily lost to the French official mind as a conse-

ment that forests were necessary to protect 'les récoltes contre la violence des vents, d'ardeur du soleil, et les sécheresses'. See Poivre's instructions in M. Delalieu, *Code des iles de France et de Bourbon*, Port Louis, 1777, pp. 222–4.
259 A. Beatson, 'Account of Mauritius': British Library, 13868.
260 Cambridge University Library, Diary of Matthew Flinders, 22 Aug. 1805. Flinders drew on the diary for his account entitled *A voyage to Terra Australis* ..., but the quotation used here does not appear in his book. I am grateful to Mr. P. J. Barnwell for pointing it out to me. Flinders made other remarks on the subject in an entry of 15 April 1805.
261 Brouard, *Woods and forests*, p. 28. The Grandes Réserves forest still exists, although it is now largely planted up with exotics.

quence of the political turmoil in France, a turmoil that was never much
reflected in the Mascarenes. There is some irony in this, as the French Revolution and the resumption of the Anglo-French conflict between 1789 and
1815 resulted in a vastly increased demand being imposed upon forests both
in metropolitan France and in its colonial possessions.[262]

In metropolitan France itself the circumstances of the Revolution put an
end to many of the Colbertian laws and to customary constraints on forest
use, and exposed the forests to the full force of urban demands. The new
dispensation also opened up the forests to pent-up peasant ambitions and
frequent episodes of incendiarism. This exposure had such a rapid and devastating effect that as early as the mid 1790s French engineers were starting
to warn of the potentially dangerous effects of increased deforestation and
slope cultivation on the incidence of flooding and soil erosion. The most influential of these warnings was made by Fabre in 1797 with the publication
of his *Essai sur la thème des torrents et des rivières*. The book was published in
the same year as the collected works of Poivre, which included the famous
discourse on the virtues of a careful use of forests and the need for a new
moral economy of nature.[263] The literature on environmental hydrology pioneered by Fabre was to have a wide following in France, where it eventually
led to the setting up of the Département des Eaux et Forêts and the foundation of the Imperial School of Forestry at Nancy in 1824. Further afield,
Fabre's work affected developments in India, mainly through the writings of
J. B. Boussingault[264] and Alexander von Humboldt, both of whom were familiar with Fabre's theories.

In North America the physiocratic conservationism of Poivre found an en-

---

262 While the Revolution meant that the direction of physiocratic colonial conservation policy
was lost in France, it was not lost on Mauritius. The island continued to be of interest to
French science after Napoleon came to power. In 1801 the explorer Baudin visited Mauritius,
and his expedition studied the geography, fauna and flora. The botanist Bory de Saint-
Vincent left the expedition here and went on to study the flora of the Mascarenes. Another
famous botanist, Dupetit Thouars, had been active in Madagascar and the Mascarenes shortly
before this, but his work was not published until 1804.

263 J. A. Fabre, *Essai sur la thème des torrents et des rivières*, Paris, 1797; Salles, *Oeuvres*. Fabre
and his French disciples (as well as Alexander von Humboldt) exercised a strong influence
over the work of John Croumbie Brown in his several books on drought and forest and water
conservation in South Africa. George Perkins Marsh referred to them frequently in his
compilation *Man and Nature*, published in 1864. French and Italian foresters, hydrologists
and water engineers of this period (1790–1820) tended to exercise an indirect influence
through their writings rather than in their projects, since they were not often employed by
the British abroad. Later, their involvement with the British became more direct, an example
being the employment of the Count Vasselot de Regne in the Cape Colony after 1872.
Moreover, for a period after 1869, at the suggestion of Hugh Cleghorn, Indian forest officers
were trained in the French Imperial Forestry School.

264 See Chapter 7 for biographical details.

thusiastic adherent in Thomas Jefferson. As a consequence of his period as a
minister in France, Jefferson entered into a long friendship with Dupont de
Nemours, Poivre's son-in-law and biographer.[265] This instilled in him a life-
long interest in agricultural science and in soil conservation and treatment in
particular. The clearest indication of his debt to Poivre consists in his remarks
on the introduction of the olive tree and upland rice to South Carolina and
Georgia. 'The greatest service', he said, echoing Poivre, 'which can be rendered any country is to add a useful plant to its culture.' His later design for
a mouldboard plough and such part as he played in attempting contour culture, or 'horizontal ploughing', on the mountain-side at Monticello have often
been quoted by historians of agriculture and conservation and are now well
remembered in a land where 'farmers in general did not come round to contour ploughing until more than a century later'.[266]

The global conflict between Britain and France led to an extraordinary
growth in demand for naval timber and to a world-wide competition to secure
reliable sources of such timbers as teak. This competition was very rapidly
won by the British, much as it had been in the analogous conflict with the
Dutch during the seventeenth century. At that time the English had still had
an advantage in being able to secure supplies from the American colonies at
a time when other European nations were forced to rely on more insecure
sources from the Baltic states and Russia. In the Napoleonic wars, however,
this ready supply of American timber was denied to the British by the loss
of the American colonies in 1776. This led in turn to a greater concentration
on the Cape and India as possible sources of shipbuilding teak and other
woods.[267] Eventually this was to lead to concern about the economic and environmental effects of forest depletion in India, particularly after 1815, and to
a repetition of the pattern which had developed in microcosm on Mauritius
under the French.

When the British assumed control of Mauritius in 1810, few of the new

265 L. S. Kaplan, *Jefferson and France: An essay in politics and ideas*, New Haven, Conn., 1967,
    pp. 99–100. On Dupont de Nemours in the United States and as a physiocrat, see Léonce
    de Lavergne, *Les économistes français du XVIIIe siècle*, Paris, 1870, pp. 381–435.
266 Russell Lord, *The care of the earth: A history of husbandry*, New York, 1962. Poivre's phy-
    siocratic influence can also be traced in the plans Jefferson drew up and in some part sub-
    mitted as legislation during his public career. These called for a library in 'every country in
    Virginia' in an Act for 'the more general diffusion of knowledge' through a free school system
    there and for a statewide scheme 'for a system of agricultural societies' that foreran by a
    century the national establishment of agricultural extension learning.
267 See N. A. M. Rodger, *Wooden Walls: An anatomy of the Georgian navy*, London, 1986, for
    details of the rise in consumption of timber during the Napoleonic period. Rodger treats the
    Royal Navy at this time as the greatest single industrial concern in the British economy,
    surpassing even the East India Company in terms of consumption of raw materials.

colonists seem to have understood the function of the forest reserves which covered many of the island mountain-sides. Clearly the fact that by that time both Matthew Flinders and Alexander Beatson had written official reports on the Mauritius forest-reserve system did not actually effect an equivalent diffusion of information at a more popular level. We know from an essay by William Chambers that 'when we took the Mauritius from the French, our enterprising colonists thought it a pity that the fine rich soil found on the tops of the hills should be given up to support what they considered useless woods; so they cut down the trees, and replaced them by cultivated fields'. However, this state of affairs did not persist for long. 'Very shortly', Chambers recounted,

> it was noticed that the streams were shrinking; that one spring after another had disappeared; that the green of the meadows was changed to a dusty brown; that the grain sown grew up thin and hungry; and that the earth, in short, ceased to be productive. Reflecting persons were not slow in discovering the cause of this great change. They noticed that the periodical rains, however abundant they might be, soon cleared away from the cultivated country, leaving it exposed to the rays of a fiery sun, which scorched and withered up everything for want of a perennial supply of moisture. The next step was with all possible speed to reclothe the mountains with forest and jungle, upon which experience had proved the fertility of the lower lands depended . . . throughout Southern India, a similar policy has been forced upon the rulers by the urgent necessity of the case.[268]

This mention of India is significant. As we shall see, the forestry policies pursued on Mauritius, like the related innovations in state environmentalism developed a little later in the Eastern Caribbean and on St Helena, became important models for the state naturalists and conservation pioneers on the Indian sub-continent after the late 1830s. In particular, the writings of Ber-

---

268 W. Chambers and R. Chambers, 'Failure of springs in the East', *Chambers Journal of Popular Literature*, 496 (1863), 1–3. This article was later referred to as part of the main supporting evidence for J. Spotswood Wilson's seminal paper on the threat of world desiccation read in 1865 at the Royal Geographical Society immediately prior to the establishment of the all-India Forest Department; see Wilson, 'On the progressive desiccation of the basin of the Orange River in Southern Africa', *Proceedings of the Royal Geographical Society*, 1865, pp. 106–9, 106–109, and 'On the general and gradual desiccation of the earth and atmosphere', *Report of the Proceedings of the British Association for the Advancement of Science (Transactions)*, 1858, pp. 155–6. Wilson's environmental polemics, supported by the example of Mauritius, were useful propaganda for the Indian conservation lobby and were also utilised by J. C. Brown, colonial botanist of the Cape Colony, particularly in his later books (much quoted in Indian conservation literature) on soil erosion and the need for conservation. See e.g. *The hydrology of South Africa*, Edinburgh, 1875.

nardin de Saint-Pierre and the experiment in conservation practised on Mauritius before 1810 exercised a direct influence on Edward Green Balfour,
probably the single most influential proponent of the enormous forest-
conservation schemes pursued by the East India Company in India after 1840.
These Indian schemes then provided the model for most forest-conservation
projects which were later pursued elsewhere in both the French and British
colonial systems.

But the significance of the physiocratic environmental policy developed by
the French in the Indian Ocean colony goes far wider than this. The conservationist policies and discourses evolved by Poivre and his colleagues actually
allow us to redefine and reinterpret the conceptual origins and essential characteristics of early western environmental concerns and the mentality surrounding them. Above all, early environmentalism emerges as a critical part
and product of an increasingly self-conscious culture and language of contact
among eighteenth-century western society, tropical nature and non-European
learning.

At the core of this environmentalism lay two linked social and physical
concerns. These were anxiety about the nature of western (particularly
French) society and anxiety about the ability of man to destroy nature and
change the climate of the earth. Implicit in both fears was a suspicion that
man might destroy his integrity and himself as a species. The sheer speed of
ecological change induced by capital-intensive agriculture in the tropics acted
to intensify the crisis in environmental perceptions. It has become a commonplace among environmental historians that the calculative and reductionist
aspects of Newtonian science were implicitly hostile to any philosophical or
practical harmony between man and nature. A close inspection of the evidence
indicates the contrary to be true. The Newtonian insights of Stephen Hales
had allowed risk to be reinterpreted in a measurable and systematic way, and
in a way that the state could find convincing, not least in a setting where
physiocrats in particular valued the application of science to the analysis of
economic problems. Similarly, the Rousseauist language of nature and the
reformist intentions of the Romantic scientists of French Mauritius were not
antagonistic to the mechanics of the new climatic thinking. Instead they made
up two interdependent elements in a new environmental discourse that engaged the colonial state to an unprecedented degree.

A whole host of other factors conspired to focus state attention on environmental risk. Most of these were personified in Poivre himself. As far as
his own conservationist antecedents and motivations are concerned, his familiarity with Chinese, Indian and Dutch systems of environmental management, his physiocratic convictions and his engagement with the island as a
Utopian social metaphor were all important constituents of his environmen-

talism. But it was the power of the new climatic concerns that emerged as decisive in the formulation of state conservationism on Mauritius. Moreover, very similar climatic arguments were becoming decisive on oceanic islands elsewhere in the tropics, not least in the Eastern Caribbean.

6

Climate, conservation and Carib resistance: The British and the forests of the Eastern Caribbean, 1760–1800

The preceding chapter documented the development of environmental awareness and a conservation policy under French rule on Mauritius. This had been made possible by the particular circumstances of the relationship between a local empirical knowledge of the ecological changes taking place in a distant colony and a sympathetic political and philosophical dispensation at the colonial centre. Both elements were essential to the development of the new environmentalism. Central to these developments had been the influence of the emergence of a specialist professional discourse connecting people, forests and climatic change.

Strategic economic and military considerations had also strongly affected the French perception of the island environment. Above all, Mauritius had become prominent in the emerging global botanical networks centred on the Jardin du Roi. At least part of the motivation for constructing such a network was economic, although there were other motivations. Pierre Poivre's principal concern had been to secure a successful system of plant transfers from the East Indies and to establish Mauritius as a centre of spice cultivation. Although the botanical network based on the Jardin du Roi was acquiring a global scope, the kind of sophisticated environmental critique of the colonial process that had developed on Mauritius remained for a long time highly specialised and specific to the colony, even though it became influential in developments in India and elsewhere during the nineteenth century. Colonial environmentalism on Mauritius was, then, still an exceptional development for the late eighteenth century.

Mauritius was not, however, the only colony where a comprehensive kind of conservation policy had developed by the early 1790s. Some comparable and connected developments had taken place in the British colonial context, although perhaps in a rather less sophisticated sense, on a number of islands in the Eastern Caribbean that had been annexed by Britain in 1763 under the conditions of the Peace of Paris.[1] These British developments stemmed largely from the same set of philosophical, scientific and economic roots that had influenced the French. As on Mauritius, a limited number of disciples of physiocratic philosophy and Enlightenment science stimulated the onset of an environmentalist colonial policy. In the Caribbean case, two figures stand out as having played a seminal role. These were Soame Jenyns, otherwise better known as a Tory writer and political commentator, and Alexander Anderson, a radical Scottish physician, botanist and first curator of the St Vincent Botanic Garden. They may seem an unlikely duo. Both men, for very different reasons, shared a highly critical attitude towards the whole project of imperialism. Anderson, for example, was especially uneasy about the treatment meted out to indigenous peoples by the colonial ruler. In this context a climatic and medical environmentalism provided a powerful discourse. The circumstances of colonial rule allowed Anderson, in particular, to make claims which closely connected an analysis of natural processes with a social critique, and to substantiate these claims in legislation and in texts which he intended to publish. Overtly religious reasons for presenting environmental claims and prescriptions are not prominent in either Jenyns's or Anderson's involvement with Caribbean forest policy. Nevertheless, we cannot neglect this element altogether. Soame Jenyns wrote extensively on the theology of evil, while Anderson was probably much affected by the dissenting science of Joseph Priestley. Subliminally, at least, environmentalism may have been a vehicle for religious messages.

This chapter explores the development of this environmentalism on Tobago and St Vincent. It also briefly surveys the cultural confrontation between a land-hungry colonial state and an indigenous culture. In this context the colonial state justified its actions through a codified and manipulated legal ideology which conferred annexation rights explicitly on those who cleared forest and 'cultivated' land. The new professional (and state) scientist, making environmentalist claims, found himself thrust into the uncomfortable and potentially subversive position of arbitrating (or simply articulating) an incompatible and entirely unequal set of competing interests. The climatic–environmentalist discourse thus emerges as a potential field of conflict between scientist and state. Ultimately, whoever controlled the terms of this powerful discourse, in science and in legislation, might also affect or even police the control of people and land. These issues remained largely unresolved in the

1 I am grateful to Dr Robert Anderson of Simon Fraser University, British Columbia, and Dr Selwyn S. Dardaine of the Forest Department of Trinidad and Tobago for first drawing my attention to the significance of the forest legislation of eighteenth-century Tobago. I have also utilised Dr Dardaine's unpublished research dissertation entitled 'The role of forestry in the development of Trinidad and Tobago', submitted to the Department of Management Studies, University of the West Indies, St Augustine, Trinidad, 1979.

Eastern Caribbean during the eighteenth century. Nevertheless, the environmentalist legislation of the period was explicit in its intentions and offers a
useful starting point to consider the growth and dynamics of colonial conservationism.

As early as 1764 a system of forest reserves and environmental legislation
was set up in the 'Ceded Islands' of St Vincent and Tobago. In later years
the forest-conservation model evolved on these islands influenced the course
of colonial forest conservation in other parts of the colonial world almost as
much as the pattern established on Mauritius. The three relevant legal instruments were the Grenada Governorate Ordinance of March 1764, the Barbados Land Ordinance of 1765 and the King's Hill Forest Act passed by the
St Vincent Assembly in 1791. All three instruments were intended quite specifically to prevent local climatic change, and they can be compared with
Poivre's *Reglement économique* of 1769, which was based on the same theoretical premises.

The local political impact of the introduction of forest reservation in the
Caribbean was dramatic, as it provoked episodes of determined resistance by
the Carib population of the islands. This was in stark contrast to Mauritius,
where resistance to forest protection had been largely confined to the protests
of European landowners. The experience of late-eighteenth-century colonial
forest reservation in the Eastern Caribbean thus bears far more resemblance
to the pattern which later developed in Western India and Southern Africa
after the 1830s than to that which had developed in the far less contentious
social context of Mauritius. In particular the connections between colonial
forest control and attempts to control indigenous colonised people became
well established on the Caribbean islands. A new framework of consensus in
international law tended to encourage, and was used to justify, this kind of
oppression. In particular Emmerich de Vattel's *Law of Nations*, first translated
into English in 1760, legitimated colonial annexation and the acquisition of
'sovereignty' by reference to the exercise of forest clearance and cultivation.
Those who did not cultivate it, Vattel claimed, had no right to retain control
of the land.[2]

Local resistance to the new environmental policies in the Caribbean is an
important but neglected field; it certainly affected colonial environmental attitudes. However, it has to be somewhat marginal, in this chapter, to our main
attempt to understand the developing colonial discourses on nature and environmental control in the region. The desiccationist origins of early Caribbean forest policy were rooted both in the climatic and arboricultural concerns
of the French agronomes and their British imitators and in the physiological

---

2 E. de Vattel, *The law of nations, or principles of natural law, applied to the conduct and affairs of
   nations and sovereigns: A work tending to display the true interest of powers*, London, 1760.

researches of Woodward, Hales and Buffon. As we have seen, Poivre's acquaintance with the work of Duhamel du Monceau and with contemporary thinking on the relations between trees and climate was closely related to broader debates among the agronomes and the physiocrats. Once on Mauritius, Poivre was able to put into practice the ideas he had expressed in his Lyons speech of 1763.

By contrast, the diffusion of French desiccationism into British colonial policy was rather more tenuous and haphazard and less determined by new Rousseauist conceptions of a moral economy of nature. It relied instead on more straightforward economic priorities and on a network of personal links established between British and French savants. In particular, British Caribbean forest-protection policies relied almost entirely for their initiation on the institutional role played by the London Society for the Encouragement of Arts, Manufactures and Commerce. Even then the transfer of the new climatic ideas was dependent on close membership connections between the Académie des Sciences, the Society of Arts and the Lords Commissioners for Trade and Plantations.[3] Such connections were, however, relatively likely to be made, as the Society of Arts had, since shortly after its inception, developed a sharp institutional (and arguably physiocratic) interest in stimulating agricultural and arboricultural development in the colonies, especially those in North America and the Caribbean. After the Peace of Paris, the Society suddenly found itself able to exert a very direct influence over colonial land-use policy. Some examination of the antecedents of the Society is therefore appropriate here.

The Society of Arts had been founded in 1754. Its philosophical justifications lay in a line of direct descent from the Baconian notion of a 'Solomon's House', in the activities of the Hartlib circle and in imitating the Royal Society itself. It had other forerunners too. In 1683 a Philosophical Society had been founded in Dublin based on the Royal Society. This had foundered, and in its ashes had arisen the Dublin Society for Improving Husbandry, Manufactures and Other Useful Arts. The Dublin society, along with a number of other groupings, may have provided William Shipley with the model for his Society of Arts, actually founded in March 1754 at a meeting in Rawthmells Coffee-house, Henrietta Street, Covent Garden.[4]

Almost from its inception, the Society became associated with tree planting. The first suggestion that the Society should involve itself in such an activity originated in the ideas of Henry Baker, who on 20 March 1755 presented the

---

3 The last was the predecessor of the Board of Trade.
4 See D. G. C. Allan, *William Shipley, founder of the Royal Society of Arts: A biography with documents*, London, 1979. The eleven founding members were Viscount Folkestone; Lord Romney; Dr Stephen Hales, F.R.S.; Henry Baker, F.R.S. (naturalist and author, married to Daniel Defoe's youngest daughter); Gustavus Brander, F.R.S.; James Short, F.R.S.; John Goodchild; Nicholas Crisp; Charles Lawrence; Husband Messiter; and William Shipley.

Society with a quarto pamphlet published by him to 'promote the planting of timber trees in the common and waste grounds of the kingdom for the supply of the Navy, the employment and advantage of the poor as well as the ornamenting the nation'. This led directly to the inclusion of three 'premiums' for tree planting in the Society of Arts prize list for 1758.[5] 'A continuous supply of useful timber', the Society's journal recorded at the time, was 'absolutely necessary as well for the ornament and conveniency as for the security of these kingdoms.'[6] In the same year prizes of £40 were offered for planting and securing the 'greatest number of Logwood trees' in the colonies, not 'less than 500 in any one plantation before the third week in December 1760'.[7] Tree planting and colonial enterprises were therefore combined in the Society's activities at an early date in its history. The Society of Arts took a particular interest in the West Indies, possibly through the influence of Sir Joshua Steele, one of the early members of the Society and later the founder and president of the Barbados Society of Arts, one of the first learned societies to be founded in a British colony.[8] The Society was especially keen (as were Pierre Poivre and the French government at exactly the same time) to promote the development of plant transfers between the Pacific, the East Indies and the West Indies. As on Mauritius, this commercial interest encouraged an official concern with environmental matters. In 1760 prizes were offered specifically for the successful introduction of cinnamon trees into the West Indies. In the same year, in one of its premium lists the Society suggested that land should be reserved in the colonies for gardens or nurseries for 'experiments in raising such rare and useful plants as are not the spontaneous growth of the kingdom or of the said colonies'. It added that if the colonial legislatures or 'other incorporate bodies would help establish such gardens' the Society would provide proper premiums for plants raised in them. The first of these gardens was started in 1765 at Kingstown, St Vincent, by General Robert Melville,

5 A gold medal and two silver medals were offered for sowing the greatest quantity of land with acorns at the rate of four bushels to the acre. Similar premiums were offered for planting Spanish chestnuts, elm and Scots pine.
6 Royal Society of Arts, *Premiums by the society, established at London, for the encouragement of arts, manufactures and commerce*, London, 16 June 1760.
7 Ibid.
8 Tree planting and the cultivation of exotic crops were among Steele's main enthusiasms; see Henry Trueman Wood, *A history of the Royal Society of Arts*, London, 1913. In the *Transactions* of the Society, vol. 4, p. 219, it is recorded that 'Steele sent the Secretary an account of an ancient Mango tree then existing in a plantation in Barbados called "The Guinea".' The tree had been imported by Edwin Lascelles in 1742. Wood notes that Portuguese missionaries had in fact introduced the mango to Brazil from the East Indies. Steele, however, was one of the first English colonists to take an interest in plant introductions and seems to have pioneered the idea of the Society of Arts' taking an active role in colonial plant transfers and the development of botanical gardens.

the new governor of the Ceded Islands, or 'Southern Caribbees'.[9] As a member of the Society of Arts, Melville appears to have decided to found the garden as a result of the Society's advertisement of 1760.[10] Dr George Young, an army surgeon on St Vincent, was appointed curator of the botanical garden. He acted as such until 1774, in which year he sent a full report on the new garden to the Society in London. As the first botanical garden in the Americas, the St Vincent establishment was to prove significant in the subsequent history of early environmentalism and in providing the institutional basis for the diffusion of desiccationist ideas about deforestation and changes in rainfall.

In 1763 the Society acquired a much more direct political influence over developments in the West Indies as a result of the territorial concessions made by the French at the Peace of Paris at the end of the Seven Years' War. The cession of St Vincent, Dominica, Grenada and Tobago to Britain as the constituent territories of the 'Grenada Governorate' meant that a whole series of decisions were required to determine land allocation and ownership in the new colonies.[11] Considerable capital was available at this date for investment in sugar cultivation, and the drive to develop sugar plantations became the main plank of official strategy in the area. Rapid deforestation was an inevitable consequence of this policy, as it had already been in other parts of the Caribbean.[12] Robert Melville was appointed first governor of the Grenada Governorate under a proclamation of 3 August 1763, and his scientific interests began immediately to play their part in events, not least through his interest in climatic theory. Climate and health on Tobago were matters of particular concern to Melville, and he soon told the Lords Commissioners for Trade that epidemics 'were an evil much to be dreaded and carefully to be provided against in the beginning of a West India settlement'.[13] Initial orders by White-

---

9 Robert Melville, F.R.S., F.R.S.A. (1723–1809), attended grammar school and the universities of Glasgow and Edinburgh. In 1744 he entered the army as an ensign in the 25th Regiment (the King's Own Scottish Borderers) and served in Flanders. He was promoted to captain in 1751 and major in 1756 and then commanded the 38th Regiment (the South Staffordsire Regiment) at Guadeloupe in 1759. In a very full life Melville became a biographer, botanist, antiquarian and ballistician. In many ways he typified the university output of the Scottish Enlightenment, particularly in his alertness to technical and cultural developments in France and its colonies.

10 R. Dossie, *Memoirs of agriculture*, 3 vols., London, 1768, III, p. 400.

11 The background to the cessions of 1763 is recorded in Jean-Claude Lorrain, *La mise en valeur de l'île de Tobago (1763–1783)*, Paris, 1969, and in Watts, *The West Indies*, pp. 240–58. For a basic political history of Tobago, see Douglas Archibald, *Tobago, 'Melancholy Isle'*, vol. 1, *1498–1771*, Port of Spain, Trinidad, 1987. A good contemporary account of the Eastern Caribbean is W. Young, *A tour through the several islands of Barbados, St Vincent, Antigua, Tobago and Grenada in the years 1791 and 1792*, published as part of Bryan Edwards, ed., *The history, civil and commercial, of the West Indies*, London, 1818.

12 See Chapter 1.

13 Public Record Office, London [henceforth cited as PRO], CO 101/9, Letter of 23 Jan. 1764.

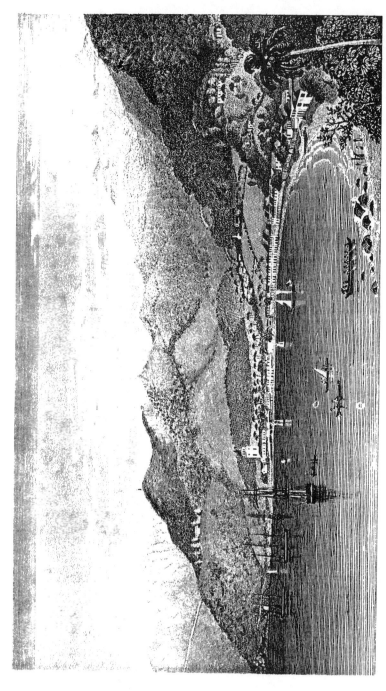

Plate 14. Kingstown, St Vincent, in about 1815. The grounds of the Botanic Garden can be seen behind the church tower. The hill summits were still forest-covered at this time. (Reproduced from Charles Shephard, *An historical account of the island of Saint Vincent*, London, 1831)

hall for the new civil authorities to take control of the island were made by Lord Egremont on 13 August 1763.[14] It was at this stage that the first formal plans were drawn up for the occupation of the Ceded Islands. Tobago, the first object of these plans, was the only one of these islands that did not have a long-standing British military presence. It was also at this stage that some of the more innovative features of the land-settlement scheme became evident.[15] The plans presented for Tobago are of considerable interest to our theme, especially with regard to the proposals for forest reservation. The area of the island was estimated at 100,000 acres. It was proposed to divide Tobago into parishes of 6,000 to 10,000 acres, with 1,000 acres set aside for an island capital. A large part of the island was deliberately to be set aside as forest reserve. Each parish, it was originally proposed, should retain a certain portion of land as uncut forest.

The settlement proposals of the Lords Commissioners for Trade were submitted to the Lords of the Committee for Plantation Affairs on 18 November 1763. In early 1764 they were laid before the Lords of Treasury and the King in Council, Lord Hillsborough representing the Lords Commissioners for Trade on the council. The proposals were issued as a proclamation on 1 March 1764. The proclamation (no. 20 of 1764) stipulated specifically that

> such a number of acres as the Commissioners should from the best of their judgement project should be reserved in woodlands to His Majesty's His Heirs and Successors in one or more different parishes in each part of each island, respectively in order to preserve the seasons so essential to the fertility of the islands and to answer all public services as may require the use and expense of timber.[16]

This order was further elaborated and its semantics and practical implications slightly altered in an ordinance issued 'by the Kings authority' on Barbados on 19 January 1765. This ordinance stated that woodlands should be preserved 'as shall seem necessary for the constitution and repair of fortifications and public buildings and *to prevent that drought which in these climates is the usual consequence of a total removal of the woods*'.[17]

14 PRO, CO 101/9, 'Order to commanding officer at Tobago', 13 Aug. 1763.

15 PRO, CO 102/1, Report of 3 Nov. 1763: 'Representations of the Commissioners to His Majesty upon the method of disposing of the lands in the islands of Grenada, Dominica, St Vincent's and Tobago'.

16 PRO, CO 101/1, no. 26, proclamation of 1764, p. 123: 'Plan for the speedy and effectual settlement of His Majesty's islands of Grenada, the Grenadines, Dominica, St Vincent's and Tobago and for the designated parts of H.M. Lands . . . to H.M. Order in Council made upon the representation of the Commissioner for Trade and Plantations dated 3rd November 1763 and the alterations proposed therein by the reports of the Lords of the Treasury and Commissioners for plantation affairs of 25 Jan. and 4th Feb. 1764'.

17 PRO, CO 106/9, Copy of printed ordinance issued in Barbados 19 Jan. 1765 (my italics).

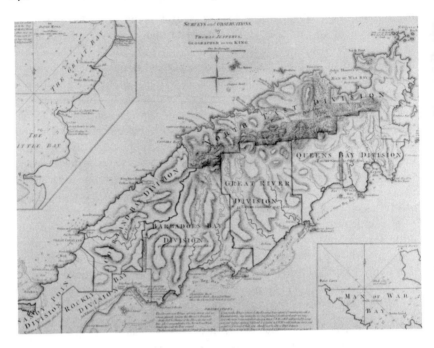

Plate 15. A map of Tobago showing the forest reserves established according to the proclamation of 1764. The reserves run along the main mountain ridge in the northeast of the island and are marked 'reserved in wood for rains'. The map, made by Thomas Jefferys, is based on the original survey of John Byres, which had first been published in 1776. (Reproduced by permission of Cambridge University Library)

Significantly, the same proclamation laid down that 'the native Caribbees of St. Vincent are to remain undisturbed in the possession of their cottages and goods'.[18] In the event, nearly a year passed before the proclamation, first issued in London in March 1764, was actually translated into policy on the ground, and the Barbados ordinance was the first effective and local step in this direction. William Young, appointed chief settlement commissioner of the Ceded Islands, soon took the process of executing the ordinance further, beginning with the survey and settlement of Tobago. However, he appears to have treated the intentions of the 1764 proclamation with some liberality, and his instructions to the surveyors on the ground reflected this. 'Settlement reservations of woodlands', Young announced, 'should be made in the most hilly parts of each parish for the construction and repair of mills, farms and public buildings and for the preservation of the seasons. Likewise', he added,

18 Ibid.

'such reservations [shall be made] in proper places along the coast as shall seem expedient for land and shipping and other public purposes . . . attention shall be paid to the nature and quality of the soil.'[19] The priority accorded to sugar production and the wish not to use cultivable lowland for forest reserve were clearly factors of importance when Young came to make the local decisions. By shifting the locations of the reserves to the 'hilly areas' he started a process of altering the original plans of the Commissioners for Trade, which ended with the plans being dropped altogether on some islands. The extent of local alterations was strongly affected by the fact that, unlike the Commissioners for Trade, local colonists often took a hostile view of the properties and influences of primeval woodland. In particular the native tropical forest cover was thought by many to promote disease and insanitary winds. Young himself, charged with reserving the forests, was actually a proponent of the view that they should be done away with. 'The rains', he said, 'are less frequent and the sea air pure and salutary by reason of its not yet being infected in its passage over hot and reeking woods . . . the heat and moisture of the woods are likely to be the chief obstructions to the [speedy settlement of the colony].'[20]

Such sentiments indicate the extent to which the notion of forest protection 'for the preservation of the seasons' was as yet a relatively controversial concept. Young seems to have accepted the view that the frequency of rains was related to the extent of the forest cover of an island. While having, of course, to follow instructions, he clung to the view that forests and their associated humidity were undesirable. Even so, by this date it was well accepted that high humidity and low wind speed were essential for the successful cultivation of sugar cane. It was this factor which had probably helped to encourage the inclusion of desiccation concepts in the settlement plans espoused by the Commissioners for Trade. However, the story behind the acceptance of desiccationist notions in the Caribbean colonial situation was a good deal more complex than this. In order to understand the background of the new policy, it is necessary to look more closely at the origins and social context of the development of desiccationism in England and in particular at the intellectual influences affecting the Lords Commissioners for Trade.

Soame Jenyns, tree planting and desiccationism

A survey of the membership of the Lords Commissioners for Trade in 1763 helps to give a number of clues to its highly unusual excursions into the

19 PRO, CO 106/9, letter/order of 22 Feb. 1765: 'Resolution of meeting of Board [of Settlement Commissioners] on board Storeship *Melvill*, Barbados Bay, Tobago'.
20 Ibid.

implications of contemporary climatic theories. At the time that the Commissioners' representations to the king were made in November 1763, the members were Lord Hillsborough (an Irish peer who was effectively secretary of state for the colonies), Soame Jenyns, Edmund Bacon, John Yorke (a member of the Hardwicke family) and one Bamber Gascoyne.[21] Among the Commissioners, Soame Jenyns and Edmund Bacon were also members of the Society of Arts. Of these two, Soame Jenyns appears to have been the key figure responsible for arousing the interest of the Commissioners in the climatic consequences of deforestation and for encouraging his colleagues to incorporate the implications of the new climatic theories into their colonial land-settlement and forest policy.[22] As we have already seen, the early development of desiccationism was bound up with the close relations between French and British science and in particular with the arboricultural writings of Duhamel du Monceau. These had in turn drawn heavily on the plant physiological insights of Stephen Hales, a fellow of Corpus Christi College, Cambridge, and probably the most distinguished Newtonian scientist in early-eighteenth-century Britain.[23] Hales had been a founder member of the Society of Arts. However, he had died in 1761 and did not himself play a direct part in promoting the practical implications of contemporary thinking about the relationship between trees and climate. The critical question to be established, therefore, is how Soame Jenyns, a friend of Stephen Hales's, was persuaded to adopt the tree-planting enthusiasms of the Society as well as to take on current desiccation ideas and lobby to institutionalise them in colonial policy.

Jenyns's interest in tree planting, by no means unusual by the 1760s, would have been reinforced by his close acquaintance with Lord Hardwicke and the Yorke family.[24] Jenyns frequently visited the Hardwicke seat at Wimpole Hall in Cambridgeshire, only twenty miles from his house at Bottisham Hall, near Cambridge, and would have been impressed by the magnificent gardens and recently planted avenues of limes and elms. Indeed, it was not long before similar lines of trees, planted by Jenyns himself, graced the grounds of Bottisham Hall. In 1755 the Hardwicke connection had furnished the Cambridgeshire landowner with a seat among the Lords Commissioners for Trade. In 1761 this social elevation was supplemented by an election to the Society of Arts. Jenyns was also by now the member of Parliament for Cambridge.[25]

21 PRO, CO 102/1, 'Representations of the Commissioners . . .'
22 For a full biography of Jenyns, see Ronald Rompkey, *Soame Jenyns*, Boston, 1984.
23 D. G. C. Allan and R. E. Schofield, *Stephen Hales: Scientist and philosopher*, London, 1983, p. 139.
24 For a fuller account of tree-planting fashion (but one that takes no account of contemporary climate theory), see Keith Thomas, *Man and the natural world*.
25 Ronald Rompkey, 'Soame Jenyns, M.P.: A curious case of membership', *Journal of the Royal Society of Arts*, 120 (1972), 532–42. This article documents Jenyns's membership of the Society

Plate 16. Soame Jenyns, painted by Sir Joshua Reynolds.
(Photo, Cambridge University Library)

By joining the Society of Arts, Jenyns would soon have come into contact
with the physiocratic enthusiasts in the Society and encountered their tree-
planting, agronomic and botanical (including plant transfer) interests. He
would also have become open to lobbying by those members of the Society
who had financial or land stakes in the colonies, and especially in the West
Indies. Chief amongst the latter was Joshua Steele, a liberal West Indies sugar
planter and later founder of the Barbados Society of Arts.[26] Jenyns may have

of Arts and attempts to identify his likeness in the mural *Human Culture*, by James Barry,
which was painted at the Society of Arts in the 1770s. See also Rompkey, 'Some uncollected
authors: XLIX, Soame Jenyns', *Book Collector*, 25 (1970), 210–11. Jenyns was M.P. for Cambridge in 1741–54 and 1758–80 and a Lord Commissioner for Trade in 1755–80. He died in
1787.

26 Letter from Joshua Steele to Secretary of the Society of Arts, 24 May 1785, Royal Society of

been convinced on straightforward economic grounds that the forests of the
Ceded Islands should be protected in order to enhance potential sugar-cane
yields. But the agenda of the Society was more complex and long-term. In
1760 the Society had made plain its commitment to the cause of interoceanic
plant transfers with its support for colonial botanical gardens and especially
the one on St Vincent. Projects for plant transfer and the cultivation of new
crops were, of course, closely tied up with the growing intellectual interest in
climate and its effects on culture, vegetation and the development of man.
Climate change, it may be argued, represented a major potential threat to
colonial economic projects. Moreover, such thinkers as Buffon often raised
fears that climate change could bring about degeneration in crops and man.
Human interventions might help to counter this threat, it was thought. By
transferring crops from one part of the world to another, or preventing rainfall
change through forest reservation, man could hope to reassert control over
the chain of natural processes and restore his supremacy. For Jenyns, schooled
in ideas about the Great Chain of Being, the project of reconstructing and
'improving' the colonial landscape in the way he had already done on his
estate near Cambridge was attractive and transferrable. With the territorial
cessions of the Peace of Paris, the West Indies colonies could, it seemed, be
improved and controlled in the same way. For a man of Jenyns's upbringing,
the idea of saving and controlling land was a familiar one. His father, Sir
Roger Jenyns, had made a fortune in fen drainage and had known Cornelius
Vermuyden.[27] Moreover, Soame Jenyns himself, alongside his more academic
works, had written extensively on the organisation of fen drainage.[28]

Why, then, did deforestation become such an apparently urgent political
issue in the West Indies during the eighteenth century? The connections between the powerful sugar lobby and the state of the Barbados economy and
landscape provide much of the answer and part of the explanation for nascent
conservatism in the colonial West Indies, quite apart from the rise to prominence of climatic theories. Quite simply, Barbados was experiencing a severe
ecological and resource crisis by the time of the Peace of Paris. As early as
1665 the island had been almost totally deforested.[29] Most of the forest clearance had taken place very rapidly, between 1625 and 1660, as sugar cultivation

Arts archives, John Adam St, London W1, Letters from West Indies, 1780–90; Wood, *History of the Royal Society of Arts*, p. 97.

27 Vermuyden stayed at the Jenyns seat in Bottisham for much of the time he was employed in fen drainage, and some of his diaries remain there. See also Darby, *The draining of the fens* for further details of Vermuyden's life.

28 E.g. Soame Jenyns, *Remarks on a bill presented in the last sessions intituled A Bill for preserving the drainage in the Middle and South Levels*, London, 1777.

29 Watts, *Man's influence on the vegetation of Barbados*, p. 45, and 'Plant introduction and land-scape change in Barbados, 1625–1836', Ph.D. diss., McGill University, 1963.

expanded over the island. A report of 1667 emphasises the almost complete loss of woodland on the island. In Barbados, it was said, 'all the trees are destroyed, so that wanting wood to boyle their sugar, they are forced to send for wood to England'. Significantly enough, the same report went on to describe the resources of Tobago as wild and untouched in comparison to Barbados.[30] There was some truth in this. Both Tobago and St Vincent remained fully forested and relatively undisturbed by Europeans until 1764–5.[31] With Barbados deforested, Tobago, in the words of John Poyntz, was still 'covered in a prodigious growth of her massy and prodigious timber trees'.[32] Poyntz's 1683 description of Tobago as a naturalistic island idyll soon attracted the attention of Daniel Defoe, who used the careful descriptions of the uncolonised 'desert island' as the basis for the descriptive setting of *Robinson Crusoe*, first published in 1719. As on Mauritius, where the cultural shadow of the 'robinsonnades' had exercised such an impact on the romanticisation of the island environment, a potential link emerged between a new typology of environmental risk and colonial perceptions of the West Indies in terms of literary constructions of tropical nature and the exotic 'other'. However, the perceptions of the Barbados colonists were at first largely utilitarian.

Since the early seventeenth century, Tobago had been used as a reliable source of supply for hardwood timbers. The Barbados timber cutters visited Tobago principally for cedar, lype, locust, mastic and other indigenous woods. A contemporary observer noted that as long as the cutters did not stay too long on the island the Cacciques (Caribs) 'gave them freedom of the axe'.[33] The contrast with Barbados and Tobago would have become more and more obvious, particularly after 1665, when only one woodland was left on the former (at Turner's Hall).[34] Furthermore, over the ensuing century as a result of the stripping of woodland, soil erosion also became a steadily more serious problem on Barbados.[35] These factors, then, must have influenced the approach taken by the Commissioners for Trade to the planning of land use on

---

30 PRO, CO1/21, 'Memorial of the island of Tobago', 1667, p. 171.
31 PRO, CO 101/18, fol. 312: Replies by George Gibbs, captain of militia in Courland (Tobago), to an enquiry by a British minister, 6 Oct. 1773. There had been some very limited phases of deforestation for sugar-cane cultivation during the Dutch occupation of Tobago from 1632 to 1667. According to Rochefort, who visited the island in 1664, there were then six well-equipped sugar factories; see C. Rochefort, *Tableau de l'Isle de Tobago*, Leiden, 1665. There is also a record of a party from Barbados led by a Captain Marshall that settled in Tobago in about 1642 but abandoned plantations of tobacco and indigo to settle in Surinam; see David L. Niddrie, *Land use and population in Tobago*, London, 1961, p. 16.
32 John Poyntz, *The present prospect of the famous and fertile island of Tobago*, London, 1683. This work was subtitled *Proposals for the enclosures of all that are minded to settle there*.
33 C. R. Ottley, *Romantic Tobago*, Port of Spain, Trinidad, 1969.
34 Watts, *Vegetation of Barbados*, p. 45.
35 See Hughes, *Natural history of Barbados*.

the Ceded Islands and on Tobago in particular. The theories diffused through from the Society of Arts would have been an additional and possibly decisive factor. The lessons of Barbados were not going to be ignored, or so it seemed.

Some mention has already been made of Soame Jenyns's connections with the Society of Arts and its effectively environmentalist agenda. But what of Soame Jenyns as an intellectual and a theological writer? Martin J. Rudwick and Stephen Jay Gould have both copiously demonstrated the critical part played by shifting religious convictions in shaping the progress of debates about geology and chronology during the late eighteenth and the early nineteenth century.[36] Similarly, there is little doubt that religious temperament and development continued to exert an influence over the evolution of environmental concerns in the late eighteenth century. This is not surprising, as the growing awareness of 'deep time' was, in fact, closely linked to the development of anxieties about species and climate change. Soame Jenyns was no exception to this pattern. His dual interest in natural theology and the Great Chain of Being are much evidenced in his prolific writings, for which he was well regarded by some of his contemporaries and much denigrated by others. The latter included Samuel Johnson, a particularly savage critic of Jenyns's theological masterpiece, *The Nature and the Origins of Evil*.[37] There is no doubt, too, that Jenyns was acutely conscious of contemporary debates on the connections between climate and culture. While he did not actually visit the West Indies or any other part of the tropics, he was still quite content to pass judgement on the risks involved in living in them. 'If the Southern Climes', he wrote, 'are gilded with a brighter sunshine . . . provided with more frequent gales and decorated with a greater profusion of plants and flowers, they are at the same time perpetually exposed to pestilential threats, infested with noxious animals, torn by hurricanes and rocked by earthquakes unknown to the rougher regions of the north.'[38] This construction of the tropical and colonial landscape as an essentially hazardous environment would have been affected by a whole variety of literary and non-literary impressions. Moreover, only a very few years had passed since the devastating Lisbon earthquake of 1755 had registered its dramatic impact on the European psyche.[39] Clearly, the notion of a chaotic and hazardous tropic may have encouraged Jenyns to favour measures which aimed to control and artificially manipulate an unstable climate. However, there is little evidence that he actually favoured the colonisation process at all. On the contrary, his writings indicate that he regarded

36 Rudwick, *The great Devonian controversy: The shaping of scientific knowledge among gentlemanly scientists*, Chicago, 1985; Gould, *Time's arrow, time's cycle*.
37 S. Jenyns, *A free enquiry into the nature and origins of evil, in six letters* . . . , London, 1757.
38 C. N. Cole, ed., *The works of Soame Jenyns*, 4 vols., London, 1788–90. A poem included in this collection is entitled 'To a young lady going to the West Indies'.
39 Glacken, *Traces on the Rhodian shore*, pp. 521–2.

the accumulation of colonies as having contributed dynamically to the severe national debt that had accumulated in Britain by the 1760s. This debt, he believed, amounted to a subtle form of revenge by the colonised territories. 'All these infallible marks of riches', Jenyns wrote, 'have committed and progressively increased with our debt and are therefore undoubtedly derived from it. No small part indeed of them has flowed in from the West and East Indies but these ought also to be placed to the same account because, without the aid of this fictitious wealth, we could never have so far extended our commerce and our conquests.' The revenge of the colonies, he thought, would take the form of the growth of corruption in the mother country.[40]

The introduction of forest reservation in this political context represented a reaction against the profligacy that had impoverished the Barbados soils and robbed the island of essential timber. By contrast, the control exercised by the Commissioners for Trade over the development of the Ceded Islands seems to represent a remarkably cautious policy. Indeed, the careful survey and subdivision of the island lands into plantation plots and forest reservations was highly reminiscent of the laying out of the East Anglian fenlands after drainage, an activity in which Jenyns and his ancestors had been intimately involved and from which they had made their fortunes.

While notions of control and exclusion (of indigenous peoples) were never far from the surface, the highly planned nature of the Grenada Governorate land settlement seems also to have represented a distinctively physiocratic response to past profligacy in the use of resources.

The innovative tree-planting policies of the Society of Arts require some explanation, as they were clearly instrumental in the new environmental planning developed for the Ceded Islands. It is possible to argue, as Simon Schama does, that the new enthusiasm for tree planting that had developed in Europe during the late sixteenth and the early seventeenth century was principally related to a cult of freedom or of liberty, co-opted, in the English case, by a royalist or statist commitment to stimulating a ready timber supply for a 'liberating' Royal Navy.[41] However, in transferring such arguments for controlled cultivation of trees to the colonial context, it is necessary to avoid explanations that are too facile or naive. In particular, one should not underestimate the novel and growing significance of trees as essential explanatory components in the new climatic theories. Furthermore, far from any associations with liberty, the Commissioners for Trade were planning for a slave-dependent plantation economy which, as parliamentary investigations of the 1790s showed, was to be almost unprecedented in its espousal of deliberate

---

40 Cole, *Works of Soame Jenyns*, III, p. 272.
41 'Primaeval forests and the cult of nature', lecture at Christ's College, Cambridge, 7 May 1991.

and cruel punishment as a way of increasing the productivity of the sugar estates. The slave-emancipation priorities of Pierre Poivre found no parallel among the British forest preservers of the West Indies. A distinction also needs to be drawn between an atavistic interest in preserving the 'natural' or the ancient and primeval and a more manipulative and power-conscious interest in constructing a new landscape by planting trees or, conceivably, marking out reservations. Mindful of the continuing association of forests with lawlessness, tree connoisseurs and landowners were usually careful in England to distinguish areas which were effectively appropriated and managed from those which were not.[42]

Soame Jenyns himself was, like many Cambridgeshire landowners of the 1760s (especially his friend Lord Hardwicke at Wimpole Hall), an enthusiastic tree planter. He left a series of long avenues of limes at Bottisham Hall that could still be seen in the 1980s. However, contemporary British colonial tree planting and forest reservation seems to have concealed a variety of other agendas, some climatic, others clearly not. In New England, colonial forest reservation had been designed, from its beginnings in 1691, largely for the purpose of securing sustainable supplies of white-pine masts and other timber for the navy. As a result, the reservation laws were actively resisted and treated by the European colonists with the contempt which they showed for other arms of an economically oppressive colonial government. During the early nineteenth century, colonial forest reservation, especially in South Africa, India and Java became part of a means of responding to anxieties about climate and the timber supply.[43] However, it also became useful in controlling unruly peoples and 'tribes', claiming territory and organising economic space. As a result, early colonial forest reservation frequently became associated with forced resettlement. It might also involve an effective biological reconstruction of the forest environment to serve the economic interests of the state. Indigenous food or material needs were rarely a priority in this process of gaining control of the biological landscape, so that impoverishment and famine often followed colonial forest reservation.

It seems very likely that this kind of historical development in the relations between colonial forest control and indigenous tropical forest-dwelling peoples found an early expression in the Eastern Caribbean after 1763. This was at a time when similar patterns of control and resistance were appearing in the German states and in colonial Java. However, the parallels should not be

---

42 K. Thomas, *Man and the natural world*, p. 215; see also S. Daniels, 'The political iconography of woodland', in D. Cosgrove and S. Daniels, *The iconography of landscape*, Cambridge, 1988.

43 See Grove, 'Colonial conservation, ecological hegemony and popular resistance'; and Nancy L. Peluso, 'The history of state forest management in colonial Java', *Forest and Conservation History*, 35 (1991), 63–73.

exaggerated. The intentions of Jenyns and his colleagues were expressed against the background of what was perceived to be an extremely hazardous tropical environment. By attempting to control atmospheric processes through rational means, a land-use strategy was adopted that was highly innovative and marked a complete break from what had gone before in the Caribbean. (Previously perhaps only the Venetians had attempted the kind of comprehensive control over the landscape that was sought by the Commissioners for Trade in the Grenada Governorate.) And there was a further item of climatic doctrine on the agenda. This was the idea that by managing to control rainfall the processes of degeneration which Buffon had so feared might be controlled. The Commissioners for Trade were familiar with land degeneration in a very specific form. In 1750 Hughes had vividly described the chaos of landslips, soil erosion and hurricanes that periodically afflicted Barbados.[44] It was this kind of disorder which the Commissioners sought to control. But, as we shall see, successive governments in the Grenada Governorate (later the Windward Islands) were faced with vigorous and long-lived indigenous opposition to their land-use policies, particularly on St Vincent.

We have already seen that the desiccation ideas and the scientific and agronomic programmes of the physiocrats were major components of environmentalism on Mauritius. Jenyns and his colleagues in the Society of Arts and among the Commissioners for Trade certainly shared in promoting the elevated status of science and specialised or professionalised knowledge that was advocated by the physiocrats. They were also institutionally linked to the Newtonian thinking of Hales, Buffon and Duhamel Monceau and, indeed, gave such thinking official credibility. However, the Commissioners for Trade do not seem, in general, to have shared in the Romantic or Utopian Edenism that had proved so important on Mauritius at the same period. This was despite the fact that seventeenth-century descriptions of Tobago had been an important inspiration to Defoe in writing *Robinson Crusoe*. However, Tobago certainly provided the raw material for a variety of commercial propaganda on plantation settlement, particularly that written by John Fowler in 1774.[45] In general, the characteristic British perception of the West Indies environment seems to have been somewhat less associated with Edenic meanings than was the case in the contemporary French context. However, the critical significance of the botanical garden in acting as a stimulus to a whole set of metaphorical as well as botanical agendas was certainly duplicated after 1765 in the Ceded Islands, specifically in the garden at Kingstown on St Vincent. Furthermore, from the first foundation of the St Vincent garden in 1765, close

44 Hughes, *Natural history of Barbados.*
45 John Fowler, *A summary account of the present flourishing state of the respectable colony of Tobago in the British West Indies,* London, 1774.

practical links were maintained between it and the garden at Pamplemousses on Mauritius, almost to the point, arguably, where they represented elements of a single institutional construct or network rather than discrete and independent intellectual entities.

In some respects, however, it has to be said that for adherents of that version of a tropical Eden that included the notion of a noble savage, Tobago, St Vincent and some of their neighbours (especially Dominica) were a field far fuller of indigenous human meaning than the previously uninhabited Mascarene Islands of the Indian Ocean. This was because, at the time of the Peace of Paris, they still sheltered a considerable population of indigenous Carib aboriginal peoples, some sections of which had long since intermixed with the descendants of escaped slaves. In this social setting, the British project of surveying and reserving town, plantation and forest lands quickly acquired a meaning distinctly different from that on Mauritius. This meant that the language of desiccationism and forest reservation soon became identified, especially on St Vincent, with an exercise in political domination, population exclusion and relocation, and eventually with open conflict among British colonists, Caribs and insurgent French revolutionaries. Particularly in the case of the latter, the whole discourse of the 'liberty tree' (insofar as it relates to the emergent eighteenth-century European interest in forest protection) took on an unexpected dimension. This new identification meant, too, that the motivations behind forest reservation on what had been conceived of as island Edens became increasingly ambiguous and confused. The construct of the forest as a desirable component of a programme for climate control and stability starkly confronted a more confused (and more antique and atavistic) image of the forest as the characteristic dwelling place of fearsome rebels and indigenous bandits. In the course of this developing confrontation as it emerged in the thirty years after 1763, the notion of the noble savage died a violent metaphorical death in the Caribbean at the same time as the indigenous social reality of the 'black Caribs' emerged as constituting one of the most effective groups of organised military (and non-military) resisters ever encountered during British colonial rule.[46] The encounter was made the more complex in that the terms of the London proclamation of March 1764 for the settlement of the Ceded Islands envisaged the creation of a whole society of plantation owners, town dwellers, slaves, and even 'poor white' settlers for whom smallholdings were to be provided in a kind of deliberately transplanted class dispensation. The large amounts of land left over from this project of landscape and social construction were to be declared forest reserve. No provision was made in this projection for land for the indigenous Caribs. In fact,

---

46 Bernard Marshall, 'The black Caribs: Native resistance to British penetration on the windward side of St. Vincent, 1763–1773', *Caribbean Quarterly*, 79 (1973).

the methodology adopted to plan the land closely resembled the strategy adopted on Mauritius during the 1760s, where there was no indigenous population. The task of map making and surveying acquired a particularly oppressive meaning in such a situation. Cartographically, what was left out of the survey became just as important as what was included in the map. On Tobago the Caribs were left out of the map-making process altogether and within twenty years had disappeared as a separate population. This deliberate and highly symbolic cartographic omission serves to indicate the need to appreciate the historic power of the act of mapmaking in shaping the nature of the discourse on colonial conservation and desiccationism in the Caribbean.[47]

The process of taking control of the government of Tobago and the process of surveying the island and designating forest reserve were almost synonymous. Ottley tells us that Alexander Brown, the first British governor, 'walked through the forest all the way to the new capital, Georgetown' (later moved to a new site and called Scarborough) to 'take up residence in the gubernatorial hut at Fort Granby'.[48] Cultivation spread quickly as new colonists mainly from Barbados arrived. In 1764 four thousand acres were planted out with sugar cane, and by 1767, a further twenty-five thousand acres. A decade later the colony exported 24,000 cwt of sugar, 100,000 gallons of rum, 150,000 lb of cotton, and 5,000 lb of indigo.

The forest reserves established by proclamation in 1764 became a permanent feature of the landscape and were little altered during the next two centuries. Even during subsequent phases of French occupation, the forest-protection legislation was recognised, and regulations continued to be enforced.[49]

In 1777 the Commissioners for Trade found it necessary to demand the repeal of a law passed by the Tobago Assembly in April 1776. This law had effectively attempted to curtail the power of the Crown to alienate land for forest reserve. Its underlying motivation, it seems, had consisted in settler resentment of the original land-use dispensation and a determination to do away with the forest reserves.[50] By this stage some Tobago colonists had clearly felt that the area gazetted for forest reserve was far too extensive and trespassed too far on opportunities for profit at a time when the sugar market was buoyant. Moreover, deforestation on other islands, as well as development on Tobago itself, sharply encouraged efforts to export the valuable timbers of the

47 For a comparable approach to the 'discourse of maps', see J. B. Harley, 'Maps, knowledge and power', in Cosgrove and Daniels, eds., *The iconography of landscape*, pp. 277–312.

48 Ottley, *Romantic Tobago*. PNM

49 Lorrain, *La mise en valeur de l'île de Tabago*.

50 PRO, CO 101/6, Report by Mr Jackson, 18 Jan. 1777; CO 102/2, Report of the Board of Trade, 18 Feb. 1777.

highland area, especially its fustic, sirmac and gumwood. Undoubtedly the forty square miles of the main forest reserve contained an enormous quantity of valuable timber.[51] Despite settler opinion, however (and the interruptions of the periods of French occupation), the boundaries of the original Tobago forest reserves were maintained with few changes.

Resisting survey and fighting from the forest: The black Caribs of St Vincent and the struggle to define the boundaries of power

The remarkably stable institutional and ecological history of the 'rain reserves' of Tobago contrasts markedly with the history of those envisaged under the same 1764 proclamation on St Vincent, Grenada and Dominica. The carto-graphic team superintended by James Simpson of Barbados had found its task to be relatively easy on Tobago. Its experiences on the other islands of the governorate were far more uncomfortable, particularly on St Vincent. Here the Caribs contrived to enforce their own alterations to the settlement and survey scheme. They thereby permanently altered and distorted the pro-gramme of colonial land allocation, forcing compromises both in the scheme and the meaning of the survey and in the connotations attached by the colo-nists to different parts of the island environment. In other words, indigenous meanings in the environment survived and even changed the colonial set of meanings, at least for some years. The process of surveying and dividing Tobago up into lots had formalized the allocation of land use and exercised a remarkable influence over later patterns of land use. Above all, no notion of common land was entertained at all, even the forest reserves being considered Crown land. The Tobago Caribs, failing to resist the new designations, were forced to become a labour pool or were ignored and finally disappeared, the victims of random killings, food shortages and imported diseases.

The survey of St Vincent, by contrast, was much longer in the making. This was principally because the indigenous black Carib population of the island put up a spirited and successful resistance to the process of survey and land allocation as a continuance of a pre-existing tradition of resistance to attempted colonial depredations. As a result, the colonial construction of the landscape, so formally adhered to on Tobago, was temporarily altered and adapted on St Vincent to suit Carib requirements. Ultimately, Carib resistance on St Vincent and latent European settler resistance to the provisions of the

---

51 Statistics on forest-reserve area are given in L. G. Hay, *A handbook of the colony of Tobago*, Scarborough, Tobago, 1882.

1764 proclamation meant that it became a dead letter, at least until the Carib rebellion of 1791.

It is worth looking at part of the background to this pattern of resistance. By the terms of the Treaty of Aix-la-Chapelle in 1748, St Vincent had been declared a neutral island by the French and English. In fact, the treaty recognised the two highly successful efforts made by the Caribs to repel French and English attempts to invade and settle the island, in 1719 and 1723 respectively. The approach taken by the English to colonisation in 1763 was, therefore, rather more hesitant than it had been on traditionally docile Tobago. We find, for example, that the likelihood that the Caribs would vigorously oppose settlement was recognised explicitly by William Young in a pamphlet published in 1764, shortly after he had been appointed chief settlement commissioner.[52] 'When the Black Caribs of St Vincent', Young wrote, 'are daily appraised of the humanity and generosity of our gracious sovereign, and *assured of the enjoyment of their lands, freedom, favour and protection*, they be gained over to our cause and even rendered useful.'[53] This degree of caution was soon extended to the plans for surveying the island. Instructions of 16 December 1764 stated that 'no survey should be made of lands occupied or claimed by the Caribs until further instructions are sent out'. By February 1764 the Caribs had in fact already appointed a missionary, the Abbé Valledares, as their public agent to negotiate with the British invader. The settlement commissioner, Young reports, 'opened an immediate correspondence with Valledares and succeeded in engaging him to cooperate with the views of the British government in settlement of the district inhabited by the Caribs'.[54] This negotiation process ran into an immediate problem, as the Caribs did not accept the concepts of private property implicit in the settlement proposals planned by the British. The areas of Carib settlement, it was reported at the time, were 'occupied mostly in common as by an erratic nation of savage warriors and hunters'. What little cultivation there was, Young went on, 'appeared merely in small disturbed spots of provision ground near to their cabins . . . worked entirely by women; for the rest of the Caribs drew their sustenance by their guns or from the seas'.[55] Young complained that the Caribs had as little idea of their 'obligation to cultivate the earth' as they had of their 'having no right to appropriate more than they could cultivate'. Furthermore, Young ambivalently observed, they understood 'the abstract reasonings of Wolfus and Vattel no more than they appreciated the grant of St

52 The existence of this pamplet is reported by William Young's son (also called William Young) in *An account of the black Caribs of St Vincent*, London, 1795, pp. 19–29. For a modern account, see Marshall, 'The black Caribs'.
53 Young, *Account of the black Caribs*, p. 23 (my italics).
54 Ibid., p. 21.
55 Ibid.

Vincent to Lords Carlisle and Willoughby by Kings Charles 1st and 2nd'.[56]
This was an important statement historically, as it gave a clear indication of
the extent to which a highly exclusionist political ideology of land use had
become an accepted part of the justification for the expropriation and colonisation of native lands. As Young implied, only cultures practising settled
agriculture could be considered legally entitled to claim sovereign rights over
land. Here, then, it may be possible to locate at least some of the antecedents
of the very long-running critique of shifting cultivation and pastoral nomad-
ism.[57]

In fact the Caribs' appreciation of the European legal standpoint on St
Vincent was a great deal more sophisticated than Young appeared to realise.
What was more, the black Caribs were quite prepared to legitimate their claims
in European terms by reference to the invited intervention of the governor of
Martinique in an old land dispute that had surfaced in 1700 between the black
(mixed-race) Caribs and the red (pure-blooded) Caribs. A geographic line, the
'Base de l'isle', had been drawn to separate the populations. As Young records,
this intervention grew shortly into a sacred prescription in 'the short memories
of a savage people and perhaps one not to be cancelled but with the strong
arm of conquest and control'.[58] The social memory of this legitimation was,
of course, long rather than 'short', as Young mistakenly thought.

All attempts to involve the Caribs in the survey, redistribution and sale of
their own long-occupied lands during 1764 and 1765 failed, despite their being
offered the carrot of 'full rights as British subjects'. In 'this situation of affairs',

56 Ibid., p. 22.
57 Vattel, *The law of nations.* The operative passages in Vattel's text are: 'The cultivation of the
   earth causes it to produce an infinite increase . . . it forms the resource and the most solid
   fund of riches and commerce for the people who enjoy a happy climate . . . the sovereign
   ought not to allow either communities or private persons to occupy large tracts of land in
   order to have it uncultivated. These rights of common, which deprive the proprietor of the
   free liberty of disposing of his lands, that will not allow him to farm them, and to cause them
   to be uncultivated in the most advantageous manner, these rights I say are contrary to the
   welfare of the state and ought to be suppressed or reduced to just bounds . . . Spain is the
   most fertile and the worst cultivated country in Europe. [p. 36] . . . China is the best cultivated
   country in the world . . . those people like the antient Germans and the modern Tartars, who
   having fertile countries, disdain to cultivate the earth and choose rather to live by rapine, are
   wanting to themselves, and *deserve to be exterminated as savage and pernicious beasts* . . . there
   are others who, to avoid agriculture, would live only by living on their flocks. This might
   doubtless be allowed in the first ages of the world, when the earth, without cultivation, produced more than was sufficient to feed its few inhabitants. But at present when the human
   race is so multiplied it could not subsist, if all nations resolved to live in that manner. Those
   who retain this life usurp more extensive territories than they would have occasion for, were
   they to use honest labour, and have therefore no reason to complain if other nations more
   laborious and closely confined come to possess a part' (p. 37: my italics).
58 Young, *Account of the black Caribs,* p. 23.

Young disingenuously tells us, 'the conduct of the Commissioners was embarrassed and undecided, but in all cases just and even favourable to the
Caribs'.[59] The operative word here was 'embarrassed'. The Caribs had provoked a crisis of sovereignty and control and persisted openly in disclaiming
allegiance to the British Crown. The Crown, the settlement commissioners
thought, 'could not with either honour or advantage, hold a divided sovereignty in an island only twenty-one miles in length'.[60] A major part of this
sovereignty dispute concerned the forests of the island and their rightful ownership. The issue emerged prominently in an agonised letter sent by the settlement commissioners to the Lords Commissioners of the Treasury in
Whitehall on 10 August 1765. In it the commissioners (William Young [the
elder], Robert Stuart and Robert Gwynne) stated that the Caribs

> live in huts scattered in an *irregular manner* at a great distance from each
> other, without any established subordination, claiming large tracts of
> woodland intervening of which they make no use; and are besides pos-
> sessed of other lands in the cleared part of the country, which interfere
> much with the large area of plantations for sale.[61]

To settle this 'problem', the commissioners suggested, alternative land should
be offered to the Caribs on the nearby island of Bequia. However, Bequia, it
was soon realised, was deficient in water and would not actually support the
Caribs at all. But the idea of compulsory resettlement had now been firmly
sown in the mind of officialdom, and the Bequia scheme accurately prefigured
the forced resettlement of the Caribs which was to take place to that island,
in much harsher circumstances, in the 1790s. Moreover, the Bequia scheme
effectively exposed the underlying intentions of the commissioners in their
attempts to survey and allocate Carib land. Theirs was, of course, an exclusionist programme of which the Carib leadership had, from the outset, been
acutely and sensitively aware. Indeed, the 1764 land proclamation, applying
to the whole Grenada Governorate, made no provision whatsoever for Carib
land interests and their mode of forest and land use. The relatively docile
Carib response to the proclamation on Tobago, in a territory where the indigenous population was anyway very low, seems to have encouraged the commissioners to expect a similar response among the very different and much
larger population on St Vincent. As it turned out, the St Vincent Caribs were,
in the medium term, able to find ways of intimidating and manipulating the
settlement commissioners so as to adapt the survey project to their own ends.
In the course of doing so, they effectively disrupted the forest-reservation

59 Ibid., p. 24.
60 Ibid.
61 Ibid., p. 27; (my italics).

schemes so beloved of the Commissioners for Trade, although less beloved of
large elements of the settler population.

In doing so, the Caribs managed also to further exacerbate the highly ambiguous situation in which the colonising power found itself vis-à-vis people
who were both 'Indian' and 'Negro' in their ancestry. While Indians had
frequently found themselves eligible for easier treatment as noble savages, the
black African affinities of the black Caribs invited cultural comparisons with
the groups then being imported to other West Indian islands as plantation
slaves at a time when the brutality meted out to slaves in the British Windward
Islands was almost unparalled in severity. This was further complicated by
the fact that the British soon developed a very healthy respect for the experience, organisation and guerilla fighting skills of the black Caribs. In February
1768, after a period of three years in which the Caribs successfully held up
the survey and land-allocation programme, new proposals were announced
that finally led to a break in the uneasy truce between Caribs and colonists.
The apparently contradictory provisions of the new proposals serve to indicate
the important change of mood that had taken place in the ranks of the now
seriously frustrated colonial power. The new settlement provisions included
two significant ideas:

> (1) That no step shall be taken towards the removal of any Charaib, till
> the whole arrangement and design should have been notified and ex-
> plained to the satisfaction of their chiefs; and that they be made to
> comprehend the conditions in which settlement was proposed and
> that the plan be carried into effect with the gentlest hand and in the
> mildest manner.
> (2) Under these terms the spots of cleared land which they now occupy
> should be sold, and made part of plantation allotments, with the
> woodlands which surround them; and on the final removal of the
> Charaibs shall make part of such plantations.[62]

It is quite clear that at this stage the Carib leadership, and above all Chief
Chatoyer, realised that, despite the interceding efforts of the Abbé Valledares,
the period of a phoney land war had come to an end.[63] The Caribs thus
determined to prevent any further road building or surveying taking place on
the island. Matters then came quickly to a head, and from December 1768
the surveying teams under James Simpson (who had surveyed Tobago without
any resistance) were continually harassed and threatened by armed Caribs. On
29 April 1768 Levi Porter, an assistant surveyor, reported that the Caribs had
burnt his house and 'stolen my maps and equipment'. They would 'not have

62 Ibid., pp. 31–7.
63 Ibid., p. 38.

Plate 17. Chief Chatoyer and his wives. (Engraving made in 1792 and taken from B. Edwards, *The history, civil and commercial, of the West Indies*, London, 1818)

the Great Road go any further', Porter told Simpson in his letter. The Caribs did not stop at this symbolic act. After burning Porter's house, three hundred well-armed Carib warriors then proceeded to demolish the new military barracks on the Great Road.[64] On 1 May forty men of the 32nd Infantry Regiment found themselves confronting the same three hundred Carib warriors. The commander, Captain Wilkin, decided to retreat and avoid any decisive engagement, which, in the confines of the forest, he was by no means sure of winning. Instead Wilkin decided to retreat south to Kingstown to consult the governor and council about the strategic situation.[65] On this occasion, on 1

64 PRO, CO 106/11, Assistant Surveyor Levi Porter to James Simpson, Kingstown, 29 April 1769.
65 PRO, CO 106/4, Letter from John Poynes to James Simpson, 3 May 1769.

May, John Byres, the government cartographer, was forced to hide his new half-made survey maps in a field.[66] However, the Caribs soon found and burnt the hidden maps, and Byres too retreated to the safety of Kingstown. A peace was then declared by the British on the basis that no further attempts would be made 'to interfere in the country or build further roads'.[67]

The situation was then reported by the settlement commissioners to the Commissioners for Trade. The report, dated July 1769, made the very specific point that the Caribs were able to use the extensive forest cover of the island in a very effective military sense. The Caribs, the commissioners said, would continue to 'be very dangerous and may at some time prove fatal to the [white] inhabitants of the country as their situation, surrounded by wood, makes any access to them impracticable'.[68] The St Vincent planters themselves, however, now revealed that they disagreed with the commissioners' bellicose stand. In a letter written by a group of settlers directly to Lord Hillsborough in early 1770 it was made clear to Whitehall that the settlers believed that any detachment of soldiers sent to reinforce the island should be used to protect settlers rather than to try to wipe out the Caribs. As the colonists pointed out, the Caribs now had the open backing of the governor of Martinique, so that any aggressive action against them might prove counterproductive and seriously affect the security of white settlers. In this connection the settlers again made the point that 'a very small proportion of the island . . . has yet been cleared of wood so that all efforts should be made to clear the forest'.[69] As the settlers' letter was addressed directly to the Earl of Hillsborough and wholly conflicted with the policy of the Commissioners for Trade, it seems to have received little attention. Indeed, their appeal contained opinions which were radical for the time and which would seem uncomfortably at odds with the attitudes of a slave-using society. 'It is not the wish of your memorialists', the settlers had added, 'that the Charaibs should be otherwise dealt with than in a manner entirely becoming humanity.'[70] The problem with the forest cover on the island was, as Young explained at length, that 'the large tracts of woodlands, from river to river, were claimed by families or tribes of Charaibs in common, and any sales made by one family would probably be disavowed by every other'.[71]

66 Byres had already by this time draughted the first settlement map of Tobago.
67 Young, *Account of the black Caribs*, p. 47.
68 Ibid.
69 Letter of the St Vincent colonists to the Earl of Hillsborough, quoted in Young, *Account of the black Caribs*, pp. 56–7.
70 Young adds his own bias here: 'The statement that the large tract of uncultivated land in wood could never be useful to the Charaibs is perfectly true; for a hunter's country can be of no use to the Indian where there is nothing to hunt' (p. 62).
71 Ibid., p. 63.

During 1770 ministers in London were even led to annul land sales already made by individual Caribs. The commissioners, moreover, were led to report on 15 December 1770 that 'His Majesty's Commissioners have found it necessary to desist from the execution of his instructions to report home a State of the Case and wait respectfully the King's further orders.' By this stage the Commissioners for Trade appear to have decided that the original proposals had been 'contrary to the facts of treaties [i.e. the neutrality provisions of the Treaty of Aix-la-Chapelle] and . . . omitted acknowledgement of any right in virtue of possession by the inhabitants'.

By determined resistance over a five-year period, the Caribs had thus brought about a fundamental shift in position by the colonial power. For one thing, the British had been forced to accept the legitimacy of the 'base de l'isle' as a European legal form that the Caribs had actively and voluntarily elicited from the French government on Martinique at the beginning of the century. Moreover, the Carib construction and perception of the landscape as common or clan rather than individual property had effectively won the day. This was partly because so much of the island remained under forest cover. So much was admitted by the commissioners in a remarkable statement:

> It may be easy to determine who are best entitled to the possession of cleared and cultivated lands, since it is equitable that those who have toiled should reap the fruits of their labour [this did not, presumably, apply to African slaves!] . . . yet it will be difficult to *prove any natural right or title to the large tracts of woodlands* in St Vincent's which certain Charaibs may presume to claim: there is apprehension of endangering the peace of the island from the disputes and contests among the Charaibs themselves. The sellers of these lands, as set forth in the memorial, are only three Charaibs, now it can no way be demonstrated that others of them do not conceive they have an equal claim to the enjoyment of the woods, perhaps esteemed amongst them a common right of nature; if so it is probable that those who have no share of the advantage rising from that sale may be dissatisfied with their comrades and oppose a precedent, which may· gradually endanger their other possessions by admitting strangers [colonists] into their neighbourhood without the general consent of the whole.[72]

Thus by 1770 even the settlement commissioners themselves opposed the original land-use plan and the idea of forcibly resettling the Caribs. As a result, all purchases of Carib land by colonists were officially set aside on 15 December 1770.

72 Quoted in ibid. (my italics).

Alexander Anderson and the official advocacy of environmentalism on St Vincent, 1784–1811

Carib resistance to the land-use allocation implied in the 1764 proclamation effectively terminated the original model of forest conservation for the British Caribbean in the form in which it had been developed on Tobago. The realities of military strategy and the economic priorities of the colonies had delivered a further fatal blow to the concept. There was, of course, an underlying weakness in the environmental policy of the governorate during the 1760s. In contrast to Mauritius at the same period, there was no local involvement by professional naturalists and thus no real continuity of ideological commitment to any form of sustainable economic development justified through climatic arguments. William Young, as we have seen, was actively hostile to the notion of forest protection, even though charged with its execution.

After the return of St Vincent to British control in 1783, a rather more committed kind of official environmentalist consciousness came to the surface. The fact that it was able to do so was due both to the effective institutionalisation of natural history on the island as a result of the development of the St Vincent Botanic Garden and to the increasing official interest in the garden taken by Sir Joseph Banks.[73] This institution in turn facilitated the introduction to the island colony of a whole spectrum of current European scientific debates and discourses in the person of Alexander Anderson, a Scottish physician and botanist who was appointed curator of the garden in 1785. While the introduction of desiccationist forest legislation had been a remarkable feature of the early settlement of Tobago, it had taken place as the remote effect of a distant debate and, indeed, as a conceptual constraint much at odds with the immediacies of colonial perceptions. Any real impetus to innovations in environmental policy had lain in specifically European ideas, whose philosophical inspiration and texts were located mainly in France and then acted upon in England. The 'centre of calculation', to use the Latourian terminology, remained firmly set in Paris (in the Académie des Sciences) or in London (in the Society of Arts).

While politically feasible on Tobago, the practical and symbolic rejection of the colonial map of St Vincent by the Caribs had provoked the loss of the dependent structure of desiccationism in favour of a compromised construct based more on indigenous social reality. As a result, the environmental opinions and policies which developed in government circles on St Vincent after 1783 were very much more indigenous and locally constrained. In particular,

---

73 For a full historical account of the garden, see Lansdown Guilding, *An account of the botanic garden in the island of St Vincent*, Glasgow, 1825.

the botanical garden on St Vincent became the site of a centre of environmental calculation which, while still partially dependent on outside networks
and intellectual structures, also incorporated a good deal of autonomous intellectual work. Above all, the coupling of the institutional setting of the botanical garden (and its networks) with the intellectual personality of Alexander
Anderson allowed the full impact of Enlightenment science and current environmental thinking to be felt on St Vincent and on its processes. But the
intellectual process went further than this. While resident on St Vincent,
Anderson produced a set of coherent environmentalist writings that were influenced both by the rapidly changing ecology of the island and by contemporary thinking in Europe. Most important among these texts were 'A
Geography and History of St Vincent' and a series of drafts of a book called
'The Delugia'. All were written between about 1799 and 1805.[74]

The principal piece of environmental legislation with which Anderson was
connected was the Kings Hill Forest Act of 1791. While in concept apparently
based on the 1764 proclamation for the Grenada Governorate, the Act was
also a specifically local development which had been much influenced by the
views of Anderson as well as other colonists. In terms of text and legislation,
the emergence of a relatively autonomous environmental consciousness on St
Vincent between 1783 and 1800 represents a cross-fertilisation between European scientific thought and the more autonomous physiocratic responses to
tropical environmental change which had evolved on Mauritius a decade earlier. These two environmentalisms were in fact closely connected. Thus the
climatic theories and desiccationist thinking current on Mauritius and in the
Eastern Caribbean by the 1780s can be seen as the first isolated indications of
what was, within a few decades, to become a more general and global environmental critique.

The 1773 treaty between the British and the Caribs meant that, at least
temporarily, survey and forest-reservation plans were abandoned on St Vincent. Instead, forest clearance and cultivation continued in the southern parts
of the island, mainly for sugar production. In much of the zone designated
for the Caribs, as well as in the European areas on the leeward side of the
island, the forest remained largely untouched. Towards the end of the French
occupation, between 1779 and 1785, the process of forest clearance resumed,
stimulated by an increasingly buoyant market for cotton. This rise had begun
at about the time that Alexander Anderson first visited the island in 1784. In

---

74 The four main texts, all MSS in the Archives of the Linnaean Society, are (1) 'The St Vincent
Botanic Garden', (2) 'The geography and history of St Vincent', (3) 'The delugia', and (4)
'Hortus St Vincenti'. The first two documents have been produced in typescript editions by
the Arnold Arboretum, Harvard College, Cambridge, Mass. Anderson's letters are also preserved in a variety of collections, esp. Kew Gardens Archives, Richmond, Surrey.

1785 he returned to St Vincent as superintendent of the St Vincent Botanic Garden at Kingstown (in succession to Dr George Young, whom he had earlier met on St Lucia) and remained in the post until his death in 1811. It was not long after Anderson's arrival that the notion of forest reservation reappeared on the official post-occupation agenda.

By 1784 cotton cultivation was already known to be damaging to the island soils. Moreover, in many of the West Indian islands, but particularly on St Kitts, Nevis and Jamaica, some limited soil-conservation measures had been adopted in response to the erosion problems caused by prolonged periods of uninterrupted sugar-cane cultivation.[75] Diffusion of awareness of the dangers of soil erosion may well have affected St Vincent by the 1780s. However, it seems likely that the consequences of the post-1785 clearance for cotton cultivation (linked to a subsequent rapid appearance of erosion and gullying) soon made an impact on local settler opinion. Detailed discussions took place, for example, in the St Vincent Assembly in January 1790 on the subject of soil erosion and the causes of gullying. Particular mention was made by members of the size of the new gullies, which were so wide that even fully harnessed ox teams could not cross them without the aid of specially constructed wooden bridges.[76] However, by this time legislation to gazette a 'climatic' forest reserve at King's Hill had already been set in train as a result of active lobbying of the St Vincent government by Alexander Anderson and a member of the Assembly, William Bannatyne. The original bill had been tabled in the Assembly on 13 November 1788. The bill, apparently drafted by Bannatyne with Anderson's advice, was intended to 'appropriate for the benefit of the neighbourhood the hill called "The Kings Hill"'[77]

Some mention is appropriate here of the precise status and characteristics of the King's Hill, a small but highly significant site in the history of colonial environmentalism. The hill is in the south-eastern section of the island where the natural vegetation is (in the twentieth century) known as 'dry woodland'.[78] It is an area peculiarly susceptible to drying winds at some seasons, a phenomenon that held particular hazards for the area of sugar-cane cultivation, which was at the time still expanding rapidly in that part of the island and

---

75 These soil-conservation methods are extensively described in Watts, *West Indies*. So-called cane holes were the main soil-conservation structure adopted.

76 PRO, CO 263/21, Assembly discussion, 28 Jan. 1790, passage on gullies.

77 PRO, CO 263/21, Assembly Proceedings, 13 Nov. 1788: 'William Bannatyne prays to have read a Bill . . . being delivered in at the table was read the first time, asked to be read a second time on the next meeting'.

78 J. S. Beard, *Natural vegetation of the Windward and Leeward Islands;* K. Rodney, A. Glasgow and N. Weekes, 'Summary of forest change at the King's Hill reserve, St Vincent, 1945–1990', paper presented at the International Conference on Environmental Institutions, Kingstown, St Vincent, April 1991.

particularly on the land of George Stubbs, adjacent to which the King's Hill Forest was located and on to which the forest drained.

The King's Hill Forest Bill experienced considerable delays and opposition in the course of its passage through the Assembly, largely because of the fears of some planters that parts of their estates might become sterilised under other forest reserves gazetted on the model of King's Hill. A committee on the bill which met on 2 January 1790 served to expose some of these fears. Some members suggested that it was entirely beneficial that 'wild and unfrequented woods' should be turned to cotton and sugar planting. Their real fear, however, appears to have been articulated in the concern that 'the Charaibs should be kept behind the line', that is, the zonal boundary line which had been established in the 1773 treaty with Chief Chatoyer.[79] Forest clearance, it was implied, would help to ensure the integrity of the boundary, whereas forest reservation might merely give the Caribs potential cover for future insurrections. These discussions make it quite apparent that the notion of forest reservation was not seen as offering support to efforts at social control of the Caribs; in fact, quite the contrary. Instead, the preferred colonial construction of the landscape for most European settlers, as it had been on Barbados, consisted in the development of a cleared and thoroughly socialised island.[80]

For these reasons, a second reading of the bill was deferred on 5 February 1790 and again on 13 March 1990. However, the bill was finally read a further time on 2 June 1790. On 8 December 1790 it was agreed to lay the bill before the governor for assent. After this the bill went through fairly smoothly. Even so, the governor, James Seton, insisted on an important final amendment. As it originally stood, the bill had aimed to appropriate the King's Hill Forest on behalf of the colony rather than on behalf of the king. This reflected the local origins of the scheme, which contrasted with the provisions of the Grenada Governorate proclamation of 1764. Once this political matter was dealt with, the bill finally received the governor's assent on 9 February 1791. The key climatic provision, as it was included in the third reading of the bill, ordained that the law would 'appropriate for the benefit of the neighbourhood the hill called The Kings Hill in the Parish of St George and for enclosing the same, preserving the timber and other trees growing thereon *in order to attract rain*'. When altered by the governor to bring it firmly back into the ambit of Whitehall, the final Act read significantly differently. Thus it was eventually

---

79 PRO, CO 263/21, 2 Jan. 1790.
80 A useful discussion of the role of a cleared and controlled landscape in creating a European 'colonial identity' appears in J. P. Greene, 'Changing identity in the British Caribbean: Barbados as a case-study', in N. Canny and A. Pagden, eds., *Colonial identity in the Atlantic world*, Princeton, N.J., 1987, pp. 213–67.

enacted by the authority aforesaid that the hill called the Kings Hill and
the timber and other trees and wood growing, or that may grow thereon,
according to the extent and bounding thereof is reserved by His Majesty's
said Commissioners [and] shall be and is hereby *reserved and appropriated
for the purpose of attracting the clouds and rain.*[81]

The addition of 'clouds' to the wording of the final Act suggests that some
detailed theoretical and meteorological debates had taken place in committee
or among Seton's advisers. Unfortunately, if there were any such discussions
at this stage, they have not been recorded. Certainly both legislators and governor seem to have been remarkably cautious in allocating land for purposes
of the Act in comparison to the generous allocation made in 1764 on Tobago.
Indeed, the King's Hill reserve as eventually gazetted was small almost to the
point of being experimental.

The precise site of the reserve was surveyed, as laid down in the 1791 Act,
on 5 June 1791 and was subsequently resurveyed in 1808, 1812, 1846, 1912
and 1991.[82] During this period the forest suffered little encroachment, despite
considerable local and sustainable use of the woods for firewood and yam
growing.[83] Despite its limited size, the principle upon which the King's Hill
reserve was established appears to have exercised a remarkable institutional
influence in the ensuing decades, particularly in the practice of tree planting
and forest reservation on St Helena and, less directly, over wide areas of India.
While part of the provenance of the King's Hill legislation can be attributed
in very general terms to the Grenada Governorate proclamation of 1764, the
revived form of desiccationism seems directly attributable to Anderson's influence and his personal agenda. But other lobbies may also have been at work,
particularly amongst the membership of the Society of Arts. It had been General Melville himself who had sponsored William Bannatyne, the original ta-
bler of the King's Hill bill, for election as a corresponding member of the
Society of Arts. As such, Bannatyne would have joined Joshua Steele of Barbados as one of a small group of influential West Indies planters who were
already Society members.[84]

81 Second paragraph of the Act as proclaimed on 2 April 1791.
82 See Michael Kidston, 'Kings Hill history: A surveyor's perspective', paper for Forestry Development Division, Ministry of Agriculture and Labour, Government of St Vincent, 1991.
83 In April 1991 Cyril Shallow, a farmer and banana grower living adjacent to the forest at
   Stubbs village, demonstrated to me the way in which the indigenous American yam is sus-
   tainably harvested in the forest, and the way in which small amounts of surplus and fallen
   timber are gathered for local use. The access allowed to continue such practices has almost
   certainly contributed to the survival of the forest for so long within the boundaries of 1791.
84 Archives of the Royal Society of Arts, John Adam Street, London SW1: Index of eighteenth-
   century sponsored candidates for membership. Bannatyne is spelt 'Banntine' in the Society
   records.

It seems likely that both Melville and some of his colleagues in the Society of Arts were keen to renew the climatic measures abandoned during the earlier disastrous conflicts with the black Caribs. However, the part played by Melville and the Society in founding the St Vincent Botanic Garden proved ultimately more decisive in promoting environmental ideas, particularly by providing Alexander Anderson with a base both for supporting the King's Hill legislation and for developing his environmentalist theories in a series of specific writings. The most important and coherent of the latter were included in his unpublished manuscript entitled 'The Geography and History of St Vincent'. This text (which can usefully be compared in scope and depth of insight with Poivre's speeches to the colonists of Mauritius in 1767 and with Bernardin de Saint-Pierre's *Studies* and *Harmonies of Nature*) allows one to place Anderson in his true historical context and to define the antecedents and terms of his eloquent and elaborate environmentalism.

A crisis of conscience and chronology: Alexander Anderson and the characteristics of his environmental critique, 1785–1811

Much like Pierre Poivre's the origins of Anderson's environmentalism emerged initially from his professional interest in plant transfer, a field of activity which the Society of Arts had sought to support by its vigorous sponsorship of the St Vincent Botanic Garden. For both men the study of the constraints on soil conditions for plant transfer had stimulated an interest in the dynamics of the wider environment and its interrelationships. In fact, Anderson precisely pinpointed the beginnings of his interest in soil conditions as having been aroused, like Poivre's, by an acquaintance with the work of the Dutch botanist Rumphius, and particularly his book *Herbarium Amboinense*.[85] It would be very difficult, however, to place an exact date upon Anderson's espousal of environmental fears and climatic anxieties. His ideas clearly evolved a great deal during his residence on St Vincent and were affected both by his own gathering of empirical data and by his dual response to the social crises on the island and the crisis taking place in natural science, particularly with regard to geological chronology and awareness of species extinctions. Anderson's wide reading would soon have made him aware of contemporary debates about vegetation, airs and climate. We know, for example, that he had read Edward Long's *History of Jamaica*, a large work that contained a very extensive analysis of theories that had recently been expounded by Joseph Priestley on air and the atmosphere, together with accounts of the work of other pioneers in atmospheric chemistry, including

85 Guilding, *Botanic garden*, p. 7.

Stephen Hales.[86] Anderson may have become acquainted with both Hales's and Priestley's theories quite independently of Edward Long's work. However, direct evidence of his familiarity with the work of Priestley emerges only after 1800, so it remains difficult to reconstruct the pattern of Anderson's intellectual development with any certainty or to specify the exact period at which he acquired a desiccationist mentality.

Conceivably, an incipient interest in the physical effects of deforestation may have developed through Anderson's friendship with Dr George Young, whose botanical correspondence with the Pamplemousses garden on Mauritius may have familiarised him with Poivre's first forest-protection and afforestation programmes. In fact, there is little doubt that both Young and Anderson would have had frequent opportunities to acquire a knowledge of developments on Mauritius, and they may actually have discussed them.

A letter written by Anderson to William Forsyth, the curator of the Chelsea Physic Garden (where Anderson had originally trained in the early 1770s), and later published by Sir George Yonge in *Philosophical Transactions of the Royal Society* indicates that Anderson was by 1784 already deeply interested in geology and meteorology and in the relationship between woodland and cloud cover.[87] The letter, written after an ascent of Souffrière, the main volcano on St Vincent, mentions that the mountain 'was surrounded by thick wood and during the night the whole of the mountain is covered with thick clouds, from which it frequently rains'.[88] 'I am sorry', Anderson remarked in the letter, 'that I had no instruments to take the state of the air.'[89] This statement provides us with a small but important key to Anderson's theoretical inclinations and especially to his interest in atmospheric dynamics. In particular, Anderson was interested in measuring the qualities of the air, attributing causes to those qualities and associating them with the character of climate. In connecting air quality, volcanoes and climate, Anderson was in illustrious company, particularly that of Benjamin Franklin. Alerted to the possibility of rapid climate change by the very severe winter of 1783–4, Franklin had reached the conclusion that a global cooling in the temperate latitudes could safely be attributed to a rise in volcanic activity. The cooling layer of dust that could be observed in the skies of France and the United States was, he

86 Priestley, 'Observations on different kinds of air', *Philosophical Transactions of the Royal Society*, 62 (1772), 147–264, *Experiments and observations*, London, 1774, and 'On the noxious quality of the effluvia of putrid marshes', *Philosophical Transactions of the Royal Society*, 64 (1774), p. 91.
87 A. Anderson, 'An ascent of Morne Garou, a mountain in the island of St Vincent, with a description of the volcano at its summit', *Philosophical Transactions of the Royal Society*, 75 (1785), 16–36.
88 Ibid., p. 20.
89 Ibid., p. 30.

thought, due to 'the vast quantity of smoke, long continuing to issue during the fumer from Hecla in Iceland'.[90] While it is difficult to prove, it is likely that Anderson would have become familiar with the theme of this paper, as during the 1780s he became more and more interested in the structure of volcanoes and their geological and climatic consequences. Dominating the island as it did, and with the effects of its frequent eruptions only too plain to see, Souffrière was bound to dominate Anderson's understanding of natural processes.

Initially, however, it was the small and circumscribed nature of the island that alerted Anderson to the rapid pace of tropical environmental change. During his long term as curator of the botanical garden, he came to know the island in great detail. He crossed and recrossed the colony collecting plants, insects, birds and geological specimens. Apart from voluminous notes on plants, his letters also comment on soils, deforestation, the need for forest protection and the desirability of diversifying away from simple sugar-cane cropping. He frequently collected plants adjacent to Carib habitations and described those which he thought had been introduced on the island by the aboriginal people.[91] This information was carefully documented in letters to William Forsyth at the Chelsea Physic Garden and other botanists. Anderson's expertise on the island was distilled in his manuscript 'The Geography and History of St Vincent', written in about 1800; it is from this text that one can adduce the main strands of his environmental thinking. His justification for writing the work was based on the simple but significant premise that 'Saint Vincent has been pitched upon for the establishment of the garden'. He added that

> as the Royal munificence has been the support of the institution [the botanical garden] it appears necessary to give some idea of the situation, structure, climate, seasons and soils of the island. The more so as the island is to be regarded as a nursery for supplying all the other islands with the useful plants that can be obtained from the different climates of the world.[92]

Here, then, was the initial stimulus to a book in which the two main topics of concern emerge as, first, the relations between people and climate and, secondly, the relations between colonist and Carib. There was a strong aes-

90 Benjamin Franklin, 'Meteorological imaginations and conjectures', *Transactions of the Manchester Philosophical Society*, 1784, pp. 373–7. This paper was written at Passy, France, in May 1784.
91 Most significant of these was the American yam, still a vital part of the diet of the population living adjacent to King's Hill (informant: Cyril Shallow, Stubbs village, King's Hill).
92 Anderson, 'Geography and history of St Vincent' (M5, Linnaean Society), transcription ed. R. A. and E. S. Howard, Harvard College, p. 5.

thetic theme to the book too, and Anderson's language is strongly reminiscent of contemporary Romantic literature. Perhaps few islands in the world, Anderson felt, displayed as great a variety of 'pleasing and romantic scenes as St Vincent'.[93] 'Its size and form', he informs us later in the text, 'very much resemble that celebrated island of Otaheite in the South seas, and when Captain Bligh approached it [St Vincent] in Providence two natives of that island on board leaped for joy and called out "Otaheite, Otaheite!", conceiving it to be their native land.'[94] Once again we are dealing here with an exact parallel to the new intellectual stereotypes transferred by Commerson (and to a lesser extent by Poivre) from Tahiti to the Mascarene Islands. Indeed, this throwaway comment in the 'Geography' goes a long way towards explaining Anderson's preconceptions with St Vincent and the role which its visual nature might perform in his personal cosmology. It also helps to account for Anderson's very disturbed and ambivalent response to the brutal treatment of the indigenous Caribs by the British. The image of Tahiti may also shed some light on Anderson's sensitivity towards the destruction of the forests in which the Caribs lived. In other words, the notion of a 'nouvelle Cythère', with all its Utopian social connotations, may be important to understanding Anderson's formulation of an environmentalism in circumstances in which it might have been least expected, at least in terms of the social context, which was one of oppression.

Nevertheless, for Anderson the decisive factor in his growing sensibility was the rapidity of the deforestation which he was able to witness even in the immediate environs of the botanical garden at Kingstown. In the course of a wide-ranging description of St Vincent in his 'Geography', Anderson carefully notes the changes in forest cover which had taken place in the years since he first arrived on the island. He records, for example, the disappearance during the 1790s of 'the thickest and most impenetrable forests in St Vincent'.[95] The whole account is coloured by the fact that Anderson had lived through the almost complete removal of the indigenous Carib population and through French insurrections against British occupation in 1795. The sense of guilt and insecurity that seems thereby to have been induced in Anderson himself may help to explain his confused and ambivalent attitude towards the Caribs, who had depended for their survival on the forests which Anderson so much valued and who had then been forcibly removed from the island at the end of the rebellion. The St Vincent government, Anderson believed, had been entirely responsible for provoking rebellion among the Caribs in the first place and had compounded this fault by expelling them from the island in what he

93 Ibid., p. 10.
94 Ibid., p. 36.
95 Ibid., p. 11.

considered to be a brutal and unjust fashion. Indeed, Anderson appears to have directly equated the unfair treatment of the Caribs with the uncontrolled deforestation of the island for sugar planting.

While he left the colonial treatment of the Caribs to the further judgement of others, the intensely religious Anderson was in no doubt about what sort of climatic retribution would be exacted for the deforestation of the windward parts of the island, where the most fertile estates were to be found. The seaside estates, he asserted, 'in some years suffer by drought and it is feared will suffer more as the interior lands are cleared of their native forests . . . the clouds are naturally attracted by the high and woody summits of the primary chain and then much condensed in passing down their leeward sides'.[96] The planters were, he complained, acting the same inconsiderate and imprudent part as the first settlers of Barbados and Antigua 'by the total extirpation of all the natural woods within their bounds. The loss of crops for many years past in these two islands, owing to the extermination of the native trees and woods', Anderson adds, 'ought to have been a warning to the planters on the windward side of St Vincent.' These remarks preface a part of the 'Geography' manuscript which amounts to a wide-ranging summary or even personal credo of Anderson's conservationist views. It is quoted here at length, since it provides us with a comprehensive account of colonial environmental notions as they had developed in the Caribbean by 1800.

'Turn all into cane' is too much the invariable maxim of the planter, and before it fall indiscriminately all woods, altho' of the greatest value. The noxious weed is eradicated; at the same time is the most useful plant. Not a tree is left to vary the scene. Nor do they consider that one day the expense of mill timber must oblige them to reproduce what they have so inconsiderately destroyed. Much fruitless labour has been bestowed in clearing tops of hills, found afterwards to be too barren for the cane or any cultivated plant. Had they been left in the natural clumps, they would have highly improved the look of the country and given a continued supply of useful wood and trees for shade, which is found to be absolutely necessary in pastures in this climate. The cattle resort to them for shelter against the sun, wind and rain, and against their stems clear themselves of the tick and insect, [which are] very troublesome and renders them lean. A proper proportion of woodland always tends to keep a country cool. How necessary then for man and beast within the tropics. Nor is there any reasonable doubt that trees have a very considerable effect in attracting rain, upon the certainty of which no crop depends so much as that of sugar cane. From the same cause they promote the circulation of the atmosphere and consequently health of the inhabitants. It is well known that [in] the back settlements Europeans from among the woods

96 Ibid., p. 18.

or in cleared spots among them where great part of the year they are enveloped with clouds, frequent rains, constant dews and damps with a cold atmosphere, the inhabitants are far more healthy, lively and robust than the seaside inhabitants. This in great measure accounts for the health and longevity of savages whose habitations are in the middle of woods and little cultivation around them . . . Mr Long in his *History of Jamaica* has the very just observation that all lands on first settling are healthy but after being cleared to a certain extent become unhealthy. This is also probably the case in extra-tropical countries. Had the planters next the sea only reserved the natural trees on the rocks and dry barren ridges, between the canes and the sea, as well as on those uncultivable hills and rocks scattered by beneficent nature on their estates, they would have preserved ornament as well as shelter to the cane from the spray of the sea, than which nothing is more injurious to it. They would have shown greater wisdom and foresight besides studying their own interest more effectually than by their destruction, if no more had been lost than the fruitless labour of clearing the barren hills and rocks of their native productions. It is astonishing the idea of ornament only did not preserve them, for surely to one never so little accustomed to such scenes and natural beauties, even to a savage a well-cultivated country interspersed with clumps of trees and woods is more pleasing to the eye than bare and bleak hills and rugged, ill-shapen rocks staring them in the face. On windward coasts during the dry season, from the strong regular sea breeze the saline particles raised by evaporation and agitation of the waves on the rocks rise like a mist, which affects vegetation for some miles back. To guard against it, it might have been supposed that art would have been called in, if possible, to affect the purpose in planting trees along the headlands, but nature on the windward coast of St Vincent had done what art never can perform. She had reared a natural and beautiful border of white cedar,[97] a valuable wood for many mechanical purposes and effectively screened the adjoining land, but strange to tell, not even a stump of a tree is to be seen along this bleak and dreary rock. On most of the seaside ridges and hills the mastick was a common tree. It is the most valuable wood for mill timber in the West Indies as well as buildings. So wantonly was it destroyed that not only negroes cut the trees up for fire wood, but they were piled in heaps and burnt on the fields. This will appear the more strange: that those very planters who thus destroyed it are now importing their mill timber from Demerary and Porto Rico at a vast expense and on a precarious footing . . . From the variety of situations and temperatures in the atmosphere, Saint Vincent produces a great variety of indigenous plants on the summits of the mountains, many rare and beautiful, several of which are nowhere else seen. What is remarkable, some of the identical species, natives of the forests of Guiana, are natives

97 *Bignonia leucoxylon.*

of its woods. This is the more striking when we regard the great distance, vast difference in the soils and face of the two countries. Had these plants, common to both, been all fruit-bearing or medicinal, then introduction into St Vincent might have readily been by the aborigines, which undoubtedly was the case with all the now common fruits of the island. By them probably have been introduced Carapa and Allamanda, as they are Indian medicines, but for others of no known use we are at a loss to account.[98]

These unedited manuscript remarks made by Anderson give us a very clear indication of his public reasons for pursuing the cause of forest protection so vigorously during the 1780s. An explicit landscape aesthetic is invoked and supplemented by a whole variety of fears about climate change, health, sustainability of timber supply and species extinctions. The notion of an ideal society in an ideal landscape is never far from the surface of this text, in much the same way as in Poivre's discourses. It would, I think, be unwise simply to attribute the character of the text to the influence of Rousseau and the French Romantics. In Anderson's case a distinctively empirical and botanical consciousness pervades and informs the idyll. He is sharply aware, for example, of the apparent equilibrium of the Caribs with the pre-colonial environment and is particularly admiring of their efforts at medicinal plant transfer. This is not surprising in view of the fact that he was himself concerned with transfer projects. A realisation of the relative harmony between Carib and the 'healthy' forest environment encouraged him to a much stronger critique of European-caused deforestation than he might otherwise have developed. As far as the climatic influence of forests was concerned, Anderson's reading of Edward Long's three-volume *History of Jamaica*, published in 1774, had clearly exercised a powerful influence over him. Through Long, Anderson would have received a thorough grounding in the writings of Halley, Dobson, Pringle and, above all, Hales and Priestley.[99] Priestley's work was still very recent when Long wrote but was frequently quoted in his discussions of the connections among forests, climate and health, much as it was to be forty years later for Edward Balfour and other members of the Indian medical service.[100] Edward Long, unlike Alexander Anderson, was chiefly concerned with the dangers posed by deforestation for the health of Europeans in the tropics. He appears to have utilised the powerful social messages of Priestley's atmospheric theories and his environmental medicine to a very particular regional purpose.[101]

98 Anderson, 'Geography', (Howard transcription), pp. 37–9.
99 Long, *History of Jamaica*, III, pp. i–viii.
100 See Chapter 8 for details of Priestley's influence on Edward Balfour.
101 Relevant studies on the social ideologies of Priestley and his associates are S. Schaffer, 'Measuring virtue: Eudiometry, enlightenment and pneumatic medicine', in A. Cunningham and

By the second half of the eighteenth century, the Hippocratic epidemiology and meteorology of an earlier period had been elaborated into a much more complex philosophy of the aerial system that directed attention to stagnation, overcrowding and dirt. These changes were related to several wider issues, including the development of cameralism (a largely German offshoot of French physiocracy) and the origins of medical police.[102] It has been suggested that British physicians during the eighteenth century increasingly looked to meteorology, pneumatics and the powers of the atmosphere to demonstrate the whole system of nature and in turn explain health and disease. This medical understanding of circulation in the atmospheric economy created a role for physicians in the policing of health and the management of sickness in society at large. In Europe the explanation of disease directed epidemiogical concerns to the sources of putrefaction, corruption and decay, where pathology resulted from stagnation of the vital circulation. In the West Indies, on the other hand, the explanation of disease directed attention to the status of vegetation and thus potentially to a policing of change in the landscape. For Edward Long (and therefore, one may surmise, for Anderson) the decisive insights of Priestley and Stephen Hales were those which dealt with the power of vegetation to ensure a healthy atmosphere. 'We owe to Dr Priestly', Long wrote,

> the suggestion of two grand resources for this salutary end; the first he assigns to the vegetable kingdom, the next to the sea, and other large collections of water; not however excluding Dr Hales's principle of ventilation from a share in this important office. He finds that the effluvia of vegetables are endued with the power of reviving common air, that has been vitiated, or fouled, by fire or respiration. That the aromatic vapours of plants, are not necessary participants in the office of restoring this purity; for that vegetables that have an offensive smell, or no smell at all, but are of quick growth, prove the very best for this purpose.[103]

By linking human health to the status of the tropical forest and to rainfall frequency, Long touched on very basic European worries about vulnerability to tropical diseases. At another level he also entered the realm of contemporary anxieties about 'degeneration' in tropical climates. All these concerns would legitimate the kinds of interventions to protect forest that were implicitly

R. French, eds., *The medical enlightenment of the eighteenth century*, Cambridge, 1990; C. J. Lawrence, 'Priestley in Tahiti', in C. J. Lawrence and R. Anderson, eds., *Science, medicine and dissent: Joseph Priestley 1733–1804*, London, 1987, pp. 1–10.

102 L. J. Jordanova, 'Earth science and environmental medicine: The synthesis of the late Enlightenment', in L. J. Jordanova and Roy Porter, eds., *Images of the earth*, BSHS Monographs, 1, Chalfont St Giles, 1978, pp. 119–46; S. Schaffer, 'Natural philosophy and public spectacle in the eighteenth century', *History of Science*, 21 (1983), 1–43.

103 Long, *History of Jamaica*, III, p. v.

advocated by Long and explicitly argued by Anderson. But the matter went further than this. Sir John Pringle, in a speech made in 1773 (quoted by Long in his publication of the next year), reinterpreted Priestley to find the preservation of vegetation as being valuable not only in a negative sense but also in a much more intrinsic and universal sense.[104] 'We are assured [implicitly by Priestley] that no vegetable grows in vain,' he wrote, but 'every individual plant is serviceable to mankind; if not always distinguishable by some private virtue, yet making a part of the whole, which cleanses and purifies the atmosphere.' This 'virtue' was worth cultivating as much in remote regions as in those which were more familiar. 'Nor is the herbage', he concluded,

> nor the woods, that flourish in the most remote and unpeopled regions, unprofitable to us, nor we to them; considering how constantly the winds convey to them our vitiated air, for our relief and their nourishment; and if ever these salutary gales rise to storms and hurricanes, let us still trace and revere the ways of a Beneficent being, who not fortuitously, but with design; not in wrath but in mercy, thus shakes the waters and the air together, to bury in the deep those putrid and pestilential effluvia, which the vegetables upon the face of the earth has been insufficient to consume.

Long developed this argument still further. These discoveries, he said, were 'noble, and open to us a new source of investigation into the wholesomeness or insalubrity of local situations in different countries, whether in the neighbourhood of large woods . . . or whether the inhabitants are deprived of some, or all these purifiers'. If it was necessary to preserve 'virtue' in the air for the good of temperate regions, still more was it necessary in the tropics. 'If such is the grand provision made for our globe at large, may we not indulge a thought, that it is dispensed in a more liberal portion to those regions, whose climate seems to require it?' As the processes of corruption were more active in the tropics, Long reasoned, then vegetal growth was 'more powerful and more abundant than in Northern countries'. But it might happen, he feared that 'the leafy cloathing of the woods may be parched, arid and juiceless'.[105] In those circumstances only 'tempests' and hurricanes could save the vegetation and restore the climate. Alexander Anderson, of course, had seen ample evidence of far more permanent vegetation change than Long apparently had on Jamaica. Moreover, the extreme events of hurricane and earthquake mentioned by Long in his *History* were supplemented on St Vincent by regular volcanic eruptions. In these circumstances any attempt to maintain stability in the landscape, through forest protection or other means, must have seemed desirable to Anderson.

104 Sir John Pringle's discourse, quoted in Long, *History of Jamaica*, III, p. vi. The discourse was made on his presentation of the Royal Society's Copley medal to Priestley in 1773.
105 Long, *History of Jamaica*, III, p. vii.

Climatic concerns and a contemporary landscape aesthetic both affected Anderson's desire to control deforestation and construct a stable environment. However, the text of the 'Geography' indicates that there was a third and related motive for landscape protection which was linked both to the rarity of the island plant species and to the extinction of the Carib population on St Vincent. In his desire to protect the forests, climate, plants and landscape of St Vincent, it seems likely that Anderson was, perhaps at a subconscious level, attempting to expiate the savage colonial repression of the black Carib and Carib population after their successive insurrections. Some clues to this are present towards the end of the text, where Anderson questioned the morality of forced resettlement:

> Altho' factions and rebellion may be the cause of extirpating a people from a government under which they might have ever remained free and happy, yet who can avoid melancholy sensations on a whole race of man-kind transported forever from their native land inhabited by them for generations and not conceive that there has been something radically wrong in the principle of government necessitated to that act?[106]

By discussing the policy of forced removal alongside an environmental cri-tique, Anderson highlights the connections between his desire for a reformed ethic of governance and his wish to reform the ethos of land management. Such notions of environmental morality, often linked with discourses on social justice, were soon to become typical of much colonial conservationism. Al-exander Anderson emerges simply as the first in a long line of Scottish colonial experts who linked together their biological, religious and social insights. To some extent, his nascent environmentalism may have served to resolve at a psychological level the conflicts that developed in Anderson's mind over the colonial treatment of the Caribs and their forest environment. But this was not the end of the story. His later unpublished writings indicate that Anderson became steadily more enmeshed in contradictions between his observations of natural and social change and his inherited religious and social preconceptions. His geological observations in particular led him to an assessment of geological time scales that conflicted with his religious beliefs. It is in this context that we need to set his concerns about plant extinctions and the extinction of a Carib population. The real threat, one may suggest, was one posed to An-derson's own 'nature'. His original interest in climate had first been expressed in a description of his ascent of Souffrière, the main volcano. The volcano had recently undergone, he emphasised, 'great convulsions of nature' and

106 Anderson, 'Geography', p. 97.

Plate 18. Anderson's drawing of the Morne Garou volcano on St Vincent, as published in *Philosophical Transactions of the Royal Society* for 1784. (Photo, Cambridge University Library)

'some terrible convulsion' of nature.[107] There are obvious risks involved in deconstructing Anderson's volcano drawing and the language of his 'Morne Garou' article. Even so, it seems safe to conclude that the evidence of recent, ongoing and even catastrophic natural changes presented in the environs of Morne Garou, within the confines of a small and intimately known island, clearly made an overwhelming and even appalling impact on Anderson. These emotions are faithfully portrayed in his drawing of the crater of the volcano. Here we see the image of a body torn apart, even of a womb rent asunder, with the lava blood flowing forth and the adjacent forest trees burnt to black skeletons. In the face of this, Anderson tells us, with the quixotic enthusiasm of the fanatical botanist, there 'was a probability of meeting with plants on it I could find in no other part of the island'.

107 Anderson, 'Ascent of Morne Garou', pp. 25, 27.

In fact, besides demonstrating the potential for catastrophic change, the volcano presented Anderson with data incompatible with his own religious beliefs and notions of geological time scales. This confrontation between belief and the evidence of process occupies hundreds of pages of tortuous and un-resolved argument in his unpublished 'Delugia' manuscript. In questioning geological time scales, an existential crisis of human origins was added to the situational crisis of defining the role of the colonist in a territory once inhab-ited by an indigenous people. However, in seeking to protect the forests An-derson may in fact have found a successful strategy to protect his own personal integrity in the context of a set of social assumptions about creation which he found himself forced increasingly to question. Climatic environmentalism, at the very least, restored the apparent power of the colonist to act amid a chaos in which old assumptions about chronology, process, origins and belief were all threatened. For Anderson, the tropical-island predicament had focussed this crisis. Nevertheless, before long the crisis was one that began to enter a geographically much wider social and scientific consciousness.

7

The beginnings of global environmentalism: Professional science, oceanic islands and the East India Company, 1768–1838

Through Forster's charming description of Otaheiti, particularly in Northern Europe, a general, I could say yearning interest had been aroused for the islands of the Pacific.

Alexander von Humboldt

Initially confined to a few small island locations, emergent state environmentalism became more global in scope over the period between the French Revolution and the Indian Mutiny. It achieved this institutional diffusion through the wide development of professional science in the colonial context and through the further diffusion of climatic and medical environmentalism among intellectuals and in government. There is no simple way to tell the story of the globalisation of an intellectual concept. Instead we need to consider a series of parallel developments.

By the end of the eighteenth century a keen awareness had developed of an impending global shortage of timber resources, and particularly of strategically serious threats to the supply of naval timber. But for a long time this awareness was not linked directly to the kinds of constructions of environmental risk explored earlier in this book. Some very large areas of the continental tropics came under colonial control during this period and then underwent very extensive ecological change.[1] Despite this, climatic environmentalism made surprisingly little impact at a state level in comparison to what had gone on in Mauritius and in the Eastern Caribbean. This was particularly the case in India and Southern Africa, where the period between 1770 and 1840 saw an unprecedented expansion in European influence and a particularly sharp ecological transition. However, after about 1840 these two

---

1 For a useful political account of this period of expansion, see C. A. Bayly, *Imperial meridian: The British empire and the world, 1780–1830*, London, 1989.

regions did begin to see a remarkable institutional development in attempts at state environmental control. Part of this half-century delay in institutional evolution must be attributed to the fact that, on a continental scale, the colonial state was not really forced seriously to confront the pressures engendered by the severely confined circumstances of a tropical-island environment. The strength of any environmentalist message had to rely, instead, on the power of ideas and the institutional influence of scientists and their state patrons. We have already seen that on the small islands of Mauritius and St Vincent the colonial state had, for a variety of reasons of fashion and economics, been compelled to privilege the ideas and social position of the scientific community. Scientists in these territories had, in turn, begun to find that, alongside their botanical expertise, the prescriptive precepts of climatic and Romantic environmentalism were highly effective in retaining and strengthening their political positions and social agendas.

This kind of privileging of the colonial scientist took place at a much more leisurely pace in the continental colonies. In these larger geographical spaces, especially in South Africa, India and the Americas, the spread of environmentalism depended on a very diverse set of intellectual influences, although the practical and metaphorical models established in the island colonies remained important at some critical junctures. Specifically, the botanical gardens at Pamplemousses, Mauritius, and Kingstown, St Vincent, exercised a disproportionate influence as institutional precedents for the location of expertise and the formation of centres of environmental calculation. What we can sensibly identify here are some specific connections between the professionalisation of the colonial naturalist and the growing dominance of particular individuals in cultivating a much more global and influential environmental discourse than had hitherto existed. Who were these individuals, and what were their circumstances?

The experience of the physiocrats on Mauritius had underlined the critical role of the great circumnavigatory expeditions in providing expertise and synthesising a more autonomous role for the scientist. These expeditions were the bedrock of colonial professionalisation, and the expeditions of Captain Cook were preeminent among them. Above all, they promoted and shaped the careers of Johann Reinhold Forster and Sir Joseph Banks, two key figures in the professionalisation of natural history. Much influenced by the French experience, these men actively advocated and then organised the development of a global network of professional naturalists and a system of colonial botanical gardens. They also provided some of the main influences and philosophical directions in the career of Alexander von Humboldt. Humboldt, for his part, emerged as the major figure behind the acceptance of a very specific kind of environmental world view. It was this view, and Humboldt's intellectual weight, which then determined much of the character and pattern of development of state environmental discourse and policy in British India, Southern Africa and elsewhere.

Sir Joseph Banks, the Cook voyages and the professionalisation of natural history

The possibilities for professionalisation and for state patronage of the naturalist were intially far more limited in the British than in the French colonial context.[2] Consequently, it was left to Sir Joseph Banks, as an individual endowed with enormous private means, to provide patronage and to promote the position of the naturalist in colonial government circles.[3] It is significant that Banks was first successful in doing so not in Britain but in the Cape Colony, and a little later under the aegis of the East India Company. His reasons for promoting professionalisation were complex, whereas they had been relatively simple in the case of the French physiocratic ministries. Banks found it convenient to pursue purely academic objectives which were often concealed in a cloak of commercial justification, a justification with which he was anyhow much in sympathy, as the more Rousseauian of the French naturalists were not.[4]

Between 1770 and 1810 Banks was able to lay the foundations for a patronage of professional naturalists which imitated, in both practice and prescription, the patronage of science by the physiocrats on Mauritius and elsewhere. Banks's strategy and the events which led up to it deserve some inspection, especially as the most outstanding characteristic of the intellectual

---

2 D. E. Allen, 'The early professionals in British natural history', in A. Wheeler and H. C. Price, eds., *From Linnaeus to Darwin: Commentaries on the history of biology and geology*, London, 1985, pp. 1–3.

3 For a fuller discussion, see Harold B. Carter, *Sir Joseph Banks, 1743–1820*, London, 1989.

4 M. Crosland, in *Science in France in the Revolution*, Cambridge, Mass., 1969, has claimed priority for the French in the evolving of a truly professionalised science, while Allen ('The early professionals in natural history', p. 3) notes that what was missing in Britain were the opportunities for full-time research careers on the scale which scientists enjoyed in France from as early as 1795, thanks to their extensive employment by the republican state. Both Crosland and Allen in this respect have failed to recognise earlier professionalisation in the colonies of both Britain and France. In the latter, developments after the Revolution were essentially a continuation of ideas set in train under the ancien régime. Developments in professionalisation in both countries were closely connected and helped to speed up a flow of information between groups of men who had more in common with each other than they did with the professional establishments in their own countries. See for instance J. M. Eyles, 'William Smith, Sir Joseph Banks and the French geologist', in Wheeler and Price, eds., *From Linnaeus to Darwin*, pp. 37–50. For a more recent view on the precocity of colonial professionalisation (closely corresponding to my own view), see J. E. McClellan, *Colonialism and Science: Saint Domingue in the old regime*, Baltimore, 1992.

network set up by Banks was the extent to which it relied not on the professional skills of English naturalists but on those of Scotland and Central Europe, particularly Germany. This was to have considerable consequences for the way in which environmental changes in India and other colonies were conceptualised, precisely as a result of the extent to which Banks ranked professionalism and training above nationality.

Banks's own role on the first Cook voyage set the scene for his later advocacy of professionalisation. The two primary objectives of the *Endeavour* voyage (1768–71) were astronomical and geographical. However, Banks was able to establish a tertiary aim for the expedition, much as Bougainville had done on *La Boudeuse*. Aside from partly financing the voyage, Banks participated in it in a way characterised by careful planning of a kind which prefigured his later very deliberate lobbying for the establishment of naturalists in the new colonial territories.[5] There were, nonetheless, professional precedents predating Banks's involvement with the Cook voyage. The British Museum had taken on Daniel Solander (Banks's assistant on the *Endeavour*) as a paid naturalist and curator as early as 1763.[6] The extension of the role of the state as a direct employer of scientists amounted to development of an established practice whereby naturalists had long been employed as the curators of collections belonging to the wealthier adherents of the growing enthusiasm for collecting and natural history.[7] However, there had been an intermediate stage in this social evolution. Linnaeus, for example, had been employed by George Clifford, a director of the Dutch East India Company, to oversee his collections and gardens at Hartecamp in Holland.[8] It is not surprising that Clifford should have provided this first alliance between naturalists attempting to incorporate organisms in global classificatory schemes and the progenitors of enterprises which were becoming increasingly global in their commercial outlook. For the latter, the collection of globally derived material on a systematic basis had a strategic and commercial attraction of a kind already appreciated by the Dutch in their promotion of the company garden at the Cape. The

---

5 H. B. Carter, 'The Banksian natural history collections of the *Endeavour* voyage and their relevance to modern taxonomy', in A. Wheeler, ed., *History in the service of systematics*, London, 1981, p. 61.

6 Allen, 'The early professionals in British natural history', p. 3.

7 An early instance of this was the bringing over from Germany of Johann Jakob Dillen, otherwise Dillenius, by William Shepherd in 1721: ibid., p. 4.

8 Clifford, a businessman who fancied himself a kind of nawab, was also a keen amateur naturalist and kept a garden of exotic plants as well as a private zoo at Hartecamp. He engaged Linnaeus as his personal physician and gave him the run of his luxury establishment. It was patronage on a grand scale, and Linnaeus recorded that he 'lived like a prince, had the greater garden under his charge, was allowed to procure all the books that were . . . required for the library, and now had the opportunity to work at Botany where he had everything that could be desired': A. C. Jenkins, *The naturalists: Pioneers of natural history*, London, 1978, p. 44.

global involvement of the EIC and VOC by the 1720s was paralleled by the search for an appropriate framework for systematic classification of all the world's fauna and flora. Linnaeus compared his 'genera' to parts of a map or chart. Grenovius wrote to him in 1788 that 'your charts are so useful, you can find any mineral, plant or animal on them, everybody should have them hanging on the wall as maps'.[9] The desire for a global botanical system of classification, a mental construct and idea much advocated by Rousseau as well as Linnaeus, looking to embrace all the organisms of the globe, was really an extension of the attempt to collect together all the plants of the world in the four 'quarters' and 'pulvillae' of the Renaissance botanical garden as part of a project to re-create Paradise.[10] One can thus see the professional system-atist and naturalist in colonial employ as the direct inheritor of the early Renaissance 'Paradise' botanists. As we saw earlier, an island (such as that on Lake Bienne) was, for Rousseau, like a 'great botanic garden', and so a further connection can be made.[11]

Through the intervention of Banks and his use of his personal fortune to finance his scientific work, the Cook voyages effectively separated the natu-ralist from a direct connection with mercantile interests and provided the setting for a new kind of scientific critique extending beyond the discovery of the empirical to embrace a detached kind of social empiricism, stimulated by the institutional and intellectual autonomy enabled by a ship circumnavigating the globe. The voyages were remarkable because of both the involvement of non-English naturalists in the enterprise and the way in which the circum-stances of the voyages caused many of their participants, including Cook him-self, to develop serious doubts about the impact of Europeans on the societies and environments they came across.[12] The empirical objectives of the Cook voyages were thus influential in providing a precedent for the basis on which the professional naturalist in the tropics might make his observations. They were also formative to Banks's conceptualisation of the role of the professional naturalist.

The instructions given to Cook in 1768 were explicitly scientific in empha-sis. He was to report on all aspects of lands discovered and to bring back specimens, drawings and surveys, very much on the lines of the 1666 and 1704 Royal Society instructions to naturalists. The expedition was to 'study nature rather than books and from the observations made of the phenomena

9 M. Janal, 'Classification of the Foraminifera: A case study in taxonomy and its history', Ph.D. diss., Cambridge University, 1987, pp. 20–1.
10 Prest, The Garden of Eden.
11 Rousseau, The reveries of a solitary, p. 104.
12 For a wider discussion of the development of this critique in the Pacific context, see Alan Moorehead, The fatal impact: An account of the invasion of the South Pacific, 1767–1840, Lon-don, 1966.

and effects she presents, to compose such a history of her as may hereafter serve to build a solid and useful philosophy upon'.[13] The public set much store by these philosophical aspects. Samuel Johnson's enthusiasm for the expedition articulated this well as he appealed for an expedition with a scientific turn of mind and for Banks and his companions to be

> not intent like merchants only on the arts of commerce, the value of commodities and the probabilities of gain, not engaged, like military officers, in the care of subsisting armies, securing passes, obviating stratagems and defeating opposition . . . but . . . vacant to the very objects of curiosity and at leisure for the most minute remarks.[14]

The Forsters and the Resolution voyage

Other than Samuel Johnson himself, it is striking that the individuals who seem to have been most aware of the long-term implications of the kind of large-scale empirical study of environments and societies carried on during the Cook journeys were the German naturalists Johann Reinhold Forster and Georg Forster, who accompanied the second voyage. The younger Forster remarked that 'what Cook added to the mass of our knowledge is such that it will strike deep roots and will long have the most decisive influence on the activity of man'.[15] This comment helps to highlight the degree to which the Cook voyages constituted the first major opportunity for naturalists from Central Europe and Germany to take advantage of British naval and exploring exploits, colonial settlement and the opportunities for employment which these enterprises offered. The growing strength and direction of German Romantic science, *Naturphilosophie* and Orientalism both encouraged the search for empirical knowledge of natural and social varieties and was stimulated by the information collected by such naturalists as the Forsters.[16] This was especially the case in Germany, where the influence of the Cook voyages was mediated directly through the Forsters. The third voyage saw the promotion as a specialist of William Anderson, the surgeon on HMS *Resolution*. In Cook's opin-

13 B. Smith, *European vision and the South Pacific 1768–1850: A study in the history of art and ideas*, 2nd ed., Oxford, 1960, p. 14.

14 Quoted in T. M. Curley, *Samuel Johnson and the age of travel*, Athens, Ga., 1976, p. 66.

15 Quoted in M. E. Hoare, *The tactless philosopher: Johann Reinhold Forster, (1729–1789)*, Melbourne, 1976, p. 114.

16 Smith, in *European vision and the South Pacific*, p. 1, comments that 'the opening of the South Pacific was one of the factors that contributed to the triumph of Romanticism and science in the nineteenth century world of values'.

ion, Anderson was 'by far the most accurate and inquisitive person on board'.[17] Devoted to natural history, philology and much else, he kept a journal of the voyage 'second in interest only to Cook's'.[18] The Cook voyages thus provided the context for two distinct types of professional naturalist to flourish: the German naturalist, in the shape of the Forsters, father and son, and the Scottish surgeon.[19] The roles of these two kinds of professionals became increasingly significant in the employ of the British over the next eighty years, while their education and philosophical and scientific background steadily imposed its mark in commentaries written on the tropical world and in the increasingly independent and critical views espoused by colonial scientists. The qualities of both types of naturalist were already recognised on the Cook voyages, the former by Banks and the latter more by Cook.

It is difficult to characterise or categorise the kinds of ideas developed by these professionals during the Cook voyages, as they were extraordinary in their diversity. Nevertheless, in the broadest sense, the innovative thinking in two areas – to develop much more in the circumstances of colonial employ – can be discerned in embryonic form on the Cook voyages, where the expression of critical views was less constrained than in the more circumscribed conditions of a settled colony. This was so especially in relation to new thinking about climate and about the relations between Europeans and the societies they encountered.

First, the opportunity to compare distant lands with the homeland directly stimulated thinking about climate, initially in its effects on living conditions and society and subsequently in connection with the relations among climate, history and society. One of his correspondents wrote to Dr Johnson, one of the main enthusiasts for the Cook voyage, that 'my great delight, like yours, would be to see how life is carried on in other countries, how various climates produce various effects and how different notions of religion and government operate upon human manners and the human mind'.[20] The linking of climate

---

17 J. C. Beaglehole, ed., *The journals of Captain James Cook on his voyages of discovery*, 6 vols., Cambridge, 1955–69, I, p. lxxiv. [Cited hereafter as Cook, *Journal*.]

18 Marshall and Williams, *The great map of mankind*, p. 200, quoting Cook, *Journal*, I, p. lxxxiv n.

19 The colonial employment of physicians trained in the Scottish universities was long established and a convenient career path for Scots, for whom employment in England was fraught with difficulty and prejudice. See C. Lloyd and J. Coulter, *Medicine and the Navy, 1200–1900*, vol. 4, Edinburgh, 1963. Many ships' officers, especially naval surgeons, were able to equip themselves as naturalists; see D. M. Knight, 'Science and professionalism in England, 1790–1830', *Proceedings of the XIVth International Congress of the History of Science*, 1 (1974), 53–67. In fact, as I established in Chapter 1, the tradition of the surgeon, through his botanical training, being able to double up as naturalist was present even at the time of Columbus.

20 Curley, *Samuel Johnson and the age of travel*, p. 69, quoted in Marshall and Williams, *The great map of mankind*, p. 282.

and human development, much mooted in debates about Asia, was now standard practice; for example, 'the hygrometer and thermometer had now become a standard part of the scholar's equipment'.[21] Among Scottish writers of the Enlightenment during the late eighteenth century, Lord Kames typified an interest in the influence of climate upon human society which was to develop more specifically among Scottish surgeons in India. In *Sketches of the History of Man*, Kames relied heavily on the accounts of the Cook expeditions complied by Nicholas Hawkesworth. The balmy climate praised by the explorers, he thought, hindered rather than stimulated the progress of man. 'Need we any other excuse', Kames asked, 'for their inferiority of understanding compared with the inhabitants of other climates, where the mind, as well as the body, is constantly at work procuring necessaries?'[22]

There was a second major development which involved the Forsters. The findings of the Cook expeditions, with their concurrent concern for understanding the relations between people and their physical environment, helped set the stage for the future development of anthropology and ethnology. These were fields in which the Forsters both pioneered and excelled. However, the voyage also laid a framework for a more generalised concern about the impact on exotic societies of alterations induced in the immediate physical environment in the course of European economic expansion. Such new concern was intimately connected with the kinds of more empirically based doubts which were developing about the supposed intellectual superiority of the European over other races. A degree of unease was also felt as to the damage which the colonial state and European 'modernity' might wreak upon tropical peoples. These doubts had surfaced among the French on Mauritius during the 1760s and were in particular voiced by such widely travelled individuals as Commerson and Poivre.

The Cook expeditions gave these anxieties a keener edge, and comparable opinions were expressed by both Cook and the Forsters. The first stage in the development of this sense of foreboding appears to have occurred as a consequence of the relatively long and studied contacts with indigenous peoples which the naturalists of the Cook expeditions were able to enjoy in Tahiti and other Pacific Ocean islands. J. R. Forster's preoccupations, for example, underwent a significant transformation in the course of the voyage, away from purely biological and towards more social concerns. His observations of the second voyage, devoted to 'remarks on the human species in the South Sea isles', began with Pope's dictum that 'the proper study of mankind is man'.[23]

---

21 Antonelli Gerbi, *The dispute of the New World: The history of a polemic, 1750–1900*, Pittsburgh, 1973, quoted in Marshall and Williams, *The great map of mankind*, p. 216.

22 Lord H. H. Kames, *Sketches of the history of man*, 2 vols., Edinburgh, 1774, I, p. 106; II, pp. 384–5, quoted in Marshall and Williams, *The great map of mankind*, p. 275.

23 *Observations made during a voyage round the world*, London, 1778, p. 1.

Ten years later he would explain that he had wanted to 'investigate closely the habits, rites, ceremonies and religious beliefs, ways of life, clothing, agriculture, commerce, arts, weapons, words of warfare, political organisation and the language of the people we met'.[24] Georg Forster, his son, contrasted the idyllic scenes he saw with the noisome realities of the poor at home, much as Poivre had contrasted the idyll of the Isle de France with the oppression of the peasantry in France. Tahiti, above all, provided in his eyes a setting for unambitious living which knew neither the 'absolute want nor the unbounded voluptuousness' of European society.

This state of affairs, Forster thought, was doomed. Like Diderot a few years earlier, he was appalled by the prospect opening before the Pacific islanders and concluded that 'if the knowledge of a few individuals can only be acquired at such a price as the happiness of nations it were better for the discoverers and the discovered that the South Seas had remained unknown to Europe and its restless inhabitants'.[25] Cook's comments on Australian aborigines ran on the same lines: They were 'far happier than we Europeans ... they live in a tranquillity which is not disturbed by the inequality of condition. The earth and sea of their own accord furnishes them with all things necessary for life.'[26] Even the worldly Banks showed a parallel sensitivity on the issue. Dismayed to discover the inaccuracy of Dampier's caricature descriptions of the Aboriginal, he noted instead that they were, in reality, 'happy people content with little nay almost nothing ... removed from the anxieties ... extending upon riches, or even upon the possession of what we Europeans call common necessities'.[27]

The dual concern with the connection between climate and society and the emergence of a critical view of the European impact on the 'new world' of the South Pacific, which developed on the Cook voyages and was characteristic of them, thus became closely associated with the emergence of the role of the professional naturalist in British colonial employ and especially with the writings of German and Scottish naturalists. Both climatic and social concerns, insofar as they affected the Forsters, were important to the subsequent evolution of German scientific thinking, not least in the attitudes inherited by Alexander von Humboldt, upon whom J. R. Forster exercised a great influence. In this way, both in an indirect sense (when Humboldt's views came to hold sway in the colonial scientific establishment) and in a direct sense (on

24 *Enchiridion historiae naturali inserviens*, Halle, 1778.

25 *A voyage round the world*, London, 1777, p. 14.

26 *Journal*, I, p. 319. Cook reserved his most acerbic comments in this vein for the matter of the transfer of sexual diseases to New Zealand women by English sailors – to 'thereby disturb that happy tranquillity they and their forefathers have enjoy'd'.

27 Quoted in Allan Frost, 'The Pacific Ocean, the eighteenth century's New World', quoted in turn in Marshall and Williams, *The great map of mankind*, p. 273.

the frequent occasions when German naturalists were employed by the British), the highly distinctive perceptions of the professional naturalists attached to the Cook voyages came to exercise a disproportionate effect. The painstaking and voluminous research carried out by the Forsters was recognised as such by Banks, despite his professional jealousy of J. R. Forster, and was also recognised specifically as the product of Forster's training and philosophical background obtained at the University of Halle.

It is the development of J. R. Forster's ideas on the Cook voyages that needs most attention, both because of the impression Forster's work made on Joseph Banks and because Forster strongly influenced the environmental thinking of German and Scottish scientists later employed by the British. Cook's replacement of Banks by Forster and his son on the *Resolution* voyage, along with the appointment of Walter Hodges as an official artist, led directly to new directions in thinking. These moves affected both the growing influence of naturalism in art and the way in which the conceptualisation of the noble savage took on a new analytical form in the work of the Forsters, encouraging new thinking about climate and the dynamics of social evolution. The voyage also gave a renewed impetus to western interest in the South Pacific as well as in the 'Oriental' world. Finally, and especially in the careers of the Forsters, their empirical and independent mode of working nurtured a spirit of reaction to European civilization and government. This was further assisted by the opportunity for social comparisons which acquaintance with a whole variety of new societies afforded. In all these developments, the experience and evolution of the two Forsters predominated, although the individual contributions of other scientists, such as, for example, William Wales in meteorology, was also important.

A more generalised cultural transition was also taking place that one should not neglect. To the early English Romantic writers, Cook's voyages had had a profoundly innovative significance. As Allan Frost has put it,

> in eighteenth century literature . . . the voyage motif usually functions only as action. The typical eighteenth century voyage is imbued with the spirit of the Grand Tour . . . in Romantic poetry on the other hand, the motif functions both as action and as profound psychological pattern. Physically, the Romantic voyage is one in which the protagonist sails into an unknown world and reaches a paradisal island. Imaginatively it is a progress from inherited and conventional views of reality to the perception of a new and very different reality. The voyager, as he proceeds, relinquishes revealed truths and comfortable ways of knowing experience. Beginning his voyage with little imagination or sensitivity, by the voyage's end he becomes aware of his own humanity, of the humanity of his fellow men, of their mutual kinship and of the variousness of the world. The

Romantic voyage is a man in search of truth and, much more than his seventeenth century counterpart, he is involved in and altered by the experience of his voyage.[28]

It is precisely this kind of shift in perception as a consequence of journeying and of the projection of ideas in a limited (island) setting that one can observe in the changing pattern of J. R. Forster's theorising on man, climate and the environment – or in the responses of the late-eighteenth-century French intellectuals on Mauritius. The thinking of the two Forsters cannot be explained simply by the circumstances of their employment on the Cook expeditions. One needs to look for a much earlier pattern of psychological development in their life histories.

Johann Reinhold Forster's education and early life provide us with important clues to his later attitude to his task as a naturalist and his formulation of a role for the future employment of scientists by the British. At an early stage in his life Forster was a frequent visitor in the home of Simon Pallas, professor of surgery at the Berlin Medico-Chirurgium.[29] Partly as a result of this acquaintance, he developed an ambition to study medicine at the Friedrichs University of Halle. Instead, submitting to his father's wishes, he commenced studies at Halle in April 1748 in Oriental and classical languages under the guise of studying theology.[30] Between 1753 and 1765 he held a living as a country parson at Nassenhüben, near Danzig. This was a period of scholarship for Forster during which he built up a library of over 2,500 volumes and began a serious study of natural history. He worked with Gottfried Regger on the flora of Danzig and was able to immerse himself in the work of Linnaeus and Buffon in particular, while at the same time carrying on a series of natural-history excursions with his son Georg. Forster's first employment as a professional naturalist occurred through his contacts with Hans Wilhelm Rehbinder, the Russian resident in Danzig, 'who seemed to be very impressed

28 'Captain Cook and the eighteenth century imagination', p. 102, quoted in P. Gathercole, 'Islands and the anthropological imagination', paper presented at the University of Hawaii, Nov. 1976, pp. 2–3.
29 M. E. Hoare, ed., *The 'Resolution' journal of Johann Reinhold Forster, 1772–1795*, 4 vols., London, 1982, I, p. 5. Hoare's introduction to the *Resolution* Journal, though short, provides one of the most useful biographies of the elder Forster, and I lean heavily here upon his analysis. Pallas's younger son, Peter Simon (1741–1811), became in the Russian service one of Europe's leading naturalists and travellers. He was, like Forster, an important pre-Humboldtian figure in German natural science.
30 Schneegass, 'Leben und Charakter des Herrn J. Reinhold Forster. . .', quoted in Hoare, *'Resolution' journal*, I, p. 5. Schneegass notes that by the time Forster entered Halle University he was already familiar with the Linnaean system, having studied it with his friend C. J. Jampert, a colleague at Halle.

by my knowledge of natural history, theoretical and practical husbandry and many European languages'.[31] Forster's membership of and relations with the Danzig Society had helped to secure his reputation in this way. By January 1765 he had received an offer from Rehbinder of an appointment as Catherine the Great's official commissioner to the Volga German colonies 'in order to examine the condition of the colonies' and as 'an eyewitness to refute certain injurious rumours which have been mischievously spread abroad concerning the new colonists'.[32]

The political background to this survey is interesting. Catherine was determined to revive Peter the Great's policies of territorial expansion, and she was also concerned to enhance the status of science in her empire.[33] In this last connection Forster was quick to see the opportunity which his commission afforded him, and when he suggested undertaking meteorological observations in the Volga region, was immediately supplied with instruments and reference books.[34] The survey was a far wider-ranging one than Catherine or the Academy of Sciences had bargained for. Forster concerned himself not only with the problems of the settlers but in making a comprehensive survey of natural history. Everywhere 'the ground, plants and animals of these regions, together with the climate, and its influence upon people, animals, plants and productions were examined'.[35] In late 1765 he presented the first of three reports to Gregory Orlov. These reports, while praised for their accuracy, were highly critical of the predicament of the German settlers. As Hoare comments, Forster, 'true to character, handed Orlov a thoroughgoing and critical report on the colonists' problems'. This willingness to pursue an independent approach became much further developed on the *Resolution* voyage. The Russian government had, in fact, been compelled to confront a conundrum which later faced British colonial administrations. They discovered that, while the benefits of employing a competent but independent foreign scientist might allow the enjoyment of technical expertise, it could also invite the submission of highly unpalatable technical and political criticism.

Orlov, in charge of Catherine's colonial and settlement policy, had not in fact employed Forster as a professional naturalist. Forster had, however, seen himself as such. In this respect there was a distinct difference between the approach taken by the Russian government and that taken by Poivre and

31 J. R. Forster, 'Ueber Georg Forster', *Annalen der Philosophie*, 1 (1795), col. 14, quoted in Hoare, '*Resolution*' journal, 1, p. 14.

32 Forster to Michaelis, 21 Jan. 1765, quoted in Hoare, '*Resolution*' journal, 1, p. 15.

33 For background on science in Russia at this time, see A. Uvcinich, *Science in Russian culture: A history to 1860*, Stanford, Calif., 1963, pp. 74–122.

34 G. Steiner, 'J. R. Forsters und G. Forsters Beziehungen zu Russland', *Veröffentlichungen des Instituts für Slawistik*, 28 (1968), 253–4, quoted in Hoare, '*Resolution*' journal, 1, p. 15.

35 Forster in *Annalen der Philosophie*, col. 15, quoted in Hoare, '*Resolution*' journal, 1, p. 16.

Poissonier, who quite clearly intended (on Mauritius only three years later) to employ Commerson and Lislet Geoffroy simply as professional naturalists. Nevertheless, another important precedent for later colonial science had been established. Forster's comprehensive land-survey technique, which embodied ethnological as well as natural-history survey elements, became more fully developed on the *Resolution* voyage. It also served in practice as the approach adopted by both the French and British governments after 1800, particularly in the encouragement of the Flinders voyage by Sir Joseph Banks and the Admiralty and the sponsorship of the Baudin voyages by Napoleon.

It is no coincidence that, when in England, Forster found much in common with Arthur Young, with whom he corresponded in 1798.[36] Forster's use of the requirements of a colonial survey in Russia, conducted largely for the purpose of improving administration and control on the part of an expansionist government, also bears a strong resemblance to the use made by Alexander Buchanan-Hamilton of the Bengal government's interest in surveys aimed primarily at improving the efficiency of the revenue service.[37] In his rigorous criticism of the colonial administration of Saratov, for which Orlov actually asked him to draw up a new constitution, Forster also bears some comparison with Poivre in his outright criticism of the corrupt Dumas and Desroches regimes. Such outspokenness won him few friends, and in October 1766 he left Germany and arrived in England, where he determined to seek his fortune through professional science and scholarship, an idea clearly influenced by his wide experience in Russia.

The career route chosen may appear strange at first, but it was one based on assumptions which were to affect later generations of German scientists seeking employment in Britain and its colonies and which led directly to the

36 Forster to Young, 1798, quoted in Hoare, *'Resolution' journal*, II, p. 245. The meeting, which Forster 'reckoned among the most lucky occurrences of his life', took place at the table of the politician William Petty, Lord Shelburne, later Marquis of Lansdowne (1734–1804), a noted radical.

37 This is borne out usefully by Marika Vicziany in 'Imperialism, botany and statistics: The surveys of Francis Buchanan', *Modern Asian Studies*, 20 (1986), 625–660. The similarities between J. R. Forster and Gilbert White are striking. It has been argued elsewhere that White's calls for the assemblage of provincial natural histories, made in *The natural history of Selborne*, lay behind the surveys of Scotland by Sir Alexander Sinclair for the Scottish Board of Agriculture: See P. F. Rehbock, 'John Fleming (1785–1857) and the economy of nature', in Wheeler and Price, eds., *From Linnaeus to Darwin*, p. 130. This helped to set a Scottish precedent, which was then followed by Buchanan-Hamilton in India after 1805. A study of the influence of the survey example set by Forster and mediated either through Arthur Young (who himself influenced Sinclair) or through Sir Joseph Banks would merit further research. The survey by Beales of St Helena in 1679 might also be considered a comparably Baconian response by the colonial power (and by the EIC) to a lack of knowledge of the resources present in an area over which political control had newly been asserted. Other similar colonial examples might be found.

infusion of German scientific philosophies into the British colonial context. Forster himself had British ancestry, and his boyhood friend Karl Woide, a Coptic scholar, had also settled in England.[38] However, there was another connection. The rise of the Hanoverians in England after 1714 meant that England held out a particular welcome for German scholars at court.[39] The presence of the Georgia Augusta University, an important centre of Enlightenment thought, in Hanoverian territory was also a factor in the development of British colonial science. The Göttingen link was made more specific by the correspondence maintained between 1766 and 1780 by Sir John Pringle (1707–82) with J. D. Michaelis, a friend of Forster's.[40] This was a relationship which would have acquainted Forster with Sir Joseph Priestley and his atmospheric theories, at least indirectly.

Equally significantly in the long run, the value of the humanistic and scientific education of the academies of Holland and Germany – Leiden, Utrecht, Halle and, above all, Göttingen – was given increasing credence and respect by academics in the Scottish universities and among dissenting academics in England at a time when the English universities were largely moribund.

In England, Forster found a particularly amenable context in the amateur intellectual setting of the Society of Antiquaries. This society had been founded in 1750 and was comparable in some respects with the Danzig Society, of which Forster had been a member. While the Society of Antiquaries launched his academic reputation and provided him with useful contacts, it was not the basis for a living. Through financial necessity Forster was driven to undertake the translation of a variety of works into English. This had the effect of allowing him a degree of familiarity with the most recent scientific work from the whole of Europe, a familiarity unmatched by any of his contemporaries. His meticulous cultivation of scientific society contacts meant that he also became very familiar with the latest in English writing and debate. The net effect of this learning was to allow Forster to emerge with a highly innovative synthesis of theory with which to deal with the overwhelming amount of empirical material and the impressions he confronted as naturalist on the *Resolution* during 1772–5. His predisposition to synthesis emerged most strongly in connection with the whole question of relations among man, cli-

---

38 Hoare, '*Resolution*' journal, I, p. 20.

39 Hoare ('*Resolution*' journal, I, pp. 34–82) relies for his opinion on J. E. Kelly, *German visitors to English theatres in the eighteenth century*, Princeton, N.J., 1936.

40 The correspondence is deposited in the Universitäts-Bibliothek, Göttingen, Cod. Mich. 327, fols. 229–390; see Hoare, '*Resolution*' journal, I, p. 21. 'We know too little about German literature', wrote Sir Joseph Priestley, who shared teaching duties with J. R. Forster at the Warrington Academy: Mclachlan, *English education under the Test Acts*, quoted in Hoare, '*Resolution*' journal, I, p. 21 n. 3.

mate, meteorology and the environment. In his references to these subjects in his *Resolution* journal, Forster's allusions to climatic matters indicate an evolution in thinking in which his breadth of reading, combined with the accumulation of empirical experience, led to conclusions which show some convergence with the thinking of French naturalists on Mauritius.

The outstanding feature of this evolution in Forster's thinking is that it moved from a doctrinaire environmental viewpoint closely allied to that of Buffon towards a more empirically based viewpoint which emphasised the indiscriminate influence of human agency, particularly when the island was the physical context under review. The observation of physical processes was not the only factor involved here. It is clear that Forster's views on the environmental impact of the European were strongly linked to his evolving pessimism about the impact of European society in general on the human and physical ecology of the South Sea islands. A juxtaposition gradually developed in this critique, as it had with Commerson, in which Europe was perceived in progressively poorer light in direct proportion to the amount of time Forster spent away from it, with its mental constraints. One can date the beginning of this transition quite accurately from the arrival of the *Resolution* in Tahiti in August 1773. There is very little doubt that throughout this process Forster was subject to the influence of William Wales and his meteorological knowledge, much as Walter Hodges, the artist on the *Resolution,* was subject to Wales's meteorological observations in the development of his innovative naturalistic paintings of the tropics.[41]

The key to Forster's climatic thinking, however, was the impression made upon him by Tahiti, an impression for which he was well schooled by his very recent translation of Bougainville's *Voyage* into English. Forster was predisposed to conceive of Tahiti in a Cytherian or paradisal fashion and was led in his first days on the island to write of it in the language of the Aeneid, precisely as Commerson had done; and indeed, like Dante himself in his description of the earthly island paradise in *Purgatorio.* After the ardours of the Pacific voyage, the crew were glad to 'have this happy island in sight . . . we could refresh ourselves and our ships' companies with vegetables and greens'. Forster remembered the 'fine shady plantations, the agreeable walks, the fine rivulets, the powerful sun, the queer vegetation, the delicious and salubrious fruit, the summer breezes blowing constantly to cool the air, the

41 This meeting of minds aboard the *Resolution* was later described by Cuvier in the following terms: 'This voyage deserves to be noted as forming an epoch for the history of science. Natural history having thus contracted an alliance with astronomy and navigation, now began to extend its researches into a wider sphere . . . governments have learnt how nearly related to each other are all the sciences and how much their value is increased by their labours' (quoted in C. Tomlinson, *Sir Joseph Banks and the Royal Society,* London, 1844, p. 66).

beautiful tropical sky at sunrising and sunsetting, and every other circumstance contributing towards the happiness of its inhabitants'.[42]

The moist atmosphere of the island, Forster believed, derived from the
mountains upon it. The high hills 'attract by their situation, all the vapours
and clouds that pass near them . . . the very tops were covered by lofty trees
. . . the surrounding valleys collect in their bosom the salutary humidity which
is not absorbed by the plants and is generally screened by them against the
sun's power; so that in every one a gentle stream is collected from these
smaller hills'.[43] Seafarers had often used the propensity of islands to collect a
conspicuous cloud cover for navigational purposes, since the bulky clouds
formed through the superior thermal radiation of the land surface compared
with the sea could be seen at a great distance. Forster became interested in
the technicalities of this phenomenon, as had Bougainville before him. In
Tahiti he was clearly already associating the moisture of the mountain-tops
with the water-retaining propensity of the tree cover. He saw an essentially
benevolent agency at work contributing to the appearance of the island as a
'flourishing and well-kept garden'.[44] In it 'the fruit trees rise at proper distances from each other, and the shade which their foliage throws shelters the
green turf below, which the rays of a tropical sun would otherwise scorch and
destroy'.[45] These comments on the protective properties of the tree cover and
the note of warning about the potency of the tropical sun if the soil were to
be more exposed constitute an advance on his initially more conventionally
paradisal comments.

As he grew to understand Tahiti better, Forster gained insights from the
methods of land management he saw pursued. For example, he commented
favourably on the irrigation practices that the Tahitians had adopted and
saw them as complementary to the protectiveness of the vegetation. Here
was a picture of harmony in which the happy working of the hydrological
cycle on the island corresponded closely to the image of an ideally working
society. Later on, this idyllic perception was increasingly questioned by both
Forster and Cook after the *Resolution* had left the island and both men had
learnt more about Tahitian society. Similarly, as the journey proceeded,
Forster acquired a steadily more cynical attitude towards human interaction
with the land than he had shown in Tahiti. This was a considerable tran-

---

42 Forster in Hoare, *'Resolution' journal*, entry for 25 Aug. 1773. Georg Forster speaks of the
   'romantic scenery' in connection with events of 22 August – probably the first time this term
   was used specifically in connection with the *Resolution* voyage and the settings encountered in
   the South Seas.
43 J. R. Forster, *Observations*, p. 106.
44 Ibid., p. 162.
45 Ibid.

sition to make and a matter over which he continued to show a marked ambiguity. Certainly in the *Observations* Forster maintained a conventional view of the beneficence of human activity in environmental terms. Thus he wrote that 'we find artificial changes made on the surface of our globe by mankind, not to be the least considerable'.[46] So much, then, was admitted. But 'where man, the Lord of Creation on this globe, has never attempted any change on it, there nature seems only to thrive; for in reality it languishes and is deformed by being left to itself... how beautiful, how useful does nature become by the industry of man and what happy changes are produced, by the moderate care of rational beings'. The provenance of these sentiments is easily determined, since Forster openly refers to Buffon's *Vue de la nature*.[47]

The *Resolution* journal, however, tells quite a different story, and one that indicates that while, for wider consumption, Forster was reluctant to break away from Buffon's idea of 'beneficent' man, his empirical observations, particularly on islands, were leading him to a privately more critical view. It was his first stay at the Cape which first stimulated him to consider the links among mountains, clouds, trees and rainfall. Table Mountain made a particular impression on him. The mountain itself resembled an island in the sense of being a circumscribed physiographic form upon which processes could be observed operating.[48] Later in the voyage Forster noted that 'when we came to Norfolk island, we experienced the same sudden gusts of wind with showers of rain, all of which seem to have been like those noticed by that intelligent observer M. de Bougainville'.[49] Clearly by this time Forster was attentive to the influence of physiography and vegetation on rainfall, but it was only on the last leg of the return voyage, at St Helena and Ascension Island, that he was able to combine these insights with observations on human influence.

46 Ibid., p. 135.
47 Ibid., p. 135, citing Buffon, *Vue de la nature*, Paris, 1764, vol. 24, p. 12.
48 Forster in Hoare, *'Resolution' journal*, 12 Feb. 1773. Here he notes that 'fogs are nothing but dense vapours . . . it is natural for them to be attracted by land, especially if somewhat elevated. When we were at the Cape we had frequent opportunities of seeing this confirmed.' The appearance of Table Mountain when Forster made these observations is coincidentally recorded in Walter Hodges' painting of Cape Town, made on the same occasion from on board *Resolution*. For details of this painting, see Smith, *European vision and the South Pacific*, pp. 41–3 and pl. 35. This painting was itself strikingly innovative and an example of the strong new influence of empirical observation on the art of nature, and thus very much a micro-analogy of the influence of the Cook voyages on the growth of interest in an empirical knowledge of the interactions of man and the environment on a wider scale.
49 *Observations*, p. 248.

Forster and St Helena

On 18 May 1775 Forster 'rode into the country to the Governor's Garden' on St Helena 'in order to dine with him there'.[50] On the way he 'observed deep gullets formed in the sides of the hill by strong rains'. Later in the journey he remarked that 'all the valleys have a little stream purling down. The hills in the midst of the isle, being high, attract the clouds and afford by their moisture a constant supply for these little rivulets, which are always shaded by some trees.'

Forster made extensive notes on the agriculture practised on St Helena. In an entry in his journal on 19 May (the day after his observations on the erosion gullies) he made specific reference to the works of Pierre Poivre. The allusion occurs in a passage in which he indicates that he was clearly puzzled by the lack of agricultural development on the island in spite of the availability of 'moisture attracted from the clouds'.[51] Forster was not able to resolve this matter in his own mind until his arrival on Ascension, where the desolate and desiccated state of the island enabled him to draw comparisons with what he had seen on St Helena, aided, one may reasonably surmise, by his own recent reading of Pierre Poivre.[52] In particular, in making comparisons with St Helena, Forster began to understand the significance of the extensive planting which had taken place in the colony as part of the scheme which had originally been started by Governor Roberts. 'In the afternoon', he wrote,

> we took the boats in, weighed and set sail again, leaving this barren island, which with very little trouble might be settled and made a very useful place of refreshment. For this purpose nothing is wanting but water and wood. I am persuaded that if the common furze, which thrives so well on St Helena, were planted on this island, it would no doubt equally thrive here, and were these Furzes everywhere growing, grass and other plants would no doubt immediately after grow between them, form a coat and of course gradually form a soil of Mould capable of bearing more and more plants. The more the surface of the Earth is covered with plants, the more would they not only evaporate but even attract the moisture of the air, and keep it within the soil and consequently if there are any springs in the soil, they would soon increase their water and perpetuate their supplies . . . after grass and water were more plentiful in the isle certainly many a tree would soon grow and thus afford fuel.[53]

50 Forster in Hoare, *'Resolution' journal*, 18 May 1775.
51 Ibid., entries for 19 May and 24 May 1775.
52 Here the connections between the difficulties of supplying ships with food and water and the development of environmental sensitivity surface again. Forster may have purchased his copy of Poivre's *Voyages d'un philosophe* in Cape Town in the spring of 1775, as he does not mention Poivre prior to that date.
53 Forster in Hoare, *'Resolution' journal*, entry for 1 June 1775.

Although Forster did not here relate the retentive power of the vegetation to the consequences which might follow from its artificial removal, all the elements for further reasoning on this basis were present. Furthermore, Ascension Island itself provided direct evidence of human destructive powers upon which Forster had commented at length two days before in connection with the wanton slaughter of turtles. From the master of 'a New York vessel' Forster had learnt that

> a Bermuda sloop had been here and taken a great number of turtles and besides these had turned and killed more than a hundred of them, merely for the wanton gratification of having their eggs, leaving the meat to rot on the shores of which some had been seen by us . . . cruelty hardly to be believed if the performer had not bragged of it himself, and several had seen the vestiges of this cruel Epicurism; which must, of course, vastly diminish the numbers of these creatures useful to navigators.[54]

A gradual transition was taking place in Forster's thinking towards a more critical awareness of both the significance of the status of vegetal cover in the tropical environment and the possible impact upon it of human activity. It seems that Forster arrived at his conclusions largely as a consequence of the empirical opportunities afforded him by the *Resolution* voyage, aided, as he was, by the descriptions of the results of deforestation he would have discovered in Poivre's *Travels of a Philosopher*. It is difficult to be sure, however, exactly how influential Poivre was on Forster's understanding. Forster had made somewhat similar observations during September 1774 when the *Resolution* called at New Caledonia. Here his thoughts on species introductions (probably also stimulated by Poivre's writings on spice-tree transfers) led him to think back to the earlier part of the voyage and to consider the possibility of restoring the landscape of Easter Island. There, Forster thought, 'seeds of various plants as yams and coconuts, with Breadfruit and all kinds of trees that love a Hilly country would do exceedingly well and cause more moisture by their shade and procure rivulets, to this now poor, parched-up island'.[55]

---

54 Ibid., 30 May 1775. In this connection it is worth noting that turtles and giant land tortoises were among the first animals to have been the subject of discussion about possible extinction at the hands of man (apart from the dodo itself). On both Mauritius and Rodriguez the declining tortoise and turtle populations were the subject of comment and some desultory and unsuccessful attempts at conservation in the mid 1750s. Specific variation in tortoises especially was understood at an early date, which contributed to insights as to their likely extinction on some islands. See North-Coombes, *Histoire des tortues de terre de Rodrigues*. In both British and French eyes the role of these animals as a food supply for ships' crews hastened awareness of their population decline.

55 Hoare, *'Resolution' journal*, entry for 10 Sept. 1774. It is somewhat ironic that in the same diary entry Forster recommends the introduction of goats and sheep to the Marquesas and New Caledonia as a way of increasing their prosperity – precisely the thinking which had

Poivre, however, was clearly not the only writer to influence Forster on the
subject of deforestation and its results. Other writers, for example Peter Kalm,
who discussed deforestation and drought in North America without clearly
linking the two phenomena, must have helped to form a composite basis of
ideas for Forster.[56] In the same way the accumulation on the voyage of impressions of various environments, principally those of islands, circumscribing
a variety of different physiognomies and climatic variables, had its effect on
Forster's perceptions.

Forster's immediate influence in terms of the development of ideas about
the human impact on the tropical environment was probably limited, even
after his early publications.[57] His long-term influence, by contrast, was considerable, and to him may be attributed many of the antecedents of the desiccationist thinking adhered to by Alexander von Humboldt and subsequently
integrated into the development of the topic by Boussingault. The writings of
the latter two scientists chiefly inspired, in turn, the environmental critiques
of the East India Company surgeons in India after 1837 and those of Ludwig
Pappe and John Croumbie Brown in the Cape Colony after 1835.[58]

In the case of Pappe, Forster's thinking was diffused through the close
personal and academic contact between Humboldt and Forster's son, Georg.
The link with Pappe was of a similarly personal and direct kind. In 1780
Forster returned to Halle to take charge of the botanical garden and herbarium
there, and Kurt Joachim Sprengel became his principal botanical collaborator,
particularly during the last years of his life. Along with such workers as Carl
Ludwig Wildenow, this man became Humboldt's chief botanical mentor.[59]

ruined St Helena and played a part in the deforestation of Easter Island. On the ecological
decline of Easter Island, see P. S. Bellwood, *Man's conquest of the Pacific*, New York, 1979,
pp. 300–38.

56 Kalm, *Travels into North America*, London, 1771. Forster translated this book, first published
in Sweden in 1749, for the English edition. It places special emphasis on the impact of artificially induced deforestation through the agency of fire.

57 Humboldt himself noted with respect to this in a letter to Charles Darwin in July 1839 that
Forster's *Observations* was not appreciated at the time of its publication because of a contemporary 'poverty of spirit'. Forster was, Humboldt thought, far ahead of his time: Humboldt
to Darwin, 18 Sept. 1839, in F. Burckhardt and S. Smith, eds., *The correspondence of Charles
Darwin*, 2 vols., Cambridge, 1983–7, II, p. 219. Similar comments were made about the novelty
of Walter Hodges' paintings made during the *Resolution* voyage. Common to both was the
critical influence on their theories of the breadth of their empirical experience – a fact not at
all appreciated by intellectuals who remained in Europe.

58 See Grove, 'Early themes in African conservation' and 'Scottish missionaries, evangelical discourses and the origins of conservation thinking in Southern Africa', *Journal of Southern
African Studies*, 15:2 (1989), 163–88.

59 Hoare, *'Resolution' journal*, pp. 88–9. Hoare remarks that 'Forster and ... Georg ... were
direct influences on the life and work of Alexander von Humboldt and many others in Germany ... their work is of seminal significance for German science and letters in the last quarter

Both men were thoroughly conversant with Forster's *Resolution* experiences. In accounts of these experiences, Forster's commentaries on the variability of vegetation and physiographic types in their relation to climate bulked large, as they clearly did in the mind of Humboldt. There is more explicit evidence for the influence of Sprengel upon Ludwig Pappe. Pappe was to observe in a letter written to Sir William Hooker in 1846 that he was 'imbued . . . with an ardent love of botany, having studied under the late Carl Sprengel, the renowned Prussian polyhistor, having even chosen the study of Physic merely on account of the relation between that science and natural history'.[60]

Forster's more immediate influence on his return from England showed itself in the developing professionalisation of natural history, and especially in the extent to which it became dominated by German scientific thought, which was itself quickly and profoundly affected by Forster's documentation of the *Resolution* voyage. Forster had played the initial exemplary role himself, and it was one explicitly recognised by Sir Joseph Banks. This was in spite of Banks's professional jealousy of Forster, which stemmed from his replacement as naturalist by Forster on the *Resolution* voyage. During the five years between the return of the *Resolution* to England in July 1775 and Forster's departure for Halle in 1780, Banks went to considerable effort to facilitate the publication of the records and results of the *Resolution* voyage. His high regard for Forster's empirical work and for the ambitious theoretical scope of his *Observations* was reflected in his specific recommendations to the East India Company that in employing professional naturalists preference should be given to those candidates trained in the universities of Northern Europe'.[61] Equally important, the very idea of stationing naturalists in the new British territories in India almost certainly owed its origin to Forster's appraisal of the value of long-term empirical observation in the tropics and in India especially, an idea which was outlined in *Observations*. Forster's statement on the subject is interesting in the way in which he manages to justify the placing of professional naturalists, not only in scientific but in ostensibly patriotic terms, even at a stage when he was rapidly losing his old Anglophilia. Indian plants, he observed, were

> chiefly known from herbals and the more inaccurate, unfruitful and unscientific accounts of the botanists of the last age; for we can hardly expect much from the few opportunities which the disciples of the great father of botany [Linnaeus] have had of snatching up a few plants, as they have been chiefly confined to the Voyage to China; during which they seldom

of the eighteenth century. Most German scholars have long recognised this. Anglo-Saxon scholars . . . have not.'

60 L. Pappe to Sir William Hooker: Kew Archives, Cape Letters, 1846 vol.
61 See n. 67.

go ashore and much less make any stay in places which are worthy the
attention of the curious observer. And this circumstance likewise shows,
how much that immense part of the globe, India, with its isles, wants the
labour of a new, accurate, and modern observer, accompanied by a faithful
draughtsman, used in the drawings of natural history in order to make
us better acquainted with the rich treasures of these extensive regions;
and it raises in each patriotic breast the hope that, as the British Empire
in India is so extensive, so much respected and its subjects there so
wealthy and powerful . . . some of them would engage men capable of
searching the treasures of nature, and examining the several objects of
sciences and arts in those climates.[62]

This prescription for the stationing of naturalists in India was almost immediately adopted as a course of action. In 1778, shortly after *Observations*
was published, John Gerhard Koenig was appointed by the East India Company (EIC) as its 'naturalist' at Madras, an appointment which can be attributed directly to the influence of Banks, reinforced both by his admiration for
the thoroughness of German natural history which he had witnessed in Forster
and by Forster's own advocacy of professional natural history in India.[63]

Forster was not, in fact, the only propagandist for the state patronage of
natural history that Banks would have been familiar with. He was, for example,
already conversant with Poivre's policy of employing naturalists on a professional basis. In early 1771, when the *Endeavour* called at Cape Town after its
circumnavigation, Banks had had the opportunity of meeting Pierre Sonnerat,
Poivre's nephew. This meeting is recorded in a letter written to Banks by
Sonnerat in 1783.[64] From Sonnerat, Banks would have learnt of the activities
of Commerson (at that time conversant with more plant species than any other
contemporary botanist) and his widespread collecting activities, and also of
the attempts made by Poivre to import spice trees to Mauritius. Banks was
soon to promote such plant transfers on a grand scale, not least in connection
with the ill-fated Bligh expedition of 1787, while as early as 1773 he would
have become aware of the French attempts to enlarge and develop the botan-

---

62 *Observations*, p. 182.
63 D. G. Crawford, *The roll of the Indian Medical Service*, Calcutta, 1930, p. 267. Koenig had
   originally been employed by the Nawab of Arcot and in 1776 came into contact with William
   Roxburgh, the (second) director of the Calcutta Botanic Garden (after 1793). K. Biswas in
   The original correspondence of Sir Joseph Banks . . . ' Calcutta, 1950, p. 13, notes that 'Koenig
   was an ardent student of Carl Linnaeus and was considered by the then great botanists Camp-
   bell, Carey, Fleming, Hardwick, Buchanan, Klein, Rottler, Sonnerat and others as a sort of
   Avatar of Linnaeus in India.' It was Roxburgh who first alerted Banks to the value of Koenig's
   work; see *Banks letters*, letter of 8 March 1779 from Roxburgh 'at Nagpore' to Banks.
64 Letter from Sonnerat to Banks, 12 April 1783, quoted in Ly-Tio-Fane, *Pierre Sonnerat*,
   p. 11.

ical garden at Pamplemousses, which had recently been described by Milon as 'one of the wonders of the world'.[65]

Concrete evidence of Banks's predilection for German rather than British botanists emerges in the context of correspondence he was engaged in with the EIC, a correspondence which became established on a regular basis in 1785.[66] In connection with the death of Koenig, Banks decided in 1787 to request the secretary of the Court of Directors to lay before the Court the 'utility of the work done by the late J. G. Koenig' and to point out that

> although his emoluments were small, he worked indefatigably and sent much valuable information on useful plants and other botanical matters to his colleagues in Europe, much of it which has been published by learned societies . . . valuable results came from his journeys to the Malacca Straits in 1780 . . . most of his papers perished in the loss of the 'General Barker'; in Bengal he made valuable additions to medical and economic botany; it is important not only for science but for the commerce of the EIC that a worthy successor should be found among the naturalists trained in the universities of Northern Europe.[67]

While the EIC did later employ such naturalists (Nathaniel Wallich was a prime example), Koenig was actually replaced by an Englishman, assistant surgeon Patrick Russell. Russell proceeded to write to Banks with his own views on the desirability of fostering natural science in India. Indeed, it seems that it was Russell who first convinced botanists in Britain (and Banks especially) of the ease with which a network of naturalists reporting to Kew might be established in India.[68]

---

65 Pridham, *Mauritius*, p. 217.

66 On 13 April 1785 Secretary to the Court of Directors Martin wrote to Banks in connection with the growing of hemp, canvassing the idea that Banks might hold experiments on Chinese hemp on behalf of the EIC at Kew: *Banks letters*.

67 Ibid., letter, 22 Feb. 1787, pp. 133–7.

68 Patrick Russell pioneered the use of the infrastructure of the new British civil administration as a means of collecting and collating systematic data on natural history – the same framework used in the 1840s by the EIC for the collection of information on rainfall and deforestation. In 1787, for example, he persuaded the Madras Council to distribute a questionnaire soliciting information on snakes which he 'hopes will elicit useful information' (ibid., letter to Banks, 16 Dec. 1787). This resulted in *Poisonous snakes of the Coromandel coast*, published in London in 1787. It was followed by a much longer (4 vols.) work on Indian snakes published in 1796–80. Like Koenig, Russell had had a colorful early career which had awoken him to the possibilities for scientific endeavour in colonial employ. During his tenure as physician to the English factory in Aleppo, he had been able to carry out the research for the two-volume *Natural history of Aleppo* published in 1794 in collaboration with his brother Alexander Russell. This was followed, in India, by a pioneering work, *Fishes of Southern India*, based on specimen material collected at Vizigapatam and published in two volumes in 1803; see Crawford, *Roll of the Indian Medical Service*. Crawford records the date of Koenig's appointment as 4 Nov. 1785. In fact his letters to Banks indicate that it was later, 12 Mar. 1786.

The initiative taken by the Court of Directors in 1785 in recognising the status of Banks as a scientist and botanist also marked an important new step in the status accorded to science generally in India. The timing of the direct approach made to Banks by the EIC can be related quite precisely to the establishment of the Asiatic Society of Bengal, a development which marked the beginnings of a long association between British aggrandisement in India and the flowering of Oriental and scientific scholarship in the early nineteenth century. It was an association which also helped to promote the flow of ideas between scientists in India and those outside the country.[69] As Commerson had recognised on Mauritius, the continuity ensured by the foundation of a scientific society counteracted the disadvantages of the short tenures normally enjoyed by colonial officials, with all the potential for losing hard-won knowledge which such tenures implied. Scientific societies also expedited the more rapid, large-scale and regular transfer of intellectual ideas, innovation and exchange.

The fear of famine and the foundation of the Calcutta Botanic Garden

The onset of professionalisation in natural history in India and the growing diffusion of climatic environmentalism after the 1760s soon combined to affect official attitudes to environmental change in the East India Company itself. During the 1770s a realisation developed gradually among a limited group of company servants in Bengal that the onset of British rule might have serious consequences for the incidence of drought and the frequency of famine. British rule, it was now said, implied a responsibility to assess and respond to growing evidence of artificial influences on rainfall levels. The principal exponent of this view was Captain Robert Kyd.[70]

69 William Roxburgh, the surgeon-botanist, was, with Sir William Jones, one of the members of the United Brotherhood.
70 Robert Kyd (1746–93) came from a Forfarshire family, entered the Bengal Engineers in 1764 and by 1786, when he first proposed the idea of a botanical garden to John Macpherson, the company's successor to Warren Hastings, was military secretary to the government. Kyd's Forfarshire connections may have provided him with an interest in tree planting, which was being carried out extensively in Eastern Scotland by the 1750s. Between 1740 and 1830 the Dukes of Atholl planted 14 million larches in Perthshire, while between 1757 and 1835 the Royal Society for the Encouragement of the Arts gave gold and silver medals to stimulate large-scale plantations (K. Thomas, *Man and the natural world*, p. 200; Thomas comments: 'More research on estate archives is likely to reveal that planting for timber, like planting for ornament, had a longer pre-history than is sometimes appreciated'). Kyd may have been influenced by such Edinburgh publications as Hamilton and Balfour's *Treatise on the manner of raising fruit trees* (1761), itself heavily derivative of Duhamel du Monceau's *Practical treatise on husbandry*, published in 1759.

Plate 19. Robert Kyd, superintendent of the East India Company's botanical garden at Sibpur, Calcutta, 1786–93. (Courtesy Cambridge University Library)

In 1776 Kyd had become interested in the idea of transferring spice trees from the Himalayan ranges on the eastern frontier to Calcutta. Building on this experience, he had then developed the idea of deliberately cultivating and bringing drought-resistant crops together in one place, with the intention of distributing them to peasants living in drought-prone regions. Company support for a colonial botanical garden would provide for such a project. The idea originated, according to Kyd, in 'the example of the great La Bourdon-nage [Labourdonnais] who importing from Brazil and introducing the growth of the manioc root into the islands of Mauritius and Bourbon rescued the inhabitants from the scourge of famine to which they were subject from the annual hurricanes which destroyed their harvest and entailed this calamity'.[71]

71 Kyd to Board, Fort William, 15 April 1786, quoted in BL, IOL Home. Misc. no. 799 (Proceedings of the Supreme Council 'relative to the establishment of a botanical garden on the site of the old fort at Machwa Tannah at Calcutta, 21 August – 6 March 1788, proposed by Colonel Robert Kyd', pp. 1–201).

While Eastern Scottish tree-planting traditions may have influenced Kyd, he was equally conversant with French agronomic ideas and would have been well aware of the works of Poivre and his disciple, Céré, and their activities, as his allusions to Mauritius indicate. In his radical approach to the potential role of the state in this field, Kyd gives some indication of having shared in European physiocratic thinking, particularly that relating to the deliberate promotion of 'scientific' agriculture.

If the new government in Bengal could not safeguard the citizens from famine, Kyd reasoned, all other benefits the British might bring were worthless. As he put it in his letter to the Board,

> Revolving in my mind the accumulated riches which have accrued to Great Britain consequent to our territorial possession in India I have sometimes been betrayed [*sic*] into reflections on the comparative benefits which we have conferred on the Nations of India . . . in this comparison I am afraid, the balance will stand greatly against us . . . while they suffer from physical causes consequent to the greatest of all calamities, that of desolation by famine, and subsequent pestilence.[72]

Kyd was acutely aware that the 'dreadful scourge' of famine had 'already in the course of twenty-two years devastated these far provinces from one extremity to the other'. He knew, too, that 'every possible means of averting these dreadful visitations' remained 'yet unthought of, untried'. Further, Kyd added,

> This reflection impresses me strongly with the idea of entailing on us the imputation of inhumanity and improvidence from the enormity of misery and wretchedness which inevitably continues to impend over the heads of the Natives whilst every provisional plan having only the semblance of rationality remains unattempted on the part of our administration. In justice to the late Governor-General [Warren Hastings] it must indeed be allowed this important aspect did not escape his foresight and the public granary, which had been erected in the province of Bihar by his direction, it is to be wished for, may remain forever a durable monument to the honour of his administration, and the Glory of our nation which prides itself in acts of popular humanity and maintaining the rights of all subject nations.

While Kyd was happy to acknowledge Warren Hastings's efforts to lessen the likelihood of famine, he made clear his disdain for the efforts of the 'administration' in this direction. Rather than establishing grain depots, he argued, the government would do better to establish a botanical garden and

72 Ibid.

form a stock of drought-resistant plants here at Calcutta to be transplanted under the influence of government to the principal provincial
towns and from thence disseminated in process of time over our territorial
possessions so that every village may maintain a stock of this valuable
tree [the sago tree] in reserve to be cut down as the exigencies of famine
shall require, being a vegetable production, not subject to the same causes
of failure as the crop of grain on which the natives now solely depend
for their subsistence.[73]

In this letter Kyd concentrated on the risks incumbent in famine and the
extent to which a large botanical garden might avert the danger altogether.
However, he omitted any discussion of the profits that might accrue to the
company through the development. 'I cannot help thinking', he wrote, 'that
the dreadful calamity in question may (if not wholly) in part be averted by
the means proposed, which will afford an everlasting resource, and be no
further chargeable to Government than its first introduction.'

The concept was a novel one, involving the prospect of intervention and
agricultural development on the part of the state on lines which clearly originated in the theories of the French agronomes and the physiocrats. Not surprisingly, the Board did not respond immediately to the plan, even though
John Macpherson, the interim governor, was personally attracted by it.[74] In
Kyd's later and more successful approaches to the Board, he was compelled
to stress the commercial advantages that might accrue to the EIC while significantly playing down the merits of the project for famine prevention. By
September 1786 the arguments and support for a Calcutta garden had become
much stronger. This was mainly a consequence of the growing reputation of
the botanical garden at St Vincent, where Alexander Anderson had become
curator in 1785 with the active support of Joseph Banks. In January 1786
Banks had received a report on the plans and needs of the St Vincent garden
from Sir George Yonge.[75] This report had been compiled by Anderson. It
encouraged Yonge to suggest to Banks that a Calcutta garden should be established, largely to cater to the new role which had been assigned to St
Vincent as an acclimatisation garden for the whole of the West Indies. The
Anderson report gave added ammunition to Kyd in his own campaign. In
September 1786 he wrote to Lord Cornwallis, the governor-general, to tell
him of requests from Yonge for Indian plants for the St Vincent garden. Such
requests could best be answered, he said, were a garden established at Cal-

73 Ibid.
74 Minute of the Governor-General on the subject of the letter from Kyd to G-G and Council,
   1 June 1786: *A short account of Colonel Kydd, the founder of the Royal Botanic Garden, Calcutta,*
   Calcutta, 1897, p. 6.
75 Letter, Banks to Sir George Yonge, *Banks letters,* p. 511. The report had been sent on 5 Jan.
   1786.

cutta, as he had previously suggested. A company botanical garden would 'greatly facilitate the production and despatch of the plants wanted as well as other useful or rare plants'.[76]

These allusions to St Vincent were decisive in persuading the authorities to approve the project. In May 1787 Banks wrote to Yonge to tell him that his (Yonge's) plan for the establishment of a Calcutta garden had been 'anticipated by the governor and council' and that his suggestions for direct communication between Calcutta and St Vincent 'had been applied'.[77] 'The Dutch', he said, 'have explored the Malabar coast, and the late Doctor Koenig was well acquainted with the Coromandel coast.' The French had preceded the British by several years in similar undertakings, he complained, as the expeditions 'from the Isle of France' demonstrated. But the abilities of Kyd in India and Anderson on St Vincent, he added, 'will ensure the success of exchanges between the two'.

In fact, between 1784 and 1786 the East India Company authorities in London and Calcutta had become increasingly aware of the advantages that might be gained from playing an active role in promoting and investing in crop experimentation and from efforts to transfer new crops and centralise them in botanical gardens in company territories. This, then, meant that the company became more conscious of the value of botanical science and began to accord a new status to botanists.[78] This in turn provided opportunities for botanists to influence company policy in a fashion which individuals such as Kyd, Russell and Banks were quick to take up, particularly by persuading the company that new crop experimentation would be carried out most suitably not in England, as the company had originally envisaged, but in India or adjacent islands instead. In this way, largely unwittingly, the company had laid itself open to important strands of new thinking in botanical science and agricultural improvement in Britain, and above all, albeit indirectly, to the influence of those who may be characterised as the English physiocrats.[79] Pre-

---

76 Letter, Kyd to Cornwallis, Sept. 1786, *Banks letters*, p. 511, Letter 4.

77 Letter, Banks to Yonge, 15 May 1787, *Banks letters*, p. 880.

78 The earliest extant communication between the EIC and Banks dates from 1785. It indicates that the initiative was taken by the EIC Court of Directors rather than by Banks, who had become president of the Royal Society. In it Thomas Martin, secretary to the Court, asked him for advice on experimentation in the growing of hemp in England. Banks turned down the EIC proposals for experiments at Kew, arguing for local experiments in Bengal: Letter, 13 April 1785: BL, Add. MS. 33978–9. This appears to be the first time the EIC actively sought expert advice in botanical matters in England itself.

79 The most useful discussion of relations between English and French physiocrats appears in K. E. Knorr, *British colonial theories*, London, 1963, pp. 236–44. Young, William Cobbett and Thomas Spence were all hostile to colonial enterprise, believing that it diverted attention away from domestic agriculture. Interestingly, Young was especially scathing about French investment in colonial sugar islands, including Mauritius, which he regarded as 'a wretched com-

eminent among them were Arthur Young, Joseph Banks and, a little later, Sir John Sinclair. All were heavily influenced by contemporary thinking in France, although they cannot be as easily stereotyped or characterised in their thinking as their French counterparts. The timing of the interchanges between Kyd, Banks and the EIC over the foundation of the Calcutta Botanic Garden was crucial, since it was at this time that Banks and other British botanists were becoming aware of the extent to which the French government had successfully promoted agricultural botany in the colonies and in particular of the progress which had been made at the botanical garden at Pamplemousses, Poivre's brainchild. The initial impetus for Banks's interest in the Mauritius garden, now under the superintendency of Céré, related to the possibility of improving the botanical gardens on St Vincent, Trinidad and Jamaica, all of which were institutions far more limited in scope and scale than the Pample-mousses establishment.[80] Banks himself was very ready to pay tribute to the French example and was to write, in commenting on the publications issued by the Jardin du Roi, that they

> not only shew the attention paid by the French nation, while under the ancient government, to the transportation of useful plants from one part of the globe to another, but set an example to our Royal Gardens at St Vincent, instituted for similar purposes, though possibly not supplied with equal funds, and will also encourage the West India planters to apply for and receive such plants, of which there are many.[81]

Banks's earlier contacts with Buffon and later with Arthur Young enabled him to become as conversant with these kinds of developments in the admin-istration of botanical gardens as he had already become with the particular qualities of German professional natural history.[82] For Banks, too, the French

mercial policy' (Knorr, *British colonial theories*, p. 239) – a sentiment with which Poivre and Saint-Pierre, with their hostility to the environmental and economic effects of plantation ag-riculture, would have agreed.

80 See Ly-Tio-Fane, *Mauritius and the spice trade*, II, p. 98.

81 Letter, Banks to Earl of Liverpool, 11 Aug. 1796, quoted in appendix to William Urban Buée, *Narrative of the successful manner of cultivating the clove tree in the Island of Dominica*, and re-quoted in Ly-Tio-Fane, *Mauritius and the spice trade*, II, p. 66. Céré himself noted in 1785 (a statement which helps to explain the timing of the interchange between the EIC and British botanists): 'Aussi-je jolies biens des foi en voyant l'étonnement des éstrangers Anglais, Por-tugais, Espagnols, Suédois, Danois, Allémands, Hollandais de trouver dans une isle aussi éloignée de la métropole et comme . . . au milieu de L'océan Indien, un lieu aussi riche, aussi célèbre; et de leur admiration surtout pour le menarques, sous le protection de qui croissent et se propagent tant de sources de richesses pour ses sujets . . .' Clearly by this time Le Reduit was considered the paragon of colonial botanical gardens and thus worthy of imitation by competing powers.

82 Banks corresponded with Buffon on several occasions. In June 1772 Buffon wrote to thank him for gifts of plants to the Jardin du Roi and sent him a copy of *Histoire naturelle*: BL,

example indicated the extent to which formal investment in botanical gardens might as a matter of course provide for the installation of professional botanists and might also thereby provide the means to carry out large-scale scientific surveys. For there is no question that the motives of both Banks and Kyd were not confined to the narrow commercial outlook of the EIC Directors in this matter. Rather the commercial interests of the EIC provided an opportunity for natural history. Kyd, incidentally, was actively hostile to the prospect of the expansion of British territorial control in India and stated in a letter of 1 June 1786 to the Governor-General and Council that he wished to

> divert the Administration not only from thinking of making further acquisitions by new settlements (except insofar as they may prove necessary for the peace and security of what we already hold) but also to embrace the opportunity of peace to reject such unprofitable parts of the Empire as have only proved useless burthens to our more valuable possessions.[83]

As Banks was more regularly consulted by the EIC in connection with botanical gardens and other matters, he felt increasingly able to make his scientific motives more overt and to voice his criticisms about the lack of any genuine commitment to scientific matters on the company's part. In 1791, for example, he had to remind the company, with some acidity, that the botanical gardens at Calcutta were designated 'for utility and for science and not as a place of retreat for officials'.[84] More important, Banks increasingly found himself able to influence the appointment of the superintendents of company botanical gardens in India. This was a development which eventually allowed him to secure the appointment of Nathaniel Wallich (a Dane trained at the universities of Copenhagen and Kiel) as superintendent at Calcutta in 1815, so ensuring that he retained the kinds of direct contact between Kew and Calcutta that had been possible during the superintendencies of Kyd and (after Kyd's death in 1793) William Roxburgh.

French physiocratic interest in crop transfers on Mauritius under Poivre had helped to promote an institutional and state interest in botanical gardens, soil conditions and the professionalisation of natural history, leading to the development of wider conservation concerns. In Bengal the influence of the English physiocrats ensured similar developments. The role of the botanical garden as the focus for environmental concerns in India, however, did not develop as quickly as it had done in Mauritius. This was quite simply because

Add. MS 8094, quoted in *Banks letters*, pp. 15–16. The early contacts between Banks and French geologists and the role of Young in promoting contacts with the French are alluded to in Eyles, 'William Smith, Sir Joseph Banks and the French geologists'.

83 Kyd to Governor-General of Bengal, 1 June 1786, *A short account of Colonel Kydd, the founder of the Royal Botanic Garden, Calcutta*, Calcutta, 1897, p. 6.
84 Banks to EIC, 17th June, *Banks letters*.

the wider environment of Bengal and Eastern India was not so easily observed or so subject to the pace of artificial alteration which had affected the oceanic islands, however much the role of the state in coping with the social impact of climatic exigency might have been stimulated by the likes of Kyd. Instead the logic of empirical environmental processes observed in the island colonies continued to exert its particular influence. Meanwhile, Kyd's dual concern for the collection of botanical rarities and the provision of alternative food crops to prevent famine proved effective in stimulating the development of the botanical-garden system in India and the wherewithal for a coterie of professional botanists.

The emergence of a system of botanical gardens in the British colonies was not, of course, a wholly random process. Nevertheless, it would be a mistake to think either that it was a highly organised phenomenon or that it was a development engineered entirely by Sir Joseph Banks. The notion of a linked set of gardens, each with its own superintendent, relied heavily on the model of the already extant French system based in Paris and Mauritius. In particular, Banks and his collaborators wished to imitate a system in which plants gathered from species-rich or little-known parts of India, South-East Asia, the Pacific and Latin America could be transferred both to gardens in Europe and, equally important, to the gardens on the islands of the Indian and Atlantic oceans and the Caribbean, where slave-labour economies already existed. In the sugar-and-slave colonies the full potential of the new species could then be exploited for plantation purposes in a way that was not possible further east. Between 1770 and 1820 the personnel involved in the botanical network built up around the gardens and centred on Sir Joseph Banks involved about 130 collectors and superintendents of gardens. By 1790 about 15 men were involved in running the network of British botanical gardens in the tropics. These included Robert Kyd in Calcutta; James Anderson at Madras; William Roxburgh at Samulcottah; Henry Porteous on St Helena; Helenus Scott at Bombay; and Thomas Dancer, Hinton East and Alexander Anderson in the West Indies.[85]

This network enabled a pattern of plant transfers to develop, with the main tropical axis running between Calcutta and St Vincent and having a central and essential transit point at St Helena. The form and function of this axis indicate why a number of botanists after the 1780s began to agitate for the foundation of a garden on St Helena to link India with the West Indies and with St Vincent specifically. Such a link would allow, for example, the kind of grandiose plan envisaged in Bligh's two breadfruit-transfer expeditions. But it also permitted the rapid diffusion of new environmental ideas, principally from west to east, in the opposite direction to the main plant transfers. It was

---

85 Mackay, *In the wake of Cook*, chap. 5, 7.

the formation of this main botanical-garden axis that underlay the globalisation of what had been an insular environmentalism. Environmental centres of calculation, one might say, were succeeded by an information network. How had this come about?

Agitation by East India Company officials for the foundation of a formal company botanical garden on St Helena (as distinct from a governor's garden, which had long existed) with professional staffing began with a letter from Robert Kyd to Sir Joseph Banks in January 1787, thus actually predating the formal founding of the garden at Calcutta and Kyd's superintendency. Kyd had complained that fruit trees sent to him from England were dead on arrival in Bengal.[86] The solution, he suggested, should involve the setting up of a way-station on St Helena. Kyd also discussed the idea with Patrick Russell, the naturalist at Madras. Russell, who clearly shared his view, also proposed the idea to Banks in a letter of October 1788, apparently indicating that no action had been taken.[87]

But Kyd's idea for a St Helena garden was not an original one. Alexander Anderson had, as early as 1785 and by the force of the same logic on plant transfers, already started to put pressure on Sir George Yonge, then secretary for war in London, to found a St Helena garden. Yonge duly obliged and in March 1787 reported to Anderson that he had been able to 'prevail with the East India Company to establish a garden in that island and also to give orders for seeds and plants of all kinds which may be useful in medicine and commerce to be brought and cultivated there in order to [have] them from thence conveyed in a favourable state to St Vincent'.[88] It was, in fact, the need to provision the St Vincent garden with Asian spices (a 'need', of course, to emulate the model established by Poivre and extended later by the French to the West Indies) that had led Banks to involve the East India Company directly in the business of plant transfers.[89]

In 1787 Sir William Jones began to interest himself in the progress and professionalisation of natural history in India and to correspond with Banks

---

86 *Banks letters*, letter, Kyd to Banks, 13 Jan. 1787 (copy, BL, IOL Bengal Public Consultations).
87 *Banks letters*, letter, Russell to Banks, 10 Oct. 1788 (from Vizigapatam). Russell's formal correspondence with Banks had begun in 1782, although he was already sending Banks specimens from Aleppo considerably earlier and seems to have influenced Banks a good deal, often mediating contacts with Roxburgh and Koenig, who worked in more inaccessible regions than Russell.
88 Letter, 31 March 1787, Sir George Yonge to Alexander Anderson, quoted in Anderson, 'The St Vincent Botanic Garden', Linnaean Society Archives, Piccadilly.
89 This is evidenced in a letter written by Robert Adair to Anderson in 1785 in which he stated that 'the King has been graciously pleased to command the Secretary at War to write to the directors of the East India Company to procure every kind of seed and plant which may be useful for your establishment, particularly the nutmeg, if it can be come at by any means': Letter, 6 Feb., in ibid.

on the matter. He offered, in effect, to add his weight to the growing pressure on the EIC actively to sponsor scientific endeavour. In September he wrote to Banks, reminding him that 'since the death of Koenig the need for a botanist is much felt'.[90] Jones's thinking on this matter later became more expansive, and in 1791 he again wrote to Banks asserting that there was 'a great need of a travelling botanist' in India. Company funding for those who might fill this role was quite inadequate, Sir William argued.[91] This letter, it later transpired, contained the seed of a concept that was later realised in the surveys of Buchanan-Hamilton. It also served to promote the empirical groundwork of ecological knowledge which was to enable the EIC surgeon-botanists of the 1840s and 1850s to demonstrate convincingly to the government of India the degree to which vegetal changes had actually occurred in the previous decades.[92] These interventions by Sir William Jones may have had some effect, since it is clear that by 1790 the company had at least decided to spend money on the training of naturalists specifically to maintain the kind of acclimatisation garden on St Helena that Kyd and Russell had recommended.[93] Thus Henry Porteous, the company gardener on St Helena, told Banks in 1790 that the Directors had 'sent out men trained in India' and had assigned them landholdings on St Helena.[94]

The foundation of a system of botanical gardens by the East India Company can be seen, at one level, as the realisation of a relatively straightforward botanical and economic agenda, carried out largely through the joint influence of Banks and Sir William Jones. But this programme also had a deeper meaning. That is, the company had finally come under the full influence of a physiocratic ideology derived from the activities and example of the French on Mauritius and in particular from the ideas of Pierre Poivre. There is little evidence that members of the Court of Directors were fully cognisant of the antecedents of this new physiocratic philosophy, even though they were aware of the economic benefits which might accrue from its practice. Instead, letters from the Court to Banks are replete with the older language of 'improvement' which was already so familiar in England at the time. Nevertheless, the per-

90 17 Sept. 1789, *Banks letters*. In this letter Jones also confides to Banks that he has been reading '*Philosophica Botanica* and other works of Linnaeus'. This reading would have alerted Jones to the significance which botanists attached to a greater knowledge of the Indian flora, which Forster had already underlined in 1778.

91 Letter of 18 Oct. 1791, *Banks letters*.

92 See e.g. H. Cleghorn, *The forests and gardens of South India*, Edinburgh, 1861, p. iii, for use made of Buchanan-Hamilton's records as an authority and reference point for discussions on rates of deforestation in 1805-55.

93 The transportation difficulties were not entirely resolved by this means. In 1791 Sir William Jones commented that there were difficulties in sending plants from India: Letter to Banks, 18 Oct. 1791, *Banks letters*.

94 Letter, 8 June 1790, ibid.

manent nature of the company botanical gardens and Banks's long-continued influence over appointments to them ensured both the continuity of the physiocratic influence and its incorporation into post-1840s conservation in India once it had been accepted by government. Equally important, the foundation of the Calcutta and St Helena botanical gardens provided an intellectual conduit for the diffusion of the climatic environmentalism that had been developed on Mauritius and St Vincent.

Between 1791 and 1833 St Helena became the site of a series of experiments in conservation, reafforestation and attempts to boost rainfall levels artificially. These experiments were important both on their own account and because of their strong influence on the beginnings of forest conservation in India. Unlike the earlier locally directed attempts to inhibit ecological decline on the island, this second phase of environmental intervention was closely linked to a conceptualisation of the processes of environmental change (particularly the relations between trees and climate) that was beginning to acquire a global aspect through the botanical network set up by the French and by Sir Joseph Banks in the wake of the *Endeavour* voyage.

Banks's interest in the degraded state of St Helena had become apparent as early as 1771. This acquaintance was renewed in 1784 as a consequence of a correspondence started by a new governor of the colony. In that year David Corneille, the Huguenot governor of the colony, wrote to Banks and sent him a specimen of a fish caught off the coast of the island.[95] The fish, Corneille believed, was probably very rare and was apparently previously undescribed. At any rate, the governor had not been able to find it in the volumes of Buffon which he had with him on the island. Corneille had, of course, reactivated an old pattern of contact between governor-naturalists on the island and an authority in London, without any direct involvement by the company. But this contact proved far more fruitful than in earlier times, and Banks was immediately interested in the association between the island and the occurrence of 'rare' species, as he had been in 1771. In so being, Banks was reactivating a connection between St Helena and 'rarity' that had been central to the much earlier concerns and collecting enthusiasms of Leonard Plukenet and Edward Bulkeley. However, St Helena had, for Banks, already acquired a rather complex symbolic significance. In 1771 he had discussed it in terms of a lost paradise, one that contrasted powerfully with the sensuous and unspoilt image of Otaheite and with the artificial paradise of the Cape. There is no evidence that this kind of imagery had lessened in significance in Banks's consciousness (or in his subconscious) in 1784. From this time on Banks was instrumental in establishing St Helena as an insular symbol of connections between ideal island, lost paradise and extinction. By protecting it, paradise might be re-

95 16 May 1784, ibid.

gained, exactly as the St Helena governors had constantly tried to revive it. This theme was continued in the lives and work of William Burchell, William Roxburgh, Alexander Beatson, William Webster and, not least, Charles Darwin. In the case of Darwin in particular, St Helena helped to create an archetypal and symbolic preoccupation with the island condition and with the possibility of extinction and competition between species on an island. This would lead to comparisons between islands and, in turn, to explanations argued in terms of time and the transformation and evolution of species. Contact among the scientists on the Cook expedition had raised a debate about the origins and survival of man which could be played out in a search for origins and connections between species or in debates about the comparative influence of climate (environmental conditions) in altering or degenerating different types of people or cultures.[96] St Helena lay – geographically in its eroded state and in its dynamic exhibition of rarity – at the Romantic centre of such debates and anxieties.

But in order for St Helena to fulfil this historic role, possibly as a very specific personal allegory of the world for both Banks and Darwin, a diametrically opposed or differentiated counterpart was needed – a role which the idyllic and uneroded state of Otaheite and other tropical islands fulfilled. But as early as 1784 St Helena was, at another level, still playing a somewhat simpler role as an environment where issues of rarity, endemism and restoration could be explored. It is this role which emerges in the extensive correspondence between Banks and the island governors.[97] There was no immediate outcome of the first exchanges between Corneille and Banks. Nevertheless, Corneille continued with his own naturalising and with some experiments in plant propagation and transplanting, probably influenced by what he knew of earlier activities on St Helena. In May 1786 he again wrote to Banks to inform him of his success in cultivating an endemic tree known as the laurel tulip and to say that he was sending a specimen of the tree to Kew.[98] In the same letter he regrets that he is 'unable to send a sample of ebony as all the trees have been destroyed by an insect'. He would, however, be able to send a sample of the (endemic) cabbage tree. The tone of regret indicates that Banks had made an explicit request for ebony pieces, and this may itself indicate a renewed interest in the forest cover of the island on his part. Corneille's later correspondence with Banks continued to deal with the subject of transplanting specimens of the laurel tulip to Kew.[99] In fact, the Corneille

96 The correspondence between Alexander Anderson and Blumenbach on the skull characteristics and skull sizes of the Caribs gives an indication of the strength of this debate.

97 See Chapter 3.

98 23 May 1786, *Banks letters*.

99 17 March and 30 July 1787, ibid. Corneille sent a parcel of plants to Banks in early 1787 through the offices of Masson, the Cape botanist. In July he wrote that he was 'highly gratified

correspondence indicates that, even before evolving a formal relationship with the East India Company, Banks had become intensely interested in the environmental status of one of its possessions, although at a time when he was concerning himself far more with the West Indies and the possibilities of plant transfer from the Pacific to the Caribbean. With the foundation in 1787 of new botanical gardens on St Helena and at Kew, it appears that both Banks, at Kew, and Henry Dundas, in Whitehall, began to link St Vincent and St Helena much more closely in policy terms. For example, when the King's Hill forest-protection legislation was introduced in the St Vincent Assembly in 1788, Sir Henry Dundas became actively involved in the matter and in the legislative amendments made by London to the initiative taken by Alexander Anderson and William Bannatyne.[100] Violent floods on St Helena in March 1787 were widely attributed to the earlier occurrence of excessive tree cutting. 'At a moderate computation,' the governor wrote to London, 'the damages to your property alone must amount to some thousands of pounds exclusive of the injury done individuals in many parts of the island.'[101] From thenceforth, with few interruptions until the end of company rule in the 1830s, official anxieties about the ecological state of the island were of a much more committed quality than had been the case prior to Banks's involvement with the island.[102] In October 1790 the company formally asked Banks to comment on a whole range of papers detailing the state of the island.[103] He returned these with his comments in March 1791. It was at this stage that Banks, in full knowledge of developments on St Vincent, stressed the need to act on the deforestation problem once again. In fact, he had already made his own arrangements on the subject directly with the St Helena government, utilising the extension to his botanical network initiated by Corneille.[104] Governor Corneille resigned in May 1787 and left the island. His successor, Robert Brooke, carried on his tree-planting activities from the very beginning. On 17 June 1787 he reported to Banks that trees planted by Corneille were 'prospering'.[105] Brooke supplemented this with his own efforts and in May 1791 recorded that he had recently sent to the Directors for full chests of tree seedlings and shrub plants for 'planting in accordance with' Banks's instructions. He was

at having sent plants acceptable to Kew', an interesting reflection of the much-increased status of Banks and botany in the eyes of a company official.

100 Public Record Office, Kew, CO 263/21 and CO 260/3 (Misc. Corr.).
101 H. R. Janisch, ed., *Extracts of St Helena records and chronicles of Cape Commanders*, Jamestown, St Helena, 1908 [henceforth *SHR*], 31 March 1787, SH Govt. to Directors.
102 *SHR*, 31 March 1787, Council letters to England.
103 Letter, 15 Oct. 1790, EIC Directors to Banks: *Banks letters*.
104 Banks to EIC Directors, 8 Jan. 1791, *Banks letters*.
105 Brooke to Banks, ibid., p. 154.

also engaged in 'planting coffee, cinnamon, cloves and other trees and shrubs'.[106]

The efforts made by Brooke and Banks to alert the company to the situation on St Helena and to encourage it to adopt the policies of the St Vincent government were reinforced during 1791 and 1792 by extended droughts on the island. These years of poor rainfall were not confined to St Helena; as Alexander Beatson recorded in 1816, 'the severe drought felt here in 1791 and 1792 was far more calamitous in India'.[107] Beatson, a Scotsman with a consuming interest in the dynamics of climate change, went on to record that 'owing to a failure of rain during the above two years, one half of the inhabitants in the Northern Circar had perished by famine and the remainder were so feeble and weak that on the report of rice coming up from the Malabar coast five thousand people left Rajahmundry and very few of them reached the seaside, although the distance is only fifty miles'.[108] But, as Beatson noted, 1791 and 1792 were also 'unusually dry in Montserrat'. The drought was, then, global in its impact in the tropics, and it soon evoked a correspondingly global, if grudging, response from the East India Company.[109] This was in

---

106 Brooke to Banks, 7 May 1791, *Banks letters*.

107 Beatson, *Tracts*, p. 198. Alexander Beatson (1759–1833) had been a lieutenant-general in the EIC service, was then governor of St Helena and became an experimental agriculturist. He was the second son of Robert Beatson, Esq., of Kilrie, Co. Fife. He obtained a cadetship in 1775 and was appointed to an ensigncy in the Madras Infantry on 21 Nov. 1776. He served as an engineer officer in the war with Hyder Ali, although he appears never to have belonged to the Engineers. As a lieutenant he served with the Guides in Lord Cornwallis's campaigns against Tippoo Sultan; and eight years after, as a field officer, was surveyor-general with the army under Lieutenant-General Harris which captured Seringapatam in 1799. He attained the rank of colonel in 1801. After he left India, Beatson served as governor of St Helena from 1808 to 1813. The population had been hit heavily by a measles epidemic just before his arrival and was in a wretched state. The acts of the home authorities in suppressing the arrack trade gave rise to much discontent, resulting in a mutiny in 1811, which Beatson put down with great vigour. After his return to England, he devoted much attention to experiments in agriculture at Knole Farm, Tunbridge Wells, and in Henley, Essex. He died in 1833. Main works: (1) 'An account of the Isle de France and Bourbon': BL, Add. MS 13868z; (2) *A view of the origin and conduct of the war against Tippoo Sultan*, London, 1800; (3) *Tracts relative to the Island of St. Helena*, London, 1816; (4) 'A new system of cultivation without lime or dung, or summer fallowing, as practised at Knole Farm, Sussex', and various other papers on agricultural improvement (*Dodswell's alphabetical lists of the Indian Army;* Vibart's *History of Madras sappers and miners*), all cited in *Dictionary of National Biography* entry for Alexander Beatson.

108 Beatson had culled this information from a letter written by Dr James Anderson, curator of the Madras botanical garden, to Colonel Kyd in Calcutta. No doubt Anderson knew of Kyd's technical interest in famine problems.

109 The global dynamics of the 1790–2 drought were due to an exceptionally strong El Niño off the coast of Peru: See William H. Quinn and Victor T. Neal, 'El Niño occurrences over the

part due to the critical importance of the St Helena garden in ensuring a smooth transfer of economically useful plants between company possessions and the botanical gardens of the West Indies. The serious drought problem was alluded to directly in a letter from the company directors to the St Helena government in March 1794. 'We are of the opinion', they stated,

> encouraging the growth of wood is of the utmost consequence to this island not only from the advantages to be derived from it as fuel but because it is well known that trees have an attractive power on the clouds especially when they pass over hills so high as those on your island and we are inclined to believe that the misfortunes this island has been subject to from drought might in some measure have been avoided had the growth of wood been properly attended to. We have been uniform in our directions for keeping Longwood securely fenced . . . should there be any parts of this enclosure that are not at present planted we direct that you immediately order the Governor to plant as many young trees there as possible.[110]

This was a definitive statement, and the first of its kind to be issued by the East India Company. Of course, it was highly derivative, and written in a language and form closely resembling earlier statements by Alexander Anderson and even the text of the King's Hill Forest Act. However, it may also have been influenced by company knowledge of events on Mauritius.

While still in Mysore, Alexander Beatson had been engaged by Arthur Wellesley in 1793 to carry out a survey of Mauritius with the long-term aim of annexing the island as a British naval base. The report of this survey, completed in 1794, was never actually published, even though a number of copies were produced in manuscript form.[111] The report was a thorough piece of work which was mainly concerned with the contemporary state of the island and the conditions of its harbours and defences. It also surveyed previous accounts by French writers of the agricultural history of the island and the history of its forest cover. Beatson had already published a book on the possibilities of agricultural improvement in Mysore and was familiar with much current English thinking on the subject. He showed a degree of interest in the agrarian activities of the French on Mauritius which Arthur Wellesley probably did not share. Not surprisingly, in the course of carrying out the literature survey for the report, Beatson began to appreciate the innovative character of the policies of Pierre Poivre for the island. These had, of course,

---

past four and a half centuries', *Journal of Geophysical Research*, 92 (1987), 14449–61. See further notes on this in Chapter 8.
110 *SHR*, Directors to Governor, 7 March 1794.
111 Beatson, 'An account of the Isle de France and Bourbon', BL, Add. MS 138682.

already exercised the interest and envy of Banks and many of his correspondents. For Beatson, however, Poivre's activities seem to have come as something quite new, and he dwelt at length on the success of Poivre and Céré in bringing nutmeg and other spice plants to Mauritius. He was impressed by Poivre's experimental approach to plant introductions and noted that 'M. Poivre had travelled all over Asia as naturalist and philosopher' and that he had distributed trial plants among the colonists so that they could experiment with their performance in different soils.[112] The 'Isle of France', Beatson declared in the preface to his report, 'must always be counted one of the most valuable possessions for any nation desirous of trading to Asia'.[113] The island, he thought, was 'strikingly picturesque . . . perpetual moisture hangs upon the summit of the mountains'.

So by early 1794 the East India Company had direct access to conservationist and desiccationist messages from two main locations: from St Vincent, via Banks and Dundas, and from Mauritius, via Beatson and through other sources (the secret report of 1761 had showed that the EIC was already well aware of French anxieties about deforestation at a time when a timber shortage was developing in the Calcutta environs). Both these accounts, we may note, originated with reports written by educated men from Eastern Scotland exposed to physiocratic influences. The desiccationist worries that were taken up by the EIC in 1794 certainly originated from insular conditions, and the Court borrowed directly from the language and terms used by Anderson and Edward Long, his mentor. In doing so they undoubtedly owed a more distant debt to Hales and Priestley. However, these were not the only sources of expertise on climatic matters to which the company might potentially have had access. There were, in fact, already company servants in India who had cultivated an interest in climatic variation and its causes. Chief among them was William Roxburgh, yet another physician from Eastern Scotland, who from 1778 to 1792 had been based at Samulcottah, the ancient location of a Mughal botanical garden, latterly a company garden for the Madras government. From the time of his arrival in India, Roxburgh kept systematic meteorological records, analyses of which he published in 1778 and 1790.[114] These records were communicated to the Royal Society by Sir John Pringle. As such,

---

112 Ibid., pp. 2–4. Beatson attempted to enumerate this and decided that '1400 nutmeg trees, 10,000 nutmegs growing or ready to grow, 70 clove trees and a chest of cloves' had been transported by Poivre from 'the least frequented parts of the Moluccas'.

113 Ibid., p. 383.

114 'A meteorological diary kept at Fort St George in the East Indies', *Philosophical Transactions of the Royal Society*, 68 (1778), 180–90, and 80 (1790). While assistant surgeon at Fort St George, Roxburgh took measurements three times a day, using a Ramsden barometer and Nairne thermometers.

they constitute part of the meteorological movement stimulated by Joseph Priestley's papers of 1772. In this sense Roxburgh can be grouped along with Edward Long, Alexander Anderson and General Melville as enthusiasts of climatic mensuration working all over the new colonial empire. Moreover, Roxburgh's Indian observations seem to have awoken an interest in Indian meteorology in Sir Joseph Banks himself, for we know that in 1788 Banks presented a seven-year diary of Bombay weather observations for publication in the Royal Society's *Transactions*.[115]

The formation of this grouping of climatic enthusiasts helps to explain Banks's ready reception of the dictums of Alexander Anderson on St Vincent and his support (and then the company's support) for tree preservation and tree-planting programmes on St Helena. It is difficult to be absolutely sure, however, whether there is a direct link between the new meteorological fervour and the contemporaneous and rapid development of tree-planting plans in Bengal under Kyd and then under Roxburgh. But it is highly likely. Certainly Roxburgh records (in 1812) that teak seedlings were brought from Rajahmundry Circar (in Southern India) to the new garden in Calcutta in 1787.[116]

In general the rationale given for the teak-planting programme which developed in Bengal, Bihar and Orissa under Roxburgh's supervision was presented as related merely to timber needs.[117] Nevertheless, we need to be aware that climatic convictions were almost certainly involved as well, particularly as Roxburgh was well acquainted with the Hippocratic corpus linking climate, topography and living conditions, a corpus that had become even more socially important and explicit in contemporary revolutionary France than it had been under Poivre and his fellow physiocrats.

But in order to discover a more rounded and comprehensive emergence of environmentalist notions at this period, it is necessary to look again at developments on St Helena, where the insular situation and the legacy of earlier land-management difficulties was leading, during the early years of the new century, to an increasing interest in policing and managing environmental processes. The deforestation and extinction concerns of earlier years grew in significance in government policy. But these elemental preoccupations were now joined by a far more learned and fashionable romanticisation of landscape and insular isolation, above all in the opinions and writings of William Burchell, the first company botanist on the island.

115 'Diary of the rain at Bombay from 1780 to 1787 and part of the year 1788', *Philosophical Transactions of the Royal Society*, 80, (1790), 590.
116 'Some account of the teak trees of the East Indies', *Journal of Natural Philosophy, Chemistry and the Arts*, 33 (1812), 348–54.
117 For further details of Roxburgh and the activities of the Bengal Government Plantation Committee under Roxburgh and Wallich, see Chapter 8.

The environmentalism of William Burchell and
Alexander Beatson

William John Burchell had been appointed schoolteacher and 'Acting Botanist' by the East India Company in 1805 at the instance of Governor Robert Patton. During his five years' tenure on St Helena, Burchell kept a detailed diary.[118] This diary is of considerable importance, as it allows one to document the emergence of a fully developed consciousness of the degree of endemism among the flora of St Helena, to evidence an awareness of the closeness to extinction of the rarer plants on the island and to appreciate a practical anxiety about the effects of deforestation on flooding and soil erosion.[119] Above all, the diary tells a story of the acute social and academic isolation of an imaginative and perceptive thinker and observer.

The idea of rarity, which is particularly prominent in Burchell's writings, was not an entirely new concept.[120] It was, for example, a major personal motive behind Kyd's enthusiastic promotion of the Calcutta Botanic Garden, to such an extent that Kyd felt the need to deny specifically that it was his real motive.[121] With a pronounced historical sense, Burchell soon became aware of the extent to which St Helena had deteriorated from its original pre-settlement condition. In many places 'not a blade of grass is here to be seen, but the few shrubs which you here and there in patches meet with, spring out of a parched soil of various colours'.[122] He noted on the same day that 'almost everyone can tell me, that they can remember the almost impassable groves of trees growing on those hills, which now offer to the eye nothing but a cindery barrenness'.[123] It is clear that by the time of Burchell's arrival many of the older plantations had become neglected, and there was little sign of the earlier attempts made at reafforestation by Governors Roberts, Byfield, Corneille, Brooke and Robson. Burchell remarked, for example, that

118 'St Helena journal', 1805–6: Hope Entomological Library, University Museum, South Parks Road, Oxford.

119 For further information on the taxonomic significance of Burchell's diary, see Q. C. B. Cronk, 'W. J. Burchell and the botany of St Helena', *Archives of Natural History*, 15 (1988), 45–60.

120 See Chapter 3.

121 Kyd had written, 'I take this opportunity of suggesting to the Board the propriety of establishing a Botanical garden not for the purpose of collecting rare plants (although they also have their use) as things of mere curiosity or furnishing articles for the gratification of luxury but for establishing a stock for the disseminating of such articles as may prove beneficial to the inhabitants': Kyd to Governor-General and Council, 6 June 1786, quoted in *A short account of Colonel Kydd*, p. 6.

122 'St Helena Journal', Dec. 1807: fasc. 9, beginning 8 Dec. 1807.

123 Ibid. Burchell may have exaggerated somewhat, since in 1805 Governor Brooke, in the course of writing his history of the island, recorded an inhabitant as stating that since the tree-planting activities of Governor Byfield in the 1740s the vegetation had somewhat recovered: Gosse, *St Helena*, p. 108.

all the way we have come is strewed with the decayed remains of trees
and shrubs which must formerly have nearly covered all these hills, and
is melancholy proof that the growth of the wood and verdure on St Helena is decreasing nor is this to be wondered at, when we hear that without
providing for posterity by young plantations, the soldiers and inhabitants
have been suffered barbarian-like, to cut down the trees with a wanton
waste only making use of the stems and thick branches, leaving the brush-
wood behind.[124]

In the same diary entry he commented on the harsh treatment meted out
to slaves, sympathising with their motives in attempting to escape. He goes
on to discuss the 'demolition of gum trees'. In Burchell's mind, as in that of
Poivre and Bernardin de Saint-Pierre, a close connection was made between
the degrading treatment of man and the treatment meted out to the helpless
vegetation by his fellow islanders. These anthropomorphic sentiments helped
to guide him to an interest in species extinctions. Such sentiments depended,
however, on an accurate botanical knowledge, able to contextualise the St
Helena environment in its global context. Thus, in recording one instance of
deforestation in these terms, Burchell wrote that he felt 'the demolition of one
of these ancient gum trees with a superstitious concern, and the feeling of a
fellow creature; for in all probability, unless St Helena should be deserted,
these trees would never again be suffered to attain so great an age, and (as
this tree is peculiar to the island) this was sacrilegiously destroying the largest
of the kind that would ever again be in the world'.[125] On another occasion
Burchell admired the 'singularity and beauty of the Dicksonias, which were
the most graceful ornaments of these scenes' (Journal, 1807, fasc. 9).

A quite unprecedented awareness of endemism is apparent here.[126] Burchell
was an accomplished artist and acute observer, often mentioning his drawing
and painting expeditions in his journals. He was also an effective writer whose
language and terminology were imbued with contemporary notions of the
'sublime' and the 'Romantic'. For Burchell, a consciously aesthetic approach
to landscape – indeed, a deliberate attempt to find the aesthetic and discover
scenes to excite the emotions – was assumed and was a consistent theme in
his remarks and writings, which are contemporary with those of Humboldt
on precisely the same theme.[127] In October 1807 he noted that 'the view from
the top of the woody precipice is very sublime, the luxuriance of the verdure

124 'St Helena Journal', Dec. 1807: fasc. 9 at 'I have'.
125 Ibid. (my italics).
126 Ibid., 13 Jan. 1808.
127 Alexander von Humboldt's Ansichten der Natur first appeared in Berlin in 1808. This was an
attempt, Humboldt explained in the introduction, to bring an artistic and literary treatment
to subjects of natural science.

Plate 20. William John Burchell, 1782–1864 (portrait dated 1854). (Reproduced by permission of Africana Museum, Johannesburg)

causes a delightful feeling strangely mixed with sensations of fear and wonder'.[128]

Burchell connected this somewhat overused language of sublimity with notions of the Scottish Romantic. 'You wind', he tells us, 'through one of the most romantic glens . . . in one of these woody glens I was struck with the beauty of a noble large Redwood, which rose exultingly above the thicket.' He added that he 'fancied this tree seemed proud of my admiration of its beauty and I lamented that its flowers should open and fade unadmired or that one should even droop without having been seen'.[129] In his own words, Burchell

128 'St Helena journal', 10 Oct. 1807.
129 Ibid.

experienced, as he frankly confessed, 'the most peculiar gratification' in the natural landscapes he found on St Helena.[130]

As an Englishman appointed by the EIC in response to the ministrations of Governor Patton, Burchell was exceptional among the ranks of the naturalists and physicians employed by the company between 1778 and 1857 in being English rather than Scottish, German or Danish. A man of sensitivity comparable with John Clare, and well versed in contemporary literature, Burchell brought with him an acculturated disposition to perceive the tropical landscape in terms of contemporary literary metaphor. This did not reduce the genuineness of his preoccupation with nature, for he was among the first in a long line of naturalists employed by the British in the tropics to value the non-artificial aspects of the landscapes they observed specifically in terms of their lack of artifice, or their 'wilderness' quality. At this period it is only in the writings of the French on Mauritius (Bernardin de Saint-Pierre in particular) that we find a comparably literary and learned appreciation of undisturbed nature and the attractions of isolation and the insular condition. In the case of Burchell this is conveyed in terms of the accepted contemporary images and metaphors of the sublime and the picturesque – that is, in highly developed and structured kinds of perception. The clearest indication of this acceptance of metaphor is to be found in an entry in Burchell's journal in January 1808 in which he described Mount Lot in the kinds of terms utilised by the Lake Poets in their eulogisation of Lake District and Alpine landscapes:

> Lot now appeared far over us and with its awful, stupendous, majestic size, affected me with feelings of wonder, comprised of fear and admiration . . . it cast its enormous shadow down the deep valley and against the mountains on its opposite side, I felt the truth of my expression, 'awful silent monarch of the Sandy Bay' in my address to Lot. It seems to overawe all the mountains round and defies the attacks of the weather and time.[131]

Mountains, weather and time, all introduced in this passage, were familiar elements in the pantheon of images that had been used by Rousseau, Wordsworth, Coleridge and Southey, among others, by the time Burchell came to attempt to convey his impressions of St Helena.[132] All three terms were firmly

---

130 Ibid.
131 Ibid., 12 Jan. 1808.
132 See Nicolson, *Mountain gloom and mountain glory*, and Stafford, *Voyage into substance*. For a detailed treatment of Wordsworth's contribution to English environmentalist sensitivities, see Jonathan Bate, *Romantic ecology; Wordsworth and the Romantic tradition*, London, 1991. It is unclear whether Burchell had read Wordsworth's *Prelude*. On the other hand, Wordsworth's vigorous denial of his having been influenced by the naturalism of Bernardin de Saint-Pierre does not seem at all credible.

connected with the steady, and even global, penetration of literary and artistic themes by the deepening preoccupations of geologists and other natural scientists with changing conceptions of the formation and age of the earth.[133]

These were concerns which brought in their train a new questioning of the place of man in a universe of rapidly changing conceptual dimensions and a corresponding instability to notions of man's place in the universe. Given these uncertainties and the reassessments of the significance of mortality and the timing of life and death which they were bound to stimulate, Burchell faithfully reflected wider social anxieties current among his intellectual peers. These seem to have found a convenient identification, or even transference, in an innovative sympathy with natural organisms that was evoked amidst an awesome landscape, symbolic of the awesome anxiety which new conceptions of time might evoke. Herein, perhaps, lay Burchell's fear that the beauty of the endemic redwoods of the islands might fade unseen.

Here also was a premonition of underlying feelings of powerlessness in the face of natural processes (as they were increasingly rationalised and understood) and a corresponding parallel empathy for nature confronted by the power of transforming man, an empathy which was to be far more frequently expressed after the publication of the *Origin of Species* in 1859. Burchell was able, unwittingly, to prefigure and represent the beginnings of such concerns, strengthened partly by the starkness of his own situation. Escaping a disastrous love affair, he had been able to seek distant refuge quite literally on a desert island, under the auspices of an East India Company committed to employing professional naturalists in its expanding domain. In this sense Burchell was indicative of a more general trend.

The professional men, generally well-educated intellectuals, whom the EIC employed in such professional positions were increasingly apt to seek individualistic answers to their personal predicaments in the context of tropical landscapes. Here they were unhindered by the social contexts from which they might have become partly alienated at home. The personal predilections of such men, often placed in positions of considerable influence in policy terms, were bound to affect the way in which they made decisions, especially where landscapes and exotic flora had acquired connotations that were other than merely utilitarian or scientific. In the particular case of Burchell on St Helena, there were no immediate consequences in terms of the way the landscape was

---

133 P. Bicknell and R. Woof, *The Lake District discovered, 1810–1850: The artists, the tourists and Wordsworth*, Grasmere, 1983, p. 16. Bicknell and Woof demonstrate here the very close intellectual relationship between Wordsworth and the geologist Adam Sedgwick. By 1840, Bicknell notes, it was clear that a new view of the history of the landscape of the Lake District was possible as a result of the pioneering work of Agassiz and Carpenter in Switzerland. It was Adam Sedgwick on his visit to Wordsworth of 1842 who first authoritatively applied their glacial theories to the English Lake District.

managed. Undoubtedly, however, his experience of land degradation on St Helena affected the prescriptions he later made for the similarly degrading Cape Colony landscape.[134]

In his close identification with the vulnerability of the trees of the island, Burchell was an early exemplar among naturalists whose preoccupation with rarity and the likelihood of the extinction of species increasingly involved them in the development of concern for one or a small group of related species. While the threat to these species might be real and demonstrable, the emphasis on particular kinds of plants or (more frequently after 1800) animals became increasingly anthropomorphic in character. The concept of rarity itself implied a threat to continued existence, even in the kind of use of 'rarity' made by Robert Kyd in Bengal in the 1780s. The threatened extinction of the observed organism mirrored the vulnerability of the European in an alien and possibly disease-ridden tropical environment. It mirrored also the increasingly earthly death of the human being, as some of the certainties of religious orthodoxy came to be questioned by natural science, especially those relating to the age of the earth and the longevity of creation. It would be wrong, nonetheless, to interpret the Romantic use of images of nature to carry metaphorical and philosophical loadings, as Burchell uses them, purely as an indigenous import from a native English cultural context transferred to the perceptions of the colonial naturalist. On the contrary, there is much evidence to suggest that the natural imagery used by a poet such as Coleridge, for example, was itself heavily derivative of the exploring, if not colonial, experience. Bernard Smith, for example, has argued that Coleridge's preoccupation with weather, clouds, the sea and sea travel owed much to his tutelage at Bluecoats School by William Wales, meteorologist on the *Resolution* and colleague of J. R. Forster.[135]

The preoccupation with 'grand' nature, with mountains, sky, thunder, the sea and deep valleys, reflected an interest in phenomena which possessed attributes threatened or lost in the minds of those concerned with them, something more than simply a renewed valuation of wild nature. The island itself was retained in the emerging naturalistic language of the early French and

---

134 W. J. Burchell, *Travels in the interior of Southern Africa*, vol. 1, London, 1822, p. 42. Burchell suggested that the eroding Cape Flats should be planted to shrubs, trees and grasses to prevent their further wearing away. He added that 'the scarcity of fire-wood in Cape Town has forced the poorer inhabitants to discover a timely resource in these underground stems and roots, which being in mere loose sand, are dug up with great ease. But, however convenient this source of fuel may be to individuals, the destroying of the bushes, root and branch, will at last become a greater inconvenience to the public, as the Isthmus will then be reduced to a sand-desert . . . trees would protect the soil from the action of strong winds.'

135 B. Smith, 'Coleridge's 'Ancient Mariner' and Cook's second voyage', *Journal of the Warburg and Courtauld Institute*, 19 (1956), 117–54.

British Romantics as an image which possessed, as we have seen, a long pedigree. Now, however, it was becoming a metaphor which was favoured in the works of Byron and Southey as much as the 'Oriental' images and symbols of India.[136] The dividing line between scientific and artistic tastes was a shadowy one, and the island, a metaphor which Burchell actualised in the location of his own career rather than by retaining it as an image of fantasy, grew more rather than less important in stimulating the minds of natural scientists. In the case of St Helena this was made more likely by the incidence of plant forms radically different from those found on the marine littoral of the adjoining continents or elsewhere.[137] Burchell was clearly conscious of the unusual character of the flora, although possibly not entirely precise about its endemic character, which would anyway have been accepted as impossible to establish at a time when large parts of sub-Saharan Africa remained unexplored. Indeed, it was only when Burchell carried out his formidable surveys of the South African flora in the years up to 1822 that this situation began to be remedied. He almost certainly passed on his anxieties about the survival of the island flora to Sir William Roxburgh in the course of the latter's visit during 1808 while on his return from the superintendency at Calcutta.[138] This in turn led to Roxburgh's publication of an annotated list of the St Helena flora in 1816, a list which Darwin was to rely upon almost exclusively in the course of his visit to the island during the *Beagle* voyage.[139] Thus the endemism of the St Helena flora was well established at such an early date that Darwin could state confidently in 1836 that the island possessed 'an entirely unique flora' without actually having carried out very much in the way of fieldwork on the island.[140] Indeed, 'unique' was a term that Darwin did not bestow on the flora of any other island. However, while Burchell's premonition of the endemism of the St Helena flora was to be influential in the formulation of Darwin's own theories during the late 1830s, his contemporary influence seems to have been confined to making Roxburgh more aware of the possibilities of endemism and the threat of species extinctions in a more global sense. This was an important development, and one which may have influenced him in his stewardship of the Calcutta Botanic Garden between 1792 and 1813. This was a period during which the role of that garden as a nursery

136 For the importance of India to Southey, see Javed Majeed, *Ungoverned imaginings: James Mill's 'The History of British India' and Orientalism*, Oxford, 1992, pp. 47–86.

137 See Q. C. B. Cronk, 'The historical and evolutionary development of the plant life of St Helena', Ph.D. diss., University of Cambridge, 1985.

138 G. King, 'A brief memoir of William Roxburgh, the author of the Flora Indica', *Annals of the Calcutta Botanic Garden*, 5 (1895), 1–3.

139 'A typological list of plants seen at St Helena in 1813–14', in Beatson, *Tracts*, pp. 295–326.

140 Letter, 18 July 1836, to Henslow 'on board Beagle bound for Ascension': Burckhardt and Smith, *Correspondence of Charles Darwin*, p. 501.

Plate 21. William Roxburgh, superintendent of the Calcutta Botanic Garden, 1793–
1813. (Reproduced from *A short account of Colonel Kydd* . . . Calcutta, 1897)

for plantation trees to replace those lost in deforestation was increasingly being
stressed. By the time Nathaniel Wallich, Roxburgh's eventual successor as
superintendent of the Calcutta Botanic Garden, made his first surveys of the
Burma forests after 1824, concern over the level of deforestation may well
have been connected with an interest in endemism first fostered on St Helena
in the context of the surveys conducted by Burchell and Roxburgh.

Nevertheless, it was in the field of active conservationist intervention that
the example of St Helena proved more directly influential in India and the
Cape Colony. Successive administrations on St Helena, as made clear above,
had pioneered attempts at countering deforestation and soil erosion by means
of tree and furze planting. However, these had lapsed by the time Burchell
arrived on the island in 1805. The arrival of Alexander Beatson as governor

in 1808 transformed the situation. During his tenure, until 1813, he put into effect a programme of 'improvement', which included irrigation, tree planting and forest protection. A comparison with Pierre Poivre is not an idle one, as Beatson was certainly impressed by the efforts the French had made to develop Mauritius. Moreover, Beatson's appointment as governor would certainly have been encouraged by the opinions he expressed in his report on the rival French colony. It was hoped, in essence, that he would carry out a similar task in rejuvenating St Helena.

Beatson set about discovering the land-use history of St Helena, just as he had done for Mauritius. The symbolic connotations of tropical-island environments so important in French and English Romantic literature and philosophy were not entirely lost on the new governor. Indeed, he noted that, partly because of the remoteness of St Helena, it was a 'proper subject for philosophical investigation'.[141] Otherwise his approach was strictly utilitarian; more specifically, his outlook on life was diametrically opposed to that of Burchell. Not surprisingly, the two men quarrelled violently and soon came to detest one another.[142]

Beatson was attracted by the example of Governor Roberts and certainly modelled his approach to the ecological management of the island on that of the Roberts period. His approach to improvement, however, was based more on his contacts with Arthur Young and through him with the kinds of innovation going on in England at the time.[143] This clearly suited the EIC, which had not remained immune to the debates about enclosure and crop improvement but had only flirted with these notions. Beatson was also widely read and was familiar with the works of the Forsters and the early writings of Alexander von Humboldt.[144] His approach in environmental matters reflected his political authoritarianism. However, his reading of Humboldt made him particularly open to notions of change in the environment over time, and he

141 Beatson, *Tracts*, p. iv.

142 These disagreements are documented in detail in Burchell's MS diary.

143 In a letter to Sir Charles Grevill (BL, Beatson Papers, 40.716, fol. 46) Beatson refers to 'Hoggeries according to Sir Arthur Young's plan'. He was also in touch with Sir John Sinclair, whom he consulted about his tree-planting plans, e.g. in a letter of 18 Sept. 1811 quoted in Beatson, *Tracts*, p. 47.

144 In *Tracts*, p. x, he notes, 'The stratum of shells and muds on the hills at Agrigentum, three miles from the harbour, and 1200 feet above the sea, the oyster shells found on the high mountains of Jamaica, the fossil bones of elephants found by Mr Humboldt in the Andes, 3240 yards above the level of the sea, and many other instances that might be adduced, serve only to furnish most incontestable proof that this globe has undergone many surprising changes since it was first created.' This new appreciation of the scale and timing of geomorphological change over time, gained from Humboldt, must have encouraged Beatson to observe contemporary processes of erosion and rainfall variation with a much keener eye than he might otherwise have done.

was quite convinced that deforestation had caused rainfall changes and consequently that a programme of tree planting would increase rainfall levels. He thus initiated a carefully planned plantation programme, adopting the idea of awarding prizes for planting trees, an idea he had adapted from the policy started by the Society of Arts in 1756. The EIC was also happy to back the idea of awarding prizes for tree planting on St Helena, a practice which continued until 1834, when the island reverted to direct Crown rule. Beatson computed the amount of rainfall that fell on the island and concluded that most of it was wasted and that ways of conserving and channelling water needed to be explored. His interest in accurately recording rainfall on the island was further encouraged by Sir Joseph Banks and contributed directly to regular collection of colonial rainfall records, partly on the lines begun by William Roxburgh at Madras (a precedent with which Beatson was familiar).[145] 'Philosophers of all ages', Beatson observed, 'have built upon a hope of being able to discover by repeated observations some rules concerning variations of seasons and changes of weather, convinced that such discoveries would be of the highest utility, especially in agriculture.'[146]

Beatson's nascent awareness of the dynamics of climatic change were reinforced by his consultations with such experts as surgeon John Berry, superintendent of the EIC botanical garden in Madras. This professional contact paralleled his reliance on Young and Sinclair for advice and information on the latest improvement and planting techniques.[147] Indeed, Beatson's official reliance on expert technical information is reminiscent of Poivre. Moreover, he drew readily on expertise from Mauritius as well as from Britain and India.[148] By his adoption of an improvement philosophy based heavily on the

---

145 Prior to this, regular monitoring of rainfall at the state level had taken place only in China, where it had been normal since the sixteenth century.

146 *Tracts*, p. 40.

147 Letter from Dr Berry, Madras, to Beatson, quoted in ibid., p. 168.

148 Beatson's response to Berry's report and letter (ibid., p. 188) was: 'Your observations on the attraction of moisture and rain appear to be judicious. Trees have usually been recommended for that purpose. I am of the opinion, however, that cultivation has also a tendency to produce the same effect and in proportion to the extension of arable fields so will be the increase in moisture.' This letter preceded a communication from Governor Farquhar of Mauritius, who seems to have reminded Beatson of the thinking of the French desiccationists and of the nature of conservation legislation on Mauritius. Moreover, he sent Beatson seeds of the bois noir tree to facilitate the plantation programme on St Helena. This was an important contact which led Beatson to comment: 'How much then have the present generation cause to lament the negligence and inattention of their fathers? If these plantations had been established fuel would have been during the last 20 years in abundance and there would have been enough to supply the numerous ships that annually touch here, whilst the aspect of the island would have been more beautiful, and in all probability an improvement in the climate effected, by the attraction of a greater degree of moisture from such extensive plantations' (ibid., p. 194).

work of the physiocrats, Beatson had managed to endorse a heavily interventionist philosophy, just as the EIC already had to a lesser extent in Bengal.

Reinforced by expert opinions and possessed of a vigorous and efficient turn of mind, Beatson was able to carry through reafforestation and irrigation policies on St Helena far more efficiently than those governors who had had no external support. He was also equipped with a knowledge of Indian semi-arid agricultural methods and was quick to see, as Poivre had, the possibilities of using the kinds of irrigation tanks which he had seen in use in Southern India.[149] Beatson viewed his contribution as one that would be important to posterity and would 'prove highly beneficial to present as well as future generations', and he drew the attention of the EIC Directors to his policy in his *Tracts* when they were published in 1816. The object of the plantations, he said,

> is indeed so important in every point of view, the certainty of success in this island so clearly established on the basis of facts and the advantageous consequences that would be felt by the Lords Proprietors, as well as individuals; so great that it deserves the most serious attention and in my opinion, ought to call forth every possible exertion both public and private (for some years to come) in order to restore wood to this long neglected and denuded spot.[150]

Beatson's *Tracts* soon became widely read in company circles and elsewhere. Furthermore, the book was published at a time when the EIC itself was becoming more open to notions of 'improvement', and it played a part in stimulating the formation of the Plantation Committee during the tenure of Nathaniel Wallich as superintendent of the Calcutta Botanic Garden. The wider potential of Beatson's work was, of course, still confined by a lack of theoretical universality in its scientific approach. Perceptions of the dynamics and extent of environmental change until the 1820s were still very limited conceptually. Thus even when Wallich, in work for the Plantation Committee after 1823, expressed anxiety about the extent of timber depredations, he failed to call in aid any really credible scientific critique to justify his anxieties, even though he could have utilised some current climatic thinking. Instead he generally chose to rely on older and purely economic arguments about timber depletion.[151] The opinions of the desiccationists, which the EIC and its governors were disposed to listen to and act upon on St Helena until 1834, seem to have been largely ignored during this period in India. Furthermore, the anxieties of a Burchell on St Helena or a Heber in India, both springing from

149 Ibid., p. 198, sect. xxix: 'In the year 1809 I made an attempt to introduce the Indian mode of forming tanks or reservoirs . . . this had long been a desiderata on St Helena.'
150 Ibid., pp. 201–3.
151 See Chapter 8.

a deep attachment to a naturalistic philosophy associated with the Romantic movement, were as insufficient in eliciting government intervention in India itself as were, at first, the improvement enthusiasms of Beatson.[152] It was this situation which the writings of Alexander von Humboldt would radically alter once they became widely known in India.

However, despite the lack of any immediate adoption of Beatson's desiccationism by the company, St Helena actually continued to play an increasingly decisive role in arguments about the mutability and formation of species and in discussions about the impact of deforestation on rainfall. Both these debates were strongly connected with the evidence of extinctions and endemism that was emerging on St Helena. Burchell and Beatson accurately personified and articulated two of the different streams of philosophical and scientific debate which St Helena so directly evoked. Burchell's thinking had been closely associated with extinctions and a romantically articulated 'ruination of Paradise', in a fitting finale to the much older associations between St Helena and Paradise. But Burchell's findings were far from romantic; they gave concrete evidence of endemism and contemporary plant distributions. Beatson, for his part, as a confident and assertive 'improver' (possibly too secure to be over-worried about his extinction or that of others), focussed more on the effects of deforestation during the colonial occupation and on a related consideration of geological and climatic changes over a much longer period, when he worried about time, chronology and a change in sea level. In these concerns Beatson, by his own admission, was deeply influenced by Humboldt and inspired by the observation of processes taking place in the isolation of St Helena.

Twenty years later Charles Darwin, who carried the *Tracts* around the world with him on the *Beagle*, appears to have taken Beatson's interests very seriously to heart, not least when on St Helena. However, Darwin was not the first learned observer of the island to systematically link the two issues of (1) endemism and extinction and (2) speed of environmental and geological change and thereby ensure that St Helena remained central to both concerns and eventually to theories of natural selection and evolution. That critical linkage was made by W. H. B. Webster, who visited the island in 1828 on an Admiralty expedition.[153]

Webster had apparently read more widely on St Helena than had Darwin a few years later, starting with the papers of Edmund Halley. 'It was this place', Webster wrote, 'that furnished Dr Halley, in 1676, with the theory of

---

152 Beatson's *Tracts* was later an important influence on G. P. Marsh; see Chapter 5.
153 W. H. B. Webster, *Narrative of the voyage to the Southern Atlantic Ocean in the years 1828, '29, '30, performed in H.M. sloop Chanticleer under the command of the late Captain Henry Foster by order of the Lords Commissioners of the Admiralty*, London, 1834.

springs and rivers.'[154] The circumstances were 'so forcibly pressed on his mind by the phenomena he witnessed here that he could not have failed to discern the cause, which he found had the same effect in other countries'. Webster went on to record that 'there have been seasons when this island has suffered most severely from drought, which has killed the cattle and withered the crops'. In fact, he said, 'so solicitous are they at St Helena for the preservation of water that all persons are interdicted from cutting trees down by a very severe penalty. Much more rain', he continued, 'as is the case everywhere, falls on the high lands than on the lower; and it is thought that the trees on the hills have considerable influence in attracting moisture.'[155]

As an eager student of Charles Lyell (who published his first major work while Webster was writing about St Helena), Webster wrote that 'theories are . . . flowers in the garden of nature . . . St Helena may be studied geologically to great advantage, the whole island is a singular phenomenon on the face of nature.'[156] Following up this comment as well as Lyell's remarks on the possibility of the mutability of species (although he was somewhat hostile to the new 'deep' geological time set out by Lyell), Webster embarked on a startling series of remarks about species which he was, nonetheless, constitutionally unable to follow to a conclusion. These related to the colonisation of the island by species from outside and the nature and meaning of endemism. Like Darwin later on, he was especially concerned with the comparative distribution and success of species that were colonising neighbouring islands. On Ascension Island, for example, he saw that 'the number of ferns which prevail upon the highlands of the small island, suggests the inquiry as from whence they came' and asked the question 'Were the minute seeds carried by the winds from Africa, or were they brought by birds?' If so, he asked, 'Why does not Ascension possess them all?' 'It has always struck me', he asserted,

> that naturalists have been somewhat at variance with geologists. They have found on or given peculiar species of plants etc. to remote islands, when these islands have been thought to be of a later origin than the continents themselves; where species have been limited to the first periods of creation. For example; if St Helena is of subsequent formation to the great continents, *then its possessing of a distinct and new species of plant or animated being whatsoever, must either be a conclusive proof that a successive creation of species goes forward,* or that the naturalists are wrong in their definition of discrimination of species; most probably the latter.[157]

154 Ibid., p. 368.
155 Ibid. Webster quoted as his authority Ray, who, he said, 'observed during a mist that the naked branches and boughs of certain trees condensed the moisture so fast that in 24 hours a hogshead of water might have been collected from its drippings'.
156 Ibid., p. 312.
157 Ibid.; my italics.

Webster somewhat discounted the effect of this very important, carefully reasoned and prophetic finding by refusing to trust his own logic and throwing
cold water on his own Lyellian assumptions, stating that he had no confidence
in 'the vagueness and blindness of geological speculation' but would rather
abide by the 'wisdom of the Apostle, who says "through faith we understand
that the worlds were formed by the word of God, and the things which were
made were not made of things which appear" '. The fact is, however, that in
his *Narrative* Webster constantly returned to this theme, focussing on the
question of long-term climate fluctations and on the 'permanence and variability of the solar influence at different epochs'.[158] The reputation of England,
he thought, would 'be advanced by such enquiries'.

When Charles Darwin arrived at St Helena in July 1836, he duly fulfilled
Webster's hopes, partly by paying great attention to the geology and climatic
history of the island and by studiously following up many of the ideas put
forward by Beatson in his writing, with which Darwin must by now have been
very familiar.

The island, as Beatson had observed in 1816, was 'a proper subject for
philosophical investigation'.[159] Consequently, one of Darwin's first acts on the
island was to reinvestigate the fossil-shell layers which Beatson, in emulating
Humboldt's investigation of the fossil layers at Agrigentum, had thought so
significant in establishing the age, climatic history and early environmental
history of the island. Beatson had thought that the snails he found were of a
marine variety. But Darwin discovered them to be land snails, 'but of a species
no longer living', as he wrote to his sister Caroline in recalling the highlights
of his St Helena visit.[160] Reinforced by his knowledge of Burchell's and Roxburgh's work on the occurrence of the island's endemic species two decades
before, Darwin was able (like Burchell) to associate the rapid speed of environmental change on the island, in both historical and geological time scales,
with the changes wrought on the endemic flora by deforestation and by the
invasion of alien species, 'which can hardly have failed to destroy some of the
native kinds'.[161] In this way St Helena provided Darwin with some of his best
data on the dynamics of island populations, endemism and extinctions. Thus
in the *Origin of Species* St Helena occupies a prominent place in the section
on the inhabitants of oceanic islands, actually being mentioned, in comparison

---

158 Ibid., p. 379.
159 *Tracts*, p. iv.
160 Written en route to Ascension, 18 July 1836: Burckhardt and Smith, *Correspondence of Charles
     Darwin*, p. 501.
161 Diary, entry for 9 July 1836, in P. H. Barrett and R. B. Freeman, eds., *The works of Charles
     Darwin*, vol. 1, London, 1986, p. 410.

with Ascension Island, much earlier in the text than the Galapagos Islands.[162]
There is no doubting the pivotal role played by St Helena in the construction
of Darwin's theories. However, St Helena appears to have acquired a rather
deeper personal significance for him. 'St Helena', he wrote, 'situated so remote
from any continent, in the midst of a great ocean, and possessing an unique
flora', was a 'little world, within itself, which excites our curiosity'.[163] The
island, he felt, now had a 'sterile condition and limited flora', compared with
which a 'glowing tropical style of landscape would have afforded a finer contrast' to the 'wild, arid rocks' of the coast.[164] It seems likely that the deleterious
impact of human occupation on the island alerted Darwin to the limitations
imposed by an island on a colonising species and the struggle for existence
that might ensue. 'I believe', he wrote, 'that there is not any account extant
of the vegetation when the island was covered with trees . . . it is not improb-
able that even at the present day similar changes may be in progress.' Since
the emancipation of the slaves, the human population was growing rapidly.
'Now that the people are blessed with freedom,' he warned, 'it seems probable
that their numbers will quickly increase: if so, what is to become of the little
state of St Helena?'[165] Here, then, was a Malthusian premonition of the eventual human impact on the island, coupled with observations of the effects of
the demands of one species on the survival of species in the endemic vegetable
kingdom. It has to be said, nevertheless, that Darwin's premonitions of ecological crisis went little further than this. Indeed, his comments on the conservation laws of the colony were confined to observing that the 'island is far
too English not to be subject to strict game laws'.[166]

If Beatson can be held responsible for many of the trains of thought which
Darwin developed on St Helena, Darwin was in turn certainly largely responsible for the deep interest taken in the island by his close colleague and
collaborator Joseph Hooker in the two visits which the latter made to the
island in 1839 and 1843 while on the Antarctic expedition of Sir James Clark
Ross.[167]

Hooker had been briefed by Darwin as to what he might expect to see. The
botany of the island, he observed, 'resembles none other in the peculiarity of

---

162 *On the origin of species by means of natural selection; or, The preservation of favoured races in
the struggle for life*, London, 1859, pp. 388–90.
163 *Diary*, p. 411.
164 Ibid., p. 410.
165 Ibid., p. 411.
166 Ibid.
167 For details of these visits, see E. Duffey, 'The terrestrial ecology of Ascension Island', *Journal
of Applied Ecology*, 1 (1967), 219–51; and J. D. Hooker, 'On insular floras', *Gardener's Chronicle*, 5 Jan. 1867.

its indigenous vegetation, in the great variety of the plants of other countries or in the number of species that have actually disappeared within the memory of living man'.[168] During his visits Hooker 'searched in vain for forest trees and shrubs that flourished in tens of thousands not a century before my visit, and still existed as individuals twenty years before that date'. A great part of his regret at these extinctions, it soon transpired, related to the part that these plants might have played as evidence for the mechanisms of evolution. Much influenced by Darwin, he wrote that every one of them was 'a link in the chain of created beings, which contained within itself evidence of the affinities of other species, both living and extinct, but which evidence is now irrecoverably lost'.[169] To Hooker, then, it became a matter of enormous and urgent importance to try to prevent the clearing and extinction from St Helena and Ascension of further endemic trees and plants and of trees that ensured a climate for the survival of the endemics. It is therefore not surprising that we find Hooker, on his 1843 visit to the two islands, recommending to the Admiralty in an official report that rainfall should be maintained on Ascension by conserving or planting trees. Beatson's plantations on St Helena, he told the Admiralty, had 'had the effect of doubling the fall of rain in St Helena within fifteen years'.[170]

By 1843 St Helena had, then, emerged as a great catalyst for evolutionists and conservationists. Joseph Hooker can, of course, be seen in both these roles. In spite of this, the immediate influence of St Helena on the development of state environmentalism further afield had to await the arrival of Hooker in India in 1847 in the company of Lord Dalhousie. In the interim (between the publication of Beatson's influential *Tracts* in 1816 and 1847) the development of a global environmental consciousness had become significantly dominated by the disciples of *Naturphilosophie* as well as by Alexander von Humboldt.

The diffusion of Humboldtian environmental ideas, 1800–37

The theoretical and practical responses of William Burchell and Alexander Beatson to the environmental degradation of St Helena serve to illustrate the

168 Hooker, 'On insular floras', p. 27.
169 Ibid.
170 Report to the Admiralty, quoted in Duffey, 'Terrestrial ecology of Ascension Island', p. 227. Hooker made four proposals: (1) plant the higher levels with trees of large growth; 'this is of first importance as thereby the fall of rain will be directly increased'; (2) clothe the steep sides of the valleys to help soil formation by accumulation of vegetable matter, reduce evaporation and conserve moisture condensed on the mountain; (3) plant the most promising spots of the lower dry valleys with trees and shrubs adapted to dry soil conditions; (4) introduce tropical and European plants to mountain gardens.

extent to which the example of the French on Mauritius and the writings of Forster had become incorporated into the physiocratic ideology of the British 'improvers'. Much of the efficacy of the response of the St Helena officials, in terms of a critique of artificially induced environmental processes, derived purely from empirical observations sharpened and circumscribed by the physical limitations and scale of that oceanic island. While the connections between deforestation and desiccation on St Helena had been accepted by the EIC, and by Burchell and Beatson in particular, they seemed relevant only where extensive deforestation with observable consequences had already taken place. This was less the case on Mauritius with the French, whose conceptual grasp of the overall implications of deforestation seems to have been stronger. Thus until after the 1820s and despite the diffusion of information between the island botanical gardens (involving also Roxburgh and his immediate successors at Calcutta), desiccationist theories continued to lack an effectively global dimension and also lacked rigour and scientific principle. Thus, despite the publication of Beatson's *Tracts,* there are very few indications that contemporary observers believed that the kinds of environmental changes observed on oceanic islands could also happen on a continental scale.

By about 1816, however, approaches towards more universalist conceptions of the impact of man on the tropical environment were developing, although not in the British context. Pre-eminent among the originators of more integrative approaches to the study of such processes was Alexander von Humboldt. Although Humboldt's environmental philosophy, insofar as its full implications were concerned, was a long time in gestation and similarly slow to make an impact, the eventual influence of his ideas was so far-reaching in the Franco-British colonial setting that a careful assessment of his intellectual antecedents and the ways in which his ideas were diffused is essential to an understanding of environmental policies and attitudes as they developed after about 1840.

On the face of it, British natural history did not constitute a fertile ground for the cultivation of Humboldtian ideas. Instead, in Britain and France, where the full impact of Kantian ideas was delayed for many years, the positivist empiricism of Hume and Lavoisier found wide acceptance and acquired considerable institutional inertia.[171] In Germany, on the other hand, a very strong opposition to positivism developed from the late eighteenth century onwards, not least in the emergence of *Naturphilosophie.*[172] The two figures most responsible for the strength of anti-positivist ideas were undoubtedly Georg Forster and Goethe, and it is no coincidence that these two men, together

171 M. Bowen, *Empiricism and geographical thought: From Francis Bacon to Alexander von Humboldt,* Cambridge, 1981, pp. 210–11.
172 Ibid., pp. 216–17.

with Johann Gottfried von Herder exercised the most formative and direct influence on Humboldt's career.[173] Georg Forster, like his father, Johann Reinhold, was precocious in his ambition to seek global explanations and comparisons in the study of natural sciences, particularly in establishing the relations among climate, peoples and organisms. Goethe, for his part, sought consistently in his writings to advocate the critical nature of the relationship between man and nature.[174] Moreover, Goethe was himself much influenced by French physiocratic writings based, as we have seen, on the 'Laws of nature'.[175] But another and quite different kind of thinking affected Goethe's environmental views, deriving from his 'Orientalist' contacts. Indeed, an 'Orientalist' preoccupation with Indic conceptions of the relationship between man and nature was an essential component of the thinking of both Georg Forster and Goethe, as well as that of Herder, all of which was to affect the philosophy of their disciple Humboldt.[176]

Humboldt's first major contribution to the disparate, but slowly growing, corpus of knowledge about the impact of forest destruction in the tropics did not, however, appear until 1819, in the course of the publication of the 'personal narrative' of his journeys in South America in 1798–1804. The fourth volume, published in French and almost immediately translated into English, dealt with the consequences of large-scale deforestation in a distinctly non-insular setting, the tropical forest of Venezuela. His comments in this volume did not at this stage attract attention in the English-speaking world, partly because they were embedded in a long discussion about the more recent ge-

173 Goethe's emotional commitment to the natural world influenced and was comparable to Humboldt's. As T. J. Reed has commented, 'Natural science elaborated his poet's intuition of the coherence and value of earthly things. He was more concerned with finding meaningful unities than finding classificatory divisions; and he was deeply hostile, as was Humboldt, to such Baconian and Linnaean preoccupations.' On 9 Sept. 1780 Goethe wrote to Charlotte von Stein imploring her to become 'a friend of the earth' (quoted in T. J. Reed, *Goethe*, Oxford, 1984, p. 44). This was a relatively novel approach to nature and helps to explain the formation of Humboldt's attitude.

174 Writing from Jena in March 1797, Goethe praised the young Humboldt as 'a positive cornucopia of the natural sciences' (quoted in Bowen, *Empiricism*, p. 216). In *Cosmos* Humboldt recalled that Goethe stimulated his contemporaries to 'solve the profound mystery of the universe' and renew the bond which in the primitive age of mankind united philosophy, physics and poetry': *Cosmos*, trans. Edward Sabine, 2 vols., London, 1848, II, p. 75. Humboldt never lost sight of the possibility of such a synthesis.

175 See Myles Jackson, chapter entitled 'Goethe's economy of nature and the nature of his economy', from Ph.D. diss., University of Cambridge, 1991.

176 Herder was undoubtedly the single most influential incorporator of Indic modes of thought in Germany, and Humboldt was much affected by him. Herder drew an idealised, paradisal, picture of India in his writings and regarded the Orient as 'the cradle of the human race': Sedlar, *India in the mind of Germany*, p. 13. I am grateful to Nigel Rubbra for pointing me to this source.

ological and hydrological history of South America. However, Humboldt's remarks on the effects of deforestation need to be considered in full, as they were often referred to, although often very inaccurately, in discussions about deforestation during the first half of the nineteenth century, particularly in discussions about India. They were first made in the course of an account of the fluctuations of the level of the lake of Valencia. The critical passage reads as follows:

> The changes which the destruction of forests, the clearing of plants and the cultivation of indigo have produced within half a century in the quantity of water flowing in on the one hand; and on the other the evaporation of the soil and the dryness of the atmosphere, present causes sufficiently powerful to explain the successive diminution of the lake of Valencia. I am not of the opinion of a traveller who has visited these countries since me, that 'to set the mind at rest, and for the honour of science', a subterranean issue must be admitted. By felling the trees that cover the tops and the sides of mountains, men in every climate prepare at once two calamities for future generations; the want of fuel and a scarcity of water. Trees, by the nature of their perspiration and the radiation from their leaves in a sky without clouds, surround themselves in an atmosphere constantly cool and misty. They affect the copiousness of springs not, as was long believed, by a peculiar attraction for the vapours diffused through the air but because, by sheltering the soil from the direct action of the sun they diminish the evaporation of the water produced by rain. When forests are destroyed, as they are everywhere in America by the European planters, with an improvident precipitation, the springs are entirely dried up, or become less abundant. The beds of rivers, remaining dry during a part of the year, are converted into torrents, whenever great rains fall on the heights. The sward and the moss disappearing with the brushwood from the sides of the mountains, the waters falling in rain are no longer impeded in their course; and instead of slowly augmenting the level of the rivers by progressive filtrations, they furrow during heavy showers the sides of the hills, beat down the loosened soil and form these sudden inundations that devastate the country. Hence it results that the destruction of forests, the want of permanent springs and the existence of torrents are three phenomena closely connected together. Countries that are situated in opposite hemispheres, Lombardy bordered by the chain of the Alps and Lower Peru inclosed between the Pacific Ocean and the Cordillera of the Andes, exhibit striking proofs of the justness of this assertion.[177]

The essential points of the analysis contained in this statement have not been superseded by more recent findings.[178] While reinforced by references to

---

177 *Personal narrative of travels to the equinoctial regions of the New Continent, 1797–1804*, trans. H. M. Williams, 6 vols., London, 1819, IV, pp. 134–5.
178 See Chapter 8 for relevant authorities on this point.

the Alps and the Andes, the analysis was in fact based on Humboldt's much more limited observations on the reasons for the fluctuations in level of the lake of Valencia in Aragua, Venezuela. Unlike other naturalists, who had assigned these fluctuations to geological causes, Humboldt was able to show by reference to earlier Spanish historical documentation of the region that human population shifts and ensuing deforestation had been directly responsible for the changes in lake level. In this sense Humboldt was able to use the system of lake, watershed and forest as a geomorphological model, much as the French and British naturalists had effectively used the oceanic island as a model for understanding physiographic processes. By virtue of his extensive travels, Humboldt was thus able to arrive at more generally, and intentionally, applicable conclusions.

The tone of these observations, characterised, for example, by his assertion that 'forests are destroyed . . . everywhere in America by the European planters', gives a clue to the reasons why Humboldt espoused an interest in deforestation. It was a process which he associated closely with the wider impact of Europeans on the tropical environment and on indigenous societies, an impact which Humboldt tended, by and large, to denigrate. While the roots of this attitude were multifarious, they had one identifiable antecedent in the philosophy of Johann Gottfried von Herder (1744–1803), a former student of Kant's and for some time an influential mentor in Goethe's circle. Humboldt drew extensively in his own writings from Herder's masterpiece entitled *Outlines of a Philosophy of the History of Man*. Herder was an arch-empiricist who argued that 'mere metaphysical speculations . . . unconnected with experience and the analogy of nature, appear to me aerial flights that seldom lead to any end'.[179] He argued for 'a geographical aetiology . . . a comprehensive view of the geography and the history of man, in order to complete for all of nature, including man, the picture of which we have but a few, though clear, outlines'.[180] Here, then, was part of the basis of the universalist approach which Humboldt was to adopt consistently, but particularly in his ambitious *Cosmos*, the first part of which was published in 1845.

In imbibing Herder's philosophy, Humboldt also took on Herder's liberalism and concern for moral progress. In particular, Herder's respect for other cultures led him to express sympathy for such indigenous groups as the North American Indians, who, he felt, had suffered particular degradation as a result of the destruction by Europeans of their traditional way of life.[181] He was critical, too, of the violent disruptions implied by the clearing of forests for

179 Herder, quoted in Bowen, *Empiricism*, p. 217.
180 Ibid.
181 In this respect Herder bears comparison with Poivre and Bernardin de Saint-Pierre. His writings were another humanistic offshoot of the archaic interest in the noble savage.

timber and cultivation. Nature, he believed, 'is everywhere a living whole and will be gently followed and improved, not mastered by force'. Drawing these social and ecological themes together, Herder spoke out vigorously against European dominance and the brutalising effects of great wealth:

> What are the objects of our living? For what does it disturb the whole world, and plunder every quarter of the globe? . . . why do the poor suffer hunger and with benumbed senses drag on a wretched life of toil and labour? That the rich and great may deaden their senses in a more delicate manner, without taste, and probably to the eternal nourishment of their brutality.[182]

These were radical sentiments and are of considerable assistance in explaining Humboldt's political stance. They were at least partly rooted in the fierce debates which had raged in the mid eighteenth century about the treatment of the American Indians by Europeans and about the extent to which the reality of European harshness contrasted with the idealistic image accorded the noble savage of the Americas by some French and German philosophers. To this extent Herder's uncompromising stance resembled that adopted by Pierre Poivre. In other words, the humanitarian sympathies expressed by Herder and subsequently by Humboldt, as well as their critiques of the European environmental impact, originated in the same cultural debates that had dictated the attitude of the French on Mauritius.

By the mid eighteenth century a conscious and deliberate naturalism was reaching its apogee in the articulations of Rousseau and Goethe, in very close proximity and relation to vehement styles of social reaction or activism. These were most pronounced in the case of Rousseau. Thus naturalism emerged not only as a strong artistic and philosophical phenomenon but also as a taste of an often deliberately moral kind. On Mauritius, for example, this had become integrated in the emergence of the natural environment as a medium on to which notions of moral economy or individual morality might be grafted. In this need for transference a very strong connection had been built up between the kinds of social reformism which inspired early critiques of slavery (and the social critiques associated with the French Revolution) and the kind of view which found expression in its criticism of the potential of man to destroy a more highly valued environment.

There is a further vital connection between the embryonic emergence of environmentalism on Mauritius and that which developed in other colonies through the writings of Humboldt and his mentor Herder. Both Bernardin de Saint-Pierre and Pierre Poivre were strongly attracted in a literary and practical sense to Orientalist learning, and this tradition had been carried on

---

182 *Outlines of a philosophy of the history of man*, trans. T. Churchill, London, 1800, pp. vi–ix.

by Pierre Sonnerat, Poivre's nephew. This learning had, of course, contributed
to the new Indian Ocean naturalism and to the emergence of an environmental
sensibility on Mauritius.

Similarly, the role played by Herder in the development of nineteenth-
century Humboldtian environmentalism seems to have been closely related to
the transmission of Hindu notions of man–nature concepts by German and
French Orientalists. The significance of this link cannot be underestimated;
Herder was the key figure in determining the relationship of the Romantic
movement to India. In this respect he is, in the Humboldtian outlook, very
much the equivalent of Rousseau in his influence on physiocratic environmentalism. Thus an integral part of Herder's conceptualisation of India involved his notion of history as the 'natural history' of 'living human force'.
For example, the development of mankind 'from the Orient to Rome' he
likened to the trunk of a tree out of which branches and shoots grow. The
'one old, simple trunk of humanity' shot up into 'boughs and twigs'. Herder's
knowledge of India was culled from a variety of sources but principally from
the writings of travellers such as Pierre Sonnerat, who was himself already
steeped in the Utopian preoccupations of Saint-Pierre, Commerson and Pierre
Poivre. Herder's overidealised and yet naturalistic view of Indian culture cannot obscure the fact that he possessed a genuine conviction that, in terms of
'harmony' between people and nature, Hindu society could not be bettered.
The Hindus, he wrote,

> are the gentlest branch of humanity. They do not with pleasure offend
> anything that lives. They honour that which gives life and nourish them-
> selves with the most innocent of foods, milk, rice, the fruit of trees, the
> healthy herbs which their motherland dispenses . . . moderation and calm,
> a soft feeling and a silent depth of the soul characterise their work and
> their pleasure, their morals and mythology, their arts and even their en-
> durance under the most extreme yoke of humanity.[183]

There are clear parallels here between Humboldt's conception of an ecological and geographical holism and Herder's conception of Hindu cosmology.
Thus Herder described the philosophy which he considered to lie at the core
of that cosmology as being the 'idea of *one* being in and behind all that there
is', highlighting the idea of 'the unity of all things in the Absolute, in God'.
'Vishnu', he quoted,

> is in you, in all things. . .
>
> It is foolish ever to feel offence.

183 Quoted in Halbfass, *India and Europe*, p. 70.

See all souls in your own,
And banish the delusion of being different.[184]

Clearly, in this vision of interdependency, the ability to equate the divine with
'all beings' marked a very significant departure from western or biblical notions of order and the primacy of man in creation. Similarly, the 'banishing'
of difference conveyed a notion of reciprocity and balance that finds direct
and powerful echoes in the thinking of Humboldt. This is partly because
Humboldt was largely dependent on Herder but is also due to the influence
of his own brother Wilhelm (who was an enthusiast for Jainism) and his
insights into Indian philosophy. Humboldt was himself able to perceive the
significance of the fanatical growth in the German Romantic interest in India
and expressed it as being an extension of an Edenic search, a quest for the
depths of being, for the original infant stage of the human race and for the
lost paradise of all religions and philosophies. 'Beyond the Homeric ocean',
Humboldt wrote, perceptively combining classical and Indological allusions,
might lie the *Loka loka* of Indian philosophy. This recurrent interest in the
dramatic transition from the Edenic to the Oriental led not just to an identification of the differences between the two notions but to a realisation that
the Oriental was in fact no more than a refined extension of the much older
and geographically more global search for the naturalistic and for the other.
Humboldt was not, among his contemporaries, entirely alone in expressing
this insight. Johann Görres, for example, believed in an essential unity of both
Utopian myth and a theory of origins in which there was 'one myth in primaeval times . . . one state and one language'. Of all documents of mankind,
he thought, none could compare 'as regards antiquity and faithful sense of
nature' to the Indian Vedas. Unsurprisingly, Görres celebrates A. H. Anque-
til-Duperron as the one to whom we 'owe the enjoyment of this milk of ancient
Oriental wisdom'.[185]

The credit, however, for translating these often highly distorted readings
of Hindu texts into a new environmental ethos should still probably be given
primarily to Herder and only secondarily to Humboldt. A resulting commitment to holism showed itself not just in a directly environmental sense but
in an entire moral philosophy and global knowledge of nature. Thus Humboldt felt compelled to combine his search for general scientific laws governing
the physical environment with adherence to the concepts of a natural moral
economy. In 1794 he referred in correspondence to his plans for a work to be

---

184 Ibid. Herder used Sir William Jones's English version of the *Mohamudgara* as his source.
185 J. Görres, *Gesammelte Schriften*, vol. 3, repr. Cologne, 1936, pp. 8–10, quoted in Halbfass,
    India and Europe, p. 477.

completed 'in twenty years' under the title 'Ideas on a future history and geography of plants or historical account of the gradual extension of vegetation over the earth's surface and its general relation to Geognosy'. This work was intended to consider plant life 'in connection with the whole of the rest of nature, along with its influence on sentient mankind'.[186] By 1796 he could write that he had 'conceived the idea of a universal science . . . but the more I feel its need the more I see how slight the foundations still are for such a vast edifice'.[187] He was concerned with developing such a study on an empirical basis, yet in accordance with the Platonic concept of 'harmony in nature' (the term used by Bernardin de Saint-Pierre in connection with Mauritius) 'to reduce experiments to natural laws, to establish harmony among the phenomena'. Humboldt's observations in Venezuela constituted such an experiment and his statement on the consequences of deforestation such a 'general law'. He was thus able to integrate concepts of moral economy and science in a manner that had, philosophically, become quite impossible in the climate of positivism which ruled in France and England among scientists at the time and which increasingly separated them from literary or artistic preoccupations. Thus in England those writers who were affected by pantheistic or universalist concepts of a Germanic kind, the Romantic poets in particular, became detached from the scientific mainstream. This meant that throughout the first half of the nineteenth century they were unable to implement, via any scientific reputation, the kinds of opinions about man–environment relationships which were now central to their naturalistic tastes. It is not surprising, in this connection, to discover that Ruskin, among other artists, admitted to being inspired quite specifically by Humboldt rather than by any British natural scientist.[188]

In Germany the Romantic school, with its roots in Goethe and Orientalism, was by 1807 gaining strength. Its leaders challenged the mechanistic science of France not only with their concept of the world as an organic whole but also with the argument that the aim of science should be not utility and control but rather wisdom and understanding.[189] In *Ansichten der Natur* Humboldt set out deliberately, as he stated in his preface, to develop this notion and bring an artistic and literary treatment to the subject of natural science.[190] In it he provided evocative descriptions of his South American journey. These 'views of nature' in the tropics of the New World, which aimed to illustrate the

---

186 Letter to J. F. Pfaff, Nov. 1794, quoted in H. Beck, *Alexander von Humboldt*, 2 vols., Wiesbaden, 1958–61, I, p. 256.
187 *Correspondence scientifique et littéraire*, p. 4, quoted in Bowen, *Empiricism*, p. 220.
188 Smith, *European vision and the South Pacific*, p. 155.
189 Bowen, *Empiricism*, p. 225. In 1807 Humboldt published *Essai sur la géographie des plantes*, which attempted to reconcile the physical and moral spheres. It was dedicated to Goethe.
190 Quoted in Bowen, *Empiricism*, p. 226.

workings of a constant order maintained through the action of diverse forces, were presented to Germans at a time of trouble and disorder in their own country, as he explained, 'to renew their enjoyment of such scenery'. He aimed to 'promote a love of the study of nature, by bringing together in a small space the results of careful observations on the most varied subjects, by showing the importance of exact numerical data and the use to be made of them by well-considered arrangement and comparison'.[191]

It may be argued that Humboldt brought to the crisis in early-nineteenth-century science a distinctly Edenic preoccupation. This was manifested in his enthusiasm for the New World and the tropics and in his desire to discover interrelationships between man and nature. In this way, yet also in a rigorous scientific sense, he broadened the scope of the Edenic discourse to include the whole of nature and more especially the natural world of the tropics. It is some irony that, ultimately, the most receptive audience for Humboldt's analyses of the human impact in the tropics emerged not in Europe but among the ranks of British colonial naturalists, principally those in India and at the Cape. Moreover, the British colonial connection had already exerted a formative influence on Humboldt. At least part of his enthusiasm for the integration of man and nature at a scientific level originated in his association with Georg Forster and early colonial English painting as much as with Herder and Goethe. The association with Georg Forster, who during the 1790s was a well-known sympathiser with the French Revolution, served also to strengthen Humboldt's radical political views. In this productive association with Forster, two major influences, a taste for the tropics and an anarchic radicalism, were taken on by Humboldt in the same short period of his early life.

These connections with George Forster are worth more detailed attention. On Forster's return from the *Resolution* voyage, he remained a few years in England and, like his father, wrote an account of the voyage. He then accepted the chair of natural history at Cassel, while his father departed for Halle. Later the younger Forster frequently visited Göttingen, where he formed a close acquaintance with Humboldt. There Forster both inspired Humboldt with a taste for the tropical world and assisted him in preparing himself for a career of scientific voyaging. In 1790 he accompanied Humboldt through a turbulent France and visited England with him. It was at this time that Humboldt saw paintings by William Hodges in the home of Warren Hastings.[192] Writing nearly forty years later, Humboldt himself described the influence which Forster's writings and Hodges' paintings had upon his career:

191 Ibid.
192 Smith, *European vision and the South Pacific*, p. 181.

> The lessons of experience . . . tell us how often impressions received by
> the senses from circumstances accidental, have so acted upon the youthful
> as to determine the whole direction of a man's course through life . . . if
> I may have recourse to my own experience, and what awakened in me
> the first beginnings of an inextinguishable longing to visit the tropics, I
> should name George Forster's description of the islands of the Pacific
> [sic] . . . paintings by Hodge [sic] in the house of Warren Hastings, in
> London, representing the banks of the Ganges, and a colossal dragon tree
> in an old tower in the Botanical gardens of Berlin.[193]

The mention made here of tropical islands, the Ganges and the familiar
connecting allusion to the botanical garden are striking. All were micro-
environments with an imagery which was fundamental to Humboldt's perceptions. By 1808 he had actually come to feel that tropical landscapes far
outstripped those of temperate lands in quality of aesthetic and scientific appeal.[194] 'In the frigid North', he asserted, 'in the midst of the barren heath,
the solitary student can appropriate mentally all that has been discovered in
the most distant regions and can create within himself a world free and in-
penetrable as the spirit by which it is conceived.'[195]

This new-found zeal for tropical landscapes, initially fired by Georg Forster, developed in Humboldt's thinking simultaneously with a growing social
radicalism accentuated by the increasing political repression in Germany following the rise of Napoleon and the reassertion of absolute rule in both France
and Prussia.[196] Censorship and persecution of republican or liberal sympath-
isers affected intellectuals such as Humboldt, even in Paris, at the same time
as research in the colonies became increasingly restricted – a phenomenon
which led Humboldt to become even more vituperative in his frequent criticisms of the brutality of European colonial rule.[197]

Humboldt had long nourished an ambition to visit India, the region which
had first inspired him to an enthusiasm for tropical landscapes through his
encounter with the paintings of Hodges. His penetrating social and environmental critique might have made itself felt much earlier and more directly
than it did had not his attempts to mount an expedition to the Himalayas and

---

193 *Cosmos*, II, p. 5. Humboldt was almost certainly referring here to Hodges' paintings of the
   River Hooghly alongside the Calcutta Botanic Garden. The remarkable significance of this
   connection speaks for itself.
194 *Aspects of nature*, trans. Mrs Sabine, 8 vols., London, 1849, II, p. 29. For a useful discussion
   of this issue, see Michael Dettelbach, 'Global physics and aesthetic empire: Humboldt's
   physical portrait of the tropics', MS chapter of *Visions of empire*, Cambridge University Press,
   forthcoming.
195 *Aspects*, II, p. 31.
196 Bowen, *Empiricism*, p. 240.
197 Ibid., p. 246.

Southern India met with such a sharp rebuff in 1814. It was in that year that Humboldt visited London as part of a diplomatic mission with Friedrich Wilhelm III. Repeated applications for permission to visit India in subsequent years also met with refusal from the East India Company.[198] This antipathy on the part of the company probably related to Humboldt's well-known radical and anti-colonial views. These were views that were now impossible to hide. Indeed, publication of the first two volumes of the *Personal Narrative*, with its unveiled criticism of the Spanish colonial empire, had made Humboldt one of the most famous and intellectually feared men in Europe.[199]

The combined ministrations of a politically suspicious East India Company and a scientific community philosophically hostile to German *Naturphilosophie* in Britain ensured that the volumes of the *Personal Narrative* published in Britain in 1819, which included the Venezuelan material, received relatively little credence. This was particularly the case in India, where, even though Nathaniel Wallich had expressed anxiety about the rate of deforestation in Burma and Malabar, Humboldtian interpretations of the long-term impact of deforestation had not yet been put forward as arguments for the control of the process.[200] Furthermore, despite the permeation of German-trained scientists throughout the empire, many of whom shared Humboldt's humanist positions, the first scientist to appreciate and provide the means to grasp the full environmental message of Humboldt's writings was Joseph Boussingault, a French agricultural chemist.[201] Boussingault's own explorations in South

198 Ibid., p. 240.
199 Ibid. 'Who is unacquainted with the colossal labours of a Humboldt?' asked Otto von Kotzebue in the introduction to his *Voyage of discovery, into the South Seas and Bering's Straits*, trans. H. E. Lloyd (quoted in Smith, *European vision and the South Pacific*, p. 155). It should be noted that Darwin, above all, respected Humboldt as the most important single influence on his work.
200 See Chapter 5. Wallich must have been familiar with the *Narrative*, but he did not utilise Humboldt's arguments with government when he concerned himself with timber depletion, presumably because he remained personally unaware of the side effects of deforestation.
201 Of the German-speaking scientists in British colonial employ outside India, the most important from the point of view of their environmental and social humanism as well as their contribution to the initiation of environmental protection in the colonies were Ernest Dieffenbach, Ludwig Pappe and Ferdinand von Mueller, all of whom flourished in the mid nineteenth century – in New Zealand, the Cape Colony and Australia, respectively. Dieffenbach, naturalist to the New Zealand Company and the translator of Darwin's works into German, travelled extensively in New Zealand and the Pacific. Through his familiarity with Darwin he was particularly conscious of the problem of species extinction and coupled this with a concern for the treatment of the Maoris by the British. His work on the threat to seals, the indigenous population of the Chatham Islands and the whale population off North Island are pioneering essays in the field; see G. Bell, *Ernst Dieffenbach: Humanist and rebel*, Palmerston North, 1976; Dieffenbach, *Travels in New Zealand*, 2 vols., London, 1843, and 'An account of the Chatham Islands', *Journal of the Royal Geographical Society*, 1 (1841),

America had followed closely in the footsteps of Humboldt, as a result of which he became very familiar with the work of the German.[202] Humboldt's comments on the relationship between deforestation and the moisture content of the air were of particular interest to a scientist primarily concerned with the chemical interactions between plants and their surroundings. As a result Boussingault decided during the early 1830s to develop in greater depth the study which Humboldt had made of the consequences which might flow from

195–214. Ludwig Pappe, an Austrian surgeon and botanist, was colonial botanist in the Cape Colony from 1858 to 1862 and was the first promoter, after William Burchell, of conservation schemes in the colony. Both Pappe and his Scottish successor, J. C. Brown, were much affected in their views by writings of the German plant scientist J. Schleiden (who was especially critical of the rate of deforestation in the United States); see Grove, 'Early themes in African conservation'; Schleiden, *Die Pflanze und ihr Leben: Populäre Vorträge*, Leipzig, 1848; J. C. Brown, *The hydrology of South Africa*, Edinburgh, 1875. Ferdinand von Mueller, the first government botanist in the state of Victoria, was an early propagandist of conservation and the founder of the Melbourne botanical garden. His great conservation polemic, 'Forest culture in its relation to industrial pursuits' (*Journal of Applied Science*, 1 [1872], 198–202, 213–16, 231–4), was an ecological tour-de-force well ahead of its time; see that work and J. M. Powell, *Environmental management in Australia, 1788–1914*, Oxford, 1976, pp. 70–2. In Australia the work of the German-speaking Polish scientist P. E. Strzelecki can be considered a product of the same intellectual tradition. Strzelecki, a critic of the misuse of the soils of South Australia by the colonists, was also an early student of aboriginal culture, believing it far superior to that of the Europeans. His work on soil erosion was instrumental in persuading the government of Natal to adopt a forest-protection strategy. Later he worked on the Irish Famine Relief Commission and became a vociferous critic of British famine policy in Ireland during the years of the Great Hunger; see his *Physical description of New South Wales and Van Diemen's Land*, London, 1845; G. Rawson, *The Count: A life of Sir P. E. Strzelecki, explorer and scientist*, London, 1954; Grove, 'Early themes in African conservation'; C. Woodham-Smith, *The Great Hunger: Ireland, 1845–1849*, London, 1962. Other German scientists who attained senior positions in British employ were J. G. Koenig (as Madras government naturalist), Dietrich Brandis, Wilhelm Schlich and Berthold Ribbentrop (the last three as successive inspectors-general of forests in India). See also S. C. Ducker, 'History of Australian phytology: Early German collectors and botanists', in A. Wheeler, ed., *History in the service of systematics*, London, 1981, pp. 43–59.

202 Jean-Baptiste Boussingault (1802–87), born in Paris, was educated at the School of Mines in Saint-Etienne. At a young age he was appointed to a professorship at the School of Mines in Bogotá, Colombia, where he joined Simón Bolívar in the rebellion against Spanish rule. After the fighting ceased, he travelled extensively and became acquainted with Humboldt on his own expedition. Humboldt warmly praised Boussingault's chemical, meteorological and astronomical accomplishments. On his return to France in 1832, Boussingault wrote papers developing Humboldt's desiccation thesis and then proceeded to carry out pioneering research on the nitrogen cycle in plants. His revolutionary sympathies, developed first with Bolívar, can be compared to Humboldt's, and they were stimulated further by his election as a deputy in the 1848 Assembly of the Bas-Rhin. 'To him all students of agricultural and nutritional bio-chemistry are indebted for his many contributions made during the nineteenth century when so many fundamental studies were being made in these areas'; see G. R. Cowgill, 'Jean-Baptiste Boussingault: A biographical sketch', *Journal of Nutrition*, 84 (1964), 3–9.

deforestation. As case studies to illustrate his major paper on the topic (first published in 1837) he chose to record his own observations of changing lake levels in Venezuela, just as Humboldt had. Unlike Humboldt, he chose also to refer to the vegetal and rainfall history of Ascension Island.[203] There is no evidence that Boussingault had himself visited Ascension Island, and it is very probable that he was aware of the speculations of Bernardin de Saint-Pierre and J. R. Forster upon the reasons for the aridity of the island. Thus, although Boussingault intended, as Humboldt had, to synthesise a universal 'law' derived from empirical observations linking deforestation with a series of physical consequences, he still depended heavily on the much more extensive historical and empirical data already extant that related to the ecological consequences of the European colonisation of oceanic islands.

Boussingault's strong interest in the consequences of deforestation stemmed not only from his academic specialisation in plant chemistry but more directly from a contemporary French preoccupation with deforestation, soil erosion and flooding. These destructive processes had become steadily more widespread and of some economic importance ever since disruption of land tenures and customary arrangements during the revolutionary period had directly accelerated deforestation. It was thus a problem which largely post-dated and was only indirectly connected with the approach taken by the French on Mauritius, even though, conversely, a knowledge of the environmental consequences of the Revolution may have affected the measures taken on that island in 1804 by Governor Decaen.[204]

203 Boussingault, 'Mémoire sur l'influence des défrichements dans la diminution des cours-d'eau', *Annales de Chimie*, 64 (1837), 113–41. Boussingault had also touched on this theme in an essay entitled 'Ascension au Chimborazo . . .' in 1835. Humboldt, too, published a paper on the ascent of Chimborazo, which appeared in the *Edinburgh New Philosophical Review* two years later.

204 Humboldt himself, in his analysis of the reasons for the changing levels of Lake Valencia and his later analyses of the run-off consequences of deforestation, relied heavily on the work of two Frenchmen: Gaspard C. F. Prony (the Baron Riche de Prony), a prolific physicist and hydrologist; and François Pons, author of travel accounts. In the *Narrative*, when discussing deforestation Humboldt refers the reader directly to a work by Prony entitled *Recherches sur les crues du valle de Po*. I cannot trace this work, and Humboldt may have been referring to a manuscript. Later in life Humboldt worked closely with Prony and co-published with him in Bologna in 1845; see Prony and Humboldt, 'Estratto dalle ricerche del Signore de Prony sul sistema idraulico dell'Italia', in F. Cardinali, ed., *Nuova raccolta di autori italiani che trattono del moto dell'acque*, vol. 7, Bologna, 1845, pp. 81–8. Prony was interested in the reasons for the siltation of the Po system, a topic which was later to interest G. P. Marsh and the Indian irrigation engineer Baird-Smith. Prony had earlier also published other works on the dynamics of river flow, e.g. *Mémoire sur le jaugeage des eaux courantes*, Paris, 1802. François Pons travelled in South America after Humboldt but published an account which, importantly, seems to have set Humboldt thinking again about the significance of the level of Lake Valencia; see Pons, *Voyage à la partie orientale de la Terre-Ferme, dans l'Amérique méridionale, fait pendant les années 1802–1804*, Paris, 1806.

It was on Mauritius, however, that the implications of Boussingault's pioneering paper in the *Annales de Chimie* in 1837 were first taken up. His conclusions and his emphasis on the need for active state intervention to ensure forest protection were the subject of a series of lectures given by Louis Bouton to the Royal Society of Arts and Sciences of Mauritius in 1837 and 1838.[205] Mauritians, Bouton said, would have to learn not to 'kill the goose that lays the golden eggs'.[206] The RSASM was an institutional descendant of Commerson's original but stillborn plan for an Académie, which had in the meantime found vigorous form.[207] Bouton's three lectures on deforestation and his campaigning advocacy of the need for conservation were taken up with enthusiasm and published immediately in consecutive issues of the *Cernéan*, one of the main island newspapers.[208] Here they received much attention and approbation among the unusually large intellectual community of the island. Perhaps for the first time, the efficacy of the newspaper as a conservationist propaganda tool, later used effectively in India and the Cape Colony, was perceived and acted upon by Bouton, who was to become a life-long propagandist for forest protection. The editor of the RSASM journal proceeded to write an editorial praising Bouton's lectures and recommending that the public peruse them carefully.[209]

In 1839 Bouton was made secretary of the RSASM, a position he was to occupy for more than thirty years. It was a position of considerable influence in which he was able to take full advantage of the international links the Society possessed, both to gain ideas and to disseminate his conservationist philosophy. Indeed, it was through the Society that Bouton had become aware of the Boussingault paper in the *Annales de Chimie* very shortly after it was published. Nevertheless, the political influence Bouton and the Society could

---

205 Louis Bouton (1799–1878). For details of Bouton's career, see *DMB*, pp. 657–8.

206 'Sur le décroissement des forêts à l'Ile Maurice', *Cernéan*, no. 814 (12 April 1838), 2. This lecture had originally been given as a paper to the Mauritius Natural History Society on 24 Aug. 1837 at its annual general meeting. Subsequently the paper was also published as a separate booklet by A. Mamarot, printer (Library of Congress copy no. SD242.M3B7) under the title *Sur le décroissement des forêts à Maurice*, Port Louis, 1838. Hence Bouton's lecture became widely read and discussed on the island.

207 For a detailed history of the antecedents of the RSASM, particularly those relating to the influence of Commerson, see Ly-Tio-Fane, 'Notice historique', pp. 1–24. This as yet unpublished MS is currently the best history of the oldest colonial scientific society.

208 The lectures to the RSASM were published as separate papers or newspaper 'features' in *Cernéan*, nos. 814 and 815, on 12 and 14 April 1838, under the broad title of the seminar which had been held at the RSASM meeting in Port Louis a few days earlier: 'Sur le décroissement des forêts à l'Ile Maurice'. They were subdivided by the editor of *Cernéan* under three headings: (1) L'état d'agriculture à Maurice; (2) Défrichement des forêts; (3) Reglements forestières sur la matière.

209 *Proceedings of the Royal Society of Arts and Sciences of Mauritius*, 1 (1838), 22–3.

exercise in the direction of conservation was limited by other economic interests on the island and above all by the powerful lobby of island sugar planters.
These men, while paying lip-service to the message of Bouton's lectures, effectively prevented the strengthening of the island's forest-protection system
under the Decaen laws. The sugar planters had, since the British annexation,
become sufficiently strong to be able to flout the 1804 laws with impunity.
Thus, in spite of Bouton's early campaigning, it was not until 1854 that further
legislative attempts were made to strengthen forest protection on the island.
Moreover, the 1854 legislation, promoted by Bouton with allies in government,
relied heavily on the success and example of the growing semi-official conservation lobby in India.[210]

Boussingault's 1837 paper had not become the subject of any effective at-
tention or remark in India until 1839, largely because it was not available in
English until late 1838, when it was published in the *Edinburgh New Philosophical Review*, a journal widely read by the officers of the EIC Medical
Service and hence by its naturalists. As on Mauritius, the formation of a
colonial scientific society, in this case the Madras Society of Literature and
Science, played a critical disseminating role. However, as a social group the
EIC surgeons enjoyed an intellectual and social status in the society and with
the government that far outstripped that of Bouton and his naturalist colleagues on Mauritius. It was in part this superior status that ensured that the
warnings of Humboldt and Boussingault eventually got an effective reception
in India.

210 In particular it relied upon the publicity given to the Cleghorn report to the British Association for the Advancement of Science. The coincidence in timing between the strengthened
   1854 forest-protection legislation on Mauritius and the Dalhousie memorandum of 1854
   outlining the plans for an all-India forest department is striking. A common origin in the
   Cleghorn report is more easily established. After his initial and largely ignored attempts to
   strengthen the Poivre and Decaen conservation laws, which had largely failed in practice,
   Bouton persisted during the 1840s in arguing his case. He resorted to print once more in
   1846; see 'Note sur le déboissement des forêts', *Rapports de la Société de l'Histoire Naturelle
   de l'Ile Maurice*, 1846, pp. 103–10, and 'Note sur l'état actuel des forêts à Maurice', ibid.,
   p. 175. Rawson W. Rawson, colonial secretary of Mauritius and an admirer of Bouton, became
   governor of the Cape Colony after 1853. The diffusion of conservation ideas on an inter-
   colonial basis was thus already significant by the early 1850s; see Grove, 'Early themes in
   African conservation', pp. 26, 31–2.

8

Diagnosing crisis: The East India Company medical services and the emergence of state conservationism in India, 1760–1857

In some respects the history of the response to colonially induced ecological change in India before 1857 followed the pattern which had developed on Mauritius, St Helena and St Vincent. In this way the experience gained in these island colonies exercised an important formative influence over the way in which environmental ideas were conceptualised and state conservation came to be developed in India. While the scale of the physical context was quite different and it took much longer for ecological changes to make an impact on European policy in India, the manner of response and the intellectual constraints upon it were essentially very similar. However, the way in which information about the environment was gathered, communicated and coordinated became much more critical to the formulation of scientific and state environmental policy.

From the point of view of the historian concerned with the broader picture of the economic and social changes contingent on East India Company rule, the ecological consequences of western penetration and the development of state responses to such changes are of considerable interest. Deforestation in particular, and the controls involved in the colonial response to it, had a direct and far-reaching impact on agricultural production and population movements. Other consequences of company rule have been much studied, and at first sight it may seem surprising that the ecological consequences of colonial rule in India and the environmental policies of the EIC have, until recently, received relatively little attention.[1] The principal difficulty to date relates to

---

1 For an important exception, see Richard Tucker, 'The depletion of India's forests under British imperialism: Planters, foresters and peasants in Assam and Kerala', in D. Worster, ed., *The ends of the earth: Essays in environmental history*, Cambridge, 1988, pp. 118–41. See also Michael Mann, *Britische Herrschaft auf Indische Boden: Landwirtschaftlichen Transformation und ökologische Destruktion des Central Doab, 1801–1854*, Stuttgart, 1992 (and University of Heidelberg 1991 Ph.D. diss. of the same title), and Mahesh Rangarajan, 'Production, desiccation and forest

the absence of accurate information on ecological change, so that the generalisations which have been made have normally been based on little more than guesswork.[2] While some reference has to be made here to the speed of ecological change under company rule, a very detailed assessment of it is at this point neither possible nor an essential part of this analysis.[3] Furthermore, under company rule the broader impact of environmental degradation on agricultural change, colonial production, migration and social change is a largely unexplored, although important, field and is necessarily and advisedly largely beyond the scope of this book.[4] Instead, the objectives of this chapter are confined to exploring early colonial anxieties about the Indian environment and the way in which an interventionist state response first developed in response to those anxieties. The chain of intellectual events principally involved the elaboration of arguments linking deforestation with rainfall and climatic alteration and the propagandising of such desiccationist arguments by specialists. As in the island colonies, the development of a distinctive group of professional scientists as environmental commentators took place, involving not only the canvassing of new scientific insights but also the often disguised

management in the Central Provinces' and other essays in R. H. Grove and V. Damodaran, eds., *Essays on the environmental history of South and South-East Asia*, Oxford University Press, New Delhi, in press.

2 Currently the only systematic attempts to survey the history of land-use change under colonial rule in India are those being conducted by John Richards, Elizabeth Flint and colleagues under the auspices of Duke University; see J. F. Richards, E. S. Haynes and J. R. Hagen, 'Changing land use in Bihar, Punjab and Haryana, 1850–1970', *Modern Asian Studies*, 19 (1985), 699–732. Unfortunately, for the earlier period of British rule, the basic data (anyway scanty) is far less easily used than for the period covered by the Duke University project. The same applies, of course, to the late seventeenth and the early eighteenth century. This is important, since the period before 1857, during which the conservation ideas discussed in this chapter emerged, probably experienced more radical vegetal changes than the period after the Mutiny.

3 In fact, in any future analysis of rates of ecological change in the period 1650–1850 a prime task will be to determine to what extent the changes caused by 'western' economic penetration under colonial rule were really new in scale. It seems particularly likely that vigorous economic transitions in some of the successor states to Mughal rule, especially in South-West India during the late seventeenth and the eighteenth century, were accompanied by corresponding changes in rates of deforestation, expansion of arable land and the assertion of monopolistic land-use practices and rights.

4 Some recent regional studies, however, are helpful in indicating the disruption caused to forest 'tribal' as well as agrarian societies by early-nineteenth-century forest felling, neglect of irrigation, expansion of arable land and revenue collection; see e.g. R. K. Gupta, *The economic life of a Bengal district: Birbhum, 1770–1857*, Burdwan, 1984, pp. 117–19, 296–307; E. Whitcombe, *Agrarian conditions in Northern India*, vol. 1, *The United Provinces under British rule, 1860–1869*, Berkeley, Calif., 1972, pp. 61–119; V. Damodaran, *Broken promises: Popular protest, Indian nationalism and the Congress Party in Bihara, 1935–1946*, Oxford, 1992; and Michael Mann, 'Ecological change in North India: Deforestation in the Ganga-Jumna Doab 1800–1850', in Grove and Damodaran, *Essays*, in press.

mediation of new or distinctive and sympathetic attitudes to nature in the tropical world. In India too the botanical garden, in close alliance with metropolitan botany, emerged as the focus for such professionalisation.[5] The founding of scientific societies and their journals also helped to stimulate the diffusion of environmental ideas. Lastly, an identification between moral or reformist sympathies and environmental concern became as characteristic among scientists in India as it had been in the island colonies.

By contrast, the Hippocratic analysis of environmental change, important on the islands and in physiocracy, was developed in a much more specific and influential way in India. However, the influence of long-established indigenous Indian conservation and tree-planting practices, critical to the thinking of van Reede at the Cape and Poivre on Mauritius, was also elaborated much further in colonial India under company rule. We have already seen how the Ezhava epistemologies of Malabar affected European constructions of nature in India and elsewhere. In a similar fashion, Hindu, Muslim and Zoroastrian concepts of man–environment relations formed an essential stimulus to colonial arboriculture and to the adoption of the Humboldtian environmental ideology which so much influenced EIC scientists.[6] In a more immediate sense the permeation of indigenous Indian knowledge about the consequences of deforestation was directly instrumental at a number of stages in the formation of colonial perceptions of rates and mechanisms of environmental change. In fact, it would probably be true to say that, on balance, indigenous knowledge, management and afforestation methods were more important to the evolution of company environmental policy than any set of ideas imported from outside India. After the end of company rule, this equation changed, and externally derived, especially German, formulations held greater sway. Possibly as a direct corollary of this shift, local resistance to state forestry and conservation policy became far more developed after the end of company rule.[7]

The role of universalist scientific arguments also came to be more significant than it had been in the island colonies. In India the relative influence of scientists, and especially medical surgeons, in their relations with the colonial state became far more developed and the conservation propaganda they wielded more sophisticated. As experts consulted by government, the surgeons were incorporated in an entirely new kind of scientific civil service, in a struc-

5 See Chapter 4 for the beginnings of this process in India.
6 See Chapter 7 for details of the Indic elements in Humboldt's thinking.
7 The pioneering essay in this area is R. Tucker, 'Forest management and imperial politics: Thana district, Bombay, 1823–1827', *Indian Economic and Social History Review*, 16 (1979), 273–300; for a development of this, see I. M. Saldanha, 'Colonial forest regulations and collective resistance: nineteenth century Thana district', in Grove and Damodaran, *Essays*, in press. For a useful small-scale study of resistance at a later period, see R. Guha, 'Forestry and social protest in British Kumaon, 1893–1921', *Subaltern Studies*, 4 (1985), 54–101.

ture that guaranteed some continuity in analysis and ensured that forest con-servation was taken on by the state in India as an accepted part of the role of colonial government. Indeed, in their emerging capacity as scientific advisers to government, the staff of the EIC Medical Service acquired a quite un-precedented institutional role as the source of local and international environ-mental expertise.[8] In its emphasis on the extent to which environmental degradation constituted a threat to the social fabric, the Hippocratic analysis of environmental change formed the basis for an important variety of thinking about the reasons for famine and food crises in India; it both argued for an interventionist instead of laissez-faire approach to land use and was unsatisfied with Malthusian analyses of famine.[9]

Part of the object of this chapter, then, is to trace the increasing degree of direct involvement by the EIC Medical Service in formulating a diagnosis of the ecological transition taking place in India under colonial rule. The so-phistication of this diagnosis helps to explain the direct part played by EIC surgeons and other actors in evolving an interventionist response to the threats to human health and economic stability posed by deforestation and land deg-radation in India. The methods adopted by the medical service in lobbying government to adopt interventionist controls on environmental change thus emerge as a particular focus of interest.

A secondary intention here is to indicate how the emergence of conservation policies can help shed some light on changing notions of the responsibility

8 It should be noted that an earlier authority on the subject does not perceive local scientific expertise as being significant in India until about 1900; see R. M. Macleod, 'Scientific advice for British India: Imperial perceptions and administrative goals, 1898–1923', *Modern Asian Studies*, 3 (1975), 345–84. This view needs to be drastically revised.

9 To date, analyses of the ecological factors connecting deforestation, water supply and climate have rarely entered into accounts of the history and causes of famine in India in the context of colonial rule. See e.g. D. Arnold, *Famine: Social crisis and historical change*, Oxford, 1988; B. M. Bhatia, *Famines in India*, London, 1967; S. Ambirajan, 'Malthusian population theory and Indian famine policy in the nineteenth century', *Population Studies*, 30 (1976), 5–14; J. Dreze, 'Famine prevention in India', paper presented at a meeting of the World Institute for Devel-opment Research, Helsinki, July 1986; and A. Sen, *Poverty and famine: An essay on entitlement and deprivation*, Oxford, 1982. However, for an important recent exception, see V. Damodaran 'Famine in a forest tract', in Grove and Damodaran, *Essays*, in press. Apart from the latter, none of these works (in common with almost all other studies of famine in India) consider the very prominent part contemporary propagandists of the connections between ecological change and famine played in the formation of policies on famine prevention, in which forest reservation was an important constituent after 1847. A great deal of this distorted emphasis may have originated in the way in which the report of the Famine Commission of 1880 in its conclusions played down the strength of those arguments favouring large-scale forest and watershed pro-tection as preventive measures, stressing instead less interventionist, short-term and more lais-sez-faire prescriptions; see Government of India, *Report of the Famine Commission*, 4 vols., Calcutta, 1880.

and role of the colonial state in India during the first half of the nineteenth century and particularly on the shifting strength of laissez-faire versus utilitarian and interventionist policies and the interest groups advocating them. Fears grew during the period that the unleashed and uncontrolled forces of local and European capitalism might actually threaten the survival of peasant agriculture and, in turn, endanger the security of the colonial state. Conservation thinking represented a stark contradiction and an impediment to short-term capital interests, so that its successful advent raises some awkward questions about the ideological stance adopted by the colonial state in relation to the control of destructive and capitalist economic forces.[10] The environmental ideas propagandised by the EIC surgeons, most of whom were trained at German or Scottish universities, had radical and influential implications which were not always appreciated by the governments of the time.[11] Colonial governments did, nevertheless, soon come to appreciate the full political advantage to be gained from the kinds of land-use control which forest protection implied, despite the hostility to state land control articulated by contemporary capital interests.

While the direct role of the surgeons as effective administrative innovators in land-use decision making dates, in the main, from the late 1830s, their role as providers of scientific expertise dates from a much earlier period. The employment of J. G. Koenig as a state naturalist by the Nawab of Arcot prior to his employment by the East India Company at Madras constitutes one of the earliest instances of a surgeon's being employed specifically as a non-medical state scientist.[12] There had always been a close association between surgeons and botanical science, and this was a connection that was actively fostered and utilised by Sir Joseph Banks.[13] It became much more specific with the appointment of William Roxburgh and Nathaniel Wallich as superintendents of the Calcutta Botanic Garden and John Berry as superintendent of the Madras Garden and the Madras Nopalry.[14] After 1792 their involve-

---

10 See in particular Washbrook, 'Law, state and agrarian society in colonial India', pp. 684–7, for a useful discussion of the hostility of the post-Mutiny government of India to many of the objectives of private capital.

11 For an account of the very close connections (in comparison with English medical schools) between the traditions of medical training in the Scottish universities in the early part of the nineteenth century and the French and German Enlightenment, see A. Chitnis, *The Scottish Enlightenment*, London, 1976, pp. 124–87.

12 A well-documented instance of such employment a little later by an indigenous Indian ruler involved the employment of J. M. Hönigsberger (a German surgeon from Kronstadt, Transylvania) at the Court of Lahore: Hönigsberger, *Thirty-five years in the East: Adventures, discoveries, experiments and historical sketches relating to the Punjab and Cashmere*, London, 1835. Further insights into the employment of surgeons as non-medical scientific experts are provided throughout the text of Crawford, *A history of the Indian Medical Service*.

13 See Chapter 8.

14 See King, 'Brief memoir on William Roxburgh', and M. Vicziany, 'Imperialism' botany and

ment in the problems posed by deforestation gradually developed in the context of the government's recognition of their botanical expertise, a recognition which was often actively sought out by the surgeons.

Beginning as a successor state among others, the East India Company had by 1818 succeeded in assuming and consolidating political leadership of the Indian sub-continent. The process had been complicated, since it involved the close cooperation and alliance of a variety of social and indigenous service groups (especially Bania bankers and Parsi merchants) and the specific interests of the British private traders.[15]

The fact of company success and the assertion of British corporate and private commercial interests generated important and identifiable changes in the Indian economy.[16] These related to the rise of new urban centres along the coast (e.g. Bombay, Madras and Calcutta) and inland (e.g. Kanpur, Mirzapur, Benares, Baroda and Hyderabad). Rapid economic changes were also associated with new patterns of trade, as was the acceleration in shipbuilding activity that followed expansion of the Calcutta and Bombay commercial fleets and the marine force of the EIC so essential to the patrolling and policing of the seas.[17] Conversely, the decay and dislocation of the traditional manufacturing sector, especially that dealing with cotton textiles, exercised its own impact. Parallel to this major overhaul of the economic system was the creation of major land-revenue systems to support the company raj: the *ryotwari*, *zamindary* and *malguzari*, which were the outcome of much deliberation and experimentation. The cumulative effects of these changes and policy decisions on the indigenous population have been studied in some detail and at many

statistics: The surveys of Francis Buchanan', *Modern Asian Studies*, 20 (1986), 625–60, on the competition between Buchanan-Hamilton and Wallich to acquire the superintendency of the Calcutta Botanic Garden. King's memoir is useful in revealing the significance of the occupancy of the post of Madras government botanist/naturalist in establishing the EIC Medical Service in the superintendency of the Calcutta garden. Koenig, Russell and Roxburgh all occupied the Madras post, which had itself arisen from company interest in the botanical and horticultural work carried out by Koenig for the Nawab of Arcot. The Dutch East India Company at the Cape had also generally employed surgeons as superintendents of the VOC company garden; see Karsten, *The Old Company's garden at the Cape*, pp. 1–45. However, there is no clear reason for believing that this constituted the basis of the practice at Calcutta. Recognition of the work of Koenig and Roxburgh by the company (with the encouragement of Sir Joseph Banks) was more significant.

15 D. Kumar and M. Desai, eds., *The Cambridge economic history of India*, vol. 2, Cambridge, 1983, pp. 3–352; L. S. Subramanian, 'The Banias and the British: The role of indigenous credit in Western India in the second half of the eighteenth century', *Modern Asian Studies*, 20 (1987), 473–511.

16 C. A. Bayly, *Rulers, townsmen and bazaars: North India in the age of British expansion*, Cambridge, 1983, pp. 229–309.

17 R. A. Wadia, *The Bombay dockyard and the Wadia masterbuilders*, Bombay, 1955; P. Nightingale, *Trade and empire in Western India, 1784–1800*, Cambridge, 1970.

levels in the social structure. However, the ecological impact which the company system produced has not received the same detailed attention.

This is in part because our knowledge of the speed and character of ecological change in pre-British India, particularly of deforestation, is still very limited and patchy, and our insights into changes in the first crucial decades of colonial rule are also very sketchy. However, those studies of deforestation that do exist for the period 500 B.C. to A.D. 1760 (and particularly for the period 1500–1760) indicate that periods of relatively rapid change did take place in pre-colonial times, particularly in connection with periods of military expansion by aspiring new state builders. Above all, very extensive early deforestation took place at a variety of dates in the Indus and Ganges river basins and in the semi-arid zones.[18]

A growing awareness of such pronounced pre-colonial deforestation episodes leads one seriously to question the objectivity of some recent historical essays that have tended to characterise the pre-British period as an ecological and pre-capitalist golden age of common property rights and sustainable resource use.[19] In some of these essays the caste system has even been characterised as an effective ecological adaptation to different habitats.[20] Such accounts would seem inherently Orientalist in the Saidian sense and are based on belief in a kind of pre-colonial 'Merrie India' that is closely akin to the romantic constructions of 'Merrie Africa' that have long been discarded by scholars.[21] In fact, far from being a paradise of so-called common property, the nonarable Indian environment has, from a very early date, been subject to attempts at management and control by both states and dominant groups, some of a geographically very extensive nature.[22]

18 See esp. Jean Filiozat, 'Ecologie historique en Inde du Sud: le pays des Kallar', *Revue des Etudes d'Extrême Orient*, 1980 (2), pp. 22–46; George Erdosy, 'Deforestation in pre- and proto-historic South Asia', in Grove and Damodaran, *Essays*, in press; Makhan Lal, 'Iron tools, forest clearance and urbanisation in the Gangetic plains', *Man and Environment*, 10 (1985), 83–90; Chetan Singh, 'Forests, pastoralists and agrarian society in North India', paper presented at Conference on Environment and History in India, Bellagio, Italy, March 1992; Irfan Habib, *Atlas of the Mughal empire*, Aligarh, 1982, pls. 10 and 10a.

19 See e.g. M. Gadgil and R. Guha, *This fissured land: An ecological history of India*, New Delhi, 1992, and 'State forestry and social conflict in British India', *Past and Present*, no. 123 (1989), 141–77.

20 See M. Gadgil, 'Towards an ecological history of India', *Economic and Political Weekly*, 20 (1985), 1909–18.

21 Said, *Orientalism*. For critiques of the 'Merrie Africa' hypothesis, see J. Lonsdale, 'Introduction', in D. Anderson and R. H. Grove, eds., *Conservation in Africa: People, policies and practices*, Cambridge, 1987, pp. 271–7; and P. Coquery-Vidrovich, *Afrique noire: Permanences et ruptures?* Paris, 1985.

22 Some idea of the early stages of this process is contained in D. Das, *Economic history of the Deccan*, New Delhi, 1976, pp. 105–15. For a more specific example of Maratha pre-colonial forest control, see H. B. Vashishta, *Land revenue and public finance in Maratha administration*,

These attempts to introduce state control became much more frequent towards the end of the seventeenth century and often involved plantation projects to safeguard timber for the construction of increasingly large navies. As Mughal control collapsed, the ascendancy of successor states and their attendant commercial elites caused dramatic rises in timber demand and the growing commoditisation of forests for revenue and state needs long before the East India Company became a significant power in the land. For example, until the end of the eighteenth century the forests of Cochin were under the control of the feudal chiefs of the Nadivazlis, who owed allegiance to the Rajah of Cochin.[23] These processes of forest annexation by pre-colonial states frequently involved the forced removal of peasant populations and the destruction of pre-existing customary forest-utilisation arrangements. Moreover, when the EIC did acquire forested territory, the management methods of the conquered states were often imitated and co-opted. The case of Sind provides an instructive example of the way in which an extensive 'pre-colonial' state-forest and hunting-reserve system could be taken over by the company and run with few changes. Between about 1690 and 1830 the Amirs of Sind were responsible for the reafforestation of over a million acres of the Indus flood plain with up to eighty-seven *shikargah*, or hunting and forest reserves, whose forest products were sold to the peasantry, many of whose villages had previously been forcibly removed to establish the reserves.[24] As Eastwick tells us, the shikargahs 'answer the double purpose of preserving game and supplying the whole country with timber of excellent quality, as well for the construction of boats and houses as for firing and every other useful purpose'.[25] The extent and revenue production of the shikargahs in pre-colonial times was remarkable. In Karachi district alone, for example, in the 1840s twenty-four forests covered an area of over 95,000 acres. By 1870 these forests were producing revenue for the British of 39,000 rupees per annum.[26] These figures indicate that the shikargahs had become a very important source of revenue to the amirs and in some sense substituted for land revenue, since the forest reserves occupied the best irrigated areas and the best soils.[27] Similar revenue consid-

Delhi, 1975, pp. 138–46; see also accounts of Maratha forest reserves in *Report of the Bombay Forest Commission*, vols. 1–2, Bombay, 1887.

23 Then in 1813 a forest department was set up under a *mellei melviharappan* ('mountain superintendent'); see H. Vishwanath, ed., *Working plan for Chakakuan*, Forest Department, Trivandrum, 1958, pp. 12–13 (Bodleian Library, Oxford, Indian Institute Archives, Trav. 0.3). For details of similar pre-colonial arrangments in Travancore, see F. Bourdillon, ed., *Report on the Travancore forests*, Trivandrum, 1886, pp. 15–16.

24 See E. H. Aitken, ed., *Gazetteer of Sind*, Lahore, 1907, p. 40, for estimates of individual forest areas; this estimate covered the full 87 government shikargah forests.

25 E. B. Eastwick, *Dry leaves from young Egypt*, London, 1849, p. 24.

26 *Gazetteer of Sind*, Lahore, 1874, p. 321.

27 This was why the planting of a shikargah tended to involve village removal. Napier noted in

erations applied to the pre-colonial state forest policy farther south. Thus, after the 1730s the heavy resource and financial demands of the Maratha armies compelled the Maratha state builders to extract high revenues from the forests under their control. The forest reserves designated to perform this function were eventually (after 1805), as in Sind, taken over and run by the EIC as the initial infrastructure of the Bombay forest-conservancy system. In other words, the onset of British colonial control seems likely to emerge as a less significant episode in Indian forest history than the phase in which the successor states to the Mughal empire started to exercise a new economic and political dispensation.

Discussions in the Governor's Council at Fort William, Calcutta, from the beginning of the 1760s indicate that timber shortage was already an important matter and had been for some decades before the company acquired full territorial control of Bengal and adjacent regions. As early as 1761 fears were being expressed that timber, as an expensive commodity needed for house and ship construction, was being misused. This anxiety lessened only temporarily when new supplies of softwood timbers were discovered by Richard Becker, a company agent, in the Morangs region of Southern Nepal; this timber could be floated down to Calcutta by river.[28] The same fears were expressed very explicitly on the west coast by the early 1780s. On one occasion company agents reported that 'timber which abounds in the interior parts of this country is an article of such important consideration that we cannot but recommend your honours attention of this object, and propose that indiscriminate lease of cutting be not granted, as it has occasioned great abuse'. For this reason they recommended that 'forests which used to supply the Mahratta Circar be now appropriated to the Revenue of the Company'.[29]

In both the Bengal and Bombay presidencies between 1760 and 1790, chronic difficulties in obtaining timber and controlling indigenous sources of supply encouraged company military plans and local adventurism. Above all, expansion by the company northwards and eastwards to the Nepal border and into the Maratha territories on the west coast was much encouraged by the

1843 that 'they occupy all the best land in Scinde; wherever good land was found a shikargah was at once planted, and the inhabitants driven away . . . it therefore became a matter for consideration whether they should be maintained': PRO 30/12/61, letter from Napier to Ellenborough, 22 May.

28 National Archives of India, New Delhi [henceforth NAI], Home Public Consultations, Foreign and Political Select Committee Proceedings, vol. 12 (6 Jan. – 29 Dec. 1767), committee meeting at Fort William, 14 July 1767, p. 232.

29 NAI, Home Public Consultations, noted 24 Sept. 1781: Letter from James Sibbald et al. in Bassein to William Hornby, President, Bombay, 2 May 1781 (letter no. 9). 'The revenue arises, it was noted, from the taxes and customs respecting the latter . . . it is necessary to observe that the whole revenue was farmed out, but those of Bassein cannot be.'

threat of a timber shortage. In fact, it may even be appropriate to argue that company expansionism was *normally* associated with timber shortage, much as the desire to control strategic timber supplies lay behind earlier episodes of British expansionism in North America and contemporary ones at the Cape. Despite this, the ambitions of private traders to gain control over forested areas were frequently thwarted by lack of political and territorial control and deliberate company reluctance to become involved in harvesting activities that might provoke conflict and confrontation with indigenous states and commercial interests. This was the case initially in Bengal in the 1760s and, more specifically, in the Godavery delta north of Madras. There, for example, in 1785 a proposal was made to the company by one Andrew Parkinson, a private trader, that it should establish a superintendent of woods in the forests of the Rajahmundry Circar alongside the Godavery River. In this case the Council at Masulipatam, adjacent to the forests, turned down this suggestion on the ground that the company simply did not control the relevant territory of the Bhadrachalam region.[30] Such debates and disputes within the company tended to underline the connections between ambitions for territorial and political control and access to forest resources. Where forest timber was needed to build and maintain the ships of the company marine, the search for timber emerged as a motive to expand and engage in the wars of neighbouring Indian states. As the Parkinson case shows, where the supply of shipbuilding timber was not a major political imperative, further expansion of controls over forests was rarely encouraged. Nevertheless, serious tensions sometimes arose between the presidencies through varying perceptions of the need to wage war in order to gain timber supplies. On several occasions, for example, Warren Hastings found cause to criticise the Bombay authorities for involvement in the Maratha wars when control of particular forest areas was the only reason given by Bombay for interventions unlicensed by the governor-general in Calcutta. On one occasion the agent of the Bombay government caused great irritation when he told Hastings that an unlicensed campaign was justified, since 'before we had the trade, but now we have the country where the articles [teak] of that trade are produced'.[31]

From the 1770s until about 1860 fluctuating demand for naval and military (plus some urban construction) timber represented the main significant commercial and demand factor in British forest policy in India. Urban demand for firewood expanded far more steadily until the 1840s. This position was

30 Madras, Tamil Nadu State Archives, Consultations, vol. XXXI: Letter, 1787: 'Mr Parkinson . . . addressed us . . . in regard to the situation of the port and river of Bandermalanka and the advantage of encouraging the trade in teak timber and clearing the woods bordering the Godavery.'
31 NAI, Secret Political Files, vol. 16: Proceedings of Council (letter of 23 Aug. 1875 from President, Bombay, considered): Bombay's agent questioned over attack by Bombay on Broach.

quickly changed when the need for railway sleepers suddenly became significant – indeed, dominant – at the beginning of the 1860s. The resulting and increasingly extensive search for timber after 1800 in remote, especially mountain, districts bestowed a double benefit on the company, since the need to acquire control over timber resources facilitated the control of unruly tribal groups. This was the case, for example, with the Dangs Bhils in the Western Ghats, the Paharia of the Rajmahal Hills of Bihar and the Rampa tribal groups in North Arcot near Madras.[32] Resistance by these and other groups to company incursions, though periodically violent and effective, could ultimately be controlled by direct suppression or by co-option of hill tribes into local police and army forces, so that timber could then be removed without further difficulty.

Even before the Napoleonic wars, political competition for the forests of India had been closely connected with the rise in demand for raw materials. But these new demands were not all externally created. In fact, there is evidence of an increasing integration of internal trade and commercial demands connected with the growing dominance of new states in Western India towards the end of the eighteenth century.[33] This was increasingly reflected in a growing requirement for shipbuilding timber on the Malabar Coast by both the company and other successor states of the Mughal empire.[34] However, these developments were soon overshadowed by the material demands of the global conflict between Britain and France. This was reflected in a rapid growth in demand for shipbuilding timber, which by 1810 had developed into a timber 'crisis' which was accompanied by a concerted and worldwide search for new timber resources.[35] One may represent this, as Rodger does, as the pioneering

32 H. D. Love, *Vestiges of Old Madras*, vol. 1, London, 1913.
33 C. A. Bayly, 'The Middle East and Asia during the age of Revolutions 1760–1830', *Itinerario*, 2 (1986), 80–1; L. S. Subramanian, 'Bombay and the west coast in the 1740s', *Indian Economic and Social History Review*, 8 (1981), 215–16.
34 Extensive references to this increase in demand can be found in the first two chapters of Wadia, *The Bombay dockyard and the Wadia masterbuilders*. The increasing interest of the EIC in the consequences of this rise in demand are documented in BL, Home Misc. IOL, (102) F/4/39: papers regarding the timber trade in Malabar Province, April 1795 – Jan. 1798; also in Home Misc. E/4/1014, draft 23 (1798–9), pp. 266–9.
35 R. Pering, 'A brief inquiry into the causes of the premature decay in our wooden bulwarks with an examination of the means best calculated to prolong their duration', *Quarterly Review*, 8 (1812), 28–41; Albion, *Forests and sea power*, pp. 346–69 (chapter entitled 'Searching the World for timber'). Albion's treatment is useful in drawing attention to the connections in the search for timber in the Cape, Madagascar and Malabar. Essentially it was the failure to establish reliable timber supplies at the Cape that focussed attention on Malabar. In both places the concerted searches and surveys of 1810 led to the development of more sophisticated ways of analysing and then managing timber reserves and towards more rigorous management by the state of forest reserves; see papers regarding the survey of forests in the Bombay Presidency in BL, IOL, F/4/347 and F/4/348, dealing respectively with reduction of the

growth of a kind of industrial consumption pattern.[36] It served for the first time to focus attention on the global strategic value of a raw material and on a deciding factor in the Franco-British contest. It also sharpened appreciation of the long-term value of the Western Indian and Burmese forests and can be seen, with hindsight, as the point of departure for the gradual sharpening and sophistication of environmental concerns on the part of both the British government and Indian landholders between 1790 and 1850. This was a phased development which took place with many regional variations, the phases reflecting both shifts in the influence of scientists and changes in the political priorities and sensitivities of the colonial state in India.[37]

The outbreak of the long naval conflict with the French, however, shifted the focus of incipient environmental concern away from Bengal and towards the Malabar Coast. At a relatively early date, the cumulative effect of early commercial deforestation began to be observed with some anxiety by British officials on the west coast. The Malabar forests, particularly after the loss of the American sources of supply after 1776, had come to be heavily drawn upon by both indigenous Indian merchants and the Royal Navy for shipbuilding purposes. Much local naval shipbuilding, especially of the Bombay Marine, was actually carried out by Parsi enterprises.[38] The defeat of Tipu Sultan enormously increased shipbuilding activity and, more important in terms of Indian forest history, for the first time allowed unimpeded access to the forests of Malabar and Mysore and thus to a steady supply of teak.[39]

The ease of access permitted to both British and Indian entrepreneurs under the East India Company as a consequence of the political demise of the old west-coast princedoms was a critical factor in accelerating deforestation. Political division and traditional controls had had the effect of cushioning Indian forests from the increasing pressures imposed by external markets and

Ramnagar Forest establishment and statistical survey returns, including an 1811 account of the Bhil forest tribes, by Captain Morier Williams, all in pp. 67–73; F/4/427 (10478), Reports on the teak plantations at Rampur (Boalia, or Bauleah), by George Ballard and Surgeon William Roxburgh, of July 1812; and two sets of papers on the 1810 surveys of the Malabar forests: F/4/427 (10507), pp. 271–97, and F/4/432 (10543). Further papers regarding the survey and supply of timber for shipbuilding: BL, IOL, Bombay Public Consultations, March 1813 – April 1814, Bom. Pub., 9 March 1815, draft 104, pp. 450–9. Exactly the same process was taking place in the United States, where naval forest reserves were again declared in 1816 after their earlier abandonment at independence; see Hough, 'Preservation of forests', p. 37.

36 Rodger, *Wooden Walls*.
37 For details of the latter, see Bayly, *Rulers, townsmen and Bazaars*, pp. 197–229.
38 Wadia, *The Bombay dockyard and the Wadia masterbuilders*, chaps. 1–2.
39 Rear-Admiral Sir Thomas Trowbridge noted in a letter to Jamsetjee Bomanjee, master shipbuilder at Bombay, on 14 June 1802, 'Timber, I presume, can now be had in abundance from Tippoo's country'; quoted in A. Siddiqi, 'The business world of Jamsedjee Jeejeebhoy', *Indian Economic and Social History Review*, 19 (1983), 302.

small private enterprises. As a single political and colonial entity, India then became much more vulnerable to both externally and internally generated economic and ecological pressures. Perhaps foremost among the latter was the financial stake exerted by Parsis in banking, shipbuilding and internal river traffic. By the late eighteenth century the Parsis were increasingly organising themselves as a body of collaborators working in close association with the agency houses of Bombay and exploiting new opportunities generated by English private and mercantile initiatives. Prominent among these was the collaboration between Jamsedjee and Jardine Matheson. The Pestonji Brothers and Pahis and Company based at Hyderabad also assumed a key role in 1807–20 in opening up the Godavery River for navigation and the adjacent forests for timber cutting.[40]

To some extent the situation in India in 1800 was analogous to that which prevailed in mid-seventeenth-century England as the land market became more fluid and large-scale felling took place.[41] Nevertheless, the English precedent of the Crown forest system, not conspicuously successful at home, was to be even less so at first in India, in part because of the sheer scale and geography of the problem and the power of the economic pressure groups anxious to secure a toehold in previously little-exploited Indian forests, where the ownership status was more nebulous and forests were therefore less protected than in Europe.

The first major European response in Western India to the fear of a naval timber shortage was the foundation of a timber syndicate on the Malabar Coast by surgeon William Maconochie in 1796. This first syndicate soon collapsed.[42] Maconochie's activities, it should be said, were commercial rather than scientific or medical. His initiative was followed, however, by attempts to start other agencies connected purely with the supply of timber for the Navy. These opened, closed and reopened from time to time in largely unsuccessful attempts to conserve the supply of teak from the coast and Ghat uplands of South-Western India.[43] The early history of British management of the teak

---

40 On this, see Siddiqi, 'The business world of Jamsedjee Jeejeebhoy', pp. 301–7.

41 Grove, 'Cressey Dymock and the draining of the Great Level'.

42 B. Ribbentrop, *Forestry in British India*, Calcutta, 1899, p. 62, and E. P. Stebbing, *The forests of India*, vol. 1, Edinburgh, 1922, p. 68.

43 Some of these efforts involved some interesting early species-selective measures to protect young teak trees. For example, in a proclamation of 9 June 1799 issued at Calicut it was noted that 'the government has much at heart to put an end to the very ruinous and wanton practice that prevails in every tract of forests in Malabar of cutting down the young teak trees for domestic and other purposes, but for which there are many other species equally well applicable ... the Commissioners have come to the resolution of prohibiting this practice in future, and to direct that no young teak trees ... under 24 inches in girth are to be cut down after the first of Karcadagom [the rainy season] ... this prohibition is not meant to extend to the

forests of Tenasserim in Burma followed roughly the same pattern.[44] During the late eighteenth and the early nineteenth century a series of timber-working leases were formalised by the East India Company which were to become 'a thorn in the side of' later administrations bent on public control.[45] First attempts to control cutting more specifically than by syndicate control were made by the Bengal–Bombay Joint Commission of the EIC in 1800, which attempted to impose regulations prohibiting the felling of teak below twenty-one inches in girth.[46] This measure, aimed at preventing wholesale clear-felling of forest, imposed virtually no formalised structure specifically to administer the regulations and therefore had little chance of success.[47]

After 1800 the state of the Indian forests became a matter for frequent and detailed strategic discussions in London. Viscount Melville, for example, in a letter to Marquis Wellesley on 4 July 1804 stated his 'conviction that with a view both to military and commercial purposes, this country must one day avail itself of the valuable resources to be had for ship-building in the ports of India'.[48] The state of oak timber, he went on, 'has rendered it a matter of indispensable necessity to look to India for material assistance'. Wellesley, replying from Bombay, asserted that that city remained the best site for ship-building.[49] The best crooked timber for the purpose came 'from Mahratta country between Surat and Bombay, where it is floated down the rivers'. However, Wellesley warned that 'it has . . . of late years become more scarce from the great consumption and dearer, as further away from rivers, and consequently incurring the charge of land carriage'. Straight timber was procured from Malabar through the port of Cochin. But here too exhaustion threatened. 'For my part', Wellesley says, 'I have great doubts if any great quantity of timber large enough for ships of the line is to be expected from Malabar.' He feared that 'consumption of late years (in Hyder's and Tippoo's time), was greater than the means of the country could afford'. One engineer

---

cutting of the other species of timbers of whatever size or growth in the said forests all of which may be cut down and carried away as usual': Diary of Mr Law, assistant in Ernaad taluk, 14 June 1799, quoted in W. Logan, ed., *A collection of treaties, engagements and other papers of importance relating to British affairs in Malabar*, Madras, 1891, p. 318.

44 Ribbentrop, *Forestry*, p. 62.

45 Ibid.

46 Ribbentrop, *Forestry*, p. 64.

47 Ibid.

48 Cambridge University Library, East India Papers, 10/719/40; sect. entitled 'Prince of Wales Island and the building of ships in India', p. 723. Melville noted that Andrew Tate, a ship-builder, had favoured construction in Rangoon, where, he said, 'the country seems to be wonderfully intersected by rivers, which of course must be highly useful in bringing wood to the coast'.

49 The largest ship constructed there, the letter says, was of 1,360 tons.

who surveyed a part of Malabar province 'had never seen the forests' but had 'seen the remains of large trees formerly cut down, and of course some still remaining at the greatest distance from the rivers'.[50]

On these grounds Wellesley suggested that 'several professional men should be sent to ensure a due survey' of the remaining forests, while warning that the 'climate is highly unhealthy and deaths must be expected'. The difficulties involved in extracting desperately needed sources of teak from areas not under company control were constantly referred to in correspondence during 1804. Wellesley pointed out, for example, that there would be 'some difficulty in getting permission from the Mahrattas to introduce European workmen into that part of the country'.[51] Particular difficulty was anticipated in getting hold of crooked teak 'of sufficient dimensions for ships of war'.[52] Philip Dundas, like Wellesley, concluded that 'the forests of Malabar have been nearly exhausted' but that 'the timber trade in Travancore' and Cochin was 'much better'. In fact, Dundas thought that the Travancore forests were 'inexhaustible', an impression probably brought about by the fact that they were intensively managed by the indigenous ruler on a sustainable-yield basis. Morever, as 'Cochin is not likely to fall into the hands of the Dutch, this place is advantageously situated as a general mart of teak timber'. More teak might also, he thought, be 'brought down the Piniary river from the Annamally [Annamalai] woods and the forests in the vicinity of Palghaut which abounds in timber trees'. But Dundas was also considering areas further afield. He noted that 'should it be deemed expedient to establish dock yards at Rangoon or its vicinity our dependence on the north of Europe for maritime stores and timber would be diminished; and we should hope that it would ultimately operate as a preventative to our [British] forests being entirely exhausted'. A shortage of teak, then, increased the political attraction involved in acquiring routes and territory in areas previously uncontrolled by the East India Company. It was this factor, and the possibility of military expansion in 'virgin areas' once exploited by, for example, Hyder Ali, which may have discouraged any embryonic ideas about intensive management of the forests of the west coast at a time when such management was already in place under the Dutch colonial government in Java.[53]

In 1805, the year of Trafalgar, the EIC Court of Directors set up a Forest Committee to consider how far the Navy could depend on its newly acquired supplies of Malabar teak, now highly valued as a raw material for building ships of the line. The committee, as a first step, enquired into proprietary

50 Ibid.
51 Ibid.: Letters, Philip Dundas to Viscount Melville, 21 and 28 June 1804.
52 Ibid., 'Enclosure 1', in Dundas letter of 28 June 1804.
53 See Peluso, 'The history of state forest management in colonial Java'.

rights in the forests. Its reports showed that the capacity of the Malabar Coast forests had been much overrated and that all accessible forest had already been heavily cut through. Further extensive extraction, it was felt, would entail expensive road construction, which would, however, be repaid in terms of an increased asset value for proprietors. In the same year, 1805, it was decided to issue a proclamation vesting in the East India Company itself all royalty rights once claimed by indigenous governments.[54] All further unlicensed felling was to be prohibited. The Forest Committee's findings were based on a memoir drawn up at the request of the governor of Bombay by one Francis Wrede, 'a gentleman from Germany long resident in Malabar'. In this memoir Wrede had argued that 'we are now brought to a crisis'. The company, he said,

> has for these thirteen years past been in possession of Malabar and during that period considerable progress has been made towards improving the administration and exploring the resources of that valuable province . . . the great importance of the teak forests known to exist in the interior part of the province was early a concern and pointed out by the first commissioner and has since been a favourite theme of speculation both in India and at home.[55]

By 1805, Wrede continued, the forests had become a subject of general interest not only to the Court of Directors and the Board of Control, but also to the 'British public at large'. He recommended that a new survey of the Malabar forests be attempted and suggested that the surveyors be accompanied by a surgeon, for health and other reasons. He also suggested that 'since Mr Maconochie [surgeon] had not taken up his post as Naval Architect in the United Kingdom . . . he should be invited to assist'.[56] In fact, it was not until 1810 that a surgeon actually participated in forest surveys. This occurred when surgeon Thomas Palmer was appointed conservator of Malabar during 1810–13 and was made responsible for completing the Malabar surveys.[57] Thus, even at this early stage, German expertise and that of the company medical

---

54 Ribbentrop, *Forestry*, p. 64.

55 BL, IOL, Home Misc. 1/493, LIII, pp. 1051–7, extract from Bombay Public Consultations, 19 Feb. 1805: Report of Herr Wrede, p. 1057.

56 Ibid., pp. 1093–6.

57 BL, IOL, Home Misc. F/4/429 (10507)(1): Paper regarding the survey of the Malabar forests (10508) 1810–13: In this paper surgeon Thomas Palmer is mentioned as 'acting Conservator of Malabar during this period'. Palmer encountered difficulty in having his services fully recompensed, a problem probably arising out of bureaucratic unwillingness to recognise the plurality of the medical and non-medical skills offered by the surgeon. See F/4/429: 'Memorial of Surgeon Thomas Palmer requesting some remuneration for his services as Surgeon to the Department of the Conservator of Forests from August 1804 to October 1813'.

service had proved indispensable to government in forest-conservation matters.

The Forest Committee of 1805 had recognised that regulation would fail without proper enforcement. Under pressure from the Court of Directors, therefore, Captain Watson of the EIC Police Service was appointed 'Conservator of Forests in India', the first holder of any such formalised position under the EIC. Watson was invested with wide-ranging powers, which he used with 'great energy and less discretion'.[58] Within two years he had established an EIC timber monopoly throughout Malabar and part of Travancore, and in so doing disregarded, as Wrede had suggested, all previously existing rights. Wrede had reasoned that

> the dominion of proprietary right of the jungles and every other part of the unoccupied land [sic] and appropriated land found in the province belongs to the Company just as it was possessed by Tippoo and transferred to us, and as in like manner all forests are unquestionably the royalty or property of the Circar in the Travancore and Cochin countries ... at any rate their presupposition of there being a royalty militates for the Company as Sovereign and the *onus probandi* that any part of it is private property lies with the claimants and hitherto none of them has been able to make out his claim in a satisfactory manner nor probably ever will. (p. 1057)

This opinion is useful in demonstrating the degree to which the company was able to rely on indigenous princely precedent in alienating any customary use made of forests. This policy had a dual effect: 'The government had a plentiful and cheap timber supply during his reign and ... a general discontent amongst proprietors as well as traders rose to a [high] pitch.'[59] The early opposition mounted by commercial interests against Watson was a first instance of the kind of strong political lobby which was to be mounted against state conservation efforts by private timber as well as state revenue interests in India throughout the nineteenth century. A fine distinction has to be drawn between the claims supported by Wrede and Maconochie on the part of the company (which were essentially monopolistic and very close to ideas of state control) and those made more successfully between 1815 and 1840 which involved the claims of independent mercantile interests with priorities very different from the company's. In fact, at root four types of claims were extant: those of the company itself; purchased private (Indian and British) claims; those of further concession claimants, mainly based on claims to old indigenous holdings; and those of the rajahs, which were themselves often based on the unilateral arrogation of older common rights for monopoly reasons – that

58 Ribbentrop, *Forestry*, p. 65.
59 Ibid.

is, the first and last claims were essentially of the same variety, as Wrede's report makes clear. All these types of claims ignored the activities of customary forest users, most of whom were poor and possessed no paper rights at all.

The exigencies of the wars with the French prevented the early political success of private and commercial claimants to the forests. However, after 1815 the conservationist position became more vulnerable, and the pioneering timber conservancies came to an end in 1823.[60] In that year the west-coast conservatorship was abolished by the EIC largely as a result of the private views of Sir Thomas Munro and public pressure put upon his office; he recommended to the Supreme Government that forest regulation was more trouble politically than it was worth. Munro himself, as architect of the southern 'Settlement',[61] a scheme designed at the very least to ensure maximum rent returns even in famine years, was certainly not a man to be easily persuaded of the value of forest protection. Besides, carefully documented evidence of forest destruction was not available during the first conservatorship in the way that it came to be during the 1830s. As a result, private timber interests were at an immediate advantage in lobbying.

There is some irony in Munro's role in the dismantling of the early conservancy, even though it was, as Ribbentrop pointed out, a 'probably unjustifiable monopoly'.[62] Munro had closed the conservancy at least partly in the belief that it was fundamentally inequitable, particularly in its trampling of indigenous 'property rights'.[63] In holding an idealised and highly inaccurate view of indigenous landholding, Munro remained blind to the already transforming influx of private timber interests and land grabbers, who had little in common with the pre-1792 dispensation and were ready to take quick advantage of the dismantling of controls and the growth of the market since 1823. Thus Munro wrote in 1823 that the owners of forest rights in Malabar were

> too proud traders not to cultivate teak or whatever wood is likely to yield a profit . . . they are so fond of planting . . . that to encourage them no regulation is wanted, but a free market . . . to restore the liberty of trade in private wood; let the public be guarded by its ancient protector; not a stranger but the Collector or Magistrate of the country, and we shall get all the wood the country can yield more certainly than by any restriction measures. Private timber will be increased by good prices and trade and agriculture be free from vexation.[64]

60 Ibid.
61 Munro was governor of Madras from 1823, the same year in which Elphinstone became governor of Bombay.
62 Ribbentrop, *Forestry*, p. 65.
63 See Thomas Munro, 'Timber monopoly in Malabar and Canara', in A. J. Arbuthnot, ed., *Major-General Sir Thomas Munro: Selections from his official minutes and other writings,*, vol. 1, London, 1881, pp. 178–87.
64 Ribbentrop, *Forestry*, p. 65.

The problem with this romanticist view was that it assumed that the forests were illimitable and that the dictates of capital and the market would encourage economy. That neither proposition was true was psychologically difficult for the anti-monopolist to accept in a continental situation. At any rate, Munro's view at this period was arguably responsible for increasing the rate of deforestation after 1823. Indeed, the dismantling of the early conservancies facilitated, for the first time, the widespread felling of teak forests far inland in Mysore. Ironically, this was an area which had fired Munro's Romantic and lyrical tastes during his first visits to the region, as he made clear in letters to his sister. In one of them he wrote that he spent

> many of my leisure hours on the highest summit of the rock on which the fort stands, under the shady bastion, built by Hyder. The spot has for me a certain charm, which I always feel but cannot easily describe . . . while seated on the rock, I am, or fancy that I am, more thoughtful than when below. The extent and grandeur of the scene raises my mind and the solitude and the silence make me think 'I am conversing with nature here.' To the East I see a romantic, well-cultivated valley leading to the wide plains of the Carnatic. To the south a continuation of the same valley, running as far as the eye can reach, into Mysore. All the rest, on every side, is a vast assemblage of hills and naked rocks, wildly heaped one above the other.[65]

Munro was strongly committed to the continuation of what he construed as an ancient Indian tradition of 'personal government'. At a stroke, nevertheless, he managed to destroy the basics of a conservancy system which, however inequitable, was inherited in all its essentials from the kinds of forest control practised by the coastal rajahs and which he might have been expected to approve of. Certainly in his remarkable essay on the timber monopoly there is no doubt that he accurately foresaw the kinds of popular peasant resistance which strong state forest controls and annexation would be likely to – and did – provoke later in the century. However, he left nothing at all in place of the pre-colonial or 1806 controls, and in so doing laid the groundwork for the unprecedented rates of deforestation which took place in Western India during the next two decades.

In the opening years of this period, an inherent contradiction developed between a naval timber policy which had seen the need for conservation even before 1800, and which continued to advocate one, and the newly emerged priorities of a settled occupying colonial government. The latter set great store by a high and increasing level of agricultural production and the extraction of

---

65 Munro in Ambore to his sister, March 1795: G. R. Gleig, *Life of Sir Thomas Munro*, vol. 1, London, 1830, pp. 86–7, quoted in E. Stokes, *The English Utilitarians and India*, Oxford, 1959, p. 12.

the maximum possible level of peasant land revenue and was unsympathetic at first to the influence of climatic or environmental variables on peasant producers and their working environment. The shift away from an interest in maintaining a firm grip on coastal trading, merchant, banking and timber-extraction concerns towards a position in which the EIC became dominantly concerned with maintaining agrarian land revenues was still a new and significant one in the 1820s. The social and economic consequences of this transition, especially in relation to the destruction of traditional buffers against and responses to crop failure did not emerge fully until later on. Meanwhile, in the 1820s, the likely environmental consequences of deforestation were simply not appreciated by the majority of European observers in India.[66] Thus, although the naval timber-conservation interest on the west coast continued to make its protests during the 1820s, these fell on deaf ears.

The end of the west-coast conservancies spelt the end of conservation attempts based solely on an interest in assuring a supply of timber for state needs. Instead, after 1823, most of the successful conservation initiatives were based primarily on arguments relating to matters other than simple timber depletion. Furthermore, the opinions of scientists gradually became more influential and were more willingly heard than the pleadings of the military and naval boards. After 1823 the focus of concerns about climate and deforestation and timber shortage shifted once more to Bengal. This was primarily an outcome of a localised company interest in the dynamics of climate and famine that had been nurtured by William Roxburgh, first in Madras and then, after 1793, in Bengal. This resulted less in an early interest in conservancy than in a state enthusiasm for tree planting that did not develop in the Bombay Presidency until the 1840s. In order to understand the development of state tree-planting efforts in Madras and Bengal, some appreciation is needed of the evolution of the environmental interests and activities of Roxburgh himself.

Early Scottish Hippocratic responses to ecological crisis in India: William Roxburgh and the study of climate and famine in Madras and Bengal, 1776–1825

A more sophisticated and intellectual response to evidence of deforestation and drought had in fact been developing simultaneously to the worries about naval and other timber shortages which we have already observed in the successor states of the Mughal empire. This had begun in 1776 with the arrival

---

66 Bishop Heber was a rare exception to this rule: R. Heber, *Narrative of a journey through the Upper Provinces of India from Calcutta to Bombay, 1824–5*, London, 1828, p. 274.

of William Roxburgh in Madras after a period spent as a surgeon on company ships. During the ensuing thirty-seven years, until his death in 1813, Roxburgh developed a series of analyses and diagnoses of the dynamics of climate and ecological change in India. All of these were contingent, and even marginal, to his main role as company surgeon, botanist and 'naturalist'. However, Roxburgh was by no means a marginal 'colonial scientist' simply articulating the narrow material interests of the company or colonialism. Instead he can be seen far more accurately as a product of a late Enlightenment interest in meteorology. In this sense he should rightly be placed in a category along with such colonial environmentalists and climate enthusiasts as Alexander Anderson and Pierre Poivre. But he also occupied a place in a scientific mainstream closely connected with such major contemporary figures in the Royal Society as Sir John Pringle and Joseph Banks, as well as other early Linnaeans working in the tropics. Roxburgh identified himself with the strongly dissenting and investigative Warrington Academy school of Joseph Priestley and Johann Reinhold Forster, two men whom he admired and imitated. More specifically, Roxburgh allied himself with the Priestleyite interest in the measurement of atmospheric 'virtue', with all that that implied in terms of attitudes to social and scientific reform and of dissent. In other words, Roxburgh linked the quality and 'virtue' of the atmosphere with the quality of a society. Through his training under John Hope, the Linnaean experimental plant physiologist and curator of the Edinburgh botanical garden, Roxburgh also became a direct inheritor of the ideological agendas of Stephen Hales and Duhamel du Monceau, the two men who had most influenced Hope and about whose theories he lectured in Edinburgh to Roxburgh and his fellow students in the early 1770s.[67] Hope brought Roxburgh, as his star student, into contact with two important networks; those of the Royal Society and the Society of Arts. From the Royal Society Roxburgh took up the contemporary enthusiasm for systematic meteorology, while from Hope and the Society of Arts he adopted a related and life-long interest in tree planting.[68]

As a company surgeon, Roxburgh integrated these meteorological and arboricultural programmes into a more specifically medical discourse and made them part of a programme of interventionist interaction with the tropical environment which he developed after 1776. Finally, he became a pioneer in the collection of tropical meteorological data, to an extent unrivalled elsewhere until the 1820s except among indigenous Chinese observers. It was detailed measurements over many years that facilitated his diagnosis of climate change

---

67 H. R. Fletcher and W. H. Brown, *The Royal Botanic Garden, Edinburgh, 1670–1970*, Edinburgh, 1970.
68 Later recognised by the Society with the award of a medal.

and famine incidence, the basis for his more generalised critique of the colonial impact on the Indian environment.[69]

A major 'centre of calculation' encouraging the collection of meteorological data was the Royal Society itself. The Society's connections with systematic meteorology dated back to 1723 and were in origin closely connected to the discoveries of Hales and the publication of *Vegetable Staticks*. In 1724 Junius Jurin, a close colleague of Isaac Newton, had published *Invitatio ad observationis meteorologicas communi consilio instituendes* in London. This appeal for data resulted in the submission of temperature and rainfall records from places as far apart as St Petersburg, the state of Massachusetts and, not least, Bengal, where some company servants had been directly involved. While important for the Royal Society as an exercise in initiating a data-collection network, these pioneering efforts were effectively disrupted by the wars of the mid eighteenth century.[70] However, after about 1770 an interest in meteorology and meteorological networks quite abruptly arose again. This time the motivation behind them was more directly connected with a widespread shift in Europe towards the collection of systematic data as a part of wider state policy, and it was more medically oriented. In essence, medical and agricultural climatology became institutionalised as European states increasingly intervened in matters of public and health welfare. In France, for example, a national network of observers was established in 1778 under the auspices of the Société Royale de Médecine, and contemporaries spoke of meteorology as 'a new science'.[71]

The work of two researchers contributed to the revival of meteorology after 1770: Jean Deluc's 1772 *Recherches sur les modifications de l'atmosphère* and Joseph Priestley's 'Observations on different kinds of air', also published in 1772. The dissenting and reformist connotations of Priestley's work meant that from 1772 onwards British meteorology involved a radical set of agendas at least as strong as the climatic 'moral economy' implicit in the ideas of Poivre and his physiocratic colleagues in Paris. Roxburgh could not have avoided the social messages of this meteorological radicalism and, indeed, seems to have embraced them with enthusiasm in a tropical region where meteorological fluctuations were so much more extreme than in Europe (and often fatal in their consequences) and where they therefore might be interpreted as signi-

---

69 Note that neither Poivre nor Anderson collected discrete and systematic meteorological data, while Banks and Beatson commenced collection of rainfall data on St Helena only after 1811.

70 Feldman, 'Late Enlightenment meteorology', in T. Frangsmyr, J. L. Heilbronn, and R. E. Rider, eds., *The quantifying spirit in the eighteenth century*, Berkeley and Los Angeles, 1990, p. 147.

71 Ibid. As far as methods were concerned, this revival in meteorology was based on the botanico-meteorological work of Duhamel du Monceau, whose influence on Mauritius and on John Hope has already been noted.

fying far more important social lessons. Roxburgh, like his compatriot on St Vincent Alexander Anderson, also became sharply aware of the new moral significance ascribed by their joint mentor, Sir John Pringle, to the atmospheric function of vegetation as it could now be interpreted in the light of Priestley's findings. Pringle, as we have seen, placed Priestley's pneumatics in the context of the aerial system of fevers and also linked it with the model of a benevolent economy which Priestley had begun to map. 'From these [Priestley's] discoveries we are assured that . . . every individual plant is serviceable to mankind, if not always distinguished by some private virtue, yet making a part of the whole which cleanses and purifies our atmosphere.' Storms and tempests (i.e. extreme meteorological events) would shake the 'waters and the air together to bury in the deep those putrid and pestilential effluvia which the vegetables upon the face of the earth have been insufficient to consume'.[72] The importance of this line of thinking to the later development of climatic environmentalism can hardly be overemphasised, as it became an essential part of the link made between environment and reformist notions of moral economy among Scottish surgeons in the Indian medical services.

While on St Vincent, Anderson eventually followed the implications of Pringle's sweeping environmentalist dictums (as relayed by Edward Long) by seeking to protect existing natural forests. Roxburgh, for his part, intended to go one significant stage further in India by cultivating new plantations and implicitly thereby serving mankind by purifying the atmosphere and increasing the social 'virtues' represented by the survival or renewal of vegetation. The gradual unfolding of Roxburgh's Priestleyite environmental programme (among many other activities, mainly botanical) can be identified almost from the date of his arrival in Madras in 1776. In that year he began a series of meteorological observations for the Coromandel Coast (using a Nairne thermometer and Ramsden barometer) which remained unbroken until his posting to Calcutta in 1793. Logic dictated that Roxburgh should send his observations back to the Royal Society, and he duly sent his records for 1777–9 to Sir John Pringle, thereby reaffirming the theoretical and ideological basis for the observations and incorporating the Indian environment into the ambit of the dissenting and reformist networks of Priestley and his associates. There were in fact great practical difficulties of time and space involved, and a letter from Roxburgh to Banks in 1782 indicates that many of the records which he sent to Pringle in London were lost en route.[73] However, Pringle ensured that

---

72 Sir John Pringle, quoted in Douglas McKie, 'Joseph Priestley and the Copley Medal', *Ambix*, 9 (1961), 1–22. See also Priestley, 'On the noxious quality of the effluvia of putrid marshes'.
73 Roxburgh to Banks, letter, 10 Dec. 1782, in *Banks letters*, p. 714. Roxburgh asked if Surgeon Sharpe could be commissioned to carry copies of weather records to John Pringle in London after the loss of earlier copies. Roxburgh had begun a correspondence with Banks in 1779,

Roxburgh's first sets of weather records from the Madras Presidency were prominently published in *Philosophical Transactions of the Royal Society* in 1778 and then much later in 1790.

During his first few years of residence in the Madras Presidency, Roxburgh spent much of his time as a surgeon at Nagore and in supervising the construction of an acclimatisation and botanical garden at Samulcottah, north of Madras.[74] Here he embarked on a long run of plant-transfer and tree-planting experiments, very much on physiocratic lines.[75] It was while resident at Nagore between 1778 and 1780 that Roxburgh first became interested in the interconnections between drought and famine. In times of scarcity, he noted, the supply of coconuts (a major food item) from Ceylon quickly dried up. He therefore advocated company sponsorship of food-tree planting along canal banks and village streets to secure supplies from coconut, sago, date, and palmyra palms as well as from plantain, jackfruit, breadfruit and opuntia trees.

Meanwhile Roxburgh's meticulous record keeping meant that he obtained a very detailed empirical view of the local impact of the globally occurring droughts that took place in 1787–92 and that particularly affected semi-arid zones in India, West Africa and the Caribbean. These drought episodes were almost certainly caused by an unusually strong El Niño phase in the current off the west coast of South America. This current is now believed to be the single most effective variable in controlling annual fluctuations in global atmospheric circulation and in particular the strength and incidence of the Indian Ocean monsoon.[76] In 1791 the world experienced one of its strongest known El Niño episodes.[77] Already devastated by a famine in 1780, the Circars of the Madras Presidency were again very badly affected in 1789–92, and many villages in the Godavery delta were entirely depopulated. The famine was much discussed in Europe; Edmund Burke referred to it. Roxburgh made a particular point of praising pre-colonial irrigation methods and, like Burke, believed that the EIC was largely responsible for the decline in artificial irrigation and for the increased vulnerability to famine that resulted from periods of drought. While there is no proof that Roxburgh was actually aware of Burke's critique of the company in this respect, there is no question that both

informing him of the research journey to the Malacca Strait and Siam being undertaken by Johann Koenig for the EIC.

74 Samulcottah is a small station about seven miles from Coconada and twenty-seven miles from the mouth of the Godavery River.

75 According to George King, he introduced coffee, cinnamon, nutmeg, arnotto and sappan wood as well as the breadfruit tree, the mulberry tree and various kinds of pepper vines. He also experimented with sugar cane.

76 Quinn and Neal, 'El Niño occurrences over the past four and a half centuries'.

77 The strength of the 1791 El Niño was recorded by, among other authorities, J. H. Unanue, in *El clima de Lima*, Madrid, 1815.

men belonged to the same party in this case.[78] In fact, since 1782, according to Buchanan, rainfall levels had deteriorated steadily in South-East India. This decline had been noticed by Roxburgh and had in fact led him to speculate on the periodicity of drought events and to compare the severity of the late 1780s rainfall deficit with that of earlier periods. The results of these investigations were reported to the company in 1793.[79] 'There are but few, if any', Roxburgh wrote, 'of the lower Maritime Provinces of India that are not subject to (I dare scarce venture to say periodical, because our knowledge of meteorological facts is but as yet very imperfect) visitations of drought, more or less according to unknown circumstances.' In recent years, he added, 'we have seen and heard of the dreadful effects of such droughts prevailing over many parts of Asia'. It was sufficient, he carried on, 'for my purpose to take notice of that which has taken place in the Circars for no less than three years successively, to the dreadful effects of which I have been a constant Eyewitness'. As noted in Chapter 7 the seriousness of the drought in Southern India was communicated by James Anderson, the curator of the Madras Nopalry garden, to Robert Kyd in Calcutta, in a communication which came to the notice of Alexander Beatson on St Helena some years later.[80] However, while this networking was important (particularly in its effect on Beatson's thinking), Roxburgh's response was far more practically significant. In essence it fell into three parts. First, he became interested in placing the 1789–93 droughts in an historical and chronological context. Secondly, he sought to blame the nature of zamindari landlordship as it had been reconstructed by the company for the seriousness of the famine that resulted from the drought. Thirdly, the famine increased his interest in planting trees both to provide famine foods and to try to increase the incidence of rainfall. This last concern would have been further stimulated as knowledge of the passing on St Vincent of the King's Hill Forest Act of 1791 started to get around among East India Company officials.

By taking an interest in the history of Indian droughts, a logical outcome of his meteorological interests, Roxburgh soon became aware of a comparable drought period one hundred years earlier, in the period 1685–8.[81] He actively

---

78 See Edmund Burke, 'Speech on the Nabob of Arcot's debts', 28 Feb. 1785, reprinted in P. Marshall, ed., *The writings and speeches of Edmund Burke*, vol. 5, Oxford, 1981.

79 William Roxburgh, 'Suggestions on the introduction of such useful trees, shrubs and other plants as are deemed the most likely to yield sustenance to the poorer classes of natives of these provinces during times of scarcity', report to President's Council, Tamil Nadu State Archives, Public Consultations, vol. CLXXXi, 8 Feb. 1793.

80 Beatson, *Tracts*, p. 15. See Chapter 7.

81 This drought, too, appears to correlate with a strong El Niño episode. See Quinn and Neal, 'El Niño'. On this occasion, according to Roxburgh, the climatic perturbation involved three exceptionally wet years followed by three very dry years.

sought out documentary and oral evidence of these earlier droughts, finding a rich source of material in an informant whom he refers to as 'the Rajah of Pittenpore's family Brahmen'.[82] This informant had found among 'the records of his grandfather an account of a most dreadful famine which prevailed over the northern provinces' during the years 1685 to 1687. During the last year 'only one shower fell', and 'very few people survived these three years'. Roxburgh noted, too, the incidence of lesser famines in other years, especially in 1737. But the severity of famine in the 1680s and 1780s seems to have made a deep impression on him, much as the 1770 famine had on Robert Kyd. The scale of mortality involved meant, he thought, that the government would have to address the issue by reforming land ownership and by tree planting. 'I fear', he commented, 'that no great deal of good can be done while the present system of renting the lands of these provinces prevails, viz., that the Sower scarcely knows whether he will reap or not, and if he mends the Bank of a water course or digs a well, he knows not but it may be for the benefit of another.' Government would have to restore permanent title to the ryots (peasants), he thought, 'that we may hope soonest to see resources for the Poor, hitherto unknown in these parts, springing up'.[83] In fact, on paper the Madras government approved these suggestions, resolving to 'procure cocoa-nuts from Colombo, sago-palms from Travancore and bread-fruit from the Nicobars for sowing and planting'.[84]

Shortly after submitting his famine report to the Madras government, Roxburgh was transferred to Calcutta as director of the botanical garden upon the death of Kyd. This meant that his policy initiatives for food security, land reform and tree planting on the Coromandel Coast were interrupted. Nevertheless, there were plenty of opportunities to develop such physiocratic policies in Bengal. In particular Roxburgh set about improving on Kyd's teak-planting experiments and expanding them into a fully developed plantation programme in Bengal, Bihar and Orissa. To aid him in this, he brought with him large supplies of teak seeds from Rajahmundry.[85] Between 1793 and 1813 (when Roxburgh died) the plantation programme was steadily expanded, and it continued to be enlarged by Nathaniel Wallich after Roxburgh's death. As the first planted trees started to mature, after about 1805, Roxburgh began to write papers dealing with their growth and comparing it with that character-istic of natural teak stands.[86] At least one of these papers was reprinted in

82 'Note' in Roxburgh, 'Suggestions' (see n. 79).
83 For further details of this, see Roxburgh correspondence quoted in Love, *Vestiges of Old Madras*, II, p. 410.
84 Ibid.
85 NAI, Fort William–India House Correspondence, p. 230: Letter from Roxburgh to Court of Directors, 7 Mar. 1796.
86 'A table of the growth of trees in the botanic garden at Calcutta', *Nicholson's Journal*, 17

Transactions of the Royal Society of Arts and is indicative of the close relationship which Roxburgh maintained with this society, its tree-planting campaigns and its environmentalist personalities. Roxburgh did not, in fact, drop his meteorological interests during this period, becoming particularly concerned with the provenance of the seasonal drying winds which caused so much agrarian havoc in deforested landscapes. Significantly, he published the results of these researches in medical journals.[87]

There are two main points to be made about Roxburgh's Bengal plantation initiatives. While undoubtedly additionally stimulated by the general ship and urban timber shortage in Bengal, the climatic and medical motivations for tree-planting activity which had first affected Roxburgh in Coromandel were still important. Secondly, the plantation methods he adopted were developed by him in India and were not derived from German or other European precedents. Indeed, Roxburgh's plantation methods predate most comparable German methods and owed nothing to them. Georg Hartig's standard German texts on forestry science, for example, postdate Roxburgh's first methodically organised plantations in Bengal by more than ten years.[88] This is not surprising, since the soil and weather conditions in Bengal could hardly have been more different from those of Central Europe. Instead Roxburgh relied heavily on indigenous skills and advice to develop the plantations, and the extant records reveal the considerable difficulties experienced before plantings were successful.[89] The most important of these experiments took place in the large forest reserves at Bauleah in Bengal.[90] By 1812 the experimental area was large, being some 715 bighas in size.[91] Roxburgh's early experiments must have been a success, since as early as 1798 he had decided to extend teak planting to Bihar, a development which the Calcutta authorities were quick to boast about

---

(1807), 110–11, 'Letters on various productions of the East Indies', ibid., 27 (1810), 69–76, and 'Some account of the teak tree of the East Indies', ibid., 33 (1812), 348–54 (the last paper was reprinted in *Transactions of the Royal Society of Arts*, vol. 30).

87 See, for example, 'Remarks on the land winds and their causes', *Transactions of the London Medical Society*, 1 (1810), 189–211.

88 Georg Ludwig Hartig, *Grundsätze der Forst-Direction*, Weimar, 1803. See also Henry E. Lowood, 'The calculating forester: Quantification, cameral science and the emergence of scientific forestry management in Germany', in Frangsmyr, Heilbronn, and Rider, *The quantifying spirit in the eighteenth century*, pp. 315–42.

89 NAI, Fort William–India House Correspondence, vol. 13, p. 31: 'Letter transmitting report of Dr Roxburgh on the teak tree with his request to be furnished annually with certain plants and seeds'.

90 BL, IOL, F/4/427 (10478): Reports on teak plantations at Bauleah by George Ballard and William Roxburgh, 1812.

91 For details of Roxburgh's experiments in plantation methods at Bauleah, see NAI, Home Public Consultation Letters, letter, 23 Oct. 1812: E. Barnett (Acting Collector of Bauleah) to Richard Rocke, Acting President and member of the Board of Revenue, Fort William, Calcutta. A bigha is about two-thirds of an acre.

to the Directors in London.[92] By 1813 further plantations had been established at Cuttack in Orissa and in outlying districts of North-West Bengal and Bihar.[93] Sometimes the police service was used as a convenient conduit for the supply of seeds and trees.[94] At other times in the period 1812–17 seed was provided direct to selected zamindars to make plantations at their own discretion, an idea that seems to have been taken up in several parts of Bengal. Other supplies of seeds and saplings were sent to the botanical gardens at Saharunpore and Agra, to 'Mr Gardner at Khatmandu', to the 'Vizier' at Lucknow and to stations as far off as the Ceded Provinces.[95] By 1817 some of the plantations set up by Roxburgh were being supplied with large allocations of convict labour, a development which he might not have approved of.

By the time Nathaniel Wallich took over as superintendent of the Calcutta Botanic Garden in 1816, a very extensive tree-supply and arboricultural information network had been set up based in Calcutta and stretching between Delhi in the East, Kathmandu in the North and Cuttack in the South. The Plantation Committee set up in 1823 by Wallich and the Marquis of Hastings was predicated on this network and provided the basis for an arboricultural role in government at a time when forest conservancy had been almost entirely abandoned on the west coast of India. However, the limitations of the plantation arboriculture established by Roxburgh need to be appreciated. Although convinced of a relationship between trees and the atmosphere, Roxburgh does not seem to have been able to conceive of climatic variation taking place on a *regional* basis, even though he could appreciate and apparently measure climatic changes in terms of observations at single geographical points. The critical transition to apprehending the possibility of actually measuring regional change probably required the kind of approach described in 1817 by Humboldt in his advocacy of the isotherm as a means to describe continental climates.[96]

92 NAI, Home Public Consultations: Letter, 31 Jan. 1798, Fort William, to Court of Directors: 'Considerable quantities of [teak] seeds have been sent to parts of Bengal and Berar.'
93 Ibid., External Revenue Dept: letter, 22 May 1813 (received 23 June), telling the Botanic Garden superintendent to take measures for disseminating the cultivation of the teak tree in the district of Cuttack; see also letter, 2 Oct. 1813 (received 11 Oct.), 'relative to cultivation of the teak tree in various districts'.
94 NAI, Home Public Consultations: letter of 14 Feb. 1817: 'Reply to orders, has selected and forwarded to the Superintendent of Police in the Western Provinces a quantity of teak seeds, with a copy of directions to forward the object contemplated.'
95 Ibid., Botanic Garden Letters, 1816–17. Supplies of trees were sometimes used as diplomatic presents by the company, as in 1811, when the Royal Gardens in Delhi were supplied with trees from Calcutta (letter, received 21 June, from External Political Dept to Supt, Botanic Garden, Calcutta).
96 Alexander von Humboldt, 'Sur les line isothermes et la distribution de la chaleur sur le globe',

By the time of his death in 1813, Roxburgh had formulated a Hippocratic and Priestleyite response to famine, timber shortages and deforestation, converting it to his own very unusual arboricultural strategy. While the strategy was widely accepted in company circles, which were apparently easily persuaded of the validity of Roxburgh's ideas, a philosophy which connected tree cover with atmospheric and medical 'virtue' actually ran counter to emerging currents in the medical and epidemiological thinking of the time – although such thinking was, admittedly, highly ambivalent with regard to the health benefits of forests. In 1807, for example, James Johnson (like Roxburgh an ex-naval surgeon), the most popular medical writer on climate and disease in India before 1850, remarked approvingly of the efforts being made on St Helena 'to spread vegetation and plant trees' to increase the availability of moisture.[97] But by 1818 Johnson had entirely changed his tune and warned unequivocally that 'mountain countries with trees give rise to fevers' and that miasmic poisons adhered to 'lofty umbrageous trees'.[98] Precisely at the time when the extensions of plantations were being planned by Roxburgh and company authorities near Calcutta, Johnson warned that 'all forests around Calcutta should be cleared'.[99] Similarly, the Western and Eastern Ghauts [mountains] of India, he said, were 'the origins of miasmata'. As the inheritor of Roxburgh's policy, Nathaniel Wallich ignored the Johnsonian theories of forest miasmata. Moreover, he had powerful political allies who also took the Roxburgh line on the benefits of trees, not least of these being Bishop Heber, a close friend of Roxburgh's and a devotee of his atmospheric philosophy. Heber it was who composed the eulogy to Roxburgh on the monument at the foot of the great banyan tree in the Calcutta Botanical Garden.[100]

A few years later, in 1824, Heber followed Roxburgh by criticising the reckless speed of deforestation in Kumaon and the Siwalik tracts for aesthetic and agricultural reasons, and on grounds which Wallich had not himself cared to utilise with government. 'Great devastations', Heber believed,

> are made in these woods, partly by the increased population, building and agriculture, partly by the wasteful habits of travellers, who cut down multitudes of young trees to make temporary huts, and for fuel, while the cattle and goats which browse on the mountains prevent a great part of the seedlings from rising. Unless some precautions are taken, the uninhabited parts of Kumaon will soon be wretchedly bare of wood and the

Mémoires de la Société d'Arcueil, 3 (1817), 462–602, quoted in Feldman, 'Late Enlightenment meteorology', p. 177.

97 J. Johnson, *The Oriental voyager*, London, 1807, pp. 380–2.

98 J. Johnson, *The influence of tropical climates on European constitutions*, London, 1813 (repr. 1818, 1827), p. 93.

99 Ibid., p. 71.

100 King, 'Memoir on William Roxburgh'.

country, already too arid, will not only lose its beauty, but its small space
of fertility.[101]

The complex scientific and symbolic loading of the botanical garden as an
institution, which in India had distinctive Mughal antecedents, provided the
practical infrastructure for a new-found appreciation of the vulnerability of
the environment to human action. This new appreciation was guided, as it
had been on Mauritius and St Vincent, by a strong medical preoccupation
with the workings and interdependence of environmental factors and human
health, underpinned by a growing awareness of the pharmacological significance of tropical plant species.[102] While encouraged by the state, ostensibly
for economic and commercial reasons, the botanical garden continued to encompass less openly expressed notions of the tropical environment as a paradise, botanical or otherwise, which most professional botanists were keen to
protect. It is true that the connections between paradisal ideas and botanical
or experimental gardens had actually been more pronounced in the Mughal
period. Indeed, the ancient Farsi term for an ornamental garden was 'para-
daeza'. However, many EIC gardens were, in fact, founded on the sites of
older Mughal imperial gardens. The garden at Saharanpur, revivified by the
Marquis of Hastings and J. Forbes-Royle, was an early example. Furthermore,
paradisal notions continued into the company period, albeit entirely Euro-
peanised in conception. Thus Heber had written of the Calcutta Botanic Garden at Sibpur that it was

> a very beautiful and well managed institution, enriched besides the noblest
> trees and most beautiful plants of India, with a vast collection of exotics,
> chiefly collected by Dr Wallich himself in Nepaul, Sumatra and Java and
> increased by contributions from the Cape, Brazil, and many different
> parts of Africa and America, as well as Australasia, and the South Sea
> Islands. It is not only a curious but a picturesque and most beautiful
> scene, and more perfectly answers Milton's idea of Paradise except that
> it is on a dead flat instead of a hill, than anything which I ever saw.

101 Heber, *Narrative*, p. 274. The reference to the 'beauty' of the country, as well as its physical
     state, is noteworthy here; according to Charlton, *New images of the natural*, p. 80, Heber was
     a pioneering inheritor of those French writers (especially Bernardin de Saint-Pierre) who
     appealed to nature's creativity as evidence of the existence of God as a loving, providing
     father. Such notions helped to increase the sensitivity of Europeans to landscape change.
102 A recognition of the pharmacological potential of tropical forest species in undisturbed forest
     is an extension of this idea and is especially apparent in H. Cleghorn, F. Royle, R. Baird-
     Smith and R. Strachey, 'Report of the committee appointed by the British Association to
     consider the probable effects in an economical and physical point of view of the destruction
     of tropical forests', *Report of the Proceedings of the British Association for the Advancement of
     Science*, 1852, pp. 78–102.

One can see here that, with Heber, the notion of the creation of an earthly paradise made up of plants derived from the 'four quarters of the world' was still very much alive.[103] It is no coincidence, perhaps, that it was Heber who had first clearly articulated anxieties about the rates of deforestation and possible aridification in Northern India during the 1820s.[104] However, the paradisal connotations of the botanical garden and its historical and textual connections with both Mughal and western Edenic discourses are not sufficient to explain the emerging environmentalism of the company medical service. It required an acquaintance both with Priestley's atmospheric theories and with the holistic conceptions of German Romantic science (and Humboldtian ideas in particular – themselves strongly connected with an emergent Orientalist 'Indic' knowledge) to give the Scottish surgeons of the EIC Medical Service the powerful arguments they needed to solicit state protection of the environment.

The career of Nathaniel Wallich well exemplifies these connections.[105] Once he was firmly established as superintendent of the Calcutta garden in 1817, the mere longevity of Wallich in office assured him the ear of the authorities.[106] Wallich was particularly impressed by Roxburgh's plantation efforts and moved quickly to replicate and institutionalise them, bringing about the formation of a Plantation Committee, chaired by the governor-general, in 1823. This method of formalising plantation activities seems to have been stimulated

---

103 Heber, *Narrative*, pp. 39–40. See also N. M. Titley, *Plants and gardens in Persian, Mughal and Turkish art*, London, 1979.

104 It should be recalled that the Calcutta Botanic Garden had also exercised a powerful formative impression in Humboldt's mind. See Chapter 4.

105 Nathaniel Wallich (1786–1854) was thirty years old when he assumed control of the Calcutta Botanic Garden, and he remained in charge until 1846, when he was succeeded by Hugh Falconer. Vicziany states that 'it never occurred to the Company that Wallich be asked to complete Buchanan's survey of Bengal because he simply lacked the talent for such a complex task' ('Imperialism, botany and statistics', p. 55 n. 127). Sir William Hooker, however, wrote that 'this gentleman, a pupil of the celebrated Hornemann of Copenhagen, entered upon the duties of office with an ardour which has rarely been excelled in any country and which has certainly never been equalled in a tropical climate': Review of *Illustrations of Indian botany*, *Hooker's Botanical Miscellany*, 1831, pp. 90–7. Heber, for his part, reported that Wallich was 'the epitome of all frankness . . . and creative zeal for the source of science, the last enriched by a greater source of curious information relating to India and the neighbouring countries than any which I have met with': *Narrative*, p. 40.

106 The relationship between the botanical-garden system in India and the EIC Medical Service had become formalised in 1793 with the appointment of Roxburgh as director of the Calcutta Botanic Garden in succession to Kyd. By 1814 the Sibpur/Calcutta garden contained 3,500 specimens. In 1831 Hooker wrote, 'The circumstances of Dr Wallich being appointed as successor to Dr Hamilton [Buchanan-Hamilton] to the Superintendence of the Calcutta Botanic Garden constitutes a new era in the Botany of India': *Hooker's Botanical Miscellany*, 1831, pp. i–ix (editorial).

by a run of correspondence in 1819 between the Marine Board at Calcutta and the Bombay government. These letters indicate the scale of difficulty involved in transporting coir and timber from the west coast to Bengal for particular shipbuilding projects, so that any state activity to encourage the timber supply must have seemed attractive.[107]

Wallich also intended the Plantation Committee to cope with a severe shortage of sissoo (*Dalbergia Sissoo*) and bamboo in rural areas of Bengal, a shortage which he considered a 'formidable evil', as 'bamboo is the universal building material for the lower orders of the natives of India', and 'a good sized bamboo has not been for many years procurable in Bengal'.[108] According to Wallich, Calcutta's construction and firewood needs had long been supplied from the Moorshedabad area. However, in 1815–16 the bamboo jungle had been 'cut down as it was supposed to be the cause of local epidemics'. Wallich clearly scorned this apparently Johnsonian forest clearing and pointed out that 'in the first place the sickness was not remedied'. It would be far better, he believed, to follow the example of the judicious 'Rajahs of Rampore and Rohilcund', who had carefully protected bamboo forests and plantations to cater for local needs. Otherwise, he thought, it would be necessary to import bamboo from the Mattaban coast of Burma. By articulating these views, Wallich brought about a distinctive 'social forestry' based on indigenous precedents and apparently concerned for the basic needs of the poorer rural communities. His ideas were taken up by government, although without a great deal of enthusiasm. In 1822 the Bengal Public Works Department took over Roxburgh's old plantations at Bauleah, Sylhet and the Jungle Mahals (in Eastern Chotanagpur) to continue planting teak, while adding sissoo and saul (*Shorea/robusta*) species to the plantations.[109] A year later Wallich formed the Plantation Committee to further develop the concept and provide assured finance for plantation staff. One immediate result of its proceedings was that Wallich's expertise in all matters relating to botany, forests and arboriculture was now recognised at the highest level.[110] This, along with the government's direct

---

107 NAI, Home Public Consultations, 1819, letters, 12 March (on despatch of coir and timber from Mangalore to Calcutta) and 20 July (from Marine Board on timber for Bengal for buoys and light vessels).

108 Nathaniel Wallich in House of Commons Select East India Committee cross-examination, 14 Aug. 1832, by T. H. Villiers, in *Parliamentary papers relating to the East Indies*, X, pt 1, pp. 193ff, esp. paras. 2335–43.

109 Ibid., 10/719/40, p. 771, 'Appendix'.

110 Dr H. F. C. Cleghorn noted in 1852: 'Three MS volumes of proceedings and reports, with two original maps of the route taken by Dr Wallich and Capt. Satchwell were placed by the Supreme Government with the Agricultural and Horticultural Society "for information and deposit". These volumes contain the labours of a body of public officers which, under the denomination of the "Plantation Committee", originated under the Marquis of Hastings and continued in existence six years. The records of its proceedings, as contained in these vol-

involvement in plantations, ensured that the superintendent's opinions were
eagerly sought as the timber shortage became more serious throughout India
in the late 1820s and early 1830s.

Before this, however, one early significant outcome of the Plantation Committee's work was the stimulus it gave to efforts to incorporate tree-planting
schemes in the canal-building projects which Hastings had encouraged. Here
plantations served a dual purpose: in bank stabilisation and in provision of
firewood. More important, tree cover came at this stage to be associated in
the official mind, even if only loosely, with the retention of water in local
water-tables.[111]

Wallich's consultative role was developed further in 1825 when he was
appointed to make a survey and report on the submontane forests of Oudh,
which were said to be undergoing extensive depredation.[112] This had caused
some anxiety in Calcutta, where shortages of firewood and construction timber
in the environs of this rapidly growing colonial capital had been a matter of
official concern since the 1760s. Wallich's consultancy was the first of a series

umes, extend over 1070 pages of manuscript. They contain much and most valuable, indeed
generally unknown information bearing on the great practical measure of forest cultivation
. . . the Sissoo localities in particular, and every effort should be made to preserve this information from destruction. The late Dr Spry [the author of *Modern India*,] Secretary of the
Agricultural and Horticultural Society, was desired to undertake the examination of these
records and favour the society with a report upon their contents.' Unfortunately, this was
never done, owing to Spry's untimely death, and I have not to date traced the Plantation
Committee records. Nevertheless, their contents were instrumental in persuading Dr Ryan,
Spry's successor as secretary, to campaign for forest conservation on the basis of an imminent
firewood crisis during 1841 (the same year as J. F. Royle, surgeon and later superintendent
of the Saharanpur Botanic Gardens, was advocating state forest protection in his *Productive
Resources of India*), thus aiding Alexander Gibson in his similar efforts. See Cleghorn et al.,
'Report of the committee', and Royle, *Essay on the productive resources of India*, London, 1840,
pp. 98–104.

111 There is an important, although tenuous, connection through the Marquis of Hastings among
canal reconstruction, the early fostering of botanical gardens and later advocates of conservation. In 1821 Hastings visited the North-West Province. The reconstructed canal carrying
water to Delhi was the primary interest of the expedition, and Hastings visited Saharanpur
at its head. Here his attention was drawn to a neglected 'fruit-garden' which had been
founded by Zabita Khan, the son of Najib ud-Daula, with the revenue of seven villages for
its maintenance. This had been reduced by the Marathas, who were less interested in botanical gardens (an interest of Persian origin in the case of Zabita Khan); the function of the
garden had been the encouragement of economic plants, especially fruit trees. Hastings decided to restore it and appointed George Govan, the EIC civil surgeon at Saharanpur, as
superintendent, to be succeeded by J. F. Royle in 1823. Royle, incidentally, had deliberately
chosen the medical profession for the purpose of pursuing his botanical interests. Saharanpur
was then used by Wallich as the forward base for his extensive surveys of Oudh, the Himalaya
foothills and the Terai. See Burkill, *Chapters*, pp. 31–3.

112 Stebbing, *Forests*, p. 126.

of assignments he fulfilled between 1825 and 1827 in Oudh and then further afield in Burma. In 1826 he was required to make an ascent of the Irrawaddy and report on the state of forests there, while in 1827 he had to travel up the Salween and Ataran rivers to their headwaters.[113] The recommendations made by Wallich after his Oudh expeditions are worthy of special attention, although their full implications were ignored by government at the time. In essence Wallich argued for extensive state intervention to save the forests in areas he had visited. Many of the forests of the Himalayan foothills were open to 'wanton destruction' and 'in every way deserving of being preserved for the exclusive use of government', which, Wallich thought, should 'interfere in the management of the forests'.[114] In this way a project that had been intended by government essentially as an auditing exercise after the attainment of (or the contemplation of, in the case of Oudh) full political control was converted by Wallich into an exercise in the advocacy of interventionism. The time was not yet ripe for interventionist prescriptions, however, and Wallich's ideas were ignored, so that, insofar as policy was concerned, he remained for a long time a conservationist voice crying in the wilderness.

From hindsight, part of the reason for this impasse lay in Wallich's apparent decision not to utilise arguments other than those concerning prospective timber shortages, irrespective of his own motives for advocating forest protection, which undoubtedly were far wider than considerations of the state timber supply and which were largely inherited from Roxburgh. Furthermore, Wallich apparently thought he lacked any credible scientific basis or statistical data to question government policy with respect to forests. This is perhaps surprising, since the Bengal government itself had experienced great difficulty in obtaining timber supplies in Bengal. However, the colonial state still appeared to think it might import timber from further afield.

But there was another factor. After the departure of the Marquis of Hastings, the EIC had become far less disposed than before to believe that the kind of scientific botany of which the Calcutta Botanic Garden was a symbol was really being of any substantial economic benefit. To this extent, Banks's successful and, arguably, dishonest advocacy of economic arguments with government had begun to fall flat. Thus in 1830 an EIC Retrenchment Committee

---

113 Burkill, *Chapters*, p. 34.
114 Reported in Royle, *Productive resources of India*, p. 189. Royle also noted: 'In his visit to the Terai . . . he particularly recommends a vast extent of forest-land in Oude, situated in the east side of the Kaureola river, and holding out the prospect of very valuable supplies, provided that means are adopted for preventing wanton depredation, and of allowing the young plants to grow up and take the place of those cut down.' While little notice was taken of Wallich's conservationist ideas during the 1820s, Royle's publication of part of his report in 1840 in a book widely read in official circles undoubtedly assisted Alexander Gibson in his later propagandisation of conservationist ideas as a servant of the Bombay government.

actually recommended that funding for the Botanic Garden should be heavily reduced. Similar moves were made in connection with the Dapoorie garden at Bombay a few years later.[115] It has, of course, been argued by Lucille Brockway that local colonial aims and policy on botanical gardens were firmly linked in objectives and ideology.[116] The successive attempts made by the EIC to reduce funding for the botanical gardens, or to eliminate it altogether, lead one to question the adequacy of this assumption. Both William and Joseph Hooker, for example, as successive directors of Kew Gardens found it necessary to ingratiate themselves with the company to an extraordinary extent simply because by the late 1820s the company had become almost entirely disillusioned with the economic potential and original promise of the botanical gardens. This made them early targets during periods of retrenchment, and it was only through the energetic efforts of the Hookers in the scientific community in Britain that the gardens in India survived this period at all.[117]

The early 1830s, therefore, were a period in which the company itself largely lost interest in both forest regulation and economic botany, despite the increasing preoccupation of contemporary metropolitan botanical science with Indian botany in a more academic sense. In the long run, however, it was the academic preoccupation, coordinated by William Hooker, professor of botany at Glasgow since 1820 and the future director of Kew Gardens, which enabled the botanical gardens in India and the role of the medical service in them to survive. Above all, Hooker saw the enormous scientific advantages in terms of plant collection and information co-ordination to be gained from the gardens and from the elaborate and growing network of surgeons stationed conveniently around India. It was his active encouragement of this institutional infrastructure, despite all the efforts of the EIC, which was to provide the basis for the development of a new kind of environmental critique and conservation policy in India.[118]

115 Burkill, *Chapters*, p. 109.
116 Brockway, *Science and colonial expansion.*
117 The same was true of the botanical gardens on St Helena and at the Cape during the 1830s. They suffered from much more serious neglect; see Grove, 'Early themes in African conservation', p.24.
118 Useful and comprehensive details of staffing, location and numbers of surgeons in the medical service are found in J. Macpherson, 'Notes on the condition of the Indian Medical Service', *Calcutta Review*, 1854, pp. 217–54; Spry, *Modern India;* and Crawford, *History of the Indian Medical Service* and *Roll of the Indian Medical Service.* Spry records that by 1838 there were at least 800 EIC surgeons based in mainland India. Burkhill (*Chapters*, p. 25) assembled the 'names of men who had studied the vegetation of India up to the year 1840' and found among them 28 surgeons, 7 army officers, 4 missionaries (not also surgeons) and 3 administrators in senior posts. The Edinburgh Medical School was the chief recruiting ground for the company's medical service. The efficiency and enthusiasm of the professor of botany determined the quality and research interests of the botanists produced. Roxburgh, Buchanan-

Part of the basis for the strength of the botanical garden system as an institutional basis for environmental thinking and lobbying derived from the high reputation which company surgeons enjoyed in government circles in England. For example, in 1831 and 1832 Wallich was interviewed on several occasions by House of Commons committees on a variety of Indian agrarian and economic matters. He took advantage of these cross-examinations, which appeared on the official record, to press home his own opinions on what now appeared to him an Indian forest crisis. Wallich's interest in state forest control seems likely to have been awoken by a four-month sojourn on Mauritius, where he had particularly approved of the intensive land-use methods and rigorous land-use planning inherited from the French.[119] His observations on Mauritius, his experiences with the Plantation Committee and the severe timber shortages in Bengal and Malabar all influenced him in his statements to an 1832 Commons committee. Unless 'speedy provision' was made for the renewal of these forests for the supply of timber, 'we shall', he said,

> within a very short time, find a most painful falling off, that the present means, speaking of Hindostan, would be so inadequate as I mentioned yesterday, that even in such an article as bamboo (which I would compare to nothing less than the seacoal of England as one of the indispensable necessities of life) there would also be a great falling off.

Even if the forests were to be 'properly managed', he told the committee, 'they should be sufficient for local wants, but not for exportation'. Finally, he recommended, 'it is quite time that means should be resorted to, to preserve those forests which are remaining and new plantations should be made'.[120]

While Wallich was clearly precocious and well informed, he was by no means the only influential individual to be thinking on these lines at the time or to be affected by what was known of pre-colonial practices in forest protection. The naturalist leanings of Bishop Heber have already been noted. However, in influencing forest policy in the long term, the ideas of W. H. Sleeman were actually much more important, since he initiated a fashion for roadside and firewood tree planting in Northern India during the 1820s that was taken up and expanded by Governor-General Lord Dalhousie and others after 1850 in a move that laid the groundwork for Dalhousie's more comprehensive forest-policy initiatives. Despite his better-known role as a suppressor of thuggee, Sleeman emerges in his writings and in his policies in North-West India as a person deeply interested in the history of the Indian landscape and

---

Hamilton and Gibson were all ex-pupils of Professor John Hope at Edinburgh, who had annually awarded a gold medal to the student who produced the best dried plant collection.

119 Evidence to House of Commons committee, in *Parliamentary Papers relating to the East Indies*, X, Paper 735 (II), 1831–2, para. 2335, pp. 198–9.

120 Ibid., para 2303, p. 198.

an appreciator of the tree-planting inclinations of rulers and ruled during the pre-colonial period. Of course, it would be possible to link his interest in eliminating the 'criminal' groups in society to an interest in maintaining 'virtue' in the atmosphere and in the landscape by preserving the tree cover and eliminating 'vitiated' air.[121] But this might be a far-fetched thesis, not least because forest *clearance* tended to be a greater preoccupation with those interested in controlling 'thugs' and dacoits. Instead it is probably better to explore other reasons for Sleeman's environmentalism, not least in the areas of 'Oriental' scholarship and aesthetics. In a letter of 1844 Sleeman himself described the avenue of trees which he had planted along the road 'from Maihar to Jubbulpore' in 1829 and 1830, and another, eighty-six miles long, from Jhansi Ghat on the Narmada River to Chaka. The trees planted were banyan (Ficus *bengalensis*), pipal (*Ficus religiosa*), mango (*Magnifera inelica*), tamarind (*Tamarindus indica*) and jaman (*Eugenia jambolana*). These trees, Sleeman asserted with a self-confessed interest in posterity, would 'last for centuries'.[122]

According to his own writings, Sleeman's motives for encouraging tree planting seem to have been much affected by his readings of Shaikh Sadi and other early Islamic poets. For example, he quoted approvingly Sadi's couplet which argued that 'every leaf of the foliage of a green tree is, in the eye of a wise man, a library to teach him the wisdom of his Creator'.[123] Sleeman was similarly affected by what he knew of the connections between Hindu mythology and the 'sacredness' of kalpa briksha (*Erythrina arborescens*), in a system that effectively contributed to forest protection in, for example, the Jabera and Hardwar parts of the Northern United Provinces.[124]

Sleeman stands out as one of the few men who were *not* members of the medical service vigorously to promote forest protection for other than straightforward strategic and timber-deficit reasons. This is undoubtedly because his official duties gave him unrivalled opportunities to travel throughout Northern India and gain access to regions not generally reached by Europeans. As a result, he was able to form an impression of the very rapid and geographically extensive deforestation that was taking place in the 1820s,

---

121 W. H. Sleeman, *Rambles and recollections of an Indian official* (1844), London, 1914, pp. 73–7, 433–52 (chapter entitled 'Tree Cultivation').

122 Ibid., p. 451, note added by Vincent A. Smith, Sleeman's 1914 editor.

123 'Sadi' was the nom-de-plume of the Persian poet whose name is supposed to have been Shaikh Maslah ud-Din, who lived ca. 1194–1292. His best works are *Gulistan* and *Bustan*. Sadi says in *Gulistan*, ii.26, 'That heart which has an ear is full of divine mystery. It is not the nightingale that alone serenades his rose; for every thorn on the rose-bush is a tongue in his or God's praise'; see editor's note in the 1914 ed. of Sleeman's *Rambles and recollections*, p. 75.

124 Ibid., p. 74.

especially in the Ganga–Jumna Doab (confluence) and in the foothills of the Himalayas in present-day Uttar Pradesh and Himachal Pradesh. This episode of deforestation had begun in about 1800 and lasted until at least the mid 1840s, by which time very large areas had been rendered treeless and salinated. Sleeman documented this process of degradation in great detail and recorded the dismal impact of British revenue policy on traditional forest and planting practices. He rightly took note of an initial period of rapid deforestation in the Ganga basin under the Mughal empire during the seventeenth and the early eighteenth century. The disappearance of many woodlands, he said, had taken place when 'the Sikhs, Marathas, the Jats and the Pathans destroyed them all during the disorders attending the decline of the Muhammedan empire'. However, the greatest damage, he found, had been done by the East India Company itself through excessive revenue levies. For example, the upkeep of mango groves, very important to the welfare of almost every North Indian village, had been made impossible because 'our government has, in effect, during the thirty-five years that it has held the dominion of the North-West Provinces, prohibited the planting of mango groves, while the old ones are every year disappearing . . . the government is not aware of the irreparable mischief they do the country when they govern by such measures'.[125] These were prophetic words, for the damage done to the Doab by deforestation was indeed irreparable. It led to steadily eroding soils, declining crop yields, a change in the local climate and the impoverishment and immiseration of the population on a grand scale.[126] Later the great North Indian irrigation schemes further exacerbated these problems through wide-scale salinisation of the now unprotected soils.[127]

Similar rates of deforestation were characterising Western India. The dismantling of the early forest conservancies by Thomas Munro on ideological grounds meant that deforestation proceeded apace throughout the late 1820s and the 1830s.[128] In areas under direct EIC control, the protection of private property rights in preference to the protection of pre-existing public or common rights meant that all government sanctions on the removal of timber by increasingly vigorous private timber interests had been removed. In those areas that remained notionally outside company control, particularly in Travancore

---

125 Ibid., p. 434.
126 For a more extensive study of the degradation of the region, see Michael Mann, 'Ecological change in North India: Deforestation and agrarian distress in the Ganga–Jumna Doab 1800–1850', in Grove and Damodaran, *Essays on the environmental history of South and South-East Asia*, in press.
127 See Elizabeth Whitcombe, *Agrarian conditions in Northern India*, vol. 1, *The United Provinces under British rule, 1860–1869*, Berkeley, Calif., 1972.
128 To date, however, it is not possible to make any very accurate assessment of this period of rapid deforestation; more research is needed.

as well as in some parts of Mysore and Malabar, the situation remained more as it was during the first conservancy period. That is, elements of indigenous forest control remained. During the 1830s, nevertheless, the Bombay and Madras governments came under first intermittent and then, after 1837, persistent pressure to alter their approach to forest management. In the Bombay Presidency this led eventually to the highly interventionist conservation approach of the late 1840s.

Strong practical pressure came, surprisingly, from those areas left under indigenous control. In 1830, not long before Wallich made his effectively futile attempts to secure government intervention in areas of unrestricted deforestation, the Nilumbur rajah had made an urgent approach to the government of Bombay.[129] He pointed out that if conditions were left as they were prices would continue to rise and the extraction of under-age timber would continue, so that complete disappearance of the forests would soon follow. This advice was taken seriously at the time, although the Bombay government seems to have been uncertain in its response, deciding on 20 April 1830 to send the observations of the rajah on to the Indian Navy Board. The Navy Board concurred with the rajah and strongly advised the restoration of the old conservancy, but to no immediate avail.[130] The government of Madras was then brought into the matter and the Nilumbur initiative communicated to the Madras Board of Revenue for comments on 22 April 1831.[131] At this point the initiative ran deep into the institutional sand of the Madras Revenue Board, which throughout the 1830s remained implacably hostile to any real form of government forest control. Between 1831 and 1837, therefore, the activities of the timber merchants expanded without any serious check on their activities, effectively defended as they were by the sympathetic stance of the revenue boards and the effective impotence of the navy and military boards. Concerned as the latter were about the deforestation rate, they remained without allies in government prepared to back their wish for new controls. Moreover, even though Wallich sought to raise the long-term strategic implications of deforestation with a House of Commons Select Committee in 1832, his efforts came to nothing, and the Revenue Board view prevailed against all conservationist arguments.[132]

This situation might have continued considerably longer, even though it is clear that in several parts of India the speed of deforestation was causing increasing disquiet among EIC officials and collectors away from the main

---

129 Stebbing, *Forests*, p. 72.
130 Ibid.
131 Ibid.
132 Wallich evidence before Select Committee, 1831–2, Q. 2365, quoted in Siddiqi, 'The business world of Jamshedjee Jeejeebhoy', p. 302.

cities. In 1837, however, the situation changed, once more as the result of an initiative from an area outside company control. In September of that year the Madras government received a report from the resident in Travancore on the forests of that province, and the subject was once more reopened.[133] Once again, when approached for its view the Madras Board of Revenue denigrated the report, which was concerned principally with illegal inroads being made by timber merchants who had previously operated, legally, outside Travancore. The Madras government then asked the board to reconsider the Nilumbur rajah's old report in the light of the complaints now being made from Travancore, which had arisen essentially because the rajah's advice had been ignored. More directly, the revenue authorities were asked to consider new measures for the protection and management of forests in their charge. The board attempted to stonewall this direction of thought, first by indicating that it 'would institute enquiries' in the matter and secondly by furnishing the government with a copy of a report received from the collector in Malabar, Mr Clementson, in 1834.[134] Unlike many reports received from collectors during 1837, this one, in response to the Nilumbur initiative and the 1831 recommendations of the Indian Navy Board, considered the notion of resuming government interference in timber cutting as an infringement of private property rights.[135] It is clear that the Revenue Board considered that Clementson's laissez-faire views, wrapped up as they were in legal arguments, would easily put paid to the Travancore report. During 1838, however, this confidence was betrayed, ironically enough, by Clementson himself, who submitted a new report in May 1838 commenting on the indiscriminate cutting of teak, irrespective of age, by all landowners, with the single exception of the Nilumbur rajah.[136]

Clementson suggested no solution to this apart from imposing a high duty

---

133 Stebbing, *Forests*, p. 73. The Travancore report had originally been submitted by one Mr Munro, a Scottish forester and conservator of the Travancore forests, to the resident, Colonel Fraser. Munro had written: 'The system of throwing open the teak forests to all who wish to cut, or giving them to contractors, is in the highest degree ruinous. They cut indiscriminately all that comes in their way; any range of forest, however extensive, would be destroyed if left to their tender mercies. They never think of planting and all that such speculators calculate on is present profit or loss, without troubling their heads about depriving future generations of the benefit they now enjoy. The teak forests of Malabar are, I am told, in this predicament, and if the British government do not oblige them to plant and also leave some large trees here and there for seed, this valuable tree will be extinct [*sic*]. There are two ranges of hills in our forests that were formerly rented to a Parsee, and if the contract had not been taken from him, before it was too late, he would not have left a teak tree standing. It will take 40 or 50 years before the forests recover from the effect of this avarice.'

134 Stebbing, *Forests*, p. 72.

135 Ibid.

136 Ibid., p. 75.

on young timber. This would have been an unenforceable policy under the best of conditions. Significantly, Clementson commented on the contrasting state of the Travancore forests, averring that the 'easier' conditions there were due to the fact that the forests belonged to the government and that restrictions on timber cutting that could be imposed there would be impossible in Malabar because of the preponderance of private ownership.

Pressure on the Madras Revenue Board as, for the time being, the arbiter of these problems continued to be built up by further unsolicited reports during 1838 from the collectors in Canara and Rajahmundry. The report made on Canara by Collector Blane roundly condemned the inability of the revenue authorities to control deforestation. It specifically raised the issue, for the first time, of the depredations made by *coomri*, or shifting cultivation, suggesting that the revenue authorities should make an attempt to control this separately. This was a somewhat far-fetched suggestion in the circumstances. The principal difficulty, the collector pointed out, was lack of anyone in the province with technical knowledge of either this issue or forest management in general.

The report from Rajahmundry in August 1838 was far more alarmist.[137] The collector, G. A. Smith, made the point that timber merchants based outside his province operated without hindrance in Rajahmundry and were entirely outside his control or surveillance. It was this report, in fact, which finally persuaded the Board of Revenue to send all the collectors' reports on deforestation to the Madras government for its perusal during September 1838. Along with the reports, they sent the extraordinary recommendation that no new independent action needed to be taken apart from prohibiting the felling of small timber. The government response on this occasion already differed significantly from the pattern earlier in the decade, and the whole problem came before the Madras Military Board as part of a government attempt to secure a new initiative in the matter. The extreme institutional reluctance to attempt any other intervention still limited the Military Board in its role, although it appointed an officer in Canara in November 1838 to report on available timber resources, while the resident in Travancore and the collector in Malabar were asked to report further on the status of timber other than teak. Effectively, then, any further action was delayed by the Madras government, as much from institutional inertia and lack of expertise in the face of an unprecedented problem as from any deliberate policy.[138] An institutional impasse had been reached.

137 Ibid., p. 77.
138 Ibid., p. 78. The Madras Military Board despatched Lieutenant Miller of the Ordnance at Canara in November 1838 to examine the forests 'with reference to the resources in Saul timber as well as teak'. The significance of this lay in the fact that saul (or sal), unlike teak, was a timber for general rather than Navy use and held the premier place in the timber markets of Central, North-East and North India.

Meanwhile in Bombay, as in Madras, the military authorities also became closely involved in the forest problem during 1838, also to no immediate effect. Essentially this new involvement of the military represented a third pressure exerted upon the government, following on that already applied by the indigenous interests and the three collectors, all requesting a new initiative. In Bombay it was the Indian Navy Board that became concerned with the specific issue of whether naval timber supplies should be secured by individual contract or through an agency. This was a direct consequence of a decision having been taken to recommence Navy shipbuilding in the Bombay yards.[139]

The Bombay government permitted the Navy to take its own action in the matter on this occasion, and the superintendent of the Navy, Admiral Sir C. Malcolm, appointed Captain John Harris to report on the state of the Malabar forests. Harris had been Navy timber agent in Malabar in 1828–9 and was therefore one of the few men qualified to carry out this task. He was unequivocal in his findings, reporting that almost all accessible forests available for water carriage had already been felled. Furthermore, he commented favourably on the views expressed by the Nilumbur rajah in his letter to the Bombay government in 1830, thus adding the weight of his approval of the rajah to Clementson's.[140] The Navy Board at this stage aligned itself firmly with the idea of conservancy, envisaging full powers being exercised to control cutting operations. In so doing, it found itself in complete contradiction to the views and indeed the interests of the Madras Revenue Board, which, even when confronted with evidence of wholesale deforestation in Malabar, still refused to countenance further controls. Instead the board talked, in procrastinating fashion, of the 'great diversity of opinion on the subject of the timber contained in the Malabar forests'.[141]

---

139 Stebbing, *Forests*, p. 78; T. Cruickshank, *The practical planter*, Edinburgh, 1830, p. 14. This decision was, in fact, probably related to the increasing difficulty experienced by the Navy in securing timber from Northern Europe, that is from forests closed to the British until 1815 which had in the years intervening between then and 1838 become overworked and the timber thus overpriced; hence the resurgence of the Malabar forests in strategic importance at the end of the 1830s. The perception of a renewed crisis in timber supply is recorded in Cruickshank, p. 14: 'Our foreign trade in timber must soon be attended with great depletion. The principal sources for which we are furnished with this article at present are Canada and the northern part of . . . Europe . . . in the course of the next 40 or 50 years it may be as uncommon to import wood from the British settlements in N. America as at present it is to bring the same commodity from the United States . . . the methods being pursued in North America, for the purpose of clearing land . . . often affect areas far beyond the limits intended by those who practise it. Whether the dreadful conflagration which took place at Miramichi in 1815 proceeded from this or some other cause does not seem to be well ascertained; but it furnishes a striking example of the mischief that may be done . . . and may be so quoted as a warning.'

140 Stebbing, *Forests*, pp. 78–9.

141 Ibid., p. 60. Nevertheless, the board recognised that 'no time should be lost in taking steps

When in January 1839 the Navy Board again requested information on the future of timber supplies and the likelihood of further controls, it received an embarrassed response from the Madras government, relayed through Bombay, that 'nothing decisive had been done'.[142] On this occasion the Navy decided, unilaterally, to station an agent, Lieutenant Williams, on the Malabar Coast, seeking Bombay government approval after the event. By this stage, then, the Madras Revenue Board had simply lost all credibility with government and Navy interests on the west coast. In the face of continuing criticism from the Navy Board and, for example, from the collector in Canara (who had complained about the lack of technical expertise available to him), the Bombay government found itself suffering from its failure to locate appropriate expertise to restore some order to what had developed, in practical and political terms, into a full-scale deforestation and timber-supply crisis. This crisis had been allowed to develop almost entirely through the intransigence of the revenue boards and inability on the part of government to grasp the implications of allowing full rein to private property rights. Earlier failures to monitor the physical facts of deforestation effectively contributed to the sense of crisis.

It is worth noting at this stage the extent to which the political initiative had passed not only from the Madras Revenue Board but also from the Madras government itself with regard to decisions about land use in its own territory. During 1838 and 1839, however, the Bombay government was better apprised of the situation, largely through the direct pressure put upon it by the Indian Navy Board and through the presence of the Bombay dockyards, with the direct interest this implied in the Malabar forests and even in forests farther away.

In fact, it seems clear that by 1838 the opinions of Alexander Gibson, superintendent of the Dapoori Botanic Garden at Poona, were already making themselves felt in government circles.[143] Stebbing notes that 'the government

to reform a system which must ultimately prove so injurious to the interests of the Province, in the destruction of one of its most valuable products'. Preoccupation with the commercial timber value of the forests was to remain a characteristic of Revenue Department policies even after 1857, and until the end of the century, at a stage when other departments of government were fully cognisant of the non-accountable economic and social benefit of forest reservation; see, for example, F. A. Pressler, 'Panchayat forestry in Madras', paper presented at World Environmental History Conference, Duke University, Durham, N.C., April 1987, and Government of India, *Famine Commission*, IV, pp. 39–53 (minutes of evidence of Sir Richard Temple).

142 Stebbing, *Forests*, p. 81.

143 Alexander Gibson (1800–67), botanist and surgeon, was born at Laurencekirk, Kincardineshire, on 24 Oct. 1800. He took his degree in medicine at Edinburgh, where he was taught by Professor John Hope, the botanist, who had also taught Roxburgh and Buchanan-Hamilton. In Jan. 1825 he was appointed assistant surgeon in the EIC Medical Service and served at least two years in the Indian Navy, a normal requirement for surgeons starting out

had been carrying out an enquiry of its own'.[144] The 'enquirer' here was almost certainly Gibson. In 1838 he had published his first major report on the natural resources of Western India, and subsequently the government seems to have become aware through his researches that royalties in the Deccan and Konkan from teak and blackwood could be considered the prerogative of government 'except in those villages where the right to timber had been specifically granted to the Mandaris by the terms of their *Sanad*.[145] It does seem likely that this information came from Gibson, keen to encourage the government to assume direct control of the forests. In fact the issue of Mandari rights may have come to Gibson's knowledge during his travels as official vaccinator in the region in the early 1830s.

By 1839 a fourth pressure had also started to act on both governments in the circumstances of the forest crisis. In a sense, this pressure had begun with the way in which the reports of the collectors in Malabar, Canara and Rajahmundry reinforced the more extensive critique despatched by the resident in Travancore. These were reports which in essence questioned the ability of government to manage important strategic and human resources at all. This initially low-level official discontent surfaced fully, especially in Madras, in the aftermath of the serious famines of 1837–9 and resulted in mounting internal criticism of governmental attitudes to famine management. A notable example of this kind of criticism came in 1838 from J. E. Thomas, a Madras government civil servant, in an issue of the new *Madras Journal of Literature and Science*.[146] Thomas's main theme in two articles he published in consec-

in company service. During this time he studied several Indian languages and became proficient in Hindustani, Marathi and Gujerati, later becoming acquainted with Konkani and Kannada. By 1836 he had been appointed a vaccinator for Deccan and Khandesh, and acquired in the course of this task a widespread field knowledge of the biota of the region and an unusually close knowledge of the rural economies of the area. At this time he also grew familiar with the rapid ecological changes taking place in the Deccan. There is some dispute about the date of his appointment to the superintendency of the Dapoori Botanic Garden. Burkill gives it as 1836, while Crawford (*Roll of the Indian Medical Service*) and the *DNB* (quoting his obituary in *Proceedings of the Linnaean Society*, 1867, p. 33) give it as 1838. His report on teak deforestation submitted to the Bombay government in 1840 led directly to his appointment as conservator of forests in the presidency. At Dapoori his successful efforts to produce drugs for the use of the medical service won him special commendations from the Court of Directors, leading it later to take his warnings about the precipitational effects of deforestation much more seriously than might otherwise have been the case. He was elected a Fellow of the Linnaean Society on 19 April 1853 and died in India on 16 Jan. 1867. His works are listed in the bibliography.

144 *Forests*, p. 28.

145 See A. Gibson, 'A general sketch of the province of Guzerat, from Deesa to Daman', *Transactions of the Medical and Physical Society of Bombay*, 1 (1838), 1–77.

146 'Notes on ryotwar or permanent money rents in South India, and on the duty of government in periods of famine', pp. 53–78, 200–21.

utive issues of the journal was that 'the followers of Adam Smith' had mis-
interpreted and mistakenly applied his theories to India when they were
intended to apply only to European conditions. Thomas believed that they
did not take into account the vagaries and character of the Indian land-tenure
systems or the variability and harshness of the climate. He quoted specific
instances of famines which he believed had been exacerbated by mistaken
government policy. Thus at 'Nagpur in 1830 it is reported to have instantly
converted scarcity into absolute famine', and 'it is not easy to conceive a wise
course even in a financial point of view'. Positive rather than negative intervention was far preferable in the context of famine. 'A Government Com-
missariat', he felt, 'should be forced to input its supplies from places where
grain was relatively abundant' rather than be allowed to rely on some notional
kind of market mechanism to assure grain supplies. Thomas then urged a
complete reassessment of government policy, noting:

> The object of these remarks is not so much to advocate particular meas-
> ures of relief, but rather to induce a full examination of the doctrine laid
> down in government orders; and to endeavour to ascertain whether it be
> an indisputable truth to be taught to all our native servants that injury
> must inevitably follow from any interference of government in seasons of
> dearth . . . in this country.[147]

Other influential commentators in and outside India were at work in a
similar vein in the last years of the 1830s. Howitt, for example, in an openly
anti-colonial tract entitled *Colonization and Christianity*, drew attention to
Abbé Guillaume Raynal's allusions to the Bengal famine of 1770, which had
so alarmed Robert Kyd and 'which [had] throughout Europe excited so much
horror of the English'. In fact, Raynal had summarised a body of travel literature and used it as the basis for a wide and slashing indictment of the
Europeans as destroyers of whole peoples, in a veritable chronicle of genocide.[148] When applied to the Indian situation, these kinds of criticism of government policy in forest, revenue and famine management found a common
feature in their critique of the long-term implications of what were essentially
laissez-faire policies. These, it was felt by many of the commentators, held
out disastrous possibilities, which the famines of 1837–9 tended only to confirm. It was this situation which propelled both the Madras and Bombay
governments, assailed by conflicting evidence from diametrically opposed interest groups within government, to seek out the expertise of the medical
service. Thus in 1840 assistant surgeon Alexander Gibson, superintendent of

---

147 Ibid., p. 54.
148 W. Howitt, *Colonization and Christianity: A popular history of the treatment of natives by the
   Europeans in all their colonies*, London, 1838, pp. 268–70; G. Raynal, *Histoire philosophique et
   politique des deux Indes*, vol. 5, Amsterdam, 1764.

the Dapoori Botanic Garden, was appointed to inspect and report on the forest 'problem', as it was now known. This was consistent with a pattern already better established in Bengal, where surgeons Buchanan-Hamilton, Wallich and Helfer had all served in comparable consultancy roles.[149]

Precisely as in Bengal, Gibson's position as superintendent of the botanical garden at Dapoori constituted the key to his selection on the grounds of professional expertise. By choosing to rely on the somewhat unknown quantity of a physician such as Gibson, the Bombay government had, largely unwittingly, exposed itself to the influence of a scientific community which during the 1830s had undergone some important changes in its character and integration. It was a community characterised by an academic, medical and ideological agenda quite distinct from that to which government had been accustomed earlier in the century. The main features of these changes are worth considering, since they determined the new parameters within which the forest problem was increasingly dealt with in the period 1840–60.

Whereas Roxburgh, Buchanan-Hamilton and Wallich had operated for much of the time in relative professional isolation, the surgeons employed as consultants and experts on natural resources from the late 1830s operated in a more complex intellectual context and one far more integrated with the world of science outside India. Internally, the growth of the medical service had been accompanied by the emergence of provincial medical and scientific societies, each with its scientific journal. Both these developments served to accelerate and enrich the diffusion of scientific ideas of all kinds amongst the European intellectual elite, not least amongst those for whom new thinking about the natural environment had become directly relevant. Specifically, they served to provide a wealth of empirical material on forests and deforestation and to offer what were in effect early ecological ideas, for which the newness of the Indian environment in scientific terms provided theoretical stimulus.

A new elite of scientists, most of them within the medical establishment, constituted a specialist intellectual renaissance that produced a stream of articles and papers on the medicine, natural history and ethnology of India.[150]

149 See Vicziany, 'Imperialism, botany and statistics', pp. 625–60, for details of Buchanan-Hamilton's employment by the EIC as a consultant.
150 The *Madras Journal of Literature and Science* commenced in 1831 under the editorship of John Cole, a surgeon in the EIC Medical Service. Other important journals making their appearance at this time that contributed to the emerging environmental debate were *Transactions of the Bombay Medical and Physical Society*, commencing in 1838; the *Indian Journal of Medical and Physical Science* (1834); the *Quarterly Medical and Surgical Journal of the North-West Provinces* (1848); the *Indian Annals of Medical Science* (1833); the *Calcutta Journal of Natural History* (1841), edited by Surgeon McClelland (ceased in 1847). The last journal is a useful exemplar of the close links between the scientific journals and the employment of EIC surgeons as EIC consultants. McClelland, who had arrived in India in 1830, had been employed by the company to study soils in the Kumaon Hills with a view to possible tea

While this was a development which had earlier foundations, the founding of
the new scientific societies in the early 1830s, especially in the South of India,
together with the expansion of the medical service, gave it an entirely new
vigour. The external relations of this community with scientific developments
in the centres of European science were characterised by the increasing preoccupation of British botanists with Indian flora and fauna. This was a development assured of continuity and potency by the appointment of Sir
William Hooker as director of Kew in 1841. Hooker had trained many of the
surgeons in the EIC Medical Service. Throughout the 1830s and 1840s he
deliberately reinforced the network of contacts and scientific channels that had
been developed by Sir Joseph Banks between Kew Gardens and surgeons
stationed in different parts of India. The developing infrastructure of the
medical service provided a ready-made information-gathering network for
Hooker, and one in large part staffed by individuals who owed allegiance to
him and his Kew establishment as much as they did to the medical service
itself.[151] After 1847 this connection was strengthened still further by the arrival
in India of Hooker's son, J. D. Hooker, as an influential member of Lord
Dalhousie's entourage.[152]

The chief implication of these developments for the Bombay government
and, a little later, for the Madras government was that, with reliance on the
medical service, the whole issue of deforestation came to be defined much less
in terms of timber depletion and much more in terms of the environmental,
species-extinction, social and even aesthetic consequences of deforestation.
Empirical evidence of the effects of deforestation was gradually accumulating

cultivation. In 1835 he went to Assam with Nathaniel Wallich and William Griffith and in
1852 produced a report on the Pegu forests which was decisive in encouraging Dalhousie to
promote state forest control on an all-India basis.

151 The way in which Sir William Hooker built up the system of patronage essential to his
information and plant-gathering network is well described in an obituary in the *Journal of
the Royal Geographical Society* (1866): 'Hooker obituary', pp. 197–8. Written by Sir Roderick
Murchison with the assistance of J. D. Hooker, it instructs us: 'In 1820 he went to Glasgow
as Professor of Botany, where he remained for twenty years. During that period he was an
admirable teacher, exciting in his pupils the highest enthusiasm by the animating style and
clearness of his lectures, and still more by the annual excursions to the highlands, in the
course of which he never failed to convey to those who accompanied him . . . his own love
of Nature and her works . . . numbers entered the army, navy and Indian Medical Service
or sought other positions in foreign countries. To all of these Sir William Hooker was ready
to lend a helping hand, guiding their studies while pupils, and furthering their interests
afterwards, well satisfied to be repaid by a share of their collections . . . thus zealous botanists
of his own training were spread almost broadcast over the face of the globe . . . indefatigable
as a letter writer, and strictly punctual in reply, he attended to all who applied to him for
information and thus knew everything which was done in his favourite science all over the
world.'

152 Leonard Huxley, *Life and Letters of Sir J. D. Hooker*, 2 vols., London, 1918, 1, p. 235.

and being disseminated through the new scientific journals. Of central significance was the gradual diffusion of a single predominating scientific argument, that is, the critique of the effects of deforestation based on the writings of Priestley, Humboldt and Boussingault. This analysis, which guided the thinking of the whole medical service by the early 1840s, was one which made its impact by stages. It relied for its acceptability not only on its predictive power but on a framework of thinking, not often made explicit, which valued the natural environment of India in terms much wider than the purely commercial. Indeed, for many of the surgeon-botanists, commercial argument can be said to have counted for little. Central to the Humboldtian analysis of environmental change as propounded by the medical service was the prospect that widespread deforestation could cause fundamental climatic and therefore agrarian and economic change. The most influential propagandists and exponents of this view after 1840 were Alexander Gibson himself in Bombay, and assistant surgeon Hugh Cleghorn and assistant surgeon Edward Balfour, the latter two active in the Madras Presidency. Other surgeons, such as Donald Butter, Robert Wight, Hugh Falconer and John Ellerton Stocks, also played a significant part in the propagandising of Humboldtian views within the company apparatus.

An analysis of the development of this kind of thinking between 1837 and the late 1840s presents some special problems. In general, however, the desiccationist argument became prominent in direct proportion to the growing political influence of the medical service in government decision making. An early product of the close association of the Bombay and Madras governments with the expertise of Gibson and his colleagues was a growing disarticulation between the increasingly sophisticated perception of deforestation at presidency level and the much less developed attitudes espoused by the government of India and the EIC Court of Directors. The main bone of contention involved an increasing divergence of views about the primacy of private property rights vis-à-vis government revenue interests in forested areas.

By the early 1840s both presidency governments had become much more inclined to question the sanctity of such rights and increasingly to consider the economic and social disbenefits of the kind of activity which the full exercise of property rights might imply. The far less evolved outlook of the Court of Directors, on the other hand, was clearly shown in February 1840 in the review it undertook of the development of forest policy between 1800 (the date of the Bengal–Bombay Joint Commission) and April 1839. First of all, the Court even questioned the need to resurvey the Malabar forests (which the Bombay government had proposed on the advice of the Navy Board), on the ground that surveys had already been carried out in 1805 and 1806![153] The

153 Stebbing, *Forests*, p. 86.

complete inability of the Court to appreciate the dynamics of land-use change and the limitability of natural resources in India was much in evidence at this time. While grudgingly admitting that land might be purchased to serve the immediate needs of government, the Court also stipulated, astonishingly in view of the events of the late 1830s, their neo-Munrovian and 'anxious wish that in the prosecution of a survey, if such a measure should appear necessary, the utmost care may be taken to avoid any infringement of the rights of or any inconvenience to . . . private persons'.[154]

Lobbying for the new conservation, 1840–7

After about 1840, an increasing divergence of views developed between levels of the EIC apparatus about the most appropriate response to the deforestation issue. At presidency level, Alexander Gibson and other surgeons were able to indicate to the Bombay and Madras governments the complexity and scale of the consequences that might follow from further deforestation. By and large, Gibson's knowledge was based (apart from the basic publications by Humboldt and Boussingault) on material which does not appear to have made an impact on either the Court of Directors or the government of India, to whom expertise comparable to that offered to the presidency governments was not immediately available. Nevertheless, a considerable amount of evidence on the consequences of deforestation was freely available in scientific circles. An understanding of the way government conservation policy evolved and the significance of the part which Gibson played in stimulating it involves an analysis of the way in which he selected appropriate information to use in lobbying government. Thus a survey of the kind of literature Gibson would have been familiar with is useful.

In 1838 Boussingault published his major paper on the effects of forest clearance and run-off in the *Edinburgh New Philosophical Journal*, in a translation of his original Paris lecture published in the *Annales de Chimie* in 1837.[155] This transfer of ideas between French and Scottish academic communities was a familiar one. It was built on the tradition of close contact between the two communities established as early as the mid eighteenth century. The *Edinburgh New Philosophical Journal* was a journal widely read among surgeons trained at the Scottish universities, as the majority of surgeons working in India were by the late 1830s. The implications of this paper were realised relatively quickly by surgeons working in India, mainly because of their pro-

---

154 Ibid.
155 Boussingault, 'Mémoire sur l'influence des défrichements dans la diminution des cours-d'eau'.

fessional and Hippocratic preoccupations with water supply and atmosphere, issues which Humboldt and Boussingault linked to forest cover. Within a year of the English translation's appearing, Boussingault's warnings made their appearance in direct and indirect form in scientific publications in India. Among the first of these was a paper published by Captain T. J. Newbold in 1839 in the recently founded *Madras Journal of Literature and Science*.[156] This was an important paper for several reasons, not least because it helped alert assistant surgeon Edward Balfour to the potential impact of deforestation on rural food supplies and local climates. Drawing on the results of interviews with villagers in the Hoogri River valley between Bellary and Bangalore, Newbold was able to make a connection between the appearance in recent memory of sand dunes, the submerging of arable fields by alluvium, flooding and recent deforestation. Newbold was the first in a line of commentators on this sort of connection, all drawing their material and field examples from the Arcot, Bellary, Ceded Districts and Bangalore areas, in a region peculiarly susceptible to periodic drought and soil erosion.[157]

The receptiveness of the surgeons of the medical service to Boussingault's paper was due principally to a growing interest within the medical profession in epidemiology and public health, particularly with regard to water-borne diseases. This was an interest which had its main origins in the context of European urbanisation. Increasing doubt was also being cast on older theories of the 'miasmic' origin of tropical diseases.[158]

Since the 1760s, Scottish medical teaching in particular had been characterised by an emphasis on the environmental context of disease. It was this new approach, as well as earlier French methods, which eventually culminated in surgeon Ranald Martin's suggestion of 1835 that officers in the medical service should be called upon to compile medico-topographical reports about the hinterlands of their stations.[159] Of these, surgeon Donald Butter's report

156 T. J. Newbold, 'Notice of river dunes on the banks of the Hoogri and Pennaur rivers', *Madras Journal of Literature and Science*, 1839, pp. 309–10. Newbold, later made a Fellow of the Royal Society, was a prolific writer in the natural sciences of India and Malaya, his outstanding book being *A political and statistical account of the British settlements in the Straits of Malacca*, London, 1839. Like Balfour, he was much interested in and knowledgeable about the hill tribes of the Eastern and Western Ghats; see e.g. 'The Chenchars: A wild tribe inhabiting the Eastern Ghauts', *Journal of the Royal Asiatic Society*, 8 (1846), 271–83.

157 F. C. Danvers, for example, in his pioneering essay on the causes of famine, entitled 'A Century of Famines', quotes at length from the writings of Sir Richard Temple on the connections between deforestation and famine in North Arcot and Chingleput: Danvers, 'A century of famines', unpublished paper, Edinburgh University Library, India Papers, category X, pp. 6–11.

158 For the traditional 'miasmic' view, see Spry, *Modern India*, pp. 184–96. Spry, a surgeon, considered forests to be fertile breeding grounds for disease, a view disputed in 1849 by Edward Balfour.

159 Crawford, *History of the Indian Medical Service*, p. 247: 'The [Medical] Board at first threw

on Awadh (Oudh) stands out as being clearly derived from Boussingault in its discourse on local forests and climate.[160] Like Sleeman, Butter warned that the imminent imposition of the 'strictly enforced revenue system' would have the almost immediate effect of 'destroying the remnants of the sylvan verdure' of Oudh, thus

> emphasising the slow, but certain process by which India, like all other semi-tropical countries, (such as Central Spain, Southern Italy and the Western territory of the United States), has its green plains – no longer capable of entangling and detaining water in the meshes of a herbaceous covering, – ploughed into barren ravines, by its sudden and violent though now short-lived rains – its mean temperature and its daily and annual range of temperature augmented – its springs and perennial streamlets dried up – and its rainfall and the volume of its rivers diminished.[161]

cold water on the scheme, whereupon Martin laid his suggestion before government, which approved; and the Board then called for reports.' Several were published; the best-known are Martin's report on Calcutta published in 1837 and Taylor's on Dakka published in 1840. Other reports published in the scheme were D. Butter on Oudh and Sultanpur, 1839; W. Dollard on Kumaon, 1840; R. H. Irvine on Ajmir, 1841; W. Jacob on Jessore, 1837; McCosh on Assam, 1837; D. A. Macleod on Bishnath, Assam, 1837; R. Rankine on Saran, 1839; F. P. Strong on Calcutta, 1844. Spry explained in *Modern India* (p. 184) that 'medical topography embraces a wide range of inquiry, and requires on the part of the medical scientist an aptitude for observation which only few men possess, while a knowledge of the subject is of such paramount importance to the well-being of a state that no-one can contemplate it without being impressed by its magnitude'. Spry added perceptively: 'Happiness is ever attendant upon health. Without the one, we can never hope to enjoy the other – so firmly fixed was this truth in the minds of men in the earliest ages that we find Homer paying the highest compliment it perhaps ever received: "A wise physician skilled in words to heal, is more than armies to the public weal". (*Iliad*, 13,xi,630) Much of what fairly comes under the name of topography has already been glanced at in the following pages, such is the natural character of the country . . . its elevations and formations, the chief productions of the soil, as well as the constitutional and characteristic peculiarities of the people . . . one fruitful source of disease in Central India is the variability of the climate . . . the experience I have had of the climate of the Saugar and Nerbudda territories convinces me that, at least among the European community, much sickness might be avoided if more consideration was given to this subject.'

160 Butter, *Outlines of the topography and statistics of the southern districts of Oudh and the cantonment of Sultanpur, Oudh*, Benares, 1839. Butter's own comments in the introduction to his work are helpful in explaining the extent to which such surveys, essential to any serious assessment of contemporary land-use change, were previously lacking: 'I have to my knowledge endeavoured to give a fruitful and unbiased description of the Southern Districts of Oudh, but the total absence of official . . . information, has rendered the attempt more arduous than, in the commencement of my task, I had expected.' Nevertheless, the report became widely distributed, and Sir Henry Laurence commented in 1844 that 'Dr Butter's "Outline" is a very creditable piece of work': H. M. Lawrence, *Essays, military and political, written in India*, London, 1859, pp. 375–427.

161 Butter, *Topography of Oudh*, p. 9.

Measures could be taken to ameliorate this process, Butter thought. However, 'artificial planting', he pointed out, 'which might if carried on systematically arrest the current deterioration of climate, is on the decline'.

This was a comprehensive statement of the desiccationist argument. Butter's belief that the climate had already started to deteriorate is an important indicator of the potency which desiccation fears had already acquired in India and of their potential as an intellectual weapon with which government might be persuaded to carry out the kinds of land-use prescriptions which the medical conservation lobby was soon to recommend. However, in 1840 this was a psychological weapon which Alexander Gibson, although certainly well aware of the arguments, did not choose to use immediately. This was partly because in 1840 he was as yet in only a consultative position and had anyway been assigned a very specific task, that is, 'to visit the forests and report on their resources and on the best means to be adopted for their preservation and improvement'.[162]

Though trained as a surgeon, Gibson had become first and foremost a botanist, and his early response to deforestation reflects the priorities of the botanical enthusiasts of the period. Soon after his appointment as a consultant to the Bombay government, he entered into correspondence with Sir William Hooker. This connection encouraged him to take steps to promote state conservation initiatives. An early letter to Hooker, written very soon after the latter was appointed director of Kew, gives a useful impression of Gibson's attitude in the early 1840s. 'The Deccan', he wrote, 'is more bare than Gujerat and the clefts of the Ghat mountains are the only situation where trees are to be found in any quantity and even there they are disappearing fast under the increased demand for land for spade husbandry . . . they are too steep for the plough.' It is a matter 'for regret', he continued, '*for the naturalist, perhaps also for the economist*, that the woods are in such rapid progress of destruction'.[163]

The text of this letter indicates that both personal scientific and public economic motives were being articulated in connection with the new advocacy of conservation in the Bombay Presidency in the early 1840s. The first kind of motive, much the more important in compelling the actions of Gibson, was not at this period put forward by the surgeons as an argument to persuade governments to take a long-term environmental view. A third set of overlap-

162 Stebbing, *Forests*, p. 78.
163 Royal Botanic Gardens Archives, Kew, India Letters: Alexander Gibson to J. D. Hooker, 24 March 1841 (letter no. 211) (my italics). This correspondence reflects the direct involvement of the Hookers, father and son, in the deforestation issue, one reinforced by the visits of J. D. Hooker to St Helena and Ascension in 1843 and to India in 1847–50. Their simultaneous involvement in early conservation in the Cape Colony should be noted: Grove, 'Early themes in African conservation', pp. 23–24, 31.

ping motives also started to make an explicit appearance in the 1840s. These
related to the maintenance of social stability in the countryside and to the
maintenance of public health and the prevention of famine. It was this last
set of motives that became most prominent during the decade after Gibson's
appointment as a consultant, both because they were associated most closely
with the anxieties of government at the time (it was beginning to recognise
the threat which the consequences of deforestation might present to social as
well as economic stability) and because they were at the heart of the Hippocratic and specifically public-health ethos espoused by the surgeons.

In 1841 Gibson made an inspection of the forest tracts near the coast in
the Northern and Southern Conkan, and in 1842 undertook an experimental
thinning of teak forests in the Rutnagherry Collectorate. During the same
period as his early survey work, two further significant reports were submitted
on the Bombay forests: by the government timber agent at Surat, Mr Boyce,
in 1841 and by Colonel Jervis, the chief engineer in Bombay, in his capacity
as a member of the Military Board in 1843.[164] Thus at this period agents of
three groups, the government of India, the military authorities at Bombay and
the government of Bombay, were concerned with the deforestation problem.
Boyce's report recommended the leasing of particular forests to the government by 'tribes' (especially the Dangs Bhils of the Western Ghats) and private
owners, and in June 1842 the government of India was minuted to this effect
by Bombay. Both reports were far wider in scope than previous surveys, and
the recommendations they made bear the imprint of Gibson's opinions. Thus
Boyce was particularly concerned with the medicinal products of the Bombay
forests and canvassed the possibility that 'a careful examination of the forests
would disclose other productions of value from a commercial as well as a
scientific point of view and at the same time allow of a large quantity of land
within this limit being brought into cultivation'.[165]

Colonel Jervis's 1843 report is noteworthy in that much of the material was
devoted to arguing that conservation might have a very positive influence on
the way of life of the agrarian population. He noted, for example, that 'the
plantations south of Songhur, scattered and of little account for external commercial purposes', were 'capable of being turned to profitable use if conserved,
so as to secure a succession of cuttings, all of which are applicable to increase
the comfort of the dwellings of the people, and this is of the more consequence
here as the country is otherwise bare of wood'.[166]

It is clear from Jervis's report that the appointment of Gibson had resulted
in some efforts to protect forests, especially those nominally in government

164 Stebbing, *Forests*, p. 111.
165 Ibid., p. 110.
166 Ibid., p. 111.

ownership. Moreover, the reports of Jervis and Boyce both stressed the social benefits that might be derived from protection. It was even proposed in 1842 that Boyce, who had unusual insights into traditional forest use, should assume a form of conservatorship of the newly leased forests in the Dangs region of the Western Ghat mountains.[167] This idea was not followed up, and it seems clear that funding was not allocated. Instead responsibility for the forests remained in the hands of separate Bombay government departments – the Military Department, the Political Department and the Board of Revenue – none of which exerted any real executive function. Jervis's report prompted the Military Board to suggest that it be invested with absolute control over the Bombay forests to provide timber for all government departments. The Bombay government in 1843 remained equivocal on this point. Instead, and here the hand of Gibson himself is evident, the Military Board was asked to submit a scheme for the establishment of a conservancy under Gibson.[168] The Military Board complied and recommended that he be appointed conservator while retaining the post of superintendent of the botanical garden. Moreover, it was suggested that as 'interim Conservator' he might also be made responsible for the administration of forests in Madras. This suggestion, not surprisingly, did not meet with the approval of the Madras government.

By 1845 the Bombay government had become fully convinced, entirely on the strength of Gibson's promptings, that an independent department should be established free of any interference by, for example, the Military Board. The arguments that seem most to have convinced the Bombay government were those relating to the serious decrease in the supply of firewood and building timber throughout the presidency. By 1845 these shortages had reached crisis point in the perception of the government. Thus in 1846 it was reported by Gibson that in the neighbourhood of Mangalore 'the article of firewood, formerly so abundant, is now one of the chief items of expense to the poorer classes of people, and is a deprivation severely felt by them'.[169] The cause of this scarcity, Gibson suggested, was 'the improvidence with which the wood was treated, every tree and bush being felled at first, and the shoots and saplings which would have grown up and supplied their places being cut down every year until the roots die off, leaving nothing but the bare laterite hills which will remain for ever afterwards utterly sterile and useless'.[170]

In November 1845 the Bombay government submitted the entire correspondence with the Military Board and Gibson to the government of India, detailing its intentions with regard to formally setting up a conservancy. The

167 Ibid., p. 114 (minute of the chief engineer, 9 Dec. 1843).
168 Stebbing, *Forests*, p. 117.
169 Ibid., p. 120.
170 Ibid., pp. 120–1.

urgency of the matter was emphasised and the sanction of the supreme government requested for establishment purposes. An optimistic forecast was made that the cost might be defrayed by the sale of thinnings from the forest.[171]

This last suggestion was presumably made in the belief that no establishment would be sanctioned unless a reasonable return on expenses could be demonstrated. An interest in 'social forestry' was clearly not expected of the government in Calcutta by the now relatively enlightened Bombay authorities. But the urgent firewood problems faced by the Bombay government do not appear to have been found convincing in Calcutta. Instead the government of India delayed any decision and made enquiries of Bombay concerning the possible inclusion of Madras in the scheme, and also enquired as to whether forests outside government ownership would be subject to government sanction from the proposed conservancy.[172]

Throughout this period a consistent campaign of lobbying for forest protection emanated from the lowest levels of the EIC up through the Bombay government to the government of India. From above, the government of India, reluctant to fund conservancy schemes in either Madras or Bombay, started to come under pressure from the members of the Court of Directors, themselves still largely ignorant of the urgency of the Indian forestry problem as it was perceived by the medical service. The response of the supreme government in March 1846 to the Bombay submission on conservancy promised yet another period of procrastination by the authorities, and it was at this stage that Gibson took matters into his own hands through scientific publication and by bypassing the company authorities in India altogether. By early 1846 he had exploited arguments about shortages of firewood to a considerable extent but without any clear success in his campaign to secure government sanction for conservancy. Now he decided to turn to quite a different strategy and emphasise the climatic dangers of deforestation. It is hard to understand why this line of argument had lain dormant so long. The medical service had been made aware of Boussingault's reasoning of over eight years before.[173] One hypothesis may be that Gibson did not feel confident from a scientific point of view in extending the line of Boussingault's reasoning too far. Specifically, he was reluctant to go beyond discussion of the impact of deforestation on catchment run-off (which Boussingault considered verifiable) to treat the relationship between forest cover and climate or precipitation, a much less verifiable matter.[174] His mind seems to have been finally changed, however, by

171 Ibid., p. 118.
172 Ibid.
173 See Butter, *Topography of Oudh*, p. 9.
174 For recent authoritative contributions to this debate in the Indian context, see V. M. Meher-

his receipt of a letter from a correspondent in Mahabaleshwar dated 21 February 1846 'in which the writer mentions the common belief in the Konkan that with the removal of wood, the small streams had more or less dried up'. The correspondent also mentioned that it was generally held by Parsi merchants resident in the Nilgiri Hills that declines in rainfall had followed local deforestation. Other reports were also quoted, all of them notable for originating with indigenous rather than European authorities.[175] By 6 March 1846, only a few days after receiving this letter, Gibson had finished compiling a manuscript report on the destruction of the forests of the Konkan in which he made specific mention of the climatic and economic consequences of deforestation. 'A change of climate', he wrote 'is by no means limited to the mere district in which the clearing has taken place, but its influence extends far inland.'[176] Deforestation in the Western Ghats, that is in the headwaters of rivers watering the fertile western coastal lowlands of the presidency, would clearly be affected by such changes, or so Gibson thought. It is important to stress that these were regions to which the company at the time attached a great deal of economic importance, particularly for large-scale cotton growing. Unlike Roxburgh before him, Gibson now saw for the first time the dangers of regional rather than just local climate change.[177] The potentially formidable indirect economic disbenefits of deforestation detailed in the report were unmistakable. Having finished it on 6 March 1846, Gibson sent the report in letter form directly to the Court of Directors in London without approaching the Bombay government with it at all. Instead he used material from the report as the basis of a short but prominent paper to be published in *Transactions of the Bombay Medical and Physical Society*,[178] a journal which enjoyed widespread readership among medical-service and other officials throughout India. The article was published later in the year. The symbolism of these actions cannot have been lost on the Bombay government; Gibson had appealed over the heads of both the Bombay authorities and the government of India directly to the Court of Directors and the Indian scientific community. This was an

Homji, 'The link between rainfall and forest clearance: Case studies from Western Karnataka', *Transactions of the Institute of Indian Geographers*, 2:1 (1980), 59–65, and 'Probable impact of deforestation on hydrological processes', *Climatic Change*, 19 (1991), 163–73. In general it is now considered by forest meteorologists that deforestation exercises a profound impact on rainfall and climate at micro and macro levels, both directly and through the effect of increased albedo (reflectivity of the denuded land surface). The subject is still a matter of vehement debate; see letter to the *Times* by Sir Charles Pereira on trees and rainfall, 3 Aug. 1992.

175 IOL., Boards Collections; v/27/560/107, incomplete letter to A. Gibson, p. 21.

176 Gibson, 'Report on the forests of the S. Conkan', unpublished MS and letter to Court of Directors, 9 March 1846, quoted in Cleghorn et al., 'Report of the committee'.

177 Ibid., p. 102.

178 'Report on deforestation in South Conkan', pp. 37–41.

indicator, if one were needed, of the weight and status which his professional medical status lent him. Nevertheless, the action was a gamble; but it was one which quickly paid off by breaking at a stroke the administrative logjam among scientific advisers, presidency governments and the government of India. Moreover, Gibson had backed the gamble by documenting his findings among his own peers in an academic forum. As a result, on 17 December 1846 the government of India authorised 'the employment of an establishment for the management of the forests under the Bombay Presidency, at a monthly charge of 295 Rupees'. This enabled the Bombay government on 22 March 1847 to add 'Conservator of Forests' to Alexander Gibson's appointment as superintendent of the Dapoori Botanic Garden; and authorised him 'to entertain the establishment which had been sanctioned' by the government of Bombay and for which Gibson had long campaigned.[179]

Implications of the formation of the Bombay Forest Department and its later consequences

The formation of a new conservancy in the Bombay Presidency in 1847 and the establishment of Gibson as its first conservator constituted a major turning point in the development of British colonial policy towards the environment and its degradation, not only in India but in a much wider context. It was important, above all, because the central rationale for establishing the conservancy was based not simply on the prospect of rapid timber depletion (as the 1805–23 conservancy under Watson and Palmer had been) but on acceptance by the East India Company of a set of much wider and longer-term environmental considerations and risks. Whilst the underpinnings of this new approach were based on a distinctively Humboldtian and ecological approach to the environment, and one which recognised the essential interdependence of its elements, this did not necessarily mean that the state had accepted a new ideology in any wholesale fashion. Instead the key factor in the decision taken by the Bombay government related to the emergence of a political situation in which a new economic balance was struck between the short-term priority of land revenue and much longer-term priorities relating to sustainability in patterns of resource use and to social stability. These were now seen as being threatened by the kind of reckless deforestation which had taken place since the 1820s. Without a doubt, the conservancy decision represented an enormous shift by the colonial government in response to a new 'scientific' and medical assessment of economic risks.

At the very least, as Sir George Arthur commented in 1848, short-term

179 Stebbing, *Forests*, p. 118.

forest-revenue interests would now have to be sacrificed, and the object of government would be

> to secure these general resources of the state, for the deficits of which no amount of revenue will compensate, and for the foundation of a system to be perfected hereafter which shall secure an adequate permanent supply of timber, future regularity being in no case risked for an excessive profit at the outset.[180]

An equally radical and possibly even more surprising transition in attitude had occurred on the part of the Court of Directors as a direct result of Gibson's communication with them in March 1846. While even in the short term this initiative was undoubtedly decisive in securing funding from the government of India for the formal establishment of the Bombay Forest Department, his intervention also had more significant long-term consequences, for in July 1847 the Court of Directors issued a highly unusual circular letter, Despatch no. 21 of 7 July 1847. This stated that a knowledge of the relationship between deforestation and climate had

> a strong practical bearing on the welfare of mankind, and we are anxious to obtain extensive and accurate information in regard to it. We desire, therefore, that you will furnish us with any that you may possess, and that you will institute enquiries in such quarters as may be likely to lead to the acquisition of particular facts bearing upon the question. It has been suggested that the circumstances of the district of Azimghur afford some illustration of the subject, and we shall be glad to receive a correct report of any facts relating either to that district or others which may be calculated to throw light upon the subject of our enquiry.[181]

The despatch was a sophisticated document, clearly based on a good deal of research and survey of literature as well as the information which Gibson had provided to the Court. It was also innovative in its breadth of approach and went far beyond the simple utilitarian statements of Sir George Arthur. The Court accepted the desiccation arguments largely on the strength of Gibson's wielding the spectre of climatic deterioration and imminent agrarian crisis on the west coast of India. It also went on to accept unquestioningly the reputation of Humboldt's South American work, despite the company's earlier hostility to Humboldt himself. The readiness of the Court to take on board the links between economic and climatic change may seem surprising

---

180 Ibid., p. 122.
181 Azimghur, it should be noted, was a district mentioned specifically by Butter in his *Topography of Dudh*, and it seems that the Court had referred to his work. The despatch is quoted in E. G. Balfour, 'The influence exercised by trees on the climate and productiveness of the Peninsula of India', in Government of India, *Famine Commission*, IV, p. 100.

when contrasted with the difficulty the surgeons had initially experienced in convincing the government of India of the dynamics of the deforestation problem. However, while one cannot adduce specific evidence, the constructive and research-oriented response of the Court to Gibson's approach can probably be attributed to an official exhumation of much earlier desiccation arguments put forward on St Helena, St Vincent and Mauritius after the 1790s.[182] In these earlier cases desiccation had already been accepted as posing a potential threat to colonial agriculture and therefore to the long-term future of the company.

The specific mention made of Azimghur in Despatch no. 21 almost certainly relates to the attention of the Directors having been drawn to Butter's report on Oudh, a report which had itself been influenced by Wallich's well-known opinions about the same region. Clearly the weight of scientific opinion had been increased by the fact that it came independently from several quarters of the global scientific community. The opinions of Butter and Gibson were by the end of 1846 also reinforced in a more contemporary way by other authorities, not least by C. S. Logan. The latter had first publicised his work on deforestation, drawn from his experiences in the Malay peninsula, in a lecture to the Asiatic Society of Bengal in 1846. While this lecture was not published until 1848, it seems clear that Logan's opinions had helped to influence the evolving view of the Directors.[183]

The significant development here lay in the extent to which the collating of examples of environmental deterioration from different parts of the world (including Penang and the Americas) put forward by a number of scientists had played a part in convincing the Directors of the gravity of the situation. Moreover, it had encouraged them to perceive the problem in India, as Butter had started to do, as part of a global phenomenon. This was a direct inheritance from Humboldt, and the holistic connotations were reflected in the opinion of the Directors that 'the subject is one having a strong practical bearing on the welfare of mankind'.[184] This was a particularly surprising statement in that it originated with a traditionally conservative body. The about-turn taken by the Directors at this stage is a clear indication of the potency of the desiccation argument as well as the extent to which the Humboldtian analysis had become acceptable to them. Even to the company the implications

182 Ibid.
183 J. S. Logan, 'The probable effects on the climate of Penang of the continual destruction of its hill jungles', *Journal of the Indian Archipelago*, 2 (1848), pp. 534–5. This was a version of his lecture to the Asiatic Society of Bengal in Calcutta in 1846. At the time, Logan, a geologist, was the editor of the *Journal of the Indian Archipelago*. He had had field experience in both Malaya and India and was able to compare deforestation in the two countries.
184 Despatch no. 21, quoted in Balfour, 'The influence exercised by trees', p. 100.

were clear: Deforestation could no longer be treated as a purely local problem amenable to local solutions.

More striking, however, was the way in which the anxiety which the new scientific insights induced in the Directors meant that the problem of timber supply as a simple raw-material problem had faded into the background, at least temporarily.[185] There were several reasons for this. First, the climatic threat, so successfully articulated by the medical service and by Gibson in particular, by implication threatened the whole fabric of the colonial enterprise and the future of company rule in India. The potential for overall agricultural failure caused by a change in rainfall went beyond supply factors to encompass famine and social breakdown. These concerns had already been pre-empted by the Bombay government in its conservationist response to the firewood crisis and in its appointment of Gibson as a scientist capable of interpreting the degree of risk and the need for a response to apparently unpredictable natural processes. These fears were now taken on by the company as a whole. The anxieties expressed about the 'welfare of mankind' by the Directors need to be seen in context. The strength of the scientific arguments, as well as the improved status of science (and this applied to the medical service in India in particular), was a major factor in explaining the vigour of the Directors' response to Gibson's initiative. However, more subtle political perceptions had provided a fertile ground for the scientific arguments. Europe itself in 1847 and 1848 was becoming increasingly turbulent politically, and Chartism and early syndicalism in England had already made a sharp political impact both domestically and in the colonies. In Ireland the famine had started to take a heavy toll, and, from the point of view of the Directors, Gibson's analysis seemed to promise more of the same for India. It should be recalled that the experience of the famines in 1837–9 in Southern India had prepared the way for changes in the attitudes of the presidency governments. By 1846, with the added lesson of the Irish famine, the Court of Directors had itself undergone a parallel transition in attitude.

On receipt of the Court of Directors' despatch, the government of India, usually tardy in its relations with the presidency governments, took uncharacteristically immediate action and asked the Madras government to provide 'information respecting the effect of trees on the climate and the productiveness of a country or district'.[186] The Madras government acceded surprisingly quickly to this request both by soliciting information on the subject through

---

185 Ribbentrop (*Forestry*, p. 68) states that by the early 1840s 'the necessity of scientific advice was beginning to be more constantly urged'.
186 Government of India to Government of Madras, 28 Aug. 1847, quoted in Balfour, 'The influence exercised by trees', p. 100.

newspaper advertisements throughout the presidency and by circularising officials, mainly through the Revenue Board and the military authorities.[187] The
alacrity of the Madras government in this case can probably be explained as
the consequence of persistent lobbying of that government by Gibson, now
conservator of forests in Bombay, in concert with Blane, the collector in Canara, with whom Gibson co-operated and corresponded extensively. During
1847 and 1848 Gibson and Blane plied the Madras government with letters
and papers that copiously documented the economic and climatic consequences of deforestation. The Madras government had, in a sense, brought
this stream of conservationist propaganda upon itself. This was because, after
refusing an offer by the Bombay government to make Gibson responsible for
the Canara and Gondah forests, it had indicated instead an interest in taking
advantage of Gibson's experience.[188]

Gibson's success in utilising the threat of agricultural failure on the west
coast were deforestation not to be controlled encouraged him to pursue a
similar strategy with the Madras government, in cooperation with Blane. This
time Gibson raised the threat posed to river and coastal trade and transport.
Both in his letters to the government and in his first report to the Bombay
Forest Department, he drew attention to the widespread and chronic siltation
of ports and rivers along the coasts of Madras as a direct consequence of
deforestation and the ensuing soil erosion.[189] This was the same kind of threat
which had proved conclusive in promoting government controls on Mauritius
fifty years earlier. Although Gibson may not have been aware of the Mauritius
experience, his deputy and afterwards successor as conservator, Dalzell, certainly was.[190] Gibson himself had had ample time to become aware of the
connections between deforestation and siltation both during his time in the
Bombay Marine (where he must have witnessed the steady decline in the
capacities of some ports and rivers) and during his extensive travels as a
vaccinator in the Deccan and Kandeish.[191]

Gibson's lobbying of the Madras authorities thus helps to explain the ready
response of the presidency government to the Court of Directors' despatch.
As the reports from the collectorates and different parts of the presidency
started to flow in, most of them tended to confirm the Court's anxieties.[192]

187 Ibid.
188 Stebbing, *Forests*, p. 119.
189 Ibid., pp. 120, 213, 215.
190 N. A. Dalzell, *Observations on the influence of forests and on the general principles of management
   as applicable to Bombay*, Byculla, 1863, p. 5.
191 Burkhill, *Chapters*, p. 101.
192 Balfour, 'The influence exercised by trees', p. 100. The first responses to the circular arrived
   very quickly from Canara, on 31 Aug. 1847 and 8 Nov. 1847, thanks principally to the
   interest of Blane, the collector, in the subject and to his earlier work with Gibson on the

(The method of acquiring information by circular throughout the presidency, while innovative, was not without precedent. Surgeon Patrick Russell [appointed Madras government naturalist after the death of Koenig in 1785] had used the same method to obtain material for his zoological surveys during the early 1790s.)[193]

The environmentalism and radicalism of Edward Green Balfour

By mid 1848 the impact of the replies from the collectorates had served to alarm and even radicalise the Madras government on the deforestation issue at least as much as the Court of Directors had been alarmed by Gibson. Most of the respondents, while confirming the high rates of deforestation (and the surveys of the late 1830s provided a convenient benchmark for these impressions), also confirmed the opinion that rainfall had declined through deforestation. The possibility that famine would result from the reduction in forest cover now became uppermost in the mind of the Madras government. This was a development reinforced by the approach made to the government by assistant surgeon Edward Green Balfour in late 1847.[194] Balfour had been alerted to the government's position by the advertisements placed in the *Madras Spectator,* and he immediately 'furnished the government with a copy of a memorandum on the subject [of deforestation–climate links] which I had written and published about the year 1840'.[195] His interest in the subject was of long standing. It had originated, as Balfour told the secretary to the Madras

topic. Other reports received were from Rajahmundry, 6 Jan. 1848; Coimbatore, 6 Jan.; Kurnool, 29 Feb.; Nellore, 4 March; Calicut, 4 March; Trichinopoly, 7 March; Bellary, 9 March; North Arcot, 26 April; Salem, 10 May.

193 See Chapter 7.

194 'Notes on the influence exercised by trees in inducing rain and preserving moisture', *Madras Journal of Literature and Science,* 25 (1849), 402–48. Edward Green Balfour (1813–89) was educated at Montrose Academy and Edinburgh University. He arrived in India in 1834 and obtained a commission as an assistant surgeon in 1836. Like Alexander Gibson, Balfour was a scholar in several Indian languages as well as Persian. He founded the Madras Government Museum and library in 1850 and compiled the *Cyclopaedia of India* in 1857. The latter followed a prolific and polymathic output of work in literature and science. From 1858 to 1861 he was political agent to the Nawab of the Carnatic and in 1875 was instrumental in the founding of the Madras Medical College for Women. He personally translated and had printed in Hindi, Telugu, Tamil and Kannada Dr T. Conquest's *Outlines of Midwifery.* His later researches were mainly in the fields of Indian indigenous medicine and forestry practice. A list of his publications is to be found in the 1885 edition of the *Cyclopaedia of India.* Balfour stands as the clearest example of an apparent duality of humanist reform and conservation concerns.

195 'The influence exercised by trees', p. 100.

government, in a 'remark in Dr Priestley's writings'. This had 'directed my attention to the influence of trees in the health of man'. It was this that had led him to 'arrange a few notes which I had collected . . . on the influence of trees in inducing rain and preserving nature'.[196]

By this stage the government of Madras had finally submitted plans to the government of India for an establishment to cover the costs of running a forest department on the Bombay model. Provoked by the lack of central government response to its application, the Madras government took the step of reprinting Balfour's 1840 article, with additions, and sending it out to the 'Governments of Bengal, Bombay and Agra' for comments.[197] On 26 May 1849 this elicited a response from the government of India that was distinctive in its complete lack of awareness of the forest problem as it was conceived by the presidency governments. The letter resurrected the old contentions about the sanctity of private property rights and assured the Madras government that landowners were 'always the best stewards of their own lands'.[198]

This unimaginative response from the government of India exasperated the governor and Council in Madras, and it was at this stage that a decision was taken to propagandise the problem by the same methods earlier used by Gibson. This was a very unusual move on the part of government and illustrates the degree to which the Madras authorities found themselves peripheralised and hampered in their ability to respond to what they saw as a crisis. Effectively driven into the same perceptual camp as the medical service, partly as a result of the successful lobbying of the latter, the Madras government found itself adopting the methods of the scientific community and becoming a lobbying interest on its own. In this way, then, a decision was taken by the Madras authorities to sponsor publication of some of the material submitted by Balfour, along with copies of some of the responses received from the collectorates, in the *Madras Journal of Literature and Science*. This initiative was applauded as being likely to promote further investigation of the subject. Certainly it won the Madras government specialist backing in its campaign for establishment of a forestry department. The editor of the journal, J. J. Losh, commenting on the reports, noted:

> Three of these having been placed at the disposal of the Literary Society for publication in their journal, the first inserted is a paper by Assistant Surgeon Balfour, whose attention having been directed to this subject for many years past, his own observations will be found to be interspersed

196 Letter, 3 Feb. 1848, Balfour to Secretary, Madras Govt. in BL, IOL, Home Consultations, V/27/560/107.
197 Minutes of consultation of 8 Sept. 1848, Madras Government, quoted in Balfour, 'The influence exercised by trees', p. 100.
198 Stebbing, *Forests*, p. 123.

with the remarks of different authors, the whole forming a summary of
all that is known regarding this very important subject . . . with this paper
before them, future enquirers will be able to prosecute their labours with
all the exactness that a scientific inquiry of such vast importance to India
demands.[199]

The editor pressed the point home with an allusion to the political influence
which scientific expertise could confer:

That the subject will now be fully investigated there can be no doubt,
for besides an interesting letter received from Surgeon Smith, a very
important one has also been received from General Cullen, whose well-
known scientific character is sufficiently appreciated to ensure the attentive perusal of any remarks that proceed from his pen.

Quoting widely from Boussingault's 1838 paper, Balfour assembled evidence with a thoroughness which had not been attempted before.[200] His report
remains valuable as a representative survey of the literature available to scientists in India in the late 1840s on the connections between forests and
climate. The paper was unashamedly global in its scope and search for precedent. In this sense Balfour showed the kind of concern to present comprehensive information which was to culminate in his compilation of the
Cyclopaedia of India in 1857.
   However, Balfour's 1849 paper is important for reasons going far beyond
the merely technical. He was undoubtedly both unusually radical and open-
minded by nature. These were characteristics which may have been encouraged in his youth by his uncle, Joseph Hume, the leader of the radical party
in the House of Commons and a man who had also at one time been an East
India Company surgeon and who continued to be an active critic of the company.[201]
   Edward Balfour's openly anti-colonialist sentiments must have owed much
to his uncle, with whom he remained in frequent contact until the latter's
death in 1855. But they also typified a set of reformist and radical attitudes
that was widespread among Scottish staff in the company medical service by
the end of the 1840s. Both Hume and Balfour were strongly affected by their
intellectual acquaintance with the physiocrats, but with greatly differing results. In Hume's case, physiocracy persuaded him towards free-trade radicalism, while for Balfour physiocracy justified a statist case for environmental
protection – both, of course, stemming from a basic concern for 'natural law'.
Moreover, both men were attracted by the ideas of Jeremy Bentham and

199 Vol. 36 (1849), 400–1.
200 Balfour, 'Notes on the influence exercised by trees'.
201 Valerie Chancellor, The political life of Joseph Hume, Stratford-on-Avon, 1986, pp. 9–17.

Francis Place. Other aspects of their radicalism were also closely related, as well as being unusual for the time. For example, Hume was an early advocate of female suffrage, a cause which brought for him the ambiguous soubriquet 'Scotland's gift to the world'.[202] Balfour, as an equally strong feminist, pioneered female medical education in India, bringing about the opening of the Madras Medical College to women in 1875. Hume advocated land reform and state intervention to avoid famine in Ireland, just as Balfour did at precisely the same time in India. Perhaps most significant, both men had an avid interest in vernacular literature: the one, of Ireland; the other, of India. While in Balfour's case this was certainly a sympathetic 'Orientalism' (he spoke and wrote several Indian languages and was at one time employed as a government translator of Persian), his enthusiasms indicate a significant and specialised interest in local knowledge and traditions. These gave rise, above all, to his expertise in indigenous medicine and environmental knowledge.[203] Like Sleeman, his contemporary, Balfour was much attracted by Islamic literatures and religion and even set up the Mohammedan Public Library in Madras. Though there is no direct evidence that his Islamic reading influenced his attitudes to the Indian environment (as it clearly did in Sleeman's case), the connection is an intriguing one.

Following a career path almost identical in its first years to that of his illustrious uncle, Balfour managed to combine careers as an acclaimed medical surgeon and a recognised writer on India. From an early date, his reading was wide and cross-disciplinary and was carried on in several European and Indian languages. As a consequence, he was able to supplement his reading on the environmental factors influencing disease (a field on which he published widely in the 1840s) with an appreciation of many of the environmentalist texts and theories already outlined in this book. By 1849 he probably possessed a more comprehensive knowledge of the available literature on climate and environment than anyone else in India or perhaps further afield. He had read from Stephen Hales through Gilbert White to Alexander von Humboldt and had covered even later and more local authorities. But his writings indicate a bias towards the more radical writers, especially those combining environmental critiques with those of the social impact of colonialism, since he quotes lavishly and approvingly from Bernardin de Saint-Pierre and Alexander von Humboldt, who, he asserts, 'must be regarded as valuable authorities'.[204] Bal-

202 *Scotsman*, 1 Sept. 1830.
203 See Balfour, *The Vydian and the Hakim, what do they know of medicine?* Madras, 1875, and *Gul-dastah; or, The bunch of roses*, Madras, 1850. The latter was a lithographed series of extracts from Persian and Hindustani poets.
204 'Notes on the influence exercised by trees', p. 421.

four's interest in Saint-Pierre and in Mauritius appears to have been aroused by a visit he made to that island in 1834, in the course of which he climbed Mount Pieter Both and explored its wet mountain forests. However, he did not confine himself to Saint-Pierre for information on the Mascarenes and quotes other lesser-known sources about Mauritius and Bourbon.[205]

From a reading of his assembled texts, but relying mainly on Bernardin de Saint-Pierre's *Studies of Nature*, Balfour listed twelve facts which he thought could be established regarding the favourable impact of trees on climate. He began his 1849 paper with some exaggeration, stating that 'with the exception of a few localities in Southern India the whole country seems destitute of trees'. Echoing Butter's opinions of 1838, Balfour advocated the widespread introduction of plantations to deal with this shortage: 'Southern India would be greatly enriched and its climate mellowed by the introduction of arboriculture.'[206] In order to achieve reconstructive measures on the scale required, Balfour did not hesitate to advocate a strongly statist solution. It was, he said, only 'the government or the civil servants of the state who could accomplish anything on a great scale, but their efforts may be seconded by every individual resident in it'. Paraphrasing the Zoroastrian sayings of Pierre Poivre, he added that 'the man who makes a few trees grow where none grew before will be a benefactor to this country'. He reinforced his analysis of deforestation-climate links by citing specific historical examples of the connections between drought caused by deforestation and the occurrence of famine in India. Although not specifically rejecting the idea that traditional responses to famine might be distorted by overexacting revenue policies, Balfour preferred to concentrate on demonstrating a link between increased famine incidence, artificially induced changes in water supply and local climatic trends. 'Famines', he wrote,

> have occurred in this country and one or two of them have been caused by wars but most of them have been owing to droughts and our efforts to prevent their recurrence must be . . . to procure an ample supply of water, for rich as the soil is in many parts of India, the soil acts as a very secondary part . . . to obtain our utmost supply of water from the atmosphere we must plant trees; to prevent the rain as soon as it falls from rushing to the rivers and hence to the ocean, in fact to retard its flow and thus be enabled for a longer period to employ it for agricultural purposes we must plant trees, and we must plant trees in order to have a few springs of water trickling from the mountainsides . . . considering

205 E.g. remarks made on moisture in the forests of Bourbon in a 1709 work by a M. de la Roque and an article by J. Hayter in the *Illustrated London News*, 2 Sept. 1848, p. 142.
206 'Notes on the influence exercised by trees', pp. 445–6.

the great numbers famines have destroyed it cannot seem an unnecessary
anxiety again to obtain a more abundant and more regular supply of rain
from the country to prevent their recurrence.[207]

Despite his caution in the main text of the 1849 paper, Balfour implied in
a footnote that he considered the 1770 famine, as had Reynal and Howitt
before him, as being a straightforward consequence of the onset of British
colonial rule and revenue policies.[208] 'Within the first five years from our first
acquisition of the technical sovereignty of the Bengal Provinces in 1765, a
famine prevailed which swept off in two years' time one-third part of the
entire population – probably an exaggeration, but which is not denied by any
party – and destroyed as many of the human race as the whole inhabitants of
the present Kingdom of Holland.'[209] Not content with this historical reference,
he cited a more recent example of famine, that of 1837–9 – the very famine
that had stimulated J. F. Thomas to write his critique of the EIC's laissez-
faire policy.[210] Balfour was here responding to opposition to tree-planting
schemes among those Europeans who believed that forests might be engines
for disease.[211] Contemporary arguments about the origins and vectors of disease were interconnected with broader environmental arguments. Balfour tried
to dismiss the apprehension about miasmic 'reservoirs' of disease in terms of
'relative misery', in which he clearly assessed the health of Europeans as far
less at risk than the vast native majority were at risk from famine. 'The dangers
to Europeans', he wrote,

> are purely imaginary and equally so, in my opinion, to the native popu-
> lation, although their spare diet and spare forms, their food and mode of
> life expose them to the influence of vitiated air. But even with every excess
> we may with full confidence assert that increased mortality which many
> most gratuitously assume as the inevitable consequence of much vegeta-
> tion, would never amount to five hundred thousand, the number of the
> native population that are said to have died in 1839 in India of famine
> alone. A famine sweeping whole cities, nay whole districts of the earth
> must far exceed, in the amount of misery and death it occasions, the
> hardships which could be entailed on a family by one of its members
> being carried from a more sickly climate, even supposing that the planting
> of trees would ever become excessive or cause a climate to change, which
> I do not believe.[212]

207 Ibid., p. 447.
208 Howitt, *Colonisation and Christianity*, p. 268.
209 'Notes on the influence exercised by trees', p. 448.
210 Thomas, 'Notes on ryotwar'.
211 See e.g. Spry, *Modern India*, pp. 184–96.
212 Balfour, 'Notes on the influence exercised by trees', p. 440.

An explicit connection made here by Balfour between forest cover and famine incidence, and the possibility which he held out that protection and planting might actually stem famine helps to explain the alacrity with which Balfour's ideas were taken up at an official level. Indeed, the governor in council 'perused with much pleasure and satisfaction the valuable and very interesting report furnished by Assistant-Surgeon Balfour', deeming it of importance that local revenue officials should be 'in possession of information so intimately concerned with the welfare of the districts under their respective charges'.[213] The paper, it was explained, had already been printed in the Fort St George Gazette for 'general transmission to the Government of India and the Governments of Bengal, Bombay, Agra and the Honourable the Court of Directors'. These statements by the Madras government tend to give the impression that Balfour's desiccationist arguments were accepted without question. In fact, this was far from the case, and some of the responses and debates printed in the *Madras Journal* indicate that his assumption that rainfall decline and deforestation were closely connected was actually strongly contested. Major-General Cullen, for example, the resident in Travancore and Cochin, disputed the forest–rainfall connection, supporting his case with a statement to the same effect made by the Dewan of Cochin.[214] The Madras government clearly sought to control the terms of this debate on rainfall causation; clearly supporting the views of the desiccationists, it sought to give prominence, for example, to views diametrically opposed to those of Cullen which were expressed in documents sent to the chief secretary by surgeon C. I. Smith of the Mysore Commission. This was not surprising, since J. F. Thomas, the Madras chief secretary, was himself a radical who, as we have seen, had advocated strong and statist interventions in famine and forest matters. Furthermore, he seemed more inclined to give credence to the views of the medical surgeons than to the anti-desiccationist views of lay army officers such as Cullen and his colleagues on the revenue boards. Personal contacts made through Thomas and his colleagues with the Madras Literary Society at its headquarters in the city may also have contributed to this government bias towards the views of trained scientists.

The high reputation which Balfour himself enjoyed with the Madras government can partly be attributed to his earlier record, since he had already achieved some prominence as an authority on public health and on the ethnology of hill and forest tribes in Central India.[215] Furthermore, earlier in

---

213 *Madras Journal of Literature and Science*, 36, (1849), p. 401 (editorial).

214 Letter from Cullen to J. F. Thomas (Chief Secretary, Madras Govt), dated at Cochin, 31 March 1849, *Madras Journal of Literature and Science*, 36 (1849), pp. 400ff.

215 'On the migratory tribes of natives of Central India', *Edinburgh New Philosophical Journal*, 1843, pp. 29–47.

1849 he had published some notable papers on the statistics of cholera incidence and on the reasons for the discharge of Indian soldiers from the army.[216]

The links between water supply and cholera, although not proven, were already suspected in 1849. Public health and disease control in general were beginning to acquire an important place in ideas on social reform at this time, particularly after the publication of the Chadwick report in 1842, and the concept of government intervention in this area had become acceptable.[217] In a broader sense, it should be noted, government intervention in health had been advocated in urban areas in Britain since as far back as 1770.[218] Bearing these evolutionary factors in mind, it should therefore come as no surprise to find that Edward Balfour found it both logical and expedient to present the 'forest problem' as being fundamentally a public-health question demanding the kinds of interventionist solutions in the countryside that were being adopted in the urban sanitary landscape. In fact, this was Balfour's major contribution to the analysis of environmental change. Advocates of forest protection could now claim the high ground of what were accepted public-health priorities in India and the metropole.[219]

In endorsing Balfour's views as part of its own propaganda campaign in favour of forest protection, the Madras Presidency had picked a figure who stands out as the most singular representative of a group of government scientists of reformist persuasion. These men, whose influence was first strongly felt in the Madras Presidency in about 1838, combined a reasonably sensitive and atypical interest in the culture and welfare of the indigenous population with an equivalent concern to develop public works specifically related to the basic resource needs of the population. Famine, disease, water supply and forest protection were inextricably linked in their minds. This concern for basic needs far outweighed more short-term commercial considerations, whose facilitation was anyway quite unrelated to the likely employment status and promotional potential of a government surgeon.

216 *Statistics of cholera*, Madras, 1849, and 'Remarks on the abstract tables showing the number of native soldiers discharged from the Madras Army, during the five years from 1842–3 to 1846–7', *Madras Journal of Literature and Science*, 36 (1849).
217 E. Chadwick, *Report on the sanitary conditions of the labouring population of Great Britain*, London, 1842.
218 R. E. Lewis, *Edwin Chadwick and the public health movement, 1832–1854*, London, 1952, p. 27.
219 Balfour himself continued to develop the interest in forest protection which he had acquired by way of a concern for adequate water supplies and through his reading of Butter, Boussingault and Humboldt. His interest in the culture and survival of the hill tribes played a part in this; see 'On the migratory tribes'. The *Cyclopaedia of India*, edited by Balfour in 1857, contained extensive references to the forest-protection problem, and he went on to publish further books on forestry in 1862 and 1885; see Balfour, *The timber trees . . . as also the forests of India*, Madras, 1870.

Retaining the full confidence of the presidency governments, and at the same time open to the most radical reforming concerns then current in Britain, the surgeons were able to take full advantage of the enormous influence which their social position conferred upon them in the company context. Ideas and information flowed quickly and easily among them as a coterie of qualified men. In relating famine incidence to deforestation, Balfour offered the possibility of an effective palliative to widespread utilitarian concern about the ills of the ryots in a way in which discussions of land-tenure problems and land revenue rating alone could not. This is why the Madras government campaign of 1849 is exceptional. It represented a tentative beginning to a structured and interventionist state response to what was by 1849 already being seen as a resource crisis and a social crisis. Moreover, it is hard to conceive of a more millennial threat than the famine-death scenario put forward by Balfour. With the important exception of the efforts of William Roxburgh in Madras in the 1780s, earlier responses to famine had consisted largely in providing granaries and limited public-works schemes for the starving, in even more limited direct relief, in pious hopes that Smithian laws of supply and demand might save the day, or, in some quarters, in a fatalistic and Malthusian acceptance of widespread famine death.[220] Forest conservation presented itself as an alternative solution and, furthermore, one which offered the government opportunities for more direct control over arable land and over unruly 'tribal' people.

It is quite conceivable that the success of the surgeons in changing the policies and views of the presidency governments was assisted by a contemporary shift in the strength of reformist, humanitarian and statist attitudes within the establishment. As suggested above, these shifts in attitude may have been speeded up by the official experiences of Indian and Irish famines, the full appalling scope of which was just beginning to be understood by British society and governments. The exchanges which took place between Hume and Balfour on such matters were simply part of a larger and increasingly anxious official response to famine.[221] Nevertheless, three more local

---

220 See Ambirajan, 'Malthusian population theory and Indian famine policy in the nineteenth century', pp. 5–8.
221 See Woodham-Smith, *The Great Hunger*, pp. 132–269. In order to understand these links further, a study of timing, diffusion of ideas and personnel would be required. Woodham-Smith notes in this respect that 'the conduct of the British government during the Famine is divided into two periods. During the first, from 1845 until the summer of 1847, the government behaved with considerable generosity. An elaborate relief organisation was set up, public works were started on a scale never attempted before . . . but during the second period, after the transfer to the Poor Law in the summer of 1847, the behaviour of the British government is difficult to defend' (p. 408). Nevertheless, in late 1846 and in 1847 the fear of total social breakdown in Ireland was manifest, and it had probably been present earlier. In 1848 Lord Monteagle warned Sir John Russell that 'the crack of the gentry is going on

factors were sufficient impetus: the close contact surgeons necessarily had with the realities of human suffering, their empirical grasp of the resource situation, and their ability through scholarship and wide reading to relate the discoveries and writings of such foreign scientists as Humboldt and Boussingault to the Indian predicament. In exposing the trends of long-term deterioration in soil quality, water supply and climate, they made plain the dangers of laissez-faire governmental strategies. More important, in hoping to husband resources, reduce hazards and promote social-welfare objectives, they allowed the pre-conditions for a 'development-oriented' governing and land-use philosophy to acquire embryonic form. In harnessing the ecological facts of forest clearance and drought to the threat of climatic change and famine as well as to possible loss of production and revenue, the surgeons had uncovered an apparently unassailable argument.[222] It was one which, although not always accepted, became more sophisticated in its formulation and policy consequences as time went on. Edward Balfour in particular continued to play a central part in propagandising desiccationist theories of famine incidence, not least when he was surgeon-general of India at the time of the famines in 1877–9.[223]

The initiatives which Balfour took in 1849 while still a junior assistant surgeon in Madras government service were not initially successful in the face of the intransigence of the government of India. The major perceptual differ-ences among levels of government persisted – an extraordinary phenomenon in view of the environmentally interventionist position adopted in 1847 by the Court of Directors. Nevertheless, it was one whose essence had been under-stood at an early stage by Alexander Gibson and Edward Balfour in their advocacy of the conservation case outside the confines of India. The key to Gibson's success with the Court of Directors and to Balfour's success with the Madras government had consisted in using the authority of internationally generated scientific expertise as an essential part of their propaganda. The essence of this scientific approach lay in its appeal to phenomena not confined to India but experienced world-wide.

right and left', a Poor Law inspector spoke of 'the dread of the break-up of all society' and said that the state of the gentry is awful', and the *Times* prophesied 'a tremendous crash . . . in which all interests and all classes will be swept away': all quoted in Woodham-Smith, p. 373.

222 In a wider social sense the obsession with climate in India and other colonies was reflected in the pages of almost every issue of the popular and scientific journals circulating amongst Europeans in India in the 1840s. Comparisons were often made in Indian medical journals with the climatic conditions in other colonies; see e.g. M. Stovell, 'Notes on the climate of the Cape of Good Hope', *Transactions of the Bombay Medical and Physical Society*, 1849, pp. 195–215. These climatic obsessions set the stage for the more widespread fears of global desiccation which became current in the 1850s; see e.g. Wilson, 'On the general and gradual desiccation of the earth and atmosphere'.

223 See Government of India, *Famine Commission*.

The reluctance of the government of India in 1849 to respond to the medical environmentalists soon led another surgeon, Hugh Cleghorn,[224] to take the political approach of Gibson and Balfour a stage further by publicising the deforestation crisis in India in an extra-Indian scientific context, with the express aim of securing a unitary state strategy for forest protection in India. He did this by raising the issue at a meeting of the British Association for the Advancement of Science (BAAS) in 1850 and then securing a grant from the BAAS to finance a year-long programme of research and a survey of the literature on the whole problem of tropical deforestation throughout India and South-East Asia. The results of the research were published as a twenty-two-page report in the proceedings of the association in 1852.[225]

The report was nominally compiled by a committee but was actually written and edited by Cleghorn himself. It reiterated all the conservation arguments of the previous fifteen years and as such represents a landmark in the history of the colonial response to environmental change. It can be compared both in scope and in the impact it had on government conservation policy with the impact of the Chadwick report of 1842 on public-health policy in Britain.[226] In both cases, a permanent extension of the role of the state was being advocated in a collective interest and in contravention of the interests of private capital. The two reports, one produced at the core of empire and the other at its periphery, were in fact more closely connected in the basis of their thinking than might at first appear. Both reports prescribed state intervention to control water and run-off, the one in the city, the other in the country, on the ground of public-health imperatives. However, although both justified state intervention on the basis of public health and disease (or famine) prevention as being a moral good, the ideological motives behind the reform

---

224 Hugh Francis Cleghorn (1820–95) was born in India, educated at the University of Edinburgh and returned to India in 1842 as assistant surgeon at Shimoga in Mysore, adjacent to the heavily forested Western Ghats. He arrived at Shimoga at a time when extensive forest clearance was taking place. The process clearly made a great impact on him, and he spent the rest of his professional life involved in matters of forest protection. He was made professor of botany and materia medica at Madras in 1851 and was appointed conservator of forests in Madras in 1855 and inspector-general of Indian forests in 1867. Cleghorn acquired his botanical interests from his father, Hugh Cleghorn (1787–1834), private secretary to the governor of Ceylon, who had himself been trained by Johann Peter Rottler, a Tranquebar medical missionary and friend of J. G. Koenig, the first Madras government naturalist. The younger Cleghorn's interest in Humboldt and his appointment of German staff to the Madras Forest Conservancy may be related to these German botanical connections. The governor of Ceylon during Cleghorn's youth there was George Walker, who had previously been governor of St Helena. Whether Cleghorn junior became acquainted with St Helena's problems thereby is open to surmise. See Cleghorn, *Forests and gardens of South India*, DNB, and Burkill, *Chapters*, pp. 76–86.

225 Cleghorn et al., 'Report of the committee'.

226 Chadwick, *Report on the sanitary conditions of the labouring population of Great Britain*.

Plate 22. Hugh Francis Cleghorn, 1820–95, conservator of forests in the Madras Presidency (1855) and inspector-general of Indian forests (1867). (Reproduced by permission of the University of St Andrews)

programmes of both Chadwick and Cleghorn need to be treated with some circumspection. In fact, it seems likely that Chadwick was inspired principally by Benthamite ideas about control and state power rather than by reformist altruism, and that elimination of the misery of poverty was not his principal objective.[227] However, the medical service's connections with Bentham were far less explicit than they were with the quite different ideology of Alexander von Humboldt. Any attempt to explain Cleghorn's environmentalism (which, like that of Balfour, influenced forest policy over several decades) would probably require, initially, some exploration of his religious background. This con-

227 See Julian Martin, 'Edwin Chadwick: Social or medical reformer?', M. Phil. diss., Dept of the History and Philosophy of Science, University of Cambridge, 1984, pp. 27–8.

sisted in almost fanatical adherence to a personal and idiosyncratic evangelical revivalism coupled with a Scott-like enthusiasm for 'romantic' scenery.[228] As an early environmentalist in India, Cleghorn could, and did, exercise both of these personal bents, in much the way that his Scottish contemporary, John Croumbie Brown, preached and practised an environmental gospel in South Africa.[229] Along with Balfour's papers, the Cleghorn report and its recommendations became the basis, in terms of analysis and prescription, for most of the subsequent colonial responses to the problems of environmental degradation in India and further afield. Before this could take place, however, it required the utilitarian efforts of yet another Scot, Lord Dalhousie, as governor-general, to convert the environmentalism of the surgeons into an all-India forest-protection policy. In the course of doing so, in his first few years as governor-general Dalhousie appears to have absorbed the tenets of the medical environmentalists and, equally important, the implications of pre-colonial models of arboricultural practice, especially those found in Sind and the Punjab.

The legacy of Balfour and the Sindhi amirs: Lord Dalhousie and the influence of pre-colonial forestry on a utilitarian project

Lord Dalhousie arrived in India in 1847. The new governor-general's utilitarian bent and his ambitions for expanding the administrative and technical role of the state quickly led him to sympathise (albeit for partially different motives) with the interventionist approach adopted by the medical service to what was now widely referred to as the 'forest problem'.[230] In fact, it seems that Dalhousie was first alerted to the significance of the forest issue through his meeting with J. D. Hooker, son of Sir William Hooker, director of the Royal Botanic Gardens at Kew. This occurred through the chance circumstance that both men travelled out to India in 1847 in the same entourage.[231]

228 See University of St Andrews Archives, Cleghorn Papers: Hugh Cleghorn's notebooks on sermons, Box 12.
229 See Grove, 'Scottish missionaries, evangelical discourses and the origins of conservation thinking in Southern Africa', *Journal of Southern African Studies*, 15 (1989), 22–39.
230 See Stokes, *The English Utilitarians and India*, pp. 248–51. While Stokes discussed Dalhousie's interest in establishing all-India authorities, he did not deal at all with what was one of Dalhousie's longest-lasting legacies: the all-India Forest Department, the basis for which was first established in 1851 in the Punjab. The department was formalised in a memorandum of 1854, the same year in which Dalhousie's famous 'education despatch' was gazetted.
231 W. B. Turrill, *Joseph Dalton Hooker: Botanist, explorer and administrator*, London, 1963, pp. 50–1; Huxley, *Life and letters of Sir Joseph Dalton Hooker*, vol. 1.

As a result, Hooker played a major role in alerting Dalhousie to the possible consequences of deforestation. He thereby perpetuated the part played by his father in lobbying both Alexander Gibson and the Cape government on the advisability of forest protection. It was Hooker's visit to St Helena and Ascension Island in 1842 that had convinced him conclusively of a dynamic relationship between forest cover and rainfall. He had been especially impressed by the alleged success of Roberts's and Beatson's reafforestation programmes on St Helena in promoting an increase in rainfall on the island.[232] These claims had been enabled by Sir Joseph Banks's efforts to promote a continuous series of meteorological observations on St Helena from 1811, in direct imitation of Roxburgh's earlier weather researches in the Madras Presidency.[233] This had led Hooker, in turn, to promote a tree-planting programme on Ascension Island with the Navy authorities, for whom the island had recently acquired a degree of strategic importance. Shortly after Dalhousie's contacts with Hooker on the subject, he was supplied by the Madras government with Balfour's 1849 paper. This would have reinforced Hooker's St Helena dictums, since Balfour had made great play of Boussingault's findings on the effects of afforestation on Ascension Island and of the reports made in the *St Helena Almanac* of 1848, which had attributed the considerable rainfall increase during the 1840s to government tree planting.[234] Dalhousie's enthusiasm for government intervention in arboriculture and forest reservation was thus given considerable initial encouragement by the example of St Helena and, even more conclusively, by the literature surveys of Edward Balfour.

By 1850, too, the continued influence of Hooker and the well-publicised efforts of the Madras government to instigate and fund a formal conservancy had helped to convince Dalhousie of the significance of deforestation and the need for a centralised state response, as he admitted in a minute he wrote in February 1851. In it he recorded that when, during the last season, he had

> traversed the plains of the Punjab . . . there was one characteristic of the
> wide tract which could not fail to strike the least observant traveller . . .
> I refer to the almost total absence of forest trees and of even fruit trees
> and of bushes leaving the whole territory unadorned by the foliage which
> is its natural cover, nor stocked with the timber requisite for a thousand
> purposes in the every-day life of the people who dwell in it . . . this is a
> manifest and will shortly be felt to be an increasing evil unless some
> measures are taken to provide at present a remedy for the future . . . the

232 Duffey, 'The terrestrial ecology of Ascension Island'; Beatson, *Tracts*, pp. 194–5.
233 Beatson, *Tracts*, p. xxxv.
234 Boussingault based his comments on Ascension Island on an essay by one Desbassyn, quoted in Balfour, 'Notes on the influence exercised by trees', p. 436. Balfour, in turn (p. 408), had used the 1848 *St Helena Almanac*, p. 5.

Government should provide some means to that end and should bring
them into operation without delay.

At this stage Dalhousie was already well aware of the climatic arguments,
as he made clear in the memorandum. As a result, he felt strongly

> the urgent duty of endeavouring to give to this country the clothing of
> forest trees from my knowledge of the well-ascertained and beneficial
> effect which trees produce on the healthiness and fertility of the tracts in
> which they are found. No power has been more clearly established than
> this salubrious and fertilizing effect of foliage in an Indian climate. It has
> been the subject of much enquiry and has been affirmed and demon-
> strated in every report submitted from different parts of India, many of
> which have passed through my hands, and one of which I forwarded to
> the local government in the Punjab some time ago ... None of us can
> live to see the complete result of that which we now propose to com-
> mence. Few of us will gather the fruit where now we plant. But if we
> succeed in framing this design and advance it in some degree towards
> completion, we may at least enjoy the satisfaction of feeling that we shall
> leave behind us an heritage for which posterity will be grateful.[235]

An examination of the language and terms used by Dalhousie in his Punjab
minute indicates a strong reliance on Balfour's environmentalist arguments,
which the governor-general clearly found convincing, supported as they were
by the authority of J. F. Thomas and the Madras government.

It was the military annexation of the Punjab in 1849 that provided the
context for a pioneering attempt at state arboriculture in North-West India.
The detailed planning for this enterprise, which provided the first field experience of state forestry for Dalhousie, is extensively documented in the
records of the Agri-Horticultural Society of the Punjab. This episode has, to
date, been entirely neglected by writers on the history of Indian state forestry.
As a consequence, the critical influence of pre-colonial forest practices in providing models (rather than just a legitimation) for early management methods
in colonial state forestry has not been properly appreciated. The history and
enormous scale of the forest system established in the Indus valley by the
Amirs of Sind has already been referred to in this chapter. The annexation
of Sind by Sir Charles Napier provided an opportunity to set up an embryonic
forest administration based directly upon the infrastructure of shikargahs, or
game and forest reserves. This development was due largely to Napier's per-

235 'Minute on agriculture' from Dalhousie to Agri-Horticultural Society of Lahore, 20 Feb.
    1850, read to the Society on 12 Aug. 1851 and published in J. L. Stewart, ed., *Select papers
    of the Agri-Horticultural Society of the Punjab from its commencement to 1862*, Lahore, 1865,
    pp. 1–5; quoted in J. Storr-Lister, 'Tree-planting in the Punjab', *Cape Monthly*, 1873, pp.
    365–8.

sonal interest in forestry matters. The shikargahs had first come to his notice
during the military campaigns against the Talpur amirs in 1843, when the
reserves had been very effectively used as coverts for guerrilla action by the
indigenous forces. In May 1843 Napier learnt that the amirs were accustomed
to sell firewood rights in some of the shikargah forests for up to 300,000 rupees
per annum for a single forest. 'If this species of property is so valuable', he
wrote, 'it may well demand a district establishment to attend to it.'[236] Napier
therefore recommended to Lord Ellenborough, the governor-general, that he
write to J. C. Loudon, a celebrated forestry expert of his acquaintance, for
advice and assistance. 'If your Lordship', he added, 'could appoint someone
acquainted with the care of forests to be at the head of an establishment it
would prove a great source of revenue . . . I formerly devoted much of my
time to this study, but it is impossible for me to attend [now] to such matters.'[237] Whoever was appointed, he thought, 'must be eternally in these woods
to regulate the cutting and pruning'. Loudon, he thought, would suggest
'someone whose character he could depend on and who would come to this
country accompanied by half a dozen assistants'.[238]

Ellenborough, however, preferred to use local expertise and suggested that
a Captain Baker, of the Bengal Engineers, should be appointed with 'several
scientific officers' to survey and administer the ancient canals and forest reserves of the amirs under a single agency.[239] Baker duly arrived in Sind in
1843, while the efficient Ellenborough despatched the necessary scientific survey instruments to Karachi by sea.[240] One of the earliest measures taken by
Napier and Baker's new forest administration was to open the forests up to
the local peasantry and small landowners to enable them to forage their animals and take forest produce free of charge. Since this represented a complete
reversal of the exclusionist policy of the pre-colonial ruler, much short-term
political credit was thereby gained, although in a fashion much criticised by
some contemporary British officials.[241]

The further development of the Sind Canal and Forest Department is of
great importance to our narrative. This is not least because two of its early

236 PRO, Ellenborough Papers, 30/12/61: Letter to Ellenborough, 22 May 1843. See also Sind
　　Archives, Karachi: Political 201, Sind file for 1843.
237 PRO, Ellenborough Papers, 30/12/61.
238 John Claudius Loudon (1783–1843) was probably the best-known arboriculturist of the time.
　　As the founder of the *Gardener's Magazine*, Loudon was John Ruskin's first publisher. He
　　also laid out the Birmingham Botanic Garden and published *Arboretum et fruticetum Britan-
　　nicum* (8 vols., London, 1838), which would have been known to Napier.
239 PRO, Ellenborough Papers, 30/12/94: Letter to Napier 16 June 1843.
240 Ibid., 13 Aug. 1843.
241 John Jacob, 'Notes on administration,' (original MS), p. 58n, quoted in H. T. Lambrick, *Sir
　　Charles Napier and Sind*, Oxford, 1952, p. 322.

administrators, John Ellerton Stocks (a company surgeon) and N. A. Dalzell, became prominent in the early development, structuring and methods of the Bombay Presidency Forest Department and (in the case of Dalzell) in establishing the theoretical desiccationist and climatic rationales for an all-India forest-conservation system.[242] Similarly, Alexander Gibson, founder of the department, possessed an intimate knowledge of the pre-colonial Sind system and incorporated many of its features in the running of the first large-scale colonial forest-reserve system outside Sind itself, where the reserves were run much as they had been under the amirs, albeit in a rather more relaxed fashion.[243] The first few years spent in working the Indus valley shikargahs as a forest department are extensively documented and indicate a constant chopping and changing of policy by a chronically undermanned forest staff, largely overwhelmed by the demands that were now made on the forests by the local inhabitants as a result of Napier's indulgent policy on access.[244] Until about 1850 the experience of the Sind Forest Department was really the only working example of formalised state forest reservation that was available to the East India Company authorities outside the plantations run on the sites marked out by Roxburgh and Wallich. Although by 1850 some experimental teak plantations had been started by Lieutenant Connolly at Nilumbur in Malabar at the suggestion of the local rajah, few of the trees were more than six years old. As a result, Dalhousie's interest in developing state arboriculture in the Punjab meant that surgeon John Stocks was soon consulted by the Punjab Board of Administration on the long-established management system of Sind. This took place at the same time as district officers throughout the Punjab were being asked to provide local forest information. Stocks, however, was the only outside expert consulted at this stage.[245] Stocks's career is clearly of some interest in considering the diffusion of the Sind forest-management system. As a surgeon and botanist, his knowledge of the Indus environment had become well developed since his transfer from Bombay to Sind in 1843. Several years later it was stated locally that 'none gave so much satisfaction as did Stocks while [the forests] were under his management . . . for works of this

---

242 See Dalzell, *Observations on the influence of forests*.

243 Gibson's expertise on the Sind forest system and the probability that he adapted it for use in the Western Ghats are attested to by Edward Balfour in his 1885 edition of the *Cyclopaedia*, entry 'Alexander Gibson'.

244 Lieutenant Walter Scott, *Report on the management of canals and forests in Scinde*, Calcutta, 1853, esp. pp. 63–7; BL, IOL, V/23/206 (or National Library of India, Calcutta, G.P. 333.5 (5431); B 639, SPB, no. 7). See also Baker, 'Report on the economic condition of roads, canals and forests in Sind', 1846, 56pp, IOL, V/23/345 (1).

245 Proceedings of the Board of Administration for the Affairs of the Punjab, 13 April 1852, and circular sent to all Commissioners, 1 March 1852, in Stewart, *Select papers of the Agri-Horticultural Society*, pp. 5–6.

description where improvements are so invaluable to the revenues, men of first rate abilities are necessary'.[246] However, this emphasis on revenue gives a somewhat misleading impression, since the forest staff in the late 1840s considered that a major part of their raison d'être was to protect the forests in order to prevent river-bank erosion and the agriculturally disastrous incidence of sand drift. Scott, for example, in his 1848 report (printed in 1853) pointed to the significant role played by the amirs' forests in this respect. 'I am clearly of the opinion', he wrote, 'that the woods in Scinde are extremely useful in preventing the drift of sand and that they ought to be extended' for this purpose, 'as I proposed in a former portion of this report'.[247] However, to do this, he thought, it would be necessary to 'exclude cattle' and remove the provision of free access Napier had allowed to the local farmers. The main advantages of this would consist in preventing sand drift and assuring a local supply of firewood. The negligible financial returns from the forests, Scott asserted, did not show by any means their value to the government'.[248]

The priority of protecting forests and preventing erosion rather than increasing revenue was reflected in the report which Stocks presented to the Punjab Board of Administration in October 1852. Stocks was particularly keen that the new government should follow the methods of the amirs, commenting that 'the mode which they took to ensure the growth of a jungle was well suited to the ends proposed'. He noted that 'by stakes or walls' they enclosed 'large tracts of ground and let the natural jungle come up unrepressed, *taking especial care that no goats and no animals got admittance, or indeed any living being as far as they could prevent it*'.[249] Such measures under the amirs, he pointed out, had required 'co-operation on the part of neighbouring Village authorities, combined with the presence of a Government Keeper, or a Fence and Keeper'.[250]

These strictures by the amirs, Stocks noted, contrasted with the much looser colonial regime, under which 'since our occupation, nothing has been done, but to keep up the wood at present existing . . . but all this within the

246 *Scindian*, 12 July 1856, quoted in Balfour, *Cyclopaedia* (1857), article entitled 'Timber and Fancy Woods of Eastern and Southern Asia', p. 1936.
247 Scott, *Report on the management of canals and forests*, pp. 63–5.
248 Initial plans to charge the grazing fees imposed by the amirs were soon abandoned, as Scott recorded: 'Captain Rathbone settled with me that as the people derived absolute and great advantages from being allowed to cultivate the forest at all, that they ought not to be allowed to graze free. He has now changed his opinion, however, and says that the charge for grazing interferes with cultivation . . . at present much of my time is taken up with forest disputes and the people are so detached [*sic*] that I cannot be certain that I even get the truth of any complaints' (ibid., p. 65).
249 'Report on the forests of Sind by Assistant Surgeon J. E. Stocks, Forest Ranger in Sind', 29 Oct. 1852, in Stewart, *Select papers of the Agri-Horticultural Society*, pp. 18–21 (my italics).
250 Ibid., p. 19.

old forest limits, which have also been encroached on by cultivators by permission of Government to a vast extent, as far as the unwooded and waste
parts of the forest are concerned'. Stocks therefore advocated a reversion to
the methods of the amirs. His opinions are important for a number of reasons,
not least because they demonstrate that the enormous reserves of the pre-
colonial regime were run a great deal more tightly and unsympathetically to
small farmers than was the case after colonial annexation. Considerations of
access by the local population were more important under the colonial regime
than in earlier times. Furthermore, Stocks's recommendations were seized
upon by Dalhousie and the Punjab authorities and seem to have formed the
basis for much of Dalhousie's later attitude towards forest administration. In
particular, he acted on Stocks's approval of the expansionist policies of the
amirs in rapidly enlarging the areas of state-controlled forest, even at the
expense of revenue-earning agriculture.

Stocks himself, along with N. A. Dalzell and Alexander Gibson, went on
quite independently to apply the exclusionist policies of the amirs in the Bombay Presidency, as Gibson's official reports reveal. Before 1865 the local subordinate officers of the Bombay Conservancy, as in Sind, were employed and
named according to indigenous usage rather than according to imported
terms.[251] Indeed, adherence to indigenous models took place to such an extent
that little recourse was made in the pre-Mutiny period to the Continental
forest-management systems of Germany and France, which have long been
supposed to have been slavishly adhered to by early colonial foresters in India.
Even Dietrich Brandis himself acknowledged the legacy, noting that 'we owe
the maintenance of forests in Sindh and of the rukhs in the Punjab entirely
to the actions taken by the former rulers; and that during the first period after
the occupation of the country, the action of the British government has not
in all cases been favourable to the preservation of forests and woodland in the
arid and dry regions of India'.[252] One could hardly hope to find a more au-

---

251 For local nomenclatures and the influence of Sindhi and Maratha pre-colonial management
   models, see Alexander Gibson, 'Description of the system adopted for the forestry conservancy of the Bombay Presidency', in Gibson, ed., *A handbook for the forests of the Bombay
   Presidency*, Byculla, 1863. E. Aitken, in the *Gazetteer of Sind* of 1847, pp. 40ff, notes that
   Scott was followed as forest ranger (conservator) by 'Capt. Crawford, Dr Stocks, Captain
   Hamilton, and Mr Dalzell' and that it was Hamilton and Dalzell who first re-marked the
   boundaries of the pre-colonial shikargahs as forest reserves. All these men, it should be noted,
   went on to join the Bombay Presidency Forest Conservancy under Gibson and then (in the
   case of Stocks and Dalzell) to succeed him as conservators. Sind was also a training ground
   for figures who later became prominent in foresty circles much later in the century. Schlich,
   for example, who later became professor of forestry at Oxford University, was made conservator of Sind in 1871.
252 D. Brandis, 'On the distribution of forests in India', *Transactions of the Scottish Arboricultural
   Society*, 7 (1873), 90, and 'Sind forests', *Indian Forester*, 4 (1879), 359–64.

thoritative testament to the significance of pre-colonial forestry methods in North-West India. Moreover, as Brandis went on to say, 'past neglect' by the British in this respect had been made good in the Punjab, 'where extensive plantations have been made . . . which now cover upwards of 12000 acres'. Of course this was a derisory figure in comparison with the area of over a million acres reafforested by the amirs between 1783 and 1843. Nevertheless, it provided Dalhousie with some important interventionist, and largely indigenously inspired, experience in the critical period before he decided on a fully fledged and utilitarian forest project for the whole of India.

A survey of the forests of Burma in the late 1840s by surgeon John McClelland, an ardent enthusiast of natural history and an advocate for the preservation of rare plants, provided a further stimulus to Dalhousie's interest in forest protection, since McClelland strongly advised rigorous state intervention and reservation to save the rapidly disintegrating forests of Pegu.[253] One part of his report was especially innovative and constituted articulate advocacy of a notion that in more modern parlance would be termed 'sustainable yield'. A forest, McClelland argued,

> may be a regarded as a growing capital, the resources of which are young trees, and unless these are preserved and guarded to maturity, it is obvious that a forest must necessarily degenerate from the nature of an improving capital to that of a sinking fund, which, given time, must become expended. The loss occasioned by the removal of an undersized tree is not merely the difference in value as compared with a full-grown tree as a piece of timber, but must be estimated by the number of years the forest may be deprived, by its removal, of the annual distribution of its seed, which period will vary according to the stage of growth at which it was cut down, and the time which it would otherwise have taken to arrive at maturity.
>
> If we fail in the comparatively simple duty of preserving the old forests, we can scarcely hope to succeed in the more difficult task of creating new ones. Planting as a means of extension, when carried out in connection with thriving forests, might, indeed, become a duty; with a view of perpetuating an object that conferred a lasting benefit on society. . .

The economic justification presented here for a programme of conservancy in *existing* forests, in preference to an arboriculture to create new forests, was

253 Burkill, *Chapters*, p. 155; Stebbing, *Forests*, p. 206. Exports of finished teak from the Moulmein district of Burma were rising rapidly at the time McClelland recommended the exclusion of private timber companies from Burma. E. O'Reilley, in 'The vegetable products of the Tenasserim Provinces', *Journal of the Indian Archipelago*, 4 (1850), 55–65, records the following exports of finished teak prior to 1850 from the Moulmein region (in net timber tons): 1840, 4,952; 1841, 6,399; 1842, 11,457; 1843, 10,528; 1844, 14,245; 1845, 13,360; 1847, 11,225; 1848, 18,000.

clearly found convincing by the authorities. Indeed, the continued influence of McClelland's report and of the slightly earlier Cleghorn report led directly to the formulation of the 'Dalhousie memorandum' of 1855 which became the main basis for the centralised forest-management policy adopted in India after 1860.[254] In the Madras Presidency, Hugh Cleghorn's increasingly senior status in the medical service and his editorship of the BAAS report led directly to his appointment by Lord Harris as conservator of forests in the Madras Presidency, the Madras Forest Department being finally established in 1855. A year later a further department, run on a co-operative basis with the princely government, was opened in Mysore. This too was headed by Cleghorn, at the request of Sir Charles Cubbon.[255] By the time of the Mutiny, therefore, the basic infrastructure of state forest conservation was in place in all presidencies as well as elsewhere in India. The significance of this development has, perhaps, been lost in much recent historical literature. This is largely because attention has been focussed on the undeniable erosion of customary patterns of access to Indian forests during the colonial period and the patterns of popular resistance that developed in some regions as a consequence. While important as part of a 'subaltern' history of colonial India, this preoccupation has served to obscure another equally interesting story. This consisted in an unusually precocious and (often literally) non-conformist response to a series of ecological, climatic and subsistence crises which were perceived to exist on a scale paralleled in more modern times only by the drought crises of sub-Saharan Africa since the 1970s.

This response was based primarily on the prescriptions and political influence exerted by six EIC surgeons, William Roxburgh, Alexander Gibson, Edward Balfour, Hugh Cleghorn, John Ellerton Stocks and John McClelland.[256] Their success in promoting environmental interventionism as part of the re-

---

254 Burkill, *Chapters*, p. 155; Stebbing, *Forests*, p. 206.
255 Cleghorn, *Forests and gardens*, p. x.
256 Of course the much later rise to prominence of Dietrich Brandis, employed after the Mutiny to set up an all-India Forest Department on the recommendation of Hugh Cleghorn, was an important development. But it took place long after the principle of a state forest-conservation service had been established throughout India. This should be borne in mind when considering some recent analyses of the history of the forest service in India, e.g. R. Guha in 'Forestry in British and post-British India: A historical analysis', *Economic and Political Weekly*, 1983, pp. 1882–96. Since Guha attributes to Brandis many of the foundations of a 'scientific' ideology used to conceal straightforward considerations of the imperial need for raw-material resources, the divergence is an important one. Brandis was in fact far less concerned with the climatic risks of deforestation than were the Scottish surgeons who first promoted state conservation. It was not, either, simply a question of the introduction of German forest methods; German foresters had been employed as early as 1856 by the Madras Forest Conservancy, and Herr Wrede had been employed as a forest consultant by the Bombay authorities as early as 1805: See Cleghorn, *Forests and gardens*, p. 19.

sponsibility of the colonial state marked the continuing, and for practical purposes permanent, influence of a mixture of physiocratic, Priestleyite, Scottish Hippocratic and Humboldtian thinking on British colonial environmental attitudes. But this was not all. Underlying their environmental critique, a radical and reformist message was being articulated in which a real concern about environmental health was used as a vehicle to express anxieties about the social and moral consequences of colonialism and industrialism. Sometimes this concern was expressed in millennial terms, so that famine and the dire physical and economic results of deforestation were actually cast as the consequences of a social transgression committed on the Indian peasantry. This idea was particularly strong with Edward Balfour and can be seen as a consequence of his effective conversion to the texts and physiocratic reformism of Bernardin de Saint-Pierre and his strong family connections with a Scottish radical tradition. But Balfour was not alone. Many of the other Scottish surgeons shared this radicalism, as well as sharing an interest in indigenous environmental knowledge and forest management.[257] Nevertheless, the rich variety of motives underlying the scientific arguments of the surgeons would have been of little avail were it not for the fact that they were fronted by climatic arguments threatening famine, economic failure and societal breakdown.

Setting the commencement of environmental protection in India in a wider perspective

The very early incorporation of conservationism as an accepted part of the role of the colonial state in India needs to be set in a broader context. There is no doubt that environmental sensibilities in Britain, for example, were, among some groups, almost as well developed by the 1860s as they were among the scientific services in India.[258] They were very different kinds of sensibilities, however, and were associated with different kinds of social critique. The biota of Europe were simply not perceived as being threatened by

257 There is no doubt, for example, of the particularly radical social opinions of Surgeon Robert Wight; see Cleghorn et al., 'Report of the Committee', p. 32.
258 See P. D. Lowe, 'Values and institutions in the history of British nature conservation', in A. Warren and F. G. Goldsmith, eds., *Conservation in perspective*, London, 1983, pp. 329–51. Lowe deals mainly with the transition from animal-protection movements to bird preservation. These movements did not involve a consciousness of the ability of man to destroy the environment on a global scale. Lowe also omits the critical part played by scientists in lobbying government and ignores the fact that systematic ecological research began in India (principally with surgeons Hugh Cleghorn and M. P. Edgeworth). See also D. E. Allen, 'The early history of plant conservation in Britain', *Transactions of the Leicester Literary and Philosophical Society*, 72 (1980), 35–50.

Plate 23. The Committee of the Madras Literary and Scientific Society in about 1860. Hugh Cleghorn (holding a symbolic staff of teak) sits at the far right. Edward Balfour (appropriately holding a fern specimen) is the standing figure. (Reproduced by permission of the Sprott family of Stravithie, Fife)

rapid ecological change of the kind that was taking place in India. As a result, embryonic worries about the destruction of rural landscapes and about species extinctions remained the concern of a largely ineffective minority. Only the cause of animal protection, strongly advocated by the Quakers, had resulted in serious legislation. As Turner has shown, this was a cause with strong institutional and personal links with anti-slavery campaigning, and it was strongly identified with an emerging urban reform movement.[259]

Interest in the aesthetics of the rural landscape in metropolitan France and Britain was already well developed by the end of the eighteenth century, as the writings of John Clare, Southey, Gilpin and some others demonstrate.[260]

---

259 J. Turner, *Reckoning with the beast: Animals, pain and the Victorian mind*, London, 1980, pp. 15–38.
260 'Within the last thirty years', wrote Southey in 1807, 'a taste for the picturesque has sprung

So too, the rise of what Raymond Williams has called the 'green language' corresponded to the emotional commitment that had developed in relation to the threat perceived to the old landscape pattern (and the rural working lives and ethos it represented) in the context of the 'agricultural industrialisation' of the late-eighteenth-century enclosures. By the 1840s what had been a minority interest at the time of John Clare had flowered into a major literary and popular preoccupation or cult.[261] In 1844, for example, Sir Robert Peel is reported to have commented at some length on the reasons why he collected pictures of 'wild' landscapes and on the solace that such landscapes were to him in his urban work.[262] In spite of this, the fact remains that where individuals did campaign against the despoliation of the landscapes they valued by the forces of capital and by the spread of railways and, above all, by the incursions of urban housing, their efforts were, until at least the mid 1850s, notably unsuccessful. The failure of the attempts made by William Wordsworth to restrain railway building in the Lake District serves to illustrate this point.[263]

Concerns about species extinctions in Europe developed much later than the preoccupation with rural landscape, as attempts to outline the intellectual history of concern about species extinction in Britain have already demonstrated.[264] Here too the early expression of concern about human depredations on species did not result in any direct involvement by the state. The idiosyncratic and exceptional efforts made by Charles Waterton to make his estate into a nature reserve constitute an interesting precedent and are an indication of the level of awareness of the human destructive potential that had developed by the 1830s in Britain.[265]

up . . . a new science for which a new language has been formed and for which the English have discovered a new sense in themselves, which assuredly was not possessed in their fathers', quoted in K. Thomas, *Man and the natural world*, p. 267.

261 R. Williams, *The country and the city*, pp. 127–42.

262 C. Brown, *Dutch paintings*, London, 1983, p. 11. Brown quotes Mrs Jameson, in *Private galleries of art in London* (1844), recording a conversation with Sir Robert Peel when he was prime minister. She remembers Peel saying, ' "I cannot express to you the feeling of tranquillity, of restoration . . . with which, in an interval of harassing official business, I look around me here." ' . . . he turned his eyes on a forest scene of Ruisdael and gazed on it for a minute or two in silence.'

263 *A complete guide to the English lakes*, London, 1842, pp. 160, 150–5.

264 Allen, 'The early history of plant conservation in Britain'.

265 N. Moore, ed., *Essays on natural history by Charles Waterton*, London, 1871, pp. 119–35. His actions were exceptional, even eccentric. One of the interesting features of Charles Waterton's initiatives is that he had travelled very extensively in South America shortly after Humboldt, and there is little doubt that his enthusiasm for natural history and for the fate of species in Britain was closely associated with his enthusiasm for tropical wildlife and tropical forests in particular; see Waterton, *Wanderings in South America, the North-West of the United States*

Consciousness of the role of man in causing extinctions had, as we saw in earlier chapters, developed much earlier among botanists stationed in tropical-island colonies and in India than it had in Europe. Certainly by as early as 1810 Saint-Pierre and Commerson on Mauritius, Alexander Anderson on St Vincent, Burchell on St Helena and Kyd and Roxburgh in Bengal had all acquired some insight into the phenomenon; and it undoubtedly affected their approach to matters affecting environmental control by the state. At a more generalised level of discourse, this early colonial awareness, particularly of processes taking place on St Helena, was vital in acquainting Charles Darwin with ideas about extinction and endemism at critical points in the voyage of the *Beagle*.

But Darwin was not alone in this. By the early 1840s Ernst Dieffenbach, in his work on the fauna of New Zealand and the Chatham Islands and then in his studies of Mauritius, had become acutely aware of the potential for further rapid extinctions as European capital-intensive economic activity spread over the whole globe.[266] Others reacted with interventionist ideas. For example, Hugh Edwin Strickland, first made aware of the extinction problem by his work on the palaeontology of the dodo and other extinct birds of the Mascarenes, actually suggested that the entire colony of New Zealand should be made a nature reserve to save its remaining indigenous fauna.[267] This was at a time when the value of rare island faunas was being recognised in the formulation of theories about species origins, not only by Darwin but also by Strickland, Dieffenbach and Joseph Hooker.[268]

The striking thing about all these early colonial concerns with extinction is that, whilst they certainly constituted a hidden motivation behind many of the other arguments used to justify forest protection in Mauritius and India before 1847, they rarely made overt appearances in scientific debates and very rarely affected government policy. There are notable exceptions to this rule, one example being the case of the measures taken to protect the elephants of Knysna Forest in the Cape Colony during 1846, although even this can prob-

and the Antilles in the years 1812–1824, 2nd ed., London, 1880, esp. pp. 289–94. Here he writes of the forests of the Americas that 'Nature is fast losing her ancient garb and putting on a new dress in these extensive regions . . . spare . . . these noble sons of the forest beautifying your landscapes beyond all description; when they are gone a century will not replace their loss, they cannot, they must not fall.'

266 *Travels in New Zealand:* on extinctions, pp. 7–12, 50–2; on forest destruction, pp. 257, 297–98; on the destructive impact of man, pp. 416–17.

267 H. E. Strickland, 'Report on the recent progress and present state of ornithology', *Report of the Proceedings of the British Association for the Advancement of Science*, 1848, pp. 170–221; Strickland and Melville, *The dodo and its kindred*.

268 See M. Di Gregorio, 'Hugh Edwin Strickland (1811–1853) on affinities and analogies, or, The case of the missing key', *Ideas and Production*, 7 (1987), 35–50.

ably be explained better in terms of previous decisions taken for quite other reasons to protect the forests in which the elephants lived.[269]

At the time that Alexander Gibson was attaining some success in securing state conservation in the Bombay Presidency in 1847, the threat of species extinction was still not a truly credible one in the eyes of most scientists in India, let alone in the eyes of the colonial state. Even in the pages of the Cleghorn report to the BAAS, the concept of species extinctions made only a veiled appearance when it was pointed out that forest destruction might entail the disappearance of many medically and potentially economically useful plants.[270]

It is true, however, that individual conservation propagandists such as surgeons Hugh Cleghorn and Robert Wight often expressed a virulent hostility to much in the way of development of a colonial infrastructure.[271] Cleghorn in his own books deprecated the extension of railways into the highlands of Southern India, largely for aesthetic reasons.[272] His opinions were later echoed by Sir Richard Temple, who also attributed some of the famines of the 1870s to the indirect effects of deforestation for railway purposes.[273] Moreover, both Cleghorn and Wight attributed the principal cause of damaging deforestation in the Nilgiri Hills to the activities of European planters, who, they believed, were the real villains of the piece.[274] Cleghorn further commented in 1869 on the high flow of 'capital' into the hills and the inevitable destruction that would result.[275] Some of this hostility to the activities of European private capital can even be identified in the operating methods of the Madras Forest Service at the time Cleghorn was its chief conservator, especially in the differential treatment accorded particular privileged groups of 'tribal' shifting cultivators in comparison with lowland Indian incomers and European plant-

269 Grove, 'Early themes in African conservation', pp. 23–9.
270 Cleghorn et al., 'Report of the committee'.
271 Cleghorn, *Forests and gardens*, pp. 3–4; Wight, quoted in Cleghorn et al., 'Report of the committee', p. 87.
272 Cleghorn, *Forests and gardens*, pp. 3–21. Cleghorn's sharp awareness of the speed of change occurring in forests once 'left to nature, thinly peopled' was enhanced 'by his reading of Anton Hove's *Travels* of 1786', Buchanan-Hamilton's *Journey through Mysore* of 1807 and Valentyn's *Travels* of 1804. The intervening forty years had wrought immense changes, Cleghorn believed, and 'the axe of the coffee planter and of the kumari cultivator have made extensive and often wanton havoc, devastating a large portion of the area of primaeval forest': *Forests and gardens*, p. 2. The word 'primaeval' was a favourite of Cleghorn's and helps to explain the nature of his interest in protecting the forests in their undisturbed 'natural' state.
273 Minute of 14 April 1878, quoted in Danvers, 'A century of famines', pp. 9–10, 18–19.
274 See e.g. Wight in a letter quoted in Cleghorn et al., 'Report of the committee', p. 37.
275 Cleghorn, in the discussion after presentation of a paper by G. Bidie, 'On the effects of forest destruction in Coorg', at the Royal Geographical Society, 25 Jan. 1869, in *Proceedings of the Royal Geographical Society*, 1869, pp. 80–3.

ers.[276] However, these kinds of attitudes and arguments, hostile to both private capital and state-sponsored 'development', were rarely directly used in attempts to secure government support for forest conservation. Instead the threat of artificially induced drought and famine was quite adequate to the needs of the conservation propagandists, particularly when combined, after the 1860s, with the threat of shortages of urban firewood and timber for railway sleepers.

Nevertheless, it was the threat posed by the consequences of artificially produced climatic change which primarily motivated the entry of government into extensive state forest control and started to bring about the exclusion of private capital from forestry activity after 1847. Imperial timber needs (largely those generated internally in India, and not so much externally, as is often supposed) certainly became a factor in forest policy after about 1862, once railway building had commenced.[277] Timber needs alone, however, were not initially the main stimulant to the extension of government forest control, as some authorities have suggested. Indeed, it might be recalled that the old conservancy system, originally founded purely to ensure a sustainable timber supply for the East India Company, the Royal Navy and the Bombay Marine, had been completely dismantled by Munro in 1823. By the time raw-material needs did actually become more urgent, the principle of state forest control for reasons of firewood supply, soil and water conservation, and famine prevention was already well established, especially in the two presidency forest departments.

The threat posed by the economic and social consequences of desiccation, first effectively promoted by Butter, Gibson, Balfour and Cleghorn, continued to preoccupy the official mind of government throughout the period 1850–80.[278] Moreover, a growing number of scientists, in and outside the medical

---

276 Cleghorn, *Forests and gardens*, pp. 54–5. Cleghorn was especially mindful of the efficacy of pre-British forest reservation, noting that 'in the days of the rajahs (in Gumsur) the felling of timber was systematically discouraged'. He was well aware of the difficulties in distinguishing between 'kumari' felling carried out by 'tribal' people and that carried out by incomers (see ibid., pp. 120–7, 140–1), a distinction not at first understood by the Madras government.

277 See e.g. C. Brownlow, 'The timber trees of Cachar', *Journal of the Agricultural and Horticultural Society of India*, 1865, pp. 336–62; he wrote that 'the future supply of sleepers for Indian railways is becoming an important question'. Cleghorn referred in 1865 to 'the wants of the Sind railway': 'Memorandum on the timber procurable by the Indus, Swat and Kabul rivers', *Journal of the Agricultural and Horticultural Society of India*, 1865, p. 73. In 1858 he had written that 'the requirements of the Indian Navy, the Madras and Bombay railways, the Public Works and Telegraph departments, have been unusually heavy' (quoted in Cleghorn, *Forest and gardens*).

278 See e.g. Government of India, *Famine Commission*, IV, pp. 505–25 (selected evidence on denudation of forests); Balfour, 'The influence exercised by trees'; minutes of evidence by

service, believed that they had found new evidence to support theories linking deforestation with run-off, rainfall and famine incidence.[279] After Cleghorn's BAAS report had been published in 1852, the issue gradually gained international recognition, leading directly to further initiatives in state conservation on Mauritius and in the Cape and Australia.[280] Supra-colonial scientific gatherings subsequent to the BAAS meeting of 1851 reinforced the impression that the colonies faced a worsening desiccation crisis, resolvable only by the wholesale extension of government forest reservation. Unfortunately, it appeared to require a famine to lend credibility to scientists in the eyes of government and to provide the required impetus for the state to intervene with measures to protect the environment. In India, for example, serious droughts in 1835–9, the early 1860s, and 1877–8 were all rapidly followed by the initiation or renewal of state programmes designed to strengthen forest protection, often with the specific aim of preventing subsequent droughts. Of course such legislation had the convenient by-product of increasing state control over land and timber supplies. This expansion in state forest control almost always took place at the expense of traditional rights and customs over forests and grazing. While the desire to control rebellious minority tribal groups and to secure a sustained supply of cheap timber encouraged this expansion, the fear of climatic change remained an important motive.

In a similar pattern in South Africa, the early pioneer of state conservation in the Cape Colony, John Croumbie Brown, was able to secure government agreement to new measures on forest conservation and the prevention of grassland burning only after the disastrous drought of 1861–3 had wrought havoc on settler agriculture throughout the colony.[281] In fact, the Southern African drought of 1862 encouraged the development of a whole school of desicca-

Sir Richard Temple, qq. 1–236 (27 February – 7 March), in Government of India, *Famine Commission*, IV, pp. 29–43. See also A. J. Stuart, *Extracts from 'Man and Nature' . . . with some notes on forests and rainfall in Madras*, Madras 1882.

279 See Stuart, *Extracts from 'Man and Nature'*; Bidie, 'Effects of forest destruction in Coorg'; Government of India, *Famine Commission*, IV, pp. 505–25; Balfour, 'The influence exercised by trees'; C. R. Markham, 'On the effects of the destruction of forests in the Western Ghauts of India on the water supply', *Proceedings of the Royal Geographical Society*, 1869, pp. 261–7. The discussion which followed the reading of the latter paper at a Royal Geographical Society meeting chaired by Sir Roderick Murchison was important in providing the opportunity for a number of scientists in the audience to debate the relative rates of desiccation in different parts of the world, including North America, Trinidad, Java, Persia, India, Australia and South Africa.

280 See Grove, 'Early themes in African conservation'; Powell, *Environmental management in Australia*, p. 80. As Powell points out, it was not until N. A. Dalzell moved from Sind to become conservator of forests in the Bombay Presidency in 1862, succeeding Alexander Gibson, that the rationales adopted by Indian conservationists made themselves felt in Australia.

281 Grove, 'Early themes in African conservation'.

tionist theory (closely related to its contemporary Indian counterpart) which was convinced that most of the semi-arid tropics were undergoing long-term aridification as part of a process aided by colonial deforestation. Theories of widespread climatic change acquired further credibility when a paper was read at the Royal Geographical Society in London in March 1865 entitled 'On the Progressing Desiccation of the Basin of the Orange River in Southern Africa', by James Fox Wilson, a naturalist and traveller. He believed that the Orange River was 'gradually becoming deprived of moisture' and that 'the Kalahari desert was gaining in extent'.[282] Wilson believed that the desiccation was due to 'the reckless burning of timber and the burning of pasture over many generations by natives'. David Livingstone, present at this lecture, disagreed strongly with Wilson's analysis. Rainfall decline, Livingstone asserted, was a natural result of geophysical phenomena. Another speaker, Francis Galton (a cousin of Charles Darwin's), believed that the introduction of cheap axes into Africa by Europeans had promoted excessive deforestation and consequent drought. Yet another member of Wilson's audience, Colonel George Balfour of the Indian Army, struck a more caustic note. Rainfall decline in India, he believed, was caused principally by the deforestation activities of the whole community, including European plantation owners. Countermeasures were necessary. He had been informed that morning, he said, that in the West Indies the government of Trinidad had 'passed a law prohibiting the cutting down of trees near the capital in order to ensure a supply of rain'. Balfour was quick to point out on this, as on other occasions, that in pre-colonial times it had been the practice of Indians to sink wells and 'plant topes [groves or clumps] of trees' to encourage water retention. In another Royal Geographical Society debate, in 1866, Balfour pointed out too that 'in the Mauritius the Government had passed laws to prevent the cutting down of trees, and the result has been to secure an abundant supply of rainfall'. The debate about climatic change had thus become international in reference and relevance by the mid 1860s. It was reinforced by more detailed research that raised the possibility that the very constitution of the atmosphere might be changing. Such views, the beginnings of the current 'greenhouse' debate, had found early advocacy in the writings of J. Spotswood Wilson, who presented a paper in 1858 to the BAAS entitled 'On the General and Gradual Desiccation of the Earth and Atmosphere'.[283] This paper had probably helped to influence the ideas of the debaters at the Royal Geographical Society in 1865–6. Upheaval of the land, 'destruction of forests and waste by irrigation' were not sufficient to explain the available facts on climate change, the author stated.

---

282 Published in *Proceedings of the Royal Geographical Society*, 1865, pp. 106–9.
283 Published in *Report of the Proceedings of the British Association for the Advancement of Science (Transactions)*, 1858, pp. 155–6.

He believed the cause lay in the changing proportions of oxygen and carbonic acid in the atmosphere.[284] Their respective ratios, he believed, were connected with the relative rates of their production and absorption by the 'animal and vegetable kingdom'.[285] The author of this precocious paper concluded with a dismal set of remarks. Changes in 'the atmosphere and water' were

> in the usual course of geological changes, slowly approaching a state in which it will be impossible for man to continue as an inhabitant . . . as inferior races preceded man and enjoyed existence before the earth had arrived at a state suitable to his constitution, it is more probable that others will succeed him when the conditions necessary for his existence have passed away.

The raising, as early as 1858, of the spectre of human extinction as a consequence of climatic change was clearly a psychologically shocking development. It was consistent, however, with fears that had been developing among the emerging world scientific community for a considerable period. By the early 1860s, therefore, long-established anxieties about artificially induced climatic change and species extinctions had reached a climax. The penetration of western-style economic development, spread initially through colonial expansion, was increasingly seen by more perceptive scientists as threatening the survival of man himself.

The publication of *Man and Nature*, by G. P. Marsh, in 1864 served only to aid the development of an already existing belief in a desiccation crisis of global dimensions, similar in its essentials to that which had been so assiduously cultivated by Balfour and Cleghorn in 1849 and 1850. Marsh himself has long been seen as the fountainhead of the North American conservation movement.[286] Certainly his work served to reinforce the already long-held and long-published opinions of such scientists as Cleghorn. The correspondence of Indian colonial scientists with Marsh (and that of their pioneering Cape Colony counterparts) and their familiarity with his ideas served only to make

284 A few years later, John Tyndall developed the concept of the 'atmospheric envelope' and the notion of 'greenhouse' retention of radiation heat by particular gases in the atmosphere. In doing so he built upon theories of heat transfer in the atmosphere first developed by Jean-Baptiste Fourier between 1807 and 1815; see Tyndall, *On radiation: The Rede lecture at the University of Cambridge, 16 May 1865*, London, 1865.
285 This theory was elaborated on by Arrhenius in 1896 when he raised the possibility that increasing concentrations of carbon dioxide due to the burning of fossil fuel could lead to global warning. He later calculated that doubling the level of carbon dioxide could raise average temperatures by 5°C.: S. A. Arrhenius, *Les atmosphères des planètes: Conférence faite de mars 1911*, Paris, 1911.
286 See e.g. Lowenthal, *George Perkins Marsh*, pp. 245–76; D. Worster, *Nature's economy*, Cambridge, 1977, p. 268; R. P. McIntosh, *The background to ecology: Concept and theory*, Cambridge, 1985, p. 292.

them more confident in their theories.[287] Nevertheless, such Indian forest conservators as N. A. Dalzell, in their writings on conservation, drew far more
inspiration from what they knew of St Helena, Mauritius and the eighteenth-
century French experience than from Marsh, to whom they rarely referred.[288]

287 Cleghorn wrote to Marsh saying, 'I have carried your book with me all along the slope of
the northern Himalaya, and into Kashmir and Tibet, and in course of my duty have endeavoured to direct the local authorities to the general changes and prospective consequences of
railway works now in progress in Upper India. The result of my observations has been
strongly corroborative of the view which you have so usefully promulgated': University of
Vermont Library, Burlington, Vt., Archives Dept, Marsh Papers: Letter from Rome, 6 March
1868, to Marsh at Florence. On 23 March Cleghorn wrote to Marsh: 'I leave for you a copy
of the Forest Report 1866–7 which will show that the Indian Forest Department is still in
an early stage of development.' This was the first of a series of documents on India sent by
Cleghorn to Marsh, who was, up to this time, largely ignorant of developments in India. In
1869 Cleghorn sent him Baird-Smith's *Irrigation in Italy* and *Irrigation in Southern Europe*,
by C. C. Scott Moncrieff, and he wrote that he would 'look for any new publications likely
to interest you': 12 Feb. 1869. Cleghorn also revealed on the latter occasion that 'I have been
employed by the Secretary of State in selecting the best of 90 candidates for Forest employment in India and hope to find 4 superior youths for training in Germany and 4 others for
the "Ecole Imperiale Forestière" in Nancy.' Much later, on 3 Feb. 1875, Cleghorn wrote: 'I
sent you the *Gardener's Chronicle* containing a biographical sketch of Dr Brandis and am glad
that you refer to the work in which he is engaged in India. Your notice may help to strengthen
his hand – I was glad to learn that he has made your formal acquaintance.' These extracts
tend to emphasise the extent to which Marsh and his American colleagues were dependent
on the initiatives of Cleghorn himself in learning anything about the Indian situation.

288 Dalzell, *Extracts on forests and forestry*, Madras, 1869, pp. 1–4, 101–5. Dalzell's main sources
on Mauritius were Brisseau-Mirbel, *Elémens de physiologie*, and articles published in the
Pioneer, quoted in *Extracts on forests and forestry*, p. 22. Dalzell noted (p. 22): 'It is interesting
to watch the change which public opinion undergoes under the gradual but certain advances
of scientific knowledge and perhaps there are few questions in which the general feeling has
undergone a greater change than the estimation in which trees and forests are held in India
. . . those who had been most prejudiced against the trees were compelled to admit the great
increase in sickness which had followed their destruction . . . we have come to regard the
trees as friends instead of enemies.' It should be noted that Dalzell does not quote Marsh at
all. Similarly, in 1917, R. S. Troup, erstwhile inspector-general of forests in India, in his
survey of authorities on forest–climate relations, noted that 'those who gave every attention
to the subject may be named as St Pierre, Dr Priestley, Humboldt and Boussingault; and in
India Dr Gibson and Mr Dalzell have been conspicuous': R. S. Troup, ed., *The work of the
Forest Department in India*, Calcutta, 1917, p. 2. Here too Marsh did not figure; the discontinuity in information flow seems to have been almost complete. What does emerge from
both Cleghorn's letters to Marsh and Troup's work of 1917 is the impression that the task
of propagandising the need for forest protection was a difficult and unpopular one – although
Dalzell conveys a more optimistic view of his experience in the Bombay Presidency. Thus
Troup wrote: 'The earlier years of forest administration were beset with difficulties which is
not surprising, considering that the department was charged with the unpopular duty of
protecting the heritage of nature from the repacity of mankind, a duty which naturally
aroused the antagonism of the population of India . . . the early years of the Forest Department were marked by a constant struggle against opposition in various forms for, although

This is not surprising, since the apparatus of Indian state forest conservation long predated that of the United States. When, stimulated partly by the work of Marsh, the United States Congress itself decided to explore the options for government forest conservation in the early 1870s, F. B. Hough, its main adviser and consultant on the subject, held up German, French and, above all, Indian methods of conservation as examples that might be imitated. Gifford Pinchot, another important campaigner for North American forest conservation, was similarly influenced by what he knew of the history of the Indian forest service.[289]

If one stands back to survey the transition from uncontrolled deforestation to the ambitious programme of state conservation that had developed by the time of the first Indian Forest Act of 1865, a number of milestones stand out. An intensive period of campaigning by the EIC Medical Service, based principally on the dangers of the climatic effects of deforestation, culminated in the establishment of the Bombay Forest Conservancy in 1847. Further lobbying by Joseph Hooker and a decisive advocacy of the economic case for sustainable forest management by McClelland served to convince Dalhousie of the case for wholesale state intervention in the forest sector, much against the wishes of private capital. As we have seen, General Napier and John Stocks ensured that the pre-colonial management methods of the Sind shikargahs by the Talpur amirs provided a convenient model for state forestry in other parts of India. After the end of company rule, the institutional strength and continuity of the earlier-established conservation policy, inimical to private interests and heavily influenced by the cumulative strength of the desiccationist case of the scientific lobby, was soon explicitly restated under Crown rule. Indeed, this restatement, expressed in a letter from the secretary of state for

Government had proclaimed its forest policy, this policy was not always appreciated by district officials many of whom were unable to discern the potential value of the forests or to see the baneful results of their destruction': ibid. In this sense, it is not surprising that the American experience was seen to offer few practical lessons for Indian forest protection.

289 F. B. Hough, ed., *Report of the Committee on the Preservation of Forests*, U.S. Congress, House of Representatives, 43rd Cong., 1st sess., House Report 259, Washington, D.C., 1874, p. 43. Hough quotes frequently in this paper from a report written on the Madras forests by C. Walker (*Reports on forest management in the Madras Presidency*, Madras, 1873). See also Hough, 'On the duty of governments in the preservation of forests', *Proceedings of the American Association for the Advancement of Science*, 72 (1873), 1–10. Hough himself was much influenced by the work of John Croumbie Brown (whom he knew personally and toured with in Scotland) in advocating state involvement in forestry. However, this close connection between British colonial forestry and the origins of the U.S. forest service has apparently gone unnoticed among American environmental historians, as has Hough's primacy in pioneering American state environmentalism. See e.g. S. Fox, *John Muir and his legacy: The American conservation movement*, Boston, 1981, and D. Worster, ed., *American environmentalism: The formative period, 1860–1915*, New York, 1973.

India to the governor-general in Calcutta, serves as an appropriate summary of the political and propaganda success of the Hippocratic conservation lobby in its relations with the colonial state in India. 'Most countries', the secretary of state pointed out in 1862,

> have suffered from similar neglect [to that in India], not only in the dearth and consequent high price of timber, but very often in the deterioration of climate, and in the barrenness of land formerly cultivable, if not fertile, situated at the base of hills, when these have been stripped of the forests which clothed them, condensed the vapours into rain and gave protection to the country below them . . . it is very satisfactory to me to learn that you have come to the same conclusion as Her Majesty's Government, that individuals cannot be relied upon for due care in the management of forests, inasmuch as private capital must be opposed in this instance to public interests.[290]

From its earlier location at the colonial periphery, the language of climatic environmentalism and reformist conservation had now assuredly moved to centre stage in the imperial apparatus.

290 Quoted in Stebbing, *Forests,* p. 551.

Conclusion: The colonial state and the origins of western environmentalism

I have aimed in this book to recount some of the main milestones in the intellectual development of the global environmental consciousness which emerged in the context of European colonial expansion between 1660 and 1860. This new kind of consciousness can now be observed to have arisen virtually simultaneously with the trade and territorial expansion of the Venetian, Dutch, English and French maritime powers. It was characterised by a connected and coherent intellectual evolution of ideas and concepts which had complex and yet identifiable roots in an Edenic and Orientalist search and in the encounters of a whole variety of innovative thinkers with the drastic ecological consequences of colonial rule and capitalist penetration.

The early phase of territorial expansion along the great trade routes to India and China undoubtedly provided the critical stimulus to the emergence of colonial environmental sensibilities. While the early oceanic island colonies provided the setting for well-documented episodes of rapid ecological deterioration, they also witnessed some of the first deliberate attempts to counteract the process artificially. The isolated settlement at the Cape Colony provided an analogous context for the formulation of conservationist attitudes.[1] The colonisation of the oceanic islands was especially significant in the evolution of remarkably sophisticated insights into the mechanisms and processes of ecological change brought about by the introduction of European settler agriculture in both freeholder and slave-plantation manifestations. Prior to 1700, episodes of deforestation and soil erosion in Europe, the Canary Islands, the Caribbean and South America had rarely elicited sophisticated insights into process, nor did they give rise to the kinds of programmes for environmental control which developed on St Helena and Mauritius and in the Eastern Caribbean during the eighteenth century.

Environmental deterioration particularly threatened the island economies and the security of supplies for the ships of the new European companies

---

1 See Grove, 'Early themes in African conservation' and 'Scottish missionaries, evangelical discourses and the origins of conservation thinking in Southern Africa'.

trading to India. The responses of the different nations and their companies to the process were not uniform in character. Nevertheless, a shared heritage of intellectual and scientific developments, the product of late Renaissance literature and science, proved an influential stimulus to a new valuing of the tropical environment in literary, scientific and economic terms. The institutional development of the colonial botanical garden, particularly as it was developed by the Dutch at the Cape, the French on Mauritius and the British on St Vincent, formed the basis for a new kind of learning, information collecting and networking in the tropical environment. This learning was global in its approach and in its aims. Above all, the colonial botanical garden provided the basis for the institutional emergence of environmentalist ideas.

Some of the first systematic attempts at forest and soil conservation in colonies began on St Helena and created significant precedents for later East India Company land-use ideology. At first, however, the lack of any credible expertise or corpus of intellectual justification to explain the ecological decline set in train by settlement meant that the English East India Company only very slowly became cognisant of the nature of the physical problems which its 'improvement' programmes and trade requirements engendered. Eventually St Helena became disproportionately significant in stimulating a wider intellectual awareness of the rate at which the European might degrade the tropical environment and bring about species extinctions.[2]

In the course of the emergence of colonial state conservation, the significance of initiatives taken by local actors on the basis of local and indigenous knowledge cannot be overestimated. By contrast, the writings of better-known western environmentalists writing outside the colonial context (G. P. Marsh is a noteworthy case in point) were of surprisingly little import in the formation of state policy. Instead the experience of perceiving and countering deforestation and land degradation at first hand, especially on tropical islands, proved to be far more influential. The centrality of the colonial periphery in stimulating environmental innovation was strongly reinforced both by the growing cultural significance of island environments and by the growing preoccupations of Orientalist and Humboldtian thinkers with the non-European 'other' of the tropics. The considerable importance of the tropical island as a cultural metaphor for the newly 'discovered' world as well as for the projection of discontents and Utopias helped to heighten awareness of the efficacy of

---

2 Taking St Helena and Ascension Island together, one can see that before 1870 the experience on those islands was taken up in turn in the theories of J. R. Forster (1774), Bernardin de Saint-Pierre (1769–96), Alexander Beatson (1816), J. B. Boussingault (1837), L. Bouton (1837), J. D. Hooker (1842), E. G. Balfour (1849), Charles Darwin (1859), C. G. B. Daubeny (1863), Etienne de Clave (1863), G. P. Marsh (1864) and N. A. Dalzell (1869) (dates refer to publication in English).

man as an environmental agent. Here again St Helena played a key role, not least in Godwin's *Man in the Moone,* in providing a model for later Utopian discourses, both scientific and otherwise, and in highlighting a new awareness of isolation, extinctions, race and gender, often coupled with increasingly global perceptions of natural processes. This literary interest in islands and isolation was crystallised ambiguously in Defoe's *Robinson Crusoe,* a work which not least provided a model for the French cult of the Utopian South Sea island which flowered in the wake of the writings of Rousseau, Commerson, Bougainville and Bernardin de Saint-Pierre in the 1760s and 1770s. The seminal influence of the works of both Godwin and Defoe was indicative of a two-way process by which particular literary discourses powerfully shaped changing perceptions of nature and the globe, and in which literature was, in its turn, increasingly influenced by new understandings and 'discoveries' in an expanding European world system of economic dominion and ruling discourses.

Thus, in the same way that European expansion entailed the encompassing of vast new territories under a European economic yoke, it also opened up a vast new mental domain. Expansion of this domain followed and facilitated the growth of trade, but it also fostered an exchange of experiences and ideas about the environment that became progressively complex and global in scope as trade and colonial dominion became global in reach. The tropical island, however, remained critical to the focussing of these ideas. The way in which this focussing occurred was largely dependent on the nature of the relationship between the emerging body of natural philosophers or scientists and the colonial states that they served. This relationship was much closer in French colonies than in those of England or the Netherlands.[3] This close relationship is one of the reasons why it was the French management of Mauritius which saw the first comprehensive attempts by colonial scientists to analyse rigorously and then to attempt to control the environmental consequences of European economic rule – or, more specifically, to control the ecological impact of a capital-intensive, slave-utilising plantation economy.

3 Of these three maritime powers, the discontinuity between science and state was greatest in England in the second half of the seventeenth and the beginning of the eighteenth century. There is some irony in this, since it was in England that Francis Bacon had first extensively elaborated on the need for natural philosophy to serve the interests of and to be controlled by the state. The onset of the Commonwealth prevented this development from taking place and ensured that the Royal Society remained relatively independent and relatively weak. In France, however (under Colbert), the Baconian approach became incorporated in state policy; hence the nature and scope of the 1669 Forest Ordinance and its colonial inheritors, including the Mauritius forest legislation of 1769. I am indebted to Dr Julian Martin for a discussion of this. One may argue that the East India Company itself acquired a more distinctly 'Baconian' role in science than the British Crown ever itself did before 1857.

The initiation of a major programme of conservation on Mauritius arose out of the coincidence of a specialised set of circumstances very specifically related to the objectives and structures of the French polity. This was due mainly to the success of physiocracy as a land-use ideology guiding the policies of the colonial state, coupled with the wish to play out a particular kind of insular and Utopian vision. Thus it is on Mauritius that one can observe the emergence of an environmental policy which, while not inspired by the state alone, increasingly relied on the state for its execution. The conservationism espoused by the physiocratic regime on Mauritius demonstrated for the first time the very significant effect of a new kind of valuing of the environment by an influential elite in checking the progress of ecological transition.

The mental image of Mauritius as both a tropical island paradise and as a hoped-for location for a physiocratic moral economy or Utopia came to occupy a surprisingly dominant role in the mainstream of intellectual discourse in France itself wherever the relationship between man and nature was the object of discussion. This philosophical nexus between Mauritius and Europe can be attributed almost entirely to the popularity of the fictional and non-fictional texts of Bernardin de Saint-Pierre. Indeed, it contributed greatly to the way in which a romantic environmentalism actually emerged as a vital precondition to the realisation of a social Utopia. However, this alone would not have been sufficient to ensure the involvement of the state in an environmentalist programme which required a set of rather more empirical justifications for obeying the 'laws of nature'. These were supplied by a physiocratic science.

Pierre Poivre, in particular, was able to perceive the vital importance of being able to utilise a society of established experts to make the new ecological risks credible and, indeed, dangerous in the eyes of the state. The strong institutional connections that developed in the French colonial system among the state, the tropical botanical garden and the Parisian botanical establishment facilitated the availability of such experts on Mauritius. Furthermore, the initiation of the physiocratic conservation programme on Mauritius demonstrated the peculiar suitability of the colonial state in providing a context within which independent scientists and conservationists could work. Placed in an alien environment, they were still able to take advantage of a considerable pool of intellectual experience. This meant that as early as 1770 the conservation lobby on Mauritius could draw upon published literature dealing with the environmental thinking of Europeans in locations as far apart as Europe, North America, South America, India and China.

Working within the milieu of the innately insecure fabric of the colonial state, the new scientific interest group, directly employed by the state for the first time on Mauritius, was able to exercise political leverage unheard of in metropolitan Europe. Environmentalism on Mauritius took advantage of two coupled phenomona: the demonstrable vulnerability of a small island to the rigours of plantation agriculture and an emerging literature on the interconnections among climate, trees and society that was used increasingly to imply a connection between climatic 'virtue' and social or political virtue. The latter connection became especially important in the years immediately preceding the French Revolution. The sense of insular vulnerability was made more concrete by the emergence, before the end of the eighteenth century, of a knowledge of plant types and distributions which was global in scope. This new expertise was personified particularly in Philibert Commerson. Apart from any Utopian and literary connection, it had its roots, as did much of the developing global awareness of the potential impact of the European on the environment and on other societies, in the scientific circumnavigations of the world by Bougainville and Cook.

While problems of forest degradation and soil erosion were easily understood on Mauritius, it was not long before the concept of species extinction also gathered a new momentum on the island. This was an important development, since it permitted the making of a direct theoretical link between perceptions of the vulnerability of the island and insights into the role of man as a destructive agent on a world scale. A third and most important component of ancien-régime conservationism concerned the re-emergence of desiccation theories. These theories, linking forest cover and deforestation to rainfall and rainfall change, had long existed, not least in the minds of Theophrastus and Christopher Columbus. On Mauritius, and also in the Eastern Caribbean, the revival of such desiccation theories formed the main justification for the participation of the state in environmental control. The close institutional connection which developed in the mid eighteenth century between the Royal Society and the Académie des Sciences was directly instrumental in the revival of desiccationism. It meant, for example, that such physiocrats as Pierre Poivre were able to reinforce climatic ideas co-opted from eastern thought by reference to the plant-physiological researches of Stephen Hales and the English Newtonians.

At another level the success of physiocratic conservation demonstrated the growing efficacy of the Hippocratic outlook. Medical perceptions were an essential component of physiocratic thinking, in which climate, environment and the human condition were closely related. In a similar way, desiccation theories had themselves originated in a medical concern with the nature of the relationship between health and the wider physical environment. On Mauritius desiccation theories were first used as a persuasive scientific and social lever by pioneering professional scientists (and were also used by individual ministers in government to secure a particular course of action by the state). In this sense the colonial state, with its overbearing economic and strategic preoccupations, actually constituted a more persuadable kind of institution than did the state in Europe. Later it only required the very deliberate and authoritative application of global climatic and atmospheric theories by Joseph Priestley and Alexander von Humboldt to make the desiccation argument politically powerful for scientists working on regional or national scales. Where the scientists were a powerful group of medically trained individuals, as they were in the Indian medical service, it was only a matter of time before global theories of desiccation became politically effective on a sub-continental scale, namely in India.

Early colonial conservation policies were almost always perceived as being a legitimate concern of the state rather than of the individual. Moreover, they often resulted in governments' attempting to restrict the activities of private capital or its direct and indirect agents in the prior, and longer-term, interests of the state. In essence, however, the emergence of a conservation policy related to a perception by the colonial authorities of the unacceptable risks implied in retaining an unrestricted status quo. In this respect one is dealing with a paradoxical kind of development, both in discovering that environmentalist ideas and policies emerged earlier at the colonial periphery than at the metropolitan centre and in the realisation that the colonial state was so readily influenced by independent groups of scientists. Moreover, it is perfectly clear that the motivations of those specialists who proposed controls (and who were critical of the ecological degradation which they saw happening) were by no means always identical to those of the state. On the contrary, they were sometimes actively anti-colonial.

Initially the European colonial invaders of the tropics were frequently forced to deal with a highly unfamiliar set of circumstances in which risks in the physical environment (in terms of disease, soils, water supply and fuel provision) were paralleled only by the dangers apprehended as being posed by an often equally poorly understood indigenous population. The instability of power relations between coloniser and colonised was thus frequently paralleled by the terms of a new dispensation of power defined in terms of an unknown ecology. In other words, an unfamiliar environment and populace might both present untold risks in knowing and controlling. This, of course, was a main part of the highly precocious message of Shakespeare's *Tempest*.

Above all, the course of future events was made unpredictable. As Mary Douglas has demonstrated, the problem of knowing about the risks which face it is a critical one in the self-regulation and stability of a society.[4] As a result, a minimal knowledge of future risks is required. It was this requirement which led to the conspicuous prominence of the scientist in the colonial context. The way in which the state treats the interpretation of risk offered by the specialist thus becomes of particular importance, since the expert has access to a knowledge of risks in the new environment not available to the lay person, or even

4 M. Douglas, *Implicit meanings: Essays in anthropology*, London, 1979, pp. 245–7.

to the lay state, for that matter. In an unfamiliar environment, empirical knowledge is at a premium. The traditional conventions evolved in a relatively stable and known relationship between people and land in Europe were not sufficient or apt when transferred to the tropics. Tradition had thus to give way to empirical knowledge or to local indigenous knowledge co-opted for colonial use. Prospero in *The Tempest*, it might be recalled, needed to undergo the transition from magician to natural scientist.[5]

One might argue that the sheer speed of ecological change implicit in the activities of capital in the context of colonial expansion made environmentalist ideas and conservation policies inevitable simply to protect European capital or settler investments. However, there are problems with this argument in its simplest form. Above all, rates of ecological change were not significant in eliciting intervention until they could be noticed, quantified and then worried about. In general, only the 'scientist' could effectively do the latter. This was why islands were important in the evolution of early environmental sensibilities and why the colonial state became so utterly dependent on the observations and then the predictions of scientists. Without observation or interpretation, any objective notion of rates of ecological change was politically irrelevant. Far more significant was the way in which the very nature of the colonial state and its privileged network of connections for the diffusion of information effectively promoted a sophisticated environmental critique, and, furthermore, one which was effective in encouraging the colonial state to enlarge its role far beyond that known to states in Europe. A growing interest in long-term environmental security ensured both continuity in policy and the evolution of an apparently contradictory role in land management for the colonial state. In this context, botanical gardens served a crucial purpose as symbolic texts, centres of calculation and repositories of information and expertise.

The social leverage acquired by the emerging scientific elite of the colonial state with respect to the environment demands some further exploration. Entirely contradictory motivations and ideologies could survive together, at least for a while, or even within the same state apparatus. For example, the extensive building of botanical gardens in the sixteenth and seventeenth centuries, first in Europe and then in the new colonies, arose out of plural motivations. On the one hand, there were medical and economic motivations; on the other, the botanical garden fulfilled a more complex sociological role in the re-creation of an earthly paradise. The early colonisation of sub-tropical and tropical islands undoubtedly involved economic motives. But, as constructed in literature, islands also served a mental and projective purpose, as the writings of Dante, Columbus, More, Godwin, Shakespeare, Marvell and Defoe

5 See Chapter 1.

are sufficient to demonstrate.[6] Increasingly, then, while the process of expansion continued to serve the purposes of capital and the European market, it also began to promote a longer-term project. This consisted, after about 1700, in the search for the normative location for social Utopias and the simultaneous formulation of an environmental critique. In other words, the attempt to reconcile the human ecological impact with the laws of nature manifested itself both in environmentalism *and* in searches for better and more 'natural' (or even revolutionary) social dispensations.

Governor Roberts, for example, advocated conservation and opposed the 'improvement' plans of the East India Company on St Helena. Later Pierre Poivre wished to create a new moral economy of nature and society on Mauritius. Similarly, Bernardin de Saint-Pierre started to couple his pleas for ecological restraint with pleas for the release of slaves. In the West Indies, Alexander Anderson argued for forest protection while criticising the treatment of the Caribs. In India, Colonel Kyd advocated the production of famine-resistant crops and opposed continued territorial expansion in areas west of Bengal. In much the same fashion, Edward Balfour (quoting Bernardin de Saint-Pierre) advocated forest protection to fight the famines provoked by colonial revenue demands. While the reforms advocated in the conservation, public-health and medical fields by the surgeons of the EIC Medical Service were ostensibly motivated by a distinctly Benthamite utilitarianism, their policy prescriptions were also undoubtedly affected by the interventionist and radical ideas of Joseph Priestley and Joseph Hume.

Quite consistently, then, those who criticised colonial laissez-faire policies pertaining to deforestation, soil erosion and species extinctions tended also to be those who deprecated colonial exacerbation of famine and disease patterns and the treatment meted out to indigenous peoples. In this respect colonial scientists such as Bernardin de Saint-Pierre on Mauritius, Balfour in India, Dieffenbach in New Zealand and Strzelecki in Australia are all good exemplars of the close connections between nascent environmentalism and the social reformism of physiocracy and the Enlightenment.[7] The fact that the scientists

---

6 See Chapter 1.

7 Thus Bernardin de Saint-Pierre was a pioneering figure in the French anti-slavery movement; Edward Balfour was a leading advocate of the medical education of women in India; and Ernst Dieffenbach and P. E. Strzelecki were both vociferous propagandists for the rights of indigenous peoples under colonial rule. Strzelecki, an advocate of soil conservation in South Australia and defender of the rights of Aborigines, was also later a severe critic of British famine policy in Ireland; see Saint-Pierre, *A voyage to the Isle of France;* Chapter 5 (for Balfour); Dieffenbach, *Travels in New Zealand,* pp. 372–91; Strzelecki, *Physical description of New South Wales and Van Diemen's Land,* pp. 355, 342, 361. All these individuals, with the possible exception of Balfour, can be described confidently as having been strongly anti-colonialist in sentiment, and Dieffenbach was also specifically anti-missionary; see *Travels in New Zealand,* p. 372.

employed by the British were frequently either Scottish or Central European, and thus inherently peripheral to the imperial social establishment, only served to strengthen this connection. Much later the same dualism was to recur at the metropole. For example, Octavia Hill, the founder of the National Trust and an early advocate of landscape protection, was also the leading figure in urban housing reform in Britain.[8] The emergence of a duality in social reform plus a mirroring environmental critique was just as distinctive at the colonial periphery. Undoubtedly, it reached its most sophisticated level on Mauritius, thanks to the combination of a physiocratic ethos and a pre-Revolutionary Rousseauist and Romantic critique of European society.

One has to recognise here that concern about the environment mirrored social concerns and positions. Thus, while the environment may be at risk, it is the social form which demands inspection.[9] Similarly, a specialised view of the environment may reflect a sectarian view of society.[10] A survey of the evolution of perceptions of the environment by colonial scientists indicates that for some groups the tropical environment had acquired a highly loaded symbolic value. The manifest threat posed by western economic transformation to this image mirrored the social threats and insecurities felt by those individuals who had promoted a high valuing of the environment in the first place and who had in some instances actively sought careers away from the European centre. The isolationist career of Burchell on St Helena, for example, can be seen in this light.[11] In Europe the growth of a 'green language' as a form of social response to the alienating social and economic consequences of capitalism has been eloquently described by Raymond Williams.[12] At the colonial periphery this 'language' was even more conspicuous. Indeed, for a highly educated intelligentsia the colonial state offered great scope for the expression of unconventional environmental views in terms of active policy and lobbying power. Moreover, whether or not scientists shared sectarian social views, the sheer tyranny of physical and mental distance from the centre

---

8 W. H. Williams, *The Commons, Open Spaces and Footpaths Preservation Society 1865–1965: A short history of the society and its work*, London, 1965, pp. 1–29; Octavia Hill, *Our common land: Open spaces and the future of the commons*, London, 1877. The connections between public health and housing reformers (such as Octavia Hill), urban liberal reformers, Quakerism and the commons-preservation movement have yet to be fully researched. Both George Shaw-Lefevre and John Stuart Mill were committee members of the Commons Preservation Society; see Lord Eversley (George Shaw-Lefevre), *Forests, commons and footpaths*, London, 1910, pp. 27, 98, 187, 319.

9 For a useful discussion of this, see Douglas, *Implicit meanings*, p. 247.

10 M. Douglas and A. Wildavsky, *Risk and culture*, London, 1982, pp. 3–55.

11 See Burchell, *Travels in the interior of Southern Africa*, pp. 1–13.

12 *The country and the city*, esp. pp. 287–306.

contributed to the growth of peripheral or even sectarian sympathies. Even colonial governments became peripheral in their attitudes.[13]

The intellectual history of environmental consciousness in the context of European colonial expansion appears to exhibit several important kinds of elements. At one level, environmentalist discourses related to physical well-being and bodily survival. This is the element developed principally as part of a medical critique of environmental change, leading to concerns about climate, disease, the hydrological state and, by extension, famine. At another level, a new valuing of the environment related more strongly to the mental domain of the (sometimes 'Orientalist') 'other' represented by the newly colonised or 'explored' world. This second set of notions was stimulated by literary evocations of Eden, Paradise, Utopia and New Cytheria and by Romantic images of the 'Sublime' and 'Wilderness'.[14] Such notions were strongly connected to ideas about a moral economy or even to more utilitarian ideals about the desirability of new state structures or roles. Both preoccupations, in the physical (medical) and the mental realms, were ultimately constructed as ways of dealing with anxieties about the survival, nature and integrity of the human individual and human society. The one might have been physically at risk; the other, at risk in a more complex existential, emotional or even political sense. Historically, a growing awareness of extinction processes, especially on islands, served to unite these concerns towards the end of the eighteenth century. Increasingly, too, the literature and environmentalist texts associated with islands stimulated thinking about the dynamics of species change and human origins. The writings of David Corneille, Alexander Anderson, William Burchell, W. H. Webster, Joseph Hooker, Hugh Strickland and, not least, Charles Darwin are indicators of this long-evolving connection between insular discourses and the dynamics of species formation and extinction processes. As in the closely related evolution of environmentalism, the actual and psychological *isolation* of organisms and people on oceanic islands played a vital part in the formulation of new ideas. By 1859 the publication by Darwin of a theory of natural selection had completed this story of exis-

---

13 The stand taken by the government of Madras after 1847 was a case in point, as was the critical position taken by Governor Roberts on St Helena after 1708. However, probably the most important tensions set up between metropolitan centre and colonial government periphery arose when colonial officials were themselves enthusiasts for natural history. The stands taken by two successive colonial secretaries on Mauritius, Rawson W. Rawson (prior to 1853) and Edward Newton (after 1862), are good examples of this; see Grove, 'Early themes in African conservation', p. 26.

14 In fact, the history and etymology of 'Wilderness' is largely irrelevant to the story of early or colonial environmentalism in the Old World. For the American context, where it is more relevant, see R. Nash, *Wilderness and the American mind*, New Haven, Conn., 1967.

tential isolation and anxiety, so that even in Europe, where the dangers of extinction in a biological sense were less easy to demonstrate, the entire social order had become threatened by a theory which questioned the whole fabric of traditional beliefs and structures justifying and explaining man's place in the world and in time.[15]

Finally, one might ask how the apparently radical or extreme opinions of a peripheral minority, albeit an intellectual and vociferous one, could so sway the policy of the colonial state in regard to the environment. The answer is that, directly, they did not. Instead the ability of peripheral conservation lobbies to carry out their social prescriptions can be seen as a measure of their success in threatening the centralised colonial state with death, disease, famine and economic ruin. Increasingly, between about 1760 and 1850, the scientific lobby was able to make these threats credible in the tropics. This was particularly so after the El Niño–caused global drought of 1791–2, an extreme event which gave a decisive advantage to environmental advocacy. In other words, the state could be made to act by persuading it of the dangers to its own survival. These dangers were easily represented on islands. At a continental scale, in India or in Southern Africa, for instance, the passage of such extreme events as famines, depletions caused by war, or disease episodes tended to

15 Darwin, *Origin of species;* see also Turner, *Reckoning with the beast,* pp. 60–6; G. Himmelfarb, *Darwin and the Darwinian revolution,* New York, 1959, pp. 236–42, 280, 290–3. The response to publication of the *Origin* became particularly conducive to the efforts of those activists anxious to promote the preservation of species, especially threatened bird species. Alfred Newton, the professor of comparative anatomy at Cambridge (and the brother of Edward Newton, colonial secretary of Mauritius and a keen enthusiast of fossil ornithology and the protection of indigenous species), was the chief architect of the first bird-protection legislation in Britain; see J. Sheail, *Nature in trust: The history of nature conservation in Britain,* London, 1976, pp. 22–6. Alfred Newton (followed a little later by J. D. Hooker and T. H. Huxley) was the first natural scientist to recognise the validity of Darwin's work and had maintained a considerable correspondence with Darwin in the years preceding publication of the *Origin;* see Newton–Darwin correspondence and papers in the Balfour Libary, Department of Zoology, Cambridge University. In this sense Newton can be compared to other early species preservationists who were affected by their extensive correspondence with Darwin – e.g. E. Dieffenbach (in New Zealand), L. Bouton (on Mauritius) and J. Forbes Royle (in India). Apart from recognising the uniqueness of the St Helena flora, Darwin was himself remarkably unconcerned, or seemingly so, to advocate the prevention of extinctions or the preservation of forests. He thus stands in stark contrast to his co-author and colleague Alfred Russell Wallace, a strong supporter of conservation ideas. Wallace wrote in 1863: If this is not done [conservation proceeded with] future ages will certainly look back upon us as a people so immersed in the pursuit of wealth as to be blind to higher considerations. They will charge us with having culpably allowed the destruction of some of these records of creation which we had it in our power to preserve and while professing to regard every living thing as the direct handiwork of the creator': A. R. Wallace, 'On the physical geography of the Malay archipelago', *Journal of the Royal Geographical Society,* 32 (1863), 127–37.

facilitate the task of a 'sectarian' scientific lobby.[16] Fears of chronic social instability in the colonies, stirred up by contemporary political events in Europe, were another facilitating factor. But more important than these factors was the growing ability of the colonial conservation lobby to appeal to the credibility of evidence of a global threat to the environment from human activity. Initially this was made possible by the emergence of an internationally diffused scientific literature. Later, international and inter-colonial contacts among scientists reinforced the growth of a sense of a global environmental crisis. The proceedings of supra-colonial scientific meetings, such as those of the British Association for the Advancement of Science in 1851 and the Royal Geographical Society in 1865 and 1866, reinforced the strength of the desiccation threats wielded by colonial scientists and gave them a new source of authority which no single colonial state could safely decide to ignore.

At some periods, departments or agents of the colonial state have themselves taken on a sectarian or peripheral role in countering the complacency of a metropolitan centre unable or undisposed to be sensitive to the environmental risks perceived in the peripheral colonial state. The governments of St Helena, for example, entered this category in their relations with the EIC Court of Directors. Later the Madras Presidency government adopted scientific conservation propaganda to press its case with the government of India. The articulation of a threat of social breakdown on top of climatic or economic disaster was an effective political weapon in these cases.

Colonial environmental policies arose, therefore, between 1650 and 1850, as a product of highly structured tensions between colonial periphery and metropolitan centre and between the insecure colonial state and the climatic environmentalism of the new scientific conservation elites. In recognising the contradictions which arose in this way, one needs to reconsider the nature of the early colonial state and its relationship with science. It may also seem prudent to question some of the simplistic assumptions that have been made about the degree to which science itself has genuinely been subordinated to

16 The famines of 1838–9 in India and 1862 in South Africa were instrumental in creating the climate for conservation legislation; see Grove, 'Early themes in African conservation', p. 28. Similarly, the great famine in India in 1877–9 brought about first the monolithic proceedings of the Famine Commission of 1880 and then a spate of related infrastructural reforms affecting environmental and famine management, such as (to name a few) the famine codes, the formation of an all-India Department of Agriculture and the Meteorological Department, and the strengthening of watershed and forest-protection legislation; see Government of India, *Famine Commission*, vol. 4. On Mauritius the serious outbreaks of malaria in the mid 1860s led almost immediately to the strengthening of forest protection; see Thompson, *Report on the forests of Mauritius*. Glacken argues, in a more general sense, that the great Lisbon earthquake of 1755 had a long-lasting influence in opening the eyes of European scientists to the vulnerability of man to natural hazards: *Traces on the Rhodian shore*, pp. 521–2.

the interests of capital and the colonial state. Clearly in so doing one needs to be aware of the variety of levels of discourse, disguise and argument with which scientific elites have historically encountered the problem of influencing governments about environmental risk. In a much broader sense, our older assumptions about the philosophical and geographical origins of current environmental concerns need to be entirely reconsidered. It is now clear that modern environmentalism, rather than being exclusively a product of European or North American predicaments and philosophies, emerged as a direct response to the destructive social and ecological conditions of colonial rule. Its colonial advocates, and their texts, were deeply influenced by a growing European consciousness of natural processes in the tropics and by a distinctive awareness of non-European epistemologies of nature.

Select bibliography

Manuscripts

PUBLISHED MANUSCRIPT COLLECTIONS AND DIARIES

Note: The collections referred to here are only those to which extensive reference has been made. Less frequently used edited or published manuscript sources are included in the main bibliography.

Dawson, W. R., ed., *The Banks letters: A calendar of the manuscript correspondence of Sir Joseph Banks preserved in the British Museum, the British Museum (Natural History) and other collections in Britain.* London, 1958. [These are noted in the text as *Banks letters*]

Beaglehole, J. C., ed., *The journals of Captain James Cook on his voyages of discovery.* 6 vols. Cambridge, 1955–69.

Beaglehole, J. C., ed., *The 'Endeavour' journal of Sir Joseph Banks, 1768–1771.* 2 vols. Sydney, 1963.

Hoare, M. E., ed., *The 'Resolution' journal of Johann Reinhold Forster, 1772–1775.* 4 vols. London, 1982.

Rocquette, M. de la, ed., *Humboldt: Correspondence scientifique et littéraire.* Paris, 1865.

Malleret, L., ed., *Un manuscrit de Pierre Poivre: Les mémoires d'un voyageur (texte réconstitué et annoté).* Ecole Française d'Extrème Orient, ser. LXV. Paris, 1968.

Janisch, H. R., ed., *Extracts of St Helena records and chronicles of Cape commanders.* Jamestown, St Helena, 1908.

UNPUBLISHED MANUSCRIPTS

France

Note: The manuscript details included here are based, in part, on the documentation utilised by Louis Malleret in *Pierre Poivre* (Paris, 1974) and *Un manuscrit de Pierre Poivre.* I have thought it appropriate to reference this material in full detail in view of the paucity of material available on Pierre Poivre in English and the extensive use I have made of my own translations of the Poivre material. Manuscripts in the archives of the Bibliothèque centrale du Muséum national d'histoire naturelle were consulted by myself. All other manuscript material listed has been personally consulted by myself in the countries concerned.

Paris

Archives Nationales (AN)
    File series: Vol. B: 201, 202
      Series C3 12–15; C4, 18, 25, 27, 29, 87; E337; F2; F8; C10, 11, 12; F2 B
      Série Marine C7, 26, 86, 263
      4JJ 127
      Section d'outre-mer: Dêpot des Fortifications des Colonies
Archives de la Bibliothèque centrale du Muséum national d'histoire naturelle
    (BCMNHN)
    Documents on l'Ile de France; Commerson; conversations of Malesherbes with
      Poivre
Bibliothèque Nationale
    Manuscrits français: Poivre; Marion Dufresne

Lyons

Bibliothèque Municipale de Lyon
    Documents on Poivre and his family; MS of Poivre's 'Mémoires d'un voyageur'
Bibliothèque du Palais des Arts, Académie de Lyon
    Documents on Poivre

Brest

Bibliothèque du Port de Brest
    'Correspondence originale des administrateurs des Iles de France et de Bourbon avec
      le Ministre de la Marine (1767–1816)'

Quimper

Bibliothèque de Quimper (Finistère)
    13 vols. of manuscripts (on Poivre and Ile de France affairs)

Nantes

Bibliothèque de la Ville de Nantes
    Poivre letters

Le Havre

Bibliothèque du Havre
    Lettres from Mme Poivre to Bernardin de Saint-Pierre

India

Bangalore

Karnataka State Archives, Vidhana Soudha
  Forest Department files, 1856–80
  Papers of Dr H. Cleghorn, 1860–70

Calcutta

National Library of India, Archives Section
  Reports of the Bombay Forest Department, 1847–70
  Reports of the Sind Forest and Canal departments, 1842–70

Dehra Dun, Uttar Pradesh

Forestry Research Institute
  Library and archives: forest working plans and miscellaneous documents relating to
    early conservators

Madras

Connemara Library, Rare Book Collection
  Miscellaneous pamphlets and Forest Department materials, some pertaining to N.
    A. Dalzell
Tamil Nadu State Archives
  Forest Department files, 1860–90

New Delhi

National Archives
  Madras Public Consultants and Governor's Correspondence, 1800–20: St Helena
    letters
  Fort William – India House Correspondence
  Secret Political Files
  Home Public Consultations (Letters)

Mauritius

National Archives of Mauritius, Coromandel, Port Louis
  Decaen files for 1803–4
  Forest Department files
  Malaria-control files
  Mauritius map collection
Mauritius Sugar Research Institute, Le Reduit

Archives of the Royal Society of Arts and Sciences of Mauritius; official papers and
    correspondence of the Society
Mauritius Institute, Port Louis
    Proceedings of the Royal Society of Arts and Sciences of Mauritius along with unbound
    copies, proof copies and portrait collections
Naval Historical Museum, Mahebourg
    Portrait collection

Netherlands

Algemeen Rijksarchief, The Hague
    Papers of the Vereinigte Oost-Indische Compagnie (VOC) Rijksarchief Utrecht
    Huydecoper family records

St Vincent and the Grenadines

National Archives, Kingstown
    Miscellaneous papers on forests and settlement

South Africa

Cape Town
The South African Library and Archives, Parliament St
    Papers of John Croumbie Brown (40 unclassified boxes)
    Reports of the Cape Colony Colonial Botanists
Cape Provincial Archives, Victoria St
    Forest Conservancy and Ranger files for Knysna, Tzitzikamma and Uitenhage
    Correspondence of the Colonial Botanists of the Cape of Good Hope, 1858–79

Pietermaritzburg

Natal Provincial Archives
    Forest Commission files, 1877–82
    Forest Department files 1878–1900

Pretoria

Transvaal Provincial Archives
    Forest Department files, 1870–1900

Trinidad and Tobago

National Archives
    Miscellaneous papers on the Tobago Forest reserve

Forest Department Archives
  Annual reports

United Kingdom

Aberdeen

University of Aberdeen: King's College Archives, King's College, Old Aberdeen
  Minutes of the Board of King's College

Cambridge

Cambridge University Library
  Manuscript diary of Matthew Flinders
  Department of Zoology: Balfour Library
  Newton Papers; Papers of Professor Alfred Newton; unclassified files, especially
    Newton–Darwin correspondence
  3 unclassified boxes

Edinburgh

Edinburgh University Library
  Cleghorn Papers; unclassified collection of the books, reports and papers of Hugh
    Cleghorn, including unpublished page proofs of reports by F. C. Danvers on
    Indian famines

London

British Library: India Office Library Records
  Home Miscelleneous Letters
  Bombay Public Consultations
  Bengal Public Consultations
  Madras Public Consultations
  Board of Directors Despatch Books, 1785–1850
  East India Company: St Helena correspondence
British Library: British Museum Library Manuscripts Collection
  Banks Letters Collection
  Beatson papers, particularly Add. Ms. 13808 et seq. and Add. Ms. 40.716
House of Lords Record Office, Westminster
  Records of the Commons, Open Spaces and Footpaths Preservation Society
Linnaean Society, Burlington House, Piccadilly
  Papers of Alexander Anderson, Curator of the St Vincent Botanic Garden
Public Record Office, Kew, Richmond, Surrey
  Ellenborough Papers
  Miscellaneous Papers on St Vincent and the Grenada Governorate

Royal Botanic Gardens, Kew, Surrey: Library/Archives
  Director's letters
  Cape letters, 1820–70
  India letters, 1800–99

Oxford

Hope Library of Entomology, University Museum, South Parks Road
  Manuscript diary of Burchell ('St. Helena Journal')
Christchurch College Library
  Unpublished manuscript of 'Elysium Britannicum', by John Evelyn

St Andrews

University of St Andrews Archives
  Papers of Hugh Francis Cleghorn, M.D.

Private Papers

Sprott/Cleghorn papers: Stravithie, near St Andrews, Fifeshire
Library and papers of the Jenyns family: Bottisham Hall, Cambridgeshire
Archives of the Royal Society of Arts, John Adam St, London SW1

United States of America

University of Vermont, Burlington, Vt.: University Library, Archives Department
  Papers of George Perkins Marsh
Library of Congress, Washington, D.C.
  Papers of Franklin Benjamin Hough

UNPUBLISHED DISSERTATIONS

Cronk, Q. C. B., 'The historical and evolutionary development of the plant life of St. Helena'. Ph.D. no. 13567, University of Cambridge, 1985.

Dardaine, S. S., 'The role of forestry in the development of Trinidad and Tobago'. M.A., Department of Mangement Studies, University of the West Indies, Trinidad, 1979.

Ellis, B., 'The impact of white settlers on the natural environment of Natal, 1845–1870'. M.Sc., University of Natal, Pietermaritzburg, 1985.

Gillott, S., 'The royal forests of England under the Commonwealth'. D.Phil. in progress, University of Oxford.

Janal, M., 'Classification of the Foraminifera: A case study in taxonomy and its history'. Ph.D., University of Cambridge, 1987.

Keymer, A., 'Plant imagery in Dante'. B.A., Faculty of Modern and Medieval Languages, University of Cambridge, 1982.

McCosh, J. B., 'J. B. Boussingault, 1802–1887: His life and work'. Ph.D., University of London, 1963.

Mandala, E. C., 'Capitalism, ecology and society: The lower Tchiri valley of Malawi, 1860–1960'. Ph.D., University of Minnesota, 1985.

Martin, J., 'Edwin Chadwick: Social or medical reformer?' M.Phil., Department of the History and Philosophy of Science, University of Cambridge, 1984.

Melville, E. G. K. 'The pastoral economy and environmental degradation in highland central Mexico 1530–1660'. Ph.D., University of Michigan, 1983.

Shaughnessy, G. L., 'Historical ecology of alien woody plants in the vicinity of Cape Town, South Africa'. Ph.D., School of Environmental Studies, University of Cape Town, 1980.

Subramanian, L., 'The west coast of India in the eighteenth century'. Ph.D., Visva Bharati University, Santiniketan, West Bengal, 1984.

Taylor, I. C., 'Black spot on Mersey: A study of environment and society in eighteenth and nineteenth century Liverpool'. Ph.D., University of Liverpool, 1976.

Watts, D., 'Plant introduction and landscape change in Barbados, 1625–1836'. Ph.D., McGill University, 1963.

UNPUBLISHED PAPERS

Carruthers, E. J., 'Attitudes to game conservation in the Transvaal, 1900–1910'. Paper presented to History Department, University of Cape Town, South Africa, 10 May 1985.

Castro, A. D. de, 'The hands and feet of the planter: The dynamics of colonial slavery'. Quoted in Wallerstein, *Modern World System* (q.v.), p. 162.

Cheke, A., 'A review of the ecological history of the Mascarene islands, with particular reference to extinctions and introductions of land vertebrates'. Typescript, 1985.

Dettelbach, M., 'Global physics and aesthetic empire: Humboldt's physical portrait of the tropics'. Typescript, 1991.

Dreze, J., 'Famine prevention in India'. Paper presented at World Institute for Development Research, Helsinki, July 1986.

'Rural public works for famine prevention: The Indian experience'. Paper presented at seminar on food strategies, World Institute for Development Research, Helsinki, July 1986.

Flint, E., 'Ecological consequences of change in land-use in South Asia'. Paper presented at World Environmental History Conference, Duke University, Durham, N.C., April 1987.

Gadgil, M., and Guha, R., 'Natural resource conflict in British India: A study in the ecological basis of agrarian protest'. Manuscript, 1988.

Gathercole, P., 'Islands and the anthropological imagination'. Paper presented at University of Hawaii, November 1976.

Grove, A. T., Rackham, O., and Moody, J., 'Crete and the South Aegean islands: Effects of climate on the environment (EC contract no. EV4C-0073-UK)'. Typescript report to the European Community (DG 12), 1991.

Hagen, J. R., 'Spatial and historical dimensions of shifting cultivation in India'. Paper presented at World Environmental History Conference, Duke University, Durham, N.C., April 1987.

Haynes, E. S., 'Lineage-based resource management on the North Indian Arid Zone Frontier, 1680–1980'. Paper presented at World Environmental History Conference, Duke University, Durham, N.C., April 1987.

'Changing land-use and land-use ethics in the Rajputana states, 1850–1970'. Manuscript, 1987.

Kidston, M., 'Kings Hill history: A surveyor's perspective'. Paper for Forestry Development Division, Ministry of Agriculture and Labour, St Vincent, 1991.

Ly-Tio-Fane, M., 'Indian Ocean islands: Some account of their natural history as depicted in the literature'. Paper presented at 2nd International Conference on India Ocean Studies, Perth, Western Australia, 5–12 December 1984.

'Notice historique'. Royal Society of Arts and Sciences of Mauritius, 150th anniversary commemoration. Typescript proof copy, 1985.

McFarland, M., 'Environmental and political history of Coimbatore and Nilgiris districts, 1680–1980'. Paper presented at World Environmental History Conference, Duke University, Durham, N.C., April 1987.

McNeill, J. R., 'Environmental deterioration in the mountain communities of the Mediterranean world, 1820 to present'. Paper presented at World Environmental History Conference, Duke University, Durham, N.C., April 1987.

Nikovski, P., et al., 'The effect of placing a ban on goats in the forests of Yugoslavia'. Mimeograph in library of the Belgrade Forestry Research Institute, Belgrade, 1982.

Pressler, F. A., 'Panchayat forestry in Madras'. Paper presented at World Environmental History Conference, Duke University, Durham, N.C., April 1987.

Rodney, K., Glasgow, A., and Weekes, N., 'Summary of forest change at the King's Hill reserve, St Vincent, 1945–1990'. Paper presented at International Conference on Environmental Institutions, Kingstown, St Vincent, April 1991.

Rubner, H., 'The beginnings of European policy on atmospheric pollution and the start of international collaboration'. Paper presented at World Environmental History Conference, Duke University, Durham, N.C., April 1987.

Spary, E., 'Climate, natural history and agriculture: The ideology of botanical networks in eighteenth century France and its colonies'. Paper presented at International Conference on Environmental Institutions, St Vincent, West Indies, April 1991.

TeBrake, W. H., 'Land reclamation and the formation of a public environmental policy in the Rijnland district of Holland, 1200–1450'. Paper presented at World Environmental History Society Conference, Duke University, Durham, N.C., April 1987.

Trapido, S., 'Poachers, proletarians and gentry in early twentieth century Transvaal'. Paper presented at African Studies Institute seminar, University of Witwatersrand, 1984.

Primary sources

PRINTED BOOKS AND REPORTS

Aitken, E. H., ed., *Gazetteer of Sind*. Lahore, 1907.

Anon, *An account of the conquest of Mauritius*. London, 1811.

Arbuthnot, A., ed., *Major-General Sir Thomas Munro: Selections from his minutes and other official writings*. 2 vols. London, 1881.

Arbuthnot, J., *An essay on the effect of air on the human body*. London, 1733.

Aublet, J.-B. Fusée, *Histoire des plantes de la Guiane françoise*. Paris, 1775.

Baird-Smith, R., *Irrigation in Italy*. Calcutta, 1852.

Balfour, E. G., *Statistics of cholera*. Madras, 1849.

Gul-dastah; or, The bunch of roses (extracts 'from Persian and Hindustani poets'). Madras, 1850.

The timber trees, timber and fancy woods, as also the forests of India and of Eastern and Southern Asia. Madras, 1870.

Balfour, E. G., ed., *Cyclopaedia of India and of Eastern and South Asia: Commercial, industrial and scientific*. Madras, 1857. (Further editions published in Edinburgh, 1865, 1883, 1910, 1911, 1930, 1935)

Beatson, A., *Tracts relative to the island of St. Helena, written during a residency of five years*. London, 1816.

Bernier, F., *The paradise of Hindostan: The history of the late evolution of the empire of the Great Mogul . . .* London, 1671.

Boerhaave, H., *A new method of chemistry*, trans. P. Shaw and E. Chambers. London, 1727.

Bontius, J. [Jacob Bondt], *An account of the diseases, natural history and medicine of the East Indies, translated from the Latin of James Bontius, physician to the Dutch settlement at Batavia, to which are added annotations by a physician*. London, 1769.

Boothby, J., *A true declaration . . . in a briefe discovery and description of the most famous island of Madagascar or St. Lawrence in Asia neare unto East India*. London, 1646.

Bory de St Vincent, J. B., *Voyage dans les quatre principles îles des mers d'Afrique: Fait par l'ordre du gouvernment, pendant les années 1801–1804*. 3 vols. Paris, 1804.

Bosman, D. B., and Thom, H. B., eds., *Journal of Jan van Riebeeck*. Amsterdam, 1952.

Bougainville, L. A. de, *A voyage around the world performed in the years 1766–1769*, trans. J. R. Forster and G. Forster. London, 1772.

Bourdillon, F., ed., *Report on the Travancore forests*. Trivandrum, 1886.

Brisseau-Mirbel, C. F., *Elémens de physiologie vegetale et de botanique*. 3 vols. Paris, 1815.

Brooksby, P., *Voyages and travels of that renowned Captain Sir Francis Drake*. London, 1683.

Brown, J. C., *The hydrology of South Africa*. Edinburgh, 1875.

Buchanan-Hamilton, F., *A journey from Madras through the countries of Mysore, Canara and Malabar*. London, 1811.

Buffon, G. L. Leclerc, Comte de, *Sur la conservation et le rétablissement des forêts*. Paris, 1739.

Sur la culture et exploitation des forêts. Paris, 1742.

Histoire naturelle: Générale et particulière. 44 vols. Paris, 1749–1804.

Vue de la nature. Paris, 1764.

Burchell, W. J., *Travels in the interior of Southern Africa,* vol. 1. London, 1822.

Burckhardt, F., and Smith, S., eds., *The correspondence of Charles Darwin.* 2 vols. Cambridge, 1983–7.

Burrell, A. C., ed., *The voyage of John Huygen van Linschoten to the East Indies, the Maldives, Moluccas and Brazil, from the translation of 1598.* Hakluyt Society, vols. 70–1. 2 vols. London, 1885.

Burrell, A. C., and Tiele, P. A., eds. and trans., *The voyage of Johann Huygen van Linschoten.* 2 vols. London, 1885.

Butter, D., *Outlines of the topography and statistics of the southern districts of Awadh and the cantonment of Sultanpur, Awadh.* Benares, 1839.

Cantillon, R., *Essai sur la nature de commerce en général.* Paris, 1755.

Cape of Good Hope, Government of the, *Statute Law of the Cape of Good Hope.* Cape Town, 1862.

Chadwick, E., *Report on the sanitary conditions of the labouring population of Great Britain.* London, 1842.

Churchill, A., and Churchill, J., eds., *A collection of voyages and travels done by A. and J. Churchill.* 4 vols. London, 1704.

Cleghorn, H., *The forests and gardens of South India.* Edinburgh, 1861.

The forests of the Punjab and Western Himalaya. Roorkee, 1864.

Clusius, *see* D'Ecluse.

Cole, C. N., ed., *The works of Soame Jenyns,* vols. 1–4. London, 1788–90.

Cole, W., *Cursory remarks on some parts of a work entitled 'Studies of nature' originally written by M. de St. Pierre, and translated into English by H. Hunter.* London, 1807.

Commerson, P., *Insularum borbonicarum florilegium . . . inceptum sub initio décembre 1768.* Paris, 1768.

Cooke, E., *A voyage to the South Seas and around the world.* London, 1712.

Corbett, A. F., *The climate and resources of Upper India.* London, 1874.

Cowley, A., *Plantarum, the third and last volume of the works of Mr Abraham Cowley, including his six books of plants.* London, 1721.

Cruickshank, T., *The practical planter.* Edinburgh, 1830.

Cuvier, G. L. C., *Mémoires sur les espèces d'éléphant vivantes et fossiles.* Paris, 1799.

Dalzell, N. A., *Observations on the influence of forests and on the general principles of management as applicable to Bombay.* Byculla, 1863.

Extracts on forests and forestry. Madras, 1869.

Dante Alighieri, *Purgatorio: The Vision, or Hell, Purgatory and Paradise, of Dante Alighieri,* ed. H. F. Cary. 3 vols. London, 1814.

Darwin, C., *Journal of researches into the geology and natural history of the various countries visited by H.M.S. Beagle from 1832–1839.* London, 1842.

On the origin of species by means of natural selection; or, The preservation of favoured races in the struggle for life. London, 1859.

Daubeny, C. G. B., *Climate: Four lectures delivered before the Natural History Society, Torquay.* Oxford, 1863.

D'Ecluse, C. [Clusius], *Exoticorum, libre decem.* Antwerp, 1605.

Defoe, D., *The life and strange surprising adventures of Robinson Crusoe*. Dublin, 1719.
A tour through the whole island of Great Britain, divided into circuits and journeys. London, 1724.

Delalieu, M., *Code des Isles de France et de Bourbon*. Port Louis, 1777. (Supplements in 1783, 1787, 1788)

Denis, J., *Natural history of Canada*, vol. 2. London, n.d.

Denstedt, A. W., *Schlüssel zum 'Hortus Malabaricus'; oder, Dreifaches Register zu diesem Werk*. Weimar, 1818.

Dieffenbach, E., *Travels in New Zealand*. 2 vols. London, 1843.

Dossie, R., *Memoirs of agriculture*. 3 vols. London, 1768.

Duhamel du Monceau, H. L., *Traité de la fabrique des manoeuvres pour les vaisseaux ou l'art de la corderie perfectionne*. 2 vols. Paris, 1747.
Traité de la culture des terres suivant les principes de M. Tull. 6 vols. Paris, 1750–61.
Practical treatise on husbandry. London, 1751.
Eléments d'architecture navale. Paris, 1752.
Avis pour la transport par mer des arbres, des plantes vivaces, des semences et de diverses autre curiosités d'histoire naturelles. Paris, 1753.
Traité de la conservation des grains et en particulier du froment. Paris, 1753.
La physique des arbres. Paris, 1758.
Moyens de conserver la santé aux équipages des vaisseaux. Paris, 1759.
Des semis et plantations des arbres et de leur culture. Paris, 1760.
Eléments d' agriculture. Paris, 1762.
Traité des arbres fruitiers. Paris, 1768.
Du transport, de la conservation et de la force des bois. Paris, 1767.
Traité général des pêches, et historie des poissons qu'elles fournissemt. 3 vols. Paris, 1769–77.

Dupont de Nemours, P. S., *Notice sur la vie de Poivre*. Philadelphia, 1786.
Mémoires sur la vie de Pierre Poivre. Paris, 1787.

du Quesne, A., *A new voyage to the East Indies in the years 1690 and 1691 to which is added a new description (by the Sieur le Maine) of the Canary Islands, Cape Verde, Senegal and Gambia*. 2 vols. London, 1696.
See also *Vie de Marquis du Quesne*. . .

Eastwick, E. B., *Dry leaves from young Egypt*. London, 1849.

Edwards, B., ed., *The history, civil and commercial, of the West Indies*. London, 1818.

Ellis, W., *The timber tree improved; or, The best practical methods of improving different lands with proper timber*. London, 1738.

Fabre, J. A., *Essai sur la thème des torrents et des rivières*. Paris, 1797.

Falconer, W., *Remarks on the influence of climate, situation, nature of country, population, nature of food and way of life on the disposition and temper, manners and behaviour . . . of mankind*. London, 1781.

Flinders, M., *A voyage to Terra Australis . . . prosecuted in the years 1801, 1802 and 1803 in H.M. ship the Investigator with an account of the shipwreck of the Porpoise*. 2 vols. London, 1814.

Foissac, P., *Meteorologie*. Leipzig, 1859.

Forster, G., *A voyage round the world*. London, 1777.

Forster, J. R., *Observations made during a voyage round the world*. London, 1778.

Enchiridion historiae naturali inserviens. Halle, 1788.

Fowler, J., *A summary account of the present flourishing state of the respectable colony of Tobago in the British West Indies*. London, 1774.

Gibson, A., ed., *A handbook for the forests of the Bombay Presidency*. Byculla, 1863.

Gibson, A., and Dalzell, N. A., *The Bombay flora*. Bombay, 1861.

Gilpin, W., *Observations . . . made in the year 1776 in . . . the Highlands of Scotland*. 2nd ed. London, 1789.

Remarks on forest scenery. London, 1791.

Godwin, F., alias Domingo Gonzales, *The man in the moone; or, A discourse of a voyage thither*. London, 1638.

Grant, C., *History of Mauritius; or, The Isle of France and the neighbouring islands from their first discovery to the present time*. London, 1801.

Gray, A., ed., *The voyage of Francis Pyrard to the East Indies*, trans. from the 3rd French edition of 1619. London, 1887.

Grimmelshausen, H. J. C., von, *Simplicissimus: Der abenteuerliche Simplicissimus*. Zurich, 1944.

Guilding, L., *An account of the botanic garden in the island of St Vincent*. Glasgow, 1825.

Hakluyt, R., *The principal navigations, voyages and discoveries of the English nation . . . whereunto is added the last most renowned English navigation round about the whole earth*. London, 1589.

Hales, S., *Vegetable staticks*. London, 1727.

Hall, R., *A general account of the first settlement and of the leaders and constitution of the island of Barbados written in 1755*. Bridgetown, Barbados, 1755.

Hamilton, G., and Balfour, J., *A treatise on the manner of raising fruit trees; in a letter from the Earl of Haddington, to which are added two memoirs; the one on preserving and repairing forests, the other on the culture of forests transl. from the French of M. de Buffon*. Edinburgh, 1761.

Hartig, G. H., *Grundsätze der Forst-Direction*. Weimar, 1803.

Hazlitt, W., *On the love of the country*. London, 1814.

Heber, R., *Narrative of a journey through the Upper Provinces of India from Calcutta to Bombay, 1824–5*. London, 1828.

Herbert, T., *A relation of some years travaile begunne anno 1626 into Afrique and the greater Asia, especially the territories of the Persian monarchie, and some parts of the Oriental Indies and Iles adjacent*. London, 1634.

Herder, J. G., *Ideen zur Philosophie der Geschichte der Menschkeit*, trans. T. Churchill as *Outlines of a philosophy of the history of man*. London, 1800.

Hill, O., *Our common land: Open spaces and the future of the commons*. London, 1877.

Home, H. (Lord Kames), *Sketches of the history of man*. 2 vols. Edinburgh, 1774.

Hönigsberger, J. M., *Thirty-five years in the East: Adventures, discoveries, experiments and historical sketches relating to the Punjab and Cashmere*. London, 1835.

Hooker, J. D., *Himalayan journals, or notes of a journalist in Bengal, Sikkim and Nepal Himalayas*. 2 vols. London, 1854.

Hough, F. B., ed., *Report of the Committee on the Preservation of Forests*. 43rd Cong., 1st sess. House Report no. 259. Washington, D.C., 1874.

Houghton, J., *A collection of letters for the improvement of husbandry and trade*. London, 1707.

Howitt, W., *Colonization and Christianity: A popular history of the treatment of natives by the Europeans in all their colonies*. London, 1838.

Hughes, G., *The natural history of Barbados*. London, 1750.

Humboldt, A. von, *Essai sur la géographie des plantes, accompagné d'un tableau physique des régions equinoxiales, et servant d'introduction á l'ouvrage*. Paris, 1807.

Ansichten der Natur. Berlin, 1808.

Personal narrative of travels to the equinoctial regions of the New Continent, 1799–1804, trans. H. M. Williams. 6 vols. London, 1819.

Cosmos, trans. Edward Sabine. 2 vols. London, 1848.

Aspects of nature, trans. Mrs Sabine. 8 vols. London, 1849.

India, Government of, *Report of the Famine Commission*. 4 vols. Calcutta, 1880.

Jenyns, S., *A free enquiry into the nature and origins of evil, in six letters. . .* London, 1757.

Remarks on a bill presented in the last sessions intituled A Bill for preserving the drainage in the Middle and South Levels. London, 1777.

Johnson, J., *The Oriental voyager*. London, 1807.

Johnson, J., *The influence of tropical climates on European constitutions*. London, 1813.

Kalm, P., *Travels into North America*, trans. J. R. Forster. London, 1771.

Kames, Lord, *see* Hume, H.

[Kyd, Robert] *A short account of Colonel Kydd, the founder of the Royal Botanic Garden, Calcutta*. Calcutta, 1897.

La Caille, Abbé de, *Journal historique du voyage*. Paris, 1763.

Lawrence, H. M., *Essays, military and political, written in India*. London, 1859.

Ligon, P., *A true and exact history of the island of Barbados*. London, 1673.

Linnaeus, C., *Hortus Cliffortianus: Plantas . . . quas in hortus . . . Hartecamp in Hollandia, coluit G. Clifford*. Amsterdam, 1737.

Flora zeylonica sistens plantus indicus zeylonicae insulae. Stockholm, 1747.

Philosophica botanica. Stockholm, 1757.

Logan, W., ed., *A collection of treaties, engagements and other papers of importance relating to British affairs in Malabar*. Madras, 1891.

Long, E., *A history of Jamaica*. 3 vols. London, 1774.

Loudon, J. C., *Arboretum et fruticetum Britannicum*. 8 vols. London, 1838.

Lyell, C., *Principles of geology*. 3 vols. London, 1830–3.

Macgillivray, A., *The travels and researches of A. von Humboldt*. Edinburgh, 1837.

Macintosh, J., *Travels into Europe, Asia and Africa*. London, 1782.

McLachlan, H., *English education under the Test Acts: Being the history of the nonconformist academies 1662–1820*. Manchester, 1934.

Mandelslo, J. A. von, *The voyages and travels of ambassadors sent by Frederick Duke of Holstein to the Grand Duke of Muscovy and the King of Persia begun in 1633 and finished in 1634 to which are added the travels of J. A. de Mandelslo*. 2nd ed. London, 1669.

Margo Liouth, H. M., ed., *The poems and letters of Andrew Marvell*. 2nd ed. Oxford, 1967.

Marsh, G. P., *Man and nature; or, Physical geography as transformed by human action.* New York, 1864.

Marshall, P., ed., *The writings and speeches of Edmund Burke,* vol. 5. Oxford, 1981.

Merryman, M., *The island of content; or, a new paradise discovered.* London, 1709.

Mirabeau, H. G. R., *L'ami des hommes, ou Traité de la population.* The Hague, 1756.

Misson, M., *Voyage et aventures de François Leguat et de ses compagnons en deux îles desertes des Indes Orientales.* London, 1721.

Moffat, R., *Missionary labours and scenes in Southern Africa.* London, 1840. Repr. New York, 1969.

Montagu, B., ed., *The works of Francis Bacon,* vol. 4. London, 1826.

Moore, N., ed., *Essays on natural history by Charles Waterton.* London, 1871.

Mundy, P., *The travels of Peter Mundy in Europe and Asia, 1658–1667,* ed. Sir R. C. Temple and L. M. Anstey. 5 vols. in 6. Cambridge, 1907; London, 1914–1930.

Natal, Government of, *Report of the commission appointed to enquire and report on the extent and condition of the forest lands of the colony.* Pietermaritzburg, 1880.

Newbold, T. J., *A political and statistical account of the British settlements in the Straits of Malacca.* London, 1839.

Orta, Garcia da, *Coloquios dos simples e drogas he cousas medicinais da India, comportos pello Doutor Garcia da Orta* (Goa, 1563), ed. and trans. Sir Clements Markham as *Colloquies on the simples and drugs of India by Garcia da Orta.* London, 1913.

Pasfield-Oliver, S., ed., *The voyage of François Le Guat of Bresse to Rodriguez, Mauritius, Java and the Cape of Good Hope.* (Transcribed from 1st ed.) 2 vols. London, 1891.

Paulini, G., *Un codice veneziano del 1600 per le acque e le foreste.* Rome, 1934.

Perry, W. C., *The German universities.* London, 1845.

Pike, N., *Sub-tropical rambles in the land of the Aphanapteryx.* London, 1873.

Piso, G., *Gulielmi Pisonis Medici, Amstelaedamensis de Indiae utriusque re naturali et medici, libri quatuordecem.* Amsterdam, 1658.

Plat, H., *The Garden of Eden; or, An accurate description of all flowers and fruits now growing in England.* London, 1653.

Pliny, *Natural history,* trans. H. Rackham. Cambridge, Mass., 1938.

Poivre, P., *Le citoyen du monde; ou lettres d'un philosophe chinois à ses amis dans l'Orient.* Amsterdam, 1763.

Voyages d'un philosophe; ou observations sur les moeurs et les arts des peuples de l'Afrique, de l'Asie et de l'Amérique. Yverdon, 1768.

Travels of a philosopher; or, Observations on the manners of various nations in Africa and Asia. Dublin and Glasgow, 1770.

De l'Amérique et des Américains, ou observations curieuses du philosophe, Le Douceur, qui a parcouru cet hémisphère pendant la dernière guerre en faisant le noble métier de tuer les hommes sans les manger. Berlin, 1771.

Pons, F., *Voyagé à la partie orientale de la Terre-Ferme, dans l'Amérique méridionale, fait pendant les années 1802–1804.* Paris, 1806.

Poyntz, J., *The present prospect of the famous and fertile island of Tobago.* London, 1683.

Pradt, D. D. de, *Les trois âges des colonies ou de leur état passé, présent et à venir.* 3 vols. Paris, 1801.

Pridham, C., *England's colonial empire: Mauritius*. London, 1846.

Priestley, J., *Experiments and observations*. London, 1774.

Prony, G. C. F., *Mémoire sur jaugeage des eaux courantes*. Paris, 1802.

Quesnay, F., *Philosophie rurale ou économie générale et politique de l'agriculture*. Amsterdam, 1764.

Randolph, B., *The present state of the islands*. Oxford, 1687.

Raynal, G., *Histoire philosophique et politique des deux Indes*, vol. 5. Amsterdam, 1772.

Ribbentrop, B., *Forestry in British India*. Calcutta, 1899.

Rochefort, C., *Tableau de l'Isle de Tabago*. Leiden, 1665.

Rousseau, J. J., *A dissertation on the origin and foundation of inequality among mankind*, trans. Edward Sabine. London, 1773–4.

Collections complète des oeuvres de J.-J. Rousseau. Geneva, 1782.

Letters on the elements of botany addressed to a lady, trans. T. Martyn. London, 1782.

Les rêveries d'un promeneur solitaire (vol. 3 of *Mémoires*). Paris, 1782. Trans. J. C. Fletcher as *The reveries of a solitary*. London, 1927.

Oeuvres complètes, avec des notes historiques. 8 vols. Paris, 1834.

Roxburgh, W. R., *Plants of the coast of Coromandel*. Serampore, 1820.

Royle, J. F., *Essay on the productive resources of India*. London, 1840.

Russell, P., *Poisonous snakes of the Coromandel coast*. London, 1787.

A treatise on the plague. London, 1791.

Saint-Pierre, J.-H. Bernardin de, *Theory of tides*, trans. H. Hunter. Bath, 1795.

Studies of nature, trans. H. Hunter. 5 vols. London, 1796.

A voyage to the Isle of France, trans. H. Hunter. London, 1800.

Harmonies of nature, trans. H. Hunter. 3 vols. London, 1815.

Paul and Virginia, trans. H. Hunter. London, 1841.

La chaumière indienne. Calcutta, 1866.

Salles, J., ed., *Oeuvres complètes de Pierre Poivre, précédées de sa vie*. Paris, 1797.

Schleiden, M. J., *Die Pflanze und ihr Leben: Populäre Vorträge*. Leipzig, 1848.

Die Landenge von Sues: Zu Beurteilung des Canal projektes und Auszugs der Israeliten aus Aegypten. Leipzig, 1858.

Ueber den materialismus de neureren deutschen Naturwissenschaft. Leipzig, 1863.

Für Baum und Wald: Eine Schutzschrift. Leipzig, 1870.

Schoepflin, J. D., *Alsatie diplomatica*, vol. 2. Mannheim, 1772.

Scott, W., *Report on the management of canals and forests in Scinde*. Calcutta, 1853.

Scott-Moncrieff, C. C., *Irrigation in Southern Europe*. London, 1868.

Shakespeare, W., *The Tempest*, in W. J. Craig, ed., *The complete works of William Shakespeare*. Oxford, 1905.

Shephard, C., *An historical account of the island of Saint Vincent*. London, 1831.

Sleeman, W. H., *Rambles and reflections of an Indian official* (1844). London, 1914.

Smith, A., *The theory of moral sentiments*. London, 1774.

Inquiry into the nature and cause of the wealth of nations. London, 1776.

Smith, J., *The generale historie of Virginia, New England and the Summer Isles*. London, 1624.

Smith, R., ed., *Hydrostatical and pneumatical lectures by Roger Cotes*. Cambridge, 1738.

Spry, H. H., *Modern India*. 2 vols. London, 1837.

Stewart, J. L., ed., *Select papers of the Agri-Horticultural Society of the Punjab from its commencement to 1862*. Lahore, 1865.

Strickland, H. E., *Travel thoughts and travel etc.* London, 1854.

Strickland, H. E., and Melville, A. G., *The dodo and its kindred*. 2 vols. London, 1848.

Strzelecki, P. E., *Physical description of New South Wales and Van Diemen's Land*. London, 1845.

    Gold and silver: A supplement to 'Physical description of New South Wales and Van Diemen's Land'. London, 1856.

Stuart, A. J., *Extracts from 'Man and Nature'* ... *with some notes on forests and rainfall in Madras*. Madras, 1882.

Stukeley, W., *The family memoirs of the Rev. William Stukeley, M.D.* 3 vols. Durham, 1882–7.

Tavernier, J. B., *Six voyages into Persia and the East Indies*. London, 1676.

Temple, R., ed., *The travels of Peter Mundy in Europe and Asia, 1658–1667*. 8 vols. Cambridge, 1897.

Theophrastus, *Enquiry into plants*, trans. Sir Arthur Loeb. 2 vols. New York, 1916.

Thompson, R., *Report on the forests of Mauritius*. Port Louis, 1880.

Thucydides, *History of the Peloponnesian wars*. Harmondsworth, 1972.

Tomlinson, C. *Sir Joseph Banks and the Royal Society*. London, 1844.

Tyndall, J., *On radiation: The Rede lectures at the University of Cambridge*. London, 1865.

Unanue, J. H., *El clima de Lima*. Madrid, 1815.

Urfe, H. d', *L'Astrée de M. d'Urfe* (Rouen, 1616), trans. 'A person of quality' as *The history of Astrea: The first part in twelve books*. London, 1670.

Valentia, Earl of (G. A. Mountnorris), *Voyages and travels to India*. 3 vols. London, 1809.

Valentyn, F., *Oud en niew Oost-Indien*. 2 vols. Dordrecht and Amsterdam, 1724–1726.

Van der Stel, S., *Simon Van der Stel's journal of his expedition to Namaqualand 1686–88*. Cape Town, 1932.

van Reede tot Drakenstein, H. A., *Hortus indicus malabaricus, continens regioni malabarici apud Indos celeberrimi omnis generis plantas rariores*. 12 vols. Amsterdam, 1678–93.

Vattel, E. de, *The law of nations, or principles of natural law, applied to the conduct and affairs of nations and sovereigns: A work tending to display the true interest of powers*. London, 1760.

Vie de Marquis du Quesne, dit Le Grand Du Quesne. Paris, 1783.

Walker, C., *Reports on forest management in the Madras Presidency*. Madras, 1873.

Waller, J., *The battle of the Summer Islands*. London, 1665.

Waterton, C., *Wanderings in South America, the North-West of the United States and the Antilles in the years 1812–1824*. 2nd ed. London, 1880.

Webster, W. H. B., *Narrative of the voyage to the Southern Atlantic Ocean in the years 1828, '29, '30, performed in H. M. sloop Chanticleer under the command of the late Captain Henry Foster by order of the Lords Commissioners of the Admiralty*. London, 1834.

White, G., *The natural history and antiquities of Selborne*. London, 1789.

Why has so much English capital been swallowed up in Mauritius? London, 1848.

Wolkern, L. C. von, *Historia diplomatica Nurnbergensis*. Nürnberg, 1738.

Woodward, J., *Brief instructions for making observations in all parts of the world, as also for collecting, preserving and sending over natural things: Drawn upon the request of a Person of Honour and presented to the Royal Society.* London, 1696.

An essay toward a natural history of the earth. London, 1702.

The state of physick and of diseases, with an enquiry into the late increase of them but more particularly of the smallpox . . . the idea is premised . . . of the nature and mechanism of man. London, 1718.

Géographie physique, ou essaye sur l'histoire naturelle de la terre de M. Woodward. Paris, 1735.

Wordsworth. W., *A complete guide to the English Lakes.* London, 1842.

Young, A., *Travels in France during the years 1787, 1788 and 1789.* London, 1793.

Young, W., *An account of the black Caribs of St Vincent.* London, 1795.

ARTICLES

American Association for the Advancement of Science, Special Committee, 'Report of the Committee on the Preservation of Forests', *Proceedings of the American Association for the Advancement of Science,* 1874, pp. 37–45.

Anderson, A., 'An ascent of Mome Garou, a mountain in the island of St Vincent, with a description of the volcano at its summit', *Philosophical Transactions of the Royal Society,* 75 (1785), 16–36.

Balfour, E. G., 'On the migratory tribes of natives of Central India', *Edinburgh New Philosophical Journal* 1843, pp. 29–47.

'Notes on the influence exercised by trees in inducing rain and preserving moisture', *Madras Journal of Literature and Science,* 25 (1849), 402–48.

'The influence exercised by trees on the climate and productiveness of the Peninsula of India', paper in evidence, 20 Feb. 1878, in Government of India, *Report of the Famine Commission,* vol. 4. Calcutta, 1880, pp. 100–4.

Banks, J., 'Diary of the rain at Bombay from 1780 to 1787 and part of the year 1788', *Philosophical Transactions of the Royal Society,* 80 (1790), 590.

Bidie, G., 'On the effects of forest destruction in Coorg', *Proceedings of the Royal Geographical Society,* 1869, pp. 74–5.

Boussingault, J. B., 'Ascension au Chimborazo exécutée le 16 décembre 1831', *Annales de Chimie,* 58 (1835), 100–9.

'Ascent of Chimborazo on 16th December', *Edinburgh New Philosophical Journal,* 19 (1835), 88–107.

'Mémoire sur l'influence des défrichements dans la diminution des cours-d'eau', *Annales de Chimie,* 64 (1837), 113–41.

'Memoir concerning the effect which the clearing of land has in diminishing the quantity of water in the streams of a district', *Edinburgh New Philosophical Journal,* 24 (1838), 85–106.

Bouton, L. C., 'Note sur les caractères de la végétation des îles Bourbon et Maurice', *Annales de Sciences Naturelles,* 24 (1831), 249–52.

'Analysis of the proceedings of the Society of Natural History on the island of Mauritius during the year 1833', *Hooker's Botanical Miscellany,* 1833, pp. 355–8.

'Observations on the different varieties of *Ziziphus jujuba*, cultivated in the Mauritius', *Hooker's Journal of Botany and Kew Garden Miscellany*, 1 (1834), 319–22.

'Résumé of papers etc. on the vegetation of Mauritius up to the publication of Bojer's *Hortus Mauritiana*', *Rapport Scientifique de la Société d'Histoire Naturelle de l'Ile Maurice*, 7 (1837), 27–34.

'Sur le décroissement des forêts à l'Ile Maurice', *Cernéan*, nos. 814–15 (12 and 14 April 1838).

'Descriptions of plants of Bojer', *Rapports de la Société de l'Histoire Naturelle de l'Ile Maurice*, 10 (1839), 19–25.

'Note sur le déboissement des forêts', *Rapports de la Société de l'Histoire Naturelle de l'Ile Maurice*, 1846, pp. 103–10.

'Note sur l'état actuel des forêts à Maurice', *Rapports de la Société d'Histoire Naturelle de l'Ile Maurice*, 1846, p. 175.

'Medicinal plants growing or cultivated in the island of Mauritius', *Transactions of the Royal Society of Arts and Sciences of Mauritius*, 1 (1857), 1–177.

'Sylviculture – l'Eucalyptus, son importance pour le réboisement', *Revue Coloniale de Maurice*, 2 (1872), 61–78.

Brandis, D., 'On the distribution of forests in India', *Transactions of the Scottish Arboricultural Society*, 7 (1873), 90.

Briggs, J., 'Report on the aboriginal tribes of India', *Report of the Proceedings of the British Association for the Advancement of Science*, 1851, pp. 169–76.

Brown, J. C., 'On South African torrential floods viewed in connection with the late inundations in the valley of the Garonne and its affluences and measures adopted in France to prevent such floods', *Report of the Proceedings of the British Association for the Advancement of Science (Transactions)*, 1875, p. 190.

Brownlow, C., 'The timber trees of Cachar', *Journal of the Agricultural and Horticultural Society of India*, 1865, pp. 336–62.

Chambers, W., and Chambers, R., 'Failure of springs in the East', *Chambers Journal of Popular Literature*, 496 (1863), 1–3.

Cleghorn, H., 'On the hedge plants of South India', *Annals of Natural History*, 6 (1850), 83–100.

'Remarks on *Calysacium longifolium* Wight', *Pharmaceutical Journal*, 10 (1851), 597–8.

'Note on the *Aegle marmelos*', *Indian Annals*, 1855, pp. 222–4.

'Note on the sand-binding plants of the Madras beach', *Hooker's Journal of Botany*, 8 (1856), 52–4.

'On the Pauchantee, or Indian Gutta Tree on the west coast of the Madras Presidency', *Edinburgh Botanical Society Transactions*, 6 (1860), 148–50.

'Expedition to the higher ranges of the Anamalai Hills, Coimbatore, in 1858', *Edinburgh Royal Society Transactions*, 22 (1861), 579–88.

'Notes upon the Coco-nut tree and its uses', *Edinburgh New Philosophical Society Transactions*, 14 (1861), 173–83.

'On the introduction of Cinchona trees (Peruvian Bark) into South India', *Edinburgh Botanical Society Transactions*, 7 (1863), 73–89.

'On the varieties of Mango fruit in Southern India', *Edinburgh Botanical Society Transactions*, 7 (1863), 111–12.

'Tea culture in South India', *Edinburgh Botanical Society Transactions*, 7 (1863), 30–2.

'Memorandum on the timber procurable by the Indus, Swat and Kabul rivers', *Journal of the Agricultural and Horticultural Society of India*, 1865, pp. 73–87.

'On the Deodar forests of the Himalaya', *Reports of the Proceedings of the British Association for the Advancement of Science*, 35 (1865), 79–80.

'Principal plants of the Sutlej valley: Together with approximate elevations and remarks', *Edinburgh Botanical Society Transactions*, 8 (1866), 77–84.

'On the distribution of the principal timber trees of India, and the progress of forest conservancy', *Report of the Proceedings of the British Association for the Advancement of Science (Transactions)*, 1868, pp. 91–4.

'Address to the opening of the thirty-fourth session (1869)', *Edinburgh Botanical Society Transactions*, 1870, pp. 261–84.

'Notes on the botany and agriculture of Malta and Sicily', *Edinburgh Botanical Society Transactions*, 10 (1870), 106–39.

'On the parasites which affect the government timber plantations in S. India', *Edinburgh Botanical Society Transactions*, 10 (1870), 245.

'On some economic plants of India', *Edinburgh Botanical Society Transactions*, 8 (1866), 63–4.

Cleghorn, H., Royle, F., Baird-Smith, R., and Strachey, R., 'Report of the committee appointed by the British Association to consider the probable effects in an economical and physical point of view of the destruction of tropical forests', *Report of the Proceedings of the British Association for the Advancement of Science*, 1852, pp. 78–102.

Cole, J., 'Editorial', *Madras Journal of Literature and Science*, 36 (1849), 400–1.

Collinson, P., 'Some account of the late excellent and eminent Stephen Hales', *Gentleman's Magazine*, 34 (1764), 273–8.

Commerson, P., 'Descriptions de Tahiti'. In J. Crassous, *Décades philosophiques*, vol. 18, p. 133. Paris, 1769.

'Lettre de M. Commerson, docteur en médecine et médecin botaniste du Roi à l'Isle de France, sur la découverte de la nouvelle Cythère', *La Mercure*, 25 Feb. 1769, pp. 196–205.

Defoe, D., 'The destruction of the Isle of St Vincent', *Mist's Journal*, 5 July 1718.

Dieffenbach, E., 'An account of the Chatham Islands', *Journal of the Royal Geographical Society*, 1 (1841), 195–214.

'The present state of Te Wanga Lake in Chatham Island', *Journal of the Royal Geographical Society*, 12 (1842), 142.

'On the geology of New Zealand', *Report of the Proceedings of the British Association for the Advancement of Science (Transactions)*, 1845, p. 50.

Falconer, H., 'On the aptitude of the Himalayan range for the culture of the Tea plant', *Journal of the Asiatic Society of Bengal*, 3 (1834), 178–87.

'Memorandum concerning timber trees used for fuel', *Journal of the Indian Agricultural and Horticultural Society*, 6 (1848), 163–7.

'Report on the teak plantations of Bengal', in *Selections from the Records of the Bengal Government*, no. 25. Calcutta, 1857.

Forster, J. R., 'Ueber George Forster', *Annalen der Philosophie*, 1 (1795), 9–16, 121–8.

Franklin, B., 'Meteorological imaginations and conjectures', *Transactions of the Manchester Philosophical Society*, 1784, pp. 373–7.

Gibson, A., 'A general sketch of the province of Guzerat, from Deesa to Daman', *Transactions of the Medical and Physical Society of Bombay*, 1 (1838), 1–77.

'Practical remarks on the culture and preparation of Senna in the Bombay Presidency', *Indian Agricultural Society Journal*, 2 (1843), 193–6.

'Report on the state and progress of agriculture in the Deccan for the year 1842', *Indian Agricultural Society Journal*, 2 (1843), 286–302.

'Further particulars connected with the cultivation of the Olive at the Government Botanic Garden at Hewra in the Deccan, with notes regarding the Ground Nut and Castor Oils', *Indian Agricultural Society Journal*, 3, (1844), 247–8.

'On the mode of cultivating the Latakia tobacco', *Indian Agricultural Society Journal*, 3 (1844), 250.

'Notes on Indian agriculture as practised in the western or Bombay provinces of India', *Asiatic Society Journal*, 8 (1846), 93–103.

'Report on deforestation in South Conkan', *Transactions of the Medical and Physical Society of Bombay*, 1846, pp. 37–41.

'Report on Teak and other forests visited in 1843–44', *Bombay Agricultural and Horticultural Society Transactions*, 1846, pp. 120–44.

'Report on the various vegetable substances used in India for the purpose of producing intoxication', *Hooker's Journal of Botany*, 5 (1853), 89–91.

Governor of St Helena, H.E. the, 'Address of H.M. Governor to the Agricultural and Horticultural Society of St Helena', *St Helena Gazette*, 1824, pp. 136–42.

Halley, E., 'An account of the circulation of watry vapours of the sea, and of the cause of springs', *Philosophical Transactions of the Royal Society*, 192:17 (1694), 468–73.

Hooker, J. D., 'On insular floras', *Gardener's Chronicle*, 5 Jan. 1867.

'Forestry', *Journal of Applied Science*, 1 (1872), 221–3.

Hooker, W., 'Editorial', *Hooker's Botanical Miscellany*, 1831, pp. i–ix.

'Review of *Illustrations of Indian botany*, *Hooker's Botanical Miscellany*, 1831, pp. 90–7.

[Hooker, W.] Obituary, by Sir Roderick Murchison with J. D. Hooker, *Journal of the Royal Geographical Society*, 1866, pp. 197–8.

Hough, F. B., 'On the duty of governments in the preservation of forests', *Proceedings of the American Association for the Advancement of Science*, 72, (1873), 1–10.

Humboldt, A. von, 'On two attempts to ascend Chimborazo', *Edinburgh New Philosophical Journal*, 23 (1837), 291–312.

Hume, D., 'Of the populousness of ancient nations'. In T. H. Green and T. H. Grose, eds., *Essays moral, political and literary*, pp. 356–60. London, 1882.

Lister, J., 'An extract of a letter of Mr Lister's concerning some observations made at Barbados by Mr Ligon', *Proceedings and Transactions of the Royal Society*, 1675, p. 399.

Logan, J. S., 'The probable effects on the climate of Penang of the continual destruction of its hill jungles', *Journal of the Indian Archipelago*, 2 (1848), 534–5.

Markham, C. R., 'On the effects of the destruction of forests in the Western Ghauts of India on the water supply', *Proceedings of the Royal Geographical Society*, 1869, pp. 261–7.

Money, W. T., 'Observations on the advantages of shipbuilding at Bombay, compared with building out of Oak in the U.K.', *Quarterly Review*, 8 (1812), 12–23.

Mueller, F. von, 'Forest culture in relation to industrial pursuits', *Journal of Applied Science*, 1 (1872), 198–202, 213–16, 231–4.

Newbold, T. J., 'Notice of river dunes on the banks of the Hoogri and Pennaur rivers', *Madras Journal of Literature and Science*, 1839, pp. 309–10.

'The Chenchars: A wild tribe inhabiting the Eastern Ghauts', *Journal of the Royal Asiatic Society*, 8 (1846), 271–83.

Newton, A., 'Second supplementary report on the extinct birds of the Mascarene Islands', *Report of the Proceedings of the British Association for the Advancement of Science*, 1872, pp. 23–4.

O'Reilly, E., 'The vegetable products of the Tenasserim provinces', *Journal of the Indian Archipelego*, 4 (1850), 55–65.

Pering, R., 'A brief inquiry into the causes of premature decay in our wooden bulwarks with an examination of the means best calculated to prolong their duration', *Quarterly Review*, 8 (1812), 28–41.

Priestley, J., 'Observations on different kinds of air', *Philosophical Transactions of the Royal Society*, 62 (1772), 147–264.

'On the noxious quality of the effluvia of putrid marshes', *Philosophical Transactions of the Royal Society*, 64 (1774).

Prony, G. C. F., and Humboldt, A. von, 'Estratto dalle ricerche del Signore de Prony sul sistema idraulico dell'Italia'. In F. Cardinale, ed., *Nuova raccolta di antori italiani che trattono del moto dell'acque*, vol. 7, pp. 81–8. Bologna, 1865.

Roxburgh W., 'A meteorological diary kept at Fort St George in the East Indies', *Philosophical Transactions of the Royal Society*, 68 (1778), 180–90; 80 (1790).

'Remarks on the land winds and their causes', *Transactions of the London Medical Society*, 1 (1810), 189–211.

Schneeglas, C. D., 'Leben und Charackter der Herrn D. Johann Reinhold Forster . . .', *Schriften der Herzoglichen Societät für die Gesammte Mineralogie zu Jena*, 1 (1804), 264.

Schouw, J. F., 'The origins of the existing vegetable creation', *Hooker's Journal of Botany*, 2, (1856), 32.

Smith, C. I., 'On the effect of trees on the climate and productiveness of a country', *Madras Journal of Literature and Science*, 25 (1849), 466–72.

Storr-Lister, J., 'Tree-planting in the Punjab', *Cape Monthly*, 1873, pp. 363–8.

Stovell, M., 'Notes on the climate of the Cape of Good Hope', *Transactions of the Bombay Medical and Physical Society*, 1849, pp. 195–215.

Strickland, H. E., 'Report on the recent progress and present state of ornithology', *Report of the Proceedings of the British Association for the Advancement of Science*, 1848, pp. 170–221.

'Surgeons in India, past and present', review of J. Macpherson, *Notes on the condition of the Indian Medical Service*, n.d., *Calcutta Review*, 1854, pp. 217–54.

Thomas, J. E., 'Notes on ryotwar or permanent money rents in South India, and on the duty of government in periods of famine', *Madras Journal of Literature and Science*, 1838, 53–78, 200–21.

Thomson, A. S., 'Could the natives of a temperate climate colonize and increase in a tropical country and vice versa?', *Transactions of the Bombay Medical and Physical Society*, 1843, pp. 112–38.

Thomson, T., 'Sketch of the climate and vegetation of the Himalaya', *Glasgow Philosophical Society Proceedings*, 3 (1848), 309–21.

Wallace, A. R., 'On the physical geography of the Malay archipelago', *Journal of the Royal Geographical Society*, 32 (1863), 127–37.

Williamson, H., 'An attempt to account for the change of climate which has been observed in the middle colonies of North America', *Transactions of the American Philosophical Society*, 1 (1770), 271–7.

Wilson, J. S., 'On the general and gradual desiccation of the earth and atmosphere', *Report of the Proceedings of the British Association for the Advancement of Science (Transactions)*, 1858, pp. 155–6.

'On the increasing desiccation of inner Southern Africa', *Report of the Proceedings of the British Association for the Advancement of Science (Transactions)*, 1864, p. 150.

'On the progressive desiccation of the basin of the Orange River in Southern Africa', *Proceedings of the Royal Geographical Society*, 1865, pp. 106–9.

'The water supply of the basin of the River Orange, or Gariep, South Africa', *Geographical Journal*, 1865, pp. 106–29.

Woodward, J., 'Some thoughts and experiments concerning vegetation', *Philosophical Transactions of the Royal Society*, 21 (1699), 196–227, and *Miscellanea Curiosa*, 1 (1708), 220.

Secondary sources

BOOKS

Abreu de Galinde, J., *Historia de Conquista de las siete islas de Canaria*, Santa Cruz de Tenerife, 1977.

Albion, R. G., *Forests and sea power: The timber problem of the Royal Navy, 1652–1862*. Cambridge, Mass., 1926.

Allan, D. G. C., *William Shipley, founder of the Royal Society of Arts: A biography with documents*. London, 1979.

Allan, D. G. C., and Schofield, R. E., *Stephen Hales: Scientist and philosopher*. London, 1983.

Allen, D., *The naturalist in Britain*. London, 1976.

Anderson, R. D., *Education and opportunity in Victorian Scotland: Schools and universities*. London, 1985.

Archibald, D., *Tobago, 'Melancholy Isle'*, vol. 1, *1498–1771*. Port of Spain, Trinidad, 1987.

Arnold, D., *Famine: Social crisis and historical change*. Oxford, 1988.

Arrhenius, S. A., *Les atmosphères des planètes: Conférence faite de mars 1911*. Paris, 1911.

Atkinson, G., *The extraordinary voyage in French literature before 1700*. London, 1922.

Bailey, H., *Zoroastrian problems in the ninth-century books*. Oxford, 1943.

Baker, E., Clark, G., and Vaucher, P., *The European inheritance*, vol. 3. London, 1954.

Bamford, P. W., *Forests and French sea power, 1660–1789*. Toronto, 1956.

Barnwell, P. J., *Visits and despatches: Mauritius, 1598–1948*. Port Louis, 1948.

Barnwell, P. J., and Toussaint, M. M. A., *A short history of Mauritius*. London, 1949.

Bayly, C. A., *Rulers, townsmen and bazaars: North India in the age of British expansion*. Cambridge, 1983.

Imperial meridian: The British empire and the world, 1780–1830. London, 1989.

Beard, J. S., *The natural vegetation of the Windward and Leeward islands*. Oxford forestry memoirs, no. 21. Oxford, 1949.

Beck, H., *Alexander von Humboldt*. 2 vols. Wiesbaden, 1958–61.

Beekman, E. M. ed., *The poison tree: Selected writings of Rumphius on the natural history of the Indies*. Amherst, Mass., 1981.

Beer, M., *An enquiry into physiocracy*. London, 1939.

Bell, G., *Ernst Dieffenbach, humanist and rebel*. Palmerston North, 1976.

Bell, J. F., *A history of economic thought*. London, 1907.

Benot, J., ed., *Voyages à Isle de France par Bernardin de Saint-Pierre*. Paris, 1983.

Beran, B., *The Chinantec and their habitat*. Mexico City, 1938.

Berkeley, E., and Berkeley, D. S., eds., *The Reverend John Clayton: His scientific writings and other related papers*. Charlottesville, Va., 1965.

Bhatia, B. M., *Famines in India*. London, 1967.

Bicknell, P., and Woof, R., *The Lake District discovered, 1810–1850: The artists, the tourists and Wordsworth*. Grasmere, 1983.

Bilsky, J., *Historical ecology: Essays on environment and social change*. New York, 1980.

Biswas, K., ed., *The original correspondence of Sir Joseph Banks, relating to the foundation of the Royal Botanic Garden, Calcutta, and the summary of the 150th anniversary volume of the Royal Botanic Garden, Calcutta*. Royal Asiatic Society of Bengal Series, vol. 4. Calcutta, 1950.

Blaikie, P., *The political economy of soil erosion in developing countries*. London, 1985.

Blaikie, P., and Brookfield, H., *Land degradation and society*. London, 1987.

Blaim, A., *Failed dynamics: The English Robinsonnades of the eighteenth century*. Lublin, 1987.

Blewett, D., *Defoe's art of fiction: Robinson Crusoe, Moll Flanders, Colonel Jack and Roxana*. Buffalo, N.Y., 1979.

Bloch, E., *The principle of hope*, trans. N. Plaice. 3 vols. Cambridge, Mass., 1986.

Blusse, L., *Strange company: Chinese settlers, mestizo women and the Dutch in VOC Batavia*. Dordrecht, 1986.

Blusse, L., and Gaastra, F., *Companies and trade: Essays on overseas trading companies during the ancien régime*. London, 1981.

Bockstoce, J. R., *Whales, ice and men: The history of whaling in the Western Arctic*. Seattle, Wash., 1987.

Bodi, L., and Jeffries, S., *The German connection: Sesquicentenary essays on German–Victorian crosscurrents*. Melbourne, 1985.

Bonyhady, T., *Images in opposition: Australian landscape painting 1801–1891*. Melbourne, 1988.

Boullée, A., *Notice sur Poivre*. Lyons, 1935.

Bourde, A. J., *The influence of England on the French agronomes, 1750–1789*. Cambridge, 1953.

Bowen, M., *Empiricism and geographical thought: From Francis Bacon to Alexander von Humboldt*. Cambridge, 1981.

Boxer, C. R., *Exotic printing and the expansion of Europe, 1492–1840*. Bloomington, Ind., 1972.

Braudel, F., *Capitalism and material life, 1400–1800*, trans. S. Reynolds. 3 vols. London, 1974.

Civilization and capitalism, trans. S. Reynolds. 3 vols. London, 1981.

Brockway, L. H., *Science and colonial expansion: The role of the British Royal Botanic Garden*. New York, 1979.

Brookes, J., *Gardens of Paradise: The history and description of the great Islam gardens*. London, 1987.

Brouard, N. R., *A history of the woods and forests of Mauritius*. Port Louis, 1963.

Brown, C., *Dutch paintings*. London, 1983.

Brown, J. C., *The French Forest Ordinance of 1669, with a historical sketch of the previous treatment of forests in France*. Edinburgh, 1873.

Bryans, R., *Madeira, pearl of Atlantic*. London, 1959.

Buarque, S., *Visão do Paraiso: Os motivos edenicos no descobrimento e colonizaciâo do Brasil*. Sâo Paulo, 1962.

Burch, W. R., *Daydreams and nightmares: A sociological essay on the American environment*. New Haven, Conn., 1977.

Burgh-Edwardes, S. B. de, *History of Mauritius*. London, 1921.

Burkill, I. H., *Chapters in the history of Indian botany*. Calcutta, 1965.

Busch, B. C., *The war against the seals: A history of the North American seal fishery*. Gloucester, Mass., 1986.

Cage, R. A., *The Scots abroad: Labour, capital and enterprise, 1750–1914*. London, 1985.

Cappe, P. A., *Philibert Commerson: Naturaliste-voyageur*. Paris, 1861.

Cardwell, D. S. L., *The organisation of science in England: A retrospect*. London, 1957.

Carter, H. B., *Sir Joseph Banks, 1743–1820*. London, 1989.

Chadwick, S. E., *The life and times of Edwin Chadwick*. London, 1953.

Chancellor, V., *The political life of Joseph Hume*. Stratford-on-Avon, 1986.

Charlton, D. G., *New images of the natural in France*. Cambridge, 1984.

Chaudhuri, K. N., *Trade and civilisation in the Indian Ocean: An economic history from the rise of Islam to 1750*. Cambridge, 1985.

Chitnis, A., *The Scottish Enlightenment*. London, 1976.

Christopher, A. J., *Southern Africa*. Folkestone, 1976.

Clark-Kennedy, A., *Stephen Hales, D.D., F.R.S.: An eighteenth-century biography*. Cambridge, 1929.

Cobban, A., *The social interpretation of the French Revolution*. Cambridge, 1964.

Copleston, W. E., *The Bombay forests*. Bombay, 1975.

Corney, B. G., *The quest and occupation of Tahiti. . . , 1772–1776*. 3 vols. London, 1913–19.

Crawford, D. G., *A history of the Indian Medical Service*. 2 vols. London, 1914.
The roll of the Indian Medical Service. Calcutta, 1930.

Crosby, A. W., *Ecological imperialism: The biological expansion of Europe, 900–1900*. Cambridge, 1986.

Crosland, M., *Science in France in the Revolution*. Cambridge, Mass., 1969.

Crowe, S., and Haywood, S., *The gardens of Mughal India*. London, 1972.

Curley, T. M., *Samuel Johnson and the age of travel*. Athens, Ga., 1976.

Curtin, P., *The image of Africa*. Oxford, 1964.

Dalloz, M. D., and Dalloz, A., *Jurisprudence forestière*, vol. 15 of *Répertoire méthodique et alphabetique de législation, de doctrines et de jurisprudence*. Paris, 1849.

Damodaran, V., *Broken promises: Popular protest, Indian nationalism and the Congress Party in Bihar, 1935–1946*. Oxford, 1992.

Darby, H.C., *The draining of the fens*. Cambridge, 1940.

Darian, S., *The Ganges in myth and history*. Honolulu, 1978.

Das Gupta, A., *Indian merchants and the decline of Surat, 1700–1750*. Wiesbaden, 1979.

Davidson, J. W., *The island of Formosa, past and present: history, people and resources*. Taipei, 1982. (Originally published 1903)

De Deer, D. R., *The sciences were never at war*. London, 1960.

Diamond, A. W., ed., *Studies of Mascarene island birds*. Cambridge, 1987.

Dorst, J., *Before nature dies*. London, 1970.

Douglas, M., *Implicit meanings: Essays in anthropology*. London, 1979.
Risk acceptability according to the social sciences. London, 1987.

Douglas, M., ed., *Essays in the sociology of perception*. London, 1982.

Douglas, M., and Wildavsky, A., *Risk and culture*. London, 1982.

Drew, J., *India and the Romantic imagination*. Oxford, 1987.

Driver, G. R., *Letters of the first Babylonian dynasty*. London, 1924.

Dubos, R., *The wooing of earth*. London, 1980.

Duncan, J. S., *The city as text: The politics of landscape interpretation in a Kandyan kingdom*. Cambridge, 1990.

Ehrmann, J., *Un paradis désespérée: L'amour et l'illusion dans 'L'Astrée'*. Paris, 1967.

Ellis, F. H., *Twentieth century interpretations of 'Robinson Crusoe': A collection of critical essays*. Englewood Cliffs, N. J., 1969.

Eversley, Lord (G. Shaw-Lefevre), *Forests, commons and footpaths*. London, 1910.

Ferdon, E. F., *Early Tahiti as the explorers saw it: 1707–1797*. Tucson, Ariz., 1980.

Fernández-Arnesto, F., *The Canary Islands after the conquest: The making of a colonial society in the early sixteenth century*. Oxford, 1982.

Fisher, W. P., *The literary relations between La Fontaine and the 'Astrée' of Honoré d'Urfé*. Philadelphia, 1913.

Fitter, R. F., and Scott, P., eds., *The penitent butchers*. Reading, 1978.

Fletcher, H. R., and Brown, W. H., *The Royal Botanic Garden, Edinburgh, 1670–1970*. Edinburgh, 1970.

Flint, V. I. J., *The imaginative landscape of Christopher Columbus*. Princeton, N.J., 1992.

Ford, J., *The role of the Trypanosomiases in African ecology.* Oxford, 1971.

Fox-Genovese, E., *The origins of physiocracy.* Ithaca, N.Y., 1976.

Fraser, D., *The evolution of the British welfare state: A history of social policy since the Industrial Revolution.* London, 1973.

Friedlander, M. J., *From Van Eyck to Bruegel.* Oxford, 1981.

Fuggle, R. F., and Rabie, M. A., *Environmental concerns in South Africa: Technical and legal perspectives.* Johannesburg, 1983.

Gadgil, M., and Guha, R., *This fissured land: An ecological history of India.* New Delhi, 1992.

Geertz, C., *Agricultural involution: The process of ecological change in Indonesia.* Los Angeles, 1963.

Gerbi, A., *The dispute of the New World: The history of a polemic, 1750–1900.* Pittsburgh, Pa., 1973.

Gillespie, J. E., *The influence of overseas expansion on England to 1700.* New York, 1920.

Glacken, C. J., *Traces on the Rhodian shore: Nature and culture in western thought, from ancient times to the end of the eighteenth century.* Berkeley, Calif., 1967.

Gleig, G. R., *Life of Sir Thomas Munro.* 3 vols. London, 1830.

Gosse, P., *St Helena, 1502–1938.* London, 1938.

Goudie, A. S., *The human impact.* Oxford, 1981.

Gould, S. J., *Time's arrow, Time's cycle: Myth and metaphor in the discovery of geological time.* Cambridge, Mass., 1987.

Gray, W. R., *Voyages to Paradise: Exploring in the wake of Captain Cook.* Washington, D.C., 1981.

Grierson, H. J. C., ed., *The poetical works of John Donne.* Oxford, 1971.

Grove, J. M., *The little ice age.* London, 1988.

Grove, R. H., and Damodaran, V., eds., *Essays on the environmental history of South and South-East Asia.* Oxford University Press, New Delhi, in press.

Guelke, J., *The early European settlement of South Africa.* Toronto, 1974.

Guhar, R., *The rule of property for Bengal.* Paris, 1963.

Gupta, R. K., *The economic life of a Bengal district: Birbhum, 1770–1857.* Burdwan, 1984.

Habib, I., *Atlas of the Mughal empire.* Aligarh, 1982.

Halbfass, W., *India and Europe: An essay in understanding.* Albany, N.Y., 1988.

Hall, G. K., Jones, L. F., and Gooden, S. W., eds., *Feminism, Utopia and narrative.* Knoxville, Tenn., 1990.

Harris, D., *Plants, animals and man in the outer Leeward Islands, West Indies.* Berkeley, Calif., 1963.

Haw, R. C., *The conservation of natural resources.* London, 1959.

Hay, L. G., *A handbook of the colony of Tobago.* Scarborough, Tobago, 1882.

Hays, S. P., *Conservation and the gospel of efficiency: The Progressive conservation movement 1890–1920.* Cambridge, Mass., 1959.

Helms, D., and Flader, S. L., *The history of soil and water conservation.* Washington, D.C., 1985.

Heniger, J., *Hendrik Adriaan van Reede tot Drakenstein and 'Hortus malabaricus': A contribution to the study of Dutch colonial botany.* Rotterdam, 1986.

Higgs, H., *The physiocrats: Six lectures on the French économistes of the eighteenth century.* London, 1897.

Himmelfarb, G., *Darwin and the Darwinian revolution.* New York, 1959.

Hobsbawm, E. J., *Industry and empire.* London, 1968.

Howe, S., *Les grands navigateurs à la recherche des épices.* Paris, 1939.

Hont, I., and Ignatieff, M., *Wealth and virtue: The shaping of political economy in the Scottish Enlightenment.* Cambridge, 1983.

Huffel, G., *Economie forestière,* vol. 1, pt 2. Paris, 1920.

Huntington, E., *Mainsprings of civilization.* New York, 1945.

Huxley, Leonard, *Life and letters of Sir Joseph Dalton Hooker.* 2 vols. London, 1918.

Jaggi, O. M., *Ayurveda: Indian system of medicine.* Delhi, 1981.

Jal, A., *Abraham du Quesne et la marine de son temps.* Paris, 1873.

Jeffreys, M. K., *Kaapse Argiefstukke: Kaapse Placaatboek,* pt 1, *1652–1707.* Cape Town, 1944.

Jenkins, A. C., *The naturalists: Pioneers of natural history.* London, 1978.

Jones, J. F., *La nouvelle Héloïse: Rousseau and Utopia.* Geneva, 1977.

Kahr, M. M., *Dutch painting in the seventeenth century.* London 1978.

Kaplan, L. S., *Jefferson and France: An essay in politics and ideas.* New Haven, Conn., 1967.

Karsten, M. C., *The Old Company's garden at the Cape and its superintendents.* Cape Town, 1951.

Karunaratna, N., *Forest conservation in Sri Lanka from British colonial times, 1818–1982.* Colombo, 1982.

Keen, B., ed., *The life of Christopher Columbus by his son Ferdinand.* New Brunswick, N.J., 1959.

Kekonnen, M. A. O., *Peter Kalm's North American journey: Its ideological background and results.* Helsinki, 1959.

Kelly, J. E., *German visitors to English theatres in the eighteenth century.* Princeton, N.J., 1936.

Kerridge, E., *The agricultural revolution.* London, 1967.

    The agrarian problem in the sixteenth century and after. London, 1969.

Kinkel, G., *Biogeography and ecology of the Canary Islands.* The Hague, 1974.

Kjeksjus, H., *Ecology, control and economic development in East African history: The case of Tanganyika, 1850–1950.* London, 1977.

Knight, D. M., *The nature of science.* London, 1976.

Knorr, K. E., *British colonial theories.* London, 1963.

Kokot, D. F., *An investigation bearing on recent climatic changes in Southern Africa.* Pretoria, 1948.

Kumar, D., and Desai, M., eds., *The Cambridge economic history of India,* vol. 2, *c. 1751–c. 1970.* Cambridge, 1983.

Lacroix, A., *Notice historique sur les membres et correspondents de l'Académie des Sciences ayant travaillé dans les colonies françaises des Mascareignes et Madagascar au XVIIIe siècle et au début du XIXe siècle.* Paris, 1934.

    Figures des savants, vol. 4. Paris, 1938.

Lambrick, H. T., *Sir Charles Napier and Sind.* Oxford, 1952.

Lane, F. C., *Venetian ships, shipbuilders and the Renaissance*. Baltimore, 1934.

Lavergne, Léonce de, *Les économistes français du XVIIIe siècle*. Paris, 1870.

Le Duc, St E., *Ile de France*. Port Louis, 1925.

Levin, H., *The myth of the Golden Age in the Renaissance*. London, 1969.

Lewis, R. E., *Edwin Chadwick and the public health movement, 1832–1854*. London, 1952.

Lindenbaum, P., *Changing landscapes: Anti-pastoral sentiment in the English Renaissance*. Athens, Ga., 1986.

Lloyd, C., and Coulter, J., *Medicine and the Navy, 1200–1900*, vol. 4. Edinburgh, 1963.

Lord, R., *The care of the earth: A history of husbandry*. New York, 1962.

Lorrain, J. C., *La mise en valeur de l'île de Tobago (1763–1783)*. Paris, 1969.

Lougnon, A., *L'île Bourbon pendant la Régence*. Paris, 1956.

Love, H. D., *Vestiges of Old Madras*. 3 vols. London, 1913.

Lowenthal, D., *George Perkins Marsh: Versatile Vermonter*. New York, 1958.

Loxley, R. M., *The problematic of islands*. London, 1990.

Ly-Tio-Fane, M., *Mauritius and the spice trade*. 2 vols. Port Louis, 1958, and Paris, 1970.

Ly-Tio-Fane, M., *Pierre Sonnerat, 1748–1814: An account of his life and work*. Port Louis, 1976.

McAlpin, M. B., *Subject to famine*. Princeton, N.J., 1983.

McClellan, J. E., *Colonialism and science: Saint Domingue in the old regime*. Baltimore, 1992.

McIntosh, R. P. *The background to ecology: Concept and theory*. Cambridge, 1985.

Mackay, D., *In the wake of Cook: Exploration, science and empire, 1780–1807*. London, 1985.

Mackenzie, J., *The empire of nature: History, conservation and British imperialism*. Manchester, 1988.

Maclean, T., *Medieval English gardens*. London, 1981.

MacPike, E. F., *Correspondence and papers of Edmond Halley*. Oxford, 1932.

Malleret, L., *Un manuscript inédit de Pierre Poivre*. Paris, 1968.

   Pierre Poivre. Paris, 1974.

Malone, J. J. *Pine trees and politics: The naval stores and forest policy*. London, 1964.

Manilal, K. S., ed., *Botany and history of 'Hortus malabaricus'*. New Delhi, 1989.

Mann, M., *Britische Herrschaft auf Indische Boden: Landwirtschaftliche Transformation und ökologische Destruktion des Central Doab, 1801–1854*. Stuttgart, 1992.

Marshall, P. J., and Williams, G., *The great map of mankind*. London, 1982.

Marx, L., *The machine in the Garden: Technology and the pastoral ideal in America*. New York, 1964.

Mauny, R., *Les navigateurs mediévales sur les côtes sahariennes antérieures à la découverte portugaise*. Lisbon, 1960.

Maury, L. F., *Les Académies d'autrefois*. Paris, 1864.

Meiggs, R., *Trees and timber in the ancient mediterranean world*. Oxford, 1982.

Mercer, J., *The Canary Islands: Their prehistory, conquest and survival*. London, 1980.

Merchant, C., *The death of nature: Women, ecology and the scientific revolution*. New York, 1983.

Merrier, J., *Christopher Columbus: The mariner and the man*. London, 1958.

Moir, E., *The discovery of Britain: The English tourists, 1540–1840*. London, 1964.

Moorehead, A., *The fatal impact: An account of the invasion of the South Pacific, 1767–1840*. London, 1966.

Morrell, J., and Thackray, A., *Gentlemen of science*. Oxford, 1981.

Morton, A. G., *A history of botanical science: An account of the development of botany from ancient times to the present day*. London, 1981.

Mummenhoff, E., *Altnürnberg*. Bamberg, 1890.

Murphy, A. E., *Richard Cantillon: Entrepreneur and economist*. Oxford, 1986.

Nash, R., *Wilderness and the American mind*. New Haven, Conn., 1967.

Needham, J., *Science and civilisation in China*, vols. 1–. Cambridge, 1954–.

Nicolson, D. H., Suresh, C. R., and Manilal, K. S., *An Interpretation of Van Rheede's 'Hortus malabaricus'*. Königstein, 1988.

Nicolson, M. H., *Mountain gloom and mountain glory*. Ithaca, N.Y., 1959.

Niddrie, D. L., *Land use and population in Tobago*. London, 1961.

Nightingale, P., *Trade and empire in Western India, 1784–1800*. Cambridge, 1970.

Niklaus, R., *A literary history of France: The eighteenth century, 1715–1789*. London, 1970.

North-Coombes, A., *La découverte des Mascareignes par les arabes et les portugaises: Rétrospective et mise au point*. Port Louis, 1979.

Histoire des tortues de terre de Rodrigues et le mouvement maritime de l'île. Port Louis, 1986.

O'Brien, C., and O'Brien, B., *The genius of the few: The story of those who founded the Garden in Eden*. Wellingborough, 1985.

O'Riordan, T., *Environmentalism*. London, 1976.

O'Riordan, T., and Watson, J. W., eds., *The American environment: Perceptions and policies*. London, 1976.

Ottley, C. R., *Romantic Tobago*. Port of Spain, Trinidad, 1969.

Pasfield-Oliver, S., *The life of Philibert Commerson*. London, 1909.

Paulson, R., *Emblem and expression: Meaning in English art of the eighteenth century*. London, 1975.

Pearson, W., *Rifled sanctuaries: Some views of the Pacific islands in western literature*. Auckland, 1984.

Pepper, D., *The roots of modern environmentalism*. London, 1984.

Perlin, F., *A forest journey: The role of wood in the development of civilization*. New York, 1989.

Powell, J. M., *Environmental management in Australia, 1788–1914*. Oxford, 1976.

Prentout, H., *L'Ile de France sous Decaen*. Paris, 1901.

Prest, J., *The Garden of Eden: The botanic garden and the re-creation of Paradise*. New Haven, Conn., 1981.

Pringle, T., *The conservationists and the killers*. Cape Town, 1983.

Pulsipher, L. M., *Seventeenth century Montserrat: An environmental impact statement*. Historical Geography Research Series, no. 17. London, 1986.

Raistrick, A., *Quakers in science and industry*. London, 1950.

Raven-Hart, R., *Before van Riebeeck: Callers at the Cape from 1488 to 1652*. Cape Town, 1967.

Rawson, G., *The Count: A life of Sir P. E. Strzelecki, explorer and scientist*. London, 1954.

Reed, T. J., *Goethe*. Oxford, 1984.

Rodger, N. A. M., *Wooden walls: An anatomy of the Georgian navy*. London, 1986.

Rompkey, R., *Soame Jenyns*. Boston, 1984.

Rudwick, M. J. *The great Devonian controversy: The shaping of scientific knowledge among gentlemanly scientists*. Chicago, 1985.

Sahlins, M., *Islands of history*. Chicago, 1987.

Said, E., *Orientalism*. Harmondsworth, 1985.

Sale, K., *The conquest of Paradise: Christopher Columbus and the Columbian legacy*. London, 1991.

Sargent, L. T., ed., *British and American Utopian literature (1516–1985): An annotated bibliography*. New York, 1988.

Schama, S., *An embarrassment of riches: An interpretation of Dutch culture in the Golden Age*. London, 1987.

Schoute, D., *De Geneeskunde in den dienst de Oost-Indische Compagnie in Nederlandisch-Indie*. Amsterdam, 1929.

Schumpeter, J., *The history of economic analysis*. London, 1955.

Secord, J., *Studies in the narrative method of Defoe*. Chicago, 1920.

Sedlar, J. W., *India in the mind of Germany: Schelling, Schopenhauer and their times*. Washington, D.C., 1982.

Seeber, E. D., *Anti-slavery opinion in France during the second half of the eighteenth century*. Baltimore, 1937.

Semple, E. C., *The geography of the Mediterranean region: Its relation to ancient history*. New York, 1931.

Sen, A., *Poverty and famine: An essay on entitlement and deprivation*. Oxford, 1982.

Sheail, J., *Nature in trust: The history of nature conservation in Britain*. London, 1976.

Sim, T. R., *The forests and forest flora of the Cape Colony*. Cape Town, 1907.

Skipp, V., *Crisis and development: An ecological case-study of the Forest of Arden, 1570–1694*. Cambridge, 1978.

Smith, B., *European vision and the South Pacific 1768–1850: A study in the history of art and ideas*. 2nd ed. Oxford, 1960.

Stafford, B. M., *Voyage into substance: Science, nature and the illustrated travel account, 1770–1840*. Cambridge, Mass., 1984.

Stafleu, F. A., *Linnaeus and the Linnaeans: The spreading of their ideas in systematic botany, 1735–1789*. Utrecht, 1971.

Stearn, W. P., *The influence of Leyder on botany in the seventeenth and eighteenth centuries*. Leidse Voordrachten 37. Leiden, 1961.

Stearns, R. P., *Science in the British colonies of North America*. Urbana, Ill., 1970.

Stebbing, E. P., *Jungle by-ways in India: Leaves from the notebook of a sportsman and a naturalist*. London, 1911.

The forests of India. 4 vols. Edinburgh, 1922 and (vol. 4) 1962.

The forests of West Africa and the Sahara: A study of modern conditions. London, 1937.

Stokes, E., *The English Utilitarians and India*. Oxford, 1959.

Strangman, E., *Early French callers at the Cape*. Cape Town, 1936.

Taillemite, E., *Bougainville et ses compagnons autour du monde, 1766–1769.* Paris, 1977.

Thacker, C., *The wildness pleases: The origins of Romanticism.* London, 1983.

Thirsk, J., *Economic policy and projects: The development of a consumer society in England.* Oxford, 1978.

Thirsk, J., ed., *The agrarian history of England and Wales,* vol. 5 in 2 pts. Cambridge, 1985.

Thomas, K., *Religion and the decline of magic: Studies in popular beliefs in sixteenth and seventeenth century England.* London, 1978.

Man and the natural world: Changing attitudes in England 1500–1800. Oxford, 1983.

Thomas, W. L., ed., *Man's role in changing the face of the earth.* Chicago, 1956.

Thornton, A., *The imperial idea and its enemies: A study in British power.* London, 1959.

Titley, N. M., *Plants and gardens in Persian, Mughal and Turkish art.* London, 1979.

Tober, J. A., *Who owns the wildlife? The political economy of conservation in nineteenth century America.* Westport, Conn., 1981.

Totman, C., *The green archipelago: Forestry and conservation in seventeenth century Japan.* Berkeley, Calif., 1989.

Toussaint, A., *Bibliography of Mauritius.* Port Louis, 1956.

Répertoire des archives de l'Ile de France pendant la régie de la Compagne des Indes 1715–1768. Nerac, 1956.

A history of the Indian Ocean, trans. J. Guichemand. London, 1966.

La route des îles: Contributions à l'histoire des îles Mascareignes. Paris, 1967.

Histoire des îles Mascareignes. Paris, 1972.

L'Océan Indien au XVIIIe siècle. Paris, 1974.

A history of Mauritius, trans. W. E. F. Ward. London, 1977.

Toussaint, A., ed., *Dictionary of Mauritian biography.* 5 vols. Port Louis, 1941–84. [Cited as *DMB*]

Troup, R. S., *Colonial forest administration.* Oxford, 1941.

Troup, R. S., ed., *The work of The Forest Department in India.* Calcutta 1917.

Tucker, R. P., and Richards, J. R., *Global deforestation and the world economy.* Durham, N.C., 1983.

Turner, J., *Reckoning with the beast: Animals, pain and the Victorian mind.* London, 1980.

Turrill, W. B., *Joseph Dalton Hooker: Botanist, explorer and administrator.* London, 1963.

Urteaga, L., *La tierra esquilmada: Las ideas sobre la conservación de la naturaleza en la cultura española del siglo XVIII.* Barcelona, 1981.

Uvcinich, A., *Science in Russian culture: A history to 1860.* Stanford, Calif., 1963.

Van Tieghem, P., *Le sentiment de la nature dans pré-romantisme.* Nizet, 1960.

Vashishta, H. B., *Land revenue and public finance in Maratha administration.* Delhi, 1975.

Verlinden, C., *The beginnings of colonialism: Eleven essays with an introduction,* trans. Yvonne Freceero. Ithaca, N.Y., 1970.

Vishwanath, H., ed., *Working plan for Chakakuan.* Forest Department, Trivandrum, 1958.

Wadia, R. A., *The Bombay dockyard and the Wadia masterbuilders.* Bombay, 1955.

Wallerstein, I., *The modern world system.* New York, 1974.

The capitalist world-economy: Essays. Cambridge, 1979.

Historical capitalism. London, 1983.

Wallerstein, I., and Hopkins, T. K., *Processes of the world-system.* Beverly Hills, Calif., 1980.

Watson, A. M., *Agricultural innovation in the early Islamic world.* Cambridge, 1983.

Watts, D., *Man's influence on the vegetation of Barbados, 1627–1800.* University of Hull Occasional Papers in Geography, no. 4. Hull, 1966.

The West Indies: Patterns of development, culture and environmental change since 1492. Cambridge, 1987.

Weatherill, L., *Consumer behaviour and material culture in Britain, 1660–1760.* London, 1988.

Weber, M., *The Protestant ethic and the spirit of capitalism,* trans. T. Parsons. London, 1930.

Wesseling, H. L., ed., *Expansion and reaction: Essays on European expansion and reaction in Asia and Africa.* Leiden, 1978.

Weulersse, G., *Le mouvement physiocratique en France de 1756 à 1770.* 2 vols. Paris, 1910.

Whitcombe, E., *Agrarian conditions in Northern India,* vol. 1, *The United Provinces under British rule, 1860–1869.* Berkeley, Calif., 1972.

Wiener, M. J., *English culture and the decline of the industrial spirit, 1850–1980.* Cambridge, 1981.

Williams, M., *The Americans and their forests: A historical geography,* Cambridge, 1989.

Williams, R., *The country and the city.* London, 1972.

Williams, W. H., *The Commons, Open Spaces and Footpaths Preservation Society 1865–1965: A short history of the Society and its work.* London, 1965.

Willis, M., *By their fruits: A life of Ferdinand von Mueller, botanist and explorer.* Sydney, 1949.

Wohl, A., *Endangered lives: Public health in Victorian Britain.* London, 1983.

Wood, H. T., *A history of the Royal Society of Arts.* London, 1913.

Woodham-Smith, C., *The Great Hunger: Ireland, 1845–1849.* London, 1962.

Worster, D., *Nature's economy: A history of ecological ideas.* Cambridge, 1977.

ARTICLES

Allen, D. E., 'The early history of plant conservation in Britain', *Transactions of the Leicester Literary and Philosophical Society,* 72 (1980), 35–50.

'The early professionals in British natural history'. In A. Wheeler and H. C. Price, eds., *From Linnaeus to Darwin: Commentaries on the history of biology and geology.* London, 1985.

Ambirajan, S., 'Malthusian population theory and Indian famine policy in the nineteenth century', *Population Studies,* 30 (1976), 5–14.

Bayly, C. A., 'The Middle East and Asia during the age of revolutions 1760–1830', *Itinerario,* 2 (1986), 69–83.

Beinart, W., 'Soil erosion, conservationism and ideas about development: A Southern

African exploration 1900–1960', *Journal of Southern African Studies*, 11 (1984), 52–83.

Boomgard, P., 'Forests and forestry in colonial Java, 1677–1942'. In J. Dargavel ed., *Changing tropical forests: Historical perspectives on today's challenges in Asia, Australia and Oceania*, pp. 54–88. Canberra, 1988.

Boxer, C. R., 'Two pioneers of tropical medicine: Garcia d'Orta and Nicolas Monardes', *Diamante*, 14 (1963), 1–33.

Brascamp, E. H. B., 'Hourleveranties onder de O.I. Compagnie; De Acte van 21 Juin door den soeshanan aan de O.I. Campagnie verleend tot het Kappen van houtweiken in de bosschen van blora [uit het Kolonial Archief No. XLXII]', *Tijdschrift voor Indische Taal, Land en Volkenkunde van het Koninklijk Bataviaasch Genootschap van Kusten en Wetenschappen*, 52 (1932), 108–12.

Burckhardt, F., 'The inspiration of Lamarck's belief in evolution', *Journal of the History of Biology*, 5 (1981), 413, 438.

Carruthers, J., 'The Pongola Game Reserve: An eco-political study', *Koedoe*, 28 (1985), 1–16.

Carter, H. B., 'The Banksian natural history collections of the *Endeavour* voyage and their relevance to modern taxonomy'. In A. Wheeler, ed., *History in the service of systematics*, pp. 61–70. Society for the Bibiliography of Natural History, Special Publication no. 1. London, 1981.

Chinard, G., 'The American Philosophical Society and the early history of forestry', *Proceedings of the American Philosophical Society*, 89 (1945), 444–8.

'Eighteenth century theories on America as a human habitat', *Proceedings of the American Philosophical Society*, 91 (1947), 25–57.

Christopher, A. S., 'Environmental perception in Southern Africa', *South African Geographical Journal*, 55 (1973), 14–22.

Cordier, H., 'Voyages de Pierre Poivre, de 1748 à 1757', *Revue Historique des Colonies Françaises*, 6 (1918), 1–88.

Cowgill, G. R., 'Jean-Baptiste Boussingault – A biographical sketch', *Journal of Nutrition*, 84 (1964), 3–9.

Cronk, Q. C. B., 'W. J. Burchell and the botany of St Helena', *Archives of Natural History*, 15 (1988), 45–60.

Crosby, A. W., 'Biotic change in nineteenth century New Zealand', *Environmental Review*, 10 (1986), 177–89.

Crosland, M., 'The rise and decline of France as a scientific centre', *Minerva*, 8 (1970), 453–84.

Curtin, P., 'The environment beyond Europe and the European theory of empire', *Journal of World History*, 1 (1990), 131–50.

Daniels, S., 'The political iconography of woodland'. In D. Cosgrove and S. Daniels, eds., *The iconography of landscape*. Cambridge, 1988.

Darby, H. C., 'The clearing of the woodland in Europe'. In W. L. Thomas, ed., *Man's role in changing the face of the earth*, pp. 183–216. Chicago, 1956.

Deogan, P. N., 'Punjab and colonization', *Indian Forester*, 68 (1942), 74–81.

Di Gregorio, M., 'Hugh Edwin Strickland (1811–1853) on affinities and analogies; or, The case of the missing key', *Ideas and Production*, 7 (1987), 35–50.

Ducker, S. C., 'The history of Australian phytology: Early German collectors and botanists'. In A. Wheeler, ed., *History in the service of systematics*, pp. 43–59. London, 1981.

Duffey, E., 'The terrestrial ecology of Ascension Island', *Journal of Applied Ecology*, 1 (1967), 219–51.

Edel, M., 'The Brazilian sugar-cycle of the seventeenth century and the rise of West Indian competition', *Caribbean Studies*, 9 (1969), 24–44.

Edwards, P. I., 'Sir Hans Sloane and his curious friends'. In A. Wheeler ed., *History in the service of systematics*, pp. 27–35. London, 1981.

Eltis, W., 'Richard Cantillon, a life of sterling service', *Times Higher Education Supplement*, 4 (1987), 16.

Elvin, M., and Vicziany, M., 'Ecology and the economic history of Asia', *Asian Studies Review*, 1990, pp. 39–72.

Erdosy, G., 'Deforestation in pre- and proto-historic South Asia'. In R. H. Grove and V. Damodaran, eds., *Essays on the environmental history of South and South-East Asia*, Oxford University Press, New Delhi, in press.

Eyles, J. M., 'William Smith, Sir Joseph Banks and the French geologists'. In A. Wheeler and H. C. Price, eds., *From Linnaeus to Darwin: Commentaries on the history of biology and geology*, pp. 37–50. London, 1985.

Feldman, T. S., 'Late Enlightenment meteorology'. In T. Frangsmyr, J. L. Heilbronn, and R. E. Rider, eds., *The quantifying spirit in the eighteenth century*, pp. 143–79. Berkeley and Los Angeles, 1990.

Fournier, M., 'Hendrik van Reede tot Drakenstein en de *Hortus malabaricus*', *Spiegel Historiael*, 13 (1978), 577–8.
'The *Hortus malabaricus* of Hendrik van Reede tot Drakenstein'. In K. Manilal, ed., *Botany and history of the 'Hortus malabaricus'*. New Delhi, 1989.

Gadgil, M., and Guha, R., 'State forestry and social conflict in British India: A study in the ecological basis of social protest', *Past and Present*, no. 123 (1989), 141–77.

George, A. S., 'The genus Banksia: A case study in Australian botany'. In A. Wheeler, ed., *History in the service of systematics*. London, 1981.

Giraud, Y., 'De l'exploration à l'Utopie: Notes sur la formation de mythe de Tahiti', *French Studies*, 31 (1977), 26–41.

Govindakutty, A., 'Some observations on seventeenth century Malayalam', *Indo-Iranian Journal*, 25 (1983), 241–73.

Greene, J. P., 'Changing identity in the British Caribbean: Barbados as a case study'. In N. Canny and A. Pagden, eds., *Colonial identity in the Atlantic world, 1660–1800*, pp. 213–67. Princeton, N.J., 1987.

Grove, R. H., 'Cressey Dymock and the draining of the Great Level: An early agricultural model', *Geographical Journal*, 147 (1981), 27–37.
'Charles Darwin and the Falkland Islands', *Polar Record*, 22 (1985), 413–20.
'Early themes in African conservation: The Cape in the nineteenth century', in D. Anderson and R.H. Grove, eds., *Conservation in Africa: People, policies and practices*, pp. 21–39. Cambridge, 1987.
'Scottish missionaries, evangelical discourses and the origins of conservation thinking in Southern Africa', *Journal of Southern African Studies*, 15 (1989), 22–39.

'Colonial conservation, ecological hegemony and popular resistance: Towards a global synthesis'. In J. Mackenzie, ed., *Imperialism and the natural world*, pp. 15–51. Manchester, 1990.

'The origins of environmentalism', *Nature* [London], 3 May 1990, pp. 11–15.

'The origins of western environmentalism', *Scientific American*, 267 (1992), 42–8.

'Conserving Eden: The (European) East India Companies and their environmental policies on St Helena, Mauritius and in Western India, 1660 to 1854', *Comparative Studies in Society and History*, 35 (1993) 318–351.

Guha, R., 'Forestry in British and post-British India: A historical analysis', *Economic and Political Weekly*, 1983, pp. 1882–96.

'Forestry and social protest in British Kumaon, 1893–1921', *Subaltern Studies*, 4 (1985), 54–101.

Hansmann, J., 'Gilgamesh, Humbaba and the land of the *Erin* trees', *Iraq*, 38 (1976), 23.

Harley, J. B., 'Maps, knowledge and power'. In D. Cosgrove and S. Daniels, eds., *The iconography of landscape*, pp. 277–312. Cambridge, 1988.

Hughes, J. D., 'Theophrastus as ecologist', *Environmental Review*, 4 (1985), 296–307.

'Mencius' prescriptions for ancient Chinese environmental problems', *Environmental Review*, 13 (1989), 12–25.

Johnson, R., 'Educating the educators: Experts and the state, 1833–1839'. In D. P. Donajgrodski, ed., *Social control in nineteenth century Britain*, pp. 77–107. London, 1977.

Johnston, N., 'Still no herbarium records for *Hortus malabaricus*', *Taxon*, 19 (1970), 665.

Jones, E. L., 'Environment and economy'. In P. Burke, ed., *The New Cambridge Modern History*, vol. 13, pp. 14–49. Cambridge, 1979.

Jordanova, L. J., 'Earth science and environmental medicine: The synthesis of the late Enlightenment'. In L. J. Jordanova and R. Porter, eds., *Images of the earth*, pp. 119–46. BSHS Monographs, 1. Chalfont St Giles, 1978.

Kapil, R. N., and Bhatnagar, A. K., 'Portuguese contributions to Indian botany', *Isis*, 67 (1976), 449–52.

Kathiramby-Wells, J., 'Socio-political, structures and South-East Asian ecosystems: A historical perspective up to the mid-nineteenth century'. In O. Bruun and A. Kalland, eds., *Asian perceptions of nature*. Nordic Institute of Asian Studies. Copenhagan, 1992.

King, G., 'A brief memoir on William Roxburgh, the author of the *Flora Indica*', *Annals of the Calcutta Botanic Garden*, 5 (1895), 2–9.

'The early history of Indian botany' *Report of the British Association for the Advancement of Science*, 1899, pp. 904–19.

Klein, I., 'When the rains failed: Famine relief and mortality in British India', *Indian Economic and Social History Review*, 21 (1984), 186–214.

Knight, D. M., 'Science and professionalism in England, 1790–1830', *Proceedings of the XIVth International Congress of the History of Science*, 1 (1974), 53–67.

Lafreniere, G. F., 'Rousseau and the European roots of environmentalism', *Environmental History Review*, 14 (1990), 41–73.

Laissus, Y., 'Note sur les manuscrits de Pierre Poivre (1719–1786) conservés à la Bibliothèque centrale du Muséum national d'histoire naturelle', *Proceedings of the Royal Society of Arts and Sciences of Mauritius*, 4:2 (1973), 31–56.

'Catalogue des manuscrits de Philibert Commerson, 1727–1773', *Cahiers du Centre Universitaire de la Réunion*, special issue: *Colloque Commerson*, 1975, pp. 76–107.

Lal, M., 'Iron tools, forest clearance and urbanisation in the Gangetic plains', *Man and Environment*, 10 (1985), 83–90.

Lambert, M., and Tourney, J., 'Les statues D, G, E, et H de Gudea', *Revue d'Assyriologie et d'Archéologie Orientale*, 47 (1953), 78–141.

Lawrence, C. J., 'Priestley in Tahiti'. In C. J. Lawrence, and R. Anderson, eds., *Science, medicine and dissent: Joseph Priestley 1733–1804*, pp. 1–10. London, 1987.

Lawrence, G. H. M., 'Herbals: Their history and significance'. In *History of botany: Two papers presented at a symposium at the Clark Memorial Library, UCLA*. Los Angeles, 1965.

Lawton, H. W., 'Bishop Godwin's *Man in the Moone*', *Review of English Studies*, 7 (1930), 23–55.

Lowe, P. D., 'Values and institutions in the history of British nature conservation'. In A. Warren and F. G. Goldsmith, eds., *Conservation in perspective*, pp. 329–51. London 1983.

Ly-Tio-Fane, M., 'Joseph Hubert and the Société des Sciences et Arts de l'Isle de France, 1801–1802', *Proceedings of the Royal Society of Arts and Sciences of Mauritius*, 11 (1961), 221–46.

'Pierre Poivre et l'expansion française dans l'Indo-Pacifique', *Bulletin Economique Française d'Extrème Orient*, 53 (1967), 453–511.

'Premiers projets d'entrepôt à l'Ile de France 1766–1788: Sociétés et compagnies de commerce en l'Orient et dans l'océan indien', *Actes du Congrès International d'Institut Maritime, Beyrouth, Sept. 1976*, 1976, pp. 487–98.

Mackenzie, J., 'Chivalry, social Darwinism and ritualised killing: The hunting ethos in central Africa up to 1914'. In D. Anderson and R. H. Grove, eds., *Conservation in Africa: People, policies and practices*, pp. 41–63. Cambridge, 1987.

Macleod, R. M., 'Scientific advice for British India: Imperial perceptions and administrative goals, 1898–1923', *Modern Asian Studies*, 3 (1975), 345–84.

Maheshwari, P., and Kapil, R. N., 'A short history of botany in India', *Journal of the University of Gauhati*, 9 (1958), 3–32.

Malleret, L., 'Pierre Poivre', *Bulletin de la Société des Etudes Indo-Chinoises*, n.s., 4 (1934), 69–70.

'Pierre Poivre, l'abbé Galloys et l'introduction d'espèces botaniques et d'oiseaux de Chine à l'Ile Maurice', *Proceedings of the Royal Society of Arts and Sciences of Mauritius*, 3 (1968), 117–30.

Manilal, K. S., 'The epigraphy of Malayalam certificates in *Hortus malabaricus*'. In K. S. Manilal, ed., *Botany and history of 'Hortus malabaricus'*, pp. 113–20. New Delhi, 1989.

Manilal, K. S., Suresh, C. R., and Sivarajan, V. V., 'A re-investigation of the plants described in Rheede's *Hortus malabaricus*: An introductory report, *Taxon*, 26 (1977), 549–50.

Marshall, B., 'The black Caribs: Native resistance to British penetration on the wind-ward side of St. Vincent, 1763–1773', *Caribbean Quarterly*, 79 (1973).

Masefield, G. B., 'Crops and livestock'. In E. E. Rich and C. H. Wilson, eds., *The Cambridge economic history of Europe*, vol. 4, pp. 275–307. Cambridge, 1967.

Meher-Homji, V. M., 'The link between rainfall and forest clearance: Case studies from Western Karnataka', *Transactions of the Institute of Indian Geographers*, 2:1 (1980), 59–65.

'Probable impact of deforestation on hydrological processes', *Climatic Change*, 19 (1991), 163–73.

Mehra, K. L., 'Portuguese introductions of fruit plants into India', *Indian Horticulture*, 10 (1965), 8–12, 19–22, 23–5.

Melville, E. G. K., 'Environmental and social change in the Valle del Mezquital, Mexico, 1521–1660', *Comparative Studies in Society and History*, 32 (1990), 24–53.

Metcalfe, S. E., 'Late Miocene human impact on lake basins in Central America', *Geoarchaeology*, 4:2 (1989), 119–41.

Mikesell, M. W., 'The deforestation of Mt. Lebanon', *Geographical Review*, 59 (1969), 1–28.

Moore, J. M., '*The Tempest* and Robinson Crusoe', *Review of English Studies*, 21 (1956), 58–66.

Myers, N., and Tucker, R., 'Deforestation in Central America: Spanish legacy and North American consumers', *Environmental Review*, 1 (1987), 55–73.

Nicolson, M., 'A world in the moon', *Smith College Studies in Modern Languages*, 17: 2 (1936), 23–55.

O'Hanlon, R., 'Cultures of rule, communities of resistance: Gender, discourse and tradition in South Asian historiographies', *Social Analysis*, no. 25 (Sept. 1989).

Olwig, K. R., 'Environmental science and its exegesis', *Journal of Historical Geography*, 13 (1987), 200–5.

Opie, J., 'Renaissance origins of the environmental crisis', *Environmental Review*, 2 (1987), 2–19.

Parsons, J. J., 'Human influences on the pine and laurel forests of the Canary Islands', *Geographical Review*, 71 (1981), 260–84.

Patterson, R., 'The Hortus Palatinus at Heidelberg and the reformation of the world', *Journal of Garden History*, 1 (1981), 67–104.

Peluso, N. L., 'The history of state forest management in colonial Java', *Forest and Conservation History*, 35 (1991), 63–73.

Quinn, W. H., and Neal, V. T., 'El Niño occurrences over the past four and a half centuries', *Journal of Geophysical Research*, 92 (1987), 14449–61.

'Records of the vestry of St Michael', *Barbados Museum and Historical Journal*, 14 (1947), 136, 173; 15 (1948), 17.

Rehbock, P. F., 'John Fleming (1785–1857) and the economy of nature'. In A. Wheeler and H. C. Price, eds., *From Linnaeus to Darwin: Commentaries on the history of biology and geology*, pp. 129–40. London, 1985.

Richards, J. F., Haynes, E. S., and Hagen, J. R., 'Changing land use in Bihar, Punjab and Haryana, 1850–1970', *Modern Asian Studies*, 19 (1985), 699–732.

Rollefson, G., and Kohler, I., 'Prehistoric people ruined their environment', *New Scientist*, 125 (24 Feb. 1990), 29.

Rompkey, R., 'Some uncollected authors: XLIX, Soame Jenyns', *Book Collector*, 25 (1970), 210–11.

'Soame Jenyns, M.P.: A curious case of membership', *Journal of the Royal Society of Arts*, 120 (1972), 532–42.

Rubner, H., 'Greek thought and forest science', *Environmental Review*, 4 (1985), 277–96.

Russell, P. E., 'Prince Henry the Navigator', *Diamante*, 11 (1960), 1–31.

Sauer, C. O., 'Man in the ecology of Middle America'. In C. Salter, ed., *The cultural landscape*. Belmont, Mass., 1971.

Schaffer, S., 'Measuring virtue: Eudiometry, enlightenment and pneumatic medicine'. In A. Cunningham and R. French, eds., *The medical enlightenment in the eighteenth century*. Cambridge, 1990.

Secord, A. W., 'Studies in the narrative method of Defoe', *University of Illinois Studies in Language and Literature*, 9 (1924), 1–248.

Shaw, T., 'Early agriculture in Africa', *Journal of the Historical Society of Nigeria*, 6 (1972), 143–92.

Sheridan, R. B., 'The plantation revolution and the industrial revolution, 1625–1775', *Caribbean Studies*, 3 (1969), 5–15.

Shiva, V., 'Afforestation in India: Problems and policies', *Ambio*, 14 (1985), 21–41.

Siddiqi, A., 'The business world of Jamsedjee Jeejeebhoy', *Indian Economic and Social History Review*, 19 (1983), 301–24.

Sinha, A. C., 'Social frame of forest history: A study in the ecological and ethnic aspects of tea plantation in the north-east Himalaya foothills', *Social Science Probings*, 1986, 236–63.

Sloan, P., 'Buffon's preface to the *Vegetable Staticks* of Stephen Hales (1736)'. In J. Lyon and P. R. Sloan, eds., *From natural history to the history of nature: Readings from Buffon and his contemporaries*, pp. 35–41. Notre Dame, Ind., 1981.

Smith, B., 'Coleridge's "Ancient Mariner" and Cook's second voyage', *Journal of the Warburg and Courtauld Institutes*, 19 (1956), 117–54.

Speiser, E., 'Arkadian myths and epics: The epic of Gilgamesh'. In J. Pritchard, ed., *Ancient Near Eastern texts*, vol. 3, p. 4. Princeton, N.J., 1955.

Steiner, G., 'J. R. Forsters und G. Forsters Beziehungen zu Russland', *Veröffentlichungen des Instituts für Slawistik*, 28 (1968), 245–311.

Steinkeller, P., 'The foresters of Umma: Towards a definition of Ur III labor'. In M. Powell, ed., *Labor in the ancient Near East*, pp. 92–3. New Haven, Conn., 1987.

Street-Perrott, F. A., 'Anthropogenic soil erosion around Lake Putzcuaro, Mexico, during the pre-classic and later post-classic Hispanic periods', *American Antiquity*, 54:4 (1989), 759–65.

Subramanian, L. S., 'Bombay and the west coast in the 1740s', *Indian Economic and Social History Review*, 8 (1981), 181–216.

'The Banias and the British: The role of indigenous credit in Western India in the second half of the eighteenth century', *Modern Asian Studies*, 20 (1987), 473–511.

Te Brake, W., 'Land drainage and public environmental policy in medieval Holland', *Environmental History Review*, 12 (1988).

Thacker, C., ' "O Tinian! O Juan Fernandez!": Rousseau's "Elysée" and Anson's desert islands', *Garden History*, 5:9 (1977), 41–7.

Thompson, K., 'Trees as a theme in medical geography and public health', *Bulletin of the New York Academy of Medicine*, 54 (1978), 517–31.

'Forests and climatic change in America: Some early views', *Climatic Change*, 3 (1983), 47–64.

Trautmann, T. R., 'Elephants and the Mauryas'. In S. N. Mukherjee, ed., *India: History and thought: Essays in honour of A. L. Basham*, pp. 254–73. Calcutta, 1982.

Tucker, R., 'Forest management and imperial politics: Thana district, Bombay, 1823–1827', *Indian Economic and Social History Review*, 16 (1979), 273–300.

'The depletion of India's forests under British imperialism: Planters, foresters and peasants in Assam and Kerala'. In D. Worster, ed., *The ends of the earth: Perspectives on modern environmental history*, pp. 118–41. Cambridge, 1988.

Vedant, C. S., 'Comment: Afforestation in India', *Ambio*, 15 (1986), 254–5.

Vicziany, M., 'Imperialism, botany and statistics: The surveys of Francis Buchanan', *Modern Asian Studies*, 20 (1986), 625–60.

Ware, N. J., 'The physiocrats', *American Economic Review*, 21:4 (1931), 607–19.

Washbrook, D., 'Law, state and agrarian society in colonial India', *Modern Asian Studies*, 15 (1981), 649–721.

White, L., 'The historic roots of our ecologic crisis', *Science*, 155 (1967), 1202–7.

Worster, D., 'The vulnerable earth: Towards an interplanetary history'. In Worster, ed., *The ends of the earth: Perspectives on modern environmental history*, pp. 3–23. Cambridge, 1988.

Zamora, M., 'Abreast of Columbus: Gender and discovery', *Cultural Critique*, 1990, pp. 127–48.

Index

527